Texts and Monographs in Computer Science

Editor

David Gries

Advisory Board

F. L. Bauer
K. S. Fu
J. J. Horning
R. Reddy
D. C. Tsichritzis
W. M. Waite

Reliable Computer Systems

Collected Papers of the Newcastle Reliability Project

Edited by S. K. Shrivastava

With 215 Figures

Springer-Verlag
Berlin Heidelberg New York Tokyo

Santosh Kumar Shrivastava
University of Newcastle upon Tyne, Computing Laboratory
Newcastle upon Tyne NE1 7RU/England

Series Editor
David Gries
Cornell University, Department of Computer Science, Upson Hall
Ithaca, New York 14859/USA

ISBN-13: 978-3-642-82472-2   e-ISBN-13: 978-3-642-82470-8
DOI: 10.1007/978-3-642-82470-8

Library of Congress Cataloging in Publication Data. Main entry under title:
Reliable computer systems.
(Texts and monographs in computer science)
Bibliography: p.
Includes index.
1. Electronic digital computers—Reliability—Addresses, essays, lectures. 2. Fault-tolerant computing—Addresses, essays,
lectures. 3. Computer software—Reliability—Addresses, essays, lectures. 4. Newcastle Reliability Project. I. Shrivastava, S. K.
(Santosh Kumar), 1946– . II. Newcastle Reliability Project. III. Series. QA76.5.R4464 1985 001.64 85-10023

© by Springer-Verlag Berlin Heidelberg 1985
Softcover reprint of the hardcover 1st edition 1985

2145/3140-543210

Preface

A research project to investigate the design and construction of reliable computing systems was initiated by B. Randell at the University of Newcastle upon Tyne in 1972. In over ten years of research on system reliability, a substantial number of papers have been produced by the members of this project. These papers have appeared in a variety of journals and conference proceedings and it is hoped that this book will prove to be a convenient reference volume for research workers active in this important area. In selecting papers published by past and present members of this project, I have used the following criteria: a paper is selected if it is concerned with fault tolerance *and* is not a review paper *and* was published before 1983. I have used these criteria (with only one or two exceptions!) in order to present a collection of papers with a common theme and, at the same time, to limit the size of the book to a reasonable length.

The papers have been grouped into seven chapters. The first chapter introduces fundamental concepts of fault tolerance and ends with the earliest Newcastle paper on reliability. The project perhaps became well known after the invention of recovery blocks − a simple yet effective means of incorporating fault tolerance in software. The second chapter contains papers on recovery blocks, starting with the paper which first introduced the concept. Chapter 3 contains papers on exception handling while chapter four includes papers that deal with fault tolerance in concurrent systems. It is now generally agreed that systems should be designed and constructed hierarchically. The papers in Chapt. 5 explore the issues of constructing recoverable objects in such 'multi-level' systems. Chapter 6 contains papers on distributed systems and reports on work done − both conceptual and experimental − in this important area. The concluding chapter comprises just a single paper. This is the only review paper in this volume and is included here since in it, its author (Randell) summarizes the principles of system structuring and fault tolerance that have emerged from the work of this project.

In a very amusing book[1], John Gall presented a 'fundamental theorem' for systems:

New Systems Mean New Problems

I can therefore confidently predict continued employment for those of us who spend our time trying to make computer systems more reliable. Indeed, I am looking forward to the appearance of a second volume of collected papers ten years hence.

In compiling this book I have had help from many people, but special thanks go to my colleagues Tom Anderson and Brian Randell for their advice and comments. Finally, it is a pleasure to acknowledge the continued financial support for the project by the UK Science and Engineering Research Council and the Ministry of Defence.

Santosh K. Shrivastava

---

1 John Gall: "Systemantics; How Systems Work and Especially How They Fail." Kangaroo Pocket Books, New York, 1977

Contents

Chapter 3.   Exception Handling

Chapter 4.   Concurrent Systems

Chapter 5. Multilevel Systems

Chapter 6. Distributed Systems

Chapter 7. Fault Tolerance and System Structuring

List of Contributors

A. A. AKINPELU, Department of Computer Science & Statistics, University College London, London, Great Britain

T. ANDERSON, University of Newcastle upon Tyne, Computing Laboratory, Claremont Tower, Claremont Road, Newcastle upon Tyne NE1 7RU, Great Britain

J. P. BANÂTRE, IRISA-INSA, Universite de Rennes, Rennes, France

E. BEST, GMD-Isf, St. Augustin, West Germany

D. R. BROWNBRIDGE, High Level Hardware, Windmill Road, Oxford, Great Britain

F. CRISTIAN, IBM Research, San Jose, California, USA

N. GHANI, MARI, Jesmond Road, Newcastle upon Tyne, Great Britain

K. HERON, University of Newcastle upon Tyne, Computing Laboratory, Claremont Tower, Claremont Road, Newcastle upon Tyne NE1 7RU, Great Britain

J. J. HORNING, Digital Equipment Corporation, Palo Alto, California, USA

M. JEGADO, IRISA-INSA, Universite de Rennes, Rennes, France

R. KERR, University of Newcastle upon Tyne, Computing Laboratory, Claremont Tower, Claremont Road, Newcastle upon Tyne NE1 7RU, Great Britain

J. C. KNIGHT, Department of Computer Science, University of Virginia, Charlottesville, Virginia, USA

H. C. LAUER, Apollo Computer Inc., Chemsford, Massachusetts, USA

P. A. LEE, Encore Computer Corporation, Wellesley, Massachusetts, USA

D. B. LOMET, IBM TJ Watson Research Centre, Yorktown Heights, New York, USA

L. F. MARSHALL, University of Newcastle upon Tyne, Computing Laboratory, Claremont Tower, Claremont Road, Newcastle upon Tyne NE1 7RU, Great Britain

P. M. MELLIAR-SMITH, Computer Science Laboratory, SRI International, Mento Park, California, USA

P. M. MERLIN, deceased

F. Panzieri, Summa Sistemi Uomo Macchina, Via Alberto Caroncini 58, Rome, Italy

B. Randell, University of Newcastle upon Tyne, Computing Laboratory, Claremont Tower, Claremont Road, Newcastle upon Tyne NE1 7RU, Great Britain

S. K. Shrivastava, University of Newcastle upon Tyne, Computing Laboratory, Claremont Tower, Claremont Road, Newcastle upon Tyne NE1 7RU, Great Britain

J. S. M. Verhofstad, Data General Corporation, Westford, Massachusetts, USA

R. W. Witty, Rutherford & Appleton Laboratories, Chilton, Didcot, Oxfordshire, Great Britain

W. G. Wood, SDA, Santa Clara, California, USA

Introduction

B. Randell

It was in January 1972 that a long term programme of research into the problems of designing highly reliable computing systems was initiated at the University of Newcastle upon Tyne. However the origins of the project can be readily traced back some years earlier.

I had joined the University on May 1969, following a period of some years in the United States at the IBM T.J. Watson Research Center. There, one of my principal interests was system design methodology, a situation which led to my participation in the 1968 NATO Conference on Software Engineering. Quite a number of the attendees have since remarked on the great influence this conference had on their subsequent work and thinking. This was certainly true in my case, aided by the fact that the task which Peter Naur and I undertook in the week following the conference of editing the conference report called for repeated listening to tapes of many stimulating and entertaining discussions and presentations. (Incidentally, I have always treasured Doug McIlroy's description of our resulting report as "a triumph of mis-applied quotation"!)

One major theme of the conference was the great disparity between the level of reliance that organizations were willing to place on complex real time systems and the very modest levels of reliability that were often being achieved — for example, it was also at about this time that there was considerable public debate over the proposed Anti-Ballistic Missile System, which we understood was to involve relying completely on a massively complicated computer system to position and detonate a nuclear device in the upper atmosphere in the path of each incoming missile!

At the NATO Conference there was thus much discussion about improved methods of software design, though there was a mainly implicit assumption that high reliability was best achieved by making a system fault-free, rather than fault-tolerant. Another much-debated topic concerned the practicality of attempting to provide rigorous correctness proofs for software systems of significant size and complexity. Such discussions, I am sure, played a large part in ensuring that, by the time I reached Newcastle, I was seeking to do something constructive about the problems of achieving high reliability from complex computing systems, and yet, was feeling rather pessimistic about the practicality of proving the correctness of other than relatively small and simple programs.

The plan for a major research project at Newcastle on system reliability in fact was developed very quickly in discussion with my colleague Jim Eve. This discussion was, I must admit, prompted by the impending visit of a delegation from the Computing Science Committee of the U.K. Science Research Council, whose aim was, we were told, to encourage the submission of new research proposals. The speed and scale of the Newcastle response to this invitation were

1

somewhat greater than the committee had bargained for. Thus our initial research proposal, submitted in March 1970, led to our being awarded just a very modest grant intended merely to enable us to prepare a report surveying the current state-of-the-art, and to refine our proposal. I managed to kill two birds with one report, since a somewhat shortened version served as the paper that I had been invited to give at IFIP71 on Operating Systems, whilst the complete version met with sufficient approval for Newcastle to be awarded, in November 1971, funds for the full project proposal. Since then, I am pleased to say, our work has continued to be supported by the Science and Engineering Research Council, as it later became known, together in more recent years with the Royal Radar and Signals Establishment of the U.K. Ministry of Defence.

From the start, our aim was to study the general problems of achieving high reliability from complex computing systems, rather than concentrate on problems specific to a particular application area or make of computer. Quoting from the original project proposal: "The intent is to investigate problems concerned with the provision of reliable service by a computing system, notwithstanding the presence of software and hardware errors. The approach will be based on the development of computer architecture and programming techniques which facilitate the structuring of complex computing systems so that the existence of errors can be detected and the extent of their ramifications be determined automatically, and so that uninterrupted service (albeit probably of degraded quality until the faulty hardware or software is repaired) can be provided ... (The proposed project) is thus parallel and complementary to work on achieving high reliability from individual hardware components, and on program validation. Both of these topics are of importance, but it is clear that for the foreseeable future, the designers of large-scale computing systems will not be able to achieve adequate system reliability be depending entirely on the reliability of the hardware and software components which make up their system."

Initially, and indeed for a number of years, the Newcastle project concentrated largely on the area that has since become known as "design fault tolerance", with particular reference to software faults. With situations such as that reported at the NATO Conference of OS/360 suffering more than 1000 separate bugs per release, there were few to challenge the reality of problems of residual design faults in software, though the notion of trying to provide means of tolerating such faults, rather than just preventing their existence, was much more controversial. In fact, though dealing mainly with software problems, we have always attempted to avoid undue separation of hardware and software issues. However it is only now that there is much general recognition of the fact that, thanks to the "opportunities" provided by VLSI to design ever more complex chips, hardware systems might suffer not only from operational faults but also design faults, even years after the first deliveries occurred.

Looking back over the course of the Newcastle project, one can see that we started by studying the problems of difficult faults in (relatively) simple systems and then gradually increased the difficulty of the systems that we were prepared to consider. Thus we started with the problem of tolerating bugs in isolated sequential programs, before dealing in turn with the difficulties associated with input/output, competition for shared resources, cooperating processes within a single computing system, and, finally, distributed computing systems. This can be contrasted with the approach which is more typical of a project concerned immediately with the complexities of some actual large computing system. This usually involves first considering just simple kinds of fault (in particular of completely predictable location and effect) and only gradually attempting to consider more complicated (but not necessarily less likely) fault situations. Each approach has its merits, but we are convinced that the approach that we followed has proved the more appropriate, given our wish to obtain results of reasonably general applicability, whilst avoiding undue design complexity.

Our eventual concentration on distributed systems arose not so much because of the challenge of the additional complications that they posed, interesting though these are, but rather from the view that all other sorts of system were merely simplified special cases — as C. T. Davies once put it: "I have yet to come across an interesting non-distributed system." In this arena we have taken as another archetypical "difficult" fault: the situation where erroneous data has entered the system and spread amongst the component computers, before being detected. In principle, such a problem could arise no matter the granularity of distribution — within a single VLSI chip, amongst a set of multiprocessing units, or in a geographically dispersed collection of computers. In practice, however, we have for convenience concentrated on the latter case. Thus, whereas in the early years of the project we worked mainly on topics related to processor architectures and programming languages, we have more recently found ourselves interacting principally with the networking, operating systems and database communities. Moreover, whereas at times we have concentrated particularly on mechanisms to be incorporated in fault tolerant systems, at other times much of our effort has concerned methodologies for the design of such systems. This in fact illustrates what is at once a great advantage, and a great difficulty, of trying to undertake a programme of general research in the area of computing system reliability — many different facets of computing science are highly relevant, and the problem is to decide what issues one can safely ignore!

Despite the above characterization of the overall progression of our research over the years, I must admit that the work of the project has not so much followed a detailed long term plan of work, but rather has evolved dynamically, not the least as the circumstances and the personnel involved with the project have changed. Nevertheless, we believe it is fair to claim that there has been a good degree of at least retrospective coherence and continuity to the work, centered as it has been from the start on a concern for structure as a means of coping with complexity. It is to be hoped that the present selection and organisation, by my colleague Santosh Shrivastava, of a representative collection of the project's publications will enable readers to gain an understanding of our overall approach, as well as provide them with details of many of the different investigations that have been carried out by the project. What such a collection of formal papers cannot do, however, is give any impression of the enjoyment and sense of exhileration that has usually typified the activities of the project.

3

Thus I would like to close these brief introductory remarks by making clear the personal debt that I owe to all the staff, students and visitors who have been involved with the project for the way in which they have made it such a stimulating and pleasant environment, over all these years.

Chapter 1
System Reliability

Introduction

In our every day conversations we tend to use the terms 'fault', 'error' and 'failure' (often interchangeably) to indicate the fact that something is 'wrong' with a system. However, in any discussion on reliability and fault tolerance, more precision is called for to avoid confusion. The definitions for these terms presented here in the first paper by Anderson and Lee owe their origins to the unpublished work of Melliar-Smith and to his collaborative work with Randell (see their joint paper in Chap. 3). In true computer science fashion, Melliar-Smith and Randell defined a system recursively as composed out of 'smaller' systems and defined the occurrence of a failure to be the event when the behaviour of a system does not agree with that required by the specification. Why does a system fail? To answer this is it necessary to examine the internal state of the system, which then leads us to the notions of 'errors' and 'faults'.

The second paper of this chapter presents basic concepts for the construction of fault-tolerant software systems. The paper contains a number of important ideas which include (i) 'recovery blocks' as a means of coping with software faults; (ii) 'conversations' for structuring the interactions between communicating processes so as to make the problem of error recovery manageable; and (iii) an approach to the construction of 'multilevel' fault-tolerant systems. Over the years, these ideas have been developed considerably, for example Chap. 5 reports in detail the work done on multilevel systems.

This chapter ends with a paper by Randell. This paper is of interest on two counts. First it reports on the survey work performed prior to the launching of the project and secondly this early paper on system reliability makes an instructive reading in the light of the previous two contributions. Randell stresses the importance of system reliability, which is matched by the importance of adequate performance, and promotes the concept of designing systems that contain effective provisions for coping with 'software bugs'. This objective is reflected in a number of papers that appear in subsequent chapters.

Fault Tolerance Terminology Proposals

T. ANDERSON and P. A. LEE

Abstract. At present, the fault tolerance community is hampered by using a set of conflicting terms to refer to closely related fault tolerance concepts. This paper presents informal, but precise, definitions and terminology for these concepts. In particular, the terms *fault, error* and *failure* are carefully defined and distinguished. The aim is to promote discussion in the hope that an agreed terminology will emerge.

Introduction

It is important that detailed technical discussions on any subject can be conducted with reference to an agreed terminology for the relevant concepts. Unfortunately, when causes of unreliability in computing systems are discussed a range of different (but rarely distinguished) terms is available, and this can be a source of confusion. Confusion also stems from attempts to isolate or combine issues relating to the hardware/software dichotomy.

For some years, members of the Reliability Project at the University of Newcastle upon Tyne have been developing and refining a set of terms with precise interpretations for use in discussions on system reliability and fault tolerance. The terms are intended to be applicable to all levels of a computing system and not just to either the hardware or the software. These terms and their definitions are presented here to promote discussion and obtain the reactions of the fault tolerance community, with the hope that a coherent and agreed terminology will emerge.

The paper first discusses the notion of a system since this is basic to all of the other definition. Next, the causes of unreliability within a system are examined, and finally, the means by which reliability can be enhanced are summarized.

On Systems

Any identifiable mechanism which maintains a pattern of behaviour at an interface with its environment can be regarded as a system. Physical systems have a hierarchical structure since they are built up from component systems, and so on. This is reflected in the following definition: a *system* consists of a set of components which interact under the control of a design. A *component* is simply another system. The *design* is also a system, but has special characteristics. In this paper, the design of a system will always refer to that part of the system which actually supports and controls the interaction of the components (and does not refer to any design document, such as a circuit diagram) or to the process by which the system was designed [1]. As a special case, a system may be considered to be *atomic*, with the implication that any further internal structure of that system is not of interest and can be ignored.

A system is said to interact with an *environment*, responding to stimuli at an interface (or interfaces) between the system and its environment. An *interface* is simply a place of interaction between two systems, and so (of course) the environment must be another system. The external behaviour of a system can be described in terms of a finite set of *external states*, together with a function defining transitions between states. The environment provides input as stimuli, and perceives the system as passing through a sequence of external states at discrete instants of time.

The external behaviour of a system is the manifestation of internal activity within the system, and for a non-atomic system this activity can be examined in more detail. The *internal state* of a system is defined to be a tuple comprising the external states of the components of the system. An abstraction function maps internal states to external states. Internal state transitions are a consequence of changes of state by the components; these changes are determined by interactions between the components. The pattern of these interactions is specified and controlled by the design of the system, which also determines the way in which interactions between the system and the environment impinge upon the components. Note that the state of a system is defined without reference to the design of the system. This is deliberate, and distinguishes the ongoing activity of the system from its internal organization, which is usually fixed − the state of the design itself will not be intended to change.

These system definitions are intended to be sufficiently general that they are applicable to any system whatsoever. In particular they cover computing systems considered as hardware or software systems and can be applied at many different levels in such systems. For example, a single printed circuit board can be regarded as a system − the components are the electronic components soldered to the board while the design is implemented as the tracks and wires which provide their interconnection. A central processor is a system with components such as registers, arithmetic, logical and control units, and has as its design the data highways linking them. A complete computing system has as components the central processor, primary and secondary storage, and peripherals, with the design implemented as the data buses and cabling which interconnect them. Note that the structure (and activity) of a system can be examined at different levels of abstraction (as opposed to levels of structure); a more abstract view of a computing system takes as components the various *processes* implemented in software, which interact through a design constructed, for example, as shared data areas controlled by means of semaphores.

A particularly important change in viewpoint can be identified at an *interpretive interface*, where a component of a system is interpreted (i.e. executed)

---

1 There are two reasons for this nonstandard use of the word "design". First, it makes it clear that a "design fault" (see next section) is a defect which is actually present in a system. Second, we have not found a better alternative.

by, and thereby governs and directs the operation of, the rest of the system. When this is the case it is natural and appropriate to regard the interpreted component as the design of a system whose components are abstractions of the other components of the original system. The paradigm here, of course, is the interface between hardware and software in a computing system. It will often be more useful to regard software as the design of an abstract system rather than merely a bit-pattern stored on some magnetic medium.

All systems are designed and built to be used, and support interfaces which can therefore be presumed to have useful properties. One unfortunate, but prevalent, consequence of the complexity of computing systems is that their behaviour may depart from that desired by their users. The unreliability of a system is usually assessed in terms of the frequency and extent of such departures, and also in terms of any costs incurred because of undesired system behaviour. However, any assessment of unreliability must surely distinguish between undesirable behaviour which is a result of deficiencies of the system itself as opposed to misunderstandings on the part of the users of the system. To make this distinction a *specification* of system behaviour is required.

In practice, a specification must serve many purposes; those of designers, builders, vendors and users of a system. As a result the specification of a system is rarely complete or precise, is open to question and change, and may even be undocumented. Such a specification cannot be used to define the reliability of a system. System reliability can only be defined and assessed with respect to an *authoritative specification* of behaviour, which can be applied as a test in any situation to determine whether the behaviour of the system should or should not be deemed acceptable. For the purpose of definition the role of the specification is absolute. (Systems and their specifications are discussed in more detail elsewhere.) [1]

Thus, a *failure* of a system is said to occur when the behaviour of the system first deviates from that required by the specification of the system. To extend this definition to include the occurrence of failures after the first deviation from specified behaviour is not completely straightforward (the specification might have to define what constitutes acceptable behaviour subsequent to a breach of the specification). However, complications can be avoided by adopting the convention that once the system has returned to satisfactory operation its subsequent behaviour can again be assessed with respect to the specification (i.e. ignoring any earlier failures).

The *reliability* of a system is usually characterized by a function $R(t)$ which expresses the probability that no failure of the system will have occured by time t.

On Faults and Errors

An authoritative specification cannot be challenged, so the occurrence of a system failure must be due to the presence of defects within the system. Such deficiencies will be referred to as *faults* when they are internal to a component or the design, and as *errors* when the system state is defective. This section provides precise definitions for these concepts, corresponding closely to established usage.

Consider a system which moves through a sequence of internal states s_1, s_2, s_3, . . . in response to the interactions of the system with its environment. Assume that while the system progressed through states s_1 to s_{n-1} its external behaviour conformed to the system specification, but that on entering state s_n its behaviour conflicted with the specification. That is, the system fails when it reaches internal state s_n. In this situation it seems natural to seek a "cause" to which the "effect" of failure can be attributed; that is, to identify some earlier (internal) event which can be held responsible for the failure. The internal state transitions are the obvious candidates.

An internal state transition is said to be either *valid* or *erroneous;* an *erroneous transition* is an internal state transition to which a subsequent failure could be attributed. That is, there exists a sequence of interactions with the system which would lead to a failure which would be attributed to the erroneous transition. An internal state of a system is said to be either *valid* or *erroneous;* an *erroneous state* is an internal state which could lead to a failure by a sequence of valid transitions.

For example, suppose that the transition from s_{i-1} to s_i was considered to be responsible for the eventual failure of the above system. Internal states $s_1, \ldots,$ s_{i-1} are then valid states while $s_i, \ldots, s_n$ are erroneous states, assuming that the only erroneous transition is that from s_{i-1} to s_i. Note that a valid transition is one which cannot be blamed for a subsequent failure – there is no implication that the system is operating as was intended. Thus the transition from s_i to s_{i+1} is valid even though states s_i and s_{i+1} are erroneous.

Having identified an erroneous transition as being the cause of a failure it is natural to ask what caused that transition to be erroneous. One explanation for an erroneous transition is the occurrence of a failure of a component of the system. If one (or more) of the components fails to meet its specification this could certainly place the system in an erroneous state. When this is the case the above discussion can be applied to the failing component considered as a system: the component has failed and must therefore itself have passed through a sequence of erroneous states as a result of an erroneous transition. And so on – the ultimate cause of a failure can be pursued as far as is considered worthwhile.

If, however, all components meet their specification when an erroneous transition takes place, the problem must lie in the design of the system. An obvious specification of behaviour for the design of a system is that it should ensure that all internal state transitions of the system are valid in the absence of any failure of the components. Then, if there is an erroneous transition and no components have failed the design of the system must be held to have failed. Thus, the design can be considered to be in an erroneous state. Although the state of the design of a system is usually not intended to change this cannot be guaranteed, and an erroneous transition within the design may result in a previously valid design becoming erroneous. Of course, there is also the possibility that the design may have been erroneous from the outset (i.e. the initial state of the design was erroneous) in which case an erroneous transition may be regarded as having occurred sometime during the design-process or the construction of the system.

These definitions are intended to reflect the situation when, after a system failure, the history of system activity is scrutinized in order to identify the cause of the failure. A post-mortem of this nature will often proceed by observing that the internal state at the time of failure is clearly erroneous, that the initial state of the system (or some other earlier state) was valid, and that there must therefore have been an erroneous transition at some stage. For the purposes of definition, it is the identification of erroneous transitions which determines whether a state is valid or erroneous. In turn, an erroneous transition must be the outcome of a failure of either a component or the design of the system. This seems quite natural: a system consists of a set of components together with a design; a failure of a system must be a consequence of a failure of either a component or the design.

When a system is in an erroneous state, an examination of the external states of the components of the system will enable a decision to be made as to which components have external states that would have to be changed for the internal state of the system to be valid. The states of such components are said to be *errors* in the system. An error is thus a part of an erroneous state which constitutes a difference from a valid state.

Even though the external state of a component may be an error in the system of which it is a part, the component need not be in an erroneous state when it is considered as a system in its own right. The internal state of the component may be perfectly valid but not be compatible with the states of other components of the containing system. To avoid confusion, an error in a component or in the design of a system will be referred to as a *fault* in the system. A *component fault* can result in an eventual component failure; a *design fault* can lead to a design failure. Either of these internal failures will produce an erroneous transition in the operation of the system and this transition can be referred to as the *manifestation of a fault*. The manifestation of a fault will produce errors in the state of the system, which could lead to a failure.

Note that the only difference between a fault and an error is with respect to the structure of the system; a fault in a system *is* an error in a component or in the design of the system. A fault is the cause of an error and an error is the cause of a failure, but the distinction between error and failure does not merely reflect system structure (though an error is part of an internal state while a failure relates to external states). Rather, the difference is that between a condition (or state) and an event. A system contains an error when its state is erroneous, whereas a system failure is the event of not producing behaviour as specified.

Examination of the possible causes of system failure has revealed an important dichotomy. The erroneous transition which gave rise to the failure must either be due to a design fault, or one of the components must have failed. On the one hand, a mistake made in designing or constructing a system can introduce a fault into the design of the system, either because of an inappropriate selection of a component or because of inappropriate (or missing) interactions between components. Precise identification of the fault, and of the resulting design failure as an event, can only be made with respect to a corrected design for the system. If, on the other hand, the design of a system is considered to be without blemish, then an erroneous transition can only occur because of a failure of one of the components of the system. These two possibilities are the only sources of an erroneous transition, and thus of errors and consequent system failure. It should be clear that although these possibilities are distinct for a system viewed as an assembly of particular components, a more refined examination of the system which considers a failing component as a system of interacting subcomponents would be expected to explain many component failures as being due to design faults within the component. Eventually, all system failures can be attributed to design faults at some level, unless a failure of a component which is considered to be atomic is held responsible. (Even failure of an atomic component may be considered to be due to a design fault in that a component of inadequate reliability was selected.)

In contrast to the definition of failure presented earlier, the definitions of erroneous transition and erroneous state, and therefore of error and fault, include a significant subjective element. This is considered to be an important (and unavoidable) feature of these definitions. Consider the attribution of a failure to an erroneous transition, which results in (or, as is more likely in practice, is a result of) the identification of a fault as the source of the problem. Such an attribution must envisage a correction to the system which would remove the fault and prevent the erroneous transition from occuring. The changes which can be made to correct a faulty system will rarely be unique; a judgement must be made as to the most appropriate correction. This subjective decision determines the fault, the erroneous transition and the errors which it introduced into the state of the system.

On Fault Tolerance

Two complementary approaches have been noted [2] for constructing highly reliable systems. The first approach, which may be termed *fault prevention*, tries to ensure that the implemented system does not and will not contain any faults. Fault prevention has two aspects:

(i) *fault avoidance* techniques are employed to avoid introducing faults into the system (e.g. design methodologies and quality control);
(ii) *fault removal* techniques are used to find and remove faults which were inadvertently introduced into the system (e.g. testing and validation).

The second approach is known as *fault tolerance* (and is, of course, the subject of this book). Fault tolerance techniques attempt to intervene and prevent faults from causing system failures – they are necessary because complex systems are certain to contain residual faults despite extensive application of fault prevention. Four constituent phases of fault tolerance can be identified [4, 1] and these are: (i) error detection; (ii) damage assessment; (iii) error recovery; and (iv) fault treatment and continued system service.

(i) Error detection: In order to tolerate a fault in a system its effects must first be detected. While a fault cannot be directly detected by a system, any manifes-

tation of the fault will generate errors somewhere in the system. Thus the usual starting point for fault tolerance techniques is the detection of an erroneous state.

(ii) Damage assessment: When an error is detected much more of the system state may be suspect than that initially discovered to be erroneous. Because of the likely delay between the manifestation of a fault and the detection of its erroneous consequences, invalid information may have spread within the system, leading to other errors which have not (yet) been detected. Thus before any attempt is made to deal with a detected error it may be necessary to assess the extent to which the system state has been damaged. This assessment will depend on decisions made by the system designer concerning damage confinement, and on exploratory techniques for identifying damage.

(iii) Error recovery: Following error detection and damage assessment, techniques for error recovery must be utilized. These techniques will aim to transform the current erroneous system state into a well defined and error-free state from which normal system operation can continue. Without such a transformation system failure is likely to ensue.

(iv) Fault treatment and continued service: Although the error recovery phase may have returned the system to an error-free state, techniques may still be required to enable the system to continue providing the service required by its specification, by ensuring that the fault whose effects have been recovered from does not immediately recur. The first aspect of fault treatment is to attempt to accurately locate the fault. Following this, steps can be taken to repair the fault or to reconfigure the rest of the system to avoid the fault; alternatively, no action is taken if the fault is thought to be transient.

These four phases form the basis for all fault tolerance techniques and thus can and should form the basis for the design and implementation of a fault tolerant system. There can be considerable interplay between the various phases which tends to blur their identification in a particular system. For example, a protection mechanism usually provides one form of error detection and can also play an important role in the design and implementation of the damage assessment phase. Similarly, any damage assessment undertaken by a system will utilize exploratory measures to identify possible damage, measures which will themselves use error detection techniques. The provision of error recovery will normally be dependent upon the damage assessment provided (or assumed) in the system, although some forms of error recovery attempt to minimize the need for damage assessment.

It should be noted that most existing fault tolerant systems are only intended to provide tolerance to a range of predicted component faults. Rarely is any provision made for the unanticipatable effects of design faults. When tolerance to design faults is required, very general strategies must be employed for each of the four phases of fault tolerance identified above.

Finally, when a system emobodies fault tolerance techniques the basic definitions of the previous section require modification. The revised definitions are:

an *erroneous transition* is a transition to which, in the absence of actions for fault tolerance, a subsequent failure could be attributed;

an *erroneous state* is an internal state which, in the absence of actions for fault tolerance, could lead to a failure by a sequence of valid transitions.

The changes are needed because the success of actions for fault tolerance in averting failure implies that a fault which could be tolerated would not be a fault according to the original definitions.

Acknowledgement. Many of the definitions presented in this paper are an elaboration and modification of those proposed by Melliar-Smith and Randell [3].

References

1. T. Anderson and P. A. Lee, Fault Tolerance: Principles and Practice, Prentice-Hall (1981).
2. A. Avizienis, "Fault-Tolerant Systems", IEEE Transactions on Computers Vol. **C-25** (12), pp. 1304−1312 (1976).
3. P. M. Melliar-Smith and B. Randell, "Software Reliability: The Role of Programmed Exception Handling", Proceedings of Conference on Language Design For Reliable Software, Sigplan Notices. Vol. **12** (3), Raleigh, pp. 95−100 (March 1977). (Also TR 95, Computing Laboratory, University of Newcastle upon Tyne.) (Also Chap. 3)
4. B. Randell, P. A. Lee, and P. C. Treleaven, "Reliability Issues in Computing System Design", Computing Surveys Vol. **10** (2), pp. 123−165 (June 1978).

System Structure for Software Fault Tolerance

B. RANDELL

Abstract. This paper presents and dicusses the rationale behind a method for structuring complex computing systems by the use of what we term "recovery blocks," "conversations," and "fault-tolerant interfaces." The aim is to facilitate the provision of dependable error detection and recovery facilities which can cope with errors caused by residual design inadequacies, particularly in the system software, rather than merely the occasional malfunctioning of hardware components.

Index Terms. Acceptance test, alternate block, checkpoint, conversation, error detection, error recovery, recovery block, recursive cache.

I. Introduction

The concept of "fault-tolerant computing" has existed for a long time. The first book on the subject [10] was published no less than ten years ago, but the notion of fault tolerance has remained almost exclusively the preserve of the hardware designer. Hardware structures have been developed which can "tolerate" faults, i.e., continue to provide the required facilities despite occasional failures, either transient or permanent, of internal components and modules. However, hardware component failures are only one source of unreliability in computing systems, decreasing in significance as component reliability improves, while software faults have become increasingly prevalent with the steadily increasing size and complexity of software systems.

In general, fault-tolerant hardware designs are expected to be correct, i.e., the tolerance applies to component failures rather than design inadequacies, although the dividing line between the two may on occasion be difficult to define. But all software faults result from design errors. The relative frequency of such errors reflects the much greater logical complexity of the typical software design compared to that of a typical hardware design. The difference in complexity arises from the fact that the "machines" that hardware designers produce have a relatively small number of distinctive internal states, whereas the designer of even a small software system has, by comparison, an enormous number of different states to consider — thus one can usually afford to treat hardware designs as being "correct," but often cannot do the same with software even after extensive validation efforts. (The difference in scale is evidenced by the fact that a software simulator of a computer, written at the level of detail required by the hardware designers to analyze and validate their logical design, is usually one or more orders of magnitude smaller than the operating system supplied with that computer.)

14

If all design inadequacies could be avoided or removed this would suffice to achieve software reliability. (We here use the term "design" to include "implementation," which is actually merely low-level design, concerning itself with detailed design decisions whose correctness nevertheless can be as vital to the correct functioning of the software as that of any high-level design decision.) Indeed many writers equate the terms "software reliability" and "program correctness." However, until *reliable* correctness proofs (relative to some correct and adequately detailed specification), which cover even implementation details, can be given for systems of a realistic size, the only alternative means of increasing software reliability is to incorporate provisions for software fault tolerance.

In fact there exist sophisticated computing systems, designed for environments requiring near-continuous service, which contain ad hoc checks and checkpointing facilities that provide a measure of tolerance against some software errors as well as hardware failures [11]. They incidentally demonstrate the fact that fault tolerance does not necessarily require diagnosing the cause of the fault, or even deciding whether it arises from the hardware or the software. However there has been comparatively little specific research into techniques for achieving software fault tolerance, and the constraints they impose on computing system design.

It was considerations such as these that led to the establishment at the University of Newcastle upon Tyne of a project on the design of highly reliable computing systems, under the sponsorship of the Science Research Council of the United Kingdom. The aims of the project were and are "to develop, and give a realistic demonstration of the utility of, computer architecture and programming techniques which will enable a system to have a very high probability of continuing to give a trustworthy service in the presence of hardware faults and/or software errors, and during their repair. A major aim will be to develop techniques which are of general utility, rather than limited to specialised environments, and to explore possible tradeoffs between reliability and performance."

A modest number of reports and papers have emanated from the project to date, including a general overview [12], papers concerned with addressing and protection [6], [7], and a preliminary account of our work on error detection and recovery [5]. The present paper endeavors to provide a rather more extensive discussion of our work on system error recovery techniques, and concentrates on techniques for system structuring which facilitate software fault tolerance. A companion paper [1] presents a proof-guided methodology for designing the error detection routines that our method requires.

II. Fault Tolerance in Software

All fault tolerance must be based on the provision of useful redundancy, both for error detection and error recovery. In software the redundancy required is not simple replication of programs but redundancy of design.

The scheme for facilitating software fault tolerance that we have developed can be regarded as analogous to what hardware designers term "stand-by sparing." As the system operates, checks are made on the acceptability of the results generated by each component. Should one of these checks fail, a spare component is switched in to take the place of the erroneous component. The spare component is, of course, not merely a copy of the main component. Rather it is of independent design, so that there can be hope that it can cope with the circumstances that caused the main component to fail. (These circumstances will comprise the data the component is provided with and, in the case of errors due to faulty process synchronization, the timing and form of its interactions with other processes.)

In contrast to the normal hardware stand-by sparing scheme, the spare software component is invoked to cope with merely the particular set of circumstances that resulted in the failure of the main component. We assume the failure of this component to be due to *residual* design inadequacies, and hence that such failures occur only in exceptional circumstances. The number of different sets of circumstances that can arise even with a software component of comparatively modest size is immense. Therefore the system can revert to the use of the main component for subsequent opertions — in hardware this would not normally be done until the main component had been repaired.

The variety of undetected errors which could have been made in the design of a nontrivial software component is essentially infinite. Due to the complexity of the component, the relationship between any such error and its effect at run time may be very obscure. For these reasons we believe that diagnosis of the original cause of software errors should be left to humans to do, and should be done in comparative leisure. Therefore our scheme for software fault tolerance in no way depends on automated diagnosis of the cause of the error — this would surely result only in greatly increasing the complexity and therefore the error proneness of the system.

The recovery block scheme for achieving software fault tolerance by means of stand-by sparing has two important characteristics.

1) It incorporates a general solution to the problem of switching to the use of the spare component, i.e., of repairing any damage done by the erroneous main component, and of transferring control to the appropriate spare component.

2) It provides a method of explicitly structuring the software system which has the effect of ensuring that the extra software involved in error detection and in the spare components does not add to the complexity of the system, and so reduce rather than increase overall system reliability.

III. Recovery Blocks

Although the basic recovery block scheme has already been described elsewhere [5], it is convenient to include a brief account of it here. We will then describe several extensions to the scheme directed at more complicated situations than the basic scheme was intended for. Thus we start be considering the problems of fault tolerance, i.e., of error detection and recovery, within a single-sequential process in which assignments to stored variables provide the only means of making recognizable progress. Considerations of the problems of communication with other processes, either within the computing system (e.g., by a system of passing messages, or the use of shared storage) or beyond the computing system (e.g., by explicit input—output statements) is deferred until a later section.

The progress of a program is by its execution of sequences of the basic operations of the computer. Clearly, error checking for each basic operation is out of the question. Apart from questions of expense, absence of an awareness of the wider scene would make it difficult to formulate the checks. We must aim at achieving a tolerable quantity of checking and exploit our knowledge of the functional structure of the system to distribute these checks to best advantage. It is standard practice to structure the text of a program of any significant complexity into a set of blocks (by which term we include module, procedure, subroutine, paragraph, etc.) in order to simplify the task of understanding and documenting the program. Such a structure allows one to provide a functional description of the purpose of the program text constituting a block. (This text may of course include calls on subsidiary blocks.) The functional description can then be used elsewhere in place of the detailed design of the block. Indeed, the structuring of the program into blocks, and the specification of the purpose of each block, is likely to precede the detailed design of each block, particularly if the programming is being performed by more than one person.

When executed on a computer, a program which is structured into blocks evokes a process which can be regarded as being structured into operations. Operations are seen to consist of sequences of smaller operations, the smallest operations being those provided by the computer itself. Our scheme of system structuring is based on the selection of a set of these operations to act as units of error detection and recovery, by providing extra information with their corresponding blocks, and so turning the blocks into *recovery blocks*.

The scheme is not dependent on the particular form of block structuring that is used, or the rules governing the scopes of variables, methods of parameter passing, etc. All that is required is that when the program is executed the acts of entering and leaving each operation are explicit, and that operations are properly nested in time. (In addition, although it is not required, considerable advantage can be taken of information which is provided indicating whether any given variable is local to a particular operation.) However, for convenience of presentation, we will assume that the program text is itself represented by a nested structure of Algol or PL/I-style blocks.

A recovery block consists of a conventional block which is provided with a means of error detection (an acceptance test) and zero or more stand-by spares (the additional alternates). A possible syntax for recovery blocks is as follows.

17

⟨recovery block⟩ ::= **ensure** ⟨acceptance test⟩ **by**

⟨primary alternate⟩

⟨other alternates⟩ **else error**

⟨primary alternate⟩ ::= ⟨alternate⟩

⟨other alternates⟩ ::= ⟨empty⟩ | ⟨other alternates⟩

else by ⟨alternate⟩

⟨alternate⟩ ::= ⟨statement list⟩

⟨acceptance test⟩ ::= ⟨logical expression⟩

The *primary alternate* corresponds exactly to the block of the equivalent conventional program, and is entered to perform the desired operation. The *acceptance test*, which is a logical expression without side effects, is evaluated on exit from any alternate to determine whether the alternate has performed acceptably. A further *alternate*, if one exists, is entered if the preceding alternate fails to complete (e.g., because it attempts to divide by zero, or exceeds a time limit), or fails the acceptance test. However *before an alternate is so entered, the state of the process is restored* to that current just before entry to the primary alternate. If the acceptance test is passed, any further alternates are ignored, and the statement following the recovery block is the next to be executed. However, if the last alternate fails to pass the acceptance test, then the entire recovery block is regarded as failed, so that the block in which it is embedded fails to complete and recovery is then attempted at that level.

In the illustration of a recovery block structure in Fig. 1, double vertical lines define the extents of recovery blocks, while single vertical lines define the extents of alternate blocks, primary or otherwise. Figure 2 shows that the alternate blocks can contain, nested within themselves, further recovery blocks.

Consider the recovery block structure shown in Fig. 2. The acceptance test *BT* will be invoked on completion of primary alternate *BP*. If the test succeeds, the recovery block *B* is left and the program text immediately following is reached. Otherwise the state of the system is reset and alternate *BQ* is entered. If *BQ* and then *BR* do not succeed in passing the acceptance test the recovery block *B* as a whole, and therefore primary alternate *AP*, are regarded as having failed. Therefore the state of the system is reset even further, to that current just before entry to *AP*, and alternate *AQ* is attempted.

Deferring for the moment questions as to how the state of the system is reset when necessary, the recovery block structure can be seen as providing a very general framework for the use of stand-by sparing which is in full accordance with the characteristics discussed earlier, in Sect. II. There is no need for, indeed no possibility of, attempts at automated error diagnosis because of the fact that the system state is reset after an error, deleting all effects of the faulty alternate. Once the system state is reset, switching to the use of an alternate is merely a matter of a simple transfer of control.

The concept of a recovery block in fact has much in common with that of a sphere of control, as described by Davies [2]. However, we have limited our-

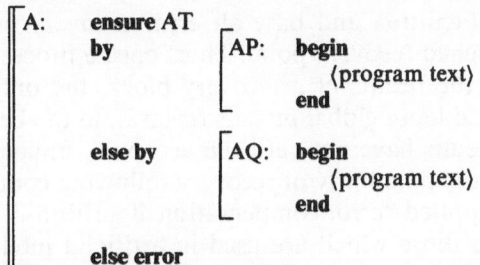

Fig. 1. Simple recovery block

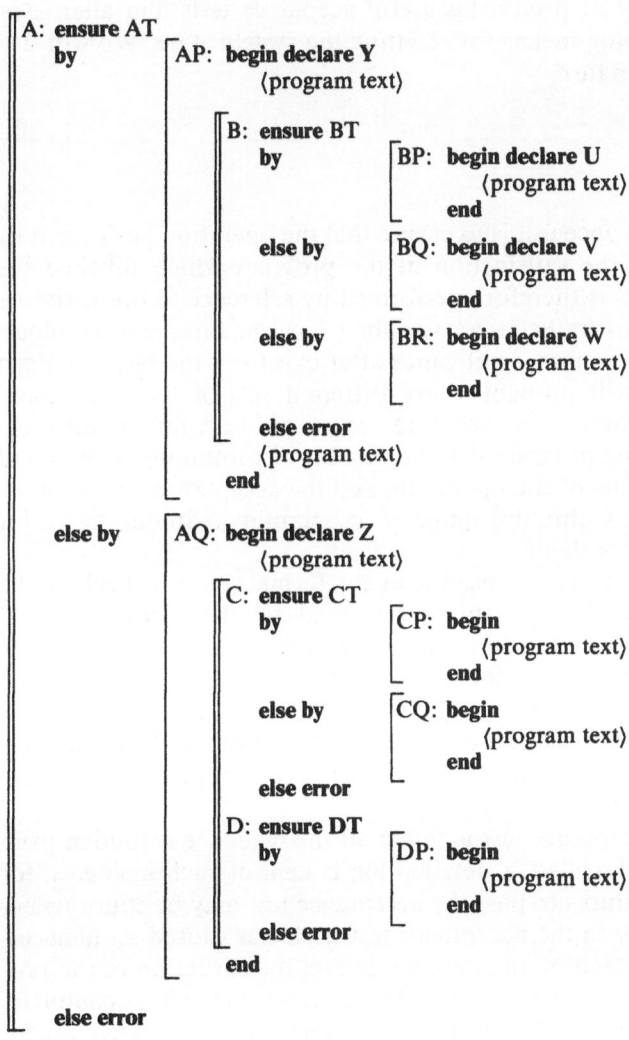

Fig. 2. More complex recovery block

19

selves to preplanned error recovery facilities, and base all error recovery on automatic reversal to a previously reached recovery point. Thus, once a process has "committed" itself by accepting the results of a recovery block, the only form of recovery we envisage involves a more global process reversal, to the beginning of a recovery block whose results have not yet been accepted. In contrast, Davies is prepared to allow for the possibility of recovery following commitment, by means of programmer-supplied "error compensation algorithms."

Although the scheme is related to those which are used in artificial intelligence-type back-tracking programs [4], there are major differences − in our scheme back up, being caused by residual design inadequacies, occurs very infrequently and is due to unforeseeable circumstances, rather than very frequently and as an essential element of the basic algorithm.

The utility of the recovery block scheme for stand-by sparing in software rests on the practicability of producing useful aceptance tests and alternates, and on the cost of providing means for resetting the system state. We will discuss each of these points in turn.

A. Acceptance Tests

The function of the acceptance test is to ensure that the operation performed by the recovery block is to the satisfaction of the program which invoked the block. The acceptance test is therefore performed by reference to the variables accessible to that program, rather than variables local to the recovery block, since these can have no effect or significance after exit from the block. Indeed the different alternates will probably have different sets of local variables. There is no question of there being separate acceptance tests for the different alternates. The surrounding program may be capable of continuing with any of a number of possible results of the operation, and the acceptance test must establish that the results are within this range of acceptability, without regard for which alternate can generate them.

There is no requirement that the test be, in any formal sense, a check on the absolute "correctness" of the operation performed by the recovery block. Rather it is for the designer to decide upon the appropriate level of rigor of the test. Ideally the test will ensure that the recovery block has met all aspects of its specification that are depended on by the program text that calls it − in practice, if only for reasons of cost and/or complexity, something less than this might have to suffice. (A methodological approach to the design of appropriate acceptance test is described by Anderson [1].)

Although when an acceptance test is failed all the evidence is hidden from the alternate which is then called, a detailed log is kept of such incidents, for off-line analysis. Some failures to pass the acceptance test may be spurious because a design inadequacy in the acceptance test itself has caused an unnecessary rejection of the operation of an alternate. In fact the execution of the program of the acceptance test itself might suffer an error and fail to complete. Such occurrences, which hopefully will be rare since the aim is to have acceptance tests which are much simpler than the alternates they check, are treated as

```
ensure sorted (S) ∧ (sum (S) = sum (prior S))
by quickersort (S)
else by quicksort (S)
else by bubblesort (S)
else error
```

Fig. 3. Fault-tolerant sort program

failures in the enclosing block. Like all other failures they are also recorded in the error log. Thus the log provides a means of finding these two forms of inadequacy in the design of the acceptance test − the remaining form of inadequacy, that which causes the acceptance of an incorrect set of results, is of course more difficult to locate.

When an acceptance test is being evaluated, any nonlocal variables that have been modified must be available in their original as well as their modified form because of the possible need to reset the system state. For convenience and increased rigor, the acceptance test is enabled to access such variables either for their modified value or for their original (prior) value. One further facility available inside an acceptance test will be a means of checking whether any of the variables that have been modified have not yet been accessed within the acceptance test − this is intended to assist in detecting sins of commission, as well as omission, on the part of the alternate.

Figure 3 shows a recovery block whose intent is to sort the elements of the vector S. The acceptance test incorporates a check that the set of items in S after operation of an alternate are indeed in order. However, rather than incur the cost of checking that these elements are a permutation of the original items, it merely requires the sum of the elements to remain the same.

B. Alternates

The primary alternate is the one which is intended to be used normally to perform the desired operation. Other alternates might attempt to perform the desired operation in some different manner, presumably less economically, and preferably more simply. Thus as long as one of these alternates succeeds the desired operation will have been completed, and only the error log will reveal any troubles that occurred.

However in many cases one might have an alternate which performs a less desirable operation, but one which is still acceptable to the enclosing block in that it will allow the block to continue properly. (One plentiful source of both these kinds of alternates might be earlier releases of the primary alternate!)

Figure 4 shows a recovery block consisting of a variety of alternates. (This figure is taken from Anderson [1].) The aim of the recovery block is to extend the sequence S of items by a further item i, but the enclosing program will be able to continue even if afterwards S is merely "consistent." The first two alternates actually try, by different methods, to join the item i onto the sequence S. The other alternates make increasingly desperate attempts to produce at least some sort of consistent sequence, providing appropriate warnings as they do so.

21

```
ensure consistent sequences (S)
by      extend S with (i)
else by concatenate to S (construct sequence (i))
else by warning ("lost item")
else by S := construct sequence (i); warning (correction, "lost sequence")
else by S := empty sequence; warning ("lost sequence and item")
else error
```

Fig. 4. Recovery block with alternates which achieve different, but still acceptable though less desirable, results

C. Restoring the System State

By making the resetting of the system state completely automatic, the programmers responsible for designing acceptance tests and alternates are shielded from the problems of this aspect of error recovery. No special restrictions are placed on the operations which are performed within the alternates, on the calling of procedures or the modification of global variables, and no special programming conventions have to be adhered to. In particular the error-prone task of explicit preservation of restart information is avoided. It is thus that the recovery block structure provides a framework which enables extra program text to be added to a conventional program, for purposes of specifying error detection and recovery actions, with good reason to believe that despite the increase in the total size of the program its overall reliability will be increased.

All this depends on being able to find a method of automating the resetting of the system state whose overheads are tolerable. Clearly, taking a copy of the entire system state on entry to each recovery block, though in theory satisfactory, would in normal practice be far too inefficient. Any method involving the saving of sufficient information during program execution for the program to be executable in reverse, instruction by instruction, would be similarly impractical.

Whenever a process has to be backed up, it is to the state it had reached just before entry to the primary alternate — therefore the only values that have to be reset are those of nonlocal variables that have been modified. Since no explicit restart information is given, it is not known beforehand which nonlocal variables should be saved. Therefore we have designed various versions of a mechanism which arranges that nonlocal variables are saved in what we term a "recursive cache" as and when it is found that this is necessary, i.e., just before they are modified. The mechanisms do this by detecting, at run time, assignments to nonlocal variables, and in particular by recognizing when an assignment to a nonlocal variable is the first to have been made to that variable within the current alternate. Thus precisely sufficient information can be preserved.

The recursive cache is divided into regions, one for each nested recovery level, i.e., for each recovery block that has been entered and not yet left. The entries in the current cache region will contain the prior values of any variables that have been modified within the current recovery block, and thus in case of

22

failure it can be used to back up the process to its most recent recovery point. The region will be discarded in its entirety after it has been used for backing up a process. However if the recovery block is completed successfully, some cache entries will be discarded, but those that relate to variables which are nonlocal to the enclosing environment will be consolidated with those in the underlying region of the cache.

A full description of one version of the mechanism has already been published [5], so we will not repeat this description here. We envisage that the mechanism would be at least partly built in hardware, at any rate if, as we have assumed here, recovery blocks are to be provided within ordinary programs working on small data items such as scalar variables. If however one were programming solely in terms of operations on large blocks of data, such as entire arrays or files, the overheads caused by a mechanism built completely from software would probably be supportable. Indeed the recursive cache scheme, which is essentially a means for secretly preventing what is sometimes termed "update in place," can be viewed as a generalization of the facility in CAP's "middleware" scheme [11] for preventing individual application programs from destructively updating files.

The various recursive cache mechanisms can all work in terms of the basic unit of assignment of the computer, e.g., a 32-bit word. Thus they ensure that just those scalar variables and array elements which are actually modified are saved. It would of course be possible to structure a program so that all its variables are declared in the outermost block, and within each recovery block each variable is modified, and so require that a maximum amount of information be saved. In practice we believe that even a moderately well-structured program will require comparatively little space for saved variables. Measurements of space requirements will be made on the prototype system now being implemented, but already we have some evidence for this from some simple experiments carried out by interpretively executing a number of Algol W programs. Even regarding each Algol block as a recovery block it was found that the amount of extra space that would be needed for saved scalar variables and array elements was in every case considerably smaller at all times than that needed for the ordinary data of the program.

The performance overheads of the different recursive cache mechanisms are in the process of being evaluated. Within a recovery block only the speed of store instructions is affected, and once a particular nonlocal variable has been saved subsequent stores to that variable take place essentially at full speed. The overheads involved in entering and leaving recovery blocks differ somewhat between the various mechanisms, but two mechanisms incur overheads which depend just linearly on the number of different nonlocal variables which are modified. It is our assessment that these overheads will also be quite modest. Certainly it would appear that the space and time overheads incurred by our mechanisms will be far smaller than would be incurred by any explicitly programmed scheme for saving and restoring the process state.

IV. Error Recovery Amongst Interacting Processes

In the mechanism described so far, the only notion of forward progress is that of assignment to a variable. In order to reset the state of a process after the failure of an acceptance test, it was necessary only to undo assignments to nonlocal variables. In practice, however, there are many other ways of making forward progress during computations, e.g., positioning a disk arm or magnetic tape, reading a card, printing a line, receiving a message, or obtaining real-time data from external sensors. These actions are difficult or even impossible to undo. However, their effects must be undone in order not to compromise the inherent "recoverability" of state provided by the recursive cache mechanisms.

Our attempts to cope with this kind of problem is based on the observation that all such forms of progress involve interaction among processes. In some cases, one or more of these processes may be mechanical, human, or otherwise external, e.g., the process representing the motion of the card-reading machinery. In other cases, the progress can be encapsulated in separate but interacting computational processes, each of which is structured by recovery blocks. In this section, we will explore the effect of this latter type of interaction on the backtracking scheme, still restricting each process to simple assignment as the only method of progress. Then in Section V we will explore the more general problem.

Consider first the case of two or more interacting processes which have the requirement that if one attempts to recover from an error, then the others must also take recovery action, "to keep in step."

For example, if one process fails after having received, and destroyed, information from another process, it will require the other process to resupply this information. Similarly, a process may have received and acted upon information subsequently discovered to have been sent to it in error and so must abandon its present activity.

Maintaining, naturally, our insistence on the dangers of attempted programmed error diagnosis, we must continue to rely on automatic backing up of processes to the special recovery points provided by recovery block entries. Each process while executing will at any moment have a sequence of recovery points available to it, the number of recovery points being given by the level of dynamic nesting of recovery blocks.

An isolated process could "use up" recovery points just one at a time by suffering a whole series of ever more serious errors. However given an arbitrary set of interacting processes, each with its own private recovery structure, a single error on the part of just one process could cause *all* the processes to use up many or even all of their recovery points, through a sort of uncontrolled domino effect.

The problem is illustrated in Fig. 5, which shows three processes, each of which has entered four recovery blocks that it has not yet left. The dotted lines indicate interactions between processes (i.e., an information flow resulting in an assignment in at least one process). Should Process 1 now fail, it will be backed up to its latest, i.e., its fourth recovery point, but the other processes will not be affected. If Process 2 fails, it will be backed up to its fourth recovery point past

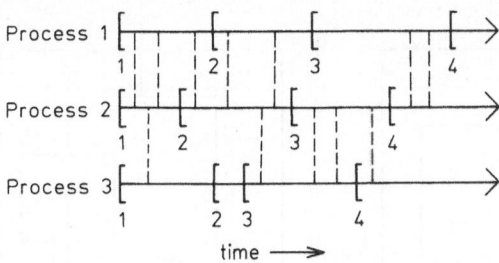

Process 1

Process 2

Process 3

time ⟶

Fig. 5. Domino effect

an interaction with Process 1, which must therefore also be backed up to the recovery point immediately prior to this interaction, i.e., its third recovery point. However if Process 3 fails, all the processes will have to be backed up right to their starting points!

The domino effect can occur when two particular circumstances exist in combination.

1) The recovery block structures of the various processes are uncoordinated, and take no account of process interdependencies caused by their interactions.

2) The processes are symmetrical with respect to failure propagation — either member of any pair of interacting processes can cause the other to back up.

By removing either of these circumstances, one can avoid the danger of the domino effect. Our technique of structuring process interactions into "conversations," which we describe next, is a means of dealing with point 1) above; the concept of multilevel processes, described in Section V of this paper, will be seen to be based on avoiding symmetry of failure propagation.

A. Process Conversations

If we are to provide guaranteed recoverability of a set of processes which by interacting have become mutually dependent on each other's progress, we must arrange that the processes cooperate in the provision of recovery points, as well as in the interchange of ordinary information. To extend the basic recovery block scheme to a set of interacting processes, we have to provide a means for coordinating the recovery block structures of the various processes, in effect to provide a recovery structure which is common to the set of processes. This structure we term a *conversation.*

Conversations, like recovery blocks, can be thought of as providing firewalls (in both time and space) which serve to limit the damage caused to a system by errors. Figure 6 represents this view of a recovery block as providing a firewall for a single process. The downward pointing arrow represents the overall progress of the process. The top edge of the recovery block represents the environment of the process on entry, which is preserved automatically and can be restored for the use of an alternate block. The bottom edge represents the acceptable state of the process on exit from the recovery block, as checked by the

25

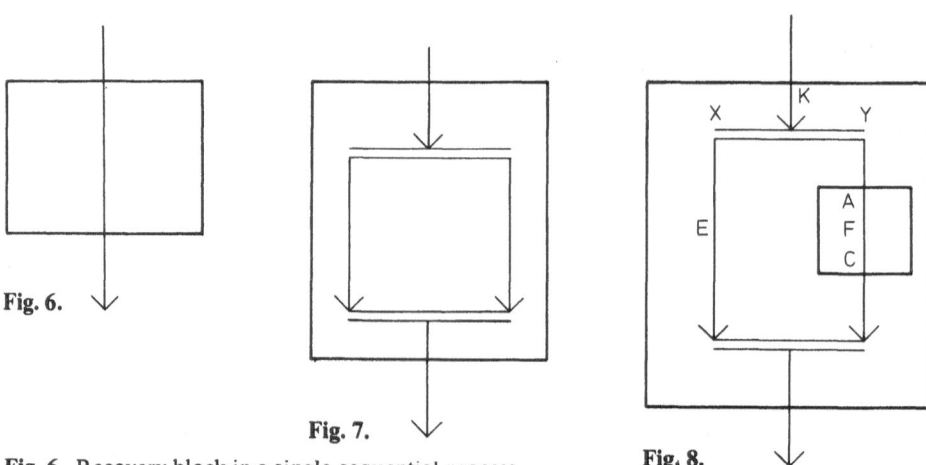

Fig. 6.

Fig. 7.

Fig. 8.

Fig. 6. Recovery block in a single-sequential process

Fig. 7. Parallel processes within a recovery block

Fig. 8. Parallel processes within a recovery block, with a further recovery block for one of the processes. Interaction between the processes at points *E* and *F* must now be prohibited

acceptance test, and beyond which it is assumed that errors internal to the recovery block should not propagate. (Of course the strength of this firewall is only as good as the rigour of the acceptance test.) The sides show that the process is isolated from other activities, i.e., that the process is not subject to external influences which cannot be recreated automatically for an alternate, and that it does not generate any results which cannot be suppressed should the acceptance test be failed. (These side firewalls are provided by some perhaps quite conventional protection mechanism, to complement the top and bottom firewalls provided by the recursive cache mechanism and acceptance test.)

The manner in which the processing is performed within the recovery block is of no concern outside it, provided that the acceptance test is satisfied. For instance, as shown in Fig. 7, the process may divide into several parallel processes within the recovery block. The recursive cache mechanisms that we have developed permit this, and place no constraints on the manner in which this parallelism is expressed, or on the means of communication between these parallel processes.

Any of the parallel processes could of course enter a further recovery block, as shown in Fig. 8. However, by doing so it must lose the ability to communicate with other processes for the duration of its recovery block. To see this, consider the consequences of an interaction between the processes at points *E* and *F*. Should process *Y* now fail its acceptance test it would resume at point *A* with an alternate block. But there is no way of causing process *X* to repeat the interaction at *E* without backing up both processes to the entry to their common recovery block at *K*. Thus communication, whether it involve explicit message passing facilities, or merely reference to common variables, would destroy the value of the inner recovery block, and hence must be prohibited.

A recovery block which spans two or more processes as is shown in Fig. 9 is termed a conversation. Two or more processes which already possess the means

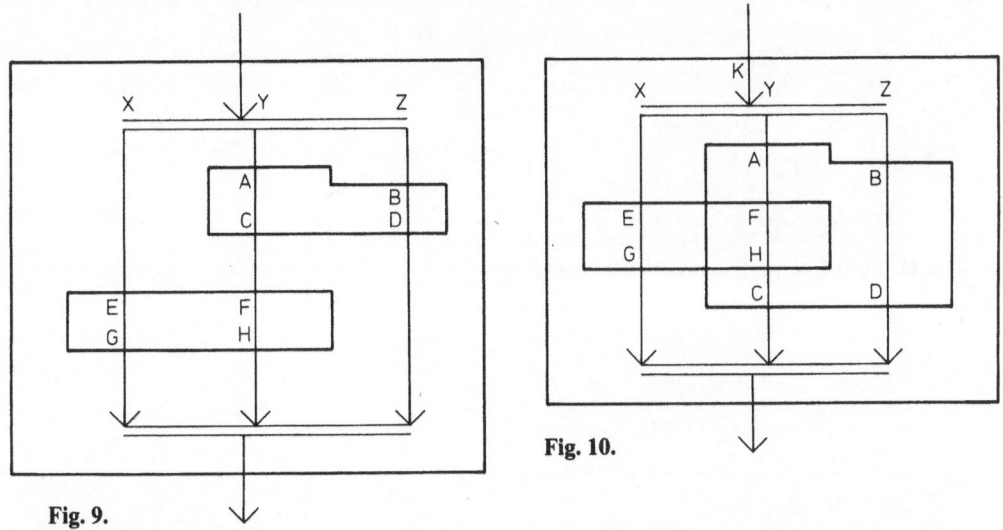

Fig. 9.

Fig. 10.

Fig. 9. Parallel processes with conversations which provide recovery blocks for local communication

Fig. 10. Example of invalid conversations which are not strictly nested

of communicating with each other may agree to enter into a conversation. Within the conversation these processes may communicate freely between themselves, but may not communicate with any other processes. At the end of the conversation *all the processes must satisfy their respective acceptance tests and none may proceed until all have done so.* Should any process fail, all the processes must automatically be backed up to the start of the conversation to attempt their alternates.

As is shown in Fig. 9, it is possible that the processes enter a conversation at differing times. However all processes must leave the conversation together, since no process dare discard its recovery point until all processes have satisfied their respective acceptance tests. In entering a conversation a process does not gain the ability to communicate with any process with which it was previously unable to communicate — rather, entry to a conversation serves only to restrict communication, in the interests of error recovery.

As with recovery blocks, conversations can of course occur within other conversations, so as to provide additional possibilities for error detection and recovery. However conversations which intersect and are not strictly nested cannot be allowed. Thus structures such as that shown in Fig. 10 must be prohibited, as can be demonstrated by an argument similar to that given in relation to Fig. 8.

V. Multilevel Systems

We turn now to a method of structuring systems which uses assymetrical failure propagation in order to avoid the uncontrolled domino effect described in

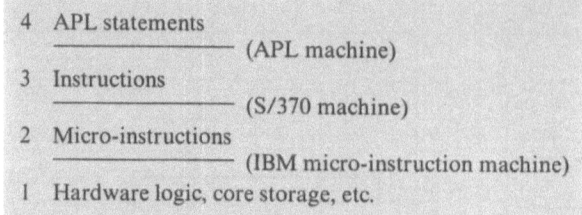

```
4   APL statements
    ───────────────────── (APL machine)
3   Instructions
    ───────────────────── (S/370 machine)
2   Micro-instructions
    ───────────────────── (IBM micro-instruction machine)
1   Hardware logic, core storage, etc.
```

Fig. 11. Fully interpretive multilevel system

8	User Program
7	Access Methods
6	Logical File System
5	Basic File System
4	File Organisation Strategy Modules
3	Device Strategy Modules
2	Input/Output Control System
1	Central Processor, Peripheral Devices, etc.

Fig. 12. Multilevel file system interpretive only at level 1 (see Madnick and Alsop [8])

Sect. IV. In so doing we extend the scope of our discussions to cover more complex means of making recognizable progress than simple assignments. Moreover, we also face for the first time the possibility of reliability problems arising from facilities used to provide the means of constructing and executing processes and of using recovery blocks and conversations. The method of structuring which permits these extensions of our facilities for fault tolerance involves the use of what we (and others) term multilevel systems.

A multilevel system is characterized by the existence of a sequence of defined "abstract" or "virtual" machines which denote the internal interfaces between the various levels. A given virtual machine provides a set of apparently atomic facilities (operations, objects, resources, etc.). These can be used to construct the set of facilities that constitute a further (higher) virtual machine interface, possibly of a very different appearance. Each virtual machine is therefore an abstraction of the virtual machine below it. Since we are concerning ourselves with computer systems, we in general expect each virtual machine to have the characteristics of a programmable computer. Thus it is capable of executing a program that specifies which operations are to be applied to which operands, and their sequencing.

Our use of the term virtual machine is quite general. In particular our concept of multilevel systems includes systems whose levels are entirely different from each other (as in Fig. 11) as well as systems whose levels have much in common with each other (as in Fig. 12), for example being constructed by applying a protection scheme on a single computer. However, in each case the operations that a given virtual machine provides can be regarded as atomic at the level above it and as implemented by the activity of the level immediately below the virtual machine interface. Thus from the viewpoint of level i of the system in Fig. 12, the whole of the file accessing operation is performed by level 7. Indeed even the operation of addition, and the whole process of instruction fetching and decoding, can be regarded as being provided by level 7. This is the case no matter which actual level below level 7 is in fact responsible for the construction of these facilities out of more basic ones.

Some virtual machine interfaces allow the facilities they provide to be used without much, or even any, knowledge of the underlying structures used to construct these facilities. Virtual machine interfaces which have this characteristic can be termed *opaque* interfaces. Such virtual machine interfaces are total (in the sense that a mathematical function which is defined for all possible arguments is total) and have associated documentation which completely defines the interface. Being total and completely documented are necessary rather than sufficient conditions for a virtual machine interface to be usefully opaque, a characteristic which only well-chosen ones possess in any great measure, but this is a subject which we will not pursue further here.

Opaque virtual machine interfaces facilitate the understanding of existing complex systems, and the design of new ones. They do this by enabling the complexity of the system to be divided and conquered, so that no single person or group of persons has to master all the details of the design. They can therefore in themselves contribute to the overall reliability of a system, by simplifying the tasks of its designers. However, if design errors are made, or operational failures of physical components occur, it will be found that existing methods of constructing opaque virtual machine interfaces are somewhat inadequate. The sought-after opacity of the interface will in many cases be lost, since error recovery (either manual or predesigned) will need an understanding of two or more levels of the system. Hence our interest in providing facilities for tolerating faults, including those due to design errors, which can be used by designers whose detailed understanding of the system is limited to that of a single level and the two virtual machine interfaces that bound it. (A very different approach to these problems, based on the use of programmer-supplied error diagnosis and recovery code, has been described by Parnas [9].)

All this presupposes that the virtual machine interfaces have some physical realization in the operational system. Conceptual levels, though of value during system design and in providing documentation of the behavior of a reliable system, typically play no part in failure situations — for example the levels in the THE system [3] have no relevance to the problem of coping with, say, an actual memory parity error. The actual physical realization in existing multilevel systems can vary widely — from, for example, the provision of physically separate storage and highways for microprograms and programs, to the use of a single control bit to distinguish between supervisor and user modes of instruction execution. What we now describe are additional general characteristics and facilities that we believe any such physical realization of a virtual machine interface should possess in order to support our techniques for system fault tolerance.

A. Errors Above a Virtual Machine Interface

Everything that appears to happen in a given level is in fact the result of activity for which the level below is (directly or indirectly) responsible. This applies not only to the ordinary operations performed at a level but also to any recovery actions which might be required. Consider for example a level i which uses our recovery block scheme to provide itself with some measure of fault tolerance, and which makes recognizable progress by means of simple assignment statements. Then it is level $i-1$ which is responsible not only for the actual assignments, but also for any saving of prior values of variables and reinstatement of them when required.

Similarly, if the virtual machine which supports level i includes any more exotic operations which change the system state as seen by level i, e.g., magnetic tape rewind, then level $i-1$ will have the responsibility of undoing their effects, e.g., repositioning the tape (whether level $i-1$ undertakes this responsibility itself, or instead delegates it to level $i-2$ is irrelevant).

Provided that level $i-1$ fulfills its responsibilities level i can thus assume that error detection will automatically be followed by a return to the most recent recovery point. This will occur whether the detection of a level i error occurs at level i itself (e.g., by means of an acceptance test) or below level i because of incorrect use by level i of one of the operations provided to it by level $i-1$ (e.g., division by zero).

It should be noted that both progress and fall back, as recognizable in the level above a virtual machine interface, are provided by progress on the level below, i.e., the level $i-1$ keeps going forwards, or at least tries to, even if it is doing so in order to enable level i to (appear to) go backwards.

For example, level i might read cards from an "abstract card reader" while level $i-1$ actually implements this abstract card reader by means of spooling. When level i encounters an error and tries to go backwards, it must appear to "unread" the cards read during the current recovery block. But level $i-1$ implements this "unreading" by merely resetting a pointer in its school buffer — a positive or forward action on its part.

All this assumes level $i-1$ is trouble free — what we must now discuss are the complications caused by level $i-1$ being unable, for various reasons, to maintain its own progress, and in particular that progress on which level i is relying.

B. Errors Below a Virtual Machine Interface

Needless to say, the programs which provide a virtual machine interface can themselves, if appropriate, incorporate recovery blocks for the purpose of local error detection and recovery. Thus when level $i-1$ makes a mistake, which is detected, while performing some operation for level i, if an alternate block manages to succeed where the primary alternate had failed the operation can nevertheless be completed. In such circumstances the program at level i need never know that any error occurred. (For example, a user process may be unaware that the operating system had to make several attempts before it succeeded in reading a magnetic tape on behalf of the user process.) But if all the alternates of the outermost recovery block of the level *i-1* program performing an operation for level *i* fail, so that the recovery capability at level *i-1* is exhausted, then the operation must be rejected and recovery action undertaken at level *i*.

This case of an error detected at level *i-1* forcing level *i* back to a recovery point in order to undertake some alternative action is very similar to the one mentioned earlier in Section V-A — namely that of an error detected at level *i-1*, but stemming from the incorrect use of an operation by level *i*. The error log which is produced for later offline analysis will indicate the difference between the two cases, but this information (leave alone further information which might be needed for diagnostic purposes) will not be available at level *i*.

The situation is much more serious if level *i-1* errs, and exhausts any recovery capability it might have, whilst performing an inverse operation on behalf of level *i*, i.e., fails to complete the act of undoing the effects of one or more operations that level *i* has used to modify its state. This possibility might seem rather small when the inverse operation is merely that of resetting the prior value of a scalar variable. However when an inverse operation is quite complex (e.g., one that involves undoing the changes a process has caused to be made to complicated data structures in a large filing system) one might have to cope with residual design inadequacies, as well as the ever-present possibility of hardware failure.

When an inverse operation cannot be completed, the level *i* cannot be backed up, so it has to be abandoned. This is perhaps the most subtle cause for level *i-1* to abandon further attempts to execute a level *i* process — more familiar ones include the sudden inability of level *i-1* to continue fetching and decoding level *i* instructions, locating level *i* operands, etc., either because of level *i-1*'s own inadequacy, or that of the level *i-2* machine on which it depends. (For example, level 3 of Fig. 11, the APL interpreter, might find that the file in which it keeps the APL program belonging to a particular user was unreadable, a fault which perhaps was first detected at level 2, by the microprogram).

There is one other important class of errors detected below a virtual machine interface which can be dealt with without necessarily abandoning level *i*, the level above the interface. After level *i* has passed an acceptance test, but before all the information constituting its recovery point has been discarded, there is the chance for level *i-1* to perform any checking that is needed on the overall acceptability, in level *i-1* terms, of the sequence of operations that have been carried out for level *i*.

For example, level *i* may have been performing operations which were, as far as it was concerned, disk storage operations. Level *i-1* could in fact have buffered the information so stored. Before the present level of fall back capability of level *i* is discarded, level *i-1* may wish to ensure that the information has been written to disk and checked. If level *i-1* finds that it cannot ensure this, but instead encounters some problem from which it itself is unable to recover, then it can in essence cause level *i* to fail, and to fall back and attempt an alternate. This will be in the hope that whatever problem it was that level *i-1* got into (on behalf of level *i*) this time, next time the sequence of operations that level *i* requests will manage to get dealt with to the satisfaction of level *i-1* as well as of level *i*.

In fact an intersting example of this case of level *i-1* inducing a failure in level *i* occurs in the mechanization of conversations. Consider a level *i* process which is involved in a conversation with some other level *i* process and which after completing its primary alternate satisfies is acceptance test. At this moment level *i-1* must determine whether the other process has also completed its primary alternate and passed its acceptance test. If necessary the process must be suspended until the other process has been completed, as discussed in Section IV-A. If the other process should fail, then the first process must also be forced to back up just as if it had failed its own acceptance test even though it had in fact passed it.

C. Fault-Tolerant Virtual Machine Interfaces

We have so far discussed the problems of failures above and below a virtual machine interface quite separately. In fact, except for the highest level and the one that we choose to regard as the lowest level, every level is of course simultaneously below one virtual machine interface and above another such interface. Therefore each interface has the responsibility for organizing the interaction between two potentially unreliable levels in a multilevel system. The aim is to embody *within the interface* all the rules about interaction across levels that we have been describing, and so simplify the task of designing the levels on either side of the interface.

If this can be done then it will be possible to design levels which are separated by opaque virtual machine interfaces independently of each other, even in the case where the possibility of failures is admitted. By enabling the design of error recovery facilities to be considered separately for different levels of the system, in the knowledge that the fault-tolerant interface will arrange their proper interaction, their design should be greatly simplified — a very important consideration if error recovery facilities in complex systems are to be really relied upon.

Various different kinds of virtual machine interfaces are provided in current multilevel systems. These range from an interface which involves complete interpretation (e.g., the APL machine interface in Fig. 11 and the lowest inferface in Fig. 12), to one where many of the basic facilities provided above the interface are in fact the same as those made available to the level immediately below the interface by some yet lower virtual machine interface (e.g., the other interfaces in Fig. 12). These latter kinds of interface, because of their performance characteristics, can be expected to predominate in systems which have many levels — in theory the multilevel file system (Fig. 12) could be built using a hierarchy of complete interpreters, but this is of course wildly impractical.

It is not appropriate within the confines of this already lengthy paper to give a fully detailed description of even a single kind, leave alone the various different kinds, of fault-tolerant virtual machine interface. However we have attempted, with Fig. 13, to show the main features of a fault-tolerant interface of the complete interpreter kind. For purposes of comparison, Fig. 14 shows the equivalent interface in a conventional complete interpreter.

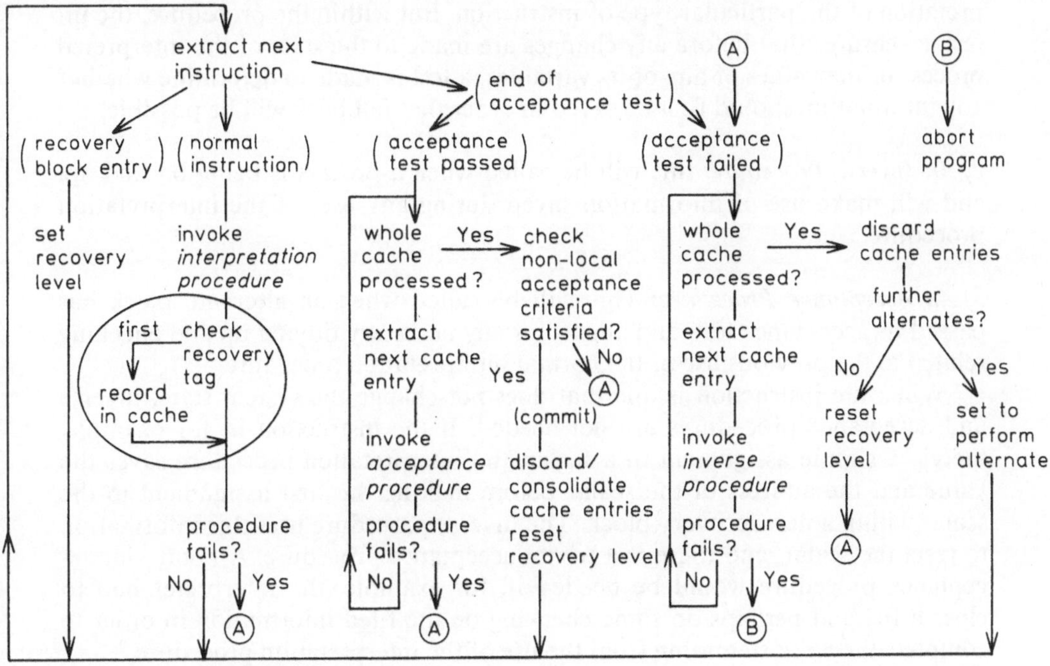

extract next
instruction

(A)   (B)

recovery
block entry   normal
instruction   end of
acceptance test   acceptance
test passed   dcceptance
test failed   abort
program

set
recovery
level   invoke
*interpretation
procedure*   whole
cache
processed?   Yes   check
non-local
acceptance
criteria
satisfied?   whole
cache
processed?   Yes   discard
cache entries

first   check
recovery
tag   extract
next cache
entry   Yes   extract
next cache
entry   further
alternates?

record
in cache   No   (A)   No   Yes

(commit)   invoke
*inverse
procedure*   reset
recovery
level   set to
perform
alternate

invoke
*acceptance
procedure*   discard/
consolidate
cache entries
reset
recovery level

procedure
fails?   procedure
fails?   procedure
fails?   procedure
fails?

No   Yes   No   Yes   No   Yes   No   Yes

(A)   (A)   (B)   (A)

Fig. 13. Fault-tolerant interpreter

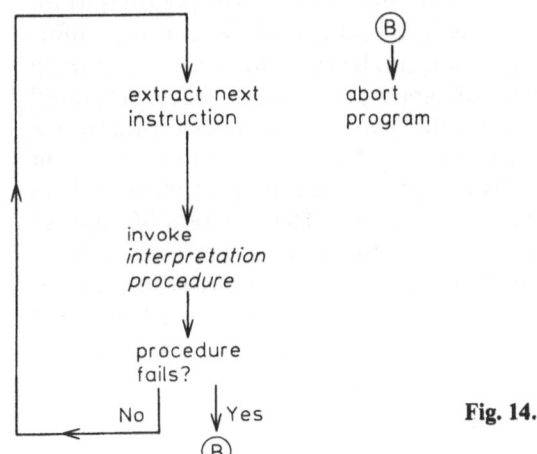

(B)

extract next
instruction   abort
program

invoke
*interpretation
procedure*

procedure
fails?

No   Yes

(B)

Fig. 14. Conventional interpreter

The basic difference between a fault-tolerant interpreter and a conventional interpreter is that, for each different type of instruction to be interpreted, the fault tolerant interpreter, in general, provides a set of three related procedures rather than just a single procedure. The three procedures are as follows.

1) An Interpretation Procedure: This is basically the same as the single procedure provided in a conventional interpreter, and provides the normal interpretation of the particular type of instruction. But within the procedure, the interface ensures that before any changes are made to the state of the interpreted process or the values of any of its variables, a test is made to determine whether any information should first be saved in order that fall back will be possible.

2) An Inverse Procedure: this will be called when a process is being backed up, and will make use of information saved during any uses of the interpretation procedure.

3) An Acceptance Procedure: This will be called when an alternate block has passed its acceptance test, and allows for any necessary tidying up and checking related to the previous use of the normal interpretation procedure.

When the instruction is one that does not change the system state, inverse and acceptance procedures are not needed. If the instruction is, for example, merely a simple assignment to a scalar, the interpretation procedure saves the value and the address of the scalar before making the first assignment to the scalar within a new recovery block. The inverse procedure uses this information to reset the scalar, and there is a trivial acceptance procedure. A nontrivial acceptance procedure would be needed if, for example, the interpreter had to close a file and perhaps do some checking on the filed information in order to complete the work stemming from the use of the interpretation procedure.

A generalization of the recursive cache, as described in Sect. III-C, is used to control the invocation of inverse and acceptance procedures. The cache records the descriptors for the inverse and acceptance procedures corresponding to interpretation procedures that have been executed and caused system state information to be saved. Indeed each cache region can be thought of as containing a linear "program," rather than just a set of saved prior values. The "program" held in the current cache region indicates the sequence of inverse procedures calls that are to be "executed" in order to back up the process to its most recent recovery point. (If the process passes its acceptance test the procedure calls in the "program" act as calls on acceptance procedures.) The program of inverse/ acceptance calls is initially null, but grows as the process performs actions which add to the task of backing it up. As with the basic recursive cache mechanism, the cache region will be discarded in its entirety after it has been used for backing up a process. Similarly, if the recovery block or conversation is completed successfully, some entries will be discarded, but those that relate to variables which are nonlocal to the enclosing environment will be consolidated with the existing "program" in the underlying region of the cache.

This then is a very brief account, ignoring various simple but important "mere optimizations," of the main characteristics of a failure-tolerant virtual machine interface of the complete interpreter kind. Being so closely related to the basic recursive cache mechanism, it will perhaps be most readily appreciated by people who are already familiar with the published description [5] of the detailed functioning of one recursive cache mechanism.

VI. Conclusions

The techniques for structuring fault-tolerant systems which we have described have been designed especially for faults arising from design errors, such as are at present all too common in complex software systems. However we believe they are also of potential applicability to hardware and in particular allow the various operational faults that hardware can suffer from to be treated as simple special cases. In fact the techniques we have sketched for fault tolerance in multilevel systems would appear to provide an appropriate means of integrating provisions for hardware reconfiguration into the overall structure of the system. Indeed as a general approach to the structuring of a complex activity where the possibility of errors is to be considered, there seems to be no *a priori* reason why the structuring should not extend past the confines of the computer system. Thus, as others have previously remarked [2], the structuring could apply to the environment and perhaps even the activity of the people surrounding the computer system.

The effectiveness of this approach to fault-tolerant system design will depend critically on the acceptance tests and additional alternate blocks that are provided. An experimental prototype systems is currently being developed which should enable us to obtain experience in the use of this approach, to evaluate its merits, and to explore possible performance−reliability tradeoffs. In our opinion, one lesson is however already clear. If it is considered important that a complex system be provided with extensive error recovery facilities whose dependability can be the subject of plausible *a priori* arguments, then the system structure will have to conform to comparatively restrictive rules. Putting this another way, it will not be sufficient for designers to argue for the use of very sophisticated control structures and intercommunication facilities on the grounds of performance characteristics and personal freedom of design, unless they can clearly demonstrate that these do not unduly compromise the recoverability of the system.

Acknowledgement. The work reported in this paper is the result of the efforts of a sizeable number of people, all associated with the Science Research Council-sponsored project on system reliability at the University of Newcastle upon Tyne. Arising out of this work, patents have been applied for by the National Research Development Corporation. Those most directly responsible for the techniques of system structuring which form the central theme of this paper are J. J. Horning, R. Kerr, H. C. Lauer, P. M. Melliar-Smith, and the author. (Professor Horning, of the University of Toronto, Toronto, Ont., Canada, held a Senior Visiting Fellowship with the project during the Summer of 1973.)

The author has great pleasure in acknowledging his indebtedness to all his colleagues on the project, several of whom, and in particular P. M. Melliar-Smith, provided many useful acceptance tests and alternates for the author's activity in preparing this paper.

References

1. T. Anderson, "Provably safe programs," Comput. Lab., Univ. Newcastle upon Tyne, Newcastle upon Tyne, England, Tech. Rep.
2. C. T. Davies, "Recovery semantics for a DB/DC system," in Proc. 1973 Ass. Comput. Mach. Nat. Conf., New York, N. Y., pp. 136−141.

3. E. W. Dijkstra, "The structure of the "THE" multiprogramming system," Commun. Ass. Comput. Mach., vol. 11, no. 5, pp. 341–346, 1968.
4. C. Hewitt, "PLANNER: A language for proving theorems in robots," in Proc. Int. Joint Conf. Artificial Intelligence, Mitre Corp., Bedford, Mass., 1969, pp. 295–301.
5. J. J. Horning, H. C. Lauer, P. M. Melliar-Smith, and B. Randell, "A program structure for error detection and recovery," in Proc. Conf. Operating Systems: Theoretical and Practical Aspects, IRIA, Apr. 23–25, 1974, pp. 177–193. (Also Chap. 2).
6. H. C. Lauer, "Protection and hierarchical addressing structures," in Proc. Int. Workshop Protection in Operating Systems, IRIA, Rocquencourt, France, 1974, pp. 137–148.
7. H. C. Lauer and D. Wyeth, "A recursive virtual machine architecture," Comput. Lab., Univ. Newcastle upon Tyne, Newcastle upon Tyne, England, Tech. Rep. 54, Sept. 1973.
8. S. E. Madnick and J. W. Alsop, II, "A modular approach to file system design," in 1969 Spring Joint Comput. Conf., AFIPS Conf. Proc., vol. 34. Montvale, N. J.: AFIPS Press, 1969, pp. 1–13.
9. D. L. Parnas, "Response to detected errors in well-structured programs," Dep. Comput. Sci., Carnegie-Mellon Univ., Pittsburgh, Pa., Tech. Rep., July 1972.
10. W. H. Pierce , Failure-Tolerant Computer Design. New York: Academic, 1965.
11. B. Randell, "Highly reliable computing systems," Comput. Lab., Univ. Newcastle upon Tyne, Newcastle upon Tyne, England, Tech. Rep. 20, July 1971.
12. —, "Research on computing system reliability at the University of Newcastle upon Tyne, 1972/73," Comput. Lab., Univ. Newcastle upon Tyne, Newcastle upon Tyne, England, Techn. Rep. 57, Jan. 1974.

Operating Systems:
The Problems of Performance and Reliability

B. RANDELL

The problems of achieving satisfactory levels of system performance and reliability are amongst the most difficult that operating system designers and implementors have to face. This is particularly the case with generic operating systems, i.e., systems intended for use in many different versions, in a wide variety of different environments. The present paper attempts to explore the reasons for these difficulties, and to discuss the interplay between performance and reliability, and, in particular, the problems of achieving high reliability in the presence of hardware failures and software errors.

1. Introduction

The task of preparing a survey paper on operating systems is daunting, to say the least. A mere catalogue of the numerous existing operating systems, and of research efforts in operating system design, would be inadequate. Moreover the subject, despite an almost frantic rate of development, is still, at least in this author's opinion, in far too disorganised and immature a state for a worthwhile analytical survey and classification to be feasible. There is not even any general agreement as to the meaning of the term "operating system". Paraphrasing Barron [3], who was in fact discussing assemblers:

"What is an operating system? Like many other things in computing it is difficult to define precisely, though any experienced programmer will recognise one when he sees it".

However, the definition given by Creech [4] is adequate for most purposes:

"An operating system can be defined to be that part of a computer system which attempts to so allocate and co-ordinate the resources of the system to achieve the optimum performance of that system. The resources involved include processors, peripheral I/O devices, operating system facilities, memory and time. The task is further complicated by the fact the operating system itself must use these resources".

This definition is better appreciated when one realises the extent of the spectrum of systems that it covers – from say, the LAP6 operating system [27] which contains less than 5000 instructions, and took less than two man years to develop, to IBM's OS/360, which contains several million lines of code, and has taken several man-millenia of effort to develop. (Incidentally, for those of you who are not familiar with LAP6, it is worth mentioning that this system provides a filling system and facilities for program preparation and assembly, and on-line editing, all on a LINC computer with 2048 12-bit words of memory.)

Rather than attempt a general survey, therefore, the present paper concentrates on just two aspects of operating systems, aspects which however are among the most important to the users of such systems, namely performance and reliability. The decision to concentrate on just these two aspects of system behaviour, and to ignore such other important aspects as functional capability, arises from the nature of the problems relating to system performance and reliability that face the operating system designer. Virtually every decision taken by the designers and implementors of an operating system has the potential of having a significant (and in the present state of our knowledge, often unforseeable) effect on the overall performance and reliability of the system. Furthermore, there are systems such as OS/360, which might be described as generic rather than specific in nature, beeing designed for a whole range of environments and machine configurations. In the case of such systems, the designers and implementors have only an indirect (though by no means small) influence on the levels of performance and reliability that will be achieved in a given installation. Even the criteria by which performance and reliability are judged will vary from installation to installation. Thus many of the problems of achieving acceptable performance and reliability at a particular installation will have to be tackled by the staff of that installation. For these reasons, and others, the problems of performance and reliability of operating systems are particularly difficult ones, and their discussion seems appropriate on an occasion such as the present one.

There is one somewhat tricky problem involved in discussing these two particular aspects of operating systems, and that is their psychological connotations. The topic of system performance can have overtones of mindless preoccupation with easily measurable (though not so easily evaluatable) attributes such as response time and storage utilization; the topic of system reliability can arouse the somewhat puritanical reaction that anything other than absolute reliability (particularly as far as software is concerned) is unacceptable. One of my aims in this talk is to convey my own, somewhat different views of these two topics.

2. System Performance and Reliability

The implication of the term "system performance" is that it is a measure of the rate at which a system is capable of doing useful work. In the same vein, "system reliability" can be regarded as a measure of the trustworthiness of the results produced by a system.

Quite crude characterizations of computing system performance (e.g. CPU utilization) and reliability can be adequate for comparing two different computing systems if their functional capabilities are identical or near-identical. However when two computing systems have very different functional capabilities it is in general very difficult to find means of characteristing performance and reliability which will facilitate meaningful comparisons of the two systems. Similarly, two different installations can have very different opinions as to the relative importance of the various aspects of a system's performance and reliability. Thus it is hardly surprising that there are no generally accepted standards for measuring performance and reliability, and it is not the intention here to propose any.

Performance and reliability are both "commodities" which are of value to users, and whose "production" will involve the incurrence of costs. Enough different computing systems have been produced and installed that one can attempt to quantify the relationship that holds between system performance (however crudely this might be measured) and cost – Grosch's "law" that performance is proportional to the square of cost, is a well-known example. Such a relationship may tell us more about a certain manufacturer's pricing policies than the realities of his development and manufacturing costs. However it does indicate that there is at least a certain level of understanding amongst customers of the need to assess their performance requirements, and of how the performance that they obtain from a system is, or should be, related to the amount that they paid for it. The situation with regard to system reliability is very different. A really naive user will not realise just how unreliable both the hardware and the software of the computing system that the manufacturer delivers to him might be. Most users will be hard put to quantify the value that they place on obtaining a certain level of reliability, leave alone have any idea how best to allocate the money that they wish to spend in order to obtain this level of reliability.

The specific role of the operating system in all this is rather interesting. It is perhaps not too cynical or misleading to regard the task of the operating system as that of enabling an installation to *achieve* the inherent performance capabilities, and *surpass* the inherent reliability capabilities, of the basic hardware. Of course it is not unknown for the amount of resources used by the operating system itself (CPU time, storage, etc.) to be so great as to cause one to question whether it is in fact making a positive contribution to the capacity of the computing system to produce useful work. Similarly, an operating system may contain so many errors that these errors become the dominant factor in the overall reliability of the computing system, rather than hardware failures, whether or not these failures are dealt with adequately by the operating system.

So far no mention has been made of any interactions between performance and reliability, but obviously these exist. Reliability is at least in part bought at the expense of performance – precautionary measures such as attempts to detect the occurrence of errors, multiple recording of data, etc., all use up resources and can impact performance. Conversely, the lack of reliability at some point within a system, can sometimes be dealt with by the system, using fallback and recovery techniques, so that the problem manifests itself to a user of the system simply as reduced performance. It is when an error goes undetected that the system will produce untrustworthy results, or perhaps no results at all (which can of course also happen even if the error is detected, if the system is not capable of coping with the situation).

Clearly, operating system designers have to be aware of these interactions between performance and reliability, and must attempt rational trade-off decisions. These decisions are very difficult for two reasons. Firstly, in our present state of knowledge, it is often difficult to predict what impact a particular feature, which is intended, say, to improve computing system reliability, will have on either reliability or performance. Secondly, it is very difficult, even when these impacts can be predicted, to judge whether the feature is worthwhile, in view of the lack, discussed earlier, of accepted norms for relating reliability to cost. This second point is more serious when one is designing a generic operating system, intended for use in various versions in many different environments, rather than a special operating system, for a specific environment, for which an assessment of the relative value of performance and reliability can be obtained. Of course the sad reality is that both the performance and reliability achieved by the early versions of most operating systems are far from adequate, and many iterations are usually needed before adequate levels are obtained.

Let me now turn from this attempt to discuss system performance and reliability in general terms, to discuss a particular problem in operating system design which illustrates the confusion which surrounds these two topics.

3. The Deadlock Problem

The problem of deadlock has been achieving ever greater attention during the last few years, and much worthwhile research has been done. However there has been a tendency to regard the problem as solely one of program correctness, and hence system reliability. In fact this problem is a very good example of the interaction between reliability and performance.

Deadlocks arise when two or more processes are allowed to proceed to the point where each reaches a situation where it is waiting for some action by one of the other processes. The standard simple example involves two processes, one having obtained resource A and requested resource B, the other having obtained resource B and requested resource A. Potential sources of deadlock problems are process communication facilities, and shared resources such as storage, I/O devices and operating system services. When viewed as an abstract problem in the theory of operating system design, the usual assumption is that the essence of the problem is to ensure that deadlocks will not occur under any circumstance. With this in mind various authors, sometimes using differing assumptions as to the amount of information that will be available to the system about the future behaviour of processes, have produced various algorithms for the scheduling of processes and the allocation of resources to processes.

Now one can in fact always avoid deadlocks by disallowing any parallel activity, but for performance reasons this is unlikely to be practicable. This fact makes it clear that deadlock avoidance strategies must be assessed not only by the extent to which they succeed in their goal of avoiding all deadlocks, but also by the extent to which they allow multiple acitivies to proceed in parallel. In fact in many cases it is feasible to provide restart facilities which enable a deadlock situation to be resolved by the rather brutal technique of abandoning one or more processes, and later restarting them. As Needham and Hartley [21] have pointed out, it is then appropriate to regard the task of the operating system designer, with respect to the deadlock problem, as being that of finding a suitable trade-off between such factors as cost and effectiveness of a scheduling and allocation algorithm, the frequency with which it fails to avoid deadlocks, and costs of restarting after a deadlock. It would be, to say the very least, aesthetically pleasing if one could satisfy oneself that the best trade-off, in terms of system performance was achieved by algorithms which guranteed the avoidance of deadlocks, but there is no reason to suppose that this is always or even often the case.

It should however be admitted that there are varying qualities of restart, the ideal restart being one whose occurrence is not noticeable to the users of the system, or at least which does not require any overt action on the part of the users. Where restart facilities fall badly below this ideal it is all too easy to justify an inadequate solution to the deadlock problem by not taking the costs to the users of restarts into account in the trade-off decisions. This is certainly the case where deadlocks can be directly caused by simple (accidental of wilful) actions by a user, as is the case in OS/360 (see Holt [15]).

4. System Performance Problems

Let us, for the moment, leave aside the problems of reliability, and concentrate on the problems of achieving acceptable performance from an operating system. As mentioned earlier, every design decision, indeed every instruction written by an implementor, is potentially the source of considerable influence on system performance. When designing a system we can have a set of preconceived ideas as to which aspects of the design, and which parts of the coding, will be most critical with respect to performance. However these intuitions can be very wrong. The reasons for this can range all the way from insufficient understanding of underlying principles, to silly coding mistakes.

For example, during recent years much work has been done on so-called "virtual memory" systems, either of the paging type, such as Atlas, or of the segmenting type, such as the B5000. Considerable effort has gone into the design and study of "replacement algorithms", i.e. algorithms for choosing which information to remove from working storage when space is needed in order to bring further information into working storage from backing storage. However it is now becoming clear that the question of which replacement algorithm is used is comparatively unimportant. Much more important, from the point of view of performance, is the problem of avoiding thrashing, the situation in which the system spends virtually all of its efforts transferring information to and from between working storage and backing storage. The usual cause of thrashing is that too many programs have been allowed to compete for CPU time and hence working storage, so that programs are excessively "space-squeezed" and continually need access to information which is not in working storage. In certain circumstances it may be regarded as acceptable for one of the duties of the operators to be that of looking out for the symptoms of thrashing, and when necessary instructing the operating system to desist from trying to run one or more currently active jobs. This is the case with, for example, the MCP operating system on the B5000 and its successors [23], and the THE system on the X8 [7]. However in general it is not acceptable to wait until thrashing has become so pronounced that it is eventually noticed by the operator; instead, strategies for avoiding thrashing by controlling the level of multiprogramming of working storage will be included in the operating system, perhaps as an extension to the basic replacement algorithm [24]. These strategies, which can often be simple to the point of naiveté, can have a far greater effect on performance than the basic replacement strategy.

At the other end of the spectrum, horror stories about the massive effects of conceptually trivial coding errors are legion. One particular one that I remember is, it so happens, also concerned with a trivial memory system. Many experiments had been conducted, and many incremental improvements had been made to the storage management strategies. In fact, by far the biggest single performance improvement was due to the eventual (and accidental) discovery of a trivial mistake in the coding of the terminal communication routine.

All this is of course a clear indication of our willingness to design and implement systems of a level of complexity which challenges, and often defeats, our ability to comprehend them. Unfortunately, the analysis of even very simple algorithms, so as to determine what their performance will be, can be extremely laborious, even when gross simplifying assmptions are made as to the statistical properties of the input data. (Such analyses can however produce quite unexpected and illuminating results, despite the simplicity of the algorithms – see Knuth [19].) Luckily, as Knuth also shows, almost equally valuable information can be obtained much more easily by experiment, using trace routines, and routines which record the frequency of execution of the various statements making up an algorithm. What is surprising is that such simple tools are not more commonly used to assist in program development.

Basically similar, but more extensive monitoring facilities, either hardware or software, are now coming into common use for "tuning" operating systems [13]. As I am sure you know, several companies now offer a service which involves spending a day or so monitoring the behaviour of an installation's operating system and standard application programs, and then making recommendations for modifications in order to improve system performance. The quite spectacular improvements which are almost always made are more an indication of the lamentable state of the original system, and of the lack of understanding of the system by the installation staff, than of any great conceptual sophistication in the tools and techniques that these companies use. Clearly this tuning process is a very worthwhile (though not necessarily as intellectually satisfying as it is demanding) method of making improvements in a complex operating system. In fact, I must admit that I think of the task as involving a kind of pathology, being concerned with trying to analyse the obscure causes of unpleasant symptoms in diseased organisms.

This type of tuning is an "after the fact" method of improving the quality of an operating system. It therefore in no sense replaces the activity, which one would like to think was a standard component of any system design and implementation project, of analysing and monitoring first the design, later the partially implemented system, and where necessary, of causing re-design and re-implementation to be undertaken. Ideally one would expect that the designer of an operating system component would be working from a detailed specification, not only of what the component was supposed to do, but also of the estimated resources (CPU time, storage space, channel time, etc.) that it was expected to need. Also available to him would be similar estimates relating to those other components with which his component would have to interact. As the system implementation proceeded, the estimates would be checked against what was achieved in practice. It would thus become clear where the redesign of a component was necessary, either because its design had been based on premises that had turned out to be untrue, or in a further attempt to make it conform more closely to the original estimates of its resource utilization.

All this may seem rather utopian at the moment. For example, in some operating systems one is forced to assume that the designers of system components which use disk access routines were as ignorant of the time taken by these routines, as the designers of the disk access routines were of the frequency with which these routines would be used. In many cases, simple back-of-the-envelope type calculations would be sufficient to expose gross disparities in the system design, but comparatively few software designers and implementors are trained or motivated to work this way. This is, I feel, indicative of how far we are from having an occupation which truly merits the title of "software engineering".

However, it is one thing to find out that a partially implemented system should be changed, and quite another to carry out the proposed changes. Comments about the need for structure and modularity, and advocating the use of (decent) high level languages, are all clearly appropriate at this point, even if they do sound like mere motherhood [22]. Perhaps as important, whenever the number of designers and implementors warrants it, are automated or semi-automated techniques for policing and co-ordinating their work. A simple example would be facilities for maintaining up to date, and accurate, lists of which system modules use, or modify, which common data structures. (Hopkins [16] has given an all too graphic account of what has happened in OS/360 due to a vast number of inadequately co-ordinated attempts to improve the performance of individual modules and groups of modules.)

Let me conclude this discussion on system design problems by returning briefly to my earlier point about the dangers of over-ambitious design goals. It is very noticeable that some of the more successful operating systems, from a practical point of view, are those whose designers have had a clear idea of the intended environment, and have resisted the temptation to attempt a giant leap in all directions at once, so to speak, by implementing the most sophisticated and general system that they could envisage. Just two examples of this are the Cambridge Multi-Access System [28] and APL/360 [9]. In the Cambridge System, it was decided that the main uses of the terminals would be for file editing and job submission, and that these facilities could be, if carefully designed, provided quite economically. On the other hand, the more general ability to interact from a terminal with any user-supplied program, which it was felt would place a heavy load on system resources, was provided only as a special mode of use, called "expensive mode", the use of which was very carefully rationed. The designers of the APL/360 system were very conscious of the need to avoid excessive information transfer between working storage and backing storage, which was a flailing-arm disk. Such information transfers could be caused by switching between users, and by user commands to load and save "workspaces" containing programs and data. Switching between users was performed under

43

the control of the system, and was calculated to be manageable – the worry was the load and save commands. By the simple expedient of allowing such commands only from a terminal, not from within APL programs, the maximum rate at which such commands can be given has been severely limited. It would be difficult to ascertain how much this decision has contributed to APL/360's undoubted efficiency, but certainly a potentially difficult bottleneck has thus been completely avoided.

5. System Reliability

As users have become (sometimes unintentionally) more dependent on their computer systems – often far more dependent than the quality of either the hardware or the software would justify – the subject of system reliability has become ever more important. However, as discussed earlier, it is no use obtaining reliability unless it is matched by adequate performance. A result that is "guaranteed" correct, produced after all need for it has passed, may well be less valuable than a timely result which has some (hopefully small, and known) probability of being incorrect.

Needless to say, a complex system will not in general be designed to produce a single result, but rather a whole set of results, to each of which a different reliability requirement might be attached. (For example, in a system which maintains a large inventory file, inserting an incorrect value into the file may be regarded as much worse than occasionally failing to answer, or answering incorrectly, requests for information from the file). In such circumstances it is only sensible to try to design the system in such a way that its more commonly occurring faults at least do not affect the more crucial of the results that the system is producing, even though they might affect the overall reliability (and performance) – the terms "graceful degradation" and "fail-soft" are the currently fashionable ones for characterising computing systems that are designed in this way. In fact a look at one of the most obviously successful projects that involved obtaining ultra-high reliability from a complex software system, the Project Apollo Ground System [2], is most instructive. One of the most striking features is the care which has been taken, in the design of the environment which surrounds the system, to minimise the extent to which reliance is put on the correct and continuous functioning of the system.

A typical dictionary definition of system is "a whole composed of components in orderly arrangement according to some scheme or plan". From this definition (and resisting the temptation to question whether the phrase "orderly arrangement" is fully applicable to complex computing systems) one is led to the view that the task of achieving reliabiltiy of a system can be split up into:
(i) that of making sure that the components of which the system is constructed are reliable;
(ii) that of coping with the consequences of any failures to achieve (i) completely.

Let us take as the level of components of interest to us in a computing system such major hardware modules as processors, memories, channels, I/O devices, etc., and the major software modules which make up the operating system, and consider what reliability one might reasonably expect from such components.

6. Hardware Reliability

Much progress has been made in achieving ultra-high reliability from hardware modules which are essentially electronic such as processors and memories; Darton [5], for example, has reported on a small demonstration computer which is to all intents and purposes absolutely reliable. (Any single failure can be detected, the offending circuit board identified, and replaced, all without interrupting the system — the time to replace a board is infinitesimal compared to the mean time between failures.) However, as I am sure you all know, much of this progress has yet to be reflected in the average present-day computing installation.

The situation is worse with electro-mechanical devices, where the levels of redundancy needed to achieve comparable reliability are much higher. Thus the "hidden" ninth spindle on an IBM 2314 disk drive, kept as a spare, although of value in increasing the probability of there being eight spindles in working order, does not prevent loss of data caused oy a head crash. To do this would require duplication of the entire set of eight spindles, and that all data be automatically recorded in duplicate. It is unlikely that this would be regarded as the most effective way of utilizing the eight extra spindels.

In summary therefore, there seems little chance that the operating system designer will be able to avoid taking at least some of the responsibility for coping with the consequences of hardware failures. It is, however, I think reasonable to expect improved hardware facilities for reporting and identifying modules that are in error, for system reconfiguration, etc., such as in the Burroughs D825 [1] and the IBM 9020 [17], to become more widespread.

7. Software Reliability

A common view of software reliability is that it is achieved solely by ensuring that the software is correct, i.e., is free of bugs. Software bugs are seen as the equivalent of design errors in hardware, with there being no equivalent to the failure that can occur after all the design errors have been removed, such as are caused by component ageing. This view is somewhat simplistic — for a start, the distinction between hardware design errors and later hardware failures can be somewhat arbitrary. However what is more to the point is that in today's cruel world it is rarely possible to wait until all the bugs have been removed from a complex software system, before it is used to provide service. (For that matter, it is not uncommon for blatant hardware design errors to be found many years after installation of a complex computing system). Indeed there are many who would deny the possibility of a large software system ever reaching a bug-free state. Certainly the current statistical evidence is on their side — it was recently stated that each release of OS/360, which is (one hopes) an extreme case, has on average over one thousand distinct errors reported in it.

It is worth examining what we mean by the term "correctness". Needless to say, the results produced by a system can only be "correct" with respect to some criterion. One would like to assume that such a criterion would be part of the detailed specification that was used to guide the design and implementation of a system. However, for other than very simple systems, such specifications are unlikely to be accurate or complete. Rather, they are often little more than an initial bargaining offer, subject to renegotiation as the system implementation proceeds and the designers and their customers start getting detailed feedback. Naturally, to a user, the fact that a system is correct with respect to some inadequate or obsolete specification will be irrelevant − to him it will be, in essence, incorrect.

It is against this background that the current research on the topic of program correctness should be assessed. Much of this work derives from that of Floyd [10], who proposed the use of automated theorem proving techniques to check the consistency of a program with programmer-supplied formal assertions about the relationships which should hold amongst the values of the variables at various stages during the execution of a program. This has in fact been done by King [18], but King's work, impressive though it is, makes it clear that, at the present state of development, even quite simple programs can tax the abilities of automated theorem proving techniques. Of direct importance to the problems of system reliability is the work of Dijkstra and his colleagues on the T.H.E. system [7], who took as their goal the task of satisfying themselves, a priori, as to the "correctness" of their design for a multiprogramming system. The degree to which they achieved their goal is indeed remarkable − however the techniques of system structuring that they developed are, I believe, of great importance in themselves, irrespective of whether they are used for facilitating the construction of correctness "proofs".

All of this is not intended to downgrade the importance of efforts to ensure that bugs are located and removed from software, or of research efforts aimed at improving our ability to specify accurately the intended behaviour of software, and to construct correct software, and at providing rigorous proofs of software correctness. Rather, the point is that for the forseeable future, complex computing systems must, I believe contain effective provisions for coping with software bugs, as well as hardware failures, if such systems are to achieve really high reliability.

8. Coping with Unreliable Components

One obvious distinction can be made between the problems of coping with unreliable hardware, and unreliable software. This is that one would expect estimates of the probability of the occurrence of the various kinds of hardware failures, based on experimental trials of prototype hardware, to be available. In contrast, predictions as to what software errors will be made must be predictions of the frailty of humans, rather than of hardware. In fact the situation with regard to coping with software errors is somewhat paradoxical; in order to know exactly what precautions to take, one would like to know what errors are likely to be made. However, if one really knew this, one would take extra care in the preparation of the relevant parts of the program, in order to avoid making the errors! In practice this distinction between hardware and software is less important than one might imagine, for various reasons:

(i)   in many cases, one has to try and cope with an error situation without knowing whether its underlying cause is a program bug or a hardware failure – indeed in some cases one may never find out;

(ii) many of the precautions that one takes because of possible software errors are quite general and not dependent on the specific type, or the location, of the error;

(iii) it is not always wise to rely too heavily on the accuracy of the hardware failure rate estimates.

The features that are built into an operating system in an effort to cope with error situations can be divided into:

(i)   preparations for the possibility of errors;

(ii) error detection facilities;

(iii) error recovery facilities.

The first category includes techniques such as multiple recording of important information, e.g. file directories, the preparation of fall-back and restart facilities such as dumps, audit trails, etc. (see for example Fraser [11]), and the provision and use of protection mechanisms. This latter topic is receiving much attention at the moment, but is I am sure still at a very early stage of development. One approach, involving the idea of "capabilities", is due to Dennis and van Horn [6], and has been developed by Lampson [20] and by Yngve and Fabry, a description of whose work has been given by Wilkes [28]. The idea is that a given process (which might be part of the activity of the operating system, or arise from the execution of a user's program) should have, at any given moment, a list of "capabilities" associated with it which indicate and delineate, what the process is permitted to do. The intention is that each process be given the minimum set of capabilities that it needs in order to perform its function. If any errors are encountered, the capability mechanism limits their possible consequences, and increases their chances of being detected. The topic of protection mechanisms is closely related to that of addressing structures – if a process cannot obtain the address of an object, even accidentally, it cannot harm the object. My own view is that this relationship has yet to be fully exploited, and that future protection mechanisms may well owe as much to work on addressing structures, such as that of the B6500 (see Hauck and Dent [14]), as to the work on the capability concept.

In general, an operating system, in addition to containing its own error detection mechanisms, should be capable of dealing with reports it receives of errors that have been detected (but which cannot be dealt with) within its components, and those that have, shall we say, escaped the vigilance of the system, and have been detected outside the system, perhaps by the operators. (In fact, this classification can be applied more finely, at every discernable level in the system.) Its own error detection mechanisms will, ideally, only be needed for errors within the system itself − in practice they might, regrettably, have to be used for attempts at detecting errors that occur inside components, even hardware components such as processors and memory. However the aim should be that all components have a reliable mechanism for error detection, if not error correction.

All error detection is based on the provision of redundant information, whose consistency can be checked. The idea of hardware and data redundancy is well-known, but program redundancy is more novel. Clearly program redundancy is something quite different from having multiple identical copies of a program − rather it involves redundancy in the specification of the intended process. (In fact Floyd's work on program correctness proofs, described earlier, uses just such redundancy, but the consistency checks are applied before, rather than during, execution.) Examples of program redundancy, some involving redundancy already implicit in the data, others involving the deliberate introduction of explicitly redundant data, include:

(i) positive checking − at a multi-way branch, where the path to be taken depends on the value of a variable, each path is taken only as the result of a positive check, leaving an extra error path to be taken if none of these checks apply;

(ii) sum checks − a typical example is to maintain a sum check on a table, adjusted with each change to a table entry, and checked at appropriate intervals;

(iii) bi-directional links − even where a uni-directional linked list would suffice, bi-directional links are used, and checks are made that an item which points at another item is itself pointed at by that item;

(iv) dog tags − a set of unique names are generated, and one is attached, for example, to each page of information. A process which accesses a page will do so by using its address. However the process will also have a copy of the dog tag, which will be checked against the dog tag kept with the page, wherever it is stored.

This list is clearly not exhaustive − techniques such as these form part of the folklore (but not, with few exceptions, such as Watson [26], the literature) of operating system design, and are probably re-invented almost daily. In fact the idea of dog tags was used by Eckert [8], and the idea of using assertions for manually checking programs can be found in the writings of both von Neumann [12] and Turing [25]!

The sorts of actions which I consider as part of error recovery include determination of the extent of the damage, reporting of the error, and, to whatever extent possible, the repairing of the damage so that the system can continue to provide service. Determination of the extent of the damage can be explicit, from a knowledge of where the error occurred (this of course is where the protection mechanism is exceedingly useful, *providing* that it itself is not involved in the error), or explicit, by tentative exploration, during which facilities are exercised and consistency checks are made on data. Error repair usually involves such acts as file recovery, the re-establishment of system data structures, etc., and in the case of identifiable hardware failure, perhaps retrying the action which caused failure, or if necessary, reconfiguring the system to isolate the failed component. In the case of software error it will often be the case that all one can do is to make sure that those services which are not affected by the error are resumed with as little delay as possible.

Perhaps it is appropriate to conclude this topic by noting that these problems of error recovery are amongst the most tricky (particularly when one tries, as one should, to allow for further errors occurring during the recovery process itself) and the most important of the whole design. Indeed one might suggest that error recovery should be amongst the first problems that are treated during the system design process, rather than, as so often happens, one of the last.

9. Conclusions

I have attempted to give you my own personal perspective on two problem areas in operating system design. These particular problems interest me because they are what I think of as "system" problem as opposed to "component" problems. As such their main enemy is complexity — the complexity that we are all too willing to build into our systems. If a system is simple enough then performance and reliability are unlikely to be too much of a problem. Complex, highly complex, systems have been created and have been made to work, but at a cost of what a decade ago would have been unbelievable amounts of programming time and effort. However there will be no easy solutions to the problems of performance and reliability unless and until we have learnt how to reduce and master this complexity.

Acknowledgements. The preparation of this paper has been greatly aided by the discussions that I have had with many friends and colleagues, in particular Jim Eve, Bob Floyd, Jim Horning, Butler Lampson, Hugh Lauer and Bill Lynch.

References

1. J. P. Anderson, S. A. Hoffman, J. Shifman and R. J. Williams, D825 — a multiple-computer system for command and control, in: AFIPS Conf. Proc., Vol. 22, 1962 FJCC (Spartan Books, Washington D.C., 1962) 86 – 96.
2. J. Aron, Apollo programming support, in: Software engineering techniques, Eds. J. N. Buxton and B. Randell, NATO Science Committee, Brussels (1970) 43 – 48.
3. D. W. Barron, Assemblers and loaders (MacDonald, London, 1969).
4. B. A. Creech, Implementation of operating systems, IEEE International Convention Digest (March 1970).
5. K. S. Darton, The Dependable process computer, Electrical Review 186,6 (6 Feb., 1970) 207 – 209.
6. J. B. Dennis and E. C. Van Horn, Programming semantics for multiprogrammed computations, Comm. ACM 9,3 (1966) 143 – 155.
7. E. W. Dijkstra, The structure of the 'THE' — multiprogramming system, Comm. ACM 11,5 (1968) 341 – 346.
8. J. P. Eckert, Reliability and checking. Theory and techniques for design of electronic digital computers, Ed, C. C. Chambers, Moore School of Electrical Engineering, Univ. of Pennsylvania, Philadelphia, Pa. (1948) 35.1 – 35.16.

9. A. D. Falkoff and K. E. Iverson, The APL/360 terminal system. Interactive systems for experimental applied mathematics, Ed. K. Klerer and J. Reinfelds (Academic Press, New York, 1968) 22−37.

10. R. W. Floyd, Assigning meanings to programs, in: Proc. Symposia in Applied Mathematics, Vol. 19, American Mathematical Society (1967), 19−32.

11. A. G. Fraser, Integrity of a mass storage filing system, Comp. J. 12, 1 (1969) 1−5.

12. H. H. Goldstine and J. von Neumann, Planning and coding problems for an electronic computing instrument, Part 2, Vol. 1, Institute for Advanced Study, Princeton, N. J. (1947). (Reprinted in: John von Neumann: Collected Works, Vol. 5, Ed. A. A. Taub (Pergamon, Oxford, 1963) 80−151.)

13. C. C. Gotlieb and G. H. MacEwen, System evaluation tools, in: Software engineering techniques, Eds. J. N. Buxton and B. Randell, NATO Science Committee, Brussels (1970) 93−99.

14. E. A. Hauck and B. A. Dent, Burroughs' B6500/B7500 stack mechanism, in: AFIPS Conf. Proc., Vol. 32, 1968 SJCC (Thompson, Washington, D. C., 1968) 245−251.

15. R. C. Holt, On deadlock in computer systems, Ph. D. Thesis, Cornell Univ. Ithaca, N. Y. (Jan. 1971).

16. M. E. Hopkins, Computer aided software design, in: Software engineering techniques, Eds. J. N. Buxton and B. Randell, NATO Science Committee, Brussels (1970) 99−101.

17. J. F. Keeley et al., An application-oriented multiprocessing system. IBM System J. 6,2 (1967) 78−132.

18. J. C. King, A Program verifier, Ph. D. Thesis, Carnegie-Mellon Univ. Pittsburgh, Pa. (Sept. 1969).

19. D. E. Knuth, The analysis of algorithms, in: The teaching of programming at university level, Ed. B. Shaw, Computing Laboratory, The University of Newcastle-upon-Tyne (1971) 49−62.

20. B. W. Lampson, Dynamic protection structures, in: AFIPS Conf. Proc. Vol. 35, 1969 FJCC (AFIPS Press, Montvale, N. J., 1969) 27−28.

21. R. M. Needham and D. F. Hartley, Theory and practice in operating system design, in: Proc, 2nd ACM Symp. on operating system principles, Princeton Univ., Princeton, N. J. (Oct. 20−22 1969) 8−12.

22. P. G. Neumann, The role of motherhood in the pop art of system programming, in: Proc. 2nd ACM Symp. on operating system principles, Princeton Univ., Princeton, N. J. (Oct. 20−22 1969) 13−18.

23. C. Oliphant, Operating system for the B5000, Datamation 10,5 (1964), 42−45.

24. A. J. Shils, The load leveller, Report RC 2233, IBM Research Center, Yorktown Heights, N.Y. (Oct. 7, 1968).

25. A. Turing, Checking a large routine, Report on a conf. on high speed automatic calculating machines, Univ. Mathematical Laboratory, Cambridge (June 22−25 2949) 67−68.

26. R. W. Watson, Timesharing system design concepts (McGraw-Hill, New York, N. Y., 1970).

27. M. A. Wilkes, Conversational access to a 2048-word machine, Comm. ACM 13,7 (1970) 407−414.

28. M. V. Wilkes, Time-sharing computer systems (MacDonald, London, 1968).

Reprinted with permission from IFIP, Information Processing 71, North Holland, Amsterdam, pp. 281−290, 1971.

Chapter 2
Recovery Blocks

Introduction

Recovery blocks provide a means of introducing a measure of tolerance against software faults. The four aspects of fault tolerance — error detection, damage assessment, error recovery and fault treatment — are embodied in a recovery block in a disciplined fashion. Acceptance tests are used for detecting errors and damage assessment for a single sequential process is particularly simple — the program in execution is assumed to be effected. (Damage assessment for concurrent processes poses complications and is the subject of Chapt. 4.) Error recovery involves restoring all modified non-local variables to their values at the beginning of the recovery block. Finally, fault treatment consists of executing an alternative module in an attempt to avoid the fault(s) that resulted in the failure of the previous module.

This chapter begins with the paper which originally presented the recovery block concept. The paper not only argued for the use of backward error recovery as the most appropriate means of coping with software faults, but also proposed a stack-like mechanism (the recursive cache, later to be termed the recovery cache) for managing recovery data. By exploiting the block structure of a language to its fullest advantage, the recovery cache manages to store minimum recovery data for any program. Lastly, the authors of the paper speculated on the possibility of 'undoing' more complex operations than memory updates (e.g. file updates, message passing) and proposed the idea of 'reverse procedures', whereby a programmer can explicitly program 'undo' operations (this concept of programmer provided 'undo' actions was later developed and incorporated in the language Concurrent Pascal, see Chapt. 4).

The second paper examines the recovery block concept in detail and answers a number of questions that are commonly asked about this approach (e.g. what types of faults are tolerated? Can realistic alternative algorithms be designed?).

The remaining five papers report on the experimental work performed to evaluate the recovery block concept. The paper by Anderson and Kerr describes the first implementation of recovery blocks, a novel recovery-cache algorithm and a computer architecture for supporting fault-tolerant programs. The following paper describes a similar experimental system in which recovery blocks were incorporated in the language Pascal. While developing programs with recovery blocks to run on these systems, we were often pleasantly surprised to find recovery blocks doing what they are supposed to do — tolerate unanticipated situations! Thus Anderson and Kerr report a genuine fault in the primary of a recovery block they had programmed which was detected by the acceptance test. The paper by Shrivastava and Akinpelu reports on some performance measurements for recovery blocks, which generally support the belief that recovery blocks do not impose any serious runtime and recovery data space overheads. The recovery cache mechanism should ideally form an integral part of a given computer; this not being possible for the existing hardware, Lee et al. describe an alternative means of providing hardware support for backward error recovery. The basic idea is simple: connect the 'recovery cache box' as a peripheral device to the processor; the box monitors the processor bus activity and converts all store 'write' cycles to 'read modify write' cycles and caches prior values. (It is necessary for this box to be located between the main store and the processor). Lastly, Verhofstad describes an experimental file system in which the concept of recovery cache is applied to disc pages, thereby making file updates recoverable.

Despite the work on recovery blocks reported here, certain doubts still linger. Can acceptance tests be designed such that subtle errors will be detected? What evidence is there that an alternative will succeed where the primary has failed? These questions can only be answered by using recovery blocks in real (or close to real) applications. Work in this direction is currently under way at Newcastle and initial results from this work are very encouraging.

A Program Structure for Error Detection and Recovery

J. J. Horning, H. C. Lauer, P. M. Melliar-Smith and B. Randell

Abstract. The paper describes a method of structuring programs which aids the design and validation of facilities for the detection of and recovery from software errors. Associated with the method is a mechanism for the automatic preservation of restart information at a level of overhead which is believed to be tolerable.

1. Introduction

Prior research into reliable computing has concentrated on the reliability of the hardware, on the detection of hardware errors, and on the configuring of systems to allow continuation of service in the presence of hardware errors. But observation of present-day large systems indicates that software faults represent a problem whose significance is at least as great as that of the hardware faults. Whilst conceding the importance of current research on improving the quality of software (e.g. work on program "correctness proofs"), the present paper is based on the view that it is also worth providing error detection and recovery facilities for both hardware and software errors. In what follows we will concentrate on software errors although we believe much of our work is of equal relevance to many types of hardware errors.

This paper describes the recovery block concept, a method of structuring programs which is aimed at aiding the design of error detection and recovery facilities, and the recursive cache, an associated mechanism which provides means for automatic "back-tracking" at a level of overhead which is believed to be tolerable.

2. Error Detection and Recovery

Reliable operation of a computing system depends on both error detection and error recovery. Several classes of error detection techniques are available, some of which operate automatically on an instruction-by-instruction basis, while others take a broader view of correct operation based on programmed checks and assertions. It is characteristic of error detection that several techniques can readily be used together, and the recovery block concept aims to provide error recovery after any kind of detected error.

Recovery and restart of the program after error detection is a difficult problem. Where instruction-by-instruction error detection is provided, the number of possible errors is too great to provide explicit recovery action for each possible case, while any automatic recovery operation which simply aims to repair the state of the program so as to allow its continuation in a valid manner cannot

53

be expected to achieve correctness rather than mere legality. Alternatively, on detection of an error by a programmed check, the number of possible ways in which the program may have erred is very large and obscure side-effects of the error may have spread into the system. The analysis, with certainty, of such an erroneous program state is in general beyond our capabilities, and therefore repair of the program state cannot be recommended.

For many applications, frequently the applications requiring the highest reliability, error recovery by repetition of whole job steps or other major program units must imply a substantial recovery overhead and a degradation of service. Such applications require a recovery mechanism which can achieve local recovery from an error whenever possible.

It is characteristic of error recovery operations that they are very much more error prone than the main programs, and are very difficult to check. It is an objective of the recovery block concept that the error recovery actions should be testable and that they should be checked with the same rigour as the main program. It is of course obvious that repetition of the operation with the same program will not always achieve recovery from a program error.

The recovery block concept is aimed at the provision of a well-structured context for explicitly considered error recovery operations. These can be constructed at various levels within the program so that if a local recovery operation should fail a more global recovery action can be substituted. Another aim is that the structure should make explicit the nature of the checks which are applied and also the nature of the action to be taken in the event of error, the number of such actions being strictly limited.

3. Recovery Blocks

A well-structured program is constructed from identifiable operations, many of which are themselves constructed from further smaller operations. The proposed scheme is based on the selection of a set of these operations upon which to base the recovery operations. These will be referred to as *Recovery Blocks*. Recovery blocks can be nested like Algol blocks, but a recovery block must have a more complex internal structure than an Algol block so as to support error recovery. Each recovery block contains a *primary block,* an *acceptance test,* and zero or more *alternate blocks.*

– The *primary block* corresponds exactly to the block of the Algol-like program, and is entered to perform the desired operation.
– The *acceptance test* is executed on exit from the primary block to confirm that the primary block has performed acceptably.
– If the primary block is detected to be in error, the *alternate block* is entered and is required to perform the desired operation in a different way or to perform some alternative action acceptable to the program as a whole. The acceptance test is then repeated.

The diagram of a recovery block's structure given in Fig. 1 is intended to be illustrative, rather than syntactically representative. The double vertical lines define the scopes of recovery block, while the single vertical lines define the

recovery block A

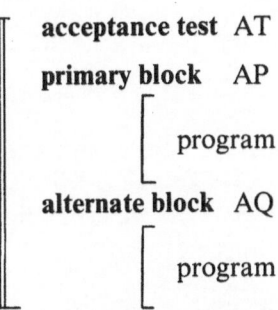

Fig. 1. A diagramatic representation of a recovery block structure. The primary block corresponds exactly to the block of the Algol-like program and is entered to perform the desired operation. The acceptance test is executed on exit from the primary block to confirm that the primary block has performed acceptably. If the primary block is detected to be in error, the alternate block is entered and is required to perform the desired operation in a different way. The acceptance test is then repeated

scopes of primary and alternate blocks. Figure 2 shows how the primary and alternate blocks can contain, nested within themselves, further recovery blocks.

4. Acceptance Tests

The acceptance test is a section of program which is invoked on exit from a primary or alternate block. This acceptance test can be regarded as an assertion of the effects of the execution of the recovery block which are required for the correct operation of the surrounding program [1]. The acceptance test provides a binary decision as to whether the assertion is satisfied and thus as to whether the recovery block has been executed in a manner acceptable to the rest of the system. There is no requirement that the test be, in any formal sense, a check on the absolute 'correctness' of the operation − it is for the designer to decide on the appropriate level of rigour of the test. For each recovery block there is a single acceptance test, invoked on exit from the primary and also on exit from the alternate should the alternate be required. Thus in Fig. 2, the acceptance test BT is invoked on completion of primary block BP, so as to check the acceptability of the results of BP.

The acceptance test does not lie within the primary block, but can be considered to be a part of the next enclosing block. Thus the acceptance test cannot access the local variables of the primary or alternate blocks; indeed there is no reason why the local declarations of these blocks should be the same. The function of the acceptance test is to ensure that the operation performed by the recovery block is to the satisfaction of the program which invoked it. The acceptance test is therefore performed by reference to the variables accessible to that program, rather than to local variables which can have no effect or significance after exit.

```
declare X
recovery block A
   acceptance test AT
   primary block   AP
      declare Y
         program
      recovery block B
            acceptance test BT
            primary block   BP
               declare U
                  program
            alternate block BQ
               declare V
                  program
            alternate block BR
               declare W
                  program
      program
   alternate block AQ
      declare W
         program
      recovery block C
            acceptance test CT
            primary block   CP
               program
            alternate block CQ
               program
      recovery block D
            acceptance test DT
            primary block   DP
               program
      program
```

Fig. 2. A more complex recovery block structure, showing how the primary and alternate blocks can contain, nested within themselves, further recovery blocks

The acceptance test can reference any variable within the current scope immediately enclosing the recovery block. The primary block may modify some of these variables. For convenience and increased rigour, the acceptance test is enabled to access such variables either for their modified value or for their original unmodified value.

5. Rejection by an Acceptance Test

There are four possible causes for the rejection of a primary or alternate block. These are:

a) an error within the block, detected explicitly by the acceptance test,

b) failure to terminate, detected by a timeout,

c) detection of an error within the block by one of the implicit error detection mechanisms (e.g. protection violation, devide by zero, etc),

d) explicit or implicit rejection within an inner recovery block which exhausts the recovery capability at that level.

If the primary of a recovery block is rejected then the recursive cache mechanism invokes an alternate. When this alternate terminates, its results are submitted to the same acceptance test, and should the acceptance test be satisfied, the program proceeds using the results generated by the alternate. If the acceptance test is again not satisfied then a further alternate is tried. Thus, in Fig. 2, if the results of primary block BP are rejected by acceptance test BT, then alternate block BQ is invoked. If the results from BQ are still unacceptable to BT, then BR must be invoked.

Should all the alternate blocks have been obeyed, and all have failed to satisfy the acceptance test, then the entire recovery block must be regarded as having failed. This causes rejection of the enclosing block which invoked the recovery block, and the alternate to that enclosing block must be attempted instead. Thus, in Fig. 2, if the results from alternate block BR are still unacceptable to acceptance test BT, then recovery block B as a whole, and therefore primary block AP, must be regarded as having failed. The next program to be attempted is alternate block AQ.

If an error occurs during the execution of the program of an acceptance test, this is regarded as an error occurring within the next enclosing recovery block. The alternate invoked is therefore that for the enclosing block rather than that for the block whose acceptability is being tested. Thus if an error is detected whilst executing the program of acceptance test BT, the alternate block AQ must be entered.

6. Primary and Alternate Blocks

It is an objective of the recovery block concept that primary blocks can be written in exactly the same manner as in a conventional system. There are no restrictions on the operations which are performed by the primary blocks, no restrictions on the calling of procedures or the modification of global variables, no requirements for the explicit preservation of restart information, and no special programming conventions.

Similarly the intention is that the alternate blocks can be written in exactly the same manner. The design of an alternate block is not affected by the prior unsuccessful execution of the primary block. The recursive cache mechanism described below ensures that an alternate block is executed as though the primary had never been entered, and as though the alternate had been substituted for the primary in a conventional program structure.

When an alternate block is entered it must therefore be presented with *exactly the same environment* as was its primary when it was entered. All the operations of the primary must have been undone, all the non-local variables altered by the primary must have been restored to their previous values. It is a requirement on the mechanisation that this recovery be achievable with reasonable efficiency both for assignments, as described below in section 8, and for more complex operations, as described in Sect. 11. The recovery block scheme provides a structuring of programs in time and space so that the recovery information can be retained with greater facility and efficiency than would be possible with, for instance, a core image checkpoint mechanism.

In particular it should be noted that the alternate has no access to the reason why the primary was rejected and no access to any results calculated by the primary. It is important that a record of each rejection is preserved for subsequent investigation, but it is envisaged that the records will lie beyond the scope of the program being run. There may be occasions when it would be convenient for the alternate to know what had gone wrong with the primary, but the number of possible error conditions is very large, and it is not always easy to distinguish one error from another. Since the alternate cannot be expected to categorise and accommodate each cause of error explicitly, it would appear preferable that the alternate should always start again from the entry to the recovery block without any record of previous rejections. Errors which are expected to be sufficiently frequent that special handling would be appropriate can perhaps be regarded as normal program conditions rather tnan unforeseeable errors.

As mentioned earlier, an alternate block might perform the desired operation in a different way, presumably less efficiently, but perhaps by a simpler and less error-prone algorithm. However the more likely case is for an alternate block to be designed to provide an operation which, though less desirable, is still acceptable to the program as a whole. Thus the recovery block structure might be used as a means of structuring the rather ad hoc error recovery facilities that many existing systems incorporate [2].

7. Orthogonality of Design

We believe that the recovery block concept should not impose any constraint on the programming or the architecture of the computer, for any design which imposes constraints may preclude, or be precluded by, other techniques intended to facilitate reliable computing.

Each primary and alternate block is programmed in exactly the same manner as a conventional program, written in any desired programming language and with any desired programming style or methodology. Extensions to existing languages are required only to define the recovery block structure, and to permit access to prior values of variables during acceptance tests.

It is natural to equate the recovery blocks with a subset of the blocks of an Algol-like program, but it is not necessary that all the Algol blocks be recovery blocks, or even that the programming language provide an Algol-like block structure. The only requirements are that the recovery blocks should be explicitly defined, that they should be dynamically nested, and that entry to and exit from recovery blocks should be explicit. Clearly, well-structured programming techniques are to be encouraged, but the recursive cache concept does not depend on them. It is applicable to programming in assembler on a S/360 as to Algol on a B6700. Thus the recovery block concept its substantially orthogonal to programming languages and methodologies.

The recursive cache mechanism, described below, operates entirely with "words" in a single linear virtual address space. The user may program with various sizes of data, may use vectors, heaps, own variables, complex list structures, parameters, or even recursive procedures. It is assumed that the computer architecture will accommodate this variety and, by a display, descriptors, indexing or other mechanisms, will convert all store references into references to words in a linear virtual address space. The address of such a word will be known as a "virtual address". The mechanism operates entirely with these words and their virtual addresses, and the significance of this data to the user program is of no concern to the cache mechanism. The description below is in terms of a classical Algol stack machine, but it is believed that conventional computer architectures can readily be accommodated, and thus the error recovery scheme is orthogonal to the architecture of the computer.

8. The Recursive Cache Mechanism

The requirement that an alternate block be presented with exactly the same environment as was its primary could be mechanised by appropriate core image check points, (or even by retaining enough information to allow programs to be executed backwards, instruction by instruction [3]), but the associated overheads would defeat the purpose of the concept. Consequently a specialised mechanisation is presented which aims to reduce the overheads to an acceptable level, while remaining invisible to the user.

The heavy overhead of recording a conventional checkpoint on entry to each recovery block is caused by the recording of the entire context of the recovery block, a substantial quantity of information. But in many cases only a few of the non-local variables will be modified by the recovery block, and all that would be needed to restore the environment are the virtual addresses and

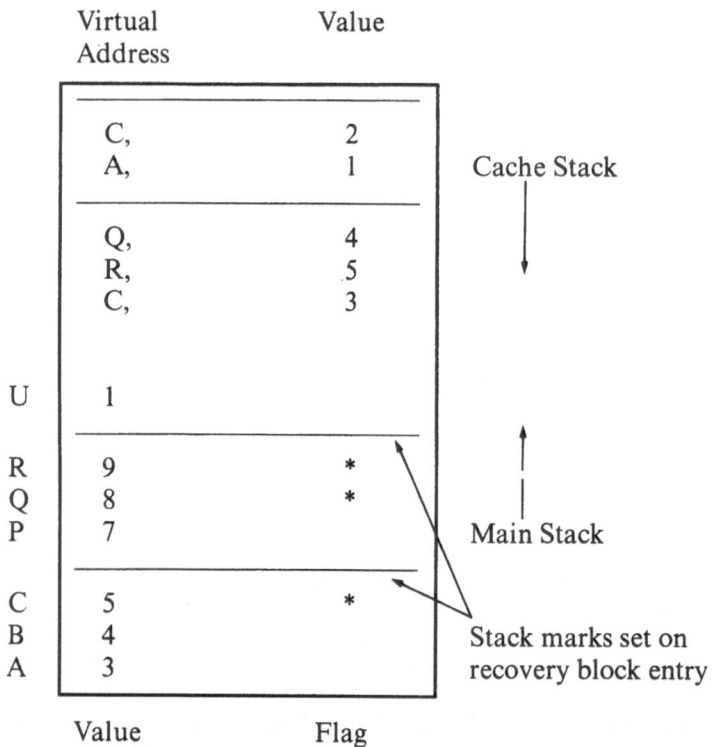

Fig. 3. A diagramatic representation of the main stack and the cache stack. Assignments to C, Q, R have been made within the current recovery block. Thus these variables have been flagged and their previous values recorded in the cache

prior values of those variables which are actually modified [4]. Thus in this mechanisation only on writing into a "word" is the virtual address and previous value of that word recorded, in an additional storage area to be called the cache.

Since only the values of the variables on entry to the recovery block need be preserved, it is appropriate to associate with each word a boolean flag to indicate that the required value has already been preserved in the cache. All these flags are cleared on entry to the recovery block, and each writing operation tests the appropriate flag. If the flag is clear, than the virtual address and current value of the word must be recorded in the cache, and the flag must be set. If it is set, then no special action is required before the write operation.

Because the recovery blocks are nested, the cache can be organised as a stack, as is shown in Fig. 3. Stack marks are placed in the cache stack to indicate recovery block entries, and similar stack marks in the main stack facilitate the recognition of variables local to the current primary or alternate block. The marks divide the main stack and cache stack into (possibly empty) regions. Each main stack word contains a value and a boolean flag which (for non-local variables) indicates modification within the current recovery block. Each cache entry contains the virtual address of a word and the value of that word on entry to the recovery block. Note that the set of words flagged in the main stack corresponds exactly to the set of words recorded within in the top region of the cache stack.

The term recursive cache was originally introduced by (inaccurate) analogy to the cache of the IBM 360/85. In fact our usage of cache can be viewed as matching its dictionary meaning of a "hiding-place", since *prior values* of variables are hidden in the cache in case they might be needed again. In contrast IBM's usage of this term, which they have now abandoned in favour of "buffer-store", was in relation to the high speed store of a demand paged virtual memory system; such a high speed store would contain *current values* of variables.

9. The Algorithm of the Mechanisation

On entry to a recovery block, stack marks are placed in the main and cache stacks, and all the flags are cleared. The flags will subsequently be reset by examination of the appropriate cache region and the same technique may be used to clear them. For examples see stages (b) or (c) in Fig. 4.

Reading any variable (local or global, whether modified or not) is done by fetching the value of the word with the appropriate virtual address, stage (e) in Fig. 4. The flag is ignored. Thus no overhead is incurred on reading, an important consideration.

Assignment to a local variable is also performed conventionally, important because many assignments are to local variables, stages (b) or (c) in Fig. 4. Local variables do not need to be cached and thus the flag is of no significance.

Assignment to a non-local variable involves testing the flag. If on assignment the flag is found to be clear, then the flag must be set and an entry, comprising the virtual address of the word and its current value, is pushed onto the cache stack. The assignment is then performed, stages (d) or (e) in Fig. 4. If the flag is set then the prior value has already been cached and the assignment proceeds conventionally, stage (f) in Fig. 4.

The performance of an acceptance test implies exit from the primary or alternate block, and therefore the deletion of all local variables from the main stack. If the acceptance test involves access to prior values of variables, these values may be obtained by searching the top region of the cache stack, though it may be appropriate first to check the flag of the word in the main stack, where the required value will be if it is actually unchanged.

If the acceptance test should reject the block then the environment must be restored to exactly the situation existing on entry. This is done by popping each entry of the top region of the cache stack, and using its value to reset the word at the virtual address cited, the flag also being cleared, stage (h) of Fig. 4. Note that this must clear all the flags, the condition established on entry to a recovery block. By removal of stack marks, this operation may be performed repeatedly to obtain recovery at an outer recovery block.

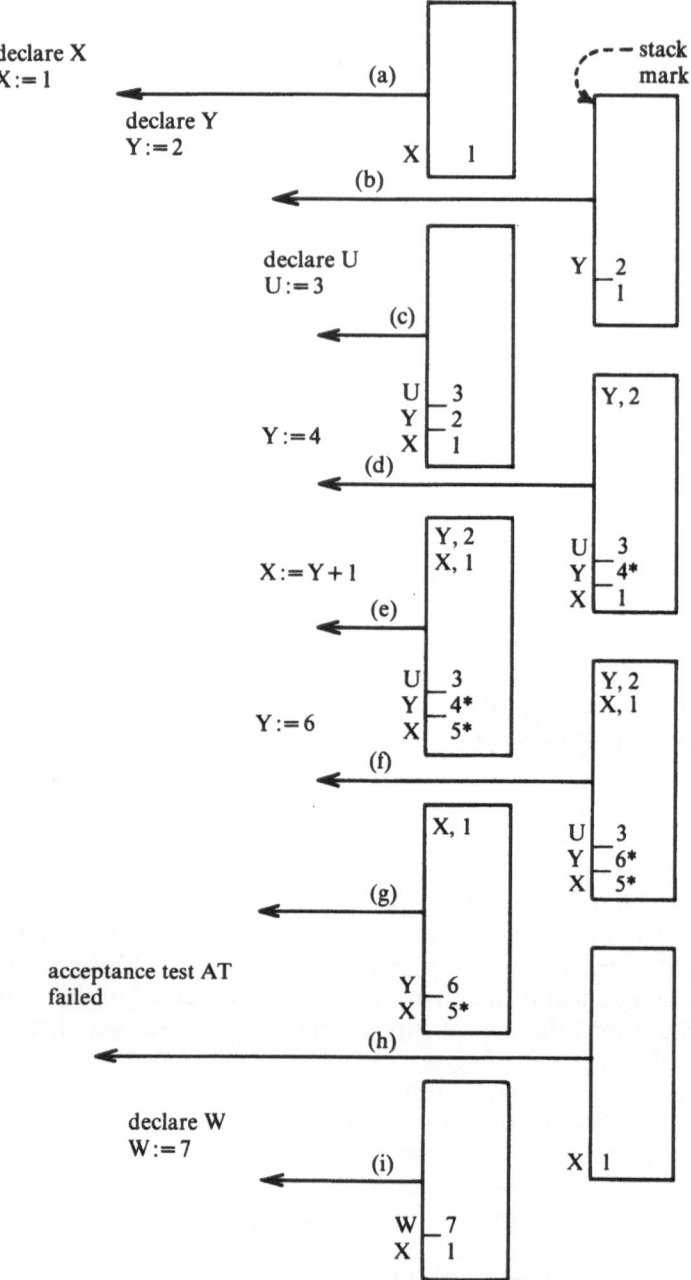

Fig. 4. The states of the stack and the cache during the execution of the program of Fig. 2. For descriptions of the various operations depicted, see the text, Sect. 9

The action if the acceptance test is passed is more complex. The aim is to set up the cache and the stack as though the accepted block had consisted solely of its non-local assignments, some of which might of course be local to the enclosing block, others of which might have been preceded by assignments to the same variables during this enclosing block. First, all the flags are cleared. Then the entries in the top-but-one region of the cache stack are accessed and the flags are set for all the words those entries address. Next the entries of the top region of the cache are processed.

If the word addressed by the cache entry is local to the enclosing recovery block then the cached value may be discarded as caching is not required for local variables. Similarly, if the flag of the word addressed is set then the cached value may be discarded, for the value cached in the lower cache region is the true value of the word on entry to that recovery block.

If the flag is not set, then the cached value is the value that a nonlocal variable had on entry to the enclosing recovery block. The cache entry must therefore be included in the top-but-one region of the cache stack, and the flag must be set.

While the top region of the cache stack is being processed it may be necessary to enlarge the top-but-one region. It is therefore appropriate to process this top region in the reverse sequence (FIFO rather than LIFO). When the top region has been fully processed and the stack marks removed, processing may resume on the enclosing, now the current, recovery block. Stage (g) of Fig. 4 shows a few of the possible circumstances. The main overheads of this implementation are incurred at block entry and block exit time, and will depend linearly on the number of different non-local assignments that have occurred. The scanning of the cache that is involved is comparatively simple, and is in our opinion quite appropriate for hardware implementation. The one instance of a search is that involved in accessing the prior value of a variable that has been changed, which occurs only in acceptance tests. The space needed in the cache will depend on the program structure, but for a given choice of recovery blocks no unnecessary information will be saved, a claim which would be very difficult to make for a system with programmer-specified check-pointing.

10. Assignments and Procedure Calls Within Acceptance Tests

In the basic scheme, an acceptance test is a transparent operation whose sole effect is to provide a binary decision on the acceptability of a recovery block. In practice however an acceptance test may be a quite complex program containing assignments and procedure calls.

Because of notational problems, it would appear to be inappropriate to allow an acceptance test to contain a recovery block. But if the acceptance test is allowed to call procedures which contain recovery blocks, then the required effect is readily achieved. The use of procedures may be very desirable for the proper structuring of complex acceptance tests.

Only minor extensions to the basic recursive cache mechanism are required to accommodate procedure calls within acceptance tests. The most significant extension required is to allow an acceptance test to pass to a procedure, as a parameter, a reference to the previous value of a variable which has been altered within the recovery block. The parameter may be of course a complex data structure, only parts of which have been altered. It would appear necessary to extend the address or reference to the parameter with a recovery block level field, which can be carried over into any subsequently derived address or reference. This level field can be used to ensure recovery of the correct values from the cache.

Modification of these original values within an ceptance test is clearly reprehensible and without any possible justification. The appending of the level number to an ddress could therefore be used to render the data thus referenced read only.

11. Recoverable Procedures

The programs discussed above generated their results entirely by assignment to storage locations, and were recovered simply by reversal of those assignments. But many programming operations generate results other than by assignments, or need to preserve some results even when the processing of the operation is abandoned and an alternate is attempted. Typical examples are operations which involve file access and input-output interfaces, accounting routines, diagnostic traces, and interactive user interfaces. It is characteristic of such programs that error recovery is more complex than automatic reversal of assignments, and an opportunity must be provided for the program designer to specify the appropriate recovery action.

It is proposed that operations requiring special recovery action should be structured into procedures, to be known as recoverable procedures. A recoverable procedure is not itself a recovery block with an acceptance test and alternates, though its body consists of a recovery block. Such a procedure may declare own variables, whose values are not automatically reset by the recursive cache mechanism in the event of error, but can be restored by program within the recoverable procedure. It may be appropriate to allow several recoverable procedures to be associated and to share a set of own variables. Such a structure would follow naturally from the classes of Simula [5] or the Type mechanism of Campbell and Habermann [6].

Just as the recovery of simple variables involves the saving of a value on first assignment within a recovery block, multiple further assignments without special action, and the restoration of the prior value in the event of an error, so the recoverable procedure must provide three entry points, the save, the normal and the reverse entry points as is shown in Fig. 5. The save entry point preserves such recovery information as the programmer specifies before performing the required action, and the mechanism will enter here the first time that the procedure is called within a recovery block. Subsequent calls of the procedure within the recovery block will enter at the normal entry point. (The assumption is that the information saved on the occasion of the first call of the procedure suffices to allow the system to be reinstated to the satisfaction of the pro-

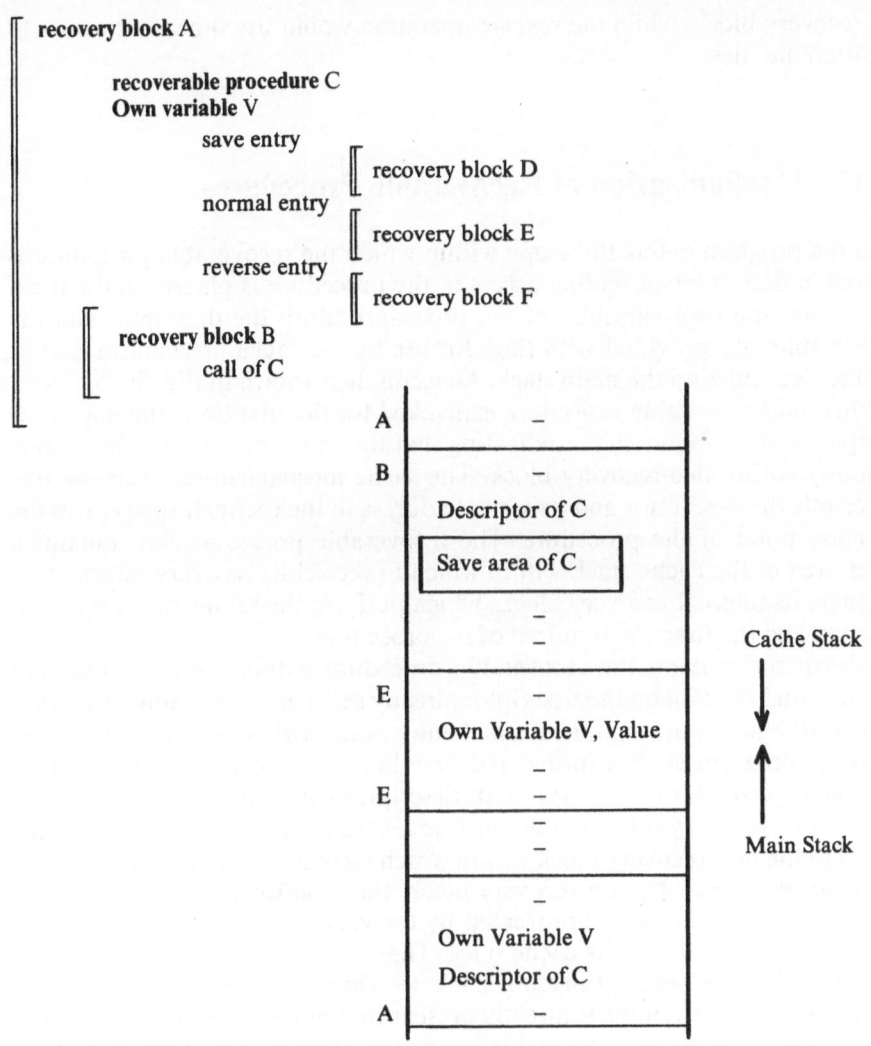

recovery block A

    recoverable procedure C
    Own variable V
        save entry

                recovery block D

      normal entry
                recovery block E

      reverse entry
                recovery block F

    recovery block B
      call of C

A –

B –

Descriptor of C

Save area of C

–

–   Cache Stack

E –

Own Variable V, Value

–

E –

–

–   Main Stack

–

Own Variable V

Descriptor of C

A –

Fig. 5. A program containing a recoverable procedure and a diagramatic representation of the stacks and their contents

grammer, even if there are many further calls). It is important to note that the program which calls the recoverable procedure is not aware of the save entry point, which is invoked automatically by the cache mechanism. The reverse entry point is also invoked automatically by the cache mechanism, in the event of an error in the block that invoked the procedure, so as to provide an opportunity to restore the recoverable procedure in accordance with the information saved on entry through the save entry point.

An example of a recoverable procedure might be a file access interface which maintains own variables indicating the current position of each file. The save operation would simply record the values of these variables on entry to each recovery block, while the reverse operation would use the saved values to reposition the files.

12. The Mechanisation of Recoverable Procedures

When the program enters the scope within which the recoverable procedure is declared, a descriptor providing access to the procedure is placed on the main stack, as are the own variables of the procedure. Both the descriptor and the own variables are provided with flags for use by the cache mechanism, just as any other variables on the main stack. An example is shown in Fig. 5.

When the recoverable procedure is invoked for the first time, the flag on its descriptor will be found clear, indicating that the procedure has not been used previously within this recovery block. The cache mechanism now sets the flag and records the descriptor and its virtual address in the cache. It then enters the save entry point of the procedure. The recoverable procedure now obtains a further area of the cache stack within which to record its recovery information and enters its internal recovery blocks which perform the saving of recovery information and the function required of the procedure.

Subsequent calls on the recoverable procedure within the same recovery block will find the flag on the descriptor already set. The recoverable procedure will then be entered through the normal entry point with no special action. But should the program enter a further recovery block before again calling the recoverable procedure, then the flag on its descriptor will have been cleared and a further set of recovery information must be recorded in the cache stack to correspond to the new recovery block within which recovery may be required.

On successful exit from a recovery block, the descriptor and its associated save area in the cache stack are treated by the cache mechanism just like any other variable recorded in the cache stack. They are transferred from one cache region to the next, resetting the main stack descriptor flag, until either they become local or the descriptor is already present in that cache region. Within the recovery blocks inside the recoverable procedure, the own variables of the procedure, and the variables within the save area in the cache stack, are regarded as non-local and can be restored just like any other variable in the event of error. But once the acceptance test of the first recovery block of the procedure is satisfied, during the exit from the recovery block these variables are regarded as local within the next recovery block, regardless of their position in the main stack, and their cached prior values are therefore discarded. Thus exit from the recoverable procedure effectively renders permanent any assignments to the own variables, and subsequent recovery can only be through the recovery program contained within the recoverable procedure. However any assignments made by the procedure to non-local variables, either directly or through some parameter mechanism, are treated normally and therefore can be undone by the cache mechanism.

After an error, the top cache stack region is processed in the conventional manner, and when the descriptor for the recoverable procedure is found, the cache mechanism invokes the reverse entry point of the procedure. The reverse entry point may involve a recovery block, further procedure calls and recovery blocks, and any other processing necessary to restore the own variables to appropriate values. (We have yet to consider the need for allowing assignments to other non-local variables from within a reverse operation.)

13. Exercising the Alternates

Within many systems containing error recovery mechanisms, the mechanisms are not tested with sufficient rigour. Adequate validation of a system's ability to cope with errors occurring in the midst of attempts to recovery from an earlier detected error can be particularly difficult. Thus errors remain within the recovery programs and the reliability of the system is adversely affected.

It is proposed that, in the recovery block system, provision should be made for the automatic exercising of the alternates, either all alternates being exercised or only a proportion on a probabilistic basis. Rejections would be recorded for subsequent analysis. This provision can be made either by an explicit mechanism, or else perhaps by appropriate programming of the acceptance tests.

14. Further Research

The recovery block scheme is only in the early stages of development, and its value has yet to be demonstrated. At present, a programmed emulator incorporating a recursive cache mechanism is being implemented for our dual processor PDP11/45, and a variety of application programs, structured into recovery blocks, will be programmed to test the concept for both efficacy and cost. Subsequently we hope to extend the recovery block concept into the code of the operating system.

We have already received encouragement from some brief experiments carried out by a colleague, David Wyeth, which involved interpretive execution of a number of Algol W programs. Even regarding each block as being a recovery block, it was found that the amount of space that would be needed for a cache was in every case considerably smaller than that needed for the stack. It would of course be possible to design a program, and its recovery block structure, so that the cache size greatly exceeded that of the stack. We believe this to be unlikely in practice, but could imagine that a scheme for removing part of the cache to backing storage, which could take advantage of the simplified patterns of access to the cache, might be worthwhile.

The most significant limitation of the recovery blocks described here is that they apply only to a single sequential process in isolation. In fact some useful progress has been made towards the recovery of asynchronous co-operating processes, and investigation continues. We hope to publish some preliminary results in this area shortly.

The recovery block concept is only one aspect of a project at the University of Newcastle upon Tyne to investigate computer system reliability. Another, closely related, aspect of this research is the design of highly structured addressing and protection schemes. A proposed 'recursive virtual machine architecture' has been documented separately [7]; a simplified version of this architecture is also being incorporated in the emulator.

15. Conclusion

Just as existing protection schemes provide error containment firewalls in space, so the recovery block concept can be thought of as providing firewalls in time. It allows programs containing provisions for error detection and recovery to be structured so as to distinguish clearly between the main program, the acceptance tests, and the action to be taken in error conditions. The provision of successive levels of error recovery permits attempts at purely local error recovery with low overheads, while the errors are contained so that the alternative programs can be run within the same environment as was the main program. The recoverable procedure concept provides a means for the extension of the recovery block concept into more complex situations. These structuring techniques are complemented by a hardware mechanism, whose overheads are in our opinion quite tolerable, which ensures that, for a given choice of recovery blocks, no unnecessary information is saved.

Acknowledgements. The development of the recovery block scheme, and the present description of it, has been greatly aided by discussions with colleagues working on or associated with the research project at the University of Newcastle upon Tyne on the Design of Highly Reliable Computer Systems. The funds for this project are provided by the Science Research Council.

References

1. R. W. Floyd, Assigning meanings to programs, in Mathematical Aspects of Computer Science, ed. Schwartz, J. T., Amer. Math. Soc. 1967.
2. B. Randell, Operating Systems: the problems of performance and reliability. IFIP Congress 1971, North Holland, pp. 281–290, August 1971. (Also Chap. 1)
3. R. M. Balzer, EXDAMS, Extendable Debugging and Monitoring Systems, SJCC 1969, p. 567.
4. C. J. Prenner et al, An Implementation of Backtracking for Programming Languages, ACM Annual Conference, 1972, p. 763.
5. G. M. Birtwistle et al., SIMULA *begin*, Student Litteratur/Auerbach 1973.
6. R. H. Campbell and A. N. Habermann, The Specification of Process Synchronisation by Path Expressions, Lecture Notes in Computer Science, Vol. 16, Springer-Verlag, 1974.
7. H. C. Lauer and D. Wyeth, A Recursive Virtual Machine Architecture, TR 54, Computing Laboratory, University of Newcastle upon Tyne, (September 1973).

Reprinted from Lecture Notes in Computer Science, Vol. 16, pp. 177–193, Springer-Verlag, 1974.

A Reconsideration of the Recovery Block Scheme

P. A. LEE

The recovery block scheme has been introduced as a method of providing fault tolerance at the software level in a computing system. From the widespread interest that has been expressed in the scheme there appears to be a standard set of questions which are posed about its implementation and utility. This paper presents a brief overview of the recovery block scheme and then examines in detail the issues that these questions raise.

The reliance which is being placed on present day computing systems has led to an increasing demand for reliability, particularly at the software levels in a system. Most techniques for producing reliable software (for instance, methodologies for program construction and testing) have concentrated on the praiseworthy aim of eliminating faults from the software before reliance is placed on its behaviour. However, it is widely recognised that complex systems are likely to contain residual design faults, both in the software and hardware. Efforts aimed at providing tolerance against such faults should have a beneficial effect on the reliability of a system. The recovery block scheme was introduced by Horning et al. (1974) as a method of providing fault tolerance at the software levels in a system, particularly against residual design faults. The concepts of the recovery block scheme have been widely presented by various members of the Science Research Council sponsored 'Reliability Project' at Newcastle University, and from the questions asked at such presentations it would appear that there is a fairly standard set of doubts and misunderstandings about the scheme. The purpose of this paper is twofold: firstly, to present these questions with their answers, in the hope of clarifying the issues they raise; and secondly, to relate the recovery block scheme to some of the recent work of the Reliability Project.

The Recovery Block Scheme

For completeness, this section presents a brief overview of the recovery block scheme. For further details the reader is referred to Horning et al. (1974), Randell (1975) and Anderson and Kerr (1976).

Recovery blocks provide a means for a programmer to specify redundancy at the software level in a system by means of standby-spare algorithms which are used, as necessary, to replace failing algorithms. The outline of a recovery block is presented in Fig. 1.

The essential components of a recovery block are a set of algorithms (called *alternates*) and an *acceptance test*. The alternates are simply statement lists, with the first or primary alternate representing the preferred algorithm. The acceptance test is a programmer-provided error detection mechanism to check on the acceptability of the results produced by the alternates. Although the recovery

69

```
ensure ⟨acceptance test⟩
by ⟨first (primary) alternate⟩
else by ⟨second alternate⟩
· · ·
· · ·
else by ⟨nth alternate⟩
else error
```

Fig. 1. Recovery block outline

block scheme fits most easily into block structured languages such as ALGOL and PL/I, it can in fact be used with other high and low level languages. Indeed, the scheme can also be used for much more abstract levels in computing systems, such as those which support job control languages and data base accessing. However, this paper concentrates on its use within individual sequential programs.

The execution of a recovery block is as follows: on initial entry, the primary alternate is entered. At the end of the alternate the acceptance test (a boolean expression) is evaluated — if this test yields 'true' (that is, the results from the alternate are acceptable) then the recovery block is exited. However, if the acceptance test yields 'false', or if an error is detected by the underlying machine during the execution of the alternate, then *backward error recovery* occurs in that the state of the program is automatically reset to the state that existed when the recovery block was entered, and then the sequence of execution described above is repeated except that the next alternate is used in place of the failing alternate. A record of the errors and acceptance test failures which occurred is produced for subsequent use by the programmer. If all of the alternates fail, then this is regarded as a failure of that recovery block and an error condition is raised. As recovery blocks can be nested to any depth (conceptually at least) the failing recovery block may itself be embedded in an alternate of an enclosing recovery block. If this is the case then the error condition will result in the failure of the enclosing alternate. Otherwise, the program is terminated.

The underlying machine which is executing the programs containing recovery blocks provides the mechanisms for switching control between alternates and to enable the backward error recovery of the objects of the program to be accomplished. (Objects for which backward error recovery is provided will be termed *recoverable objects*.) These mechanisms will be transparent to the program and, for example, could be built into the hardware of the machine. A mechanism called the *recursive or recovery cache* has been proposed to implement the backward error recovery. The recovery cache essentially provides three functions: (a) recording recovery data; (b) performing recovery; and (c) discarding recovery data when recovery is no longer required. There are several ways in which the recording of recovery data can be implemented. The basis of the method proposed in the three papers referenced above is as follows: when an object which is not local to an alternate is updated for the first time from within that alternate, the original value of that object together with its address will be stored in the recovery cache, and will be used to restore the state of that object if recovery is invoked. Thus a minimum of recovery data is maintained in the recovery cache. (This method implemented in hardware would be appropriate for providing backward error recovery for simple objects such as integers, reals and characters, and structures of the same.) Other implementations for recording recovery data will be discussed subsequently. The underlying machine will also provide mechanisms to detect errors in the execution of programs. Typical errors detected would include illegal instructions, division by zero and memory access violations.

Doubts and Misunderstandings

Q1. What types of fault are recovery blocks intended to provide tolerance against?

A1. There are essentially two types of fault that can occur in a system: (a) component faults, when a component does not function according to its specification; and (b) algorithmic faults, which are faults in the interrelationships between components. (This fault classification is discussed in more detail by Randell, Lee and Treleaven (1978).) At the hardware level in a system both component and algorithmic faults can occur, algorithmic faults being missing or incorrect connections between components. At the software level, faults are algorithmic (although can be regarded as component faults at another level of abstraction). Algorithmic faults are residual design faults in a system. The location and effects of such faults are unanticipatable, since in general they arise from unmastered complexity in the design of the system. Recovery blocks are designed to provide tolerance against algorithmic faults in both the software (program 'bugs') and in the hardware. After recovery, such faults are avoided by switching to the next alternate in the hope, perhaps vain, that the set of circumstances that led to the failure of the previous alternate are not repeated. Treatment of the fault is left for manual off-line diagnosis (aided by the error record mentioned previously) and repair.

A recovery block can also provide tolerance against some anticipated component faults in the underlying machine. If the underlying machine detects an error which it can attribute to a fault in its operation but which may have caused damage to the executing program, than an automatic *retry* facility can be provided — the error recovery for the program can be invoked to rectify any damage that may have been caused to the data of the program, and the same alternate re-entered. In this way, a recovery block can provide tolerance against the damage that has been caused either by transient component failures or by permanent component failures which result in reconfiguration or replacement of components at the hardware level.

Q2. As recovery blocks increase the size of the programming task, in that the alternates have to be programmed, surely the use of recovery blocks will increase the complexity of the program and therefore detract from, rather than increase, the overall reliability?

A2. It is true that the use of recovery blocks increases the size of the programming task. However, each alternate in a recovery block, when executed, starts from exactly the same state because of the error recovery capability that is provided. Thus the design of each alternate can (and preferably should) be independent of any other. The designer of one alternate need have no knowledge of the design of the other alternates, leave alone any responsibility for coping with any damage that a previous alternate might have caused. Equally, the designer of a program containing recovery blocks does not necessarily have to be concerned with which of the various alternates was eventually used. It is therefore argued that the increase of size in programs containing recovery blocks does not provide a corresponding increase in complexity. Indeed, the structure of recovery blocks may provide a means of reducing the complexity found in systems which have extensive ad hoc error detection and recovery facilities.

Q3. Is it always possible to generate alternative algorithms for a particular problem?

A3. The simple answer to this question is yes. The justification for this answer is as follows: there are essentially two different ways in which a recovery block can be used. The first and obvious situation is when it is required that each alternate of the recovery block produces exactly the same results. For some problems it is comparatively easy to obtain different algorithms for the alternates − sorting and mathematical functions such as integration are obvious examples. However, for other problems it may be difficult for a programmer to design different algorithms, particularly without making the same mistakes in each algorithm. To overcome this difficulty it is likely that separate programmers will be required, each working independently on a specification of the problem to provide an alternate to be incorporated in the final program. This is not a new concept and, for example, has been advocated by Gilb (1974) and Fischler et al. (1975).

A further source of alternates may be obtained from previous versions of an algorithm. A common occurrence with software products is that a new version is introduced, often simply for performance considerations. Clearly, there will be situations in which the previous version can be used as a secondary alternate enabling the new version to be introduced into the system with the knowledge that if (when) it failed, then the original version was still available as a backup.

The second situation in which recovery blocks can be used is to provide what may be termed *graceful degradation in software*. It is not necessary that each alternate of a recovery block produces exactly the same results; the constraint on the alternates is that they produce acceptable results, as defined by the acceptance test. Thus, while the primary alternate attempts to produce the desired results, the second and subsequent alternates may only attempt to provide an increasingly degraded service. The more degraded the service, the simpler the alternate may be and consequently the greater the hope that it does not contain any design faults. Similarly, as each alternate is essentially different, it is more likely that a design fault will not be repeated in all alternates, whether produced by the same programmer or not. As an example of a recovery block

```
ensure ⟨consistency of disc transfer queue⟩
by ⟨algorithm which enters request in optimal queue position⟩
else by ⟨algorithm which enters request at end of queue⟩
else by ⟨send warning 'request ignored'⟩
else error
```

Fig. 2. Recovery block example

designed in this manner, consider the part of a program that has to enter a disc-to-core transfer request into a queue of outstanding requests. The outline of such a program is presented in Fig. 2.

The acceptance test for this recovery block simply checks that the transfer queue is in a consistent state. The primary alternate attempts to place the new transfer request in the optimal position in the queue, for example, to minimise disc head movement. The second alternate avoids the complications of the primary alternate by simply placing the new request at the end of the queue. The third alternate is more desperate, and leaves the existing queue alone, providing a warning that the new request has been ignored. While this may cause problems for the program requesting the transfer, at least the rest of the system is allowed to proceed without disruption. If this alternate fails, indicating that the queue was inconsistent when the recovery block was entered, then recovery has to take place at a more global level.

It should be noted that while the recovery block scheme enables redundancy to be specified at the algorithmic level in programs, it does not provide for redundancy in the data structures of programs. Thus, while an alternate can define any data structures local to its environment, the structures which are global to the recovery block must be fixed and their structure invariant. Therefore, there may be situations in which the static structure of global data adds to the problems of designing alternates.

Q4. It is common in fault tolerant hardware systems that a component is replaced when it fails. Does the recovery block scheme provide a software equivalent to this?

A4. An analogy can certainly be drawn between the replacement of faulty hardware components and the replacement of faulty alternates in the recovery block scheme. Borgerson (1973) has defined two terms for fault tolerant hardware: spontaneous replacement, in which the failing component is detected and replaced by an identical component; and spontaneous reconfiguration, which results in some degradation of the system. The two different ways in which recovery blocks can be used, as discussed above, could be described as providing spontaneous replacement and spontaneous reconfiguration at the software level. However, two points should be noted: firstly, a hardware component is usually replaced with one of identical design and construction − this is not usually the case with alternates. Secondly, the replacement of a hardware component is usually permanent; the replaced component may be repaired, but then kept as a standby-spare until needed. With recovery blocks, however, the failing alternate is only temporarily replaced, just for that execution of the block. On subsequent entries to the block that alternate will again be used in the hope that the new set of inputs does not cause the fault to manifest itself again.

The use of alternates of differing design and construction can be contrasted with another common feature in fault tolerant hardware systems, namely triple modular redundancy (and its variants). In TMR systems three identical components and voting circuits which examine the outputs from the components are used in order to mask the effects of any single component failure. In theory, a TMR system could be used to provide a means of tolerating design faults, as discussed by Avizienis (1975). This would involve the provision of three different versions of each component which, although designed independently, would all be intended to produce identical answers, preferably all at the same speed. The utility of such a scheme seems limited.

Q5. How should acceptance tests be designed?

A5. The acceptance test is a programmer-provided error detection mechanism which provides a check on the results of an alternate at the last possible moment, that is just before the recovery block is left and a set of recovery data is discarded. Clearly, a programmer can provide as little or as much checking as he considers necessary. Ideally, the acceptance test should test for the absolute correctness of the results. However, even if such a strict test could be designed, it may not be appropriate for four reasons: (a) because of performance considerations; (b) because the test for correctness may involve objects external to the computing system — for example, a stock control data base system may not be able to check its internal representation of the stock level against that actually in the warehouse; (c) because the alternates provide an increasingly degraded service and hence their results will not be exactly the same; and (d) because the likely complexity of such a test would make the acceptance test prone to design faults which would detract from the usefulness of the recovery block by rejecting correct results, or causing their rejection through the occurrence of errors during the execution of the acceptance test.

Thus in general the acceptance test will, as its name suggests, be a test on the acceptability of the results of the alternate rather than a test of their absolute correctness. For example, an acceptance test on a sorting algorithm might only check that the sorted elements were in order and their checksum was equal to the original value, but because of performance considerations would not check that any items from the original set had been modified or lost.

When the alternates of a recovery block have been designed to provide gracefully degradable software it is clear that the acceptance test can only be as rigorous as a check on the results from the weakest alternate. This has led some people to suggest that there should be a separate acceptance test for each alternate. Such a structure can be easily obtained by nesting recovery blocks, as illustrated in Fig. 3.

While this structure may appear satisfactory in isolation, it must be recognised that, in general, a recovery block will form only part of a program and

```
ensure ⟨true⟩
by      ensure ⟨best acceptance test⟩
        by ⟨best algorithm⟩ else error;
else by ensure ⟨next best acceptance test⟩
        by ⟨next best algorithm⟩ else error;
. . .
. . .
else error;
```

Fig. 3. Multiple acceptance tests

that the acceptance test provides a check on the consistency of the results which are to be used by the rest of that program. (Indeed, it can be argued that the acceptance test should be the first part of the recovery block program to be designed.) Hence, it is likely that a single test of acceptance will often be required whether the alternates produce the same or different results.

The recovery cache mechanism can provide some run time assistance which may aid the design and implementation of acceptance tests: firstly, it can enable the prior values of objects to be referenced, so that the acceptance test can compare the current state with that on entry to the recovery block; and secondly, it can be designed to monitor the behaviour of the acceptance test with respect to the variables that had and had not been updated by an alternate. For example, it could raise an error condition if the acceptance test did not access all of the variables that had been updated by an alternate – this can ensure that the acceptance test performs at least some minimal checking of the new states of all updated objects and enables unintended updates to be detected.

The design of acceptance tests is a difficult area and still requires further research. While acceptance tests for specific problems can usually be specified, it is not yet clear whether a general methodology can be obtained, although there is some hope that the proof-directed methodology suggested by Anderson (1975) will provide some guidelines. It may also be noted that while the acceptance test is important, it will not be the only error detection mechanism in the system. As discussed previously, the underlying machine will provide mechanisms to detect errors in the execution of the program containing recovery blocks. Further programmer-provided checks could be incorporated into the alternates by means of assert statements, which raise an error condition if an error is detected. (Indeed, the structure depicted in Fig. 3 can be obtained through the use of assert statements instead of the nested recovery block, as described by Shrivastava and Akinpelu (1977).)

Q6. Can the recovery cache provide backward error recovery for all of the objects provided by the underlying machine?

A6. It is likely that there will be objects on the interface presented by the underlying machine for which backward error recovery is not available (for instance, the pages on a disc) or appropriate (for instance, objects shared by parallel processes). One method of dealing with such unrecoverable objects is to construct multi-level systems, whereby a new interface is constructed by soft-

75

ware to provide new recoverable objects which are abstractions of unrecoverable objects. The implementation of the recovery for these new objects, although achieved by programmer-provided actions, will be transparent to the programs running on the new interface and extensions to the recovery cache mechanism can ensure that this recovery is automatically invoked as required. Two systems have been constructed at Newcastle demonstrating this approach. In the system described by Verhofstad (1977), the unrecoverable disc pages provided by a machine are used to provide a recoverable filing system for user programs. The second system (Shrivastava and Banatre, 1978) provides backward error recovery for processes sharing data for the purpose of competing for the resources of the system. It is beyond the scope of this paper to describe the implementation of such multi-level systems. The interested reader is referred to the paper by Anderson, Lee and Shrivastava (1977) which describes a conceptual model of recovery in such multi-level systems.

Q7. What happens if the recovery cache fails?

A7. In any fault tolerant system there have to be some components which are reliable in that the correct operation of these components is necessary for the correct operation of the fault tolerant aspects of the system. For hardware systems, such components are referred to as the 'hardcore'. The recovery cache is a major part of the 'hardcore' for the recovery block scheme, and it is assumed that its operation will be reliable. There are two justifications for placing so much reliance on the recovery cache: firstly, it would appear that the design of the recovery cache is sufficiently simple that standard hardware design practices can ensure that there are no residual faults in its design. The second justification is that in such circumstances any hardware component can be made as reliable as is necessary, through the application of fault tolerance techniques — cost is usually the only limiting factor. The recovery cache should only be a small part of a complete system, and hence the cost incurred in making it reliable should be acceptable.

Q8. What are the run time overheads involved in the use of recovery blocks?

A8. As with any system that provides redundancy and fault tolerance, the use of recovery blocks incurs run time space and time overheads which may not be present in fault intolerant programs. (It must be noted that the costs involved in a priori testing and validation of reliable fault intolerant programs may be substantial, and have led Hecht (1976) to suggest the adoption of the recovery block scheme to reduce these costs.) The space overheads for programs using recovery blocks stems from the extra storage required for the alternates, the acceptance tests and for use by the recovery cache. As discussed previously, the recovery cache can record a minimum of recovery data, which it is hoped will in general be a small percentage of the data space of a program. Shrivastava and Akinpelu (1977) report on experiments in which the figures for programs containing a single recovery block were between 3% and 39% (with an average of 17%), which are considerably less than the 100% overhead that recording the complete data space of the program would have entailed.

The execution time overheads required to support recovery blocks will depend on the time required to evaluate the acceptance test and on the recovery cache implementation. As discussed previously, the acceptance test overhead is the responsibility of the programmer, although Kim and Ramamoorthy (1976) have proposed an architecture which attempts to mitigate this overhead. The overheads imposed by the recovery cache will depend in the main on the implementation of the mechanism used to record recovery data. There are many implementations known for this function, each of which has different tradeoffs. Tha algorithm discussed previously, which records the old values of objects just before they were updated, optimises the normal progress of a program at the expense of the extra time required to restore the state if recovery is invoked. An algorithm which inhibited the update of an object, and recorded the new value of the object in the recovery cache would optimise the time required for recovery. (Indeed, with this organisation the recovery cache could act as a high speed buffer store and also possibly increase the speed of the normal execution of the program.) Also, at the expense of extra space, the time to record recovery data can be minimised or vice versa, as exemplified by the schemes described by Horning et al. (1974) and Anderson and Kerr (1976). It must also be noted that the recovery cache is intended to be provided as part of the underlying machine (for example, to be built in hardware) and should therefore be fast, particularly as some of its operations could be performed in parallel with the execution of the program. Thus it is felt that for a given set of constraints, a suitable implementation of the recovery cache can be specified. The programmer also has some control over the recovery time – recovery blocks can be nested to provide as fine a grain of recovery as is desired so as to minimise recovery time, at the expense of course of increased recording of recovery data.

In all of the above mechanisms the execution speed of the majority of instructions provided by the underlying machine will not be affected at all by the recovery block scheme. Apart from the instructions specific to the utilisation of recovery blocks (for example, start recovery block, end recovery block) the only instructions incurring any extra overhead will be those that write to the objects of a program and therefore require intervention by the recovery cache mechanism. Indeed, further optimisations can be applied so that only those instructions which write to an object that is external to an alternate are intercepted.

Although the overheads of a given mechanism can be quantified, it is difficult (impossible) to quantify the increased reliability that is obtained through the use of recovery blocks, since this is totally dependent on their effective deployment by the programmer. However, it is felt that the overheads associated with their use and implementation can be organised to be tolerable and acceptable.

Q9. Is the recovery block scheme the best technique for providing fault tolerant software?

A9. Exception handling (for example, as proposed by Goodenough (1975)) is often advocated as an alternative to the recovery block scheme. Exception handling can be thought of as a method of programming (forward) error recovery for anticipated faults. Thus for specific faults which can be anticipated and whose full consequences can be foreseen, exception handling can provide efficient recovery for it only involves correcting the known (anticipated) errors; in contrast, backward error recovery involves complete state restoration (albeit efficiently implemented by the recovery cache), not just restoration of the erroneous parts. However, the recovery block scheme can provide tolerance against unanticipated faults, while backward error recovery need make no assumptions about the fault and the damage it may have caused, and is in consequence a general recovery technique. Thus recovery blocks and exception handling techniques should be regarded as complementary rather than competitive approaches to achieving fault tolerant software. These topics are discussed further by Melliar-Smith and Randell (1977) who also present an example of a program combining both methods, using exception handlers to deal with simple anticipated faults, such as invalid input data, while utilising recovery blocks to deal with unanticipated faults, including those in the exception handlers themselves.

Conclusion

This paper has discussed the concepts and implementation of the recovery block scheme and has attempted to answer the questions which most frequently arise in discussions of the scheme. There is no other scheme known to the author which attacks effectively the area of fault tolerant computing that recovery blocks address, namely the tolerance of unanticipated design faults, particularly in the software level of a system. Experimentation with the implementation and utilisation of recovery blocks is being continued both at Newcastle and elsewhere and should shed further light on the scheme and determine its actual effectiveness.

Acknowledgments. This paper owes much to the work of past and present members of the Science Research Council sponsored 'Reliability Project' at the Computing Laboratory, University of Newcastle upon Tyne. In particular, I would like to thank Tom Anderson and Brian Randell for critical readings of earlier drafts of this paper.

References

Anderson, T. (1975). Provably Safe Programs, Technical Report No. 70, Computing Laboratory, University of Newcastle upon Tyne.

Anderson, T. and Kerr, R. (1976). Recovery Blocks in Action: A System Supporting High Reliability, Proceedings of Second International Conference on Software Engineering, pp. 447–457. (Also Chap. 2)

Anderson, T., Lee, P. A. and Shrivastava, S. K. (1978). A Model of Recoverability in Multi-level Systems, IEEE Trans. on Software Engineering, SE-4, 6, pp. 486–494. (Also Chap. 5)

Avizienis, A. (1975). Fault-Tolerance and Fault-Intolerance: Complementary Approaches to Reliable Computing, Proceedings of 1975 Conference on Reliable Software, pp. 458–463.

Borgerson, B. R. (1973). Spontaneous Reconfiguration in a Fail-Softly Computer Utility, Datafair 73, pp. 326–331.

Fischler, M. A., Firnschein, O. and Drew, D. L. (1975). Distinct Software: An Approach to Reliable Computing, Proceedings of Second USA-Japan Computer Conference, pp. 573–579.

Gilb, T. (1974). Parallel Programming, Datamation, October 1974, pp. 160–161.

Goodenough, J. B. (1975). Exception Handling: Issues and a Proposed Notation, CACM, 18, 12, pp. 683–696.

Hecht, H. (1976). Fault Tolerant Software for a Fault Tolerant Computer, Software Systems Engineering, Online, Uxbridge, pp. 235–248.

Horning, J. J., Lauer, H. C., Melliar-Smith, P. M. and Randell, B. (1974). A Program Structure for Error Detection and Recovery, Lecture Notes in Computer Science 16, Springer Verlag, pp. 177–193. (Also Chap. 2)

Kim, K. H. and Ramamoorthy, C. V. (1976). Failure-Tolerant Parallel Programming and its Supporting System Architecture, AFIPS Proceedings Vol. 45, pp. 413–423.

Melliar-Smith, P. M. and Randell, B. (1977). Software Reliability: The Role of Programmed Exception Handling, Proceedings of ACM Conference on Language Design for Reliable Software, pp. 95–100. (Also Chap. 3)

Randell, B. (1975). System Structure for Software Fault Tolerance. IEEE Transactions on Software Eingineering, Vol. 1, pp. 220–232. (Also Chap. 1)

Randell, B., Lee, P. A. and Treleaven, P. C. (1978). Reliable Computing Systems, Lecture Notes in Computer Science 60, Springer Verlag, pp. 282–393.

Shrivastava, S. K. and Akinpelu, A. A. (1978). Fault Tolerant Sequential Programming, Digest of Papers, FTCS 8, pp. 207–208. (Also Chap. 2)

Shrivastava, S. K. and Banatre, J-P. (1978). Reliable Resource Allocation Between Unreliable Processes, IEEE Transactions on Software Engineering, Vol. 4, pp. 230–241. (Also Chap. 4)

Verhofstad, J. S. M. (1977). Recovery and Crash Resistance in a Filing System, Proceedings ACM SIGMOD Conference, Toronto, pp. 158–167. (Also Chap. 2)

Reprinted with permission from the British Computer Society, The Computer Journal, Vol. 21, No. 4, pp. 306–310, November 1978.

Recovery Blocks in Action:
A System Supporting High Reliability

T. ANDERSON and R. KERR

Keywords and Phrases. Error detection, error recovery, recovery block, recovery cache, reliability, software fault-tolerance.

Abstract. The need for reliable complex systems motivates the development of techniques by which acceptable service can be maintained, even in the presence of residual errors. Recovery blocks allow a software designer to include tests on the acceptability of the various phases of a system's operation, and to specify alternative actions should the acceptance tests fail. This approach relies on certain architectural features, ideally implemented in hardware, by which control and data structures can be retrieved after errors.

A brief account is presented of the recovery block scheme, together with a description of a new implementation of the underlying cache mechanism. The salient features of a proposed computer architecture are described, which incorporates this implementation and also provides a high level of detection for errors such as the corruption of code and data. A prototype system has been constructed to test the viability of these techniques by executing programs containing recovery blocks on an emulator for the proposed architecture. Experience in running this system are recounted with respect to the execution of programs based on erroneous algorithms and also with respect to errors introduced by deliberate attempts to corrupt the system.

Introduction

Complex computing systems can never be guaranteed to be entirely error-free. Techniques by which systems can be made to withstand the effects of errors and continue to provide acceptable service are therefore necessary. There are three key issues involved in providing an acceptable service in the presence of errors. These are:

- the ability to detect errors before an intolerable degree of damage is incurred,
- the ability to discard faulty information arising from the error and to retrieve a valid system state,
- the ability to continue, with the expectation that further useful work can be performed.

A group of research workers at Newcastle is actively engaged in developing techniques which bear upon these issues from two complementary standpoints, namely architectural and methodological. A system embodying the architectural features in order to support programs which adopt a methodological approach to the attainment of reliability has been implemented.

This paper describes techniques developed by the Newcastle reliability group and recounts our experiences in running the system.

Recovery Blocks

Recovery blocks have been proposed [Horning et al. (1974)] as a notation by which a programmer can make provision in the design of his program for checks on the acceptability of intermediate stages in the execution of the program, and also for alternative courses of action should these checks prove negative. Ways in which recovery blocks can be used in systems which aim to provide software fault tolerance have been reported [Randell (1975)], as has a proof-guided methodology for constructing the checks for acceptable program behaviour [Anderson (1975)].

Because recovery blocks play such a central role in our approach to obtaining greater program reliability, this section provides a summary of the basic recovery block scheme.

A recovery block may be represented as:

> **ensure** ⟨acceptance test⟩
>   **by** ⟨1st (primary) alternate⟩
>   **else by** ⟨2nd alternate⟩
>   .
>   .
>   .
>   **else by** ⟨nth alternate⟩
>   **else error**

where $n \geqq 1$. The acceptance test yields a logical value, and its evaluation should have no side effect. All of the alternates are statement lists. Each alternate is executed in turn until the acceptance test holds. Before an alternate is entered the state of the program is set to what it was on entry to the recovery block.

A more precise description can be given by considering the recovery block as a means of providing recovery from detected error conditions. An error condition is raised whenever the underlying system detects an erroneous situation, such as an attempt to divide by zero or to reference an invalid memory location. Moreover, if an acceptance test is evaluated and yields the value *false* then an erroneous situation has arisen and the system will again raise an error condition. Whenever an error condition is raised it is recorded by the system to form an error log which accompanies the output from the program.

A recovery block is executed by performing each alternate in turn, starting with the primary alternate, until for some alternate the acceptance test is satisfied. Error-free execution of an alternate is followed by evaluation of the acceptance test. If this evaluation is also error-free (which requires that the test yield the value *true*) then the acceptance test has been satisfied and execution of the recovery block is complete. Otherwise an error condition will have been raised, to which the system responds by restoring the state of the program to that current just before entry to the primary alternate, and then execution resumes with the next alternate in sequence, if one exists. If, however, all the alternates have been attempted and none has satisfied the acceptance test then an error condition is raised external to the recovery block, in that any further recovery can only be performed by an enclosing recovery block.

In the event of an error condition being raised for which there is no enclosing recovery block then the system terminates the execution of the program.

For both convenience and increased rigour in acceptance testing, the ability to access the value that a variable had on entry to a recovery block is helpful. The notation *prior* ⟨variable⟩ is employed for this purpose.

The acceptance test of the recovery block thus provides a means by which the programmer can incorporate his own checks for erroneous behavior to augment the basic checks that are undertaken by the underlying system. The second and subsequent alternates all endeavour to pass the same test of acceptability but the programmer is free to employ completely different algorithms to achieve this end. Although two alternates will often encode different algorithms to compute the same function this need not be the case. A subsequent alternate may be intended to have very different effects to the primary alternate, but still with the intention of satisfying the acceptance test. The greater the degree of independence between alternates the less is the risk that they all embody a common design inadequacy. Each alternate is able to operate independently of the others since all are designed to start execution from the same situation. Any effects that earlier alternates may have had on the initial situation are nullified by the restoration of the program state.

An outline of a simple recovery block is presented as an example.

```
ensure  data still valid
        by apply fast update
  else by apply slow but sure update
  else by warning ('update has not been applied')
else error
```

Acceptable behaviour for this recovery block is that the data on which it operates must remain valid (by some unspecified criterion). The recovery block is also intended to update the data, but presumably the enclosing program can continue as long as validity of the data is maintained. The primary alternate attempts to perform the update by means of an efficient, but possibly suspect, technique. If as a result the data under consideration becomes invalid, then the effects of the fast update are undone, and the second alternate is invoked. This alternate applies a less efficient algorithm in which, for some reason, greater confidence is placed − for instance the method might be very simple. If the acceptance test is again failed, then (after back-up) the third alternate performs no update at all and merely issues a warning message, leaving the data as it was on entry to the recovery block. A third failure of the acceptance test could only be due to the data being invalid originally and the system's only recourse would be to raise an error condition to be handled externally.

Recovery block notation can be regarded as a major extension of the *assert* statement employed in programming languages such as ALGOL W. An acceptance test itself behaves very like *assert* ⟨acceptance test⟩ but, in the event of the test being negative, the recovery block provides both automatic backing up and alternative code to be executed. Recovery blocks can be nested to produce a hierarchy of self-checking program modules which provide the programmer with a structured and disciplined approach for incorporating the (apparently) redundant program components needed to enhance reliability.

The Recovery Cache

To implement recovery blocks, the underlying system must be able to perform the required state restoration, and this must be done without incurring a prohibitive level of overhead. An architectural device called the "recovery cache" has been designed for this purpose. Earlier publications have called this device the "recursive cache". Our use of the term "cache" as a hiding place for prior values matches the dictionary definition and is not to be confused with IBM's former terminology for a buffer store. The recovery cache offers certain advantages over conventional checkpointing techniques. It ensures that all and only values which might be required to be reinstated are preserved for the lifetimes of the appropriate recovery blocks. The preservation and reinstatement of such values is entirely automatic and therefore not susceptible to human errors of omission, nor is it needlessly extravagant.

A possible implementation of a cache mechanism has been described in an earlier exposition on recovery blocks [Horning et al. (1974)]. That implementation, although very economic in storage requirements, displayed several undesirable speed characteristics. For example, one would hope that acceptance tests be passed more frequently than failed, yet in the early implementation the logic of the cache was much more complicated and time-consuming for acceptance than for rejection. We describe here an alternative implementation which rectifies this situation. Although slightly more extravagant in storage the complexity is reduced resulting in a potentially more reliable and less expensive design.

Since recovery blocks may be nested, the recovery cache can be organised as a stack. At any time it has the appearance of a number of regions, each corresponding to entry to a recovery block and containing the prior values of variables whose values have been altered within that recovery block. Adjacent regions are separated from each other by "barriers". The inefficiency of the original recovery cache implementation stemmed partly from the fact that it hinged on the locality of variables. The amount of work involved in determining locality depends upon the organisation of the main store of the system. For a stack organisation, locality is comparatively simple to determine; for other organisations it could be quite complicated, possibly even to the extent of limiting the number of practicable storage methods available. The implementation described here exploits the locality of values, a property which is much easier to establish and which is independent of any particular storage organisation.

We consider the main store to be composed of addressable words, each containing its own recovery level field. Apart from the barriers which demarcate the regions, each cache entry contains two fields of which one contains the ad-

```
begin declare a, b;  ─ ─ ─ ─ ─ ─ ─ ─ ─ ─  α
        a := 1; b := 2;  ─ ─ ─ ─ ─ ─ ─ ─ ─  β
        ensure b > prior b  ─ ─ ─ ─ ─ ─ ─  π
        by  ─ ─ ─ ─ ─ ─ ─ ─ ─ ─ ─ ─  γ
                begin declare c;  ─ ─ ─ ─ ─  δ
                        c := 3;
                        a := 4;  ─ ─ ─ ─ ─ ─ ─  ε
                        ensure . . .
                        by a := 5;
                                b := 6;
                                c := 7  ─ ─ ─  ξ
                        else by  ─ ─ ─ ─  θ
                                .
                                .
                        else error;
                        ─ ─ ─ ─ ─ ─ ─ ─ ─ ─ ─  η
                end
        else by
                .
                .
        else error
end
```

Fig. 1. Recovery block structure

In Figs. 2–9,
main store entry: − value, recovery level.
cache entry: − main store address, value, recovery level

Main Store

b	–	0
a	–	0

Cache

Recovery Level (RL) = 0
α: storage allocation

Fig. 2.

dress of a word in main store and the other preserves a copy of the prior contents of that word which may subsequently require to be reinstated. A special machine register is required whose purpose is to record the current recovery level. This recovery level register is incremented and decremented by one on recovery block entry and exit respectively, thereby indicating the current depth of dynamic nesting of recovery blocks. When a program is loaded the recovery level is initialised to zero.

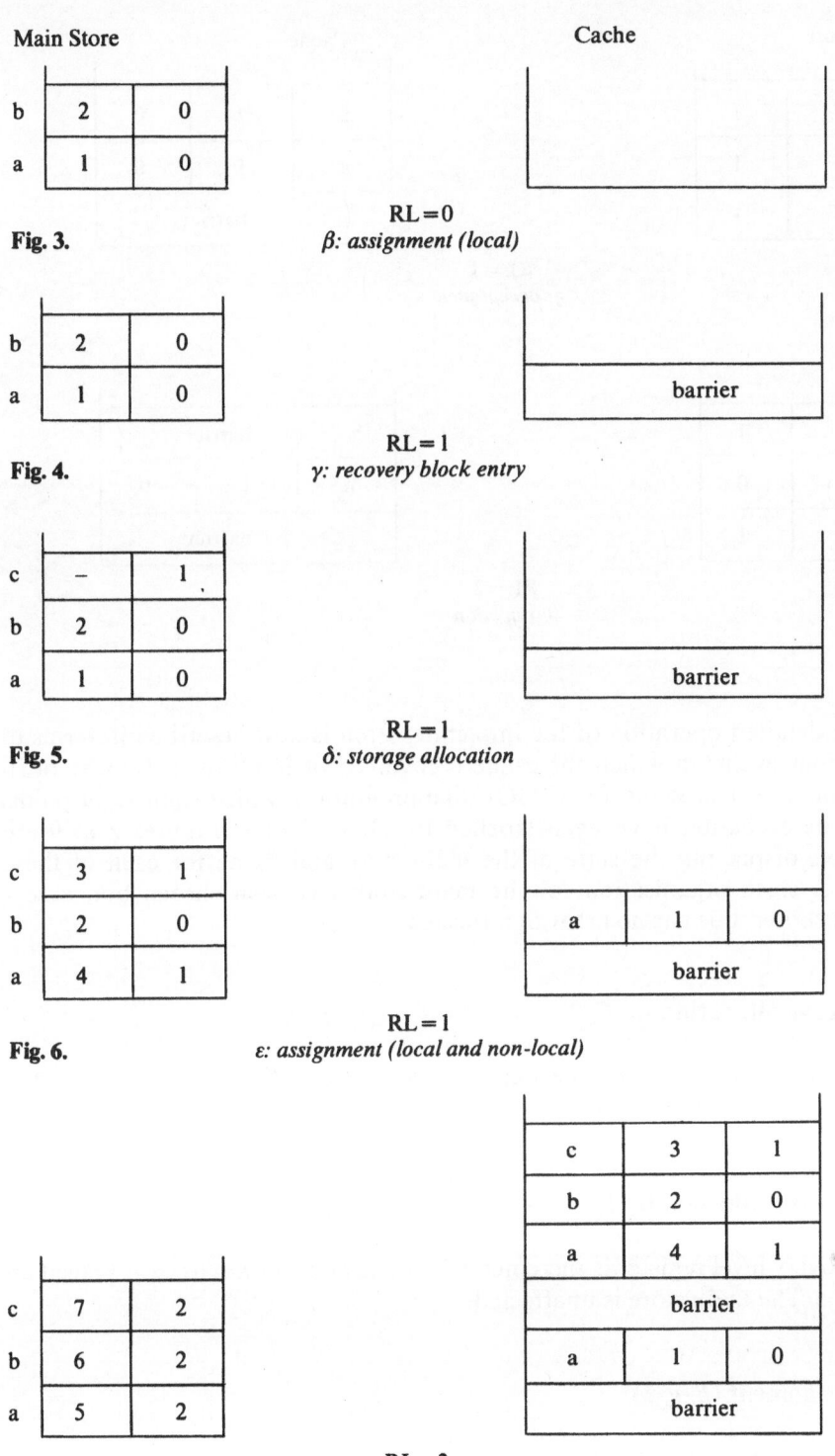

Main Store

b	2	0
a	1	0

Cache

RL = 0

Fig. 3. *β: assignment (local)*

b	2	0
a	1	0

| | | barrier |

RL = 1

Fig. 4. *γ: recovery block entry*

c	–	1
b	2	0
a	1	0

| | | barrier |

RL = 1

Fig. 5. *δ: storage allocation*

c	3	1
b	2	0
a	4	1

| a | 1 | 0 |
| | barrier | |

RL = 1

Fig. 6. *ε: assignment (local and non-local)*

c	3	1
b	2	0
a	4	1
	barrier	
a	1	0
	barrier	

c	7	2
b	6	2
a	5	2

RL = 2

Fig. 7. *ξ: assignment (non-local)*

85

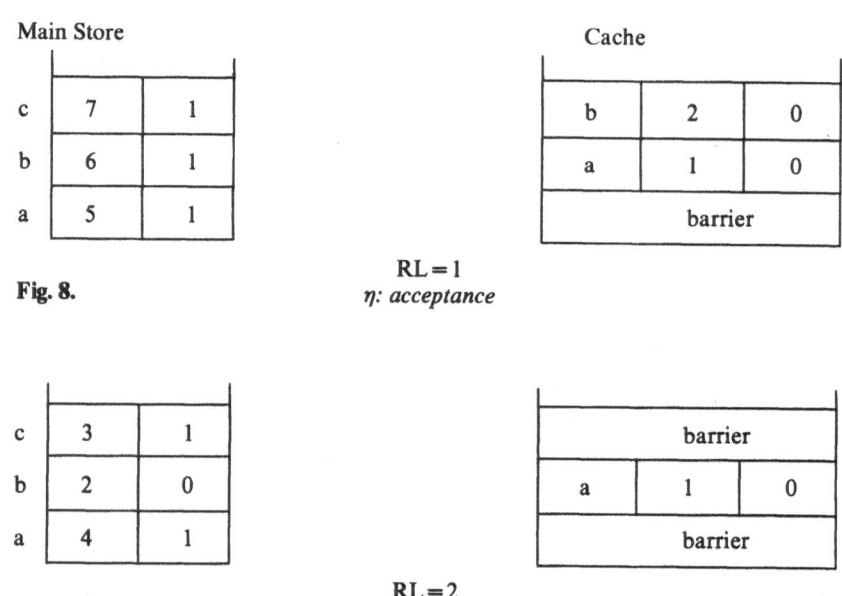

Main Store

c	7	1
b	6	1
a	5	1

Cache

b	2	0
a	1	0
barrier		

RL = 1
η: acceptance

Fig. 8.

c	3	1
b	2	0
a	4	1

barrier		
a	1	0
barrier		

RL = 2
θ: rejection

Fig. 9.

The detailed operation of the implementation is now described in terms of the various events in which the cache is involved or implicated. By way of illustration, Fig. 1 presents an ALGOL-like program in which significant points during its execution have been labelled by Greek letters. Figures 2 to 9 are snapshots displaying the state of the main store and cache for each of these points. A stack organisation for the main store has been chosen but, as explained earlier, this nas no great significance.

(i) Storage allocation (α, δ)

When a main store word is allocated, its recovery level field is initialised to the current recovery level.

(ii) Recovery block entry (γ)

The recovery level register is incremented by one and a new barrier is placed on the cache. The main store is unaffected.

(iii) Assignment (β, ε, ξ)

The recovery level of the word to which a new value is to be assigned is examined. If this equals the current value of the recovery level register, the new value

86

is assigned directly to the value field of the word and no encachement is performed. The recovery level field of the word is unaffected. If the recovery level of the word differs from the current value of the recovery level register, a new entry is placed on the cache. This entry contains a copy of the entire contents of the word (i.e. value and recovery level fields) together with the main store address of the word. The recovery level of the word in main store is now set equal to the current recovery level and, finally, the new value is assigned.

In a sense, the recovery level field of a word indicates the locality of the word's current value relative to the recovery block nest. It reveals at which recovery level the word acquired its value. There are two situations in which the recovery level field can equal the current recovery level. The first is when the word involved has already been the subject of assignment at the current recovery level. The second is when the word has been allocated at the current level but has not yet been assigned to. This can be viewed as equivalent to having had a value "undefined" assigned at the current level. In either case, encachement is not appropriate. If the word's recovery level does not equal the current recovery level, the word is neither local to this recovery block nor has it already been assigned to within it and therefore encachement of the word prior to assignment is necessary.

(iv) Failure of an Acceptance Test (θ)

The failure of an acceptance test means that the most recently executed alternate has not functioned satisfactorily. Before another alternate can be entered, the main store must be returned to the state it was in on entry to the current recovery block. This is possible since preserved in the top region of the cache are the prior values of all main store words to which assignments have been made by the faulty alternate. For each cache entry in the top region, the value and recovery level fields are copied back to the main store locations designated by the main store address. As each entry is copied it is discarded from the cache. The value in the recovery level register remains unaltered since an attempt will now be made to invoke another alternate of the same recovery block.

(v) Passing of an Acceptance Test (η)

The recovery level register is decremented by one and now indicates the recovery level to which we are about to return. The entries in the top region of the cache are then processed one by one in the following way. The recovery level of the corresponding main store word is set equal to the value in the recovery level register, thus recording that the net effect of assignments to that word at the recovery level we are leaving is equivalent to an assignment at the level to which we are returning. If the recovery level of the cache entry equals the value in the recovery level register, this indicates that the main store word involved is either local to the recovery block to which we are returning or has already been assigned to in that recovery block (in which latter case a prior value has already been preserved in the cache region for that recovery block). The cache entry is therefore discarded. If the recovery level field of the cache entry is not equal to the value in the recovery level register, this means that, in effect, a non-local assignment to the word involved has now been made for the first time in the recovery block to which we are returning and therefore, in order to preserve the prior value, the cache entry is moved down into the cache region for that recovery block. The movement of entries from the top cache region to the next is achieved easily if the processing of the top cache region is performed from bottom to top.

(vi) Access to Prior Values (π)

The main store address of the variable involved is used as the key in a search of the top region of the cache. If a find is made, the value preserved in that cache entry is returned, otherwise the result is taken from the value field of the main store location. In the case of variables which have not been cached, an optimisation could be achieved by first comparing the recovery level field of the main store word with the current recovery level. If the values are not equal the result can be taken directly from the main store location.

The only respect in which the recovery cache implementation described here is inferior to the one presented in the earlier paper [Horning et al. (1974)] is that the state of encachement of each word is represented by its recovery level field instead of by a single bit. The size of this field increases the storage overhead and limits the number of levels of recovery possible. However, we believe that, in practice, a modest number of bits (≤ 5) would suffice and be an acceptable trade-off for the considerable simplification in the cache logic.

For the sake of clarity, we have used an example expressed in a high level language and have illustrated the mechanics of the recovery cache in terms of identified variables. There is a tendency to associate assignment with variables identified explicitly in the source program. However, erroneous assignments may involve storage locations which are not explicitly named at source level and which may be reserved for some other purpose, for example static links. Since the process of encachement is bound to the storage location involved and not to any particular operation which may alter its value, prior values of that location are preserved, regardless of the cause of assignment or of the purpose which that location serves.

A Computer Architecture to Aid Error Detection

The section on the recovery block scheme explained that all errors are handled in precisely the same fashion, be they failures of acceptance tests or any other kind of error condition. However, to explore the topic of error detection we must distinguish the class of errors which are not purely algorithmic but which violate, in some way, the machine specification and cause many conventional systems to abandon the computation. We call such an error an "internal error".

The detection of internal errors is clearly important. Since it would be naive to believe that acceptance tests can always be measures of absolute correctness, there is a danger that internal error conditions could, if ignored, nevertheless produce plausible and therefore acceptable results. There is also the danger that undetected or unsignalled internal errors could damage the information structures upon which the recovery mechanisms depend. We have therefore postulated a machine architecture in which the checking of data consistency and control structure integrity figures prominently. This architecture is largely due to R. M. Simpson (1974).

The design is based on the kind of error detection afforded by the better high level languages. Such languages demand of the programmer a certain degree of so-called redundant information by which the self-consistency of his program can be checked. Disciplines are imposed by which arbitrary and error-prone control structures are disallowed. Of course, the user of lower level programming systems denies himself these benefits. Moreover, if we examine the object code emitted by typical compilers we see that the redundancy has been compiled out and that certain of the disfavoured control structures have been compiled back in. The object program therefore lacks the ability to detect errors which may have arisen through faulty compilation or malfunction of the machine. It is our belief that the safest time to check an operation is immediately before it is performed and we have therefore incorporated into our machine design many of the checks normally performed at source level. Since our experimentation with the hypothetical architecture has been by software emulation, we have probably been more extravagant with our provisions for error checking than we could otherwise have afforded. We do not know how much redundant redundancy we have incorporated.

The major parts of the storage occupied by a program can be regarded as a data segment and a program segment. The bases of these segments are addressed by separate machine registers. Any memory reference is relocated by the code or data base register determined by the context of the reference. There is no way in which a data location can be specified instead of a code location, and vice versa.

(i) Code Segment Structure

The layout of the code segment is such that it retains the control structure of the source program. There is thus a very high probability that erroneous behaviour or corruption resulting in arbitrary branching will be detected. Individual operations are either simple or composite and sequences of these form code fragments. A simple operation is one which is executed directly. A composite operation is one which transfers control to a new fragment. Typically, code fragments represent the bodies of control structures such as cycles, case alternatives, etc., and the composite instructions invoke these fragments in a controlled fashion. There is no facility for undisciplined branching. A valid program thus

```
begin declare (1 to 10000) (a, b, c);
        a := 632;  b := 249;  c := 0;
        cycle upto a times;
                exit when a < b;
                a := a − b;
                c := c + 1
        end
end
```

Fig. 10. Source language program for integer division

α: start alternative; end alternative;
β: start alternative; exit (l); end alternative;
γ: start cycle; load (a); load (b); less; case (α, β); load (a); load (b); subtract; store (a); load (c); load literal (l); add; store (c); end cycle;

start program; block begin; declare (a, b, c); load literal (632); store (a); load literal (249); store (b); load literal (0); store (c); load (a); cycle (γ); block end;
end program;

Fig. 11. Symbolic form of emulated machine language

has a tree structure in which the nodes are instructions. The leaf nodes are simple operations and the composite operations are the roots of the sub-trees. Figure 11 shows symbolically the code structure for a trivial source program (Fig. 10).

The execution of a fragment is under the control of a program point register. In addition to addressing the current point of execution, the program point register records the type and length of the fragment and, in the case of iterations, certain information relating to the number of repetitions. A program point register is loaded with this information when a composite operation is executed, causing the appropriate fragment to be entered. The fragment body is bracketed by start and end fragment instructions which check consistency with the fragment type in the program point register. The fragment length ensures that, in the event of corruption of the control structure, an error will be signalled if execution proceeds beyond the end of a fragment.

The control sequencing is administered by a control stack which is a stack of program point registers. The top entry on the control stack is the one currently active and through which the machine receives its instructions for interpretation. The execution of a composite operation causes a new program point register to be loaded and pushed on to the control stack. When the code fragment for a noniterative composite instruction, e.g. case alternative, is being executed, the occurrence of an end fragment instruction causes the top entry of the control stack to be discarded. Execution thus resumes under control of the program point register now at the top of the control stack. The control stack contains the same kind of information as the dynamic link and return information in typical ALGOL implementations, but for a much finer degree of control structure.

(ii) Data Segment Structure

The data segment is organised as a typical ALGOL stack. There are no special working registers. Instead, all expression evaluation is performed on the top of the data stack. All data stack cells are tagged such that entries of different kinds can be disinguished and checked for consistency with the operations in which they are involved. Unallocated data stack cells have the tag "unused", ensuring that certain classes of invalid data stack references can be recognised.

At any moment, the data stack is composed of a number of activation records. These are linked together appropriately by special stack entries tagged "static link" and "dynamic link" All other stack entries are concerned with the storage or description of data. The various kinds of data entry, each with its identifying tag, are: integer, logical, character, index, control variable, pointer, array descriptor, record descriptor. The tag "control variable" is one which is temporarily given to a variable used for counting the iterations of a loop and prohibits the overwriting of that variable by the program.

In addition to their tag and value fields, all data entries possess two extra fields, viz. a null-bit and a type field. The null-bit is used to distinguish allocated but uninitialised data entries from initialised entries and thereby to prevent computations involving uninitialised data. The type field contains an index into a run-time type table. The entries in the type table provide a more detailed description of the various data entries than is provided by the tag fields. For simple variables, the type table entries describe the range of values the variables may acquire. The type table entry for an array descriptor describes the array bounds and provides the index of the type table entry describing the array elements. The record descriptor entry similarly supplies the type table index for each of the fields. While the tags are used to check that only permitted operations are performed on the data specified, e.g. arithmetic on numeric items, indexing on arrays, etc., the type descriptions ensure that operands and results have magnitudes within expected ranges.

All data stack cells are provided with a recovery level field whose purpose has been described in the section on the recovery cache implementation. Any form of assignment into the data stack, be it to a variable, descriptor, static link or to a value field, tag field, etc., is preceded by an activation of the cache mechanism which may result in the encachement of the data stack cell involved. Thus a data stack assignment involving an erroneous address is always retrievable.

(iii) Instruction Types

The nature of the instructions reflects the stack organisation of the data segment and the desire to retain control structure at run-time. Data can be moved

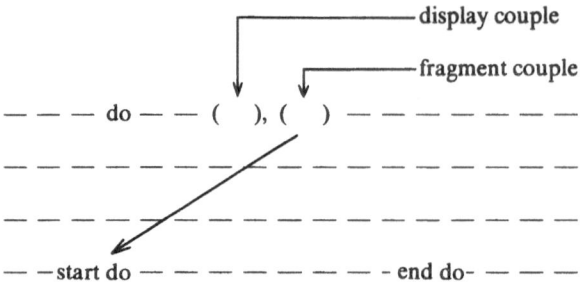

Fig. 12. "do" – a typical composite operation

to and from the top of the stack by "load" and "store" instructions in which checks are performed to detect uninitialised variables, tag and type incompatibilities, etc. Access to variables is achieved by maintaining a conventional ALGOL display vector which serves to translate display couples into data stack addresses. Computations are performed by zero-address instructions such as "add", which expect their operands in the top cells of the data stack. Checks are performed on admissability of tags, overflow, etc.

The use of high level instructions enables us to retain the control structure at run-time. These high level instructions are in fact the composite operations which enable the control of execution to be transferred from the main stream to another code fragment in order to perform a subsidiary computation. A typical composite operation is "do" which is used to perform an iteration a predetermined number of times. The parameters of the instruction are a display couple identifying a variable to be used as control variable and a fragment couple specifying the code fragment containing the body of the loop. Figure 12 illustrates.

The "do" statement requires the initial and final control variable values to be on the top of the stack. During the execution of the "do", the control variable is given a temporary tag which causes an error if any attempt is made within the "do" fragment to alter the value of the variable. The occurrence of the "do" instruction causes a new program point register to be loaded on to the control stack and the execution of the "do" fragment proceeds under its control. The "start do" and "end do" instructions bracket the "do" fragment and each checks that the top entry in the control stack is indeed a "do". In addition, "end do" checks the termination condition and, if it has been attained, terminates the iteration by popping the control stack and restoring the control variable's original tag.

Similar to the "do" instruction is the "cycle" which is intended for iterating an unspecified number of times. It has no control variable but in order to prevent infinite loops an upper limit on the number of iterations must be specified. If this limit is exceeded an error condition is raised. Only an "exit" instruction can return control successfully from a "cycle". Exit from nested cycles is catered for by a parameter. The "exit" instruction pops the control stack until the specified number of "cycle" entries has been removed. Only certain of the other control constructs may be popped on the way. For instance, an "exit" is not allowed to return control from within a "do" fragment or a recovery block.

A further composite operation is the "case" instruction. This takes a variable-length parameter list consisting of fragment couples, each designating one of the case alternatives. The case instruction expects to find the case selector loaded on the top of the stack. We are not entirely satisfied with our implementation of the case instruction because of its variable-length parameter list.

Block entry and exit are handled by "block begin" and "block end" instructions. These are responsible for creating and deleting activation records and for managing the display. Variables are allocated dynamically by the "declare" instruction which reserves data stack cells, setting the tag, type and null-bit fields. There was a very early decision not to make "block begin" a composite operation. This has proved to be a bad decision which has caused slight complications in several situations including recovery from errors occurring in blocks within recovery blocks.

Recovery blocks are catered for by "recovery", "start recovery block", "recovery case" and "end recovery block" instructions. In certain respects, the structure of a recovery block resembles a cycle whose body consists of a case instruction which selects the appropriate alternate followed by the evaluation of the acceptance test. The operation of the recovery block instructions reflects this. The role of the "end recovery block" instruction is to examine the truth value resulting from the evaluation of the acceptance predicate. If the value is *true,* the control stack is popped, otherwise an error condition is raised. The detection of an error condition initiates the recovery actions. The relevant recovery block structure is reflected by the recovery block entries in the control stack and these are used to direct the reinstatement of data values and program control.

Additional load and store instructions are provided for accessing array elements and record fields but are not described in detail here. For each type of load instruction there is a "load prior" counterpart for accessing prior values. There are no store prior instructions!

The Prototype System

The preceding sections of this paper have described the basic recovery block scheme, a high level machine architecture which includes this recovery technique, and a new design of the recovery cache mechanism. Advantages of speed and simplicity are claimed for the new design of the cache.

An initial implementation of these facilities has been constructed. Programs containing recovery blocks can be written and then tested on this prototype system and, it is hoped, can provide evidence in support of the claims made for the recovery block approach. Further motivation for the implementation stems from a need to measure the costs imposed by various aspects of the design (such as the recovery cache and the redundant information maintained by the machine architecture), and to try to estimate the utility of these aspects. Extensions to the basic recovery scheme are being investigated and the existence of the prototype permits this to be done from a firmer base than would otherwise be possible. It has been recognised that the design and organisation of the acceptance tests in a program is of major significance if recovery blocks are to be used effectively. The ability to execute programs containing recovery blocks should assist in studies of how acceptance tests should be constructed. Finally, it was expected that the detailed design decisions needed to construct an implementation could have some impact on the overall abstract design — and this proved to be the case.

The hardware configuration available to the reliability group at Newcastle comprises two DEC PDP-11/45 processors with a total of 128 K bytes of main memory. Peripherals include consoles, a line printer and disk storage. There is also a synchronous link to the University's main computer, an IBM 370/168.

A program has been written which runs on one of the PDP-11/45s and emulates the high level architecture described in the previous section. Basic support for the emulator is provided either by a stand alone monitor or via the DOS-11 operating system. The emulator operates by first reading in a prepared memory image and then interpreting the code segment of the image. Interpretation can be at full speed or in one of a number of debugging modes. Facilities are available for conveniently modifying the code segment being interpreted, usually for the purpose of deliberately corrupting the code so as to induce errors. The machine language interpreted by the emulator is simply referred to as EML (from emulator machine language).

Programs to be executed on the high level machine architecture are first encoded in a variant of a subset of the system implementation language developed by the Sue project at Toronto University [Clark and Ham (1974)]. At present the subset of the Sue system language available remains fairly restricted, but some extensions to this may be made. The current language can be summarised as providing: scoped declarations, integer subrange variables, arrays, integer and logical expressions, assignment, selection, repetition, simple input and output, and recovery blocks. This language is referred to as SUE.EML, which is also the name given to the compiler which translates the language into EML code. The SUE.EML compiler is a cross-compiler which runs on the IBM 370/168. It was constructed by modifying the code generation routines of the SUE.360 compiler distributed by Toronto Computer Systems Research Group. An EML code segment together with a run-time type table produced by the SUE.EML compiler is inserted into a memory image for the emulator and the image is sent over the link to one of the PDP-11/45s.

Extensive use has been made of Sue compilers from Toronto. The emulator and the program which prepares memory images are both written in the Sue language, and are compiled using the SUE.11 and SUE.360 compilers respectively.

Recoverability of the Prototype System

The prototype system makes available to a programmer the opportunity to include recovery blocks in his programs. To determine whether such a system does indeed enable significantly more reliable programs to be produced would require very extensive (and expensive) experimentation. The investment of effort involved is considered inappropriate for a system still under development. Even the performance of a carefully designed set of trials will probably be postponed until a more complete system has been constructed, incorporating modifications suggested from consideration of the present system and extensions deriving from current research into, for example, recoverable type structures. What can be done is to observe, at least qualitatively, the extent to which the prototype system meets its basic design aim of providing a high level of recoverability. Our experiments to date have consisted of running on the emulator programs which were believed to be correct, programs which were known to contain source errors and programs whose object code had been corrupted deliberately.

This section merely attempts to summarise our initial experiences in using the prototype system, and to report any conclusions that can be drawn. It is stressed that these experiences are mainly drawn from the (fairly haphazard) testing and experimentation the system has undergone during its development, and are in no sense part of any controlled experiments on the system.

When an EML program is interpreted by the emulator, one possible outcome is that the program executes satisfactorily without any erroneous situations being detected, and hence without making any use of recovery facilities. That this did happen on a number of occasions is perhaps more a consequence of the elementary nature of various test programs than of any programming skill possessed by the authors.

A second possibility is that the program executes unsatisfactorily in that the results generated by the program are unacceptable to the writer of the program. One explanation for such an outcome is that the program is itself defective in one of the following ways:

in certain recovery blocks, no alternate computes acceptable results,
acceptance tests are too weak enabling results generated by faulty alternates to be accepted.

If the fault does not lie in the program then the presence of a bug in the emulator has been detected. For instance, if the system collapses with a forced return to its basic support system, the unsatisfactory behaviour can be blamed on the emulator.

Not surprisingly, in view of the circumstances, many of the test programs initially executed unsatisfactorily. Any extension of the emulator and SUE.EML compiler carried the risk of introducing new errors into the system, some of which could be revealed in subsequent testing. Only rarely could unsatisfactory behaviour be attributed to the program, and on those occasions when it could the fault clearly lay with the programmer rather than with the recovery block approach.

Of much more interest is the third possibility, namely that the program executes satisfactorily despite the detection of one or more erroneous situations. Detection can either be due to the extensive basic error checking provided by the system, or to an acceptance test included by the programmer not being satisfied. A more useful categorisation is obtained by considering the error to have one of three possible sources.

(i)   A planned inadequacy in the program.

(ii) An unanticipated inadequacy in the program.

(iii) An inadequacy of the system.

These are examined in turn, with examples drawn from the three programs outlined in figures 13 to 15.

```
do n := 0 to 99;
    ensure i² ≤ n and (i + 1)² > n and n = prior n
            by try previous value of i
        else by calculate a value for i using Newton's method
        else by step i upwards from zero until (i + 1)² > n
    else error;
    write n, i
end
```

Fig. 13. The program SQRT

```
n := read;
do i := 1 to n;
    A(i) := read
end;
ensure A(j + 1) ≥ A(j) for j = 1, ..., n − 1
        n
    and ∑ (A(j) − prior A(j)) = 0
       j=1
            by order the values in A using Shell's sorting method
        else by order the values in A using linear selection
    else error;
do i := 1 to n;
    write A(i)
end
```

Fig. 14. The program SQRT

```
ensure A(i) = prior A(j)  and  A(j) = prior A(i)
            by A(i) := A(i) − A(j);  A(j) := A(i) + A(j);
                A(i) := A(j) − A(i)
        else by w := A(i);  A(i) := A(j);  A(j) := w
else error
```

Fig. 15. The recovery block EXCHANGE

(i) Planned Program Inadequacy

In an attempt to model the situation which occurs when a program contains a genuine bug, programs containing deliberate mistakes were executed on the emulator.

Figure 13 shows the program SQRT which has been used extensively to test the emulator. This program is intended to print out a table of integer approximations to the square roots of the numbers 0 to 99. Each alternate of the recovery block attempts to place the correct value in the variable i. The acceptance test checks explicitly that i contains the largest integer not greater than $\sqrt{n}$, and that the value of n has not been changed.

The primary alternate in SQRT is based on the principle that the largest integer not greater than $\sqrt{n}$ might well be equal to the largest integer not greater than $\sqrt{n-1}$, and so does nothing at all. Unfortunately, whenever the value of n is a perfect square this does not succeed, and in these cases the acceptance test rejects the erroneous value left in i. Furthermore, when n is zero at the first execution of the recovery block, the variable i has never been used and has no previous value. In this case an error condition is raised during the evaluation of the acceptance test since the emulator rejects any attempts to use the value of an uninitialised variable. This rather frivolous primary alternate was added to an earlier version of the SQRT program in order to exercise the recovery mechanisms of the emulator. Although clearly defective in general, on those many occasions when it is successful the primary alternate is exceedingly efficient. There may be some justification, in particular contexts, for employing a primary alternate for which it is known that there exist circumstances in which it will fail, if for most cases the alternate has the virtues of simplicity and efficiency. Reliability may still be enhanced as a result of the alternate's simplicity and independence from the other alternates.

The second alternate in SQRT employs a conventional root finding algorithm, modified to use integer arithmetic. It was known that the encoding of the algorithm is such that when n equals zero the value computed is incorrect, and should therefore be rejected by the acceptance test. Unlike the faulty primary alternate, this error did in fact arise from a genuine programming mistake and so may be regarded as a little more authentic.

The third alternate is programmed very simply with the aim of increasing dependability at the expense of efficiency and is expected always to be able to satisfy the acceptance test.

Next, consider the second example program, SORT, given in Fig. 14. This program is intended to read in a value for n, then read in n integers, sort them into ascending order in the array A, and then print them out in order. The alternates of the recovery block implement different well-known sorting algorithms, and both make use of the recovery block EXCHANGE shown in Fig. 15. The acceptance test confirms that the entries in the array are in ascending order and attempts to verify, by means of a sum check, that no values have been changed.

The primary alternate in SORT is an encoding of Shell's sorting method. The encoding was obtained by very casually translating an ALGOL 60 version (taken from a programming manual) into SUE.EML in the hope and expectation of introducing an error. In fact two errors were made. The first of these had the effect of assigning the value zero to a variable declared to be always positive. Detection of this by the emulator led to the second alternate being invoked. After correcting this error, a second bug was uncovered (the *step* component of a *for* statement had been omitted) which has the effect of leaving the array only partially sorted. Unless the integers are almost in order initially they are left out of order – which is detected by the acceptance test.

The second alternate is a straightforward encoding of linear selection and is thought to contain no errors.

The SORT program contains a nested recovery block, EXCHANGE, used by both alternates to interchange the values of $A(i)$ and $A(j)$. The acceptance test checks explicitly that the values have been interchanged. The second alternate is just the usual cyclic exchange using an auxiliary work variable, but the primary alternate exchanges the values without using the additional variable. In addition to its drawbacks of slowness and obscurity, the primary alternate is interesting in that it may fail because of overflow (very easily in fact since the array elements are declared to hold values from a fixed integer subrange) and this is why it was chosen.

Both of these programs, SQRT and SORT, are executed correctly by the emulator; despite their deficiencies they produce the desired results.

Another approach to modelling the effects of genuine programmer errors is to corrupt the code segment of an otherwise satisfactory program and the emulator is equipped accordingly with a special mechanism for injecting errors. Given that the program contains provision for error recovery, there is some prospect that the program will continue to give service. With more stringent provisos much more can be claimed. Consider again the SQRT program, which has been subjected to considerable corruption in this way. The recovery block in SQRT has the property that its final alternate is designed in such a way that the programmer has a very high degree of confidence that it will always pass the acceptance test, and also has the property that the acceptance test is complete in the sense that passing the test in itself guarantees satisfactory results (this last is not usually attainable except at prohibitive cost, c.f. the sum check in SORT). So, for the SQRT program, the stringency of the test and confidence in the final alternate lead to the claim that no matter what is encoded in the earlier alternates the program will still run satisfactorily. As a corollary to this claim, arbitrary corruption of the code fragments corresponding to the primary and second alternates of SQRT should not prevent the program from completing its execution successfully.

Project members and visitors to the department have risen to the implicit challenge and with ingenious penetration techniques attempted to refute this claim. Although it has to be conceded that their efforts have on rare occasions met with some limited successes, a considerable time has elapsed since the program last failed to produce its now rather tedious table of square roots. About 100 bytes of EML code are available for modification. Random changes are almost always detected immediately by virtue of the redundancy retained in the EML code. More sophisticated and structured attacks, probing for weaknesses in the emulator's implementation, are usually employed. Even so, in the vast majority of cases, the recovery mechanisms have successfully detected and recovered from any damage done to the system, often to the amazement (initially) of the authors. The damage was often much more extensive than was anticipated, largely because of the difficulty in appreciating beforehand all of the implications which a change made at the EML level could have, particularly when the change impinged directly on the recovery mechanisms. When a successful penetration has been made this has been, with one exception, attributable to an implementation error which was then rectified. Errors detected in this way have usually been rather obscure. The exception involved exploitation of a weak acceptance test in an earlier version of SQRT written before *prior* was available.

The technique of modifying the EML code to introduce errors into a program has been considered as a form of planned program inadequacy, which it certainly is. However, as has been mentioned, the errors so introduced are rarely as well understood as those built into the source version of a program. Consequently the detection and recovery mechanisms are tested against situations which are not fully anticipated; since the erroneous situations which arise as a result of authentic programming errors cannot be studied in advance, the success of the recovery techniques during these experiments is encouraging.

(ii) Unanticipated Program Inadequacy

A principle aim of the techniques provided by the prototype system is to help programmers construct defences against the residual programming errors known to remain in complex software systems. Some doubt must attach to conclusions drawn from observing the success of the recovery techniques in handling more or less contrived errors in small test programs, but this is unavoidable until experimentation on a larger scale can be contemplated.

It is therefore pleasant to record one example of a completely unplanned programming error which was handled successfully by the system. It was not realised that the primary alternate of the EXCHANGE recovery block is completely defective for the special case $i = j$, when the two variables to be exchanged are in fact the same variable. In this situation the effect of the primary alternate is to set the variable $A(i)$ to zero. The acceptance test detects this to be erroneous (unless *prior* $A(i) = 0$), the value of $A(i)$ is restored and the second alternate correctly exchanges $A(i)$ with itself.

Whether this authentic example of a programming error is in any real sense a better test of the recovery techniques than the more contrived examples presented earlier is highly dubious, but it was certainly rewarding to observe (after the event) that the prototype system had functioned as intended and recovered from a totally unexpected error. The error itself is typical of most programming mistakes − a special case or unusual combination of circumstances is so often overlooked.

(iii) System Inadequacy

Because the emulator program is itself a substantial piece of software, the presence of errors in the system is not surprising, particularly in view of the numerous extensions and modifications which have been made in the course of its construction. It has already been stated that errors in the emulator often led to unsatisfactory behaviour of a program being interpreted. Of much greater interest were a number of occasions on which an error in the emulator resulted in considerable corruption of the state of a program being interpreted but which was then detected as being erroneous and successfully recovered from. In fact, if the faulty emulator continued to observe the constraints imposed by its own basic support system (otherwise the emulator collapsed) then satisfactory program behaviour was usually achieved. Data corruption due to faulty emulator behaviour must be confined to data defining the state of the interpreted program, and that program must contain adequate recovery provision if it is to execute satisfactorily. In these circumstances the emulator is able to recover from its own deficiencies because of its ability to permit the program being interpreted to recover.

Two typical examples are recounted which occurred during penetration attempts on the program SQRT.

It was discovered that the emulator did not ensure that expression evaluation was confined to temporary locations at the head of the data stack. By modifying the EML code of SQRT so as to set up a series of "add" instructions (which decrement the data stack pointer) it was possible to delete from the data variables declared in the current block. When an attempt to access a deleted variable raised an error condition, the variables were restored from the recovery cache which, of course, records all relevant changes made to the data stack, irrespective of the reason for the change.

The second example was a consequence of the emulator not checking for overflow of the control stack. A control transfer was altered to transfer control to a code fragment containing the transfer, thus creating a recursive loop (with some difficulty because of the need to match transfer and fragment). Each pass around the loop placed additional entries on the control stack, which eventually overflowed, overwriting the data stack display. When the display was next used an error was raised, followed by the restoration of data stack and display, and by the retraction of the control stack.

In summary, we have been very gratified by the extent to which the prototype system has achieved its basic design aims. Program recovery from both artificially contrived and accidental programming errors, and from faulty behaviour due to errors in the emulator (on one occasion the fault in the emulator was due to an error in the SUE.11 compiler) has been impressive. The most important feature of the facilities supported by the system seems to be that they can be used to implement recovery capability which is not designed to meet specific error situations, and as a result is able to deal with the unexpected situations caused by errors.

The detailed design decisions entailed in implementing a system which provides error recovery have led to a better understanding of the proposed error detection and recovery facilities. Two points can be made here. It now seems preferable to regard the failure of an acceptance test as a run-time error rather than to consider a run-time error as equivalent to the premature failure of an acceptance test. The former view leads to a cleaner and more secure implementation, and has been adopted throughout this paper and in the prototype system. Secondly, we now see that a complete separation could be made between the recovery structures and the other structures (for data and control) defining the state of a program. If this were done, recovery could be made more comprehensive and more uniform than is the case with the present system.

A limitation of the basic recovery scheme implemented by the prototype system is that it provides recoverability for a single sequential process in isolation from any other processes with which it interacts. Some progress has been made in removing this restriction [Randell (1974)] and research is continuing with the aim of extending the recovery techniques to a set of mutually dependent processes. However, the present implementation is not likely to be extended in this direction. Rather we would wish to draw on the experience gained from building and using the prototype system in any future, more general, implementation.

Acknowledgements. The work described here was carried out at the University of Newcastle upon Tyne as part of a research project entitled "The Design of Highly Reliable Computing Systems". This project is funded by the Science Research Council of Great Britain whose interest and support are greatly appreciated. We acknowledge also the enthusiastic and good-humoured co-operation of all our colleagues on this project.

References

T. Anderson (1975). Provably Safe Programs. Tech. Report 70, Computing Laboratory, University of Newcastle upon Tyne.

B. L. Clark and F. J. B. Ham (1974). The Project Sue System Language Reference Manual. Tech. Report CSRG-42, Computer Systems Research Group, University of Toronto.

J. J. Horning, H. C. Lauer, P. M. Melliar-Smith and B. Randell (1974). A Program Structure for Error Detection and Recovery. Lecture Notes in Computer Science 16, Springer Verlag, pp. 177–193. (Also Chap. 2)

B. Randell (1975). System Structure for Software Fault Tolerance. IEEE Trans. on Software Engineering, 1, 2, pp. 220–232. (Also Chap. 1)

R. M. Simpson (1974). A Study in the Design of High Integrity Systems. Tech. Report 67, Computing Laboratory, University of Newcastle upon Tyne.

Sequential Pascal with Recovery Blocks

S. K. SHRIVASTAVA

Summary. The programming language Sequential Pascal has been extended to include recovery blocks. This paper describes the modifications made to the kernel and interpreter of Brinch Hansen's Pascal system to support recovery blocks and the associated recovery caches needed for state restoration.

Key Words: Sequential Pascal   Recovery blocks   Recovery cache   Fault-tolerant software

Introduction

A program structure called *recovery block* has been proposed in the literature as a means of constructing fault-tolerant software [1, 2] (defined to be software that produces acceptable results despite faults in the hardware and software). This paper describes an implementation of recovery blocks using Sequential Pascal [3] as the host language. The objectives of this paper are twofold: firstly, the implementation details are believed to be sufficiently interesting in their own right and, secondly, recovery blocks have attracted wide attention (for example, they are actively being evaluated for aerospace applications [4]); thus, an account of a method of inclusion in Sequential Pascal, a language that is widely used for research in programming methodology, should prove interesting to workers in the field of fault-tolerant programming. The paper also demonstrates that the inclusion of recovery blocks into existing programming systems can be a practical proposition.

Recovery blocks were first implemented by my colleagues [5], one of the aims of their work was to investigate a suitable computer architecture for directly supporting recovery blocks. The resulting system could however support only relatively simple sequential programs. A second experiment was therefore started with the aim of developing a system capable of supporting realistic sequential and concurrent programs incorporating recovery blocks. This paper describes the first phase of this experiment – the development of a system that is capable of supporting realistic sequential programs with recovery blocks. Work is underway to extend this system to support the features necessary for fault-tolerant concurrent programming [6]. While recovery blocks are described briefly in the next section, a familiarity with the concepts presented elsewhere [1, 2] would be helpful to the reader.

Recovery Blocks

The syntax as incorporated in Sequential Pascal is as shown. The acceptance test (a Boolean expression) is evaluated after the execution of the primary.

ENSURE ⟨acceptance test⟩ **BY**
  ⟨statement⟩ "primary"
ELSE-BY ⟨statement⟩ "first alternative"
    · · ·
ELSE-BY ⟨statement⟩ "*n*th alternative"
ELSE-ERROR;
    · · ·

If the result is true, the statement following the recovery block is executed. However, if the result is false, the state of the computation is restored to that at entry to the recovery block and the first alternative is tried and so on. If all the alternatives fail to produce acceptable results, then this is regarded as a failure of the entire recovery block — any recovery actions must be undertaken by the enclosing recovery block, if any (recovery blocks may be nested). A 'recovery cache' is used for recording the state of the computation and restoring it when the primary or the current alternative fails. The recovery cache is organized as a stack and contains recovery data for the recovery blocks entered but not yet exited. The recovery data consist of the addresses and the prior values of the global variables updated inside a given recovery block, so that the act of state restoration merely consists of copying the prior values into the variables. When an acceptance test is passed, some of the recovery data of this recovery block may have to be merged with the recovery data of the enclosing recovery block (if any). Precise details of this merging and other related aspects of recovery cache are discussed elsewhere [1, 5].

The Pascal System

The Pascal System, as developed by Brinch Hansen's group [11], is capable of supporting a number of concurrent processes programmed in Concurrent Pascal [7]. A process is capable of executing sequential programs written in Sequential Pascal (this language is closely similar to Pascal [8], from which it has been derived).

A process can make available some of its procedures to the sequential program it is running — this forms the basis of the interface between user programs (written in Sequential Pascal) and the operating system (written in Concurrent Pascal). Such procedures have been called prefix procedures (as a consequence of prefix procedures, no input–output has been defined for Sequential Pascal; rather, a system designer can program appropriate input–output procedures in Concurrent Pascal as prefix procedures). Both the concurrent program and sequential programs are executed interpretively by a simple stack machine programmed to run on the host hardware (PDP 11/45). Certain details of this interpreter and related programs are of interest within the context of this paper.

The Kernel and Interpreter

The kernel is the initial piece of software written to run on the base machine and it implements processes, synchronizing primitives, queues, basic input and

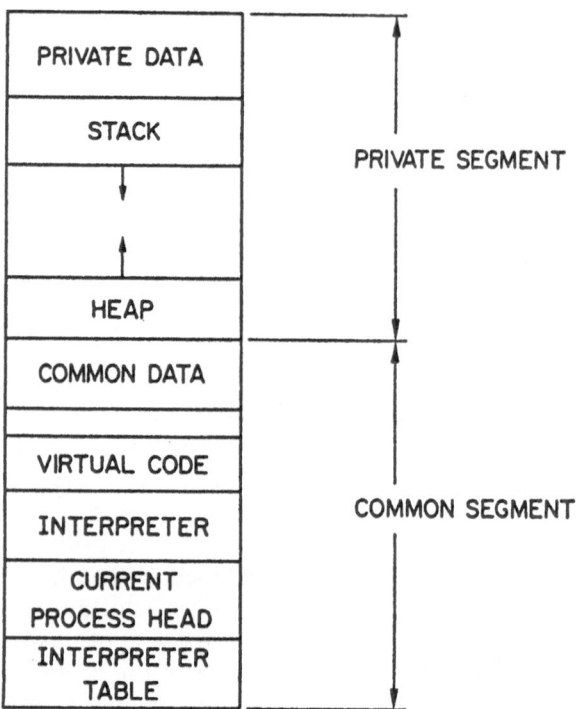

Fig. 1. Address space of a process

output and other features as required by Concurrent Pascal. It also implements a virtual storage system. The virtual address space of a process is shown in Fig. 1. The space is divided into two regions. The common segment is common to all the processes in the system. The virtual code is the code produced by the Concurrent Pascal compiler and is executed by the interpreter. The interpreter table contains, for all the virtual instructions, pointers to the interpreter areas where the appropriate interpretive procedures are stored. The stack and heap in the private segment are maintained and used by the interpreter (the heap is needed for the implementation of dynamic store allocation features of Sequential Pascal). The private data in the private segment can contain any virtual code produced by the Sequential Pascal compiler; it is also executed by the same interpreter. The kernel maintains a *process head* for every process in the system. The process head contains such details as the processor time used by the process, priority, an area for saving the contents of the processor registers etc. When the kernel selects a particular process for running, it copies its process head into the current process head area of the common segment and hands over control to the interpreter. The current process head acts as an interface between the interpreter and the kernel. Finally, the common data in the common segment contain the data (monitor variables) needed for interprocess co-ordination.

Exception Handling by the Interpreter

The execution of a program is terminated either because it terminates properly or because some predefined error condition is detected by the interpreter (such conditions include range error, stack limit, heap limit etc.). In either case, the interpreter executes an *exception program;* the essential features of this program are as shown. An entry in the current process head, 'result', is used to record the cause of the termination (result = 0 means 'proper termination', result = 1 means 'overflow error' etc.).

```
exception: if program = concurrent & result ≠ proper then
               begin
                   print ('system error');
                   stop "failure in the concurrent program (i.e. operating
                       system), so stop further processing"
               end else
               begin
                   restore stack;
                   return
               end;
```

Recovery Block Implementation

A number of changes were made to the kernel and interpreter to support recovery blocks and associated recovery caches. Despite the fact that the kernel and interpreter have been programmed in the assembly language of PDP 11/45 (MACRO assembler on DOS operating system), no particular difficulty was encountered in these modifications. This is because the Pascal system was found to be an outstandingly well-engineered product.

The Sequential Pascal compiler was modified to accept the recovery block construct shown previously and to generate the following code, where only the recovery block virtual instructions are shown explicitly. The particular control structure was selected after studying the code generation characteristics of the compiler.

```
    ENTER RECOVERY (NUMBER); "enter recovery block"
        goto 12;
11: evaluate acceptance test;
        if true then goto 13;
        ATFAIL; "acceptance test failed, the control goes to the exception
            handler"
12: case next of
        0: ⟨primary⟩; goto 11;
            ...
        n: ⟨nth alternative⟩; goto 11; "n = NUMBER-1"
        end;
13: ATPASS; "acceptance test passed"
```

'Number-1' equals the number of alternatives and 'next' indicates the statement to be executed.

The heaps in the private segments of processes (Fig. 1) were replaced by caches. Two reasons are given for this decision: (i) there does not appear to be any straightforward method of arranging the recovery of heap variables (since they do not allow the normal block structured rules), hence it was decided not to incorporate them in this modified version of Sequential Pascal; (ii) it is necessary to associate a cache with each process in the system; the most suitable place for its incorporation is the private segment of each process. Figure 2 shows the structure and organization of the recovery cache of a process; the starred entries in the current process head show the additions made to the process head of every process to support the corresponding recovery cache (in the actual implemented version, a few more entries have been included in the process heads and the caches, with a view to future use for recovery for concurrent programs; for simplicity these have been ignored in this discussion). The details of the various virtual instructions and related programs will now be described.

Enter Recovery Block

The algorithm of the virtual instruction ENTER RECOVERY (NUMBER) is as shown. The data for recovery blocks that have been entered but not yet exited are separated by barriers as shown in Fig. 2 (which shows the data for two recovery blocks). The *cachbr* entry points to the barrier of the current recovery block; the barriers are linked as shown. The interpreter uses four processor registers for pointing to the stack top (S), local variables (B), global variables (G) and the next virtual instruction to be executed (Q). These registers are saved as shown.

```
procedure enter recovery (number: integer);
    begin
        if heaptop ≥ (S "stack top" + 14 "bytes") then
        begin
            result := 'heap limit'; "ie, cache limit"
            goto exception
        end else
        begin
            Using heaptop, store current
            S, B, G and Q in the cache (= heap);
            store number; next := 0;
            push this value of next on the stack;
            "to be used by the 'case' instruction of the
            recovery block virtual code"
            create a barrier and link it to the previous one;
            cachbr := location of the new barrier
            nest := nest + 1; "counts the nesting of recovery blocks"
        end
    end;
```

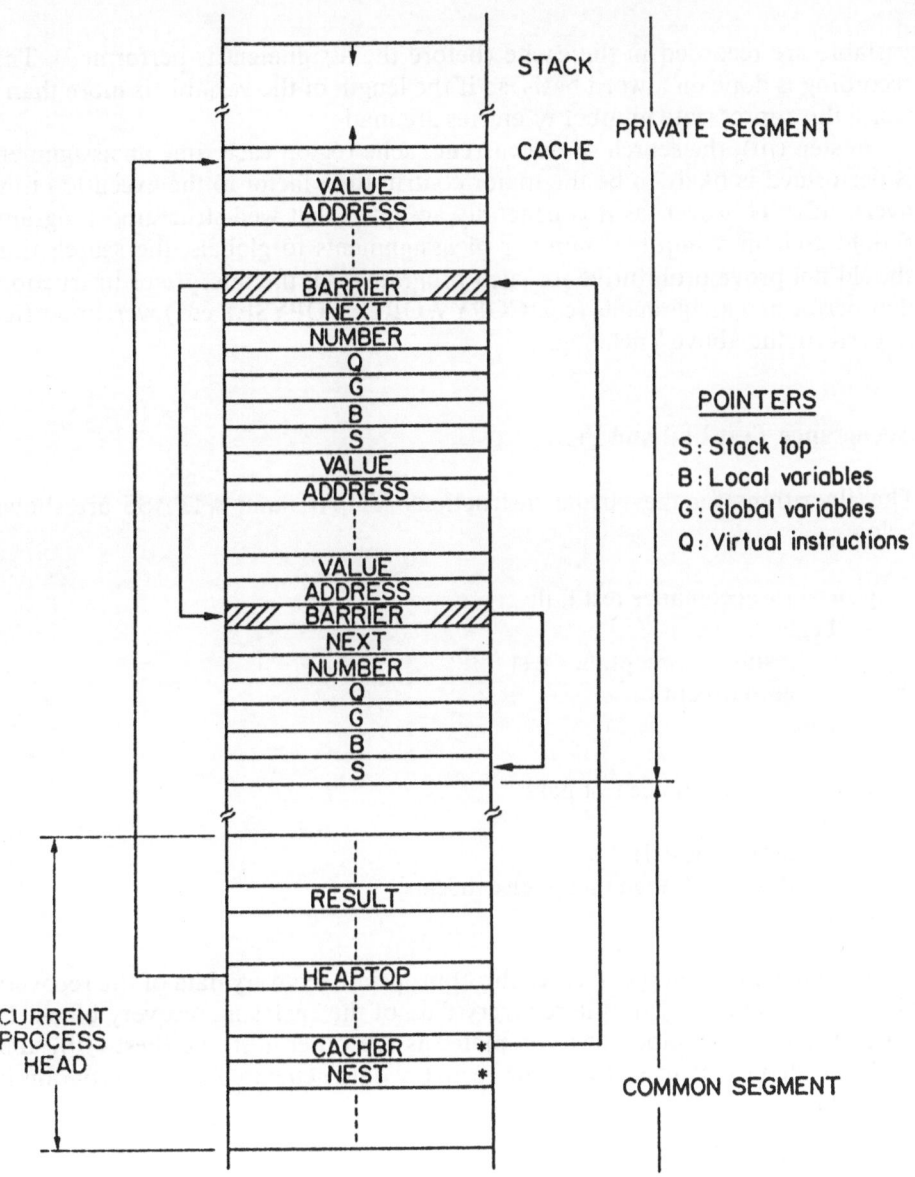

Fig. 2. Recovery cache organization

Assignments

Whenever a sequential program performs an assignment, it is necessary to check the following: (i) is it being performed from within a recovery block? (ii) if so, is the variable global? (iii) if so, does the current recovery data in the cache include the value—address pair(s) for this variable? If the answers to the first two questions are yes, and no to the third, the value and the address of the

107

variable are recorded in the cache (before the assignment is performed). This recording is done on a word basis, so if the length of the variable is more than a word, the appropriate number of entries are made.

In step (iii), the search of the current cache region each time an assignment is performed is likely to be the major contributing factor to the execution time overheads[1]. However, as it is generally accepted that well-structured programs should contain a minimal number of assignments to globals, the search time should not prove prohibitive for such programs. All the interpreter instructions that performed assignments (e.g. COPYWORD, COPYSET etc.) were modified to perform the above 'cacheing'.

Acceptance Test Fail and Pass

The algorithms for the virtual instructions ATFAIL and ATPASS are shown below.

```
procedure acceptance test fail;
    begin
        result := 'acceptance test fail';
        goto exception
    end;

procedure acceptance test pass;
    begin
        nest := nest-1;
        if nest > 0 then merge else discard
    end;
```

The procedure 'merge' merges the appropriate recovery data of the recovery block just completed with the recovery data of the enclosing recovery block [1]. When the recovery block just completed is the outermost one (nest = 0), 'discard' is called to throw away all the recovery data generated for the program in execution.

Exception Handling

From the algorithm given previously for exception handling, we see that the execution of a sequential program is terminated as soon as an abnormal condition is detected. This is no longer the case with recovery blocks: if an abnormal condition is detected while executing a recovery block, it is merely regarded as a failure of the primary or the alternative, as the case may be, and the same re-

---

1 When recovery caches are hardware implemented, extra bits can be added to the store words [1, 5] and utilized such that no search overheads are involved.

```
0001 PROGRAM TOY;
0002 TYPE M = 1..10;
0003 VAR N : ARRAY(.M,) OF INTEGER;
0004     I,J : INTEGER;
0005 BEGIN
0006         ENSURE (I = 2) & (J = 2) BY        USER LINE 11 RANGE ERROR
0007      BEGIN
0008         ENSURE J=10 BY                     USER LINE 9 A.T. FAIL
0009            BEGIN
0010             J:=0;                          USER LINE 9 R BLOCK FAIL
0011             N(.J,):=0
0012            END ELSE BY                     USER LINE 7 A.T. FAIL
0013             J:=9
0014           ELSE ERROR;
0015           I:=2
0016      END ELSE BY
0017      BEGIN
0018        I:=3; J:=45
0019      END ELSE BY
0020      BEGIN
0021        I:=2; J:=2
0022      END ELSE ERROR
0023 END,
```
(a)   (b)

Fig. 3. (a) A toy program; (b) error messages

covery actions are invoked as in the case of acceptance test failure. When the current program terminates properly, nest = 0 will also hold; from the new exception handling algorithm we see that the stack will be restored and a return made to the appropriate point in the executing process. If result ≠ proper, then nest > 0 implies that recovery capability exists. From the algorithm, we see that S, B, G and Q are restored and procedure 'restore' is called. This procedure restores the prior values of the cached variables. If an alternative exists (next < number) then this alternative will be executed when an exit is made from the exception handler. Otherwise, state restoration is carried out for the enclosing recovery block (if any), and so on. A number of error reporting messages have also been included in the handler. For example, when result ≠ proper and nest = 0 then this implies that no recovery is available, so a message 're-covery exhausted' is printed. Figure 3 shows a toy program with recovery blocks and the error messages produced.

Concluding Remarks

In the modifications described here, care has been taken to see that programs that do not use recovery blocks are not affected. Thus, the SOLO operating system [9] and all the application programs available on it run on the modified kernel and interpreter. The SOLO system can be used to develop Sequential Pascal programs with recovery blocks.

Only a few modifications to the kernel were needed — those concerned with the changes in process heads and error reporting facilities. The majority of the

109

```
exception: var recovery: boolean;
                recovery := false;
    if result ≠ proper then print (result type);
    if nest > 0 then
      begin
          while nest > 0 & ~ recovery do
          begin
              using cachbr, copy back S, B, G and Q;
              restore; next := next + 1; if next < number then
                  begin
                      push the value of next
                      on the stack;
                      recovery := true
                  end else
                  begin print ('recovery block fail');
                          nest := nest-1;
                          cachbr := location of the previous barrier
                  end
          end
      end;
          if ~ recovery then
        begin
        if result ≠ proper & nest = 0 then
        begin print ('recovery exhausted');
            if program = concurrent then
                begin print ('system stop');
                    stop
                end
          end; restore stack;
              return
          end;
```

The modified exception handler

modifications were confined to the interpreter. The size of the original interpreter was about 1 K words, the new size is $1 \cdot 8$ K words.

Since it is possible now to develop realistic programs with recovery blocks, several interesting questions arise regarding the design and performance of such programs (e.g. how should a unit of recovery be chosen? what is the time needed for state restoration? etc.). An attempt has been made to answer some of these questions elsewhere [10]. However, two results should be of interest to the readers of this paper. Firstly, timing measurements taken for a few programs without recovery blocks and with recovery blocks (containing from about 5 to 50 global assignments) indicated that the time overhead for collecting and maintaining recovery data for a recovery block ranged from about 1 to 7 per cent. Secondly, state restoration time for these programs ranged from 10 to 30 per cent of the execution time of the primaries. It is thus seen that, while a hardware implementation of caches is the best method, even the simple method of implementing caches by software as described here can be quite practical for many applications.

Acknowledgements. It is a pleasure to acknowledge the efforts of two of my colleagues: P. C. Treleaven who modified the Sequential Pascal compiler and P. A. Lee who developed the support software needed for transferring data from the DOS system to the Pascal system. His constructive criticisms on all aspects of this work are also gratefully acknowledged. Acknowledgement is also due to R. Kerr whose critical comments led to the improvement of this paper. This work was supported by the Science Research Council as a part of the 'Highly Reliable Computing Systems' project at the Newcastle University.

References

1. J. J. Horning, H. C. Lauer, P. M. Melliar-Smith and B. Randell, 'A program structure for error detection and recovery', Lecture Notes in Computer Science, 16, 177−193 (1974). (Also Chap. 2)
2. B. Randell, 'System structure for software fault tolerance', IEEE Trans. on Software Engineering, 1, No. 2, 220−232 (1975). (Also Chap. 1)
3. P. Brinch Hansen, 'Sequential Pascal report', Tech. Report, Information Science, California Institute of Technology (1975).
4. H. Hect, 'Fault tolerant software for real-time applications', ACM Comput. Surv., 8, No. 4, 391−407 (1976).
5. T. Anderson and R. Kerr, 'Recovery blocks in action: a system supporting high reliability', Proc. Second Int. Conf. on Software Engineering (October 1976). (Also Chap. 2)
6. S. K. Shrivastava and J. P. Banatre, 'Reliable resource allocation between unreliable processes', IEEE Trans. on Software Engineering, 4, No. 3, 230−241 (1978). (Also Chap. 4)
7. P. Brinch Hansen, 'The programming language Concurrent Pascal', IEEE Trans. on Software Engineering, 1, No. 2, 199−207 (1975).
8. N. Wirth, 'The programming language Pascal', Acta Informatica, 1, No. 1, 35−63 (1971).
9. P. Brinch Hansen, 'The SOLO operating system: a Concurrent Pascal program', Software − Practice and Experience, 6, 141−149 (1976).
10. S. K. Shrivastava and A. A. Akinpelu, 'Fault-tolerant sequential programming', Digest of Papers, FTCS-8, p. 207 (June 1978). (Also Chap. 2)
11. P. Brinch Hansen, The Architecture of Concurrent Programs, Prentice-Hall Inc., Englewood Cliffs, N. J., 1977.

Fault-Tolerant Sequential Programming Using Recovery Blocks

S. K. SHRIVASTAVA and A. A. AKINPELU

1. Programming Using Recovery Blocks

When using recovery blocks [1], it is desirable to structure a program such that no unrecoverable operations (e.g. I/O) appear within a recovery block − thus ensuring that a recovery action will generate a consistent prior state. The figure below shows one case where only assignments are recoverable and a large file is to be processed (the merge sort example of the next section illustrates this approach):

copy parts of files into program data area	→	process data	→	update files
unrecoverable action		recoverable action		unrecoverable action

There can be two ways of designing the different algorithms for the primary and the alternatives of a recovery block: algorithms that are different but produce identical results (see the median example below) or algorithms for alternatives that are designed to provide a degraded service (producing different but nevertheless acceptable results, see the stable marriage example). In the latter situation the acceptance test can only be as strong as the test needed to check the adequacy of the 'weakest' alternative. Sometimes, this may prove unacceptable where a stronger test is needed for the primary (or even some of the alternatives). The following figure suggests a simple way of including both of these tests. 'I' represents the acceptance test and 'Q' represents a stronger test for the primary. It is assumed that if 'Q' is false, the primary will fail.

ensure I *by begin. . ; assert* Q *end else by . . .*

2. Experimental Work

For experimental purposes, the programming language Sequential Pascal was extended to include recovery blocks [2]. The code produced by the compiler is executed by an interpreter programmed to run on the host hardware (PDP11/45). This interpreter was modified to support recovery caches and their associated operations. Thus the relative timing figures to be given later should be

112

No.	T1	T2	T3	T4	%TCM	%TRC	NG	NR	%C
1	0.6	0.62	0.64	1.31	3.33	9.33	30	8	26.7
	3.8	4	4.1	9.3	5.3	30.5	138	54	39.1
2	0.36	0.4	1.2	1.68	11.1	21.9	58	8	13.8
	1.8	1.9	5.8	8.3	7.8	31	234	32	13.7
3	4.7	4.74	14.3	20.4	1.28	28.3	227	8	3.5
	39	39.6	118.8	170	1.5	30	482	20	4
3*	–	–	4.6	10.5	1.2	25	–	–	–
	–	–	37.7	87.7	1	31.4	–	–	–
4	2	2.05	0.18	2.3	3	0.7	257	40	15.6
	16	16.2	2.6	19	1	1	307	72	22

Note: Execution times are given in seconds; T1 — time without any recovery facilities; T2 — time for a primary; T3 — time for an alternative; T4 — time with primary failing the acceptance test; $\%TCM = (T2 - T1) \times 100/T1$, time to collect and maintain recovery data expressed as a % of T1; $\%TRC = (T4 - (T2 + T3)) \times 100/T1$, time to restore system state expressed as a % of T1; NG — number of global variable 'words'; NR — number of words recorded in the cache; $\%C = (NR \times 100)/NG$.

taken as indicative of the performance of hardware implemented recovery caches. A few programs were written and their performance was evaluated:

(1) *To find the median of n items* — The primary algorithm was the 'partition' method, the alternative was a simple scanning method. The acceptance test checked that the number of items smaller than or equal to (greater than or equal to) the median was at least $(n - 1)/2$ (see entry 1 in the table; the bottom entries are for a larger input data).

(2) *Internal sort* — To sort lines of text into alphabetical order. The primary algorithm utilised the 'Quicksort' method; the alternative adopted the 'Shellsort' method. The acceptance test ensured that the lines of text were in ascending order (see entry 2).

(3) *Merge sort* — To sort lines of text residing in secondary storage. Parts of the file were sorted using internal sort developed earlier, and stored on temporary files. These files were then merged to produce a single sorted file. The merging algorithm used 'Heapsort' for the primary and 'Quicksort' for the alternative (entry 3 shows the performance with the primary of internal sort failing while entry 3 * shows the case with the primary of merge failing).

(4) *The stable marriage problem* — The primary was chosen to be the optimal solution satisfying a certain constraint while the secondary was an algorithm that produced the first possible solution. The acceptance test checked that there was no 'polygamy' (see entry 4).

The number of words actually recorded in the recovery cache for the primaries was calculated (for every word occupied by a variable, there will be two words — address and value — in the cache) and compared with the case of complete checkpointing (where the state of all global words will be recorded; note that only values need be recorded). The time to evaluate acceptance tests were also measured; they turned out to be negligibly small. From the data presented, the following conclusions can be drawn:

(1) Assuming failure to be a rare event, it is important to know the overheads for recovery data collection and maintenance when no errors are detected. The table shows that %TCM ranged between 1 to about 11% of T1.

(2) When a primary does fail, it is of interest to know the time taken to restore system state. For the sample programs, %TRC was up to about 30% of T1.

(3) A comparison with complete checkpointing shows that a substantial saving in space was made by the recovery cache. This experiment thus shows that recovery caches could provide acceptable recovery performance for many applications.

References

1. B. Randell, System structure for software fault tolerance, IEEE Trans. on SE, June 1975, pp. 220−232. (Also Chap. 1)
2. S. K. Shrivastava, Sequential Pascal with recovery blocks, Software-Practice & Experience, Vol. 8, pp. 177−185, 1978. (Also Chap. 2)

A Recovery Cache for the PDP-11

P. A. LEE, N. GHANI, and K. HERON

Abstract — Backward error recovery is an integral part of the recovery block scheme that has been advanced as a method for providing tolerance against faults in software; the recovery cache has been proposed as a mechanism for providing this error recovery capability. This paper describes a recovery cache that has been built for the PDP-11 family of machines. This recovery cache has been designed to be an "add-on" unit which requires no hardware alterations to the host CPU but which intersects the bus between the CPU and the memory modules. Specially designed hardware enables concurrent operation of the recovery cache and the host system, and aims to minimize the overheads imposed on the host.

Index Terms — Backward error recovery, fault-tolerant software, recovery blocks.

Introduction

While fault tolerance at the hardware level is common in computing systems, fault tolerant software, that is, software that can produce acceptable results despite design faults in that software, is rare. The *recovery block scheme* has been proposed as a method of introducing redundancy at the software levels in a computing system in order to provide tolerance against such design faults. (It is beyond the scope of this paper to discuss the details of recovery blocks, although a knowledge of the scheme is assumed for this paper. The interested reader is referred to [1], [4], [5], [7].)

Design faults in a program will lead to the generation of erroneous states (errors) in the variables of that program. One of the features of recovery blocks is that if an error is detected within a recovery block then *backward error recovery* occurs in that the states of the variables of that program are reset to the states that existed just prior to entry of that block. By this means, the errors generated by the failing algorithm are recovered from and not allowed to propagate. In order to support this state restoration, a mechanism termed the *recovery cache* has been proposed for providing the necessary recovery capability in an efficient (and reliable) manner; in its simplest form the recovery cache can provide, by hardware, recovery for those variables that reside in the main store of the computer. This paper discusses the design of a recovery cache which can be incorporated into existing computer systems, and describes an experimental version which has been built at the Computing Laboratory of the University of Newcastle upon Tyne for the PDP-11 family of machines.

Overview of the Recovery Cache

The main purpose of the recovery cache is to record *recovery data* so that backward error recovery can be provided for the variables of a program containing

115

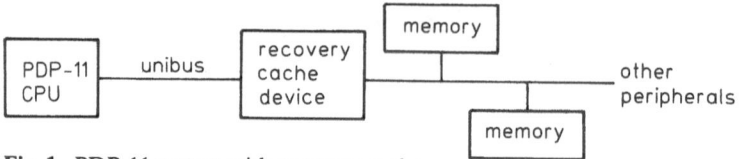

Fig. 1. PDP-11 system with recovery cache

recovery blocks. The basic functioning of the recovery cache is as follows: when a recovery block has been entered and an object is about to be written to (for the first time), the original value of that object is retrieved and stored away (together with its address) by the recovery cache, before the object is actually updated. By this means the recovery cache maintains a minimum of recovery data, and backward error recovery simply involves restoring those changed obects using the values and addresses retained in the recovery cache. (Several methods have been devised for the implementation of the recovery cache algorithms – two examples are presented by Horning et al. [4] and by Anderson and Kerr [1].)

Ideally, the recovery cache would be designed as an integral part of the computer's architecture and incorporated in the CPU and memory hardware. However, it is also desirable to have a recovery cache that could be added to existing computer systems to enable recovery blocks to be used realistically on those systems.

This paper presents the design of an "add-on" recovery cache that can be incorporated into an existing system with no changes to the CPU, memory or other peripheral device, and will not affect the existing software running on that system. Many of the aspects of the design are independent from the host system to which it is to be attached. However, for our initial experiments the host system is a PDP-11, and this will be assumed in the rest of this document. The host-dependent features are discussed elsewhere [6].

The way in which the recovery cache is added to a PDP-11 system is depicted in Fig. 1. The recovery cache intersects the Unibus between the CPU and the memory. In this position the recovery cache can monitor all of the CPU activity on the Unibus, although it is not able to monitor activity between the memory and any other peripheral device (i.e., those to the right of the memories in Fig. 1). This would only cause trouble with DMA devices which can autonomously overwrite memory. While I/O devices appear as memory locations to the PDP-11 CPU and accesses to them could therefore be monitored, the state restoration provided by the recovery cache is usually not appropriate for achieving recovery from these accesses, for instance, if the access resulted in a character being printed on a terminal. A further point to note is that the recovery cache is not able to directly access the registers which are internal to the CPU, namely the program counter, the stack pointer, the program status word, and the other six general purpose registers. Direct access to these quantities would require alterations to the CPU itself, which was not considered desirable. Nevertheless, this is the simplest method of adding the recovery cache to a system and it has been designed to be flexible enough that these problems can be circumvented by software extensions to the basic recovery cache mechanism.

It may also be noted that in this position the recovery cache has to work in terms of real addresses. Thus, application programs which made use of overlays would be difficult to handle. Similarly, concurrent use of the recovery cache by multiple parallel processes would produce extra difficulties. Therefore, for the experimental version of the recovery cache, recovery is provided only for a single core-resident program, and the recovery cache contains base-limit address registers to define the (real) addressing range for which recovery is provided. Extensions to the recovery cache mechanism to deal with some of the problems mentioned above have been discussed in other papers [2], [3], [7], [8]. The incorporation of these extensions with the hardware recovery cache described here will be investigated in a later phase.

Host Software Organization

The software running on the host is divided into two parts: 1) the application program which contains the recovery blocks; and 2) a small kernel providing some minimal set of operating system-like functions for the application program. The kernel contains the routines to interface with the recovery cache and provides recovery actions for the objects for which the recovery cache cannot provide recovery (e.g., saving and restoring the internal registers). Thus, the application programs do not need to be concerned with the provision of recovery nor with some of the finer details of controlling the recovery cache. The kernel also generates the error log which indicates the progress of the program, using one of the peripheral devices on the host system.

Figure 2(a) depicts a high-level language form of a recovery block as it might appear in an application program. The execution of this recovery block would be as follows: when the recovery block is entered, the primary alternate (alt 1) is executed. At the end of the alternate the acceptance test (a Boolean expression) is evaluated. If the acceptance test is "true" then the recovery block is exited. However, if the acceptance test is "false" then recovery occurs to restore the state of the program and the second alternate (alt 2) is entered. This sequence is repeated until either the acceptance test is "true" or the set of alternates has been exhausted. The way in which this recovery block will be represented on the host system is depicted in Fig. 2(b), where the upper case names refer to recovery cache instructions. The semantics of these instructions are discussed below.

Recovery Cache Instructions

The recovery cache has been designed to be as automatic as possible and to require a minimum of control from the program that is utilizing its features. For example, all of the CPU-memory activity on the Unibus will be automatically

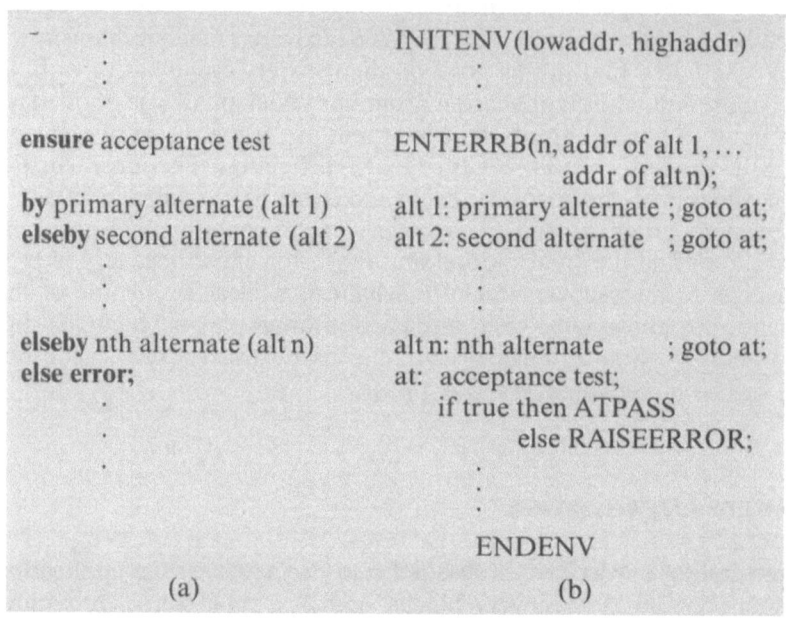

```
          ·                    INITENV(lowaddr, highaddr)
          ·                                ·
          ·                                ·
          ·                                ·

ensure acceptance test            ENTERRB(n, addr of alt 1, ...
                                              addr of alt n);
by primary alternate (alt 1)      alt 1: primary alternate ; goto at;
elseby second alternate (alt 2)   alt 2: second alternate   ; goto at;
          ·                                ·
          ·                                ·
          ·                                ·

elseby nth alternate (alt n)      alt n: nth alternate      ; goto at;
else error;                       at: acceptance test;
          ·                              if true then ATPASS
          ·                                    else RAISEERROR;
          ·                                ·
                                           ·
                                           ·

                                      ENDENV
        (a)                              (b)
```

Fig. 2. Recovery blocks in a program. (a) High-level language format. (b) Low-level language format

intercepted by the recovery cache and will not require nor be dependent upon explicit actions by the program.

To make use of the recovery cache some new "instructions" have to be added to the instruction set of the CPU. As alterations to the CPU are to be avoided, these new "instructions" are most easily obtained by making the recovery cache look like a normal Unibus peripheral device which is controlled by writing to its status registers. Similarly, parameters to "instructions" are passed through device registers.

In general, operation of the CPU should be held up once an "instruction" has been sent to the recovery cache, in order that it has time to complete its actions before the CPU continues. This is not easy to achieve in the present design, and a simple solution involving a "done" bit in the status register has been adopted.

The instructions for the recovery cache reflect the control structure required for recovery blocks. The recovery cache cannot easily directly access the program counter of the CPU; hence most of the desired control structure has to be present in the program containing recovery blocks. The proposed instructions aim to provide as much assistance as possible from the recovery cache.

INIT

This instruction causes the recovery cache to assume an initialized inactive state. This effect is also achieved when the "START" key on the host system is pressed.

118

INITENV (lowaddr, highaddr)

For this paper, "recovery environment" refers to that set of memory words for which backward error recovery is to be provided when a recovery block is entered. This instruction marks the start of a new recovery environment, and causes the recovery cache to store the state of the environment it is currently monitoring (e.g., addressing range), and sets the (real) address range which is to be monitored when activated by the ENTERRB instruction.

ENDENV

This instruction indicates the end of a recovery environment and causes the recovery cache to restore its state and restart monitoring the previous environment.

ENTERRB (number of alts, address of alt1, address of alt 2 . . .)

This instruction indicates the start of a new recovery block. The parameters indicate the number of alternates together with their starting address.

ATPASS

This instruction, indicating the successful termination of a recovery block by the passing of the acceptance test, causes the recovery cache to process and discard as necessary the recovery data that it had recorded for the current recovery block.

RECOVER

This instruction causes the recovery actions provided by the recovery cache to be invoked. It also causes the address of the next alternate to be made available (see below), or indicates an error if all of the alternates have been attempted.

RAISEERROR

This instruction is used to raise an error indication for the currently executing program, and has the effect of initiating the ERRORINT interrupt discussed below.

PRIOR (address)

This instruction causes the prior value of the variable whose address is specified to be made available by the recovery cache.

Recovery Cache Provided Information

The following (read-only) information is provided by the recovery cache via its registers:

REC.LEVEL

The current depth of nesting of recovery blocks. Zero indicates that no recovery is available.

ALT.NUMBER
The number of the next alternate to be obeyed.

NEXTADDR
The address of the next alternate to be entered.

CACHEDONE
When set this bit indicates that the recovery cache has completed its actions and is ready to receive further instructions.

Note that these quanties are maintained automatically by the recovery cache. Other status and monitoring information will also be provided to enable the performance of the recovery cache to be monitored.

Recovery Cache Generated Interrupts

Each recovery cache instruction causes an interrupt to be immediately generated in the host system. Thus routines in the kernel of the host can be provided and automatically invoked to ensure that the program using recovery blocks is properly synchronized with the actions of the recovery cache and, for instance, is not resumed until the recovery cache has completed its actions. These interrupts also provide the means through which the recovery actions provided in the kernel can be invoked to supplement the recovery provided by the recovery cache. Some examples of such actions are given below.

ENTERRB INTERRUPT
This interrupt is generated from the ENTERRB instruction, and allows for kernel-provided recovery data recording to be initiated. For example, the kernel can record recovery data to preserve the states of the internal registers.

ATPASS INTERRUPT
This interrupt, generated from the ATPASS instruction, can be used to invoke any processing of kernel-provided recovery actions. For example, the kernel can discard the recovery data it had recorded for restoring the internal registers.

ERRORINT INTERRUPT
This interrupt is generated by the recovery cache to indicate that it had detected (or had been informed) that an error condition existed. The interrupt is used to force the CPU to initiate recovery actions and enter the next alternate, as well as allowing for the initiation of any kernel-provided recovery actions (e.g., the restoration of the internal registers).

The code sequence in the CPU to handle the ERRORINT is of the form as indicated in the following (where upper case names refer to the recovery cache instructions and information).

```
if REC.LEVEL ≤ 0
   then terminate program
   else begin
      perform error logging;
      perform any kernel-provided recovery;
      RECOVER;
      wait for CACHEDONE;
      if REC.LEVEL = 0
      then terminate program
      else begin
         record recovery data for any
         kernel-provided recovery actions;
         return from interrupt but use
         address specified in NEXTADDR;
         end;
      end;
```

Recovery Cache Hardware

The experimental version of the recovery cache is based on an LSI-11 micro-computer with a number of special purpose peripherals (see Fig. 3). This results in simple low-cost hardware with many of the functions carried out by microprocessor software, and provides a flexible research vehicle which will allow further studies to be made in optimization of the recovery cache algorithms and in extensions of the techniques to more sophisticated environments.

While there will of necessity be some overheads associated with the recovery cache (discussed later on), it is anticipated that the overheads imposed on the host system will be minimal, particularly as use is made of specially de-

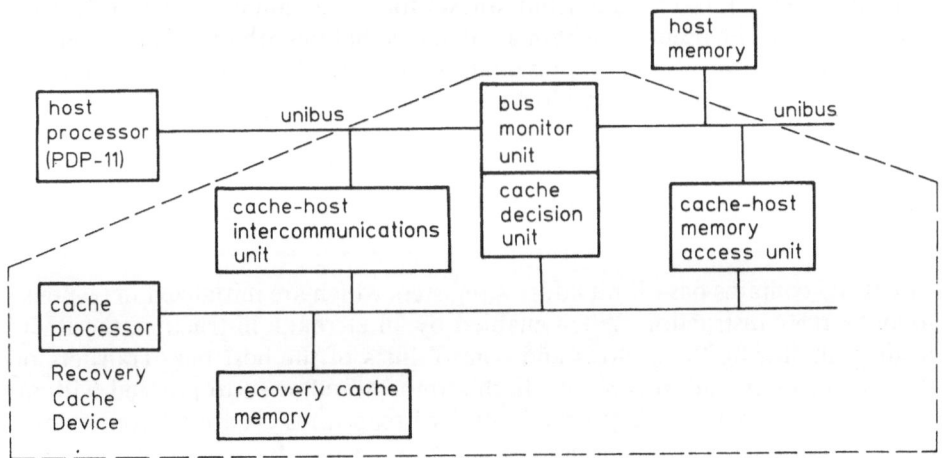

Fig. 3. Hardware organization of the add-on recovery cache

signed hardware to enable concurrent operation of the recovery cache and the host system. Moreover, the design of the recovery cache is such that the transfer of functions from microcomputer software into hardware could be easily achieved in order to reduce further any overheads that the experimental system demonstrates. For example, it is envisaged that the LSI-11 could be simply replaced by a special purpose processor capable of executing the recovery cache algorithms at high speed.

The peripherals shown in Fig. 3 have the following functions.

1) The CHIU (Cache Host Intercommunication Unit) appears to the host PDP-11 as a peripheral device and provides the interface to the host software as described above. It allows the recovery kernel in the host and the recovery cache to interact explicitly.

2) The CHMAU (Cache Host Memory Access Unit) allows the recovery cache to access the host memory directly through the normal Unibus mechanism. It is used mainly for restoring old values to the memory when recovery is invoked.

3) The BMU (Bus Monitor Unit) performs hardware monitoring of all data transfers between the host processor and its memory. It is able to prevent the host from writing into a memory location until the old value from that location has been saved, as necessary, by the recovery cache. The BMU is transparent to the host, and appears to the recovery cache processor as a device which provides a stream of address–value pairs.

4) The CDU (Cache Decision Unit) is a hardware unit which executes the decision process necessary to establish whether an address–value pair should be saved in the recovery cache and transfers the data into the appropriate place in the recovery cache memory, as necessary. The decision is based on information contained in 4-bit fields which reside within the CDU, with one field for each memory location of the host machine. Currently, the CDU implements two different algorithms which interrogate these fields. The algorithm presently being investigated uses these fields in a unary-coded fashion, bit n ($n = 0$, 1, 2, 3) being set if the associated word has already been written to (and cached) at recovery level $n + 1$. This algorithm allows for a maximum nesting of four recovery blocks. The other algorithm available is that described by Anderson and Kerr [1] which uses a binary representation in the fields, thereby allowing up to 31 levels of nesting of recovery blocks.

Recovery Cache Operation

The BMU contains base-limit address registers which are initialized in response to an INITENV instruction. When enabled by an ENTERRB instruction, the BMU begins monitoring the address and control lines of the host bus. Transfers on this bus involving addresses outside the limits are allowed to proceed without interference. Otherwise only straightforward read transfers are allowed to proceed and write transfers are intercepted. A write transfer may or may not require the original value of an object to be saved by the recovery cache (for instance, an address—value pair may only need recording the first time an object is updated; subsequent updates of that object can then be ignored by the recovery cache). While this decision process is relatively simple, the time taken for its execution may be comparable with the cycle time of the host memory. Therefore, in the proposed design this decision process is executed concurrently with the read of the original value from the host memory. If an address—value pair is to be saved in the recovery cache then the CDU initiates the necessary direct memory transfers to store this recovery data in the memory of the recovery cache; during this time the write transfer from the host system can be allowed to proceed.

On the Unibus there are in fact two types of write transfer: read—modify—write transfers and simple write transfers. The read—modify—write transfer automatically generates the information required by the recovery cache — when the memory location is read, the value can be captured by the BMU; the following write part of the transfer can then be ignored by the BMU. Conceptually, simple write transfers have to be delayed by the BMU until the original value has been read from memory. In practice, the write transfer is converted to a read—modify—write transfer by the BMU to achieve the desired effect.

Performance Considerations

The recovery cache slows down the host system in two main ways. Firstly, there is the time needed to interpret the recovery cache instructions such as ENTERRB, as the application program cannot be allowed to proceed until such instructions have been completed. Such instructions are expected to form only a small percentage of the executed instructions of the application program. Hence, the delay caused by their execution should not be significant, although it should be noted that the time to interpret the ATPASS and RECOVER instructions will in general depend on the behavior of the application program.

The second source of delays are those introduced through the interference of the BMU with memory transfer cycles of the host system. These delays are more significant as every memory cycle is delayed to some extent. The minimum level of degradation is defined by the delays introduced by the address and control line checking. In the experimental (nonoptimized) system this delay is approximately 100 ns per transfer.

The BMU performs its saving operations on both read—modify—write and pure write cycles that are within the address range defined by the INITENV instruction; normally only write cycles need to be extended, as explained above, resulting in an extra delay of 600 ns on the current host system which contains core storage with a cycle time of 900 ns. Monitoring the activity on a PDP-11 Unibus has indicated that in general approximately 8 percent of transfers are write transfers and 2 percent are read—modify—write transfers, figures which agree with those published elsewhere [9]. These figures suggest that the extra overhead on the host system would be of the order of 8 percent, caused by the need to precede each write by a read. If memory with destructive readout is used, the fact that a write cycle is converted into a read—modify—write cycle means that the additional delay is less than that incurred by forcing a separate read cycle. In this case the extra overhead would be expected to be of the order of 4 percent. Of course, these overheads will depend critically on the behavior of the application program and these percentage figures only provide a general indication of the overheads which it is hoped will occur in practice.

The above figures assume that the time required to execute the cacheing decision and to record the address—value pair is comparable with the time between write transfers on the host system. The monitoring figures discussed above indicate that, on average, the time available is equivalent to the time for 9 memory reads by the host CPU. The CDU has been designed to satisfy this criterion. Clearly, if successive write transfers occur on the Unibus then some extra delay is inevitable. In practice, most write transfers are followed by at least one read transfer (the instruction fetch), and it is therefore anticipated that this extra delay will only occur on rare occasions. Further "smoothing out" of successive write transfers is achieved by a first-in first-out buffer in the BMU.

Other performance issues would arise if the host system included a "high-speed" cache — that is, a high-speed look aside buffer. In this case the system configuration would be CPU → high-speed cache → recovery cache → memory, and the recovery cache would not degrade accesses to the high-speed cache. If the high-speed cache was write-through, then these memory writes would be caught (and delayed) as described above. If it was not write-through, then it is likely that the system degradation caused by the recovery cache would be less since a number of writes to the same object would only result (eventually) in a single write to memory. (The host kernel would also require slight alteration to ensure that the high-speed cache was flushed out at appropriate times, for instance, when a recovery point is established.)

The high-speed cache and the recovery cache can be regarded as performing related tasks, and could therefore be incorporated into a single device providing both speed-up and recovery [5], [10]. This has not yet been investigated in the current design.

Summary

This paper has presented the design of an add-on recovery cache and has discussed an experimental version that has been built for a PDP-11 host system. While the overheads imposed on the host by the recovery cache will depend on the behavior of the application program, the paper has shown how the delays can be minimized. Measurements of the experimental system will indicate where optimizations should be applied, and this will be reported in a later paper.

Acknowledgement. We would like to express our gratitude to the fellow members of the Reliability Project, which is sponsored by the U.K. Science Research Council, at the University of Newcastle upon Tyne.

References

1. T. Anderson and R. Kerr, "Recovery blocks in action: a system supporting high reliability," in Proc. 2nd Int. Conf. Software Engineering, San Francisco, CA, Oct. 1976, pp. 447–457. (Also Chap. 2)
2. T. Anderson, P. A. Lee, and S. K. Shrivastava, "A model of recoverability in multilevel systems," IEEE Trans. Software Eng., vol. SE-4, pp. 486–494, Nov. 1978. (Also Chap. 5)
3. T. Anderson and P. A. Lee, "The provision of recoverable interfaces," in Dig. Papers FTCS9, WI, June 20–22, 1978, pp. 87–94. (Also Chap. 5)
4. J. J. Horning et al., "A program structure for error detection and recovery," in Lecture Notes in Computer Science 16. Berlin: Springer, 1974, pp. 177–193. (Also Chap. 2)
5. P. A. Lee, "A reconsideration of the recovery block scheme," Computer J., vol. 20, pp. 306–310, Nov. 1978. (Also Chap. 2)
6. P. A. Lee, N. Ghani, and K. Heron, "A recovery cache for the PDP-11," in Dig. Papers FTCS9, WI, June 20–22, 1978, pp. 3–8.
7. B. Randell, "System structure for software fault tolerance," IEEE Trans. Software Eng., vol. SE-1, pp. 220–232, June 1976. (Also Chap. 1)
8. S. K. Shrivastava and J.-P. Banatre, "Reliable resource allocation between unreliable processes," IEEE Trans. Software Eng., vol. SE-4, pp. 230–241, May 1978. (Also Chap. 4)
9. W. D. Strecker, "Cache memories for PDP-11 family computers," in Proc. 3rd Symp. Computer Architecture, Jan. 1976, pp. 155–158.
10. Y. S. Vong, "A recovery cache mechanism using a high-speed buffer," M.Sc. thesis, University of Newcastle-upon-Tyne, Newcastle-upon-Tyne, England, 1976.

Recovery and Crash Resistance in a Filing System

J. S. M. VERHOFSTAD

Abstract. This paper describes mechanisms that provide the user of a filing system the dynamic facility for defining a scope within which backing out can be done on request.

Check points (defining the beginning of a new scope) can dynamically be established and procedures for 'acceptance' (at the end of the scope) or 'undoing' (within or at the end of the scope) can be invoked. These scopes can be nested.

It is also shown that these mechanisms can be used to provide crash resistance. After a crash the system will be left in the state it was in before it entered the current scope (or outermost scope if scopes are nested).

Keywords and Phrases: audit trial, backing out, consistency, crash resistance, error recovery, fault tolerance, filing system, recovery block, recovery cache (= recursive cache).

1. Introduction

This paper presents mechanisms extending earlier work on recovery blocks [Randell 75] to include recovery for a filing system. These mechanisms provide the user of the filing system the dynamic facility for defining a scope within which backing out can be done on request or will be done automatically in case an error occurs.

These same mechanisms can be used to provide crash resistance.

Earlier research on recovery blocks has concentrated on mechanisms that provide recoverability for simple variables, for example integers, reals and booleans [Horning et al. 74] [Anderson, Kerr 76].

The mechanisms presented here are the result of work that has been done in trying to find mechanisms for the implementation of the recovery block scheme for more complex data types and for filing systems in particular. A full report on the problems encountered and possible alternative solutions has been published elsewhere [Verhofstad 76].

The notion of a *recoverable* file (or filing system) and *recoverability provided for* a file (or filing system) will be used to mean that the state of that file (or filing system) can be restored to the state it was in at the most recent checkpoint made at the time of entering the current recovery block, at user request. This restoring will be done automatically if an error occurs during the execution of the recovery block. Recovery blocks can be nested.

In order to implement the described recoverable filing system, the filing system of OS6 [Stoy, Strachey 72a, b, c, d] has been redesigned. The user interface has been kept unchanged. The Computing Laboratory at the University of Newcastle upon Tyne possesses a version of OS6, which is running on a B1700 computer [Snow 76].

Section two gives definitions for the most important notions used in this paper.

Section three describes those circumstances in which the scheme will be useful and illustrates this with a brief example.

Section four describes the basic strategy used for providing a recoverable filing system.

Section five describes a specific implementation of a recoverable filing system. This example is used to illustrate the principles.

Section six describes the recovery mechanisms. The implemented filing system described in section five is used to illustrate these mechanisms.

Section seven describes the role of redundancy in systems in which recovery as described in this paper is to be provided.

Section eight describes how the recovery mechanisms can also be used to maintain consistency and provide crash resistance.

Section nine gives the main conclusions.

2. Definitions

A *recovery block* is a program structure consisting of an *acceptance test* and several alternative pieces of program. The alternatives are algorithms which are implementations of the same abstract specifications. The state of the system at entering a recovery block is the state to which the system will be "rolled back" in case an error occurs inside the scope of the recovery block or if the corresponding acceptance test fails. The first alternative will be executed when the recovery block is entered. If the execution of this alternative ends normally then the acceptance test will be performed. After an acceptance test has been performed successfully the state of the system at the time the recovery block was entered is forgotten and the recovery block is exited. If the acceptance test fails or an error occurs during the execution of a given alternative then all the operations done in the latest or current alternative will be undone (i.e. the alternative is backed out) and the next alternative will be invoked. If there are no remaining alternatives then an error occurs.

Recovery blocks can be nested so *commitment* of the operations only takes place when the outermost recovery block is exited. If an inner recovery block exhausts its alternatives then the current alternative of the recovery block in which this will generate an error, will be backed out and the next alternative of that recovery block will be invoked.

The acceptance test has no side-effects and is specified by the writer of the program. The acceptance test may test whether the abstract specifications were met by the alternative just executed. The acceptance test does not have to be complete (i.e. test all the effects of the alternative).

The use of a recovery block ensures the programmer that if the current alternative is not executed successfully either because the acceptance test fails or because a hardware or software error occurs before the execution of the current recovery block alternative is finished, then all the effects of the current recovery block will be undone. An acceptance test fails if the recovery block alternative did not perform as intended.

127

A full description of an interpreter providing the recovery block control structure (a fault tolerant interpreter) has been published elsewhere [Randell 75].

The term *cache* will be used to include the storing of any data to aid later recovery. Cacheing in the fault tolerant interpreter developed in Newcastle upon Tyne is simply done by storing the value of a variable (as it was at the checkpoint, i.e. the time of entering the recovery block) before it is updated. This only needs to be done the first time a variable is updated within a recovery block alternative [Horning et al. 74]. The data structure in which cached information is kept is called the *recovery cache* (or recursive cache).

The term 'recovery block' will be used in this paper to define the *scope* within which the user can require the undoing of the filing system operation performed so far inside that recovery block. The mechanisms described are general and not necessarily implemented in terms of recovery blocks.

3. The Advantages and Applicability of the Recovery Mechanisms

This section describes those circumstances in which the described mechanisms can be used and illustrates their applicability and usefulness in an example.

The recovery scheme described has been implemented in a system supporting a single user at a time. The implementation of the scheme in systems with multiple concurrent updates by simultaneously executing processes is outside the scope of this paper. Randell [Randell 75] has shown that recovery in those cases in general may lead to the so-called 'domino'-effect; this is the backing out of all the processes involved plus all the processes that share data with these processes and so on. A locking scheme possibly providing degrees of consistency, as for example is used in System R [Gray et al. 76], could be used to solve or avoid these problems.

The scheme described in this paper provides the general recovery block facilities to users of the filing system. The advantages, use of and applicability of recovery blocks, in general, have been described elsewhere [Horning et al. 74] [Randell 75].

Acceptance tests could for example be used to test the continued validity of invariants or predicates after relevant objects have been operated upon (see for example the invariants and predicates as used in ALPHARD [Wulf et al. 77] and SEQUEL [Astrahan et al. 75]). In systems manipulating complex data types several type mappings are generally defined. This may mean that procedures implementing operations on the most abstract types involve procedures on less abstract types and so on. Each of these procedures may contain recovery blocks thus checking consistency at all levels of abstraction.

For example, in a relational data base system an invariant for a relation may have been specified. Operations on this relation may be performed inside recovery blocks which check the continued validity of the invariant. However, unknown to the user, the system may maintain and use several inversions (these are auxiliary diectories, see for example the use of inversions in the PRTV relational data base system [Verhofstad 76a]). An update of the relation will cause the inversion to be updated. The procedure implementing the update of the relation may invoke another procedure which updates the possibly existing inversions. Both procedures may contain recovery blocks, causing the nesting of recovery blocks. If an update of the inversions goes wrong then the effects of that operation will be undone and an alternative will be tried. If none of the alternatives is successful, for whatever reason, then all of the effects of the update of the relation so far, will be undone and an alternative to this operation will be tried. The second alternative of the operation that updates the relation could for example, first destroy all the inversions; this would not affect the abstract view provided.

4. The Basic Strategy

The updates for the filing system are made in such a way that the state of the filing system can be restored to what it was at a certain programmer determined point (i.e. at the point of entering the current recovery block). The way in which this has been implemented is as follows:

A file consists of a collection of data pages in which the contents of the file are stored.

Whenever a file is updated, the pages to be updated are copied into newly allocated pages and the updates are made there. In this way two versions of the file are kept, whose pages can be shared where possible. (This scheme could be regarded as a variation of the scheme using differential files as described by Severance and Lohman [Severance, Lohman 76].) If the operations pass an acceptance test (i.e. the acceptance procedure is invoked) then the original copies (i.e. pages which are not shared with the new versions) can be destroyed. If the operations fail the acceptance test (i.e. the undoing procedure is invoked) then the same will be done for the new versions and the files will be restored to what they were when entering the recovery block.

Obviously more than two copies can be maintained in case several recovery blocks are nested.

The general principles upon which the filing system and mechanisms are based are:

1) A minimum of information is to be kept in order to restore the state of the filing system (as seen by the user) to the state it was in at recovery block entry.

The information must be sufficient to restore the state no matter which operations have been performed in the meantime.

Consequently an audit trail scheme or "reverse audit trail" scheme, which keeps track of the operations performed and executes the reverse operations in the reversed order in which the original operations were performed, are unsuitable. Recovery is to be linked with data structures and values rather than with operations.

2) Cacheing is to be done at the appropriate level. For example for file bodies, disk blocks are cached rather than disk words.
3) The original cache scheme updates all objects "in place" and old values of those objects are cached [Horning et al. 74]. While appropriate for simple data types (e.g. integers), the following strategies are sometimes more appropriate for complex data types:

a) Leave the original values in the original objects and copy the new values into new objects the first time these objects are assigned to inside a recovery block.

b) Cache the name (i.e. a pointer) of the copy.

c) Do not cache the objects but retain enough information in the cache to retrieve the original values of the objects at recovery block entry.

4) An alternative scheme which provides crash resistance does not cache the old values of objects (or names or pointers) when it is first altered, but caches the new value instead, leaving the originals unchanged. Subsequent assignments are redirected to affect the cached values rather than the original values. Unlike the original scheme (3), reads, as well as writes trigger a search through the cache.

5. The Structure of the Recoverable Filing System

Files are regarded as sequences of consecutive words which can have any possible value.

User programs running under OS6 may create files and destroy files. Files can also be freely assigned to variables, and be passed as parameters or be the result of a function call within a single program.

A bottom-up description of a file is given below (see also Fig. 1):

- The file body.
  A file body consists of a hierarchical structure of data pages and one or more directory pages. A directory page is used to point to data pages or lower level directory pages. Both a directory page and a data page occupy one disk block each.
- The header.
  For each file there is a unique header which contains general information about the file, such as: address top directory, date last accessed and owner.
  These headers have a variable length and are kept in a special file: *the header file*.
- The file index.
  Each file is associated with a unique index in a table which contains the addresses of the headers for all files in the system (an address is a tuple: page in header file, offset). This table is called the Master File List and is kept in a special file: *the MFL file*.
  The disk address of the first page of the MFL file is known by the filing system (a constant which is initialised when the system is set up and is built in the code).

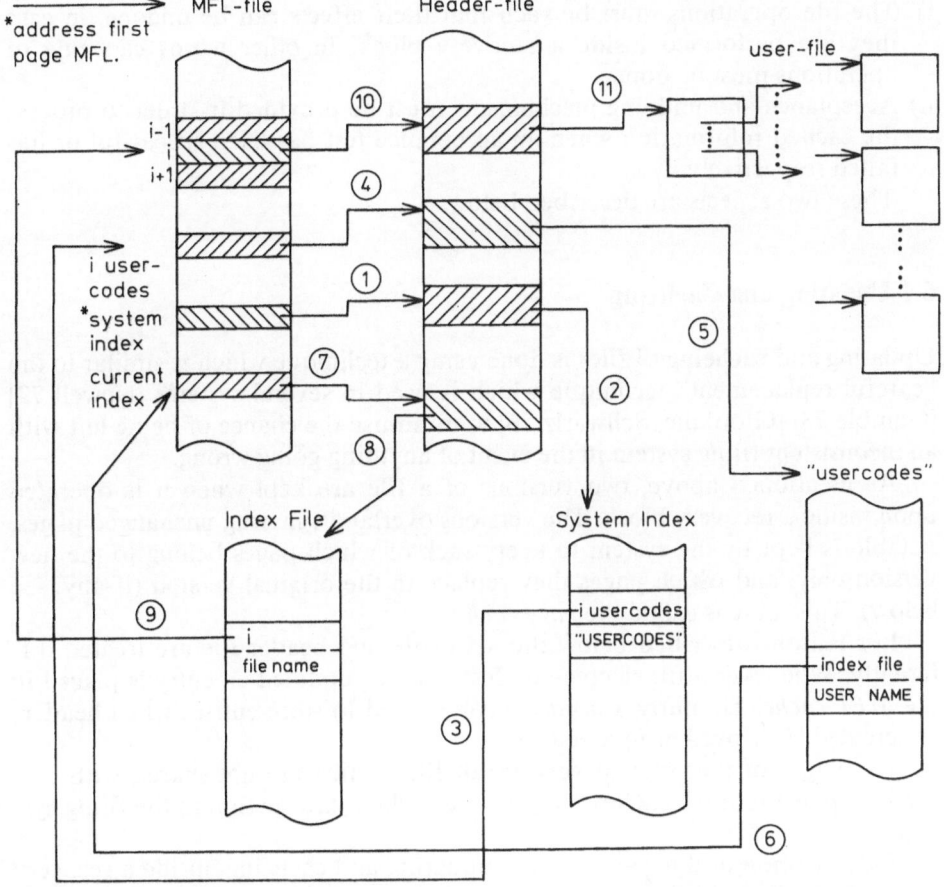

The two variables marked by a '*' are known to the system and set during system initialisation. The value 'current index' is set when the user logs on, so after that the search for a user file starts in MPL from 'current index'.

Accesses 1–6 are made when a user logs on in order to set up the current index.
Accesses 7–11 are made when the current user wishes to access one of his files.

Fig. 1. The structure of the prototype filing system

— A file name.

In order to be able to use a file in other programs *index files* are used to associate names with file indexes. The *System Index* is the index file which contains all the entries for all system files. The file index of this file (the system index) is known to the filing system (a constant initialised when the system is set up and is built in the code).

6. The Recovery Mechanisms

In order to provide recoverability for files the following two aspects are required:

i) The file operations must be such that their effects can be undone, in case they are performed inside a recovery block. In other words cacheing of operations must be done.

ii) Acceptance and undoing mechanisms must be provided in order to process the cached information when an acceptance test has been successful or has failed respectively.

These two aspects are described below:

6.1 Updating and Cacheing

Updating and cacheing of files is done using a technique which is similar to the "careful replacement" technique which is used in several systems [Newell 72] [Gamble 73] [Giordane, Schwartz 76] to minimise the chance of being left with an inconsistent filing system in the event of anything going wrong.

As mentioned above, two versions of a file are kept when it is operated upon inside a recovery block. The versions overlap in sharing unchanged pages. A table is kept by the system to keep track of which pages belong to the new version only, and which pages they replace in the original version (if any, see below). This table is called the *page cache*.

For reasons described below the MFL-file and header file are treated differently. Whenever a file is created, destroyed or updated an entry is placed in the *MFL-cache*. Similarly a *header-cache* is used to store entries when headers are created, destroyed or updated.

The pages of the original versions of files which are not shared with new versions plus the three caches form all the cached information in the filing system.

A description of the way in which updating and cacheing, inside a recovery block, is done in the filing system is given below:

After a recovery block has been entered each first operation on a file body data page is done as follows:

i) The data page is copied into a new disk page and the change will be made in this new page.

(This is for the case when a data page is updated; the file can also be extended by a data page in which case that new page is the newly created one. When a data page is deleted from a file, that data page will remain unaltered and not be copied into a new page).

ii) The same is done for the directory page pointing to the original data page (or for the directory in which a pointer is to be added or deleted in case a data page has been newly created or deleted respectively).

Higher level directories are treated the same way.

iii) For each replaced page the tuple ⟨old page i, new page j⟩ is put in the page cache. If the old page is to be deleted or the new psge has been newly allocated then new page j will have the value "deleted" and old page i will have value "new" respectively.

iv) a change in a file within a recovery block causes its top directory to be changed. Consequently the header of the file has to be changed. If the header file is to be treated as an ordinary file then this means that the disk page in which the header is stored (in the header file) is to be updated by replacement. As a result of this the addresses of other headers in that replaced disk page of the header file change. The header of the header file also changes as a result of this and consequently several other headers may get a new begin address. This means that for all these headers the MFL entries will have to be changed. If the MFL file is treated as an ordinary file then this implies that all pages in MFL in which an entry is to be changed, have to be replaced. Obviously the header of the MFL-file also has to be changed and again the header file must be changed.

Thus each first change on the filing system within a recovery block may cause a large part of the filing system to be replaced.

In order to avoid this the MFL-file and header file are treated differently.

The header of the changed file is copied into a header-cache, and the *new value* of the address of the new top directory is placed in that header in the cache.

Similarly the MFL-cache is used to contain tuples ⟨file index, tag⟩, where "tag" has value "changed", new or "deleted".

The following notes on this scheme can be made:

- The original files are unaltered on disk. The new versions are defined by the new headers kept in the header cache. Consequently the access path definition as shown in Fig. 1 is changed to include a search for a header in the cache before trying to read it from disk.
- A minimum of information is kept in caches as outlined in section 4. If a page i has been updated within a recovery block and therefore been replaced by page j, then every subsequent change to page j (within the same recovery block) can be done straightaway because it already belongs to the new version. Similarly if a file is created and subsequently destroyed within the same recovery block then no cached information about the file will remain in the cache.
- Under certain circumstances (i.e. if on average only a few words per page are updated) file words could be cached rather than file pages. It could also be feasible to cache directory entries like headers, instead of replacing complete directory pages. At present this is not done, but suggests two points which relate to the level of cacheing. These points are:

   1) A methodological one, namely: it appears that from some level onwards in a multi-level data structure, recoverability must be provided per type rather than per physical object used [Verhofstad 76].

   2) An efficiency issue, namely: It may be useful to allow the cacheing strategy to vary, depending upon the circumstances in which objects of the multi-level data type are used.

6.2 Acceptance and Undoing Mechanisms

The processing of the caches and the files at the end of a recovery block is described below.

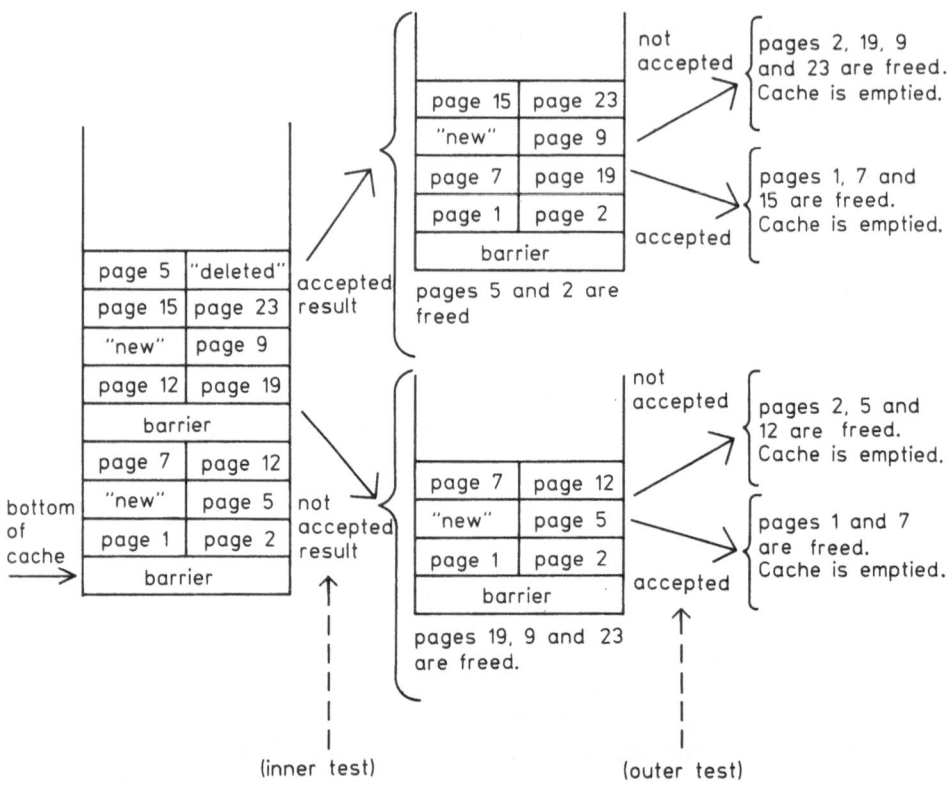

This assumes that no cacheing occurs between the execution of the inner test and outer test.

Fig. 2. Page cache processing: an example

One little note has to be made first, namely that a *barrier* is placed in the caches each time a new recovery block is entered. Thus at the end of the recovery block the information in the caches subsequent to the latest barrier will be processed.

I The page cache

The page cache is used to free pages (and update the file containing the list of free pages). It is important to note that changes to the file containing the list of free pages are not cached. The page cache is processed, at the end of a recovery block, as follows (see also Fig. 2).

i) In case the acceptance test failed (backing out is wanted and the undoing procedure is invoked):

All the "new pages" in the tuples ⟨old page, new page⟩ up to the latest barrier in the cache are freed.

The cache is cleared up to the barrier.

ii) In case the acceptance test was successful (the acceptance procedure is invoked).

a) In case the outermost recovery block is exited (recovery blocks can be nested):

All the "old pages" in the tuples $\langle$old page, new page$\rangle$ in the cache are freed. The whole cache is emptied.

b) In case an inner recovery block is exited:

The latest barrier is removed and all the tuples are moved up. Pairs of tuples up to the next barrier are combined as follows:

T1) $\langle$page 1, page 2$\rangle$ & $\langle$page 2, page 3$\rangle$ $\Rightarrow$ $\langle$page 1, page 3$\rangle$
   page 2 is freed.

T2) $\langle$"new", page 1$\rangle$ & $\langle$page 1, page 2$\rangle$ $\Rightarrow$ $\langle$"new", page 2$\rangle$
   page 1 is freed.

T3) $\langle$page 1, page 2$\rangle$ & $\langle$page 2, "deleted"$\rangle$ $\Rightarrow$ $\langle$page 1, "deleted"$\rangle$
   page 2 is freed.

T4) $\langle$"new", page 1$\rangle$ & $\langle$page 1, "deleted"$\rangle$ $\Rightarrow$ page 1 is freed.

II The header cache

If the acceptance test failed then the cache is emptied upto and including the barrier.

If the acceptance test was successful and the outermost recovery block is exited then the header file is updated to contain the new values of the headers cached.

If the acceptance test was successful and an inner recovery block is exited, then the latest barrier in the header cache is removed and headers just move up. If the same header appears both before and after the barrier, but after the next latest barrier, the earlier header in the cache is replaced by the most recent one.

III The MFL-cache

The MFL-cache is processed like the header cache. The MFL-file is updated if the acceptance test of the outermost recovery block has been successful. The cache is emptied upto and including the next barrier if the acceptance test was unsuccessful. If an inner recovery block is exited and the acceptance test was successful then the cached entries are moved up like headers in the header cache. Cache entries are combined as follows:

T5) $\langle$i, "new"$\rangle$ & $\langle$i, "changed"$\rangle$ $\Rightarrow$ $\langle$i, "new"$\rangle$.

T6) $\langle$i, "new"$\rangle$ & $\langle$i, "deleted"$\rangle$ $\Rightarrow$ nothing.

T7) $\langle$i, "changed"$\rangle$ & $\langle$i, "changed"$\rangle$ $\Rightarrow$ $\langle$i, "changed"$\rangle$.

T8) $\langle$i, "changed"$\rangle$ & $\langle$i, "deleted"$\rangle$ $\Rightarrow$ $\langle$i, "deleted"$\rangle$.

Final remarks

– The given design and definition of files is rather neat in the sense that many versions of a file can be kept without any unnecessary duplication of information or messy definition of files. Each version has the same structure and is defined by its index and header.

The mechanisms described provide the recoverability as required.

– Files are regarded as globals for each program, even if they are created inside an inner block. So only when the outermost recovery block acceptance test has been successful is the file system on disk updated. This is because files are components of a filing system, which is global.

7. The Role of Redundancy

It appears to be important to make sure that redundant information is always used as 'hints' [Lampson 75]. *Hints* are redundant data items which are always checked against some 'absolutes' and are used to optimise the efficiency of operations on data structures. In other words the correct working of programs will never depend on the correctness of hints. Hints are solely used to improve the efficiency of the implementation. For example pointers in data pages could be used to link the pages in order to make a linear search more efficient. If these links would always have to be correct (i.e. not used as hints) then this would mean that if a given page is replaced because of an update inside a recovery block, then the page pointing to the given page has to be updated too. Consequently this page has to be replaced and therefore the page pointing to it requires updating, and so on. So a whole chain of pages would have to be updated, which is of course unacceptable. Again a link-cache could be maintained to contain the changed links, however this would make the definition of files very messy. So far no mechanisms are known to implement these kinds of schemes neatly.

8. Maintaining Consistency and Providing Crash Resistance

8.1 Crash Resistance

The consistency this paper is dealing with simply requires that user operations must completely and correctly be performed or not be performed at all, no matter when a system crash occurs.

The kind of consistency this paper is dealing with is explained by the following example:

If a header is partially in disk page x and partially in disk page y, the situation whereby x has been updated and y has not been updated yet and a subsequent crash occurs leaving the header in neither its original nor in the new state, must be impossible.

Crashes are classified in either one of the following three classes:

1) No disk page is corrupted. For example if the system crashes while no disk write is in progress.
2) One disk page is corrupted. For example if a disk write is interrupted or is unsuccessful.
3) More than one disk page are corrupted. For example because of a head crash or the disk head does not position itself correctly or the operating system gets tied up and goes on writing to disk for a while.

The only way in which recovery from crashes of class 3 is possible is by keeping back-up versions of files. Good descriptions of a widely used method for filing systems and data bases, i.e. incremental dumping and audit trail schemes, are given elsewhere [Daley, Neumann 65] [Fraser 69] [Bjork, Davies 72] [Bjork 74], see also the annotated bibliography in [Tonik 75].

If a system can cope with crashes of class 1 and 2 then it is called *crash resistant*.

8.2 The Critical Updates

If the filing system, as described above, is updated inside a recovery block then only some free pages will be used to contain new values of data and directory pages, but the filing system will remain unchanged, because the MFL-file and header file remain unchanged. Consequently if a crash of class 1 or 2 will occur inside a recovery block then the filing system will remain unchanged and left behind in the state it was in before the outermost recovery block was entered. The filing system is only updated when the acceptance procedure of the outermost recovery block is executed. The header and MFL-entries are updated "in place". This updating is called the critical update. If this update goes wrong or is interrupted then the filing system can be left in an inconsistant state.

Several approaches to this problem are possible, some of these are discussed below:
a) The principle of majority voting could be used for the MFL-file and header file (see [Sklaroff 76] for a good application of this principle).
b) By using extra levels of indirection the amount of information to be updated "in place" can always be reduced to one object (see also [Newell 72]). This object in the described filing system would be "first page MFL-file", which would thus become a variable rather than a constant which could be built in the code. This one object has to be updated "in place" and this could be done in several ways, for example:

   i) Use majority voting.

   ii) Show probabilistically that the system can afford to take the risk to update it "in plane".

   iii) Use an external device or type the new value on the console before updating the constant.

c) The probability of a crash occuring during the critical update may be so small that we can afford to do this critical update "in place". If a crash does occur during this critical update then it will be treated as a class 3 crash.

(Strategy c) has been chosen in the implemented filing system described above.

9. Conclusions

Cacheing and updating mechanisms that provide the user with the facility to define scopes within which the filing system can be backed out on request (i.e. if an acceptance test fails) have been presented, and have been implemented successfully as described in this paper.

The kind of information cached and the way in which updates are made appeared to be of extreme importance if recoverability is to be provided in a reasonably efficient way, and if consistency of the data structures after a crash are to be guaranteed.

The system on disk is always kept in a consistent and coherent structure. Only during the critical update the structure may be in an inconsistent state. Several possible solutions to this problem have been discussed.

It appeared that from a certain level onwards in a multi-level data structure, cacheing has to be done "per type" rather than "per physical object" used for the implementation of the multilevel data structure.

Crash resistance is provided by never updating original versions of files. Instead the file bodies are copied and the new copies are updated. The versions of file bodies thus created overlap in identical data and directory pages. A new file header for the file, pointing to the most recent version of the file body, is kept in a cache.

Acknowledgements. The author wishes to acknowledge the many comments and critisims received from Mr. P. M. Melliar-Smith during discussions on the ideas, which led to the results presented here.

Thanks are also due to Ellis Cohen and Roger Gimson for reading earlier versions of this paper.

I also wish to thank Professor B. Randell and the referees for their many valuable comments.

References

[Anderson, Kerr 76]
Anderson, T., Kerr, R. Recovery blocks in action: a system supporting high reliability. Proc. 2nd. Int. Conf. on Software Engineering, San Francisco, Oct. 1976. (Also Chap. 2)
[Astrahan et al. 75]
Astrahan, M. M. et al. SEQUEL, Release 2. IBM Research Laboratory, San Jose, California. February 1975.
[Bjork, Davies 72]
Bjork, L. A., Davies Jr., C. T. The semantics of the presentation and recovery of integrity in a data system. IBM-Technical Report, TR 02.540, Dec., 22, 1972.
[Bjork 74]
Bjork, L. A. Generalised audit trail (Ledger) concepts for data base applications, IBM – Technical Report, TR 02-641, Sept. 16, 1974.
[Daley, Neumann 65]
Daley, D. C., Neumann, P. G. A general purpose file system for secondary storage. F. J. C. C. 1965, pp 213–229.
[Fraser 69]
Fraser, A. G. Integrity of a mass storage filing system. The Computer Journal, Vol. 12,7, Feb. 1969.
[Gamble 73]
Gamble, J. N. A file storage system for a multi-machine environment. Ph. D. Thesis, Victoria University, Manchester, England. Oct. 1973.
[Giordano, Schwartz 76]
Giordano, N. J., Schwartz, M. S. Data Base Recovery at GMIC. Proc. 1976 SIGMOD Int. Conf. on Management of Data, June 2–4, 1976, Washington D. C., pp 33–42.
[Gray et al. 76]
Gray, J. N., Lorie, R. A., Putzolu, G. R., Traiger, I. L. Granularity of locks and degrees of consistency in a shared data base. In: Modelling in data base management systems, G. M. Nijssen (ed.) North Holland Publishing Company 1976, pp 365–394.

[Horning et al. 74]
    Horning, J. J., Lauer, H. C., Melliar-Smith, P.M., Randell, B. A program structure for error detection and recovery. Lecture Notes in Computer Science, Vol. 16, Springer Verlag, pp. 177–193, 1974. (Also Chap. 2)
[Lampson 75]
    Lampson, B. W. An open operating system for a single-user machine. Xerox Palo Alto Research Centre, Palo Alto, U.S.A. January, 1977.
[Newell 72]
    Newell, G. B. (Chief Technical Officer) Security and Resilience in Large Scale Operating Systems, 1900 Series Operating Systems Division. International Computers Limited, London, S. W. 15., England, 1972.
[Randell 75]
    Randell, B. System structure for software fault tolerance. IEEE Trans. on Software Engineering, SE-1, 2, June 1975, pp. 220–232. (Also Chap. 1)
[Severance, Lohman 76]
    Severance, D. G., Lohman, G. M. Differential files: their application to the maintenance of large databases. ACM Trans. on Database Syst. 1, 3, pp. 256–267, Sept. 1976.
[Skaroff 76]
    Skaroff, J. R. Redundancy Management Technique for Space Shuttle Computers. IBM Journal of Research and Development. Vol. 20, No. 1, Jan. 1976, pp. 20–28.
[Snow 76]
    Snow, C. R. An exercise in the transportation of an operating system. Technical Report 94, Dec. 1976. Computing Laboratory, University of Newcastle upon Tyne, England.
[Stoy, Strachey 72a]
    Stoy, J. E., Strachey, C. OS6 – An experimental operating system for a small computer. Part 1: general principles and structure. The Computer Journal, Vol. 15, 1972, pp. 117–124.
[Stoy, Strachey 72b]
    Stoy, J. E., Strachey, C. OS6 – An experimental operating system for a small computer. Part 2: input/output and filing system. The Computer Journal, Vol. 15, 1972, pp. 195–201.
[Stoy, Strachey 72c]
    Stoy, J. E., Strachey, C. The text of OS Pub. Oxford University Computing Laboratory. Programming Research Group, July 1972. Technical Monograph PRG – g [t].
[Stoy, Strachey 72d]
    Stoy, J. E., Strachey, C. The text of OS Pub. Oxford University Computing Laboratory. Programming Research Group, July 1972. Technical Monograph PRG – g [C].
[Tonik 75]
    Tonik, A. B. Checkpoint, Restart and Recovery: Selected annotated Bibliography. FDT, Bulletin of ACM – SIGMOD, Vol. 7, No. 3–4, 1975, pp. 72–76.
[Verhofstad 76]
    Verhofstad, J. S. M. Recovery for multi-level data structures. Technical Report No. 96, Computing Laboratory, University of Newcastle upon Tyne, England.
[Verhofstad 76a]
    Verhofstad, J. S. M. The PRTV optimiser: the current state. Report UKSC 83. IBM U. K. Scientific Centre, Peterlee Co. Durham, England, May 1976.
[Wulf et al. 77]
    Wulf, W. A., Shaw, M., London, R. L. An introduction to the construction and verification of Alphard programs. IEEE Transactions on Software Engineering SE-2, 4, pp. 253–265, 1977.

Chapter 3
Exception Handling

Introduction

The recovery block approach discussed earlier is a means of coping with residual software faults in a system. Manifestation of such a fault can cause the program module under execution to produce an unexpected and undesired response. The possible responses obtainable from a module can be classified as: (i) expected and desired; (ii) expected and undesired; and (iii) unexpected and undesired.

To investigate this topic further, assume that the software system under consideration is structured as a hierarchy of modules with well-defined interfaces. When a module calls a procedure exported by a lower-level module, then either that call terminates normally (the expected desired response is obtained) or an *exceptional* return is obtained (which could be either expected and undesired or unexpected and undesired). A module should in general contain exceptional algorithms to cope with such undesirable events. During the design of a module we should carefully analyse the cases that could prevent the module from providing the normal desired services. Specific *exception handlers* can then be provided to deal with these exceptions.

There can be two situations under which control can pass to the exceptional part of a module: (i) the aforementioned case, when an exceptional return is obtained from a module called by this module; and (ii) a Boolean expression in the normal part of the module – inserted specifically for detecting an exception – evaluates to true. If despite the occurrence of such exceptions the module provides a normal service to its caller, then we say that the exceptions have been *masked*. On the other hand, if an exception cannot be masked then a specific exceptional return is made to the caller of the module.

It is certainly possible to write specific exception handlers for coping with expected undesired events, but what strategy should be adopted for dealing with events that were not expected? A sensible approach is to provide a default exception handler that undoes any side-effects produced by the program and then either signals a *fail* exception to the caller of the module or invokes an alternative program in an attempt to mask the exception. The similarity with the recovery block approach is not accidental. Indeed it is possible to define the semantics of recovery blocks in terms of the exception handling framework presented here. (The recovery block notation is in fact really just a convenient means of expressing the implied default exception handling.)

In the first paper of this chapter, Melliar-Smith and Randell explore this relationship between exception handling and recovery blocks and present a simple example to illustrate the complementary roles of programmed exception handling and recovery blocks. In the second paper Cristian presents a rigorous treatment of this subject. In particular he defines the *standard domain,* SD, of a program such that execution of the program beginning in a state in SD, terminates with the intended standard result. If the program is executed with the initial state not in SD, then obviously the standard service may not be obtained (an exception will occur during its execution); the set of such input states is termed the exceptional domain, ED. The designer's task is to ensure that even if a program is invoked with its initial state in ED, it still provides a specified exceptional service. The exceptional domain ED can be subdivided into the anticipated exceptional domain, AED, and the unanticipated exceptional domain, UED (see the figure). If a program is invoked with its initial state in AED

AED	SD
UED	

(UED) then an expected exception (unexpected exception) will occur. In the third paper of this chapter, also by Cristian, these ideas are applied to the design of abstract data types such that the operations provided by a data type are *total* (i.e. so that invocation of a given operation always terminates with either a standard or an exceptional service return). Proof techniques are presented for proving the correctness of programs constructed from such 'robust' data types.

An important problem encountered during the design of a program is that of how to determine where to insert checks for the detection of exceptions. Suppose the set ED for the program in question is known. Then in principle it is possible to insert a test at the beginning of the program to determine whether the program has been invoked with its state in ED. However, such a test may be as complex as the program itself. Hence it is desirable to design simple tests that are inserted at appropriate places within a program. In the fourth paper of this chapter, Best and Cristian discuss, for a given program and its specification, how the sets SD and ED can be determined and where to insert tests for the detection of exceptions. A runtime test should also be *precise:* it should be true iff the program has been invoked with its state in ED. The authors develop a mathematical framework based on the 'relational semantics' of programs and present a simple but practical example to illustrate their approach.

The last paper, by Anderson and Witty, is also concerned with the design of programs that terminate as specified. They propose the following methodology: when a program is designed and constructed in an attempt to meet its specification P, its designer should at least establish rigorously the 'safeness' of that program to meet a weaker specification Q expressed as 'P *or* error ( )' where 'error ( )' indicates an exceptional response. Experience gained from practical applications of safe programming lead authors to conclude that "safeness-directed program design and construction really works".

Software Reliability:
The Role of Programmed Exception Handling

P. M. MELLIAR-SMITH and B. RANDELL

The paper discusses the basic concepts underlying the issue of software reliability, and argues that programmed exception handling is inappropriate for dealing with suspected software errors. Instead it is shown, using an example program, how exception handling can be combined with the recovery block structure. The result is to improve the effectiveness with which problems due to anticipated faulty input data, hardware components, etc., are dealt with, while continuing to provide means for recovering from unanticipated faults, including ones due to residual software design errors.

1. Introduction

Discussions of software reliability are frequently marred by misunderstandings arising from incompatible preconceptions and terminology — for example some people have equated the terms 'software reliability' and 'program correctness' while others have assumed that 'software reliability' encompasses such concerns as the design of appropriate forms of system response to invalid input data.

The purpose of the present paper is twofold — to propose a set of terms and their definitions which might obviate further misunderstandings, and to discuss the relevance of programmed 'exception handling' to the problem of coping with residual design errors (or 'bugs') in programs.

Our informal, but hopefully precise, definitions are based closely on those given in [5]. To avoid needless specialisation the terminology is defined in general terms, and is not specific to computer programs. Rather it is relevant to all types of system, hardware as well as software. The terminology we use is intended to correspond broadly to conventional usage, but the definitions of some of the terms differ from previous practice, which typically has paid little attention to design inadequacies as a potential source of unreliability.

2. Systems and Their Failures

We define a *system* as a set of components together with their interrelationships, which system has been designed to provide a specified service. The *components* of the system are themselves systems, and we term their interrelationships the *algorithm* of the system. There is no requirement that a component provide service to a single system; it may be a component of several distinct systems. The algorithm of the system is however specific to each system individually.

This definition of 'system' with its insistence that the service provided must be specified (but not necessarily prespecified), is intended to exclude systems which are "intelligent" in the sense of being capable of determining their own goals and algorithms. At present intelligent systems are not understood sufficiently to permit consideration of their reliability.

The *internal state* of a system is the aggregation of the external states of all its components. The *external state* of a system is the result of a conceptual abstraction function applied to its internal state. During a transition from one external state to another external state, the system may pass through a number of internal states for which the abstraction function, and hence the external state, are not defined. The specification defines only the external states of the system, the operations that can be applied to the system, the results of these operations, and the transitions between external states caused by these operations, the internal states being inaccessible from outside the system.

The service provided by a system is regarded as being provided to one or more *environments*. Within a particular system, the environment of a given component consists of those other components with which it is directly interrelated.

A *failure* of a system occurs when that system does not perform its service in the manner specified, whether because it is unable to perform the service at all, or because the results and the external state are not in accordance with the specifications. A failure is thus an event. There is however no implication that the event is actually recognised as having occurred. For example, if an environment does not make full use of the specifications of a system (i.e. if what Parnas [6] terms the environment's 'assumptions' are a proper subset of the specifications) certain types of failures will have no effect.

3. Errors and Faults

In contrast to the simple, albeit very broad, definition of 'failure' given above, the definitions we now present of 'error' and 'fault' are not so straightforward. This is because they aim to capture the element of subjective judgement which we believe is a necessary aspect of these concepts, particularly when they relate to problems which could have been caused by design inadequacies in the algorithm of a system.

We term an internal state of a system an *erroneous state* when that state is such that there exist circumstances (within the specification of the use of the system) in which further processing, by the normal algorithms of the system, will lead to a failure which we do not attribute to a subsequent fault. (The subjective judgement that we wish to associate with the classification of a state as being an erroneous one derives from the use of the phrases "normal algorithms" and "which we do not attribute" in this definition — however further definitions are required before these matters can be discussed properly.)

The term error is used to designate that part of the state which is "incorrect". An error is thus an item of information, and the terms *error, error detection* and *error recovery* are used as casual equivalents for erroneous state, erroneous state detection and erroneous state recovery.

A *fault* is the mechanical or algorithmic cause of an error, while a *potential fault* is a mechanical or algorithmic construction within a system such that (under some circumstances within the specification of the use of the system) that construction will cause the system to assume an erroneous state. It is evident that the failure of a component of a system is (or rather, may be) a mechanical fault from the point of view of the system as a whole.

Hopefully it will now be clear that the generality of our definitions of failure and fault has the intended effect that the notion of fault encompasses such design inadequacies as a mistaken choice of component, a misunderstood or inadequate specification (of either the component, or the service required from the system) or an incorrect interrelationship amongst components (such as a wrong or missing interconnection, in the use of hardware systems, or a program bug in software systems), as well as, say, hardware component failure due to ageing.

Note that the definition of an erroneous state depends on the subdivision of the algorithm of the system into normal algorithms and abnormal algorithms. These abnormal algorithms will typically be the error recovery algorithms. There are many systems in which that subdivision, and hence the designation of states as erroneous, is a matter of judgement.

For example, in a storage system utilising a Hamming Code, one may regard the correction circuits as error recovery mechanisms and a single incorrect bit as an error. Alternatively (particularly with semiconductor storage) the correction circuits may be regarded as normal mechanism, and thus a single incorrect bit would not be regarded as an error, though two incorrect bits would be.

Note also that a demonstration that further processing can lead to a failure of the system indicates the presence of an error, but does not suffice to locate a specific item of information as the error. Consider a system affected by an algorithmic fault. The sequence of internal states adopted by this system will diverge from that of the "correct" system at some point, the algorithmic fault being the cause of this transition into an erroneous state. But there can be no unique correct algorithm. It may be that any one of several changes to the algorithms of the system could have precluded the failure. A subjective judgement as to which of these algorithms is the intended algorithm determines the fault, the items of information in error, and the moment at which the state becomes erroneous. Some such judgements may of course be more useful than others.

The significance of the distinction between faults and errors may be seen by considering the repair of a data base system. Repair of a fault may consist of the replacement of a failing program (or hardware) component by a correctly functioning one. Repair of an error requires that the information in the data base be changed from its currently erroneous state to a state which will permit the correct operation of the system. In most systems, recovery from errors is required, but repair of the faults which cause these errors although very desirable is not necessarily essential for continued operation.

4. Fault-Tolerant Computing Systems

A system can be designed to be *fault-tolerant* by incorporating into it abnormal algorithms which attempt to ensure that occurrences of erroneous states do not result in later system failures. The degree of fault-tolerance will depend on the success with which erroneous states corresponding to likely faults are identified and detected, and with which such states are repaired.

The software of a computing system serves to structure that system by expressing how some of the storage locations are to be set up with information which represents programs. These will then control some of the interrelationships amongst hardware components, for example, that the potential communication path between two I/O devices via working store is actually usable. Such software can of course be designed so that the computing system as a whole is tolerant of faults due to certain types of hardware failures.

However the software can itself be viewed as a system, and its components and their interrelationships discussed in terms of the programming language that was used to construct it. Thus in a block-structured language each block can be regarded as a component, which is itself composed out of, and expresses the interrelationships amongst, smaller components such as declarations and statements (including blocks).

The only faults that can be present in a nonphysical system such as a software system are algorithmic faults. However from the earlier discussion of such faults, it will be seen that the term covers much more than 'conventional' program bugs.

Algorithmic faults arise from unmastered design complexity, and can of course exist in the hardware as well as the software of a computing system. However due to such matters as the differing relative costs of modifications to hardware and to software, it is traditional for very complex design issues to be relegated to the software area, where they all too often give rise to algorithmic faults.

The idea of attempting to design computing systems which can tolerate algorithmic as well as mechanical faults is fairly novel. There is a tendency to assume that delivered hardware is free from algorithmic faults, and that what is needed is a means of ensuring that the software is also free from such faults — research to this end includes that on formal specification and validation of programs, and on methodologies for program testing and debugging. (Incidentally, the general assumption that hardware designs are correct may well not survive for much longer, given the ever increasing complexity of function that is being incorporated into a single LSI chip!)

In our research at the University of Newcastle upon Tyne on system reliability [1, 4, 5, 8] we have adopted as a basic premise that all large scale computing systems at all times contain multiple potential faults, and that these will include algorithmic as well as mechanical ones. There will be faults in the hardware, in the peripherals and in the operating system, in the logic design and in the hardware components, in the basic systems design, in the application programs and in the information stored; in the actions of the operations staff and the maintenance engineers; and in the environment of the computer system.

146

These faults may be due to the wearing out of a component, to a design inadequacy, to a statistical uncertainty (noise), to human frailty, or to an evolution of the requirements on the system as yet unmatched in the implementation.

We have been investigating the practicability of incorporating abnormal algorithms into such computing systems in order that all such types of fault can be tolerated, so that a system can provide continuous and trustworthy service to its environment without the need for any human intervention. Some of these types of fault are susceptible to existing techniques for error detection and recovery; others are not, particularly those faults of design inadequacy. Many approaches to reliable operation depend on the correct design of the system, together with complete knowledge of the possible failure modes of the components of the system. In contrast, we have chosen to investigate techniques which do not assume the absolute correctness of the algorithms. Moreover, since the number of possible failure modes of a component increases very rapidly as the component becomes more complex, much more rapidly than the number of correct modes of operation, we have felt it impracticable to rely on enumerating the possible failure modes of components, let alone design algorithms to detect or accommodate each possible component failure mode individually.

Thus the techniques of fault-tolerant system design that we have been developing, such as recovery blocks and conversations [8], do not assume correct algorithms or make any assumptions about the nature of faults. They aim to provide error detection and recovery strategies which should be applicable whenever a system fails to provide its specified service, for whatever reason.

These techniques do not attempt to diagnose the fault responsible for the errors which are detected, or to repair such faults. The error symptoms of a residual fault may be obscure and misleading, while the correct diagnosis and repair is not necessarily unique. Consequently we regard diagnosis and repair as operations to be performed off-line, and requiring human intelligence.

We do however assume that the faults to be recovered from are those residual faults remaining after reasonable efforts to obtain a reliable system. In particular we assume that the software has been designed as well as possible, using well-chosen design methodologies, together with validation techniques such as formal proofs of correctness and systematic testing. It can of course be argued that such validation techniques, which using Azivienis' terminology [2] could be described as the method of "software fault intolerance", are more productive of software reliability than attempts such as ours at software fault tolerance. Our view is that each has its place.

The argument for this viewpoint is not solely that of disbelief in the completeness with which a complex software system can be validated. Rather, it also concerns the significance that can be attributed to the experience one obtains from using such a system. Extensive usage of a hardware system whose failures are caused by faults arising from component ageing and the like provides statistics which can be a useful predictor of the likely frequency and seriousness of further failures. In contrast, the statistics gathered of failures of a software system relate merely to the history of its modification and usage (i.e. the particular sets of input data, the relative timings of input activities, etc.). Over the life of a system of any complexity whatsoever (eg. a 64-bit multiplier), only an infinitesimal proportion of the possible uses can actually occur. Thus, other than to the extent that future use will exactly match past use, failure statistics from a complex software system are not a useful predictor of the frequency of further failures. More importantly, particularly if the designer has relied totally on software fault intolerance, these statistics will not even predict the possible seriousness of further failures.

5. Exceptions

Just as we do not regard our techniques for tolerating algorithmic faults as a substitute for efforts to reduce the incidence of such faults in a system, so also do we not regard them as a complete substitute for explicit recovery from errors caused by anticipated faults. In a software system the sections of the program text that relate to such explicit recovery actions are sometimes termed "exception handlers". However the concept of an "exception" (as for example, described by Goodenough [3]) is by no means necessarily limited to such use, and is indeed quite separate from our concepts of error, fault and failures as the following discussion and definitions attempt to make clear.

The specified service that a component of a system is designed to provide might include activities of widely differing value to its environments. No matter how undesirable, none that fall within the specifications will be termed failures. However the specification can be structured so as to differentiate between a *standard* service, and zero or more *exceptional* services. For example, the standard service to be provided by an adder would be to return the sum of its inputs, exceptional services to indicate that an arithmetic overflow has occurred, or that an input had incorrect parity.

Within a system, a particular *exception* is said to have occurred when a component explicitly provides the corresponding exceptional service. The algorithm of the system can be made to reflect these potential occurrences by incorporating *exception handlers* for each exception.

These definitions match the intent, but not the form of the definitions given by Goodenough, who states:

"Of the conditions detected while attempting to perform some operation, *exception conditions* are those brought to the attention of the operation's invoker ... In essence, exceptions permit the user of an operation to extend an operation's domain (the set of inputs for which effects are defined) or its range (the effects obtained when certain inputs are processed)."

However, in contrast to Goodenough, we have taken care to avoid the use of the word 'failure' in discussing exceptions. This is not mere pendantry. Rather it is a consequence of the very basic view we take of failures, namely as occurring when and only when a system or component does not perform as specified. Although a system designer might choose to treat certain exceptions as component failures (which he might or might not provide abnormal algorithms to deal with), we regard the various schemes for exception handling (e.g. Parnas [7], Goodenough [3] and Wasserman [9]) and our technique of recovery blocks as complementary rather than competitive.

148

A basic feature of the recovery block scheme is that, because no attempt is made to diagnose the particular fault that caused an error, or to assess the extent of any other damage the fault may have caused, recovery actions have to start by returning the system to a prior state, which it is hoped precedes the introduction of the error, before calling an alternate block. Should this prior state not precede the introduction of the error, more global error detection, and more drastic error recovery, is likely to occur later. (The associated 'recovery cache' mechanisms [1, 4] automate the state saving required for this scheme.)

When exceptions are treated as component failures in a software system that uses recovery blocks, they will lead to the system being backed up to a prior state and an alternate block being called. This will be appropriate when the exception is undesirable, and the system designer does not wish to provide an individual means of dealing with it.

Putting this the other way, exceptions can be introduced into the structure of a system which uses recovery blocks, in order to cause some of what would otherwise be regarded as component failures (leading to automatic back-up) to be treated as part of the normal algorithm of the system, by whatever explicit mechanisms the designer wishes to introduce for this purpose. Failures might of course still occur, in either the main part of the algorithm, or in any of the exception handlers, and if they do they will lead to automatic back-up. Such introduction of exception can therefore be thought of as a way of dealing with special or frequently occurring types of failure, in the knowledge that the recovery block structure remains available as a "back-stop".

However we would argue strongly against relying on exception handling as a means of dealing with algorithmic faults. Programmed exception handling involves predicting faults and their consequences, and providing pre-designed means of on-line fault diagnosis. Thus although it can be of value in dealing with foreseen undesirable behaviour by hardware components, users, operations staff, etc., it is surely not appropriate for dealing with software faults — *predictable software faults should be removed rather than tolerated.* Indeed the incorporation of programmed exception handlers to deal with likely software faults would in all probability, because of the extra complexity it would add to the software, be the cause of introducing further faults, rather than a means of coping with those that already exist. On the other hand when used appropriately for anticipated faults of other types they can provide a useful means of simplifying the overall structure of the software, and hence contribute to reducing the incidence of residual design faults.

As described in [8], the recovery block scheme can be applied to any programming language in which a program which is structured into blocks evokes a process which can be regarded as structured into operations, where the acts of entering and leaving each operation are explicit, and are properly nested in time. The scheme does not depend on the particular form of block structuring that is used, or the rules governing the scopes of variables, methods of parameter passing, etc. Thus there is no particular difficulty in combining the scheme with programming language facilities for exceptions and exception handlers. By way of illustration, an example program which uses recovery blocks and procedure-oriented exception handling [9] is given in the Appendix.

6. Conclusions

Exception handling is one of many programming language design issues which is the subject of current debate, in this case a debate which has not been helped by a lack of agreement on a terminology for discussing the various basic issues concerning system and software reliability. The aim of this paper has been to clarify these issues, and to argue that despite the views that have been argued to the contrary elsewhere (eg. Parnas [7] and Wasserman [9]), explicit exception handling is not an appropriate means for providing software fault tolerance. Instead we view it as a potentially valuable adjunct to any viable scheme for detecting and recovering from software errors, which could improve the effectiveness with which anticipated faults due to input data, operators, hardware components, and the like were dealt with.

Acknowledgements. The writing of this paper has been aided by numerous discussions with colleagues on the reliability project at the University of Newcastle upon Tyne, and in the Computer Systems Research Group at the University of Toronto, and also at meetings of the IFIP Working Group 2.3 on Programming Methodology.

References

1. T. Anderson and R. Kerr. Recovery Blocks in Action: a system supporting high reliability. Proc. Int. Conf. on Software Engineering, San Francisco (13–15 Oct. 1976). (Also Chap. 2)
2. A. Avizienis. Fault-Tolerance and Fault-Tolerance: Complementary Approaches to Reliable Computing. Proc. Int. Conf. on Reliable Software. Sigplan Notices 10, 6 (June 1975) pp. 458–464.
3. J. B. Goodenough. Exception Handling: Issues and a Proposed Notation. Comm. ACM 18, 12 (1975) pp. 683–696.
4. J. J. Horning, H. C. Lauer, P. M. Melliar-Smith, and B. Randell. A Program Structure for Error Detection and Recovery. Lecture Notes in Computer Science, Vol. 16. Springer Verlag, New York (1974) pp. 177–193. (Also Chap. 2)
5. P. M. Melliar-Smith. Error Recovery for Resource Managers. Technical Report, Computing Laboratory, University of Newcastle upon Tyne
6. D. L. Parnas. Information Distribution Aspects of Design Methodology. Proc. IFIP Congress 1971 pp. TA26–30.
7. D. L. Parnas. Response to Detected Errors in Well-Structured Programs. Dept. of Computer Science, Carnegie-Mellon Univ. (July 1972).
8. B. Randell. System Structure for Software Fault Tolerance. IEEE Trans. on Software Engineering SE-1,2 (June 1975) pp. 220–232. (Also Chap. 1)
9. A. I. Wasserman. Procedure-Oriented Exception Handling. Medical Information Science, University of California, San Francisco (1976).

Appendix

Figure 1 shows a section of program text which incorporates programmed exception handling within a recovery block structure. The example, and the form of exception handling shown, are based on that given by Wasserman [9].

```
1    . . .
2    ensure consistent_inventory by
3    process_updates: begin integer num;
4                              exception goof = overflow or underflow or con-
                                     version;
5                              procedure checknum (integer j);
6                                    global integer count = 0;
7                                    procedure message;
8                                        begin count := count + 1;
9                                              write ("please try again");
10                                             if count ≥ 3 then
11                                                  begin write ("three strikes −
                                                         you're out);
12                                                       signal error
13                                                  end
14                                             else retry;
15                                       end message;
16                                    begin/* body of checknum */
17                                             . . .
18                                             read (j) [goof: message, ioerr: error]
19                                    end checknum;
20                              begin/* start of main body */
21                                             . . .
22                                    while updates_remain do
23                                             begin update_no := update_no + 1;
24                                                  . . .
25                                             checknum(num);
26                                                  . . .
27                                             end
28                                             . . .
29                              end main body
30                         end process_updates
31   else by
32   refuse_updates: begin write ("sorry − last update accepted was number");
33                         write (update_no)
34                   end
35   else error;
36    . . .
```

Fig. 1. An example of a program which incorporates programmed exception handling within a recovery block structure

151

The basic form of the example is

ensure consistent_inventory
by process_updates
else by refuse_updates
else error

The implicit assumption is that the program is maintaining an inventory file whose consistency is to be checked after each related sequence of updates, to determine whether this sequence can be incorporated. The updating process uses the procedure 'checknum' to read and check the updates. This procedure provides an exception handler for some of the exceptions that can be raised by the 'read' routine, so that the person providing the inputs can have two chances of correcting each input.

The procedure 'checknum' is taken directly from Wasserman [9], but has been simplified to take account for error recovery facilities provided by the recovery block structure in which it is used. More detailed notes on the example follow.

Line 2 The Boolean expression 'consistent_inventory' will be evaluated if and when 'process_updates' reaches its final *'end'*. If the expression is *true,* the alternate block 'refuse_updates' will be ignored and the information stored by the underlying recovery cache mechanism, in case the effects of 'process_updates' had to be undone, will be discarded. Otherwise this information will be used to nullify these effects, before 'refuse_updates' is called, after which the Boolean expression 'consistent_inventory' is checked again.

Line 4 In Wasserman's scheme a group of separate exceptions can be gathered together, as here to define the exception 'goof', using the exceptions 'overflow', 'underflow' or 'conversion'. It is assumed that all three can be signalled by the routine 'read' − the first two perhaps being built-in exceptions that the hardware signals, the third being implemented by the routine 'read' itself.

Line 7 The procedure 'message' is an exception handler defined within 'checknum'. The first two occasions on which it is called it used Wasserman's scheme for retrying the procedure which raised the exception (see line 14), but on the next occasion it signals *error.* (In Wasserman's version of this routine, 'message' raised the special exception called 'fail' which caused the whole program to be aborted. Here we assume that *error* just causes the current alternate block to be abandoned.)

Line 18 Here 'checknum' calls 'read' and arranges that the exception 'goof' (i.e. the exceptions 'overflow', 'underflow' or 'conversion') will be handled by the procedure 'message', but that if 'read' signals 'ioerror' this will cause 'process_updates' to be abandoned. In the original version of the example a further exception handler was provided, for use when 'ioerror' was signalled. This exception handler indicated that, but did not explain how, "any required cleanup" was to be done.

Line 20 All that is illustrated of the main body of 'process_updates' is that it counts the number of updates, which it reads and checks using the routine 'checknum'.

Line 32 The second alternate block 'refuse_updates' is called if the first alternate block 'process_updates' abandons its task, or fails to pass the acceptance test, for any reason (including of course, any residual design error within its code). If this happens, all changes that 'process_update' has made to the inventory will be undone, and the integer 'update_no' will be reset. This integer is then used for an apologetic message to the user.

Exception Handling and Software Fault Tolerance

F. Cristian

Abstract – Some basic concepts underlying the issue of fault-tolerant software design are investigated. Relying on these concepts, a unified point of view on programmed exception handling and default exception handling based on automatic backward recovery is constructed. The cause–effect relationship between software design faults and failure occurrences is explored and a class of faults for which default exception handling can provide effective fault tolerance is characterized. It is also shown that there exists a second class of design faults which cannot be tolerated by using default exception handling. The role that software verification methods can play in avoiding the production of such faults is discussed.

Index Terms – Exception, exception handling, failure, fault, fault avoidance, fault tolerance, hierarchical structure, module, procedure, recovery.

I. Introduction

Current research in programming aims at providing methods and tools for the construction of correct and robust software. Much effort is devoted to the design of programming languages (e.g., [12], [14], [24]), which encourage software designers to structure a system in terms of modules [18] implementing data abstractions [10]. For each data abstraction, exceptions have to be specified as a response to run-time attempts to violate its inherent invariant properties [6], [14], [16], [18]. Language mechanisms for exception handling [4], [12], [14] have been devised to help designers to program the specified exceptional responses correctly [6], [7], [16].

However, beyond a certain complexity level, it is likely that a system will contain algorithmic faults. These software design faults can (and almost certainly will) cause system failures. In order to cope with such faults, a default exception handling technique based on the use of automatic backward recovery has been proposed [11], [21]. The programming language construct devised for the systematic application of this technique is called a recovery block. (The inclusion of recovery blocks within a more general class of default exception handling mechanisms will be justified later.)

It has been argued that programmed exception handling and recovery blocks are complementary rather than competitive techniques, and that in order to obtain highly reliable software, both should be used in combination [17]. However, as these two exception handling techniques were devised and developed independently, a unified understanding of both is needed in order to achieve such an integration. The aim of this paper is twofold: to present rigorous definitions for the basic concepts which underly both approaches (and thus to highlight the unity which exists between them), and to discuss the relevance

154

of default exception handling to the problem of coping with residual design faults in programs. Most of the definitions to be given are informal accounts of formal developments reported in [6] and [7].

Attention will be focused on a specific class of faults: design faults in the sequential algorithms of a software system. This topic is sufficiently complex to deserve consideration separate from other interesting areas like tolerance to hardware or synchronization faults, or tolerance to design faults in the basic support software (e.g., compiler, link-editor). Default exception handling can cope occasionally [1] with such faults, but the result of using it as the only protection against them is difficult to predict. For example, it is difficult to predict the behavior of a recovery block if the hardware instruction decoding machinery is faulty. Our opinion is that responsibility for coping with faults specific to each interpretation level must fall on the designers of the level concerned. In what follows, it is assumed that the basic data types and operations, specified for the (deterministic [8]) language used to program a system, are correctly implemented by the compiler and that the hardware is able to detect and signal its own internal physical faults. Recent developments show that such assumptions are not as unrealistic as they appeared to be 10 years ago [19], [20].

II. Software Structure

The use of data abstraction in program development [6], [10], [14], [24] leads to programs which are structured into a *hierarchy* of *modules* [18]. Visually, such a hierarchy may be represented by an acyclic graph as in Fig. 1. Modules are represented by nodes and an arrow from a node N to a node M means that N is a *user* of M, that is, the successful completion of (at least) an operation $N.R$ exported [12] by N depends on the successful completion of some operation $M.P$ exported by M.

When observed from a user's point of view (e.g., N), a module M is perceived as being an (abstract) variable of some abstract data type. In order to make use of a module M, it is only necessary to know the set of abstract states which may be assumed by M and the set of abstract state transitions which are produced when the operations exported by M are invoked. The internal structure of a module is not visible to a user. When seen from inside, a module M is

Fig. 1.

155

a set of state variables and a set of procedures [18]. A state variable may be either of a predefined type (e.g., integer, array) directly provided by the programming language being used, or may be of some programmer defined abstract type, in which case it is implemented by some lower level module (e.g., L).

The *internal state* of a module M is the aggregation of the abstract states of its state-variables. The *abstract state* of M is the result of applying an abstraction function A to its internal state [6], [10], [17], [24]. In general, A is a partial function, defined only over the set of those internal states which satisfy an *invariant* predicate I. Such states are said to be *consistent* with the abstraction that the module is intended to implement. During a procedure execution a module may pass through a set of intermediate internal states which do not satify I, and for which A, and hence the abstract state, are not defined.

A procedure P exported by a module M is designed to accomplish a service: some internal, and hence abstract, state transition. This *intended service* can be specified by a (binary) relation *post* over states: a pair of states (s', s) is in *post* if the final internal state s is an intended outcome of invoking P in the initial internal state s'. We require this specification to be strong enough to exclude an inconsistent state being an intended outcome when P is invoked in a consistent state (remember that we are interested in algorithmic, not specification faults). Usually, the intended service of P is not defined by enumerating all the component pairs of *post*, but by giving its characteristic predicate, to be called (for reasons to become clear later) the *standard postcondition* of P. On the other hand, P itself is a sequence of operations on the state variables of M, and as such has an actual meaning which is imposed by the semantics of these operations. This *actual meaning* can be understood as being another state transition relation which contains all the pairs (s', s) such that, if P is invoked in s', then its execution terminates (normally) in s [2], [3], [6].

The set of states s', for which the execution of P terminates (normally) in states s such that $post(s', s)$, will be called the *standard domain SD* of P with respect to the specification *post*. The characteristic predicate of SD can be calculated as being the weakest precondition associated with P and *post* [2], [3], [6], [8]. The notion of a standard domain of an operation P is an important one since it characterizes all the states for which the execution of P *can* provide the specified standard service. If an execution of P starts outside this domain, then the standard service specified by *post* *cannot* be provided.

III. Exception Occurrences

An *exception occurs* when an operation P is invoked in a state outside its standard domain SD. The set of states which do not belong to SD will be termed the *exceptional domain ED* of P. A pictorial representation of the partitioning determined by the ED and SD domains over the set of states which may exist when an operation P is invoked is given in Fig. 2.

As an example, consider that among the state variables of a module M there are two variables i, j of type positive integer and that the standard service speci-

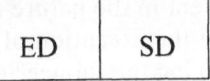

ED	SD

Fig. 2.

fied for a procedure P of M is $post \equiv i = i' + j'$ (primed symbols denote initial variable states and unprimed symbols final states). Suppose that the body of P is

$$i := i + j.$$

and let PI denote the set of machine representable positive integers. If $i' + j' \in PI$, then an $i \in PI$ satisfying post exists and the standard service specified for P can be provided. Otherwise, if $i' + j' \notin PI$, no $i \in PI$ satisfying post exists, i.e., an arithmetic overflow exception occurs. The characteristic predicates of the standard and exceptional domains are

$$SD = i' + j' \in PI \quad ED = i' + j' \notin PI.$$

Now suppose that the designer of P mistakenly types a "*" instead of a "+" in the body of P

$$(c1') \ i := i * j.$$

The characteristic predicates of the standard and exceptional domains (with respect of *post*) will be

$$SD = (i' = j') \ \& \ (i' = 0 \lor i' = 2) \quad ED = \neg SD.$$

Whenever P is invoked in a state within the exceptional domain ED a result which fails [17] to satisfy the specification of P is produced.

It is believed that the definition proposed above for the notion of an exception occurrence corresponds to the intuitive meanings associated with this term is [12], [14], [16], [17], and [21], with the term run-time error occurrence in [1], [11], and [18] and with the term failure occurrence in [17] and [21] (the relationship which exists between exception and failure occurrences is investigated in Sect. VI).

Other authors have different points of view about the notion of an exception. For example, in [9] operations which on every invocation signal an "exception occurrence" are considered. That is, the intended result of an operation invocation is no longer seen as being its normal termination with some postcondition, but rather as being an "exception" notification. Such (somewhat systematic) "exceptions" are called in [9] "monitoring type exceptions." The example given in order top illustrate their use (in connection with the programming practice referred to as "monitoring") is that of a SCAN procedure, which scans an array of positive integers and notifies than an "exception occurs" every time a positive array entry is encountered. Inherent in the nature of such "monitoring type exceptions" is the need for resuming the execution of a procedure after an "exception detection." While acknowledging the pioneering work described in [9], we would strongly argue against using exceptions for "monitoring" purposes. Other control structures (e.g., coroutines, iterators [14], [24]) offer exactly the facilities required for the implementation of monitoring, and we consider that the complexity of the exception mechanism proposed in [9] is a drawback directly attributable to a confusion between "monitoring" and exception handling. Therefore, we deliberately do not consider the "monitoring type exceptions" of [9] as being exceptions.

IV. Anticipated Exception Occurrences

The designer of a procedure P exported by a module M may anticipate the possibility of P being invoked in its exceptional domain. He may take measures for detecting this, for example, by inserting run-time checks in P (Boolean expressions which should evaluate to *true* whenever P is invoked in its *ED* [2]). However, there exist situations in which one relies on run-time checks integrated into lower level operations used by a procedure P in order to detect whether P is invoked in its *ED*. For example, suppose that among the state variables of M there are three variables i, j, k of type positive integer and that the hardware interpreter checks for each integer addition if an overflow occurs. Suppose also that the standard specification of P is $post \equiv i = i' + j' + k'$ and that the body of P is the sequential composition of the operations

$$(c1) \quad i := i + j;$$
$$(c2) \quad i := i + k.$$

If the invariant I of M is not strong enough to imply that $i' + j' \in PI$, an invocation of $c1$ may lead to an overflow. To insert a run-time check before $c1$ (for detecting whether $i' + j' \notin PI$ is true) would be redundant with the overflow check which is anyhow (efficiently) performed by the hardware. Now suppose that an overflow is detected when $c1$ is invoked. In such a case it does not make any sense to take the normal continuation of $c1$ (invoke the $c2$ operation following the ";" after $c1$), since this overflow reveals the impossibility of achieving *post* (if $i' + j' \notin PI$, then there exists no $i \in PI$ satisfying *post*).

This example illustrates something very characteristic about exception occurrences, namely that once such an event is actually detected as having occurred, it is no longer sensible to continue the standard execution of a program. Thus, in order to handle such events, it is necessary to allow for an occasional (i.e., exceptional) alteration of the usual (i.e., standard) sequential composition rule for operation invocations. An *exception mechanism* is a language control structure allowing one to express that the standard continuation of an operation is to be replaced by an exceptional continuation when an exception is detected. In what follows we (briefly) sketch the exception mechanism proposed in [4] (similar to some extent to those of [12] and [14]). A detailed syntactic and formal semantic description of this mechanism is presented in [7].

Exceptional continuations for detected exception occurrences can be defined by using exception labels. For example, the designer of an operation P can declare that an exception label E is signaled (if P is invoked outside its SD) by writing

proc P **signals** E.

Such a declaration warns a user that P has two exit points: a standard one, which can be thought of as being the semicolon following a P invocation, and an exceptional one, which will be represented by an "$[E \rightarrow$ " symbol following a P invocation. The user of P can define the exceptional continuation (if E is signaled) to be some operation K by writing

$P[E \rightarrow K]$.

In order to detect and handle the occurrence of E, the designer of P may explicitly insert in the body of P the following syntactic constructs:

(a) $[B \rightarrow H]$;
(b) $O[D \rightarrow H]$.

In the first, B stands for a Boolean expression (run-time check). In the second, O stands for some (lower level) operation invoked from P, and D stands for an exception label which may be signaled by O. The handler H may be a (possibly empty) sequence of operations and may end up with a *signal E* exceptional sequencer. The meaning of an (a) or (b) construct inserted in the body of P may be explained informally as follows. If B evaluates to *true* or O signals D, then H is invoked. If H terminates with a *signal E*, then the standard continuation of the (a) or (b) construct (what follows after the ";" standard sequencer) is abandoned in favor of an exceptional continuation (e.g., K) associated with the "$[E \rightarrow$" exit point of P. In the remaining cases, i.e., if B evaluates to *false* or O terminates normally or the execution of H does not terminate with a *signal E*, the standard continuation of the (a) or (b) construct is taken [4], [7].

As an example, consider the use of this mechanism to program the addition procedure mentioned at the beginning of this section. Assume that an overflow exception label OV is signaled if the $c1$, $c2$ operations are invoked outside their standard domains. Both operations will thus have two exit points: ";" and "$[OV \rightarrow .$" The addition procedure P can be programmed as shown in Fig. 3.

If P is invoked in a state $i' + j' + k' \in PI$ of its standard domain, then the termination of P is standard in a state satisfying *post*. If P is invoked in a state $i' + j' + k' \notin PI$ outside the standard domain, then there exist two possibilities: either $i' + j' \notin PI$, in which case the first statement of P will terminate exceptionally, or $i' + j' \in PI$ and $i' + j' + k' \notin PI$, in which case the first statement terminates normally, but the second statement terminates exceptionally. If the semantic definition of the assignment operator ":=" specifies that whenever the

```
proc  P  signals  OW;
begin  i := i + j [OV → signal  OW];
       i := i + k [OV → i := i − j;  signal  OW];
end;
```

Fig. 3.

evaluation of the right-hand side expression terminates exceptionally, no new value is assigned to the left-hand side variable [7], then in both cases P will terminate exceptionally by signaling an OW exception label in a final state satisfying $post(OW) \equiv (i = i') \& (j = j') \& (k = k')$. The exceptional postcondition $post(OW)$ specifies the (exceptional) service that P provides whenever the standard service $post \equiv i = i' + j' + k'$ cannot be provided.

If for any possible initial state on operation P provides either its specified standard service or a specified exceptional service, then P is a *total operation*. For example, the procedure of Fig. 3 is total since $(i' + j' + k' \in PI)$ $(i' + j' + k' \notin PI) = true$, that is, any possible initial state is either in SD or in the (anticipated) exceptional domain ED. Total operations for which the exceptional postconditions are of the form $A(s') = A(s)$, where A is some abstraction function, will be called *atomic* (in the sense that for an external observer, their invocation has an "all or nothing" effect: either the standard state transition is produced or the visible (abstract) state remains unchanged). For example, the procedure of Fig. 3 is atomic.

Remark: The adjective "atomic" is also used in a multiprocessing context to qualify the interference-free execution of operations [15]. In parallel programs, in which exception detections may signal attemps to violate invariants maintained by communicating processes, atomicity with respect to exceptions and atomicity with respect to synchronization become interrelated concepts [15], [21].

V. Programmed Exception Handling

Assume that the designer of a procedure P exported by a module M declares that P may signal an exception E, and that the intended state transition to be produced in such circumstances is specified by an *exceptional postcondition* $post(E)$.

As discussed in Sect. IV, an occurrence of E may be *detected*: a) either by a run-time check, or b) because a lower level exception D is propagated in P. In the latter case (illustrated by the example of Fig. 3), the detection of E *coincides* with the propagation of D in P, that is, with the invocation of a handler H of E. Although this handler is syntactically *associated* with a lower level propagated exception D by using a (b) construct, it is essential to understand that its semantics (the exceptional state transition it has to accomplish) is determined by the exceptional specification $post(E)$ of P. Thus, the phrase "handler associated

160

with" reflects a syntactic fact, while the phrase "handler of" reflects a semantic knowledge [6].

When an exception occurrence is detected, an intermediate *inconsistent state* (i.e., not satisfying the invariant I of M) may exist. In [6] it is shown that further invocations of a module left in such a state (by some exception occurrence not appropriately handled) can lead to unpredictable (i.e., unspecified) results and to subsequent unanticipated exception propagations. In order to avoid such consequences, it is essential that measures for the recovery of a consistent state are taken.

Let s' be the consistent state prior to the invocation of P and let i be the inconsistent state when the occurrence of E is detected. A set of state variables of M is called a *recovery set RS* if by modifying the state that these variables have in i, a final state s such that $I(s)$ & $post(E)(s', s)$ can be reached. In general, there exist several recovery sets for an exception detection [6]. From a performance point of view, the most interesting are those with the fewest elements. An *inconsistency set IS* is a recovery set such that for any other recovery set RS: $|IS| \leq |RS|$ ($|\quad|$ denotes set cardinality). Because of this minimality property, an IS can be regarded as characterizing that part of the state which is "really" inconsistent when the occurrence of E is detected. Thus, an inconsistency set corresponds to what in [17] and [21] is called an error. The terms "exception," "inconsistent state," and "inconsistency set" are used here in preference to "run-time error," "erroneous state," and "error" in order to avoid the negative psychological connotation usually associated with the term "error." After all, the aim of studying the behavior of operations outside their standard domains is to render these "errors" as controllable and subject to rigorous study as is now the standard behavior of operations. For nontrivial examples of inconsistency and recovery sets the interested reader is referred to [6].

If the decision is taken that module operations should behave atomically when exceptions occur, then two other kinds of recovery sets may be of interest. Let us define the *inconsistency closure IC* associated with the intermediate state i (which exists when E is detected) to be the set of all state variables modified between the entry in P and the detection of E [5]. An IC is a recovery set (for any abstraction function A and any invariant I), since by resetting all the modified variables to their initial (abstract) states, a final internal state s identical to the initial state s' is obtained, and the specification $I(s)$ & $(A(s') = A(s))$ is trivially satisfied. The second kind of recovery set we want to mention is the crudest approximation one can imagine for an IS (an inconsistency closure is a better one). This approximation is obtained by taking the whole set of state variables of M (with their state in s') to form a complete *checkpoint CP* of the initial state of M.

After the above discussion on recovery sets, we can now describe the task of a handler H of E as being to *recover* some RS before *signaling E*. Of course, if the state s in which E is detected already satisfies the $I(s)$ & $post(E)(s', s)$ predicate then no recovery action is necessary, that is, the IS associated with such an exception detection is empty.

If the exceptional postcondition $post(E)$ is not $A(s') = A(s)$, i.e., P is not intended to behave atomically, then *forward recovery* has to be used [21]. From an internal point of view, the recovery of an RS is "forward" if the final state of at least one variable in RS is different from its initial state. A forward recovery action is based on knowledge about the semantics of P [captured by I, A, $post(E)$] and has to be explicitly programmed by the designer, of P. However, if P is intended to have an atomic behavior, then the determination of the IC or CP recovery sets (which are independent of I, A) can be done automatically. Checkpointing techniques have long been used for recovering consistent system states. More recently, it has been proposed [11] to leave the task of computing the inconsistency closures, associated with the intermediate inconsistent states i through which a system may pass, to a special device called a recovery cache [1], [5], [11], [13], [23]. The (automatic) recovery of inconsistency closures or checkpoints has been called *backward recovery* in [21]. More generally, one can view the recovery of some RS as being "backward" if all the variables in RS recover their prior states (e.g., the recovery action "$i := i - j$" in the example of Fig. 3 can be seen as being "backward"). In order to avoid confusion between explicitly programmed "backward" recovery and that performed by a recovery cache or a checkpointing mechanism, we will call the latter *automatic backward recovery*.

To conclude this discussion on the detection and recovery issues raised by the handling of an exception E in a procedure P, let us denote by "[DET →" the "[B →" or "$O[D$ →" syntactic component used to detect an occurrence of E. If in P there is only one detection point for E (the case when several detection points exist is discussed in [2] and [7]), then the handling of E may be summarized as shown in Fig. 4.

Let us now investigate the consequences that a *propagation* of E by $M.P$ may have for the invoking procedure $N.R$ (Fig. 1). In some cases, the propagation of a lower level exception E in a procedure R is a consequence of invoking R within its own exceptional domain. Such a situation was illustrated by the example of Fig. 3. However, there exist cases in which a lower level exception may be propagated in a procedure even though that procedure was invoked within its standard domain (the rules for determining the standard domains of programs which contain the (a, b) syntactic constructs introduced in Sect. IV do not exclude this possibility [7]). As an example, suppose that N is a file management module which exports a procedure "CREATE a file containing Z blocks," where Z is of type positive integer. Assume that the files are stored either on a disk d_1 or on a disk d_2 and that M_1, M_2 are the modules which manage the free

```
proc  P    signals   E;
begin  .
             .
             [DET → recover RS;   signal   E];
             .
             .
end;
```

Fig. 4.

162

```
proc   CREATE (Z: positive_integer)  signals  NS;
begin  .
       .
       $M_1 \cdot AL(Z)$ [DO → $M_2 \cdot AL(Z)$ [DO → recover RS;  signal  NS]];
       .
end;
```

Fig. 5.

blocks left on d_1 and d_2, respectively. An initial state in which at least one disk has more than Z free blocks will be in the standard domain of CREATE and a state in which both disk have less than Z free blocks will be in the exceptional domain. Suppose that the space allocation within CREATE is programmed as shown in Fig. 5.

If CREATE is invoked in a state in which d_1 has less than Z free blocks, then the handler associated with the "[DO →" (Disk Overflow) exit point of the space allocation procedure $M_1.AL$ will be invoked. Now there remain two possibilities. If the initial state was in the standard domain, that is, d_2 has at least Z free blocks, then $M_2.AL$ terminates normally and the continuation is standard (i.e., the handler associated with the "[DO →" exit point of $M_2.AL$, and hence the *signal NS* exceptional sequencer are not invoked). Otherwise, if the initial state was in the exceptional domain of CREATE, the disk overflow exception which will be propagated by $M_2.AL$ will coincide with the detection of the NS (No Space) exception specified for CREATE. The handler of NS (the sequence "recover RS; *signal NS*" recovers a consistent state before propagating NS higher up in the hierarchy.

This example illustrates two things. First, the "[DET →" symbol used previously in Fig. 4 may sometimes be a sequence of "[B →" and "O[D →" symbols (this is frequently the case when dealing with exceptions due to transient input/output faults [4]). Second, lower level exception propagations can be stopped by higher lever procedures.

If a procedure R can provide its standard service in spite of a lower level exception E which is propagated in R, we say that the propagation of E is *masked* by R.

VI. Failure Exceptions

In [6] and [7] a set of proof rules for verifying the total correctness of programs with exceptions are developed. Such rules allow one to prove, for example, that the operations exported by a module are total (that is, the module is *robust* [6], in the sense that it will behave as specified in spite of possible exception occurrences). The design of total operations is, however, not a very easy task, and it is known that program verification methods are difficult to apply in practice. At present, software designers rely upon their intuition and experience in order

163

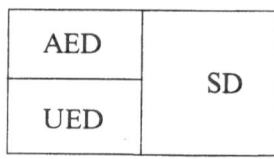

Fig. 6.

to deal with possible exception occurrences, and therefore the identification of the exceptional situations which may occur is often just as (un)reliable as human intuition is.

Assume that after having designed a procedure P which is exported by a module M, the reality is as follows. P terminates as its standard exit point in a state satisfying *post* when invoked in its standard domain *SD*. (This "real" standard domain may be different from that which exists in the designer's mind.) P terminates at a specified exceptional exit point "$[E \rightarrow$" in a state satisfying *post*(E) when invoked in an *anticipated exceptional domain AED $\subset$ ED* (this inclusion is a consequence of the fact that within *AED*, P does not terminate at its standard exit point). There exist possible initial states which are neither in *SD* nor in *AED*, i.e., are in *ED−AED*. Let us call *UED = ED−AED* the *unanticipated exceptional domain* of P. A representation of the partitioning determined by the *SD, AED, UED* domains over the set of states which may exist when P is invoked is given in Fig. 6.

As an example, suppose that M has the i, j state variables of the type positive integer and that the specification of P is *post* $\equiv i = i' + j'$, *post*(OW) $\equiv (i = i')$ & $(j = j')$. If the designer of P makes the mistake of typing a "$*$" instead of a "$+$" in the body of P

```
proc P signals OW;
i := i * j[OV → signal OW]
```

then the actual partitioning determined over the set of states which may exist when P is invoked is

$$SD = (i' = j') \ \& \ (i' = 0 \lor i' = 2) \quad ED = \neg \ SD$$
$$AED = \neg \ SD \ \& \ (i' * j' \notin PI)$$
$$UED = \neg SD \ \& \ (i' * j' \in PI).$$

In general, if a procedure P is invoked within its unanticipated exceptional domain, the following outcomes are possible:

1) the execution of P does not terminate (an infinite loop is entered),

2) a lower level exception U (whose possible propagation was not anticipated by the designer of P) is detected and there exists no handler explicitly associated with U in P,

3) the execution of P terminates normally (i.e., at the standard exit point of P) in a final state which does not satisfy the standard specification *post*,

4) the execution of P terminates with the exception label E being signaled (i.e., at the "$[E \rightarrow$" exit point of P) in a final state which does not satisfy the exceptional specification $post(E)$.

If one considers that the termination of P within a finite amount of time at some declared (standard or exceptional) exit point is part of the specification of P, then all the above outcomes are *violations* of the specification of P. According to terminology proposed in [17] and [21], we will call an invocation of an operation outside its standard or anticipated exceptional domains a *failure* occurrence. Thus, a failure occurrence when some operation P is invoked, is a particular kind of exception occurrence, namely one which was not anticipated by the designer of P. This definition does not imply that failure occurrences are actually recognized. For example, it is possible that the above violations remain unrecognized for some time (until a human user discovers that there is a discrepancy between the specified and the actual behavior of the system which contains P).

Let us assume for the moment that the occurrence of a failure when some procedure $M.P$ is invoked from a higher level procedure $N.R$ (Fig. 1) is detectable because an unanticipated exception U is propagated by a lower level procedure $L.O.$ in $M.P$. (In particular, U may be a TIME-OUT exception if L is a timer module armed at the entry in P [11]). The case when a failure occurrence remains undetected will be discussed in Sect. IX.

Now, what is a sensible reaction to such a situation? For example, what exceptional continuation should be associated with the exception propagated from a lower level? One possible solution (adopted in ADA [12]) is to continue the propagation of U in the higher level module N. Such free exception propagations across module boundaries may have dangerous consequences. First, according to the "information hiding principle" of modular programming [18], the designer of N is not supposed to know anything about the modules L used by M. Thus, an exception label U, declared for an operation O of a lower level module L is likely to be meaningless to the designer of N and it is probable that there will be no handler explicitly associated with U in $N.R$. Second, propagating U from $L.O$ directly into $N.R$ violates the basic principle that after any procedure invocation control should return back to the invoking procedure. Indeed, any $L.O$ invocation which results in a propagation of U is a definitive exit from $M.P$ (through an exit point which has not been declared for $M.P$!). Third, and this is perhaps the most serious consequence, if the lower level procedure $L.O$ was invoked when M was in an intermediate inconsistent state, then the propagation of U ind $N.R$ leaves M in that inconsistent state. Thus, there is a danger that later invocations of M will lead to unpredictable results and to additional unanticipated exception propagations.

A different approach to the problem of handling detectable failure occurrences is discussed in [4], [11], and [14]. The basic idea is quite simple: with any lower level (unanticipated) exception U propagated in a procedure P exported by a module M associate automatically some *default handler DH*, implicitly provided by the compiler (Fig. 7).

The " " before the "$\rightarrow$" symbol stands for any exception label which can be propagated in P and which has no explicitly associated handler in P. The

```
proc   P   signals   E;
begin  .
       .
       .
end [  → DH];
```

Fig. 7.

exceptional service that such a handler will attempt to provide can be identified by some language defined exception label FAILURE [4], [14] or ERROR [11]. The systematic addition of default handlers to all the procedures which are exported by the modules of a system has the following consequences. For any lower level exception which may be propagated in a procedure $M.P$ there exists an exceptional continuation in $M.P$ (either one explicitly defined or the default continuation DH). A FAILURE (or ERROR) exit point is implicitly added to any procedure.

VII. Default Exception Handling

Default exception handlers can be designed to solve the same problems as those mentioned in Sect. V for programmed exception handlers. These are: 1) *masking*, 2) consistent state *recovery*, and 3) *signaling*. But while the programmer of a handler H, explicitly inserted in a procedure $M.P$, knows what the intended semantics [captured by $I, A, post, post(E)$] of $M.P$ is, and therefore can provide a specific masking algorithm or determine an inconsistency set to be recovered, this knowledge is not available to the programming language designer who decides on a general default exception handling strategy.

The default exception handling strategy embodied in the CLU programming language developed at MIT [14] is oriented towards solving problem 3), related to the (proper) propagation of FAILURE exceptions across module boundaries, i.e., each default handler is of the form $DH \equiv signal$ FAILURE. In CLU, a suitable error message may be passed as a parameter to a *signal* FAILURE sequencer in order to help in fixing the cause of a failure detection. However, according to terminology introduced in [17] and [21], tolerance to FAILURE detections implies at least the resolution of problems 2) and 3). Thus, one can regard the default exception handling strategy of CLU as being more oriented towards debugging rather than towards the provision of software fault tolerance.

The default exception handling strategy proposed for the SESAME programming language developed at the University of Grenoble [4] was oriented towards solving the consistent state recovery 2) and propagation 3) problems. (The masking problem 1) can also be solved by using our mechanism, as will be shown later, but we have not dealt with this issue in [4].) The solution proposed to problem 2) is based on the fact that for any exception which can be detected in a procedure $M.P$ there exists a recovery set, i.e., the *inconsistency closure*, which can be determined at run-time without having any knowledge about the semantics of *M.P.* A recovery cache mechanism (more simple than that of [11] because of the modular visibility rules of SESAME) could be designed for the automatic update of the inconsistency closures associated with all the intermediate states through which a system may pass. A detailed description of this mechanism has already been published [5], so we will not repeat it here. In order to enable the automatic recovery of inconsistency closures, a *reset* primitive was made available in the language (as a compilation option). When invoked, *reset* recovers the "current" *IC* and returns normally. This primitive is mainly used in default handlers, but is also available to a programmer. (If the exceptional state transition *post(E)* specified for some anticipated exception *E* is $A(s') = A(s)$, then by inserting a *reset* primitive in the handler of *E*, the programmer is relieved from the burden of explicitly identifying some recovery set.) Problem 3) is solved by requiring the propagation of FAILURE exceptions to obey the same rules as the propagation of anticipated exceptions [4]. Thus, a *DH* handler (Fig. 7) is defined as $DH \equiv$ *reset*; signal FAILURE. Default handlers can be inserted only by the complier, i.e., FAILURE exceptions cannot be explicitly handled.

The recovery block mechanism, devised at the University of Newcastle upon Tyne [11], was designed to solve all the problems $1) - 3)$ mentioned above. Unlike the mechanisms described in [4] and [14] which support both explicit and default exception handling, the recovery block mechanism is a pure default exception handling mechanism based on automatic backward recovery. In order to deal with a possible FAILURE (the label ERROR is used in [1], [11], [13], [17], [21] and [23]) detection in a procedure *P* designed to provide some specified standard service post, a programmer can define *P* to be the primary block P_0 of a recovery block with zero or more alternate blocks $P_1, P_2, \cdots, P_k$. Assume (for simplicity reasons) that a single alternate P_1 is provided. The syntax of a recovery block construct *RB* in this case is

$RB \equiv$ **ensure** post **by** P_0 **else by** P_1 **else** FAILURE.

Let us use the notation we have established to exhibit what is hidden behind the syntax above:

$RB \equiv P'_0 [\rightarrow$ **reset**; $P'_1 [\rightarrow$ **reset; signal** FAILURE]]

where

$P'_i \equiv$ **begin** P_i; $[\neg$ post $\rightarrow$ **signal** FAILURE] **end,** $i = 0,1$.

If a FAILURE exception is detected during the execution of $P_0 = P$ procedure (because some lower level exception is propagated in P_0 or because the acceptance test *post* evaluates to false when P_0 terminates), then the *inconsistency closure* associated with this FAILURE detection is retored by a recovery cache device and the alternate P_1 is invoked. The aim of the alternate is to *mask* the failure detected in P'_0 by achieving the specified state transition *post* in a different way. Since no attempt is made at elucidating the reason why P_0 could not achieve *post*, the construction of an alternate P_1 is based on the single assumption that, when invoked, P_1 starts in the same state as the primary P_0. If the invocation of P_1 leads to another FAILURE exception detection, then the masking problem 1) cannot be successfully solved at the level of *RB*. Problem 2) is solved by invoking again the recovery cache to restore the inconsistency closure associated with the FAILURE exception detected in P_1'. Problem 3) is dealt with by propagating a FAILURE signal to the user of *RB*. The termination of an *RB* is standard if no FAILURE is detected during the execution of P_0' or if a FAILURE detection in P_0' can be masked by the termination of P_1 with *post*.

The view about recovery blocks presented above is somewhat idealistic however. For example, we have assumed that a precise [2] monolithic run-time chek $\neg$ *post* can be programmed for the exceptional domains of the P_0, P_1 components. In practice, postconditions may contain logical quantifiers and other expressions not directly interpretable on a machine. Thus, to program a Boolean (executable) expression with the same truth value as *post* may turn out to be a very difficult task. (In [2] the idea of splitting the monolithic acceptance check into a set of simpler assertions, without quantifiers, spread among the intermediate operations which compose P_0, P_1 is investigated; but pursuing such a verification-oriented approach leads naturally to a programmed, rather than default, exception handling style.) What is likely to happen in practice is that an acceptance test is an approximation of *post*: some, but not all, invocations of P_0, P_1 outside their standard domains will be detected, that is, the probability of the unwanted 3) outcome discussed in Sect. VI will be nonzero.

VIII. Programmed and Default Exception Handling in Hierarchies of Data Abstractions

Consider a software system structured into a hierarchy of data abstractions (Fig. 1). Let $\{T_i\}$ be the set of operations defined on those component data abstractions which are visible to a user of the system. (These data abstractions, storing information which is significant to the users, are generally implemented by high-level modules.) Let us distinguish a T_i operation from other (lower level) hidden operations by calling T_i a system *transaction*. The purpose of (both programmed and default) exception handling is to ensure that transaction executions will preserve the invariant properties inherent to the data abstractions which compose a system in spite of possible exception occurrences.

Suppose that the invocation of a system transaction T_i leads to the occurrence of an (anticipated or unanticipated) exception D when some lower level operation $L.O$ is invoked. The operation $L.O$ will be said to be *weakly tolerant* to the occurrence of D if D is detected and the (programmed or default) handler of D recovers a consistent state for L before propagating D to the invoking procedure $M.P$. If this procedure can mask the propagation of D, then $M.P$ is said to be *strongly tolerant* to the occurrence of D. Otherwise, if the propagation of D coincides with the detection of a higher level exception E in $M.P$, then $M.P$ in its turn must be weakly tolerant to E. In general, if an exception propagation D, E, F. $\cdots$ takes place across modules L, M, N, $\cdots$, and none of the traversed modules can perform a successful masking, then each module must be weakly tolerant with respect to that propagation (i.e., each must contain a programmed or default handler able to recover a consistent module state and continue the propagation).

Default exception handling based on automatic backward recovery can be used to render the transactions of a system weakly or strongly tolerant to detected unanticipated exception occurrences. After a transaction execution is terminated, the recovery data maintained by the recovery cache have to be discarded in order to allow the cache to keep track of the inconsistency closures associated will potential exception detections during the next transaction execution. The operation of discarding the information accumulated in the cache when a transaction is terminated is the *commitment* of that transaction [21].

IX. Tolerance of Design Faults

If the unanticipated exceptional domain *UED* of a procedure P is not empty, we will say that P contains a *design fault* (or algorithmic fault). A failure occurrence when P is invoked (in some state within its *UED*) will be called a *manifestation* of the fault. Between a manifestation and a detection of the consequences of this manifestation (either by a run-time check or by a human user who observes a discrepancy between the actual and the specified behavior of the system which contains P) a design fault will be called *latent*.

If the transactions implemented by a system are weakly or strongly tolerant to failure occurrences caused by design faults, then the system can be termed *design fault tolerant*. As discussed in Sect. VII and VIII, default exception handling based on automatic backward recovery can be used to provide design fault tolerance, but the question is: to what extent can one rely on this technique to make tolerable the consequences of human mistakes made during the design (or debugging) of a system?

Let us call the time interval between the beginning and the end of a transaction execution a *commitment interval* and let us call the time elapsed between a manifestation of a design fault and a detection of the consequences of this manifestation a *latency interval*. Suppose that when a transaction T_i is started, the internal states of the system modules are consistent, and that during the execution of T_i a design fault manifests itself. If this manifestation leads to a FAILURE exception detection before the termination of T_i, then by invoking automatic backward recovery it is possible to restore, for all the system modules invoked since the beginning of T_i, internal states which are equivalent to those which existed at the beginning of T_i. These recovered internal states are then consistent, and the danger of later additional unanticipated exception detections is avoided.

However, it is possible that the manifestation of a design fault does not cause some explicitly checked invariant property to be violated, so that not

FAILURE exception is detected during the execution of the T_i transaction. Thus, at the commitment of T_i (when the recovery information enabling a return to the consistent system state which existed at the beginning of T_i is discarded) some of the component modules of the system will be in an inconsistent state. It is then possible that a FAILURE exception caused by the design fault which has manifested itself during T_i is detected during some later transaction execution T_j. The invocation of automatic backward recovery will then restore, for the system modules, internal states which are equivalent to those which existed at the beginning of T_j. But since these states were already inconsistent, the recovered system state will be inconsistent and the danger of further unpredictable behavior and additional unanticipated exception detections persists.

Thus, while default exception handling based on automatic backward recovery *can* provide effective fault tolerance for design faults with latency intervals contained within the commitment intervals associated with transaction executions, it is *not adequate* for coping with design faults having latency intervals which stretch over successive transaction executions.

One of the key problems to be solved by software designers in order to avoid the production of design faults with long latency intervals is the systematic identification of the exceptional domains associated with operations and the design of precise run-time checks for detecting any invocation within these domains. Mathematically, the *ED* of an operation can be calculated as being a solution of a fixed point semantic equation associated with that operation [3]. It is known that this solution exists and it is also known that it can be calculated by successive approximations. The trouble is that such a solution is obtained as a limit of an infinite approximation sequence and that machines (and human beings as well for nontrivial cases) are unable to guess suitable induction hypotheses which can be used to prove the convergence of such iterations. Thus, an automatic determination of the exceptional domains associated with operations and their specified postconditions does not seem to be practically feasible within the current state of the art in machine aided programming.

A more pragmatic approach to the problem of identifying and detecting exception occurrences is investigated in [2], [6], and [7]. A designer is left to identify what he believes to be the standard and exceptional domains of an operation. In doing so, some guidelines (discussed in [2] and [6]) can be of help, but the identification of these domains is regarded as being a craft. The goal of the work reported in [2], [6], and [7] is to provide systematic verification procedures which allow one to check whether, within the identified standard and exceptional domains, an operation will indeed behave as specified. The design of systems which can help to carry out such verifications seems to be feasible within the current state of the art in machine aided program verification. Now, if after having checked the behavior of an operation within the identified exceptional and standard domains one can prove that the disjunction of their characteristic predicates is *true* (i.e., that the operation is total, or equivalently, that its *UED* is empty), it follows that there should be no surprises when that operation is invoked.

X. Conclusion

During a recent conference on Reliable Computing and Fault Tolerance [20], a general consensus was reached: "that it is quite unclear how to balance fault avoidance and fault tolerance in the case of design faults." It was decided there that "the proper treatment (of this problem) is of urgent and increasing importance for the 1980's."

The subject discussed in this paper is at the boundary between fault avoidance and fault tolerance. Fault avoidance concepts (e.g., invariants, weakest preconditions) have been used to investigate some basic issues underlying the design of fault-tolerant software systems (e.g., the use of the exceptions to structure the design of such systems, exception handling, etc). A unified point of view on programmed exception handling (a fault avoidance technique) and default exception handling based on automatic backward recovery (a fault tolerance technique) has been proposed.

The purpose of (programmed and default) exception handling is to ensure that system transaction executions will preserve the invariant properties inherent to the component system modules in spite of possible exception occurrences (anticipated as well as unanticipated). It has been shown that the problem to be solved by programmed or default exception handlers are basically the same (i.e., masking, consistent state recovery, and signaling) and that the handling of exceptions by default (for fault tolerance purposes) is based on the fact that automatic backward recovery can be used to recover consistent system states in a manner which is independent of the semantics of the operations implemented by that system. The cause—effect relationship between software design faults and failure occurrences has been investigated and it has been shown that default exception handling based on automatic backward recovery can provide effective fault tolerance only for those design faults which have latency intervals contained with the commitment intervals associated with system transaction executions.

Among the problems to be solved in order to avoid the production of design faults with long latency intervals, the systematic identification and detection of exceptions associated with system operations plays a key role. It has been suggested that progress in solving this problem may be achieved by concentrating research efforts towards the construction of interactive support systems, which can help software designers to check that the detection of exception occurrences is performed reliably.

References

1. T. Anderson and R. Kerr, "Recovery blocks in action," in Proc. 2nd Int. Conf. on Software Eng., San Francisco, pp. 447–457, October 1976. (Also Chap. 2)
2. E. Best and F. Cristian, "Systematic detection of exception occurrences," in Science of Computer Programming, vol. 1, no. 1. Amsterdam, The Netherlands: North-Holland, 1981, pp. 115–144. (Also Chap. 3)
3. P. Cousot, "Semantic foundations of program analysis," in Program Flow Analysis – Theory and Applications, S. Muchnick and N. Jones, Eds. Englewood Cliffs, NJ: Prentice-Hall, 1981, pp. 303–342.

4. F. Cristian, "Le traitement des exceptions dans les programmes modulaires," Ph.D. dissertation, Univ. of Grenoble, Grenoble, France, 1979.

5. —, "A recovery mechanism for modular software," in Proc. 4th Int. Conf. on Software Eng., Munich, 1979.

6. —, "Robust data types," Acta Informatica, Vol. 7, pp. 365–397, October 1982. (Also Chap. 3)

7. —, "Verifying the total correctness of programs with exceptions," Univ. of Newcastle upon Tyne, Tech. Rep., 1982.

8. E. W. Dijkstra, A Discipline of Programming. Englewood Cliffs, NJ: Prentice-Hall, 1976.

9. J. Goodenough, "Exception handling, issues and a proposed notation," Commun. Ass. Comput. Mach., vol. 18, no. 12, pp. 683–696, 1975.

10. C. A. R. Hoare, "Proof of correctness of data representations," Acta Informatica, vol. 1, no. 4, pp. 271–281, 1972.

11. J. J. Horning, H. C. Lauer, P. M. Melliar-Smith, and B. Randell, "A program structure for error detection and recovery," in Lecture Notes in Computer Science, vol. 16. New York: Springer-Verlag, 1974, pp. 177–193. (Also Chap. 2)

12. J. Ichbiah et al., "Rationale for the design of the ADA programming language," SIGPLAN Notices, vol. 14, no. 6, 1979.

13. P. A. Lee, K. Heron, and D. Gani, "A recovery cache for the PDP-11," IEEE Trans. Comput., vol. C-29, pp. 546–549, June 1980. (Also Chap. 2)

14. B. H. Liskov and A. Snyder, "Exception handling in CLU," IEEE Trans. Software Eng., vol. SE-5, pp. 546–558, 1979.

15. D. Lomet, "Process structuring, synchronisation and recovery using atomic actions," in Proc. ACM Conf. on Lang. Design for Reliable Software: also in SIGPLAN Notices, vol. 12, no. 3, 1977. (Also Chap. 4)

16. D. C. Luckham and W. Polak, "ADA exception handling: An axiomatic approach," ACM Trans. Progr. Lang. Syst., vol. 2, no. 2, pp. 225–233, 1980.

17. P. M. Melliar-Smith and B. Randell, "Software reliability, The role of programmed exception handling," in Proc. ACM Conf. on Lang. Design for Reliable Software: also in SIGPLAN Notices, vol. 12, no. 3, 1977. (Also Chap. 3)

18. D. L. Parnas, "A technique for software module specification with examples," Commun. Ass. Comput. Mach., vol. 15, no. 5, pp. 330–336, 1972.

19. W. Polak, "Verification of a Pascal compiler," Ph.D. dissertation, Stanford Univ., Stanford CA, 1980.

20. B. Randell, "Report on the IFIP working conference on reliable computing and fault tolerance in the 1980's, London," Univ. of Newcastle upon Tyne, Newcastle upon Tyne, England, Int. Rep., 1979.

21. B. Randell, P. A. Lee, and P. C. Treleaven, "Reliability issues in computing systems design," Comput. Surveys, vol. 10, no. 2, pp. 123–165, 1978.

22. R. M. Sedmak and H. L. Liebergot, "Fault tolerance of a general purpose computer implemented by very large scale integration," IEEE Trans. Comput., vol. C-29, pp. 492–500, June 1980.

23. S. K. Shrivastava, "Sequential Pascal with recovery blocks," Software Practice and Experience, vol. 8, pp. 177–185, 1978. (Also Chap. 2)

24. W. A. Wulf, R. L. London, and M. Shaw, "An introduction to the construction and verification of Alphard programs," IEEE Trans. Software Eng., vol. SE-2, pp. 253–265, July 1976.

Robust Data Types

F. CRISTIAN

Summary. Data types with total operations and exceptions are proposed as basic building blocks for the construction of modular robust software. A notation for specifying such data types is presented and the issues underlying their correct implementation in a programming language supporting data abstraction and exception handling are discussed and illustrated by examples. New light is shed on some important aspects of exception handling such as the identification and specification of exceptions, the precise detection of exception occurrences, recovery of consistent states after exception detections and verification of the correct implementation of specified exceptional effects for operations.

1. Introduction

It is customary in current approaches to data abstraction to leave the result of an operation invocation unspecified if certain preconditions do not hold [13, 21, 3, 16, 12]. For example, the result of invoking the top operation on a stack may be specified to be the top element of the stack if the stack is not empty. Troubles arise when the stack is empty, since then there does not exist a top-element. This situation is commonly referred to as an exception occurrence [5, 15, 17, 18].

The need for taking into account exceptions is not even explicitly recognised in certain academic spheres. Software engineers, on the other hand, know that substantial parts of the programs they usually write are devoted to detecting and handling exceptions. The argument most often advanced for not specifying what happens if exceptions occur is that static verification methods can be used to guarantee that such situations never arise, provided the environments in which the programs run satisfy certain hypotheses. In reality, strong assumptions about the behaviour of these environments can rarely be made, especially if their correctness is not verified or verifiable (e.g., human users). It is then essential to specify what should happen if exceptions occur.

One possibility is to specify that an exception occurrence leads to program abortion. This (somewhat radical) solution is simple and has been modelled mathematically by several authors (e.g. [8, 10]). While it may be satisfactory for certain kinds of programs (e.g. student programs) it is certainly not satisfactory for other kinds of programs (e.g. operating systems, data base systems, process control systems).

In this paper we show how exceptions may be used to structure the specification, implementation and verification of programs which are robust, i.e. can continue to behave as specified in spite of exception occurrences. The goal is to demonstrate that the construction of robust programs can be made subject to rigorous design methods similar to those (e.g. [13, 8, 21, 3, 16]) proposed for the development of programs without any provision for exception handling.

173

As we consider the notion of a data type to be one of the most important software structuring tools, the focus will be on the design of robust data types. These may be used as building blocks for larger robust systems. Exceptions are rigorously defined, a notation for specifying data types with total operations and exceptions is proposed, and it is shown how such data types may be implemented in a programming language supporting encapsulation and exception mechanisms. The elaboration of these issues sheds new light on some basic aspects of exception handling, such as the identification and specification of exceptions for operations, the precise detection of exception occurrences, the recovery of consistent states after exception detections and the propagation of exceptions. A method for proving the correctness of implementations with respect to specifications is also proposed. By this method the verification of a program which may signal $k \geqq 0$ exceptions is factored into $k + 1$ independent proofs: one (classical) proof of correct standard behaviour and k proofs of correct exceptional behaviour. This separation of concerns can be taken as an indication that the effort required for producing robust programs is not much greater than that required for producing programs which deliver their specified result only if they do not have some other unpredictable behaviour.

The paper is composed of two main parts. In the first, we introduce the notion of a robust data type together with a simple example and sketch criteria for verifying the total correctness of data type implementations with specifications. By total correctness it is meant that the implemented operations terminate cleanly (without unanticipated exception detections). In the second part, we use the simple example to construct a more elaborate hierarchically structured example. This allows a natural generalisation of the earlier correctness criteria and presents some important aspects of exception handling in hierarchies of data abstractions.

2. Robust Data Types

For a definition of a data type with exceptions to be precise, it is first necessary to have a clear idea of what is meant by a data type with partial operations. Thus, although the main interest is in data types with total operations and exceptions, the Sects. 2.1, 2.2, 2.3 of this first part of the paper are devoted to discuss issues related to the specification, implementation and total correctness of data types with partial operations. Section 2.4 defines what we mean by an exception occurrence and Sect. 2.5 describes briefly the exception mechanism we use. The last three sections take up the issues discussed in the first three sections (i.e. specification, implementation, total correctness) for data types with total operations and exceptions.

2.1. Data Types with Partial Operations

Data abstraction has emerged from recent research in programming as a means of extending the data definition and manipulation facilities of a programming language with new (abstract) data types. In an imperative programming language, like that considered in this paper, one can view a *data type* as being a (finite) set of *values* plus a (finite) set of *operations* [21]. These values and operations are usually specified in terms of some underlying *data space*. By a data space we mean a *mathematical structure* consisting of several *sorts of sets* and *operators* among those sets [11]. The semantics of the operations of a data type is expressed by formulae in the language of this structure, and a distinguished 'sort of interest' can be used to specify the set of values of the type [12, 9].

The data spaces which underly the data types of an imperative language may either be defined *implicitly* by axioms [11, 22, 12, 9, 4] or may be constructed *explicitly* from a fixed repertoire of well-known basic data spaces like integers, sequences, sets of integers and so on [13, 21, 3, 16, 1]. The second definition method (to be used in this paper) leads to shorter presentations since it relies on the reader's familiarity with the concepts used when describing new data spaces. However, as our solution to exception handling is entirely at an imperative programming language level, it can accommodate with any particular data space definition method.

We assume that an instance of a data type T is declared in a program as being a *variable* of type T. A mapping from program variables to values (of their type) is a program *state*. When we speak about the state (or value) of a variable we mean the result of applying a state function to it. Only programs with a finite number of variables which may take a finite number of distinct values are considered, so the set S of distinct states of any program is finite.

Let OP be an operation specified for a data type T. The purpose of invoking OP on a variable of type T is to produce a state transition. Thus, the semantics of an operation OP is generally taken to be a *state transition relation* [13, 21, 3, 16, 9]. A pair states $(s', s) \in S \times S$ is in this relation if the final state $s \in S$ is an *intended* outcome of invoking OP in the initial state $s' \in S$. (As in [21, 9], states prior to operation invocations are primed.) In practice, such a relation is not defined by enumerating all its component pairs, but by giving its characteristic (binary) predicate:

$$post \in S \times S \leadsto \{true, false\}$$

called (for reasons to become clear later) the *abstract standard* postcondition of OP. In general *post* is a partial relation: there exist initial states which do not have successors in *post*. A total unary predicate, the *abstract standard precondition* of OP:

$$pre \in S \to \{true, false\}$$

will be used in what follows to characterise the domain of *post*, that is, the set of those initial states which have successors in *post*:

$$pre(s') = true \equiv s' \in dom(post)$$

where

$$dom(post) \equiv \{s' \in S | \exists s \in S: post(s', s) = true\}.$$

175

An operation is called *partial* if its semantics is a partial state transition relation. We wait unit Sect. 2.6 to see how exceptions can be used to build total operations.

In order to illustrate the notions discussed so far we specify a simple data type *RESOURCES*, often used in operating systems to manage a finite number $n > 0$ of resources. The positive (machine representable) integer n is a generic parameter of the type. The resources are identified by the set of integer constants $\{1, 2, \ldots, n\}$ denoted $[n]$. The mathematical data space underlying the *RESOURCES* data type contains three sorts of sets (booleans, machine representable integers and the set of subsets of $[n]$ denoted $P[n]$) together with a collection of operators among these sets. Some of the operators are total and others partial. Among the former we mention: "$\in$" (membership), "$\cup$" (set union), "$-$" (set difference), "$||$" (cardinality), etc. Among the latter there is the partial (nondeterministic) choice operator "*oneof*" which for a subset r of $[n]$ yields an element of r if r is not empty, i.e. $\forall r \in P[n]: |r| > 0 \Rightarrow oneof(r) \in r$. With partial operators we associate total predicates "*def*" indicating whether they are applied to elements of their domain or not (e.g. $def(oneof(r)) \equiv |r| > 0$). For the finite data spaces needed to specify finite (machine representable) data types such total predicates always exist. When proving correctness properties about programs which use the *RESOURCES* data type, we assume the mathematical properties of its underlying data space to be well-known. For example properties like $|r| < n \Rightarrow r \cup \{oneof([n]-r)\} \in P[n]$, $|r| < n \Rightarrow |r \cup \{oneof([n]-r)\}| = |r| + 1$, etc. will be taken to be true without any further explanation of *why* they are true.

A notation close to that of [21] is used in Fig. 1 to specify the *RESOURCES* type. In order to avoid explicit mention of state functions, we write variable identifiers in capital letters and variable values in lower case letters (e.g. if V is a program variable v stands for a value of V). Also, if an operation does not change the state of a variable we *omit* explicit mention of this fact (e.g. the term $i = I$ indicating that the *RELEASE* operation does not alter the value parameter I is omitted in line 10 and in line 9 we have written $i \in r'$ instead of $i' \in r'$).

Line 2 defines a value of an arbitrary variable R of type *RESOURCES(N)* to be a subset of $[n]$. The predicate in line 3 specifies the initial value assumed by such a variable after its declaration to be the empty subset. The intention is

```
1    specification of type RESOURCES (generic N: INTEGER > 0)
2    values r ∈ P [n]
3    initial value r = { }
4    operations
5        procedure GET returns I: INTEGER
6        pre |r'| < n
7        post i = oneof ([n] − r') & r = r' ∪ {i}
8        procedure RELEASE (I: INTEGER)
9        pre i ∈ r'
10       post i ∈ r' & r = r' − {i}
```

Fig. 1. Specification of a data type with partial operations

to make the value of R be the subset of those resources which are allocated
Lines 5 and 8 define the syntax for invoking the operations GET and RE-$LEASE$. Following [13] this syntax will be $I := R.GET$ and $R.RELEASE(I)$.
Line 7 states that the standard result of GET is to return an integer value i identifying a resource which was previously free, i.e. $i = oneof([n] - r')$, and which
after the invocation becomes allocated, i.e. $r = r' \cup \{i\}$. The standard result
of invoking $RELEASE$ with a parameter I (line 10) is to deallocate the resource
i, i.e. $r = r' - \{i\}$, if it was previously allocated, i.e. $i \in r'$. The preconditions in
lines 6, 9 characterise the domains of the postconditions in lines 7, 10. As these
abstract standard domains are strictly included in the set of (abstract) states
which can exist for the pair of variables R, I, the operations GET and RE-$LEASE$ are partial.

2.2. Implementation

We assume a PASCAL-like (deterministic) programming language providing a
SIMULA class like construct [13] for the *implementation* of abstract data types.
An implementation of a data type T defines a concrete *internal representation*
for the set of values specified for T, the bodies $B(OP)$ of the *procedures* implementing the specified operations OP and an *internal state initialisation algorithm INIT*. We assume that the internal state of an instance of T cannot be accessed otherwise than through the operations defined for T and that $INIT$ is
automatically invoked at instance creation.

Let C be the set of internal states associated with the variables of an implementation. The intended semantics of a procedure $B(OP)$ can be specified
by a *concrete standard postcondition*

$$cpost \in C \times C \rightsquigarrow \{true, false\}.$$

A pair of states (c', c) is in $cpost$ if c is an *intended* outcome of invoking $B(OP)$
in the initial state c'. On the other hand, each procedure is a sequence of commands available in the programming language being used, and as such has an
actual meaning which is imposed by the semantic definition of this language.

The actual standard semantics of $B(OP)$ can be defined to be another (partial) relation

$$reachable\ (B(OP)) \in C \times C \rightsquigarrow \{true, false\}$$

with the understanding that a pair (c', c) is in this relation if when invoked in
the state c' $B(OP)$ terminates cleanly in c [2]. However for program proofs, one
is interested in knowing not only if a program terminates, but if it terminates in
a state satisfying a given postcondition [8]. For this purpose, the use of the
backward predicate transformer semantics given in [2] is more suitable. This
semantics is similiar to that of [8]. One difference is that the predicates we
consider are binary, i.e. primed states may occur in them. A more important
difference is that in predicates we use *noncommutative* logical con-

nectives & (conditional and) and ∨ (conditional or) and that we take special care in dealing with data types (e.g. bounded integers, finite arrays) with partial operations. For example, let T be a language defined type with a partial unary operator f in its underlying data space. If the standard effect of invoking an operation OP on a variable V of type T is the assignment of a new value $f(v)$ to V, then the standard semantics of OP is given in [2] as

$$wp(``V.OP", Q) \equiv def(f(v)) \;\&\; Q[f(v)/v]$$

where Q is an arbitrary predicate and $Q[f(v)/v]$ stands for the result of substituting all free occurrences of v in Q by $f(v)$, after all the usual precautionary measures for avoiding name clashes. The guard $def(f(v))$ at the left of the non-commutative "&" is essential for ensuring that the term $f(v)$ to be substituted is well defined, i.e. is obtained by applying f to an element of its domain. A detailed discussion of the technical issues related to the use of such a non-commutative logic is beyond the scope of this paper. We limit ourselves to state that its use seems to be necessary whenever one wishes to avoid the occurrence of undefined terms in the verification conditions generated during program proofs.

Returning now to our discussion about the actual standard semantics of a procedure, we define it to be its backward predicate transformer (derivable as the composition of the predicate transformers associated with its component commands). In particular, we define the *concrete standard precondition cpre* of a procedure to be the weakest precondition associated with its body and its concrete standard postcondition:

$$cpre \equiv wp(``B(OP)", cpost)$$

where

$$wp(``B(OP)", cpost)(c') \equiv \exists\, c \in C: reachable(B(OP))(c', c) \;\&\; \\ cpost(c', c).$$

Thus, *cpre* characterises the set of initial states c' for which $B(OP)$ terminates cleanly in a final state c satisfying $cpost(c', c)$.

An implementation of the *RESOURCES* data type is given in Fig. 2.

We assume that the positivity of the generic parameter N is checked by the compiler. The *AND, OR* operations of the *BOOLEAN* language defined data type are noncommutative as their corresponding logical connectives & and v (e.g. if the loop guard in line 9 is evaluated in a state $j = n + 1$ then the well defined result *false* is obtained even though $\neg def(t(n + 1) = used)$). The concrete standard postconditions stated as comments (between % symbols) in lines 12, 16 specify the intended semantics of the *GET* and *RELEASE* procedures. The concrete standard preconditions in lines 7, 14 have been derived using the programming language semantics given in [2].

```
 1   type RESOURCES =
 2   class (generic N: INTEGER > 0);
 3     type RESOURCE-STATE = (FREE, USED);
 4     var T: ARRAY (1 ... N) of RESOURCE-STATE;
 5     procedure GET returns I: INTEGER;
 6     var J: INTEGER;
 7     begin % cpre = ∃j: 1 ≦ j ≦ n & t′ (j) = free %
 8        J := 1;
 9        while (J ≦ N) AND (T (J) = USED) do J := J + 1;
10        T (J) := USED;
11        I := J;
12     end; % cpost ≡ 1 ≦ i ≦ n & t′ (i) = free & t (i) = used %
13     procedure RELEASE (I: INTEGER);
14     begin % cpre = 1 ≦ i ≦ n & t′ (i) = used %
15        T (I) := FREE;
16     end; % cpost ≡ 1 ≦ i ≦ n & t′ (i) = used & t (i) = free %
17   begin for I := 1 to N do T (I) := FREE % INIT %
18   end RESOURCES
```

Fig. 2. Implementation of a data type with partial operations

2.3. Correctness

In order to prove the correctness of a data type implementation with respect to
a specification, one has to establish a correspondence between internal and abstract states. Following [13] this correspondence will be defined by an *abstraction function* denoted *A*.

In our example, the *A* function is defined[1] on any value *t* that the state variable *T* declared in Fig. 2 may reach:

$$A(t) \equiv \{j \,|(1 \leq j \leq n)\ \&\ t(j) = used\}$$

Clearly, for every reachable t, $A(t) \in P[n]$ holds.

Criteria for establishing the consistency of a data type implementation with
a specification (within a partial correctness semantic framework) have been
proposed in [13]. Such a proof of correctness guarantees that whenever an
operation is invoked in an initial state satisfying its precondition, either it terminates in a state satisfying the postcondition or it does not terminate properly,
i.e. loops indefinitely or leads to an (unanticipated) exception detection. Our
interest is in clean termination, so we need to strengthen the criteria given in
[13] as follows.

---

1 As all the procedures of this paper have parameters or return values of language defined
  types and the abstraction functions for them are identity functions we omit their explicit
  mention

179

Let C be the set of internal states reachable by an instance of a data type T, $INIT$ be the initialisation algorithm, and A be the abstraction function. First, A is necessary to verify that the constraints on the generic parameters of T guarantee that $INIT$ yields a state c for which $A(c)$ satisfies the 'initial value' predicate of T:

$(VC0)$ $constraints\ on\ generic\ parameters \Rightarrow wp(\text{``}INIT\text{''}, initial\text{-}value(A(c)))$.

Furthermore, for each operation OP of T it is necessary to show that its concrete semantics is consistent with its abstract semantics. Let $post$ be the abstract standard postcondition of OP and pre characterise the domain of $post$. At the implementation level, let $cpost$ be the concrete standard postcondition of $B(OP)$ and $cpre = wp(\text{``}B(OP)\text{''}, cpost)$ characterise the initial states c' for which $B(OP)$ yields final states c such that $cpost(c', c)$. The first verification condition ensures that whenever OP is invoked in a state c' for which $A(c')$ has a successor in $post$, then for c' there exists a reachable successor in $cpost$:

$(VC1)$ $pre(A(c')) \Rightarrow cpre(c')$.

The second verification condition ensures that the successor c reached after the (clean) termination of $B(OP)$ corresponds through A to a specified abstract successor of $A(c')$:

$(VC2)$ $cpost(c', c) \Rightarrow post(A(c'), A(c))$.

As an example, we state below (without proof) the verification conditions which ensure that the implementation of Fig. 2 is totally correct with respect to the specification of Fig. 1.

1) Correct initialisation

(I) $n > 0 \Rightarrow wp(\text{``}INIT\text{''}, A(t) = \{\ \})$.

2) Correctness of the standard effect of GET

$(G1)$ $|A(t')| < n \Rightarrow cpre(GET)(t')$
$(G2)$ $cpost(GET)(t', t) \Rightarrow i = oneof([n]-A(t'))\ \&\ A(t) = A(t') \cup \{i\}$.

3) Correctness of the standard effect of $RELEASE$:

$(R1)$ $i \in A(t') \Rightarrow cpre(RELEASE)(t')$
$(R2)$ $cpost(RELEASE)(t', t) \Rightarrow i \in A(t')\ \&\ A(t) = A(t') - \{i\}$.

In deriving the above verification conditions we have used the predicate transformer semantics [2] of a language supporting predefined data types such as $BOOLEAN, INTEGER, ARRAY$. Now that we have extended this language with the $RESOURCES$ data type, it would be interesting to express the semantics of its operations in terms of predicate transformers also. That would allow

180

programs using *RESOURCES* to be verified in the same manner as if only pre-defined types were used (a main idea in data abstraction is to place abstract and predefined data types on an equal footing). The last part of this section investigates this point briefly.

We assume in what follows that whenever an operation *OP* of a data type *T* is invoked on a variable *V* in a state outside the standard domain, i.e. $\neg\,pre(v')$ then *OP* does not terminate normally (a systematic method for enforcing this behaviour is given later). Our second assumption is that the abstract post-condition of *OP* describes explicitly how the new state v is obtained by applying a (generally partial) operator f of the underlying data space to v', i.e. $post \equiv v = f(v')$ where $pre(v') \Rightarrow def(f(v))$[2]. Under the above assumptions, the truth of the (*VC0, VC1, VC2*) verification conditions ensures that $pre(v')$ is the necessary and sufficient condition for the standard termination of *V.OP* in a state satisfying $v = f(v')$. Another way of saying this is the following: the necessary and sufficient condition for the standard termination of *V.OP* in a state satisfying an arbitrary predicate Q is the truth of $pre(v)$ & $Q[f(v)/v]$ before the invocation of *V.OP*:

$$wp(``V.OP", Q) \equiv pre(v)\ \&\ Q[f(v)/v].$$

Thus, under the assumption that the operations specified for *RESOURCES* do not terminate normally outside their standard domains, their predicate transformer semantics can be given as follows:

(1) $\quad wp(``I := R.GET", Q) \equiv |r| < n\ \&\ Q[x/i, r \cup \{x\}/r]$
$$\textbf{where } x = oneof([n]-r),$$
(2) $\quad wp(``R.RELEASE(I)", Q) \equiv i \in r\ \&\ Q[r-\{i\}/r].$

The expression $Q[a/b,\ c/d]$ stands for the result of simultaneously substituting in Q all free occurrences of b by a and all free occurrences of d by c.

As an example, let us use (1) to derive the necessary and sufficient condition for the program

```
C1      I := R.GET;
C2      J := R.GET;
```

to terminate normally. This is:

$$
\begin{array}{ll}
wp(``C1", wp(``C2", true)) & \text{(by 1 with } Q = true) \\
= wp(``C1", |r| < n) & \text{(by 1 with } Q = |r| < n) \\
= |r| < n\ \&\ |r \cup \{oneof([n]-r)\}| < n & \text{(properties of underlying} \\
= |r| \leq n-2. & \text{data space)}
\end{array}
$$

Thus, *C1; C2* terminates normally iff initially they are at least two free resources.

---

2 The case when *OP* has parameters or returns some value can be dealt with similarly

2.4. Exceptions

Let D be an integer array with domain $1 \ldots N$ and I, R be variables of type *INTEGER* and *RESOURCES*(N) respectively. Suppose that in order to achieve some desired state transition one composes the following two commands into a program:

$C1$	$I := R.GET$;
$C2$	$D(I) := 1$;

Such sequential compositions are based on the (most often implicitly made) assumption that when the 'next' command $C2$ is invoked, the standard state transition specified for the 'preceding' command $C2$ has been accomplished. Here the invocation of $C2$ makes sense only if the state $s2$ after $C1$ is such that $s2(I) = i$ is a newly allocated resource name and hence is a valid index for accessing D. If the state $s1$ prior to the invocation of $C1$ was such that $s1(R) = [n]$, then a state $s2$ such that $post(GET)(s1, s2)$ cannot be reached (because such a state does not exist!). In such circumstances, the initial assumption that the execution of $C1$ should be followed by that of the 'next' command $C2$ has to be revised. Problems arise not only in programs which use data types, but also in those which implement them. For example, if the *GET* procedure of Fig. 2 is invoked in an initial state in which all the entries of the array T are used, the loop in line 9 terminates with $j = n + 1$ and the invocation of the 'next' command in line 10 results in an array bounds violation.

A possible solution to the above difficulties is to *abort* a program whenever one of its component operations is invoked outside its standard domain. Conceptually that can be modelled by specifying that such an invocation does not produce a successor state (the operation "fails to terminate" [8]) or that some error value — and hence error state — is produced and the program remains for ever in it (the following operations produce error values from error values [10]). This paper is devoted to the discussion of another possible solution.

Let us define an invocation of an operation outside its standard domain to be an *exception occurrence*. By the definition of this domain it follows that once the goal of an operation invocation is specified to be some (partial) state transition relation *post*, the set of initial states which lead to exception occurrences (the *exceptional domain* of the operation) is uniquely determined as the complement of the standard domain *dom(post)*.

The solution to exception handling we want to explore is based on the following idea: an exception occurrence should cause an (exceptional) alteration of the (standard) sequential composition rule for operation invocations. A programming language control structure which allows to express that the standard continuation of an operation invocation is to be replaced by an exceptional continuation when an exception occurrence is detected will be referred to as an *exception mechanism*. In what follows we assume that the exception mechanism introduced in [5] (similar to some extent to those of [17, 15]) is available in our programming language. Because of space limitations, we present here only those features of the mechanism which are needed for understanding this paper.

2.5. Exception Mechanism

Exceptional continuations for exception occurrences can be defined by using exception labels. The designer of a procedure OP can declare that whenever OP is invoked in its exceptional domain an exceptional label E is signalled:

procedure OP **signals** E

and an invoker of OP can define the exceptional continuation, if E is signalled, to be some exception handler K by writing:

$OP[E; K]$.

In order to detect and handle the occurrence of the (by now labelled) E exception, the implementor of OP can insert in $B(OP)$ one of the following syntactic constructs:

(b) $[B; H]$
(c) $C[F; H]$.

In (b), B stands for a *b*oolean expression without side effects. In (c), F stands for an exception label which may be signalled by the *c*ommand C. H stands for an exception handler. All the handlers to be used in this paper follow the syntax:

$H = H1$; **signal** E

where $H1$ is a (possibly empty) sequence of commands [3]. Exceptional continuations can be associated with operation invocations and exception labels only by using (c) constructs (e.g. $OP[E; K]$ is an instance of such a construct).

The concept of a continuation function used in denotational semantics [20] can be used to express formally the meaning of the **signal** sequencer used in (b, c) constructs. However, in what follows we choose (for simplicity reasons) to remain within the traditional data abstraction approach to programming in which to abstract from such 'control' issues (in order to better concentrate on data representation issues) is an integral part of the 'divide and conquer' underlying philosophy. We therefore limit ourselves to giving a 'local' predicate transformer semantic characterisation of the (b, c) constructs. This characterisation captures that part of their semantics which can be described in terms of program states, and is sufficient for proving the correctness of programs which implement data types with exceptions, provided certain context-sensitive syntactic constraints (to be described below) are satisfied by these programs.

---

3 Issues related to standard handler terminations (corresponding to exception propagations being stopped – or masked) are discussed in [5, 7] and will not be considered in this presentation

Let us first present informally that part of the (b, c) constructs which will not be described in terms of predicate transformers: the **signal** E sequencer. Two context-sensitive syntactic rules have to be obeyed when using it in a procedure: it can occur only in an exceptional construct surrounded by square brackets and the signalled label E must be declared in the header of the procedure (so that invokers may define exceptional continuations for occurrences of E). These constraints can be checked by a compiler without difficulty. Let us denote by

$$C[P; H]$$

either a (b) or a (c) construct (if C is empty then P stands for a boolean expression B and otherwise it stands for a label F which may be signalled by C). We assume in this paper that **signal** E sequencers are used in procedure bodies only according to the syntactic pattern (u) given below:

(u)
```
procedure OP signals E;
begin C 1;
    C[P; H1; signal E];
    C 2;
end;
```

where $C1$ and $C2$ are (possibly empty) sequences of commands. The effect of executing the **signal** E sequencer is the following: the standard continuation of the $C[P; H]$ construct (the 'next' $C2$) is ignored and OP terminates exceptionally with E being signalled, i.e. an exception handler K associated (by using a (c) syntactic construct) with E in the invocation context of OP is activated. Thus, a **signal** E inside a procedure OP is a (restricted kind) of forward jump to a handler (statically) associated with E in the invocation context of OP [5, 17]. We assume that if OP is a value returning procedure used in an assignment $V := OP$, no new value is assigned to V if OP terminates by signalling E. An exception mechanism must be designed so as to guarantee that exceptional continuations for command invocations always exist and are uniquely defined. For a detailed discussion of these exception mechanism design issues the interested reader is referred to [5, 17].

We now come to those aspects of the (b, c) constructs which can be described in terms of predicate transformers (under the assumption that the above constraints relative to **signal** commands and exceptional continuations are enforced). Consider a (b) construct inserted in a procedure according to the (u) pattern and suppose that B always has a well-defined value. The local effect of inserting the construct in $B(OP)$ can be described as follows. If the preceding command $(C1)$ terminates normally in a state s in which the value $b = s(B)$ of B is *false*, then the following command $(C2)$ is invoked in the same state s (independently of what the meaning of $H1$ might be):

(bs) $\qquad wp(\text{``}[B; H]\text{''}, Q) \equiv \neg b \, \& \, Q.$

Otherwise, i.e. if the preceding command $(C1)$ terminates in a state e in which $e(B) = b$ is *true*, the exception handler following the "[B" syntactic fragment is invoked in the (same) state e:

(be) $wp("[B", Q) \equiv b \& Q.$

Thus, a (b) construct acts as a switching point. By using it one can write in a linear notation two sequentially composed programs which share their entry points but have distinct exit points and perform different state transitions: $C1$; $[B; H]$; $C2$ behaves like $C1$; $C2$ in the standard case $(b\,s)$ and like $C1$; H in the exceptional case $(b\,e)$. One could remark that the program $C1$; **if** B **then** H **else** $C2$ can do the same job. We prefer the (b) syntax for several reasons. First, it leads to a clear separation between what is standard and what is exceptional in programs. Second, it provides a means for forbidding **signal** sequencers to occur 'hidden' within standard programming constructs (like the previous "**if** B **then** H **else** $C2$"). If the **signal** sequencer could occur within them, then the semantic definition of every standard construct would have to be modified to reflect this possibility. Our opinion is that the need to define an exceptional semantics for programming constructs should not interfere with, but rather be a completion of, their standard semantics, which should remain unchanged. This point is further elaborated when the predicate transformer characterisation of the (c) construct is given. We also show that the restriction to use signals only in exception programming constructs surrounded by square brackets enables one to prove *separately* properties relative to the standard and exceptional behaviour of programs.

As a first example of such a proof, let us use the $(b\,s, b\,e)$ clauses to derive the conditions for standard and exceptional termination of a (slightly modified) version of the *GET* procedure of Fig. 2 in which the exceptional construct

$$[J > N; \textbf{signal } OV]$$

is inserted as shown in Fig. 4 of Sect. 2.7. Let $C1$ and $C2$ be the sequential compositions of the commands preceding (lines 7, 9) and following (lines 10, 11) this exceptional construct:

$$C1 \equiv J := 1; \textbf{while } (J \leq N) \, AND(T(J) = USED) \textbf{ do } J := J + 1$$
$$C2 \equiv T(J) := USED; I := J.$$

The modified *GET* procedure terminates in a state $t = t'$ by signalling the OV (erflow) exception label iff the following precondition holds:

$$wp("C1; [J > N", t = t') = \qquad \text{(by the } b\,e \text{ clause)}$$
$$= wp("C1", (j > n) \& (t = t'))$$
$$= \forall j: (1 \leq j \leq n) \Rightarrow (t'(j) = used).$$

The condition for standard termination with the internal state being changed as specified by *cpost* (*GET*) is

$$
\begin{aligned}
wp(\text{``}C1;\ [J > N;\ \textbf{signal}\ OV];\ C2\text{''}, cpost(GET)) &= \\
= wp(\text{``}C1;\ [J > N;\ \textbf{signal}\ OV]\text{''}, & \\
(1 \leq j \leq n)\ \&\ (t'(j) = free)) & \qquad\qquad \text{(by the } b\,s \text{ clause)} \\
= wp(\text{``}C1\text{''}, (1 \leq j \leq n)\ \&\ (t'(j) = free)) & \\
= \exists\, j\colon (1 \leq j \leq n)\ \&\ (t'(j) = free). &
\end{aligned}
$$

Thus, the insertion of the exceptional construct of *OV* in *GET* does not alter the standard properties of this procedure. However, if the procedure is now invoked in an initial state for which *cpre*(*GET*) does not hold, the invocation of *C2* is replaced by that of the handler *of* the *OV* exception, in this example a simple **signal** *OV* sequencer. This causes the exceptional termination of *GET* and the invocation of a handler *K associated* with the label *OV* in the invocation context of *GET*:

$$
I := R.GET[OV;\ K].
$$

K may in its turn handle the occurrence *of* another exception specified for the program which invoked *GET*. We postpone a discussion of the issues related to exception propagations until Sect. 3.5 and content ourselves for the moment to emphasise that the phrases 'handler of *E*' and 'handler associated with *E*' are used to designate distinct handlers.

Predicate transformer characterisations similar to (*b s, b e*) can be given also for (*c*) constructs. Assume that such a construct is used in a procedure according to the (*u*) pattern and that *F* is signalled by *C* iff *C* is invoked outside its standard domain. The necessary and sufficient condition for the command (*C2*) following the *C*[*F*; *H*] construct to be invoked in a state satisfying a predicate *Q* is the standard termination of *C* in such a state (independently of what the meaning of *H1* might be):

$$(cs) \qquad wp(\text{``}C[F;\ H]\text{''},\ Q) \equiv wp(\text{``}C\text{''},\ Q).$$

Thus, by adjoining in a program an [*F*; *H*] exceptional construct to a command *C*, one does not change the standard behaviour of that program. For example the standard semantics of *I* := *R.GET*[*OV*; *K*] is the same as that of *I* := *R.GET*:

$$
\begin{aligned}
(1') \qquad & wp(\text{``}I := R.GET[OV;\ K]\text{''},\ Q) \\
& \equiv |r| < n\ \&\ Q[x/i,\ r \cup \{x\}/r]\ \textbf{where}\ x = oneof([n] - r).
\end{aligned}
$$

If an invocation of *C* is an *F* exception occurrence, the presence of [*F*; *H*] triggers· the invocation of *H*. Assume that the (exceptional) state transition produced by *C* in such circumstances is specified to be the identity relation over states. Then the necessary and sufficient condition for *H* to be invoked in a state satisfying some predicate *Q* is the exceptional termination of *C* when invoked

186

in such a state:

$$(c\ e) \qquad wp(\text{``}C[F\text{''}, Q) \equiv \neg\ wp(\text{``}C\text{''}, true)\ \&\ Q.$$

For example, we want an OV exception occurrence to leave the state of the program variables unchanged and just trigger the invocation of a handler associated with the OV label:

$$(l\ e) \qquad wp(\text{``}I := R.GET[OV\text{''}, Q) \equiv |r| = n\ \&\ Q.$$

The next sections will discuss how such operations can be specified and correctly implemented.

2.6. Data Types with Total Operations and Exceptions

A specification method should allow the description of not just the standard effect of operations, but also of possible exceptional effects. The specification of exceptional effects should state when exceptions should be signalled and what state transitions should occur in such cases.

Let S be a set of abstract states for some data type T and let OP be an operation of T with abstract standard postcondition $post$ and standard domain pre. Let E be an exception label to be signalled if OP is invoked in the exceptional domain $pre(E) \equiv \neg\ pre$ and let $post(E)$ be a (possibly partial) state transition relation such that every initial state satisfying $pre(E)$ is in the domain of $post(E)$. The construct

$$E: pre(E) \rightarrow post(E), \quad pre \rightarrow post$$

will be used to specify the meaning of the operation OP as a *pair* of (exceptional and standard) state transition relations. If at the invocation of OP the initial state $s' \in S$ satisfies $pre(E)$, the exceptional state transition labelled by E occurs: the relation between s' and the successor state $s \in S$ is $post(E)$ and the continuation in the invocation context of OP is exceptional, i.e. a handler associated with E is invoked instead of the 'next' statement in that context. If at the invocation of OP the initial state s' satisfies pre, the standard state transition occurs: the relation between s' and s is $post$ and the continuation in the invocation context is standard.

Because by definition $pre(E) \vee pre = true$, it follows that an operation specified as indicated above is *total* (every possible initial state has a successor either in $post(E)$ or in $post$).

If all the operations specified for a data type are total then the data type will be termed *robust* (its operations have a well defined behaviour for any possible initial state and exception occurrences do not cause program abortion [8] or a subsequent cascade of error notifications [10]).

Total operations for which the abstract exceptional postconditions are identity state transition relations, i.e. $post(E) \equiv (s = s')$, will be called *atomic* (in

```
1    specification of type RESOURCES (generic N: INTEGER > 0)
2    values r ∈ P [n]
3    initial value r = { }
4    operations
5       procedure GET returns I: INTEGER signals OV
6       OV: | r' | = n,
7       i = oneof ([n] − r') & r = r' ∪ {i}
8       procedure RELEASE (I: INTEGER) signals ILL
9       ILL: i ∉ r',
10      i ∈ r' & r = r' − {i}
```

Fig. 3. Specification of a data type with atomic operations

the sense that their invocation has for an external observer an 'all or nothing' effect: either the standard state transition takes place or the state remains unchanged).

As far as the robustness of programs is concerned, the fundamental concept is that of a total operation. However, in what follows we choose (for simplicity reasons) to give only examples of atomic operations. When specifying such operations we omit to write their exceptional postconditions and their standard preconditions (which can be immediately retrieved by negating the written exceptional preconditions).

Figure 3 presents a robust version of the *RESOURCES* data type. The two operations *GET* and *RELEASE* are now total (when invoked outside their standard domains the exceptions OV (erflow) and ILL (illegal) are signalled). The data space in terms of which this specification is given is the same as that presented in Sect. 2.1. In order to define a data type with *total operations* and exceptions one can use an underlying data space with *partial operators*. In our example the partiality of the *"oneof"* operator does not create any inconvenience: this operator cannot be invoked directly by a user of the *RESOURCES* data type, so it need not be made total. The *"oneof"* operator can be applied to elements of $P[n]$ in program proofs, but the non-commutative "&" of (1, $1'$) ensures that it will never be applied to { }, that is, the 'error terms' studied in [10], will never be generated.

2.7. Implementation

Suppose that in order to implement an operation OP, which may signal an exception E, an exceptional construct is inserted in $B(OP.)$ according to the (u) syntactic pattern. This has the effect of adding to the standard meaning $wp("B(OP)", Q)$ of OP an exceptional meaning $wp("C1; C[P; H1]", Q)$ where Q stands for an arbitrary predicate. Thus, the actual semantics of $B(OP)$ becomes a *pair* of (standard and exceptional) predicate transformers. If $cpost$ is the concrete standard postcondition specified for $B(OP)$, then the concrete standard precondition *cpre* is defined (as in Sect. 2.3) to be

$$cpre \equiv wp(\text{``}B(OP)\text{''}, cpost).$$

The *cpre* predicate can be derived by using the $(b\,s,\,c\,s)$ semantic clauses given in Sect. 2.5. A *concrete exceptional postcondition* $cpost(E)$ can be used to specify the internal state transition *intended* to be produced when E occurs. Under the assumption (u) that in $B(OP)$ there exists one occurrence of the **signal** E sequencer, the *concrete exceptional precondition* is defined to be

$$cpre(E) \equiv wp(\text{``}C\,1;\ C[P;\ H1\text{''}, cpost(E)).$$

The $cpre(E)$ precondition can be derived by using the $(b\,e,\ c\,e)$ semantic clauses. While *cpre* still characterises the initial states for which the termination of $B(OP)$ in a state satisfying *cpost* is standard, $cpre(E)$ becomes the characteristic predicate of the initial states for which $B(OP)$ terminates exceptionally by signalling E in a state satisfying $cpost(E)$. In both cases the termination will be called *clean*, since infinite looping or unanticipated (i.e. unspecified) exception detections are excluded.

An implementation of the robust version of *RESOURCES* specified in Fig. 3 is given in Fig. 4. The only additions made to the implementation given in Fig. 2 are the exception label declarations in lines 5, 13 and the exceptional constructs in lines 9, 14. The standard algorithms, obtainable by removing the next between square brackets, are the same.

```
1   type RESOURCES =
2   class (generic N: INTEGER > 0);
3      type RESOURCE-STATE = (FREE, USED);
4      var T: ARRAY (1 ... N) of RESOURCE-STATE;
5      procedure GET returns I: INTEGER signals OV;
6      var J: INTEGER;
7      begin J := 1;
8         while (J ≤ N) AND (T (J) = USED) do J := J + 1;
9            [J > N; signal OV];
10           T (J) := USED;
11           I := J
12     end;
13     procedure RELEASE (I: INTEGER) signals ILL;
14     begin [(I < 1) OR (I > N) OR (R (I) = FREE); signal ILL];
15        T (I) := FREE
16     end;
17     begin for I := 1 to N do T (I) := FREE
18  end RESOURCES
```

Fig. 4. Implementation of a data type with atomic operations

Each of the exceptional constructs of Fig. 4 contains a boolean expression (a run-time check) and a corresponding **signal** sequencer. We want such checks to be *precise* in the sense that they become *true* whenever the initial state is in the exceptional domain and they remain *false* if the initial state is in the standard domain. A second property should be *efficiency*. The place for inserting checks should be chosen so as to minimise their evaluation cost. For example the insertion of a check for OV at the entry of GET (by using a loop similar to that of line 8) would not be optimal since its evaluation would be redundant with the following search for a free entry in T. The placement of the check after the loop is better. Intuitively one might say that if there is a choice between testing a predicate with quantifiers and a predicate without quantifiers, the latter is to be preferred. Issues related to the derivation and placement of precise checks in programs which are written in a language having both backward and forward predicate transformer semantics are discussed in [2].

2.8. Correctness Criteria

In order to prove that a data type T with total operations and exceptions is correctly implemented, two new verification conditions (for correct exceptional behaviour) have to be added to those of Sect. 2.3.

The first verification condition concerning the correct internal state initialisation is the same as that given in Sect. 2.3.:

$(VC0)$ *constraints on generic parameters* $\Rightarrow wp(\text{``}INIT\text{''}, initial\text{-}value(A(c)))$.

Let now OP be an arbitrary total operation of T specified by

$$E: pre(E) \rightarrow post(E), \quad pre \rightarrow post$$

where $pre = dom(post) = \neg\, pre(E)$. Assume that the implementor of OP has decided that the best place for inserting an exceptional construct in the body of OP is as shown below:

$$B(OP) = C1; [B; H]; C2$$

where B is the check for, and $H = H1$; **signal** E is the handler of, E. $H1$ may be empty as in the examples of Fig. 4. Also $C1$ or $C2$ may be empty; a check may be placed at the entry or at the exit of a procedure. Let $cpost$ be the standard concrete postcondition of OP and $cpost(E)$ be the concrete exceptional postcondition to hold just before E is signalled. Let furthermore $cpre$, $cpre(E)$ be the concrete standard and exceptional preconditions as defined in Sect. 2.7. The verification conditions for correct standard behaviour are the same as those of Sect. 2.3:

$(VC1)$ $pre(A(c')) \Rightarrow cpre(c')$
$(VC2)$ $cpost(c', c) \Rightarrow post(A(c'), A(c))$.

190

The verification conditions for correct exceptional behaviour ensure that whenever OP is invoked outside its abstract standard domain, the occurrence of the specified E exception is detected and the resulting exceptional concrete state transition is consistent with that specific:

$(VCE\,1)\quad pre(E)(A(c')) \Rightarrow cpre(E)(c')$
$(VCE\,2)\quad cpost(E)(c', c) \Rightarrow post(E)(A(c'), A(c)).$

The derivation of $cpre$ and $cpre(E)$, as well as the proofs of the above verification conditions can be carried out *completely separately*. If OP has been specified to be atomic, then the proof of $(VCE\,2)$ is often trivial. This is the case in our *RESOURCES* example.

The verification conditions $(VC\,1)$ and $(VCE\,1)$ ensure in particular that B is a precise run-time check for the occurrence of E: $(VCE\,1)$ states that the handler H of E is activated if the initial state is exceptional and $(VC\,1)$ states that H is not activated if the initial state is in the standard domain. In fact, whenever these two verification conditions hold, $cpre$ and $cpre(E)$ determine a (strict) partition over the set of initial internal states which may exist when the procedure OP is invoked. Indeed, from $pre(E) \vee pre = true$, $(VC\,1)$ and $(VCE\,1)$ it follows that $cpre(E) \vee cpre = true$, and from $cpre(E) \Rightarrow wp("C\,1", b)$ and $cpre \Rightarrow wp("C\,1", \neg b)$ it follows that $cpre(E)\ \&\ cpre \Rightarrow wp("C\,1", b\ \&\ \neg b)$ $= false$, i.e. $cpre(E)\ \&\ cpre = false$.

Conversely, assume that classical proof methods have been used to show that the standard algorithm $C\,1; C\,2$ of OP is totally correct with respect to $cpre$, $cpost$. If the preciseness of the check B is established by

$$\neg\ cpre = wp("C\,1; [B", true)$$

then by the $(b\ s,\ b\ e)$ clauses it follows that the robust algorithm $B(OP)$ has the same standard behaviour as $C\,1; C\,2$. Thus, the proof of correct standard behaviour can be retained for the extended $B(OP)$ unchanged. This is a significant point since it shows that exceptional constructs can be inserted for robustness purposes in non-robust programs without altering the correctness of their standard behaviour.

Returning now to the implementation of Fig. 4, we can apply the semantic clause $(b\ e)$ to show that the run-time check for ILL is precise:

$$\neg\ cpre\ (RELEASE) = wp("[(I < 1)OR(I > N)OR(T(I) = FREE)",$$
$$t = t').$$

The preciseness of the check for OV has already been discussed in Sect. 2.5. It is not difficult to check that the verification conditions $(VCE\,1, VCE\,2)$ hold for GET and $RELEASE$:

$(GE\,1)\quad |A(t')| = n \Rightarrow \neg\ cpre(GET)(t')$
$(GE\,2)\quad t = t' \Rightarrow A(t) = A(t')$
$(RE\,1)\quad i \notin A(t') \Rightarrow \neg\ cpre(RELEASE)(t')$
$(RE\,2)\quad t = t' \Rightarrow A(t) = A(t').$

The above conditions together with the conditions $(I, G1, G2, R1, R2)$ of Sect. 2.3 establish the total correctness of the implementation of Fig. 4 with respect to the specification of Fig. 3. In particular the conditions $(GE1, RE1)$ for the GET and $RELEASE$ operations ensure that the assumption of Sect. 2.3 concerning their exceptional termination holds. Thus, the standard predicate transformer semantics of the operations of Fig. 3 is that given by the formulae $(1, 2)$ of Sect. 2.3. Their exceptional semantics is:

$(1e) \qquad wp(\text{``}I := R.GET[OV\text{''}, Q) \equiv |r| = n \ \& \ Q$
$(2e) \qquad wp(\text{``}R.RELEASE(I)[ILL\text{''}, Q) \equiv i \notin r \ \& \ Q.$

Before ending this introduction to robust data types we would like to discuss on their use in the design of robust algorithms. More specifically, we will show on a simple example how the semantic clauses of Sect. 2.5 may be used to derive conditions for the exceptional termination of such algorithms. Aspects related to exception occurrences in loops will also be briefly discussed.

Assume we want to design a robust version of the two-resources allocation program given in Sect. 2.3:

$C1 \qquad I := R.GET[OV; H];$
$C2 \qquad J := R.GET[OV; K].$

We are interested knowing under which condition the above program terminates exceptionally. The condition for OV to be signalled by $C1$ is:

$$wp(\text{``}I := R.GET[OV\text{''}, true) = |r| = n. \qquad \text{(by } 1e)$$

The condition for OV to be signalled by $C2$ is:

$$
\begin{aligned}
& wp(\text{``}C1; J := R.GET[OV\text{''}, true) && \text{(by } 1e) \\
& = wp(\text{``}C1\text{''}, |r| = n) && \text{(by } 1') \\
& = |r| < n \ \& \ |r \cup \{oneof([n]-r)\}| = n \text{ (properties of underlying data} \\
& && \text{space)} \\
& = |r| = n-1.
\end{aligned}
$$

It follows that $C1; C2$ terminates exceptionally whenever initially there exists at most one free resource.

In general, if a command C which may signal an exception E has to be iteratively invoked, the syntactic construct

$(L) \qquad \textbf{while } B \textbf{ do } C[E; H]$

can be used [5] to define the scope of the association of H with E to be the whole loop, i.e. if E is detected during some iteration the exceptional continuation is H. The insertion of $[E; H]$ does not change the standard behaviour of the loop: the condition for standard termination in a state satisfying some predicate Q (if B is always well-defined) is that defined in [8]

(Ls) $wp(\text{“\textbf{while } } B \text{ \textbf{do} } C[E; H]\text{”}, Q)$
           $\equiv wp(\text{“\textbf{while } } B \text{ \textbf{do} } C\text{”}, Q) = \exists\, i \geq 0: S_i$
           $S_0 = \neg\, b\; \&\; Q, \quad S_{i+1} = b\; \&\; wp(\text{“}C\text{”}, S_i)$

where S_i is the condition for standard termination after exactly i iterations. The necessary and sufficient condition for exceptional termination can be defined similarly:

(Le) $wp(\text{“\textbf{while } } B \text{ \textbf{do} } C[E\text{”}, Q) \equiv \exists\, j \geq 1: E_j$
           $E_1 = b\; \&\; wp(\text{“}C[E\text{”}, Q), \;\; E_{j+1} = b\; \&\; wp(\text{“}C\text{”}, E_j)$

where E_j is the condition for exceptional termination with E being signalled during the jth iteration. If for every integer n, both S_n and E_n are false, then the loop will never terminate.

Using the $(Le, 1, 1e)$ clauses one can show for example that the loop

     while $TRUE$ **do** $I := R.GET[OV; H]$

always terminates exceptionally, since

     $wp(\text{“\textbf{while } } TRUE \text{ \textbf{do} } I := R.GET[OV\text{”}}, true) = \exists\, k \geq 0: |r| + k = n$

holds for any initial state $r \in P[n]$. The two-resources example can be similarly generalised to the case when $k \geq 1$ resources need to be allocated and recorded in some integer array D with index domain $1 \ldots P, k \leq p$:

     $wp(\text{“\textbf{for } } I := 1 \text{ \textbf{to} } K \text{ \textbf{do} } D(I) := R.GET[OV; H]\text{”}, true) = |r| + k \leq n$
     $wp(\text{“\textbf{for } } I := 1 \text{ \textbf{to} } K \text{ \textbf{do} } D(I) := R.GET[OV\text{”}, true) = |r| + k > n.$

These examples will (it is hoped) convince the reader that the derivation of conditions for the exceptional termination of programs bears a great similarity to, and is not more complicated than, the derivation of conditions for standard termination [8]. Other examples are to be found in [6].

3. Exception Handling in Hierarchies of Data Abstractions

Programming with abstract data types leads to hierarchically structured programs. Rather than give an abstract general presentation of the problems encountered when handling exceptions in such programs, we prefer to introduce them through an example. We therefore devote the first sections of this second part of the paper to present a top-down hierarchically constructed program which implements the abstraction of a pool of $SEGMENTS$ in terms of the RE-$SOURCES$ data type and some other language provided data types such as AR-

RAY, RECORD, etc. This example allows to introduce in Sect. 3.5 general total correctness criteria for the implementation of robust data types with partitioned exceptional domains and representation invariants. The example is further used in the remaining sections to discuss some important aspects of exception handling in hierarchies of data abstractions, such as exception propagation and recovery of consistent states after exception occurrences.

3.1. An Example

The data space underlying the *SEGMENTS* data type contains all the sorts of mathematical objects mentioned in Sect. 2.1, as well as a new sort of objects: functions. It also contains all the operators mentioned in Sect. 2.1 together with some new operators on functions. The notation which will be used to denote this new objects and operators is briefly introduced in what follows.

Let A, B be finite sets. A partial function f from A to B is a subset $f \subseteq A \times B$ such that if $(a, b_1) \in f$ and $(a, b_2) \in f$ then $b_1 = b_2$. $f(a)$ stands for the unique b which corresponds to a. The domain of f is $dom(f) = \{a \in A | \exists b \in B: f(a) = b\}$ and its range is $ran(f) = \{f(a) | a \in dom(f)\}$. If $dom(f) = A$ then f is total. If $|dom(f)| = |ran(f)|$ then f is injective. The set of partial functions from A to B is denoted $A \rightsquigarrow B$, the set of total functions from A to B is denoted $A \rightarrow B$ and the set of total and injective functions from A to B is denoted $A \leftrightarrow B$. If $f \in A \rightsquigarrow B$ then we write $f = oneof(A \rightsquigarrow B)$. B can itself be a set of functions $B = C \rightsquigarrow D$. In such a case, if $x \in dom(f)$ then $f(x)$ is a function. If $y \in dom(f(x))$ then $f(x)(y)$ denotes the application of $f(x)$ to y and $rran(f)$ denotes the union of the ranges of the $f(x)$ functions:

$$rran(f) \equiv \bigcup_{x \in dom(f)} ran(f(x)).$$

Two operators (function extension "$\sqcup$" and function restriction "$\backslash$") will be used to construct new functions from old functions. If $x \notin dom(f)$ and $y \in B$ then $f \cup x, y$ is the extension of f to the domain $dom(f) \cup \{x\}$ defined by $(f \cup x, y)(a) = $ if $a \in dom(f)$ then $f(a)$ else if $a = x$ then y. If $x \in dom(f)$ then $f \backslash x$ is the restriction of f to the domain $dom(f) - \{x\}$ defined by $(f \backslash x)(a) = $ if $a \in dom(f) - \{x\}$ then $f(a)$.

The *SEGMENTS* data type is often used in operating systems to create contiguous (virtual) memory spaces composed of pages from a set of available (real) memory blocks. In its specification (Fig. 5) we consider three generic parameters that may vary from one system to another: $x s$ – the maximum number of segments, $x p$ – the maximum number of pages that a segment can have, and $x b$ – the maximum number of available memory blocks.

If $o \leq z \leq xp$ is a segment size, then a segment of this size is a function $f \in [z] \leftrightarrow [x b]$ (recall $[n]$ is used to denote $\{1, 2, \ldots, n\}$). The set of pages of f is $dom(f) = [z]$ and its blocks are $ran(f) \in P[x b]$. If a segment has a domain $[0]$ then it is empty. Consider now the set of all *non*-empty segments:

$$nes = \bigcup_{z \in [x p]} [z] \leftrightarrow [x b].$$

194

```
1    specification of type SEGMENTS (generic XS, XP, XB: INTEGER > 0)
2    values s ∈ [x s] ⤳ ⋃ [z] ↦ [x b]
                        z∈[xp]
3    initial value dom (s) = { }
4    operations
5       procedure NEW (Z: INTEGER) returns N: INTEGER signals NOV,
                                                       BSZ, BOV
6       NOV: |dom (s')| = x s,
7       BSZ: z ∉ [x p],
8       BOV: |rran (s')| + z > x b,
9       n = oneof ([x s] − dom (s')) & s = s' ⊔ n, oneof ([z] ↦ ([x b] − rran (s')))
10      procedure DESTROY (N: INTEGER) signals BN
11      BN: n ∉ dom (s'),
12      n ∈ dom (s') & s = s'\n
13      procedure READ (N, P: INTEGER) returns·B: INTEGER signals BN, BP
14      BN: n ∉ dom (s'),
15      BP: n ∈ dom (s') & p ∉ dom (s' (n))
16      b = s (n) (p)
```

Fig. 5. The specification of SEGMENTS

We want the *SEGMENTS* data type to maintain a correspondence between segment names in [$x\,s$] and non-empty segments in *nes*, so that these can be retrieved if their name is known. Thus an abstract value of this type is defined (line 2) to be an element s of [$x\,s$] ⤳ *nes*.

3.2. Partitioned Exceptional Domains

As for the *RESOURCES* example of Fig. 3, the *NEW, DESTROY* and *READ* operations specified for *SEGMENTS* are atomic. What is new is that two of them (*NEW* and *READ*) can signal more than one exception. Let us look at *NEW*. Its standard effect (Fig. 5, line 9) is to extend to previous state s' with a new segment name and a new segment of the required z size. The returned result is the new segment name. The standard domain is

$$pre(NEW) \equiv \neg\, pre(NOV)\; \&\; \neg\, pre(BSZ)\; \&\; \neg\, pre(BOV).$$

Indeed, a successor state satisfying the abstract postcondition of *NEW* exists if the following conditions are satisfied. First, $\neg\, pre(NOV) \equiv |dom(s')| < x\,s$ should hold, so that a new segment name from [$x\,s$] − $dom(s')$ can be chosen. Otherwise, the exception *names overflow* (*NOV*) may be signalled. Second, $\neg\, pre(BSZ) \equiv z \in [x\,p]$ should hold, so that the required size is a legal one. Otherwise the exception *bad size* (*BSZ*) is signalled. Third, $\neg\, pre(BOV) \equiv |rran(s')| + z \leq x\,b$ should also hold, so that a segment in [z] ↦ ([$x\,b$] − $rran(s')$)

with z distinct new blocks can be chosen. Otherwise we have the exception blocks *overflow* (*BOV*).

Such *partitionings* of the exceptional domains are frequently encountered in practice, whenever the intention is to convey (through distinct exception labels) more information about the particular circumstances of an exception occurrence. This can be useful for diagnostic purposes, or for allowing the association of distinct handlers with different exception labels so that different recovery actions may be taken [5, 17, 15, 2].

Often, the different exception preconditions do not determine a strict partition of the exceptional domain (e.g. *NEW* can be invoked with a bad size in a state $dom(s') = [x\ s]$). To impose at the specification level some a priori order on the actual evaluation of the concrete exception preconditions would restrain the freedom of an implementor to choose the best places for inserting exceptional constructs. Thus, a specification should allow for some non-determinism on the order in which exception preconditions are evaluated, similar to that of the guarded commands [8].

We define the meaning of a total operation specification

$$E_1: pre(E_1) \rightarrow post(E_1), \ldots, E_k: pre(E_k) \rightarrow post(E_k), pre \rightarrow post$$

where $\neg pre(E_1) \& \ldots \& \neg pre(E_k) = pre = dom(post)$ as follows. If the operation is invoked in an initial state s' outside the standard domain *pre*, then some exception E_i, for which $pre(E_i)(s')$ was true initially, is signalled, and the relation between s' and the successor state s is $post(E_i)$. Otherwise the standard service specified by *post* is provided. For example if *NEW* is invoked in some initial state satisfying $pre(NOV) \& pre(BSZ)$, then according to the specification of Fig. 5 either the *NOV* or *BSZ* exceptions may be signalled.

3.3. Implementation

Let us focus now on providing an implementation for *SEGMENTS*. First, we need to decide on some internal state representation. The abstract integer intervals $[x\ s]$, $[x\ p]$, $[x\ b]$ can be represented by using language provided scalar types.

 type *S-NAME* $= 1 \ldots XS$; *P-NAME* $= 1 \ldots XP$; *B-NAME* $= 1 \ldots XB$;

and the set of functions $[x\ p] \rightsquigarrow [x\ b]$ can be represented by an array

 type *FUNC* $= ARRAY(P\text{-}NAME)$ **of** *B-NAME*;

A segment is a restriction of such a function to an interval $[s\ z]$ where $s\ z$ is a value of **type** $SIZE = 0 \ldots XP$. Such a restriction can be described by its domain and the corresponding 'pages – blocks' mapping, i.e. by an element of the Cartesian product 'sizes' × 'mappings'. Abstract Cartesian products can be conveniently represented by records

 type *S-DESCRIPTOR* $= RECORD\ SZ:SIZE$; *B:FUNC* **end**;

196

The set of allocated segment names $dom(s)$ is a subset of $[x\ s]$. Thus we have a good opportunity to use our *RESOURCES* data type to represent $dom(s) \in P[x\ s]$ as a possible state of

var *NAMES*: *RESOURCES(XS)*;

We can represent the set of allocated blocks $rran(s) \in P[x\ b]$ in a similar manner by using another state variable of type *RESOURCES*

var *BLOCKS*: *RESOURCES(XB)*;

Finally, by using another array, we can represent an arbitrary function from segment names to segments as a possible state of

var *SG*: *ARRAY(S-NAME)* **of** *S-DESCRIPTOR*;

A complete implementation of *SEGMENTS* in terms of the above internal state representation is given in Fig. 6.

Concretely, the procedures work as follows. When a segment of *size z* has to be created, *NEW* requests a new segment name m (Fig. 6, line 11), allocates z unused blocks, updates the descriptor $SG(m)$ (lines 12, 13) and returns m (line 14). *DESTROY* first checks that the name n of the segment to be deleted corresponds to some previously created segment. If so, the blocks of that segment are released (line 18), the size of the corresponding segment descriptor is set to 0 and n is also released. Otherwise the exception *bad name BN* is signalled. *READ* just returns the pth block of the segment with name n if possible, otherwise signals *BN* or *BP* (*bad page*).

3.4. Representation Invariant

The data definition facilities of the PASCAL like language (extended with the *RESOURCES* types) used to represent the internal states of *SEGMENTS* do not allow for a direct expression of all our intentions: the set C of states which may be assumed by the state variables *NAMES, BLOCKS* and *SG* is much bigger than the set of internal states we really want. When chosing the internal state representation for *SEGMENTS* the intention has been to make every reachable internal state satisfy the following properties:

1) Only the segments whose *names* are recorded in the *NAMES* state variable are non-empty:

$$I_{sn} = \forall\ n \in [x\ s]:\ n \in names \Leftrightarrow s\,g(n).s\,z > 0.$$

2) Every non-empty segment n is a *total* function from its set of pages $[s\,g(n).s\,z]$ to the set of allocated blocks:

$$I_{st} = \forall\ n \in names:\ B(n) \subseteq blocks$$

197

```
1   type SEGMENTS =
2   class (generic XS, XP, XB: INTEGER > 0);
3     type S-NAME = 1 ... XS; P-NAME = 1 ... XP; B-NAME = 1 ... XB;
                                                      SIZE = 0 ... XP;
4       FUNC = ARRAY (P-NAME) of B-NAME;
5       S-DESCRIPTOR = RECORD SZ: SIZE; B: FUNC end;
6     var NAMES: RESOURCES (XS); BLOCKS: RESOURCES (XB);
7       SG: ARRAY (S-NAME) of S-DESCRIPTOR;
8     procedure NEW (Z: INTEGER) returns N: INTEGER signals NOV,
                                                      BSZ, BOV;
9       var M: INTEGER;
10      begin [(Z < 1) OR (Z > XP);  signal BSZ];
11        M := NAMES. GET [OV;  signal NOV];
12        SG (M). SZ := Z;
13        for I := 1 to Z do SG (M). B (I) := BLOCKS. GET [OV; HBOV];
14        N := M
15      end;
16      procedure DESTROY (N: INTEGER) signals BN;
17      begin [(N < 1) OR (N > XS) OR (SG (N).SZ = 0);  signal BN];
18        for I := 1 to SG (N).SZ do BLOCKS.RELEASE (SG (N).B (I));
19        SG (N).SZ := 0;
20        NAMES.RELEASE (N)
21      end;
22      procedure READ (N, P: INTEGER) returns B: INTEGER signals BN, BP;
23      begin [(N < 1) OR (N > XS) OR (SG (N).SZ = 0);  signal BN];
24        [(P < 1) OR (P > SG (N).SZ);  signal BP];
25        B := SG (N). B (P)
26      end;
27    begin %NAMES and BLOCKS do not need to be explicitly initialised %
28      for I := 1 to XS do SG (I). SZ := 0
29    end SEGMENTS
```

Fig. 6. An implementation of SEGMENTS

where

$$B(n) = \{s\,g(n).b(p)\,|\,1 \leq p \leq s\,g(n).s\,z\}$$

denotes the set of blocks of the segment with name n.

3) Every non empty segment is injective:

$$I_{si} = \forall\ n \in names{:}\ |B(n)| = s\,g(n).s\,z.$$

4) Only those physical blocks which are actually allocated to non-empty segments are recorded in the *BLOCKS* state variable:

$$I_{ba} = blocks \subseteq \bigcup_{n \in names} B(n).$$

5) Two distinct segments have disjoint sets of blocks:

$$I_{sd} = \forall\ n, m \in names: n \neq m \Rightarrow B(n) \cap B(m) = \{\ \}.$$

Let I_c be the conjunction of all the above constraints:

$$I_c = I_{sn}\ \&\ I_{st}\ \&\ I_{si}\ \&\ I_{ba}\ \&\ I_{sd}\ .$$

A proof that the initial internal state of *SEGMENTS* satisfies I_c and that any invocation of the *NEW*, *DESTROY* and *READ* operations preserves I_c is given in [6]. It follows by induction on the length of invocation sequences that I_c is a *concrete* (or *representation*) *invariant* [21] of the implementation of Fig. 6. The abstraction function A for *SEGMENTS* will be defined only on those internal states $c \in C$ which satisfy I_c (this partiality of A is not inconvenient since all the reachable internal states satisfy I_c). Let c be such a reachable internal state. The truth of $I_c(c)$ implies that for every $n \in names$ the relation

$$f(n) \subset [s\ g(n).s\ z] \times \{s\ g(n).b(p)|1 \leq p \leq s\ g(n).s\ z\}$$

defined by

$$\forall\ p \in [s\ g(n).s\ z]: (p, s\ g(n).b(p)) \in f(n)$$

is a total and injective function $f(n) \in nes$. We therefore can define the result of applying A to c to be that element of $[x\ s] \rightsquigarrow nes$ which has the domain $c(NAMES) = names$ and maps every $n \in names$ to $f(n)$:

$$\forall\ c \in C: I_c(c) \Rightarrow dom(A(c)) = names\ \&$$
$$\forall\ n \in names: dom(A(c)(n)) \equiv [s\ g(n).s\ z]\ \&$$
$$\forall\ p \in dom(A(c)(n)): A(c)(n)(p) \equiv s\ g(n).b(p).$$

Thus, all the internal states satisfying I_c correspond through A to possible abstract states of *SEGMENTS*:

$$\forall\ c \in C: I_c(c) \Rightarrow A(c) \in [x\ s] \rightsquigarrow nes.$$

We call such internal states *consistent* (with the abstraction we want them to represent).

3.5. General Correctness Criteria

In order to prove that the implementation of Fig. 6 is consistent with the specification of Fig. 5, we cannot directly apply the criteria given in Sect. 2.8, since at that stage we did not take into account the possible existence of representation invariants or partitioned exceptional domains. The verification conditions given there will now be generalised to cover also this case.

199

Let S be the set of abstract states specified for some data type T and C be the set of internal states of an implementation of T. If A is the abstraction function, then it is first necessary to ensure that every state satisfying the concrete invariant I_c is a *valid* [21] representation of some possible abstract state:

$$\forall\, c \in C\colon I_c(c) \Rightarrow A(c) \in S.$$

After initialisation, the internal state must be consistent with that specified:

(*VC0*) *constraints on generic parameters*
  $\Rightarrow wp(\text{``}INIT\text{''}, I_c(c) \,\&\, initial\text{-}value(A(c))).$

Let OP be an arbitrary operation of T specified by

$$E_1\colon pre(E_1) \to post(E_1), \ldots, E_k\colon pre(E_k) \to post(E_k), pre \to post$$

where $dom(post) = pre = \neg\, pre(E_1) \,\&\, \ldots \,\&\, \neg\, pre(E_k)$. Let $B(OP)$ be the body of the procedure implementing OP, *cpost* be its concrete standard postcondition and $cpre = wp(\text{``}B(OP)\text{''}, cpost)$ be the standard concrete precondition of OP. The verification conditions for correct standard behaviour ensure that whenever OP is invoked in its standard domain a concrete state transition consistent with that specified takes place:

(*VC1*) $I_c(c') \,\&\, pre(A(c')) \Rightarrow cpre(c')$
(*VC2*) $I_c(c') \,\&\, post(c', c) \Rightarrow I_c(c) \,\&\, post(A(c'), A(c)).$

Assume that for each specified exception E_i an exceptional construct is inserted in $B(OP)$ according to the (u) pattern of Sect. 2.5:

$$B(OP) = C1;\ C[P;\ H_i;\ \textbf{signal}\ E_i];\ C2$$

Let $cpost(E_i)$ be the concrete postcondition intended to hold before E_i is signalled and

$$cpre(E_i) = wp(\text{``}C1;\ C[P;\ H_i\text{''}, cpost(E_i))$$

be the corresponding concrete exceptional precondition. By the definition of $cpre(E_i)$ it follows that any invocation of OP in an internal state c' satisfying $cpre(E_i)$ leads to the exceptional termination of OP in a state satisfying $cpost(E_i)$. In order to prove the correct implementation of the exceptional effects specified for OP, it is necessary to ensure that whenever OP is invoked outside its abstract standard domain some specified exception is detected:

(*VCE1*) $I_c(c') \,\&\, \neg\, pre(A(c')) \Rightarrow (cpre(E_1) \vee \ldots \vee pre\ (E_k))(c').$

One has also to make sure that only an exception whose abstract precondition

200

was true at the invocation of OP can be signalled:

$$(VCE\,1')\quad I_c(c')\ \&\ cpre(E_i)(c') \Rightarrow pre(E_i)(A(c')).$$

(Remark: when the exceptional domain is not partitioned this condition is always satisfied.) Finally, it is necessary to ensure that the internal (exceptional) state transition produced when E_i is signalled is consistent with that specified:

$$(VCE\,2)\quad I_c(c')\ \&\ cpost(E_i)(c', c) \Rightarrow \dot{I}_c(c)\ \&\ post(E_i)(A\,(c'), A(c)).$$

A proof that the implementation of $SEGMENTS$ (Figs. 6, 7) is consistent with the specification of Fig. 5 is given in [6].

The above verification conditions ensure in particular that *any* reachable internal state is consistent: $(VC\,0)$ ensures that the initial state is consistent, $(VC\,1,$ $VCE\,1)$ ensure that whenever an operation is invoked in a consistent state then the only possible state transitions are those specified by $cpost$ or $cpost(E_i)$ and $(VC\,2, VCE\,2)$ ensure that all these state transitions preserve I_c.

The invariance of I_c over *any* sequence of operation invocations – even if some are exception occurrences – is essential for a data type implementation to behave in a predictable manner (an example in the next section shows that if an inconsistent state is reached after an exception occurrence not appropriately handled, then unpredictable behaviour, usually revealed by later exception detections, follows). Thus, a correct implementation of a data type T with total operations and exceptions is *robust* because its internal state consistency no longer depends on the assumption that the users will always invoke the operations of T within their standard domains, as was the case in most previous approaches to data abstraction in imperative languages [13, 21, 3, 12, 16, 9].

In order to achieve robustness, however, it is not required that exceptional constructs be inserted in programs wherever possible. The existence of invariant properties can be used to avoid unnecessary insertions. For example, in Fig. 6 we have not associated any handlers with the ILL exception of $RELEASE$ since the truth of I_c whenever $DESTROY$ is invoked guarantees that this exception cannot occur (for more details see [6]). If the $RELEASE$ operation of the $NAMES$ and $BLOCKS$ variables cannot be invoked from other programs than that of Fig. 6, then one can also remove the exceptional construct for ILL from the body of the $RELEASE$ procedure of these instances. The approach to exception handling presented here is of use when the known invariants are too weak to rule out possible exception occurrences. We therefore consider it to be complementary to those oriented towards proving the absence of exception occurrences.

3.6. Exception Detection

For an exception occurrence to be *detected*, it is necessary in principle that some (precise) run-time check evaluates to *true*. For example, an occurrence of the BSZ exception (Fig. 6) is detected if the boolean expression in line 10 evaluates to *true*. The value of this expression depends only on the state of the Z parameter and this state can be directly accessed in the context of the NEW procedure. The use of an encapsulation mechanism for data abstraction purposes may sometimes forbid direct access to the state of a variable belonging to an abstract type. For example the evaluation of the concrete precondition $|names'| = x \, s$ of NOV cannot be performed in the context of NEW since direct access to the internal state of $NAMES$ is prohibited in accordance with the 'information hiding principle'. However, by the semantic definition of GET we have

$$wp(\text{"}M := NAMES.GET[OV\text{"}, true) = |names'| = x \, s.$$

Thus, at the level of $SEGMENTS$, an occurrence of NOV is actually detected if the lower level exception OV is propagated by the statement $M := NAMES.$ GET in the NEW procedure, that is, if the handler of NOV in line 11 is invoked. Similarly, the loop in line 13 can signal an exception OV if the concrete precondition $|blocks'| + z > x \, b$ corresponding to $pre(BOV)$ was true at the invocation of NEW. Thus an occurrence of BOV is also detected as a result of the propagation of a lower level exception. A proof that the detection of the BSZ, NOV and BOV exceptions by the above means is precise is given in [6].

Exception propagation is a general technique which can be used to detect the occurrence of (higher level) exceptions in hierarchically structured systems. The general pattern is as follows:

procedure $OP1$ **signals** $E1$
begin
⋮
$OP[E; HE1]$
⋮
end

An invocation of a (higher level) operation $OP1$ in its exceptional domain $pre(E1)$ causes a lower level operation OP to be invoked in its exceptional domain $pre(E)$. Thus, the propagation of E in $OP1$ *coincides* with the detection of the higher level exception $E1$ in $OP1$. Although the handler $HE1$ of $E1$ is syntactically associated with the E exception label by using a (c) construct, it is essential to understand that its semantics (the exceptional state transition it performs) is determined by the specification of the $E1$ exceptional effect of $OP1$. Thus the phrase 'handler associated with' reflects a syntactic fact while the phrase 'handler of' reflects a semantic knowledge.

When an exception occurrence is detected (either by the evaluation of a run-time check or as a result of a lower level exception propagation) an *intermediate* internal state, not satisfying a representation invariant, may exist. For example when the occurrence of the BOV exception is detected by the exceptional termination of the **"for"** loop in line 13 Fig. 6, the internal state is

$$m \in names$$
$$s \, g(m).s \, z = z$$

$$s\,g(m).b(1) \in blocks$$
$$\vdots$$
$$s\,g(m).b(i-1) \in blocks$$
$$s\,g(m).b(i) = ?$$
$$\vdots$$
$$s\,g(m).b(z) = ?$$

where $i = x\,b - |blocks'|$ is the value of the loop counter when the handler *HBOV* of *BOV* is invoked (for more details see [6]). Clearly, such an internal state does not satisfy the I_{st} invariant defined in Sect. 3.4 and hence is *inconsistent*.

If an instance of a data type is left in an inconsistent internal state (because an exception occurrence is not appropriately handled), then further operation invocations can lead to unpredictable (i.e. unspecified) results and to later unanticipated exception detections. For example, if an instance of *SEGMENTS* were left in the above state, then during a next invocation of *READ* or *DE-STROY* with an actual parameter m, there would be a possibility of detecting either a language defined exception *UNINITIALISED* (when some variable $SG(m).B(j)$, $i \leq j \leq z$, is accessed) or an *ILL* exception (if the *RELEASE* operation on *BLOCKS* is invoked with such a parameter). Another possible outcome is that no exception is immediately detected, and incorrect state transitions continue to take place until the state of the system using *SEGMENTS* becomes seriously corrupted.

In order to avoid the occurrence of such dangerous situations, it is essential for the designer of a handler to know if an inconsistent state may exist when the handler is invoked. If that is the case, he should provide for the recovery of a consistent state (so that the *VCE 2* condition is satisfied). The need for such recovery actions is recognised in recent exception mechanism proposals: in [17] such actions are called "clean-up" actions and in [15] these are said to be "the last wishes of a procedure before disappearing". However, no precise guidelines for programming them are given. The next section is an attempt at clarifying this issue.

3.7. Recovery of Internal Consistent States

Assume that an operation *OP* specified for a data type T may signal an exception E and that a handler of E is inserted in the body of *OP* according to the (u) pattern of Sect. 2.5:

$$B(OP) = C\,1;\ C[P;\ H\,1;\ \textbf{signal}\ E];\ C\,2.$$

Assume also that, when *OP* is invoked, the internal state c' is consistent and when the occurrence of E is detected (i.e. $H\,1$ is invoked) the intermediate state i is inconsistent. The task of $H\,1$ is to change i into a consistent state c. The unit of internal state change will be considered to be the change of a simple variable, i.e. a variable whose type is not an *ARRAY* or *RECORD* structured type.

203

Variables belonging to such types will be considered to be aggregates of simple variables accessible through the selector functions specified for these types.

A set of simple state variables RS will be called a *recovery set* for the inconsistent state i which exists when E is detected, if by modifying the values that these variables have in i, a final state c such that $I_c(c)$ & $post(E)(A(c'), A(c))$ can be reached. In general there exist several RS for an exception detection. For example, the set of simple state variables $\{NAMES, BLOCKS, SG(m).SZ, SG(m).B(1), \ldots, SG(m).B(x\,p)\}$ is a recovery set for a BOV exception detection, since if the values $\{names', blocks', 0, 0, \ldots, 0\}$ are assigned to them, a state c such that $I_c(c)$ & $(A(c) = A(c'))$ can be reached. This is possible because the values of the I_c and A functions defined in Sect. 3.4 do not depend on the values of $SG(m).B(j)$, $\leq j \leq x\,p$, when $s\,g(m).s\,z = 0$. However, a decision that the handler $HBOV$ of BOV (Fig. 6, line 13) should recover this RS would not be the best, since too much work would be done. From a performance point of view, the most interesting recovery sets are those with the fewest elements.

A recovery set IS such that for any other recovery set RS: $|IS| \leq |RS|$ will be called an *inconsistency set*. Because of this minimality property, one can think of an inconsistency set as containing only those simple state variables which are 'really' inconsistent with respect to the I_c and A functions of T (inconsistency sets have been called "errors" in [19]). For a BOV exception detection there is a unique inconsistency set $IS = \{NAMES, BLOCKS, SG(m).SZ\}$. The handler $HBOV$ of BOV given in Fig. 7 recovers for the variables of this IS the values $\{names', blocks', 0\}$ before signalling the occurrence of BOV.

A proof that the final state c reached after the execution of $HBOV$ satisfies I_c & $(A(c) = A(c'))$ is given in [6].

If the decision is taken by the system designers that all the data types used to structure a system should have atomic operations, then two other kinds of recovery sets may be of interest. Let us define the *inconsistency closure IC* associated with the intermediate state i which exists when E is detected, to be the set of all simple state variables modified between the entry in OP and the detection of E. For a BOV exception detection, the inconsistency closure is $IC = \{NAMES, BLOCKS, SG(m).SZ, SG(m).B(1), \ldots, SG(m).B(i-1)\}$. As the NEW operation has been specified to be atomic, clearly IC is a recovery set, since if all the modified variables recover their previous values a state c identical to the initial c' is obtained and the $I_c(c)$ & $(A(c) = A(c'))$ property is trivially satisfied. The second kind of recovery set we want to mention is the crudest approximation one can imagine for an IS (an inconsistency closure is a better one). This approximation is obtained by taking the whole set of state variables with their respective previous values to form a *check-point CP* of the internal state c' which existed when OP was invoked.

```
13.1   %HBOV ≡ %for J := 1 to I − 1 do BLOCKS. RELEASE (SG (M). B (J));
13.2              SG (M). SZ := 0;  NAMES. RELEASE (M);
13.3              signal BOV
```

Fig. 7. The handler of the BOV exception

After the above discussion on recovery sets, we can now describe the task of a handler *HE* of an exception *E* as being to *recover* some *RS* before *signalling* *E*. Of course, if the state c in which the occurrence of *E* is detected already satisfies the $I_c(c)$ & $post(E)(c', c)$ predicate, no recovery action is necessary, that is, the *IS* associated with such an exception detection is empty.

If *post(E)* is not the identity state transition relation (*OP* is not atomic) then *forward recovery* [19] has to be used. The recovery of some *RS* is 'forward' if, after recovery, the final value v of at least some $V \in RS$ is different from its initial value v'. The determination of an *RS* (preferably an *IS*) for forward recovery requires knowledge of *post(E)*, I_c, *A*. Thus, handlers for forward recovery have to be *explicitly* inserted by humans. However, if the operations are intended to have an atomic behaviour, then the determination of either the *IC* or *CP* recovery sets can be performed independently of such knowledge and can be automatised. Check-pointing techniques have long been used for that. More recently, the idea of leaving the task of continuously updating the inconsistency closures associated with all potential exception detections to a recovery cache device has been proposed [14]. Automatic recovery of inconsistency closures or check-points is known as *backward recovery* [19]. More generally, a recovery action can be termed 'backward' if every variable V of the recovered *RS* is restored to its previous value v'. For example, the recovery action performed by *HBOV* is backward. Automatic backward recovery does more work than strictly necessary since in general $|IS| < |IC| < |CP|$) but this seems to be the price to be paid if the intention is to provide *default* exception handling for fault tolerance purposes [7].

Default exception handling attempts at providing a solution to the following problem: if the exceptional domain of some operation *OP* is not accurately identified by its designer, or the checks for detecting exception occurrences are not precise, then for some exception occurrences (if they are detected because of lower level propagated exceptions) there will be no explicitly provided exception handlers. The idea is then to force the invocation of a default handler able to recover an inconsistency closure or checkpoint. If subsequent masking attempts (e.g. invocation of alternate algorithms [14]) are not successful, then the 'unanticipated' acceptional state transition which occurs is identified for the invoker of *OP* by some *FAILURE* or *ERROR* predefined exception label. The aim of introducing such a label in a programming language is, on one hand, to guarantee the existence of a (default) exceptional continuation for every possible exception detection [5], and, on the other hand, to try and make non-total operations 'total' in the following sense:

$$\ldots, E_i: pre(E_i) \rightarrow post(E_i), \ldots, FAILURE:$$

$$\neg (\bigvee_{i=1}^{n} pre(E_i) \vee pre) \rightarrow s = s', \quad pre \rightarrow post.$$

A general model for explicit [17, 15] and default [14] exception handling in hierarchies of data abstractions is presented in [7]. The definitions introduced in this paper are used there to show the unity exists between these complementary exception handling techniques, developed independently for the same purpose: the production of robust software systems.

4. Conclusion

This paper has investigated the problems of specifying and handling the exceptions inherent in the data types which exist in, or may be added to, imperative languages supporting data abstraction and exception handling [5, 17, 15]. Our goal was to define data type operations in such a way as to ensure that the following conditions are satisfied. First, exception occurrences should not mean program abortion. Second, the semantics of the operations of a data type should be well-defined when exceptions occur. Third, this semantics should be defined so as to ensure that, in the verification conditions obtainable in program proofs, the operators of the specification language are always applied to elements of their domains (i.e. the "error terms" studied in [10] are never generated). Another goal has been the achievement of a proper separation between standard and exceptional aspects of program behaviour. In that sense, we consider the concept of an exception to be a useful software structuring tool, which should take its place alongside such established structuring concepts like procedures, parameters, processes, etc.

An approach similar to that presented in this paper, but using a partial correctness semantic framework is presented in [18]. The use of such a framework ensures that, if an operation invocation does not lead to an infinite loop or to an unanticipated exception detection, the specified standard and exceptional effects are correctly provided. Our interest was in robustness properties. We therefore have used the stronger predicate transformer semantic framework introduced in [2]. Present verification systems use partial correctness programming logics, and the ability to use them in proving the partial correctness of the standard and exceptional algorithms of operations may well counterbalance the fact that such verification tools do not provide any guarantee of robustness. The question of how to construct verification systems able to guarantee the robustness of the verified programs is a matter of future research. The ever increasing needs for highly available and reliable computer systems may well make the availability of such tools a necessity.

Acknowledgements. The author would like to thank E. Best, P. Cousot, S. Gerhart, J. Horning, C. Jones, S. Krakowiak, J. Mitchell, B. Randell, J. Rushby and J. Thatcher for discussions valuable in clarifying the ideas presented in this paper. The reported research has been successively sponsored by the French National Center for Scientific Research and by the U.K. Science Research Council.

References

1. Abrial, J. R.: The Specification Language Z — Syntax and Semantics. Programming Research Group, Oxford University, 1980
2. Best, E., Cristian, F.: Systematic Detection of Exception Occurrences. Sci. Comput. Progr. **1** (1), 115–155, North Holland Pub. Comp. (1981). (Also Chap. 3)
3. Björner, D.: Formalisation of Data Base Models. In: Abstract Software Specification. D. Björner (ed.), Lecture Notes in Comp. Sci., pp. 144–215 (1979) Springer Berlin-Heidelberg-New York
4. Broy, M., Wirsing, M.: Initial versus Terminal Algebra Semantics for Partially Defined Abstract Types. TUM-I8018, Technical University Munich, 1980

5. Cristian, F.: Le Traitement des Exceptions dans les Programmes Modulaires. Doctoral Thesis, University of Grenoble, 1979
6. Cristian, F.: Robust Data Types. Technical Report 170, Computing Laboratory, University of Newcastle upon Tyne, 1981
7. Cristian, F.: Exception Handling and Software Fault Tolerance. IEEE Transact. Comput. C-31 (6), 531 – 540 (1982). (Also Chap. 3)
8. Dijkstra, E. W.: A Discipline of Programming. New York: Prentice Hall, 1976
9. Gerhart, S. L., et al.: An Overview of AFFIRM – a Specification and Verification System, Proc. IFIP80 Congress, Tokyo, 1980
10. Goguen, J. A.: Abstract Errors for Abstract Data Types. In: Formal Description of Programming Concepts. Neuhold, E. J. (ed.) North Holland, pp. 492 – 525 (1978)
11. Goguen, J. A., Thatcher, J. W., Wagner, E. G.: An Initial Algebra Approach of the Specification, Correctness and Implementation of Abstract Data Types. In: Current Trends Progr. Methodology. Yeh, R. T. (ed.) New York: Prentice-Hall, pp. 80 – 149 (1978)
12. Guttag, J., Horning, J. J.: Formal Specification as a Design Tool. Proc. 7th ACM Symp. Principles Progr. Lang., Las Vegas, 1980
13. Hoare, C. A. R.: Proof of Correctness of Data Representations. Acta Informat 1 (4), 271 – 281 (1972)
14. Horning, J. J., Lauer, H. C., Melliar-Smith, P. M., Randell, B.: A Program Structure for Error Detection and Recovery. Proc. Conf. Operat. Syst. Theor. Pract. Aspects, IRIA, (reprinted in Lecture Notes in Comput. Sci. Vol. 16, Springer) (1974). (Also Chap. 2)
15. Ichbiah, J., et al.: Rationale for the Design of the ADA Programming Language. SIGPLAN Notices 14 (6), (1979)
16. Jones, C. B.: Software Development: A Rigorous Approach. New York: Prentice-Hall, 1980
17. Liskov, B. H., Snyder, A.: Exception Handling in CLU. IEEE Trans. Softw. Eng. SE-5 (6), 546 – 558 (1979)
18. Luckham, D. C., Polak, W.: ADA Exception Handling: An Axiomatic Approach. ACM Trans. Progr. Lang. Syst. 2 (2), 225 – 233 (1980)
19. Randell, B., Lee, P.-A., Treleaven, P. C.: Reliability Issues in Computing System Design. Comput. Surveys 10 (2), 123 – 165 (1978)
20. Stoy, J. E.: Denotational Semantics: The Scott-Strachey Approach to Programming Language Theory. Cambridge: MIT Press, 1977
21. Wulf, W. A., London, R. L., Shaw, M.: An Introduction to the Construction and Verification of Alphard programs. IEEE Trans. Softw. Eng. SE-2 (4), 253 – 265 (1976)
22. Zilles, S. N.: An Introduction to Data Algebras. In: Abstract Software Specifications. Björner, D. (ed.). Lecture Notes in Comput. Sci., pp. 248 – 272 (1979), Springer Berlin, Heidelberg, New York

Systematic Detection of Exception Occurrences

E. BEST and F. CRISTIAN

1. Introduction

In proving the correctness of a program, a common stratagem is to consider only initial states in which certain properties are satisfied. For example, in the knowledge that a given array contains at least one positive element, one might prove a program for finding, say, the first positive element in that array, even though the program may otherwise (i.e. if the array does not contain any positive elements) lead to unpredictable results.

In practice there is however a strong demand for 'robust' software, having a well-defined behaviour even in circumstances in which certain initial assumptions are no longer true. Such 'exceptional' circumstances can occur whenever the inputs of the program cannot be guaranteed to have the properties they may be expected to have.

An example of this is a compiler where a syntactically well-formed program is expected as standard input, but where it cannot be guaranteed that all input programs are indeed well-formed. Another example would be a program requesting the exclusive use of a resource, expecting that at least one resource is free. In both cases provisions are needed for the treatment of unexpected (or exceptional) input. The need for a theory which can provide a basis for the systematic identification, detection and handling of exceptions has been expressed several times in the literature [7, 14]. This paper explores ways of adapting previously developed semantic and correctness theories of programs [3, 4, 6, 9, 12] for the design of robust programs.

We focus specifically on two questions. Firstly, given a program and its specification, how can one characterise its standard and exceptional input domains? Secondly, how can one design appropriate run-time checks for the detection of any possible exception occurrence? We shall not deal with the question of actually handling an exception once it has been detected; for such a discussion the reader is referred to [2] and [11].

Once the exceptional domain of a program is found, nothing would be easier in principle than to test at the beginning of the program whether or not the initial state falls into the exceptional domain, thus making the program robust. However frequently such a test would of necessity duplicate some of the work performed by the program itself, and it may therefore be much more natural and economical to insert tests within, or even at the end of the program.

For instance, in order to test whether or not two given input values violate a bound restriction when added, one has to actually add them together. Similarly, it is the duty of a substantial part of a compiler to check whether or not an input program is well-formed, and it would be ridiculous to separate this checking entirely from the other tasks of the compiler. In this paper we derive verification conditions for robustness checks to be inserted anywhere in the program, as well as heuristic guidelines for choosing the place where to put such tests.

The paper is organised as follows. A mathematical framework integrating and generalising relational semantics, predicate transformer semantics and program correctness criteria is described in Sect. 2, where our first question concerning exceptional input domains is also discussed. In Sect. 3 we turn to our second question concerning the design of appropriate run-time checks for the detection of exception occurrences.

Sections 2.1 and 2.2 contain brief descriptions, respectively, of our programming language and our specification language. In Sects. 2.3–2.5 three equivalent types of semantics are defined, all of which are useful in deriving robustness tests. In Sect. 3.1 we consider the sequential composition of two programs and the tests that can be inserted between them. In Sect. 3.2 we discuss the circumstances in which such tests would have to involve the initial values of variables, and in Sect. 3.3 we go on to consider checks in conditionals and iterative statements. Finally, in Sect. 3.4 we apply all of this to the simplified but still practical example of a bracket matching program.

2. Intended and Actual Meanings of Programs

2.1. Programming Language

We use a modified version of guarded commands [4]. Our programs have the following general form:

$$\langle\text{program}\rangle :: = \langle\text{variable declarations}\rangle; \langle\text{command}\rangle.$$

We assume that to every variable there is associated a specific set of values which it may take. We define the state of a program to be a mapping from the variables used in the program to their values. The set of all possible states is denoted by S.

We use the following (hopefully self-explanatory) syntax for commands:

$$\langle\text{command}\rangle :: = \text{skip} \mid \text{abort} \mid \langle\text{assign}\rangle \mid \langle\text{if}\rangle \mid \langle\text{do}\rangle \mid$$
$$\langle\text{command}\rangle; \langle\text{command}\rangle$$
$$\langle\text{assign}\rangle :: = \langle\text{var}\rangle := \langle\text{expr}\rangle$$
$$\langle\text{if}\rangle :: = \textbf{if} \langle\text{bool}_1\rangle \rightarrow \langle\text{command}\rangle \square \ldots \square \langle\text{bool}_n\rangle \rightarrow \langle\text{command}\rangle \textbf{ fi}$$
$$\langle\text{do}\rangle :: = \textbf{do} \langle\text{bool}\rangle \rightarrow \langle\text{command}\rangle \textbf{ od}.$$

We consider only deterministic programs (i.e. in $\langle\text{if}\rangle$, $\langle\text{bool}_1\rangle$, ..., $\langle\text{bool}_n\rangle$ are mutually exclusive) but some of the formulae that follow remain valid in the non-deterministic case.

As we are interested in exceptional effects, we specifically allow expressions to be partial rather than total functions of variables. For instance,

$$x := x + 1$$

may be undefined if $x = \text{MAXINT}$ initially. For any state s, variable x and expression E we therefore introduce a predicate

defined (x, E, s)

to denote the fact that in state s, the evaluation of E will lead to a value that lies within the value domain of x. This predicate will be used in the semantic definition of our language in Appendix A.2.

2.2. Specifications

We define the specification G (for 'goal') of a program as a relation

$$G \subseteq S \times S \tag{1}$$

over the state space S. G describes the intended effect of the program, the understanding being that for an initial state $s' \in S$, $(s', s) \in G$ if s could be a corresponding final state.

A specification may be non-deterministic in that several final states may correspond to a single initial state. We call G 'undefined' for initial states to which no final state corresponds, and we define the domain of G as the set of initial states for which G is defined (for notation see Appendix A.1):

$$\text{dom}(G) \equiv \{s' \in S \mid s' \, G \neq \emptyset\}. \tag{2}$$

In practice a specification is not usually given by enumerating its member pairs, but rather by its characteristic binary predicate which for reasons of simplicity we also denoted by G:

$$G : S \times S \rightarrow \{\text{true, false}\},$$
$$G(s', s) = \text{true} \Leftrightarrow (s', s) \in G.$$

A specification can make reference to the value of a program variable, say x, in the initial state s' and in the final state s. In order to simplify the notation, throughout the paper we adopt the convention of writing x' instead of $s'(x)$ to denote the initial value of x, and x instead of $s(x)$ to refer to the final value of x.

We use binary predicates involving both primed and unprimed variables in an analogous way in which unary predicates are used in [9] and [4]. The difference is that the former represent relations over the state space while the latter represent subsets of the state space. A unary predicate can be seen as a special case of a binary predicate, involving either only primed variables ('precondition') or only unprimed variables ('postcondition').

As an example, assume that a program for the management of N resources (e.g. disk blocks) has to be written, where $N \geq 1$. The two services the program is to provide are: ALLOCATE some free resource and RELEASE a previously allocated resource. Suppose the variables are

> **var** I: integer;
> A: **array** $(0 \ldots N - 1)$ **of** $0 \ldots 1$,

and that for $0 \leq j \leq N - 1$, the jth resource is free iff $A[j] = 0$.

If the intended effect of the ALLOCATE command is to assign to the variable I the name of a previously free resource then the (non-deterministic!) specification of ALLOCATE can be described by the following binary predicate:

$$G(\text{ALLOCATE}) \equiv (0 \leq I \leq N - 1) \ \& \ (A'[I] = 0) \ \& \ (A[I] = 1). \tag{3}$$

All initial states satisfying

$$\exists j: 0 \leq j \leq N - 1 \ \& \ A'[j] = 0 \tag{4}$$

have at least one corresponding final state making (3) true; and conversely, if (4) does not hold initially, then (3) cannot be made true. In other words, (4) is (the characteristic unary predicate of) the domain of $G(\text{ALLOCATE})$. Input states violating (4) (i.e. states in which no resource is free) require exceptional treatment by the ALLOCATE procedure.

2.3. Relational Semantics

Once the goal of a program has been stated as its specification, one has to compose it from the available primitives and hope − or prove − that it realises that goal. We define the actual meaning of a program c again as a relation

$$R(c) \subseteq S \times S \tag{5}$$

over the state space. $R(c)$ can be defined by induction on the syntactic structure of c using the semantic clauses given in Appendix A.2.

Our interpretation of $R(c)$ is that c, started in an initial state s', must terminate in some $s \in s' R(c)$. If it may fail to terminate when started in s', then $s' R(c) = \emptyset$ [13]. Perhaps this understanding appears unbecoming in that possible non-termination, infinite looping and aborting are all put into the same 'bag' $s' R(c) = \emptyset$. However, as we shall see it is perfectly possible to base our formalism on this understanding which is related to the wp formalism of [4], as shown below in Sect. 2.4.

As already mentioned, we consider only deterministic programs. That is, we impose on $R(c)$ the condition

$$R^{-1}(c) \circ R(c) \subseteq \text{Id} \qquad (6)$$

(see Appendix A.1). Thus, for deterministic c, $s' R(c) s$ if and only if c, when started in s', terminates in s.

As an example, consider the program

```
ALLOCATE1 ≡ I := 0;
            do (I ≤ N − 1) & (A[I] = 1) → I := I + 1 od;
            A[I] := 1,
```

Fig. 1

which is supposed to implement the specification (3) above. In order to show this, one has to relate the concrete meaning $R(\text{ALLOCATE}1)$ to the intended meaning $G(\text{ALLOCATE})$. One has to show that whenever the intended goal can be achieved a priori (i.e. (4) holds initially) then $R(\text{ALLOCATE}1)$ actually yields a final state satisfying (3).

In general a command c will be said to implement a specification G iff

$$\forall s' \in \text{dom}(G): \emptyset \subset s' R(c) \subseteq s' G. \qquad (7)$$

That is, for all inputs s' in the domain of G the program terminates ($\emptyset \subset s' R(c)$) and produces a final state satisfying G ($s' R(c) \subseteq s' G$). (7) corresponds to what is known as 'total correctness' [12].

The definition (7) is weak in the sense that it allows a deterministic program such as ALLOCATE1 to implement a non-deterministic specification such as $G(\text{ALLOCATE})$. It is also weak in the sense that nothing is required of the behaviour of c outside the domain of G. We show in the next section how to prove that ALLOCATE1 implements the specification (3).

The next two sections introduce backward and forward semantics (the latter being a generalisation of the relational semantics just defined). We need both of these semantics in the determination of the run-time tests to be inserted in a program.

2.4. Backward Specification-Transformer Semantics

The well-known process of "backsubstituting a postcondition through the text of a program" [4] in order to derive properties of the program can readily be generalised for specifications as defined in Sect. 2.2. The idea is to use relations over the state space not only as a means of globally describing a program c, but also as a means of describing the effect that components of c must have in order to ensure that c will indeed accomplish the overall goal.

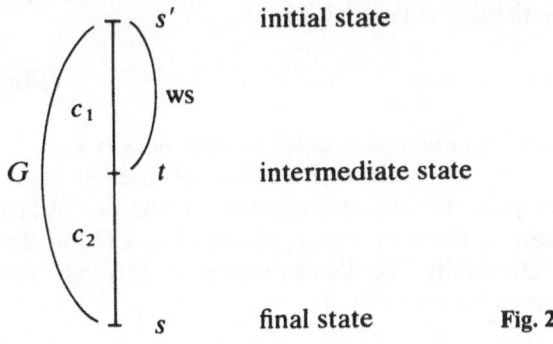

s'	initial state	
t	intermediate state	
s	final state	Fig. 2

For instance, if c is sequentially composed of c_1 and c_2 (see Fig. 2), one is interested in the intermediate specification of c_1 needed to ensure that c_2 will accomplish the goal G. In this situation we define the 'weakest' specification for c_1 which guarantees that G is implemented by $c = c_1; c_2$ is a relation $ws(c_2, G) \subseteq S \times S$ satisfying

$$s' \, ws(c_2, G) \, t \Leftrightarrow \emptyset \subset t \, R(c_2) \subseteq s' G. \tag{8}$$

An initial state s' and an intermediate state t thus stand in relation $ws(c_2, G)$ iff c_2, when started in t, terminates in some final state s satisfying the global goal $s' G$.

To see that $ws(c, G)$ as defined in (8) generalises the wp (weakest precondition) semantics of [4], let $X \subseteq S$ be a subset of the state space and define

$$wp(c, X) = \{s \in S \mid \emptyset \subset s \, R(c) \subseteq X\} \tag{9}$$

(compare also [13]). Our interpretation of $R(c)$ implies that $wp(c, X)$ contains all initial states guaranteeing the termination of c in a state in X, which is precisely the interpretation of the wp operator in [4]. The connection between ws and wp can then be expressed as

$$wp(c, \operatorname{cod}(G)) = \operatorname{cod}(ws(c, G)).$$

What is different is that in our definition (8) both the second argument of ws and ws itself are considered binary rather than unary predicates.

The operator ws has properties similar to those of wp. From (8) one derives

$$ws(c, \emptyset) = \emptyset, \tag{10a}$$

$$ws(c, G_1 \cap G_2) = ws(c, G_1) \cap ws(c, G_2), \tag{10b}$$

and for deterministic programs satisfying (6) one also has

$$\text{ws}(c, G_1 \cup G_2) = \text{ws}(c, G_1) \cup \text{ws}(c, G_2). \tag{10c}$$

The ws semantics of our programming language is given in Appendix A.2.

As an example of its use we prove the correctness of the program ALLOCATE 1 (Fig. 1) with respect to its specification G(ALLOCATE) (formula (3) in Sect. 2.2). This can be done by writing G(ALLOCATE) at the end of the program and 'mechanically' backsubstituting it through the program using the rules of Appendix A.2 (see Fig. 3).

0	$\{\exists j: (0 \leq j \leq N-1) \,\&\, (A'[j]=0) \,\&\, (A[j]=0)\}$
1	$I := 0;$
2	$\{\exists j: (I \leq j \leq N-1) \,\&\, (A'[j]=0) \,\&\, (A[j]=0)\}$
3	$\textbf{do}\,(I \leq N-1) \,\&\, (A[I]=1) \to I := I+1\,\textbf{od};$
4	$\{(0 \leq I \leq N-1) \,\&\, (A'[I]=0)\}$
5	$A[I] := 1$
6	$\{(0 \leq I \leq N-1) \,\&\, (A'[I]=0) \,\&\, (A[I]=1)\} = G(\text{ALLOCATE})$

Fig. 3

In each step of this backsubstitution one obtains from a given binary predicate a new binary predicate, again containing a mixture of primed and unprimed quantities; in fact, if c denotes the statement in line k in Fig. 3 and G denotes the specification in line $k+1$, then the specification in line $k-1$ equals $\text{ws}(c, G)$.

When the backsubstitution has come to an end (i.e. in line 0) one can identify initial and 'current' states, simply by 'priming' all unprimed variables. By this identification one obtains a unary predicate, namely the characteristic predicate of the set

$$\text{st\_dom}(c, G) \equiv \{s' \in S \mid s' \,\text{ws}(c, G)\,s'\} \tag{11a}$$

containing precisely those initial states for which c is guaranteed to terminate in a final state satisfying G.

The set (11a) is by definition (8) a subset of dom (G). All initial states s' outside st_dom (c, G), i.e. in

$$\text{ex\_dom}(c, G) \equiv S \backslash \text{st\_dom}(c, G) \tag{11b}$$

must be treated as exceptional w.r.t. the given specification G and program c. We therefore call st_dom (c, G) the 'standard domain' or the 'implementation domain' of c with respect to G, and its complement, i.e. ex_dom (c, G), is called the 'exceptional domain'.

The set $st\_dom(c, G)$ equals the domain of G iff c implements G as defined in formula (7); formally,

$$c \text{ implements } G \Leftrightarrow dom(G) = st\_dom(c, G) \tag{12}$$

which can easily be proved from the definitions. In our example (Fig. 3), if 'priming' is actually applied to the specification in line 0, we obtain the characteristic predicate (4) of the domain of G; which, by (12), proves the correctness of ALLOCATE 1.

2.5. Forward Specification-Transformer Semantics

Instead of asking for the weakest specification for c_1 which guarantees that $c = c_1; c_2$ implements some specification G, one could also ask for the strongest transition (abbreviated 'st') relation which can be derived for c by knowing that the component command c_1 implements a specification G_1 (see Fig. 4):

$$s' \, st(c_2, G_1) \, s \equiv \exists t : s' \, G_1 \, t \ \& \ t \, R(c_2) \, s$$

i.e.,

$$st(c_2, G_1) = G_1 \circ R(c_2). \tag{13}$$

The strongest 'post'-specification of G_1 is thus simply the relational composition of G_1 and $R(c_2)$.

Using (13), the correctness of c with respect to G can be established by proving that

$$\forall s' \in dom(G): \emptyset \subset s' \, st(c, \text{Id}) \subseteq s' \, G. \tag{14}$$

For example, by using the rules for st (see Appendix A.2), the fact that ALLOCATE 1 implements $G(\text{ALLOCATE})$ can be established by 'pushing'

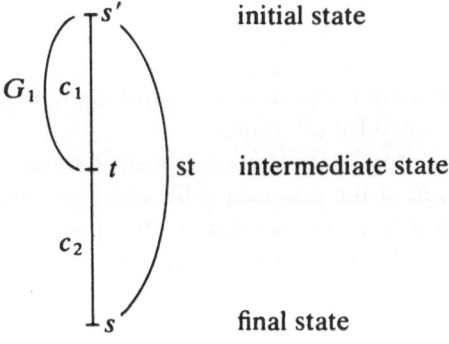

initial state

st   intermediate state

final state   Fig. 4

215

$$
\begin{array}{ll}
0 & \{\text{Id}\} \\
1 & \left(\begin{array}{l} I := 0; \end{array}\right. \\
2 & \{I = 0\} \\
3 & \left(\mathbf{do}\ (I \leqslant N-1)\ \&\ (A[I]=1) \to I := I+1\ \mathbf{od}; \right. \\
4 & \{(I = N\ \mathbf{or}\ (0 \leqslant I \leqslant N-1\ \&\ A'[I]=0\ \&\ A[I]=0))\ \& \\
  & \quad (\forall j: 0 \leqslant j < I \Rightarrow (A'[j]=1\ \&\ A[j]=1))\} \\
5 & A[I] := 1 \\
6 & \{(0 \leqslant I \leqslant N-1)\ \&\ (A'[I]=0)\ \&\ (A[I]=1)\ \& \\
  & \quad (\forall j: 0 \leqslant j < I \Rightarrow (A'[j]=1\ \&\ A[j]=1))\}
\end{array}
$$

Fig. 5

the relation Id forward through the program as shown in Fig. 5. As the last relation is non-empty and implies $G(\text{ALLOCATE})$, we have established again that the command ALLOCATE 1 correctly implements its specification. We shall in the next section use a similar method to derive exceptional tests.

3. Run-Time Checks for the Detection of Exception Occurrences

3.1. Preciseness of Run-Time Tests

Consider a specification G and a program c. We have seen that (whether or not c implements G) the set of input states S can be partitioned into the set of 'standard inputs' st_dom (c, G) on the one hand and its complementary 'exceptional domain' ex_dom (c, G) on the other hand (cf. formulae (11a) and (11b) in Sect. 2.4). For inputs in the standard domain (which may be empty), c does implement G whereas for inputs in the exceptional domain (which may of course also be empty), c may either not terminate properly or end up in a final state not satisfying G. Moreover, if (and only if) the standard domain equals the entire domain of G then c does correctly implement G, as defined in formula (7) in Sect. 2.3.

Exception handling aims at extending a program c in such a way that whenever c is started in an initial state outside the standard domain, then during its execution a specially designed piece of program (an 'exception handler') becomes activated. We call such extended programs 'robust' or 'tolerant to exception occurrences' [1]. The main purpose of exception handling is thus to make programs 'total', or well-defined for all inputs.

In order to find out whether or not the input state is exceptional, there has to be a test somewhere during the execution of the program. This test does not necessarily have to take place at the beginning. For instance, in the program ALLOCATE 1 (see Fig. 1), rather than to test the exceptional condition

$$
\forall j: 0 \leq j \leq N-1 \Rightarrow A'[j] = 1 \tag{15}
$$

at the beginning of the program, it is more economical, as well as more natural, to place the test after the loop as follows:

```
1    I := 0;
2    do (I ≤ N − 1) & (A[I] = 1) → I := I + 1 od;
3    [I > N − 1 → 'exception handler']
4    A[I] := 1
```
Fig. 6

The meaning of the exceptional clause in line 3 it that the Boolean expression $I > N - 1$ is evaluated and if found false, execution continues with the next statement; if found true, control is given to the exception handler whose exact working does not concern us here. We do not worry either about what precisely "economical" means in the context of tests; intuitively, one might say that predicates not involving quantifiers (such as $I > N - 1$ in Fig. 6) should normally be considered as more economical than predicates which do involve quantifiers (such as (15)).

We can easily convince ourselves that in line 3 in Fig. 6, the test "$I > N - 1$" evaluates to 'true' if and only if the initial state lies in the exceptional domain (15). For this reason we call it a 'precise run-time test': it activates the exception handler when, and only when, an exception occurs.

In this section we characterise the precise tests that can be inserted in a program. It is important that such tests be precise because if they are too strong then it is possible that no exception handler is activated even though the input is exceptional, and if they are too weak then certain acceptable input states may find themselves being treated as cases of failure.

Before defining precise tests formally, we make a few observations. The first is that the requirement for a test to be precise may not uniquely determine that test. For instance, the line

$[I = N \rightarrow$ 'exception handler'],

if inserted instead of line 3 in Fig. 6, would also 'catch' precisely all exceptional inputs. This is due to the fact that the relation $I < N + 1$ is part of the strongest postcondition after the loop (see Fig. 5).

Our next observation is that not all locations in a program are equally appropriate in supporting exception detection. For instance, there is no way of catching an exception *after* the least assignment $A[I] := 1$ in Fig. 6, because the exception will by this time already have led to an array bound violation when the expression $A[I]$ is evaluated in line 4 with $I = N$.

Our third (and last) observation is that if one allows tests to refer also to the initial state rather than just to the current state then in some cases exceptional tests could be inserted where otherwise they could not. As an example, we consider the following alternative implementation of G(ALLO-CATE) which differs from ALLOCATE 1 in the loop condition:

217

```
ALLOCATE2 ≡ I := 0;
          do (I < N − 1) & (A[I] = 1) → I := I + 1 od;
          [A[I] = 1 → 'exception handler']
          A[I] := 1
```
Fig. 7

Again, $A[I] = 1$ can be shown to be a precise exceptional test. By allowing the test to make reference to initial values (by using primes) one can in ALLOCATE2 (in contrast to the previous program) insert a precise test at the end of the program:

```
I := 0;
do (I < N − 1) & (A[I] = 1) → I := I + 1 od;
A[I] := 1;
[A'[I] = 1 → 'exception handler']
```
Fig. 8

Although in this example there is little point in doing so, for generality and uniformity we allow tests to refer to the initial states, as advocated, for example, in [10]. Thus, we define a test T formally as a binary predicate

$$T: S \times S \rightarrow \{\text{true, false}\} \tag{16}$$

where the first S refers to the initial state and the second S to the current state. We return to the question of binary versus unary tests in the next section.

Consider now a general sequential decomposition of a program c:

$$c = c_1; c_2.$$

We wish to determine,

(a) whether a precise exceptional test can be inserted between c_1 and c_2, and
(b) if so, to characterise the set of all such tests.

Question (a) is easy to answer. It has to be ensured that for every exceptional initial state, control actually reaches the point between c_1 and c_2 (unless there are different kinds of exceptions, a case which will be discussed below); in other words the following relation must hold:

$$\text{ex\_dom}(c, G) \subseteq \text{wp}(c_1, S) \tag{17}$$

(where wp is as defined in (9)).

As to question (b), let T denote the test to be inserted between c_1 and c_2. We call T a 'precise exceptional test' iff the following holds:

$$\forall (s', t) \in R(c_1) : s' T t \Leftrightarrow \textbf{not } s' \text{ ws}(c_2, G) t. \tag{18}$$

218

Relation (18) expresses formally our intuitive understanding that the test T should evaluate to 'true' if and only if the pair of states (s', t) under consideration cannot be guaranteed to lead to a final state satisfying G.

With the two definitions

$$T_s \equiv R(c_1) \ \& \ \textbf{not} \ \text{ws}(c_2, G), \tag{19a}$$

$$T_w \equiv \textbf{not} \ R(c_1) \lor \textbf{not} \ \text{ws}(c_2, G) \tag{19b}$$

formula (18) can be rewritten as the equation

$$R(c_1) \ \& \ T = T_s \tag{20}$$

and (20) can further be equivalently reformulated as a set of two implications

$$T_s \Rightarrow T, \tag{21a}$$

$$T \Rightarrow T_w. \tag{21b}$$

(21a) and (21b) imply that the set of precise tests equals the sublattice between T_s and T_w of the lattice of binary predicates, so that one is justified in calling T_s the 'strongest precise test' and T_w the 'weakest precise test'. Fig. 9 is a representation of the relationship between T_s and T_w.

The formulae (21) can be interpreted as follows. Formula (21a) means that all pairs of (initial state, current state) such that c_2 is not guaranteed to establish G must imply the truth of T; thus T must be weak enough actually to activate an exception handler in case of an exception occurrence. T_s itself may be too strong in the sense that too much is tested (an example of this will follow). Formula (21b), on the other hand, means that the truth of T must ioply either something impossible (**not** $R(c_1)$) or that c_2 cannot be guaranteed to establish G; thus T must be strong enough not to treat any acceptable state as an exception. T_w itself may be too weak in the sense that it may 'catch' a lot of exceptional situations which never occur (again, an example follows).

Because $\text{st}(c, \text{Id}) = R(c)$ for all programs c (see formula (13) in Sect. 2.5), a general method of deriving precise tests T is to backsubstitute (as exemplified

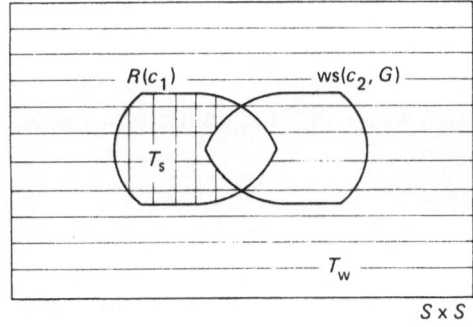

Fig. 9

in Sect. 2.4) the specification G through c_2 up to the point where T is to be inserted and simultaneously to push (as exemplified in Sect. 2.5) the relation Id forward through c_1 up to the same point. Where the two meet we can form their difference (19a) to derive the strongest test T_s, or the union (19b) to derive the weakest test T_w, and we can use (20) as a verification condition for an arbitrary test T to be precise.

We illustrate this method on our example. Let us choose the following partitioning of ALLOCATE 1:

$$
\begin{aligned}
c_1 &\equiv I := 0; \\
&\quad \textbf{do } (I \leq N - 1) \,\&\, (A[I] = 1) \rightarrow I := I + 1 \textbf{ od}; \\
&\quad (*) \\
c_2 &\equiv A[I] := 1
\end{aligned}
$$

Fig. 10

and assume a test is to be inserted at point $(*)$.

We first note that (17) is satisfied because c_1 always terminates. We then derive (compare Fig. 3, line 4 and Fig. 5, line 4):

$$
\begin{aligned}
R(c_1) &= \mathrm{st}(c_1, \mathrm{Id}) \\
&= (I = N \textbf{ or } (0 \leq I \leq N - 1 \,\&\, A'[I] = 0 \,\&\, A[I] = 0)) \,\& \\
&\quad (\forall j: 0 \leq j < I \Rightarrow (A'[j] = 1 \,\&\, A[j] = 1))
\end{aligned} \tag{22a}
$$

$$
\mathrm{ws}(c_2, G(\text{ALLOCATE})) = (0 \leq I \leq N - 1) \,\&\, (A'[I] = 0). \tag{22b}
$$

States satisfying (22a) but not (22b) are described by

$$
T_s \equiv (I = N) \,\&\, (\forall j: 0 \leq j \leq N - 1 \Rightarrow (A'[j] = 1 \,\&\, A[j] = 1)) \tag{23a}
$$

and states violating either (22a) or (22b) by

$$
\begin{aligned}
T_w \equiv{}& (I < 0) \vee (I > N - 1) \vee (A'[I] = 1) \vee (A[I] = 1) \vee \\
& (\exists j: 0 \leq j \leq I \,\&\, A'[j] = 0 \,\&\, A[j] = 0).
\end{aligned} \tag{23b}
$$

Examining (23) we see that both in T_s and in T_w some terms are redundant. The second term in T_s, for instance, is implied by the first term "$I = N$" in combination with (22a). Similarly, (22a) implies that the first term in T_w can never be true. All in all, we have thus shown that $I = N$ and $I > N - 1$ are precise tests, and that $I = N$ is the strongest non-redundant precise test that can be inserted at point $(*)$ in Fig. 10.

We also mention the following theorem whose proof is omitted for reasons of brevity. For deterministic programs,

$$
T_s = \mathrm{st}(c_1, \mathrm{Id} \,\&\, \textbf{not } \mathrm{ws}(c, G)). \tag{24}
$$

This means that instead of simultaneously backsubstituting G and pushing Id forward until they meet between c_1 and c_2, one can also backsubstitute G to the beginning of the whole program, negate the resulting predicate, identify 'initial state' and 'current state' (Id & ...), and push the result forward through c_1. This may sometimes be simpler than the other method.

We end this section with two remarks. Firstly we note that the condition (17) gives an indication about the location to choose for T. Since $st\_(c, G) \subseteq wp(c_1, S)$ by definition, (17) means nothing less than that c_1 is required to terminate for *all* inputs. Thus the tests must not be inserted 'too late' in the program. Note that there always exists at least one decomposition of c in which c_1 terminates, namely the trivial $c = skip; c$. The reader is invited to derive the special cases of formulae $(17)-(21)$ for $c = skip; c = c; skip$.

The second remark is that it is often natural for the exceptional domain $ex\_dom(c, G)$ to be partitioned into further subsets $E_1, E_2, \ldots$ etc. If these subsets are mutually disjoint then our formulae can easily be generalised. All that needs to be done is to refine the definition of 'precise test' to that of a test T being 'precise for exceptions in E_i' and to change $(17)-(21)$ appropriately. This question will be discussed further in Sect. 3.4.

3.2. Unary Versus Binary Checks

In this section we discuss under which circumstances a binary rather than a unary exceptional test is required. It is desirable that the test be unary rather than binary because otherwise the initial values of variables would in some way have to be kept saved in store.

Let us reconsider the program ALLOCATE 2 of Figs. 7 and 8:

```
I := 0;
do (I < N − 1) & (A[I] = 1) → I + 1 od;
A[I] := 1
(∗)
```

Fig. 11

A precise test $A'[I] = 1$ involving the initial value of A can be inserted at $(\ast)$. However no precise test involving just the current state of A (which in this case is also the final state) can be inserted there.

The reason that no unary test can be inserted at $(\ast)$ is the existence of two different initial states s', s'' leading to the *same* final state t at $(\ast)$, such that the pair $(s'\ t)$ satisfies the goal but (s'', t) does not. To see this, define s' such that $s'(A[N-1]) = 0$ and $s'(A[j]) = 1$ for all $0 \le j < N - 1$ (in which case (s', t) happens to satisfy the goal $G(\text{ALLOCATE})$), as compared to s'' such that $s''(A[j]) = 1$ for all $0 \le j \le N - 1$ (in which case the state at $(\ast)$ is the same t as before, but (s'', t) does *not* satisfy $G(\text{ALLOCATE})$).

Generally, we define for $c = c_1; c_2$ the following condition:

There are no two initial states s', s'' and current state t s.t.

$$(s', t) \in R(c_1), (s'', t) \in R(c_1), t R(c_2) \subseteq s' G \text{ and } t R(c_2) \not\subseteq s'' G. \quad (25)$$

It is possible to show that if, and only if, (25) holds then the test between c_1 and c_2 can be unary rather than binary. This gives a second indication of where to put the test: namely, the partitioning $c_1 ; c_2$ should be chosen such that (25) holds. We are not considering the question further whether the rather cumbersome property (25) can be made equivalent to, or at least a consequence of, a 'nicer' property.

3.3. Checks in Conditionals and in Loops

In this section we derive analogues of the verification conditions (17)–(21) for precise tests in conditionals and in loops. For conditionals there is little to define. One has to ensure that the 'if clause'

$$\textbf{if } B_1 \rightarrow c_1 \;\square \dots \square\; B_n \rightarrow c_n \textbf{ fi}$$

cannot abort due to the non-existence of a true B_i, and that every chosen alternative accomplishes the overall goal. Hence with

$$T = \textbf{not } B_1 \; \& \dots \& \; \textbf{not } B_n$$

and

$$T_i = \textbf{not } \mathrm{ws}\,(c_i, G)\,,$$

the modified program

$$
\begin{aligned}
&[T \rightarrow \text{'exception handler'}] \\
&\textbf{if } B_1 \rightarrow [T_1 \rightarrow \text{'exception handler'}] \\
&\qquad\quad c_1 \\
&\square \\
&\quad \dots \\
&\square\; B_n \rightarrow [T_n \rightarrow \text{'exception handler'}] \\
&\qquad\quad c_n \\
&\textbf{fi}
\end{aligned}
$$

is a robust version of the above 'if clause'.

On the other hand, we consider a loop

$$c = \textbf{do } B \rightarrow c' \textbf{ od} \tag{26}$$

in which a test T is to be inserted such that the modified program

$$
\begin{aligned}
&\textbf{do } B \rightarrow [T \rightarrow \text{'exception handler''}] \\
&\qquad\quad c' \\
&\textbf{od}
\end{aligned}
$$

is a robust version of c with respect to a global goal G. Again it has to be ensured

(a) that control actually enters the body of the loop and

(b) that T becomes true in some iteration iff the input was exceptional.

Property (a) can be ensured by postulating that B is true for every state in the exceptional domain, or in set notation that:

$$\text{ex\_dom}\,(c, G) \subseteq B. \tag{27}$$

(27) is an analogue of (17) for loops.

Property (b) can be analysed as follows. We 'cut' the loop (26) between B and c', i.e. at the point at which the test T is to be inserted. Let us define the states at this point to be the 'intermediate' states. The transition relation giving the set of intermediate states reachable from a given intermediate state by an unspecified number of repetitions of the loop can be described in general by (for notation see Appendix A.2):

$$R_0 = (R\,(c') \circ R\,(B))^*. \tag{28a}$$

On the other hand, the relation between initial states and intermediate states and the relation between intermediate states and final states can be described, respectively, by the following two relations R_1 and R_2:

$$R_1 = R\,(B) \circ R_0, \tag{28b}$$

$$R_2 = R_0 \circ R\,(c') \circ R\,(\textbf{not}\ B). \tag{28c}$$

Pictorially, we may represent the relationship between these relations as shown in Fig. 12.

Property (b) can be ensured iff for all intermediate states t for which R_2 is not guaranteed to satisfy the overall goal G, another intermediate state, say x, is reachable from t such that the test T will hold in x. This underlies the following definition. We call a (binary) test T 'precise' for (26) iff

$$\forall\,(s', t) \in R_1 \colon \textbf{not}\ s'\ \text{ws}\,(R_2, G)\ t \Leftrightarrow \exists\ x \colon t\,R_0\,x\ \&\ s'\,T\,x \tag{29}$$

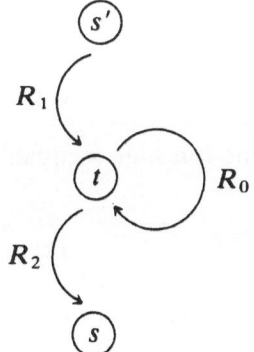

Fig. 12

223

where $\mathrm{ws}(R, G)$ for two relations R and G is the obvious extension of formula (8) in Sect. 2.4:

$$s' \, \mathrm{ws}(R, G) \, t \Leftrightarrow \emptyset \subset t \, R \subseteq s' \, G.$$

Formula (29) is the analogue of (18) for loops. Using relational algebra, (29) can be rewritten as the equation

$$R_1 \, \& \, \mathbf{not} \, \mathrm{ws}(R_2, G) = R_1 \, \& \, (T \circ R_0^{-1}). \tag{30}$$

Formula (30) is the analogue of (20) for loops. Since, by our overall assumption (6), R_0 is deterministic, R_0^{-1} is injective (see Appendix A.1). Using this fact it may be proved that if two tests T_1 and T_2 satisfy (30), then so do $T_1 \, \& \, T_2$ and $T_1 \vee T_2$. Hence the set of tests satisfying (30) is again a sublattice of the lattice of binary predicates.

As an example we prove that the test $I = N - 1$ in the following alternative implementation of G (ALLOCATE) is again a precise test:

```
ALLOCATE3 ≡ I := 0;
            do A[I] = 1 → [I = N − 1 → 'exception handler']
               I := I + 1
            od;
            A[I] := 1
```

Fig. 13

(27) is fulfilled because, taking into account the initial assignment of 0 to I, the truth of the exceptional condition

$$\forall j: 0 \le j \le N - 1 \Rightarrow A'[j] = 1 \tag{15}$$

implies in particular that $A[I] = 1$ on loop entry.

To prove (29), we consider an initial state s' and an intermediate state t. We denote by $I' = t(I)$ the value of I in state t. $(s', t) \in R_1$ implies that

$$I' \in \{0, \ldots, N - 1\} \, \& \, \forall j: 0 \le j \le I' \Rightarrow A[j] = 1. \tag{31a}$$

On the other hand, $\mathbf{not} \, s' \, \mathrm{ws}(R_2, G) \, t$ means that

$$\forall j: I' < j \le N - 1 \Rightarrow A[j] = 1. \tag{31b}$$

For another intermediate state x, $s' \, T x$ means that the value I in state x equals $N - 1$, and $t R_0 x$ then means that

$$\forall j: I' < j \le N - 1 \Rightarrow j \in \{0, \ldots, N - 1\} \, \& \, A[j] = 1. \tag{31c}$$

This proves (29) because under the assumption that the first clause in (31a) holds, (31b) and (31c) are equivalent.

We end this section with two remarks. It might be objected that the procedure outlined in the last paragraphs breaks down if, say, the search of the array A is begun with the index 1 rather than 0, because in this case the initial state in which the very first, but no other, resource is free ($A[0] = 0$ and $A[j] = 1$ for $1 \leq j \leq N - 1$) will give rise to an exception. However a program in which the search begins with 1 does not itself implement the specification G (ALLOCATE), as defined in Sect. 2.2 and 2.3. The initial state just mentioned would therefore belong to the exeptional domain rather than to the standard domain, which justifies the detection of an exception.

Our second remark concerns the design of the last version of the allocation algorithm. In contrast to the previous two versions, in ALLOCATE 3, the tests on A and on I are separated out in such a way that all testing on I occurs just immediately before I is actually changed. This seems indeed the most natural location for the test to be placed, because the inside of the loop can now be regarded as an 'action on I' by itself, indicating proper program structure. This leads no only to a (however slight) gain in the average amount of testing done, but also to the desirable property that I never actually assumes any values outside its 'natural' domain between 0 and $N - 1$.

It may well be possible that this line of reasoning can be generalised to derive a third, albeit more heuristic, indication of where to put tests in a program; namely, to try and separate them out in such a way that the test of an exceptional precondition coincides with testing one of the variables of the program for transgression of its 'natural' value domain. We shall return to this point in the next section.

3.4. An Example: Bracket Matching

The purpose of this section is to illustrate an application of our formalism to a non-trivial example. We have chosen the example because it occurred in the programming experience of one of the authors and because it is one of those fairly typical examples in which a whole variety of exception testing occurs spread all over the text of a program. After describing the problem informally and formally in Sect. 3.4.1, we present the design of an implementation in Sect. 3.4.2. Sect. 3.4.3 contains the design of a robust version of the implementation and Sect. 3.4.4 outlines a proof that the tests inserted in the robust version are indeed precise.

3.4.1. Specification of the Problem

Assume a stream W of characters is given as input to a bracket matching (BM) program. Some of the characters are 'B' (for 'begin') and some of them are 'E' (for 'end'). The string W may, for example, represent the internal encoding of an Algol program. The program BM is then required to analyse the block structure of that program by finding all matching 'begin'–'end' pairs.

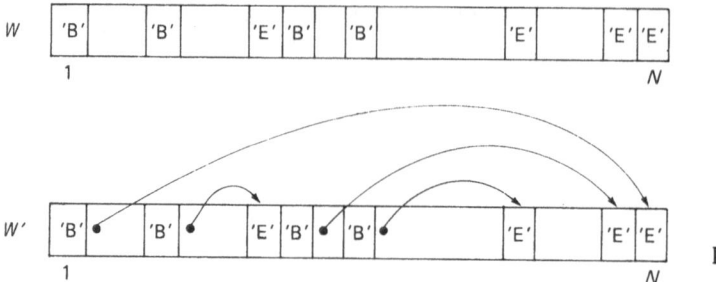

Fig. 14

In this situation the following is assumed (see Fig. 14). The first character of W is a 'B' and the last character in W is its matching 'E'. Furthermore, after every 'B' a 'space' is provided in W for the index of its matching 'E' to be inserted. We further assume that the depth of nesting of 'B'–'E' pairs must not exceed a positive constant $C > 0$ (reflecting, for example, dynamic memory allocation constraints imposed by a host operating system).

Let the input stream W be represented by an array W containing integer encodings for characters 'B', 'E', etc., with bounds 1 and $N > 0$:

var W: **array** $(1 \dots N)$ **of** integer.

We assume 0 to be the encoding for the 'space'.

In order to state the specification of BM formally, we first have to define what it means for a 'B'–'E' pair to 'match'. Because 'to match' is a symmetric property, we shall take care in this definition to proceed as symmetrically as possible. A necessary condition for a 'B' and a succeeding 'E' to match is that between the two there is an equal number of other 'B's and 'E's. They must furthermore be close enough together so as not to encompass two or more blocks.

This yields the following definitions, in which we always assume $1 \leq i \leq j \leq N$. Let $\text{nb}(K, i, j)$ be the number of occurrences of an arbitrary integer constant K between two indices i and j (inclusively) of W:

$$\text{nb}(K, i, j) \equiv \text{card} \{l \mid i \leq l \leq j \,\&\, W'[l] = K\}.$$

Then

$$D(i, j) \equiv \text{nb}(\text{'B'}, i, j) - \text{nb}(\text{'E'}, i, j)$$

denotes the difference between the number of 'B's and the number of 'E's between i and j. We can now define the matching of 'B' and 'E' as a predicate

$$\text{Match}(i, j) \equiv W'[i] = \text{'B'} \,\&\, W'[j] = \text{'E'} \,\&\, D(i, j) = 0 \,\&$$
$$(\neg \exists k: i < k < j \,\&\, W'[k] = \text{'E'} \,\&\, D(i, k) = 0). \tag{32}$$

226

The last term in (32) expresses the requirement that the 'B' and 'E' in question must be near enough together. It could have been replaced by its symmetric counterpart involving 'B' rather than 'E'. There is in principle no reason why the one definition should be preferred rather than the other. However we are already envisaging a sequential scan of W from 1 to N, in which case it is natural to search for the first 'E' which matches a given 'B'. This is why we 'cheat' and prefer (32).

The formal specification of the BM program as a relation between initial and final states can be stated as a conjunction of four simpler constraints:

$$G\,(\mathrm{BM}) = P1\ \&\ P2\ \&\ P3\ \&\ P4 \tag{33}$$

where

> $P1 \equiv \mathrm{Match}\,(1, N)$
> requires that the first and the last character in W are a matching 'B'–'E' pair;

> $P2 \equiv \forall i: (1 < i \le N)\ \&\ (W'\,[i-1] = \text{'B'}) \Rightarrow$
> $\qquad (W'\,[i] = 0)\ \&\ \mathrm{Match}\,(i-1, W\,[i])$
> requires that matching indices have to be inserted after each 'B' in place of the 'space' reserved for this purpose;

> $P3 \equiv \forall i: (1 \le i \le N) \Rightarrow D\,(1, i) \le D$
> limits the depth of possible nesting of 'B'–'E' pairs;

> $P4 \equiv \forall i: (1 < i \le N)\ \&\ (W'\,[i] \ne W\,[i]) \Rightarrow (W'\,[i-1] = \text{'B'})$
> represents the requirement that all entries other than 'spaces' must remain untouched.

Both $P1$ and $P3$ impose a direct constraint on W'. This remark, together with a part of $P2$ (the constraint that each 'B' has to be followed in W' by a 0) leads us to advance

$$
\begin{aligned}
\mathrm{DBM} \equiv\ &\mathrm{Match}\,(1, N)\ \&\\
&(\forall i: (1 < i \le N)\ \&\ (W'\,[i-1] = \text{'B'}) \Rightarrow W'\,[i] = 0)\ \&\\
&(\forall i: (1 \le i \le N) \Rightarrow D\,(1, i) \le D)
\end{aligned}
\tag{34}
$$

as a necessary condition for the existence of a final state W satisfying $G\,(\mathrm{BM})$.

The condition is also sufficient. Indeed, if $D\,(1, N) = 0$ (which is implied by $\mathrm{Match}\,(1, N)$) then one can prove that for every index i such that $1 \le i < N$ and $W'\,[i] = \text{'B'}$ there exists a j with $\mathrm{Match}\,(i, j)$, and it is therefore possible to define a W with the 'spaces' following the 'B's replaced by their appropriate matching indices and all the other entries unmodified. Therefore (34) is the characteristic predicate of $\mathrm{dom}\,(G\,(\mathrm{BM}))$.

3.4.2. Design of BM Standard Implementation

In order to implement G(BM) our only obligation is to establish the second part of P2 by filling the 'spaces' after all 'B's. We envisage a sequential scan of W and use the well-known methods of varying a constant [5] and weakening a predicate [8] in order to turn a specification into an invariant. Thus we replace the constant N in P2 by a variable I, omit the precondition $W'[i] = 0$ and add another term R:

$$\forall i: 1 < i \leq I \,\&\, W'[i-1] = \text{'B'} \Rightarrow (R \vee \text{Match}(i-1, W[i])).$$

Our objective is to choose R such that it is true for $I = 1$ or $I = 2$ and false for $I = N$, thus establishing P2 on termination of the envisaged program. For a given i with $W'[i-1] = \text{'B'}$, the "space" at i can be filled as soon as the index of the matching 'E' is contained in I. This happens (supposing a sequential scan) as soon as the quantity $D(i-1, I)$ ceases to be positive. "$D(i-1, I) > 0$" is therefore the natural choice for R:

$$\forall i: 1 < i \leq I \,\&\, W'[i-1] = \text{'B'} \Rightarrow (D(i-1, I) > 0 \vee \text{Match}(i-1, W[i])). \tag{35}$$

The most convenient way in which the 'space' indices can be kept in memory so as to be accessible when their matching 'E's become known is of course by using a stack (which we call ST with pointer P). Because the stack is 'pushed' on encountering a 'B' and is 'popped' on encountering an 'E', its pointer P can be taken to satisfy the equation $P = D(1, I)$. As the quantity $D(1, I)$ may vary from 0 to D and becomes zero iff the 'E' matching the very first 'B' has been found, it is natural to let P range from 0 to D and take "$P=0$" as the termination condition. Thus we have the further invariant:

$$0 \leq P = D(1, I) \leq N. \tag{36}$$

Our implementation is shown in full in Fig. 15.

In order to prove that the BM program implements G(BM), one has to establish that

$$\text{DBM} \subseteq \text{st\_dom}(\text{BM}, G(\text{BM})). \tag{37}$$

This proof can be conducted by showing that under the assumption DBM, both (35) and (36) are indeed loop invariants and imply P2 on termination. It is left to the reader to convince himself of this fact.

3.4.3. Design of a Robust Version

Once the correct behaviour of the program within the domain of its specification has been established, one can concentrate on its behaviour outside this domain. In our example, having established the correctness

```
        var I: 1..N;
            P: 0..D;
            ST: array 1..D of 1..N;
 10     I := 2;
 20     P := 1;
 30     ST[P] := I;
 40     do P ≠ 0 → I := I + 1;
 50         if W[I] = 'B' → I := I + 1;
 60                     P := P + 1;
 70                     ST[P] := I
 80         □ W[I] = 'E' → W[ST[P]] := I;
 90                     P := P - 1
100         □ else → skip
110         fi
120     od
```

Fig. 15.
BM standard algorithm

property (37) and hence the equality DBM = st_dom(BM, G(BM)), we may obtain the exceptional domain of BM with respect to G(BM) by negating (34):

$$\text{ex\_dom}(\text{BM}, G(\text{BM})) = E_1 \vee E_2 \vee E_3 \tag{38}$$

where

$E_1 \equiv \neg \text{Match}(1, N)$
corresponds to the nonexistence of a matching 'B'–'E' pair in the first and last entries of W;

$E_2 \equiv \exists i: (1 < i \leq N) \ \& \ (W'[i-1] = \text{'B'}) \ \& \ (W'[i] \neq 0)$
corresponds to the case where a 'B' is not immediately followed by a 'space' as required.

$E_3 \equiv \exists i: (1 \leq i \leq N) \ \& \ (D(1, i) > D)$
corresponds to the level of nesting exceeding the limit D.

Our objective is to insert a set of tests in BM such that altogether these tests can detect all possible exceptions in (38), i.e. are precise of (38). Following the heuristics set out at the end of Sect. 3.3, we attempt to match the variables used in the program with the terms in (38), so that the various tests in the program can correspond in some meaningful way to all terms in (38) and thus 'cover' the exceptional domain.

For example, because of the construction of the two local variables I and P in Sect. 3.4.2, these two variables cannot be allowed to transgress their respective value domains. More concretely, P is only to be increased under the condition $P < D$. We need to know in what way such tests correspond to terms in (38), in order to find out whether or not (38) is indeed covered. Because via (37), (34) and (33) the expression (38) relates to the specification G(BM), such

```
1      [W[1] ≠ 'B' → HE₁₁]
4      [N = 1 → HE₁₃]
7      [W[2] ≠ 0 → HE₂]
10     I := 2;
20     P := 1;
30     ST[P] := I;
40a    do P ≠ 0 → [I = N → HE₁₃]
40b             I := I + 1;
50a             if W[I] = 'B' → [I = N → HE₁₃]
50b                            I := I + 1;
54                             [W[I] ≠ 0 → HE₂]
57                             [P = D → HE₃]
60                             P := P + 1;
70                             ST[P] := I
80a             ▯ W[I] = 'E' → {1 < ST[P] ≤ N & W[ST[P]] = 0 &
                                 W[ST[P] − 1] = 'B' & Match(ST[P] − 1, I)}
80b                            W[ST[P]] := I;
90                             P := P − 1
100             ▯ else → skip
110             fi
120    od;
130    {P = 0 & Match(1, I)}
140    [I < N → HE₁₄]
```

Fig. 16. Robust BM program

correspondences can be expected to be the closer, the clearer the program specification is reflected in the program variables.

Figure 16 gives our solution in full. We will continue with the justification for each one of the test it contains.

The shorthand 'HE$_j$' is used for 'handler of the exception E_j'. In what way these handlers correspond to the exceptions is discussed informally in this section and formally in the next section.

In our justification for the tests inserted in Fig. 16 we start with E_3 (38). We see that $D(1, i)$ already corresponds to P via (36). Therefore, whenever P may exceed its limit, i.e. just before line 60, an occurrence of E_3 can be detected. This shows that the test in line 57 corresponds to E_3. This is one of the cases in which the single testing of a program variable precisely covers a term in the expression of the exceptional domain (this will be made more formal in Sect. 3.4.4). Underflow of P (line 90) cannot occur because of the guard of the loop.

E_2 mentions the values of W and can therefore be taken care of by testing W itself. We can make use of the fact that a test for $W[I] = 'B'$ already exists in line 50. Thus it is most natural to insert a test on $W[I] = 0$ after the ensuing incrementation of I, i.e. after line 50; this leads to line 54. Because every 'B' (except the first one) is screened by line 50, line 54 takes care of every 'space' except the very first one which is conveniently tested at the beginning (line 7).

E_1 is the only part of (38) not immediately expressible in terms of program variables. We reconsider the definition (32) of Match (i, j) and split E_1 into four smaller terms:

$$E_1 = E_{11} \lor E_{12} \lor E_{13} \lor E_{14}, \tag{39}$$
$$E_{11} \equiv W'[1] \neq \text{'B'},$$
$$E_{12} \equiv W'[N] \neq \text{'E'},$$
$$E_{13} \equiv D(1, N) \neq 0$$
$$E_{14} \equiv \exists k: 1 < k < N \,\&\, W'[k] = \text{'E'} \,\&\, D(1, k) = 0.$$

E_{13} corresponds to an unbalanced number of 'B's and 'E's in W, while E_{14} corresponds to the case that the 'E' matching the first 'B' is situated before the end of W.

E_{11} can easily be tested at the beginning (line 1). E_{12} could be tested on termination, but this is unnecessary since the loop can only be left via lines 80–90, which ensures that $W[I] = \text{'E'}$ on termination (see also line 130). In fact something curious happens to E_{12}: it does not have a handler. This can be attributed to the fact that E_{12} can entirely be covered by other exceptions:

$$E_{12} \Rightarrow (E_{13} \lor E_{14}).$$

Of course, is we were interested in having a special treatment for E_{12}, a special exception clause could be inserted to detect it (say at the beginning).

E_{13} contains the term $D(1, N)$ which corresponds to P via (36). The condition $D(1, N) \neq 0$ can be detected as soon as I reaches N. This, in turn, can only arise at the very beginning (line 4) or if the variable I exceeds its limit during the execution of the loop (lines 40a and 50a).

Finally, the term $D(1, k)$ again appears in E_{14}. The matter of interest is here that this quantity equals 0 *before* N has been reached. It follows that a test whether $I < N$ at the end of the loop (i.e. when $P = 0$) will detect this condition (line 140). This concludes our informal derivation of the tests to be inserted.

In conclusion, the design of these tests can perhaps best be described as an attempt to cover the exceptional domain term by term. If the variables of the program already correspond in a clean way to these terms (which they do in our case) then there is also likely to be a close correspondence between these terms and the tests whether those variables exceed their natural domains. Some tests, such as the one in line 54, cannot be motivated in terms of local variables. However, there again the placement of such tests can be influenced by the way the standard algorithms work (in this case the test on 'B' in line 50).

In all cases the wish could be discerned to place the test for an exceptional subdomain such that the corresponding exceptional condition is detected as soon as it 'arises' in terms of the program at hand. This is perhaps the most general heuristic statement about the placement of tests that can be extracted from our considerations.

3.4.4. Proof of Preciseness

Our aim in this section is to show that the total set of tests in lines 1, 4, 7, 40a, 50a, 54, 57 and 140 of Fig. 16 is precise for the exceptional domain (38), satisfying:

(i) whenever a test is true then an exceptional input state has been detected;
(ii) conversely, every exceptional input state leads to an intermediate state in which some test is true.

In proving this we encounter the following complication. It would be nice to show, using say (29), that for each individual exceptional domain E_i, the corresponding exception handler HE_i becomes activated if and only if the input state was in E_i. However, as remarked at the end of Sect. 3.1, such a strategy is possible only for *disjoint* subdomains.

In our situation we have six non-disjoint exceptional sub-domains in (38) and (39). As a result, if an input state is in two or more of those domains, it cannot a priori be determined which exception will be detected first (if at all). For example, if the input of the BM program shown in Fig. 16 satisfies both E_2 and E_3, either E_2 or E_3 can be detected first, depending on the particular shape of W'.

However, for every individual exceptional sub-domain we can prove a slightly weaker property than full preciseness, namely:

(i)   if an exception handler HE_i is activated then the input state was in E_i;
(ii') for every input state in E_i, either the corresponding handler HE_i eventually becomes activated, or another exception E_j is detected prior to that (indicating that the input state lies in the intersection E_i & E_j).

If (i) and (ii') can be proved for all (overlapping) exceptional sub-domains then the truth of (i) and (ii) follows directly for the union of these sub-domains; i.e. in combination the tests are precise for the full exceptional domain.

In the sequel we prove (i) and (ii') for the expection E_3 of our example. For $E_1 - E_2$, the demonstration is analogous. The proof which follows is not entirely formal but, we hope, precise enough to avoid any misunderstanding.

(i) Assume that during the execution of the loop, an intermediate state has been reached such that the test $P = D$ of line 57 evaluates to true. From the loop invariant $P = D(1, I)$, which was true at the end of the previous iteration, and from the fact that the two most recently visited array elements contain 'B' and 0, respectively, (lines 50–54), we can infer that $D(1, I) = D + 1$ holds for the actual value of I. It follows that E_3 was true initially.

(ii') Conversely, assume E_3 is true initially. Define

$$i_0 = \min \{i \,|\, (1 \le i \le N \,\&\, D(1, i) > D\}.$$

By this definition, i_0 always 'points' to a 'B', i.e. $W'[i_0] = $ 'B' (otherwise the minimality of i_0 would be contradicted). As I is only incremented by 1 in BM, we have to consider the following two cases:

(a) During the execution of the loop, I reaches the value i_0. This can only be a consequence of executing the statements in line 40b (sub-case a1) or in line 50b (sub-case a2).

(a1) If $i_0 = N$ the guard of HE_{13} in line 50a leads to the detection of E_{13}. If $i_0 < N$ and $W'[i_0 + 1] \neq 0$ the guard of HE_2 leads to the detection of E_2. If $i_0 < N$ and $W'[i_0 + 1] = 0$ the exception E_3 is detected in line 57. No other possibilities remain.

(a2) Since $W[i_0] = $ 'B' the guard of HE_2 in line 54 is true and the exception E_3 is detected.

(b) I never reaches the value i_0 during the normal execution of the BM program. Two sub-cases have to be considered.

(b1) The loop is not entered. As the execution of the statements in lines 10, 20, 30 cannot lead to the occurrence of a language defined exception, it follows that one of the guards of the lines 1, 4, 7 was true and an exception E_{11}, E_{13} or E_2 has been detected.

(b2) The loop is entered. Two outcomes are possible.

(b21) The loop terminates normally. If $I < N$, then E_{14} is detected in line 140. $I = N$ implies $i_0 < 2$ which together with $D > 0$ contradicts the definition of i_0.

(b22) The loop terminates abnormally. As a result of their design, the tests in the exceptional clauses in Fig. 16 provide a set of 'local'arguments that none of the expressions and statements in the standard algorithm can lead to the occurrence of language defined exceptions. For instance, incrementing P in line 60 cannot lead outside the domain $0 \ldots D$ of P because of the immediately preceding test. Similarly, the well-definedness of the statement in line 80b can be inferred from the immediately preceding assertion; etc. It follows that the abnormal termination of the loop must be due to a guard for HE_{13}, HE_2 or HE_3 being true in some intermediate state.

Thus (i) and (ii') are established for E_3. Proving (i) and (ii') for all of $E_1 - E_3$ establishes the preciseness of the total set of tests for the exceptional domain (38).

We point out that for the argument in case (b) above to be 'easy', it has been important that every individual component statement in the program could easily ('locally') be examined to discover whether or not it would lead to the occurrence of a language defined exception. This in turn has been a consequence of our design decisions to let the tests correspond to individual program variables.

Because of the 'vagueness' of this kind of heuristics, however, we consider the proof just given to be less than satisfactory. However as experience with similar 'preciseness' proofs can be expected to increase, we are confident that a stricter framework for the insertion an verification of exceptional clauses in a program will evolve. We hope that the considerations of this paper can be seen as providing first steps in this direction.

4. Conclusion

Although the identification and detection of possible exception occurrences are important problems in the design of robust software [7], we scarcely know of any other attempt of establishing a framework both rigorous and practical for solving them. In practice, programmers rely upon their intuition and experience in dealing with them, and therefore the identification and detection of possible exceptional conditions is often just as (un)reliable as human intuition is.

The paper proposes a systematic approach for solving the above mentioned problems. It is a part of an on-going effort aiming at providing a rigorous framework for the design of correct and robust software. In this paper we have concentrated on the exceptional preconditions of an exception handler, at the expense of the programming of such a handler itself. This latter issue is investigated in [1, 2]. We have also illustrated our approach on two examples, both being of a kind likely to arise in practice.

Except in very simple cases, we do not propose to use our method as an automatic means of deriving exceptional preconditions. As is well known, the determination of forward and backward predicate transformers for loops (in terms of which the precise run-time checks were expressed) is usually a hard problem, requiring the use of inductive reasoning. The preciseness formulae given in this paper are not a substitute for experience in, and heuristics for, the appropriate placement of tests in a program, just as correctness formulae are not a substitute for the design of correct programs. Rather, our formulae should be taken as verification conditions for precise tests. We have however also exhibited a number of statements which are candidates for heuristics in the placement of exceptional tests, and we are confident that a more comprehensive heuristic framework for this purpose will evolve.

This paper should not be mistaken as a case for inserting run-time checks in a program whenever possible. Of course, run-time checks are superfluous when the constant falsehood of an exception precondition can be proved, and the overhead of checking for things that cannot happen should be avoided. The approach presented here is of use in the other case in which the assumptions about the environment in which a program will run do not rule out possible exception occurrences. We therefore consider our approach to be complementary to those oriented towards proving the absence of exception occurrences.

We have used binary predicates (relations) rather than unary predicates (subsets) for describing the intended meaning of programs. Another possible approach would be to duplicate the state space with 'auxiliary' or 'logical' variables which store the initial values of the 'real' variables, and allow predicates to involve both 'real' and 'logical' variables, while the commands would be allowed to modify only the 'real' variables. The two approaches seem to be in principle equivalent, since a specification (relation) in our approach would correspond to a unary predicate (subset) over the duplicated state space (i.e. the cartesian product) of the other approach. We consider our approach to be conceptually at least as clean.

The expression of the exact run-time checks were given under the simplifying assumption that the exceptional input domain is not partitioned. In practice however (as the Bracket Matching program or examples in [2] show) the exceptional domain can often naturally be partitioned into several exceptional sub-domains. If these sub-domains are disjoint then the formulae given in this paper can immediately be generalised. The other case, i.e. when the exceptional domains overlap, requires a modification of the proof method, whereby the formulae given have to be slightly weakened for the sub-domains themselves. Such a modification presents little difficulty; we have illustrated it on the Bracket Matching example and refer the reader to [2] for a more formal treatment.

A. Appendices

A.1. Relation Algebra

Throughout the paper, the connectives $\&$ and $\vee$ are not commutative; we define

$a \& b \equiv$ **if** a **then** b,
$a \vee b \equiv$ **if** a **then** true **else** b.

However the $\&$ and $\vee$ connectives inherit associativity and most other properties of the classical logical connectives.

Let S be a set, $x, y \in S$ and G, H binary relations over S. The basic operations over binary relations are:

(binary)	$x \, G \circ H \, y \equiv \exists z : x \, G \, z \, \& \, z \, H \, y$	(composition)
	$x \, G \cup H \, y \equiv x \, G \, y \vee x \, H \, y$	(union)
	$x \, G \cap H \, y \equiv x \, G \, y \, \& \, x \, H \, y$	(intersection)
	$x \, G \backslash H \, y \equiv x \, G \, y \, \& \, \textbf{not} \, x \, H \, y$	(difference)
(unary)	$x \, G^{-1} \, y \equiv y \, G \, x$	(inverse)
	$x \, \bar{G} \, y \equiv \textbf{not} \, x \, G \, y$	(complement)
	$x \, G^* \, y \equiv \exists n \geq 0 : x \, G^n \, y$	(star)
	where G^n is defined inductively:	
	$G^0 = \mathrm{Id}, \ G^n = G \circ G^{n-1}$	
(nullary)	Id: $\quad x \, \mathrm{Id} \, y \equiv x = y$	(identity)
	$\emptyset$	(empty relation)

Operations from relations into the set S:

$\mathrm{dom}\,(G) = \{x \in S \mid \exists y : x \, G \, y\}$	(domain)
$\mathrm{cod}\,(G) = \{y \in S \mid \exists x : x \, G \, y\}$	(codomain)
$x \, G = \{y \in S \mid x \, G \, y\}$	
$G \, y = \{x \in S \mid x \, G \, y\}$	

Special classes of relations:

G is deterministic   if $G^{-1} \circ G \subseteq \mathrm{Id}$
     injective   if $G \circ G^{-1} \subseteq \mathrm{Id}$
     surjective   if $\mathrm{cod}\,(G) = S$
     total   if $\mathrm{dom}\,(G) = S$

A.2. Semantics of the Programming Language

Relational semantics (see Sect. 2.3)

$R\,(\text{skip}) \equiv \mathrm{Id}$
$R\,(\text{abort}) \equiv \emptyset$
$R\,(x := E) \equiv \{(s', s) \mid \text{defined}\,(x, E, s') \,\&\, s\,(x) = \text{value of } E \text{ in } s' \,\&$
$\qquad\qquad\qquad \forall y \neq x\colon s\,(y) = s'\,(y)\}$
$R\,(\textbf{if } B_1 \rightarrow c_1 \,\square \ldots \square\, B_n \rightarrow c_n \textbf{ fi})$
$\quad \equiv R\,(B_1) \circ R\,(c_1) \cup \ldots \cup R\,(B_n) \circ R\,(c_n)$
where $R\,(B) = \{(s, s) \mid \text{defined}\,(B, s) \,\&\, B\,(s) = \text{true}\}$
$R\,(\textbf{do } B \rightarrow c \textbf{ od}) \equiv (R\,(B) \circ R\,(c))^* \circ R\,(\textbf{not } B)$
$R\,(c_1; c_2) \equiv R\,(c_1) \circ R\,(c_2)$

(the last three formulae hold only for deterministic commands).

Weakest specification-transformer semantics (Sect. 2.4)

$\text{ws}\,(\text{skip}, G) = G$
$\text{ws}\,(\text{abort}, G) = \emptyset$
$\text{ws}\,(x := E, G) = \text{Def}\,(x, E) \,\&\, G\,[E/x]$
where $\text{Def}\,(x, E) = \{(s, s) \mid \text{defined}\,(x, E, s)\}$
   and $G\,[E/x]$ stands for the specification obtained from G
   by substituting all free occurrences of x by E.
$\text{ws}\,(\textbf{if } B_1 \rightarrow c_1 \,\square \ldots \square\, B_n \rightarrow c_n \textbf{ fi}, G)$
$\quad \equiv \exists j \in \{1, \ldots, n\}\colon B_j \,\&\, \forall j \in \{1, \ldots, n\}\colon B_j \Rightarrow \text{ws}\,(c_j, G)$
$\text{ws}\,(\textbf{do } B \rightarrow c \textbf{ od}, G) \equiv \exists G_i$
$\quad$ where $G_0 \equiv \textbf{not } R\,(B) \,\&\, G,$
$\qquad\quad G_{i+1} \equiv R\,(B) \,\&\, \text{ws}\,(c, G_i)$
$\text{ws}\,(c_1; c_2, G) = \text{ws}\,(c_1, \text{ws}\,(c_2, G))$

Strongest specification-transformer semantics (Sect. 2.5)

$\text{st}\,(\text{skip}, G) \equiv G$
$\text{st}\,(\text{abort}, G) \equiv \emptyset$
$\text{st}\,(x := E, G) \equiv G \circ R\,(x := E)$ as above
$\text{st}\,(c_1; c_2, G) \equiv \text{st}\,(c_2, \text{st}\,(c_1, G))$
$\text{st}\,(\textbf{if } B_1 \rightarrow c_1 \,\square \ldots \square\, B_n \rightarrow c_n \textbf{ fi})$
$\quad \equiv G \circ (R\,(B_1) \circ \text{st}\,(c_1, \mathrm{Id}) \cup \ldots \cup R\,(B_n) \circ \text{st}\,(c_n, \mathrm{Id}))$
$\text{st}\,(\textbf{do } B \rightarrow c \textbf{ od}, G) \equiv \textbf{not } R\,(B) \,\&\, (\exists G_i)$
$\quad$ where $G_0 = G, \; G_{i+1} = \text{st}\,(c, R\,(B) \,\&\, G_i)$.

Again, the last three formulae hold only for deterministic commands.

Connections Between These Semantics

Given $R(c)$, then $\text{st}(c, G)$ can be obtained from formula (13) in Sect. 2.5, while $\text{ws}(c, G)$ can be obtained from formula (8) in Sect. 2.4.

Conversely, for deterministic commands, $R(c)$ can be retrieved from $\text{ws}(c, G)$ by

$$s' R(c) t \Leftrightarrow s' \text{ws}(c, \{(s', t)\}) s',$$

and from $\text{st}(c, G)$ by

$$R(c) \equiv \text{st}(c, \text{Id}).$$

Acknowledgement. The authors are indebted to their colleagues in the Reliability Project, in particular to Brian Randell and Graham Wood. This work has been supported by the Science Research Council of Great Britain.

References

1. F. Cristian, Exception handling and software fault tolerance, Proc. 10th International Symposium on Fault Tolerant Computing, Kyoto (1980). [Also Chap. 3]
2. F. Cristian, Robust data types, Chap. 3.
3. J. de Bakker, Mathematical Theory of Program Correctness (Prentice-Hall, Englewood Cliffs, NJ, 1980).
4. E. W. Dijkstra, A Discipline of Programming (Prentice-Hall, Englewood Cliffs, NJ, 1976).
5. E. W. Dijkstra, A theorem on odd powers of odd integers, in: Program Construction, Lecture Notes in Computer Science **69** (Springer, Berlin, 1979) 47–48.
6. R. W. Floyd, Assigning Meanings to Programs, Applied Mathematics **19** (AMS, Providence, RI, 1967).
7. S. L. Gerhart, Program verification in the 80's: Problems, perspectives and opportunities, ISI/RR-78-71, USC-ISI (1978).
8. D. Gries, Is 'sometimes' ever better than always?, in: Program Construction, Lecture Notes in Computer Science **69** (Springer, Berlin, 1979) 113–124.
9. C. A. R. Hoare, An axiomatic basis for computer programming, Comm. ACM **12** (1969).
10. J. Horning, H. C. Lauer, P. M. Melliar-Smith and B. Randell, A program structure for error detection and recovery, Proc. Conference On Operating Systems: Theoretical and Practical Aspects, IRIA (1974); also: Lecture Notes in Computer Science **16** (Springer, Berlin). [Also Chap. 2]
11. D. Luckham and W. Polak, ADA exception handling – An axiomatic approach, ACM TOPLAS **2** (2) (1980).
12. Z. Manna, Mathematical Theory of Computation (McGraw-Hill, New York, 1974).
13. M. Wand, A characterisation of weakest preconditions, J. Comput. System Sci. **15** (1977).
14. W. Wulf, Abstract data types – A retrospective and prospective view, Proc. MFCS'80, Lecture Notes in Computer Science **83** (Springer, Berlin, 1980) 94–112.

Safe Programming

T. ANDERSON and R. W. WITTY

Abstract. Safe specifications and programs are advocated as a simple way of enhancing the reliability of software. The behaviour of a safe program can be more easily certified as being correct with respect to its safe specification, which implies guaranteed termination. This paper describes the theory of safe programming, demonstrates the building of a safe program and summarises the experience gained from practical applications of safe programming.

Key Words. Bounded repetition, Correctness, Reliability, Termination.

Introduction

The provision of a certification of the correctness of a program is intended to increase confidence that the behaviour of the executed program will conform to what is required of the program. Such a certification should consist of:

(a) a specification of the intended behaviour of the program, and
(b) an argument to show that, when executed, the program will always meet this specification.

The argument often breaks down into two parts; one part to show that all executions of the program terminate and the other to show that on termination the required results have been obtained. To be convinced that the program is indeed correct it is necessary to be satisfied that the specification is appropriate and that the argument (usually called a proof) is valid. Unfortunately, current experience indicates that correctness proofs constructed for even quite short programs can be lengthy, complex and (as demonstrated by Gerhard and Yelowitz [5] and Anderson [1]) invalid. For a proof to be of real value it should be clearer and simpler than the associated program.

To illustrate the above remarks a conventional proof of correctness will be presented for a small program. Then, in contrast, the specification will be altered to what is termed a safe specification, a safe program constructed, and a short, clear proof of safeness given. The practical application of safe programming is the discussed.

A Correct Program

Consider the following specification:

Using only integer arithmetic, find the largest integer i less than or equal to the square root of a given non-negative integer constant n (find $i = [\sqrt{n}]$). That

238

is, given $n \geq 0$ find i such that

$$(i^2 \leq n) \wedge ((i + 1)^2 > n).$$

The following solution is based on the Newton-Raphson root finding method.

```
SOLUTION 1:
  begin
  i := [(n + 1)/2] {initial value};
  while i² > n do
    begin
    i := [(n + i²)/(2 i)] {next estimate};
    end;
  end SOLUTION 1;
```

A proof of correctness can be given as:

Proof of Termination. On entry to the loop body $i^2 > n$ which together with $i > 0$ implies that $i > [(n + i^2)/2\,i]$. The assignment $i := [(n + i^2)/2\,i]$ at each iteration ensures that the value of i must strictly decrease, and as it is always non-negative, only a bounded number of iterations can therefore occur.

Proof of Correct Behaviour.

1. After initialisation, $(i + 1)^2 > n$ since $([(n + 1)/2] + 1)^2 > n$.
2. For any positive i, $([(n + i^2)/2\,i] + 1)^2 > n$ and so $(i + 1)^2 > n$ after each assignment in the body of the loop.
3. Thus $(i + 1)^2 > n$ always, and after termination $i^2 \leq n$ also (from the **while** test).

The above proof is very informal, and some simple lemmas on integers have been omitted. However, it fails to inspire a great deal of confidence. If a proof is to be of real value it should be clearer and easier to understand than the associated program. For just as a simple program is more likely to be correct than a complex program, so a simple proof is more likely to be valid than a complex proof.

Adequate Programs

Proof guided program design methodologies, as advocated by Dijkstra [3, 4], help to create simpler proofs. A variation of these techniques is possible; instead of attempting to prove the correctness of a program with respect to its original specification, some weaker criterion of acceptable behaviour is selected. That is, if the original specification is denoted by P then a specification Q is chosen such that:
(a) any program which conforms to P will also conform to Q, and
(b) Q prescribes an acceptable behaviour of the program.

The program is the designed and constructed in an attempt to conform to P, but so as to facilitate the provision of a much simpler proof of correctness with respect to Q than would be possible using P. Such a proof will be termed a proof that the program is *adequate*.

Safe Programs

In the context of software reliability a special case of adequacy, termed safeness, is relevant. As a weaker specification for a program intended to satisfy P, take Q to be $P \vee$ "error", meaning that the program should either behave as was originally intended or should terminate with an explicit indication of the reason for failure. A proof of adequacy for this particular form of Q will be termed a proof that the program is *safe*.

Ideally, a program should be designed so that its proof of safeness can be substantially simpler than a corresponding correctness proof. One way of achieving this objective is shown in the following solution to the largest square root problem introduced above.

Safe specification:

Given $n \geq 0$ find i such that
$((i^2 \leq n) \wedge ((i + 1)^2 > n)) \vee$ "error"
Program:

SOLUTION 2:
```
begin
i := [(n + 1)/2] {initial value};
iteration_counter := 0;
while (i² > n) and iteration_counter < iteration_limit do
    begin
        i := [(n + i²)/(2 i)] {next estimate};
        iteration_counter := iteration_counter + 1;
    end;
{safety check 1}
if iteration_counter > iteration_limit then error ("loop limit");
{safety check 2}
if not (i² ≤ n) and ((i + 1)² > n)) then error ("wrong answer");
end SOLUTION 2;
```

Proof of Safeness. *Termination:* Guaranteed by testing of iteration_counter.

Adequacy: After termination either an error will have been detected or a correct answer will have been calculated since an explicit test of correctness is included.

The simple nature of this proof leaves little opportunity for error which justifies a high level of confidence in the safeness of the program.

240

Note that the proof does not depend on the particular expressions used as "initial value" and "next estimate", or on the value of the iteration_limit (as yet unspecified). However, the requirement that the program be designed to also conform to the original specification demands that appropriate expressions are chosen (the proof of termination for SOLUTION 1 suggests $[(n + 1)/2]$ as the iteration_limit). Except for this requirement, the program below would be an acceptable solution since it is safe for all specifications P.

begin error ("wrong answer"); **end**;

An argument for safeness can be made independent of any assumptions about the input to a program, since any necessary assumptions can be checked at run time. Hence, safe behaviour can be guaranteed even with invalid input data, whereas correctness proofs conventionally assume valid input.

More generally, the adoption of a safe programming specification enables a programmer to introduce redundancy into a program specifically as a means of simplifying the proof of the program with respect to that specification. Redundancy included in a program for this purpose will often be in the form of **assert** statements (eg Algol-W[9]); a proof of safeness can rely on all such assertions holding when the program is executed since otherwise a failure indication would be generated.

It should be noted that an over stringent or otherwise ill-chosen assertion may generate a failure indication when the same program without the assertion would have executed correctly. Such an occurrence is indicative of a lack of understanding on the part of the programmer and, in practice, rectification of such an occurrence always leads to a deeper understanding of the program's specification and a more reliable program. The consequences of an over stringent assertion may be contrasted favourably with those resulting from the failure of a weak (or non-existent) assertion to detect an erroneous execution of the program.

By augmenting a safe program with routines which take corrective action in the even of an erroneous situation being detected, a significant enhancement of the reliability of the program can be obtained. The recovery block notation described by Randell [8] can be used to achieve this augmentation without increasing the complexity of the program. Anderson [1] has elaborated on these points.

Bounded Repetition

The above program is atypical in that the explicit testing of the results of a program is rarely feasible in practice. However, it seems perfectly feasible to eliminate the need for a proof of termination simply by programming in languages which ensure that all programs must halt, thereby greatly simplifying the overall proof.

Such languages do not provide explicit control transfer and impose constraints on all iterative and recursive facilities. Consequently they cannot be use to program all of the recursive (computable) functions, and are known as sub-recursive languages. The work of Constable and Borodin [2] indicates that such languages can provide all of the functions actually used in computing and this seems to be borne out in practice (see below). Indeed, these restrictions are an advantage of the subrecursive languages.

An iterative facility provided by many languages can be denoted by:

repeat *S* **possibly forever**

where *S* denotes a statement list which may or may not include conditional **exit**s. *S* is repeatedly executed until an **exit** is taken whereupon the construct is terminated. The **while** loop is a typical example of this type of iteration.

Consider two special cases of the construct.

repeat *S* **forever**

S contains no **exit**s and is repeated infinitely. This special case is rarely needed, and would deserve careful consideration if it were.

repeat *S* **exactly** *n* **times**

Here *n* denotes a non-negative integer value; *S* contains no **exit**s and is executed precisely *n* times. This special case is frequently needed. Its termination is guaranteed.

The main criticism of the more powerful **possibly forever** construct is that it permits infinite repetition when in all probability the programmer did not intend this to occur. By analogy with the two special cases above an alternative version is suggested which prevents infinite repetition.

repeat *S* **upto** *n* **times**

S contains one or more conditional **exit**s and is executed at most *n* times, the construct being terminated earlier if an exit is taken.

A sub-recursive language only provides bounded iteration constructs.

repeat *S* **upto** *n* **times** (*S* contains one or more **exit**s)
repeat *S* **exactly** *n* **times** (*S* contains no **exit**s)

If potentially infinite iteration is to be included in a programming language then a separate construct should be specially provided.

Recursive constructs may be constrained in a similar manner to the iterative constructs discussed above.

Luckham and Suzuki have reported [6] on work related to the proposals of this section. They advocate the use of repetition counters as a means of formally establishing termination within a weak logic of programs.

Experience with Adequate Programs

An attempt has been made to demonstrate the possibility of writing a practical piece of software so as to obtain a simple proof of adequacy, by a postgraduate student at Newcastle University (M. S. Reynolds). A file system was implemented with specification P: "All user commands to the file system are correctly processed". A proof of adequacy was provided for the specification Q: "All user commands to the file system are either correctly processed, or if not, the user is sent a warning message and the integrity of all previously filed data is maintained". By means of isolating those routines which actually modified the file structures, and incorporating run time checks to verify their actions, a reasonably simple proof of Q was obtained. A large portion of the software could be ignored completely when establishing adequacy, a considerable benefit. Another encouraging feature of this experiment was that throughout the debugging phase, when the program was patently not correct, its behaviour was, however, always adequate.

Experience with Safe Programs

The Rutherford Laboratory has a small, primitive mini-computer (used to control a graphics system) whose only software tools are an assembler, a loader and a debugging tool which allows the examination and alteration of the contents of absolute memory addresses. The machine has no supervisor program, no memory partitioning or protection hardware and no printer. A major difficulty in programming this machine is that erroneous programs generally overwrite themselves, thereby making debugging extremely difficult. It was therefore decided to construct all new software according to the principles of safe programming.

Several programs have been constructed including a multi-tasking system. The first program was built from 8000 lines of hand coded assembler statements and has never failed. It has been in constant use since September 1975 logging details about the resources consumed by the users of the graphics system. The multi-tasking program to actually control the graphics system was built by cross-compiling over 20,000 lines of a simple systems implementation language which included multiple exit loops based on Zahn's construct [10]. These proved a success as they eliminated the need to follow each loop by additional, redundant tests to determine which of the possible exit conditions actually terminated the loop (see below).

None of the safe programs written so far has overwritten itself or failed to terminate, even during development when bugs were obviously present. The need to place a bound on each loop proved beneficial rather than restrictive. The very act of determining the loop limit caught errors at the design stage. It was surprising how small most of the loop bounds were in practice, and how most loops had natural bound anyway. For example, in the multi-tasking

243

program there is a routine which reads characters from a terminal until a carriage return character is encountered. This could have been coded as:

```
I := 0;
loop
    I := I + 1;
    BUFFER (I) := readnextchar (teletype);
repeat unless
    BUFFER (I) eq Carriage Return;
endloop;
```

Simple, elegant, efficient and lethal because the inputting of too many characters before the carriage return could have caused overwriting of the memory area after the end of the buffer. The natural loop limit here was the number of characters making up a line on the terminal, 72 on an ordinary teletype, which led to an easy proof of safeness. This gave rise to the version:

```
I := 0;
loop
    I := I + 1;
    BUFFER (I) := readnextchar (teletype);
    terminate gotline if BUFFER (I) eq Carriage Return;
    terminate snag if done 72 times;
repeat
    situation gotline causes OK;
    situation snag causes error ("line too long");
endloop;
```

which utilises the form of Zahn loop contained in the systems implementation language mentioned above. The run time overheads associated with bounded repetition proved negligible as the "**if done** $\langle limit \rangle$ **times**" construct allowed very compact and efficient code to be generated. An extra add and test instruction per loop was a small price to pay for the increased reliability.

Meissner [7] has reported favourably on bounded loops and has suggested a template from which bounded loops may be constructed in FORTRAN.

Using Meissner's template, the above example would lead to the following FORTRAN solution:

```
      I = 0
      DO 7 J = 1,72
      I = I + 1
      BUFFER (I) = READCH (TTY)
      IF (BUFFER (I).EQ.CRET) GOTO 8
7     CONTINUE
      CALL ERROR ("LINE TOO LONG")
8     CONTINUE
```

244

The knowledge that a program will terminate safely whatever its input has greatly increased confidence in the programs; it has saved hours of debugging time and has increased enormously the programmers' peace of mind.

Conclusion

Safeness directed program design and construction really works.

Acknowledgement. The authors would like to acknowledge the support of the Science Research Council of Great Britain.

References

1. T. Anderson, Provably Safe Programs, Tech. Rep. 70, Computing Laboratory, University of Newcastle upon Tyne (February 1975).
2. R. L. Constable and A. B. Borodin, Subrecursive Programming Languages, Part I: Efficiency and Program Structure, J. ACM 19 (July 1972), 526–568.
3. E. W. Dijkstra, Concern for Correctness as a Guiding Principle for Program Composition, Infotech State of the Art Report 1: The Fourth Generation (1971), 357–367.
4. E. W. Dijkstra, A Discipline of Programming, Prentice-Hall (1976).
5. S. L. Gerhart and L. Yelowitz, Observations of Fallibility in Applications of Modern Programming Methodologies, IEEE Trans. on Software Engineering 2 (September 1976), 195–207.
6. D. C. Luckham and N. Suzuki, Proof of Termination within a Weak Logic of Programs, Acta Informatica 8 (1977), 21–36.
7. L. P. Meissner, Bounded Loops, FOR-WORD 3 (January 1977).
8. B. Randell, System Structure for Software Fault Tolerance, Current Trends in Programming Methodology 1, Prentice-Hall (1977), 195–219. [Also Chap. 1]
9. E. H. Satterthwaite, Debugging Tools for High Level Languages, Software – Practice & Experience 2 (July 1972), 197–217.
10. C. T. Zahn, A Control Statement for Natural Top-Down Structured Programming, Lecture Notes in Computer Science 19, Springer Verlag (1974), 170–180.

Reprinted with permission from BIT, Vol. 18, pp. 1–8, 1978.

Chapter 4
Concurrent Systems

Introduction

Atomic actions are now regarded as an important structuring concept for concurrent systems. Given a system of interacting processes (e.g. processes that share data), we would like execution of a program by a process to be 'free of interference' from ('indivisible' with respect to) other such executions. The so-called serializability property of atomic actions guarantees just that. Atomic actions can also be embellished with the 'failure atomicity' property: they can be provided with backward recovery capability such that an action in execution can be terminated without producing any side effects. The Newcastle papers collected in this chapter are concerned with the development of atomic action concept and discuss programming language features and recovery facilities for the construction reliable concurrent systems.

The first paper is the one in which Lomet introduced the concept of atomic actions by giving three 'equivalent' definitions. These definitions capture intuitively what we mean when we say that a process (within an atomic action) does not 'interact' with other processes (outside the atomic action). By imposing a restriction that any results produced by an action become visible to other actions only after the action terminates, it is possible to make the backward recovery of atomic actions independent from each other. Lomet describes how atomic actions can be made a unit of backward recovery. The paper by Best and Randell presents a precise characterization of atomicity. *Occurrence graphs* are used to model computations. A given computation − represented by a subgraph − can then be regarded as atomic if and only if it can be 'collapsed' into a single event without introducing a cycle in the graph. The idea of replacing a subgraph by a single event naturally leads to the concept of nested atomic actions, whose structure can be represented by extending occurrence graphs to *structured occurrence graphs*. Best and Randell then introduce the notion of *inherently atomic occurrences* (*contractions*) and show that the 'two phase' locking technique as employed in many data base systems to ensure atomicity of user programs is in fact a means of ensuring that these programs are contractions. Finally, structured occurrence graphs are used to model recovery in distributed systems.

As mentioned earlier, it is possible to make the recovery actions of processes independent from each other. Papers three to five are concerned with the design and implementation of a programming system for constructing a system of such independently recoverable concurrent processes. We have seen that (Randell, Chapter 1) backward recovery of a process that has interacted with other processes can start a cascade of recovery actions. In the third paper Shrivastava and Banatre argue that a simple technique of performing recovery exists even if

247

there are interactions between processes, provided these interactions are confined to those necessary for harmonious sharing of resources (i.e. when processes are competing for resources). So, while at a lower level of abstraction these processes do interact, at a higher level they appear to be logically independent.

The recovery actions of such competing processes are discussed in detail in the third paper. A data type *port* is developed for specifying resource acquisition, use of the resource, 'unuse' of the resource in case recovery is required and release of the resource. Papers four and five describe how these ideas have been incorporated in the programming language Concurrent Pascal. Both Concurrent and Sequential Pascal were extended with recovery blocks and further, *ports* were included in Concurrent Pascal. A number of working examples are presented in the fourth paper to illustrate how seemingly complex recovery actions can be performed with some ease. The details of the recovery system that supports the recovery features of ports are presented in the fifth paper.

In the last paper of this chapter, Anderson and Knight develop a methodology for introducing software fault tolerance in real-time systems. They observe that a large class of real-time systems possess a similar iterative structure consisting of a group of cyclic communicating processes with well defined synchronization points. Thus, the group of processes between two synchronization points can be made recoverable by enclosing their activities inside a *conversation*-like recovery structure (see Randell, Chapter 1, where conversations are introduced; note also that a conversation is an atomic action). For real-time systems the authors have developed a restricted version of the conversation concept, termed an *exchange*. The four aspects of fault tolerance − error detection, damage assessment, recovery and provision of continued service − are then discussed with special reference to real-time systems.

Process Structuring, Synchronization, and Recovery Using Atomic Actions

D. B. LOMET

This paper explores the notion of an atomic *action* as a method of process structuring. This notion, first introduced explicitly by Eswaren et al. [6] in the context of data base systems, reduces the problem of coping with many processes to that of coping with a single process within the atomic *action*. A form of process synchronization, the *await* statement, is adapted to work naturally with atomic actions. System recovery is also considered and we show how atomic actions can be used to isolate recovery action to a single process. Explicit control of recovery is provided by a *reset* procedure that permits information from rejected control paths to be passed to subsequent alternative paths.

Key Words and Phrases. Multiprocessing, synchronization, recovery, mutual exclusion

1. Atomic Actions

Introduction

It has long been realized that some way of restricting process interaction is required if programs involving multiple processes are to be correctly implemented. Ideas similar to atomic actions have been suggested for this purpose as far back as Dijkstra's famous paper [5]. Thus Dijkstra postulates that certain primitive operations "are to be regarded as indivisible, non-interfering actions...". Brinch Hansen states [1], even more emphatically that "It is impossible to make meaningful statements about the effects of concurrent computations unless operations on common variables exclude one another in time. So, in the end, our understanding of concurrent processes is based on our ability to execute their interactions strictly sequentially." An atomic action, as we use the term, is merely a device for permitting the writer of a procedure to secure the same benefits of atomicity, i.e. indivisibility, non-interference, strict sequencing, as is enjoyed by the primitive operations.

The important properties of atomic actions can be expressed in a number of equivalent ways. We illustrate three.

1. An action is atomic if the process performing it is not aware of the existence of any other active process (can detect no spontaneous state change) and no other process is aware of the activity of this process (its state changes are concealed) during the time the process is performing the action.

2. An action is atomic if the process performing it does not communicate with other processes while it is executing the action.

3. Actions are atomic if they can be considered, so far as other processes are concerned, to be indivisible and instantaneous, such that the effects on the system are as if they were interleaved as opposed to concurrent.

249

Background

The current widely known process structuring mechanisms do not provide the programmer with the ability to specify atomic actions. We review some of these below.

Dijkstra [5] proposed semaphores as a mechanism by which a programmer could assure that a sequence of actions could be regarded as indivisible. The idea is to use semaphores to assure that code intended to be indivisible is executed by only a single process at a time. A semaphore is used to guard the code. So long as process interactions can only occur in the "critical section" guarded by the semaphore, the code will function as an atomic (indivisible) action.

When processes can interact by means of several common variables and while executing several different sections of code, mutual exclusion by means of a semaphore guarding a critical section no longer can assure atomicity. Consider first the case of a single common or *shared* variable v that is accessed by several sections of code executed by different processes. One now needs a convention by which a semaphore can be associated with a shared variable so that all code accessing the variable is required to test the same semaphore. Such a semaphore has been called a lock [4]. Locks provide a way of assuring that only one process has access to a shared variable at a time.

Brinch Hansen [1] introduced the idea of a critical region as a means of structuring the seizing and releasing of lock semaphores. Thus, to access a common (*shared*) variable "v", one specifies a critical region

1.(1) **region** v **do** S

where only code in S is permitted access to "v". Further, if one process is in a critical region associated with shared variable "v", all other processes are excluded from regions associated with "v".

Problems arise for critical regions as soon as one is interested in accessing more than one variable. Not only is deadlock a potential problem but one may have difficulty assuring that the critical regions are atomic. Consider the code fragment below:

1.(2) **region** v **do**
　　　　region w **do** S1;

　　　　† .

　　　　region w **do** S2;
　　　　end;

The outer critical region (i.e. for "v") is no longer atomic. A second process can examine "w" at (†) and change "w" so that S2 sees the change, thus communicating with the process in *"region v"* and destroying the atomic nature of the region.

250

Such code sequences can be transformed, of course, into ones in which the variables are held for the duration of the outer region and these will be atomic. However, subtle cases can arise that require much more knowledge and care if atomicity is to be preserved. Consider the skeletal program of 1.(3).

1.(3)   b: **procedure;**   a: **procedure;**
       region w **do**   **region** v **do**
        begin;   S;
          a;   **end** a;
           ·
     † ·
           ·
          a;
        end;
    end b;

Unless the writer of procedure "b" is fully aware of the code in procedure "a" (an unfortunate requirement, to say the least) and seizes "v" as well as "w", then, as shown in 1.(3), the procedure "b" will not be atomic since communication can occur at (†).

A way of assuring that some actions can be guaranteed to be atomic is to make use of monitors as expounded by Brinch Hansen [1] and Hoare [8]. A monitor is similar to an instance of a SIMULA class [3], i.e. it is a data object that possesses not only variable components but also procedure components. Then additional constraints are placed on the use of these components in a multiprocessing environment. These are, quoting [8]

1. "only one program [process] at a time [can] succeed in entering a monitor procedure..."
2. "procedures local to a monitor should not access any non-local variables other than those local to the same monitor."
3. "these [local] variables of the monitor should be inaccessible from outside the monitor".

These constraints assure that the monitor procedures are atomic.

There are two problems with monitors. One, atomic actions involving more than one monitor must be implemented in an indirect way, perhaps by using monitors to realize semaphores. Two, the first constraint on monitors, i.e. that only one process can be executing any of the collection of monitor procedures, is more restrictive than necessary. What is required, simply and directly, is that monitor procedures be atomic.

Data base systems present many of the same problems as operating systems. In some respects, however, the problems are even more severe. In particular, the set of records (shared variables) that are to be accessed during a "transaction" may be very hard to determine ahead of time. Nonetheless, users desire to be presented with a consistent view of the data, i.e. one in which each of them appears to be the sole user of the system. It is for this reason that transactions possessing the attribute of being atomic were introduced by Eswaren et al. [6]. A number of interesting properties of such transactions were established in [6]

251

but the terminology used is data base oriented and no concrete notation is suggested. The next section presents and motivates a notation, which will subsequently be augmented by a notation for process synchronization and recovery.

Action Procedures

What is needed is a facility by which the writer of a procedure can directly state his intention that a procedure be atomic. We regard the procedure mechanism as the extension mechanism for operations. Therefore, any property that is possessed by a primitive operation should be expressible when a user provides a procedure. In particular, it should be possible for a user to write a procedure that exactly reproduces the effect of any given operation. For this reason, it is essential that a mechanism be provided that permits the writing of atomic procedures. It is this line of reasoning, along with considerations of system recovery, that led us, independently of [6], to the notion of atomic actions and action procedures.

We suggest the following notation for *action* procedures.

1.(4) $\langle$identifier$\rangle$: **action** ($\langle$parameter-list$\rangle$);
            $\langle$statement-list$\rangle$
         end;

The semantics of actions are the same as those of procedures except that *actions* are to be performed as atomic actions, i.e. they are to be indivisible, etc. It should be clear that the difficulties of 1.(3) can then be avoided by writing:

1.(5)   b: **action;**   a: **action;**
            a;   S;
            .   **end;**
            .
            .
            a;
         end;

That "b" is an action assures that it is atomic regardless of the procedures or actions it may call. The effect of this is to shift the responsibility for resource acquisition and release to the implementor of *actions* rather than being the responsibility of the programmer using *actions*.

The shift of resource acquisition and release from user to implementation is simultaneously a great responsibility and a great opportunity. The implementation must now assure that deadlock does not occur (or can be overcome) while maximizing the amount of concurrency. The opportunity arises because the implementation is no longer constrained by explicit directions from the user. The user benefits enormously by having this entire messy area removed from his concern, thus enabling him to concentrate on the remaining program logic.

It should be clear that resources that can only be referenced by a single process require no special protection in order to assure that actions are atomic. This observation suggests that we syntactically distinguish *shared* and *private* resources. Doing this greatly eases the implementation burden by identifying those variables for which there is contention, i.e. the *shared* variables. Brinch Hansen [1] has previously made this suggestion though coupled with critical regions. By declaring variables as *shared* or *private*, the implementation problems for atomic actions should be comparable to those for critical regions.

The *shared* (or *private*) attribute applies to an object as a whole and not to its separate components. Local variables of a procedure are, of course, always private. To enforce that *private* objects not be accessible to other processes, we must insist that references to *private* objects not be assigned to *shared* objects. Of course, references to *shared* objects can be assigned to *private* objects. They would not otherwise be accessible.

The *shared/private* attribute is useful in other ways as well. First, it serves as valuable documentation, identifying the variables that are potential communication links between processes. Second, it is useful in memory management. One can garbage collect *private* resources that are no longer accessible by their associated process. One need not examine all processes in the system looking for additional references since none can exist. Further, when a process terminates, all its private resources can be reclaimed.

Implementation Issues

There are a number of ways that atomic actions might be realized. A particularly simple one in a multiprogramming system is to execute an *action* with interrupts disabled. That is, no interrupts are taken and the action retains control of the system until it completes. In effect, it seizes all system resources during its execution. This strategem exploits the property that *actions* can be interleaved, i.e. concurrent processing in which several processes execute simultaneously is not required in order for an action to complete.

In a multiprocessor system, if we wish to exploit resources efficiently, then it is important to attempt to maximize concurrency. This requires that only resources actually needed by an *action* during its excution be acquired. Other processes wishing to use these resources must wait for them to be released.

Eswaren et al. [6] has identified the pattern of resource acquisition and release required to support atomic actions. Such a pattern is called two phased. It arises as follows. As a process executing an atomic *action* proceeds, it acquires the *shared* resources it needs. This is called the "growing phase". The set of resources held is constantly increasing since a process must not release any resources so long as there may be additional resources that it will need. [See 1.(3)] Once any resource is released, no others may be acquired and the set of held resources is constantly decreasing. This is called the "shrinking phase". The conceptual "instant of time" *ta* at which the *action* occurs can be regarded as

253

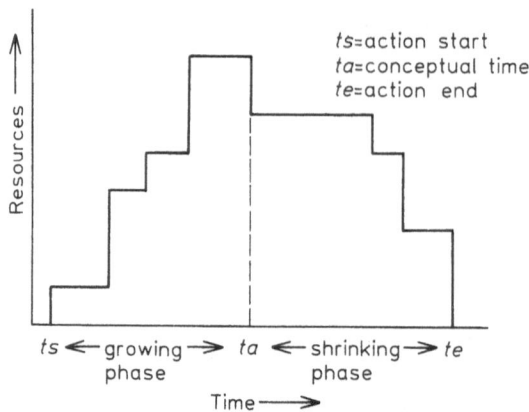

Fig. 1. Resource acquisition and release as a function of time for atomic actions

the time at which the first resource is released. It is established in [6] that this discipline of resource acquisition and release guarantees that actions have a serial schedule, i.e. their effects are as if they are interleaved. Figure 1 illustrates this strategem.

It is possible to refine this strategy. Observe that resources that are merely examined by an *action* need not be concealed from other processes. It is sufficient if other processes are prevented from changing these resources. Acquisition of resources such that other processes can examine but not change them is called "locking in the shared mode" [7]. Resources that are updated by an action must, of course, have these updates concealed from other processes. Thus, when these resources are acquired, no other process must be permitted to examine them. Such resource acquisition is called "locking in the exclusive mode" [7]. Both forms of locking must be two phased with the same *ta* [6, 7].

The resource acquisition and release strategy described above does not constitute a resource management algorithm. A user cannot determine whether he executes alone or concurrently. How resource contention is handled if concurrent execution is to be achieved is not stated. Nor have we described a method for coping with deadlock or indefinite postponement. The analysis above has merely provided the framework in which a resource management algorithm must operate.

2. Process Synchronization

Synchronization using Actions

The sufficiency of atomic actions to provide synchronization can be demonstrated by presenting an implementation of semaphores in terms of atomic actions. Since semaphores are capable of realizing critical regions, conditional critical regions, and monitors, there can be no doubts about the functional adequacy of atomic actions for providing synchronization.

We provide semaphores by means of a SIMULA like class [3], the component procedures of which either are or contain action procedures. The semaphore class is defined in 2.(1).

The code for "V" needs no particular explanation. It is an *action* procedure and hence performs its effects as an atomic operation. The code for "P" is somewhat more complicated. First, "P" is not itself an atomic action. Rather it loops continuously, the body of the loop being atomic but each cycle of the loop providing an opportunity for changes to be made to "sem". Within the *action* body, "sem" is tested. If found to be greater than zero, the continuously testing loop is terminated with "sem" decremented by one. The loop termination is accomplished by calling the *escape* procedure "proceed". This construct is a variation of the "label" procedures of Landin [9] and Clint and Hoare [2]. When an *escape* procedure terminates, it returns control to the caller of its lexically enclosing procedure. Thus, when "proceed" terminates, control returns to the caller of "P".

There are two difficulties with this semaphore class definition, in particular with the body of P.

1. The repeated testing of "sem" constitutes busy waiting, consuming real processor time.

```
2.(1)      semaphore: class;
              sem: integer initial (0)
              V: action;
                sem := sem + 1;
                return;
                end;
              P: procedure;
                proceed: escape; †
                  return;
                  end proceed;
                repeat (
                  action; ‡
                    if sem ≥ 0 then
                      begin;
                        sem := sem − 1;
                        proceed;
                        end;
                      end;)
                end P;
            end semaphore;
```

† An unnamed **action** procedure is written here where it is to be executed, in the same way as a **begin** block.

‡ An **escape** procedure named "proceed", not an "escape" statement. See the text.

2. If several processes are testing the same semaphore, a race exists and there is no guarantee that some processes will not be subjected to indefinite delay. This is so because no scheduling policy is provided.

Busy waiting has yet a third difficulty if we wish to provide synchronization within an atomic action. Notice that the busy waiting in P involves time slots in which "sem" is accessible to other processes because the "wait" loop consists of a succession of atomic actions rather than being embedded in one large action. In a single atomic action the variables within the action, once examined, cannot be changed by other processes. Thus, busy waiting within a single action would be in vain.

It might be argued that, as with the procedure P, one can always provide for the busy waiting to involve many atomic actions, with other processes thus capable of changing the tested variables. This is extremely difficult to arrange, however. Let us suppose that "A" is an *action* procedure, that "B" is an an ordinary procedure, and that "B" uses semaphores. So far as "B" is concerned, such use of semaphores should result in a workable program. If, however, "B" is called from "A", it becomes part of an atomic action, and hence, so does the busy waiting in "B". Now, however, the busy waiting will never detect changes in "sem" and the program will loop forever. If "sem" is permitted to change, then a communication link has been established between the process executing A and B and the process changing "sem", thus destroying the atomic nature of *action* procedures.

The Await Statement

The problem with permitting "sem" to change is the fear that communication will be established with a process inside an *action* procedure. But if such a process does not remember that it has seen previous values for "sem", i.e. if there is no way for it to subsequently determine whether the test was satisfied the first time or only after many repetitions, then we can take a different view. This view is that an action procedure "A" did not commence its execution until after "sem" had changed.

What we need in order to realize this view in which the entire *action* is delayed until the test can be satisfied on its first execution, is a mechanism that informs the system that this is our intent and permits the system to enforce the required constraints. For this purpose, the *await* statement is introduced. The intent of *await* is similar to that suggested for it in [1, 8], but the description of it is different in order to maintain the integrity of atomic actions.

The await statement has the following syntax:

2.(2) **await** (⟨boolean expr⟩) **then** ⟨procedure⟩

Following our view that all executable constructs should be describable as some form of procedure, we produce 2.(3) as the semantics of the *await* statement.

2.(3)   await: **action** (test: **boolean function,** body: **procedure**);
        ‡ **delay** (atomic action until prescience
        tells us that "test" is true, or that
        it escapes, then immediately execute
        the following)
        if test **then**
            begin;
            body;
            return;
            end;
        else error; †
        end await;

† "error" might be, for example, an **escape** procedure.

It is, of course, true that such a procedure could not be written which is why *await* must be primitive. The *"delay"* at (‡) represents a bit of magic that cannot be expressed otherwise. It must be guaranteed that no subsequent testing on the part of a process can determine how many times the "test" expression is executed. In order to assure this, it is required that "test" have no side effects. This prevents the retention of any state change other than the result of the expression, which will be *true* when control finally passes to the *then* clause. Notice that "test" is evaluated in the *action* procedure with "body". This assures that there is no possibility of the variables in "test" changing between the evaluation of "test" and the execution of "body" and hence guarantees that "test" remains true until (or unless) "body" changes those variables. When *await* is itself executed within an *action* procedure, the evaluation of "test" ensures that the variables upon which "test" depends can no longer be changed, except by the process executing this *action*. Two *awaits*, one with "test" and the other with "test" as below:

2.(4)   **action;**

        .
        await test **then** S1;
        .

        † **await** ¬ test **then** S2;
        .

        end;

in which both are within the same action, will result in the process executing this action being indefinitely delayed at (†), provided the process itself did not change the variables of "test". Of course, if the variables of "test" cannot be changed by some other process, then the process executing 2.(4) cannot complete. Such situations can never be completely eliminated without drastically reducing the power of the language. This is true whether or not *await* is provided. One can, in fact regard endless looping or recursion as instances of the same problem.

257

Implementation Issues

The preceding section introduced *await* statements without placing any constraints on the form of the boolean expression that was used for synchronization. To reduce implementation problems, it may be desirable to restrict the boolean expression.

Whenever an *await* expression is not satisfied immediately, it is necessary to suspend the executing process and place it on a queue of waiting processes. Many strategies for this are available, particularly if we are not concerned with whether our waiting processes resume as quickly as possible. However, it seems desirable for the implementation to attempt re-execution of an *await* expression whenever one of its variables changes. One would like, therefore, to identify those variables that might cause the resumption of some waiting process.

One could interpretively test some indicator associated with every *shared* variable to determine whether a process waits on this variable. However, one can greatly reduce such interpretation while enhancing program readability if variables used for synchronization are explicitly designated. Thus, we suggest that at least one of the variables in an *await* expression be designated as a *synchronizing* variable, i.e. be declared with the *synchronizing* attribute. Our implementation problem is then confined to *synchronizing* variables. Only *synchronizing* variables need be permitted to change during the repeated evaluations of the *await* expression, and only the updating of *synchronizing* variables need result in interpretation to discover whether waiting processes should be resumed. With respect to acquiring and releasing resources, only *synchronizing* variables might ever be acquired and released several times by an atomic action, and then only during the repeated evaluations of the first *await* expression in which they occur.

Additional restrictions might be required in terms of the number of variables and the operations permitted upon them in order to reduce implementation cost and improve efficiency. The most restrictive requirement would be for each *await* expression to consist solely of a single *synchronizing* boolean variable. Less severe restrictions should also be feasible.

One important feature of the *await* statement in conjunction with action procedures is that, unlike the case for monitors and conditional critical regions, the concepts do not require the exposure of an underlying implementation in order for them to be understood. Thus, no explicit mention (at the conceptual level) of process queues is required, though obviously, an implementation will exploit queues and will require a scheduling strategy. Further, one need not be concerned with maintaining invariants at the point where an *await* statement occurs. Those parts that have become temporarily invalid because of updates preceding an *await* are exactly those parts of the system state that are not accessible to other processes. The components available to other processes, since they are unchanged, still satisfy their required invariants.

An Example: Buffers

Buffering is a common technique for optimizing the performance of parallel processes of the producer-consumer variety. While a consumer cannot consume what a producer has not yet produced, a buffer permits a producer to "race ahead" of the consumer, producing results that are retained in the buffer for subsequent consumption. Thus, in addition, buffers reduce the possibility that a consumer will be delayed by waiting for a result from a producer.

We wish to provide buffers by means of *actions* and *await* statements. Our first attempt will be to modify slightly previous solutions in terms of conditional critical regions or monitors. This is shown in 2.(5).

2.(5)   buffer: **class shared;**
        frame: **array** $(0: N-1)$ **of T;**
        count: **integer initial** (0) **synchronizing;**
        head: **integer initial** (0);
        send: **action** $(x: T)$;
          await (count $\leq N-1$) **then**
            begin;
              frame (head $\square$ count) := x; †
              count := count + 1;
            end;
          end send;
        receive: **action** $(y: T)$;
          await (count > 0) **then**
            begin;
              y := frame (head);
              head := head $\square$ 1; †
              count := count − 1;
            end;
          end receive;
        end buffer;

† $\square$ is addition modulo N.

This solution is adequate when the use of the buffers occurs outside of all atomic actions. Unfortunately, a problem arises when "send" or "receive" are used within atomic actions. Consider "receive". When a process P executes "receive" in an atomic action, the changes it makes to "head" and "count" cannot be seen by other processes. Hence, these processes cannot execute "send" (or "receive"), and in particular, cannot refill the buffer, until P completes its atomic action.

Thus, only as many messages can be received in an atomic action as are in the buffer at the time that the first "receive" executed. This is highly unfortunate as it introduces a large measure of time dependence, and hence, uncertainty. One would like to exploit the full potential of the buffer, i.e. all its frames, whether the buffer is used outside of or within an atomic action.

Another pitfall must be avoided. In an atomic action, it should not be possible to receive more messages than can be contained at one time in the buffer. Otherwise, we will have established communication into the atomic action. The desired solution allows the maximum flexibility in sending and receiving messages consistent with the constraints imposed by the atomicity of actions of the communicating processes. The class defined in 2.(6) provides precisely that.

2.(6)   buffer: **class shared;**
      frame: **array** $(0: N-1)$ **of T;**
      empty: **array** $(0: N-1)$ **of boolean**
        initial (true) synchronizing;
      head: **integer initial** (0);
      tail: **integer initial** (0);
      send: **action** (x: T);
        await (empty (tail)) **then**
          begin;
            frame (tail) := x;
            empty (tail) := **false;**
            tail := tail □ 1; †
          end;
        end send;
      receive: **action** (y: T);
        await (¬ empty (head)) **then**
          begin;
            y := frame (head);
            empty (head) := **true;**
            head := head □ 1; †
          end;
        end receive;
      end buffer;

† □ is addition modulo N.

Each buffer frame is only accessed if it is actually needed and the control information governing the buffer is distributed as separate information for each frame. Further, importantly, the pointers "head" and "tail" are distributed to consumer ("receive") and producer ("send"), respectively. This distribution of control information can be readily seen by examining Fig. 2 below which illustrates the relations between the various components of the buffer as implemented in 2.(6).

Note that once a frame has been accessed, it cannot be reused until the action is complete (except by the action itself). The "send" and "receive" procedures are almost completely symmetric, and hence, the flexibility provided to receivers is also provided to senders. Thus, merely because a buffer is full (or almost so) when the first send is issued within an action does not prevent it from ultimately sending as many messages as there are buffer frames. Other processes can continue to read messages deposited in the buffer by prior actions, making those frames ultimately available to the sending action.

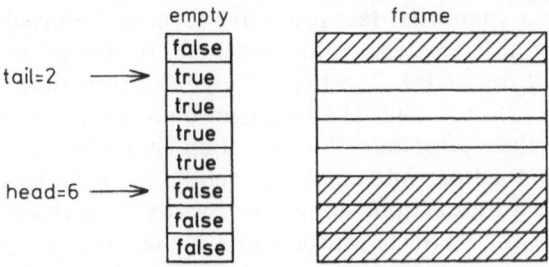

Fig. 2. The bounded (circular) buffer described by the program of 2.(6). The shaded elements of "frame" contain data

3. System Recovery

A Unit of Recovery

By system recovery we mean the undoing of errors as opposed to their correction. This is usually thought of as consisting of two phases:
1. the rolling back of the system to a previous state, assumed to be valid, by undoing some set of actions, presumably including the erroneous ones.
2. the re-performance of the actions undone in 1. that were not (known to be) erroneous.

An error is usually associated with or detected in some process while recovery to a "checkpointed" state may involve many other processes. Thus, step 2. is needed so that correct actions are not lost. It should be clear that with a sufficiently comprehensive system log, such system recovery is always possible, though at rather great expense, so long as errors have not escaped to the "outside world".

One need not back up the entire system to provide a method of undoing errors. In an appropriately structured system, in which a programmer identifies the units of recovery, it becomes possible to restrict the undoing of errors to the process (or unit) in which they occurred. A mechanism for so structuring systems has been introduced by Randell [10] who calls this unit a recovery block.

The idea of a recovery block, in so far as undoing errors is concerned, is to isolate the process executing it from other processes. Randell states [10] that "communication, whether it involves explicit message passing or merely reference to common variables, would destroy the value of the ... recovery block, and hence must be prohibited." This restriction assures that recovery blocks are, in fact, atomic.

By preventing other processes from becoming dependent upon the effects of an atomic action until the action is complete, only the process executing the action is affected by errors in the action. Hence, only this process needs to be restored to a previous state. And restoring this process involves restoring to a previous state only that part of the system that is modified by this process during the execution of the atomic action. It is unnecessary to re-perform actions of other processes since none of these were undone.

Gray et al. [7] point out that a somewhat less restrictive form of "transaction" than atomic transactions also possesses this attribute of being independently recoverable. These "transactions", called "degree 2 transactions" (atomic "transactions" are degree 3) only conceal all changes until completion. Atomic actions not only prevent this communication out of an action but also prevent communication from other actions into an atomic action. Being subject to this weaker restriction, degree 2 transactions do not necessarily, as a result, possess a serial schedule nor are their effects reproducible if they are re-executed.

Recovery Bookkeeping

In order to permit atomic actions to be recoverable, their implementation must be such that

1. updated resources, i.e. those locked in the exclusive mode, are not released until the action is completed. Once a modified resource is released, independent recovery can no longer be assured as another process may examine the resource and hence become dependent upon it.
2. the initial states of all resources modified by the action can be reconstructed. This usually involves maintaining a time ordered log of update operations on which overwritten information is recorded together with its location.

In [10], recovery is realized by means of a mechanism called a "recursive cache". Rather than recording all modifications and then undoing them in reverse time order, only the first change in any location is recorded. All modifications to the system state must first be checked, interpretively at run time, to determine if a previous change has already been recorded. This means, of course, that only the starting state of a recovery block can be restored, and not intermediate ones, but this is all that is required.

A "recursive cache" is but one of a number of methods for providing recovery. A compiler could, in a large number of cases, identify updates that do not represent initial changes in a recoverable atomic action and permit these updates to run without additional interpretive overhead. Updates that might represent initial changes in an atomic action could be logged. One might, as with the "recursive cache", try to eliminate from the log all changes after the first one, but there is no need to do so. Further, strategies that are only partially successful in eliminating redundant log entries are also possible. One might employ, for example, a small associative store with recently logged items and eliminate additional potential log entries already in this associative memory. This is quite similar to dynamic address translation is a virtual memory. These recovery strategies all need to be evaluated carefully.

Reset Procedures

Recovery facilities are, in effect, means of providing backtracking. Such backtracking is usually presented at the programming language interface in a more or less implicit guise, e.g. recovery blocks, backtrack programming, etc. There are important advantages to explicit invocation of recovery facilities, particularly if the ability to communicate information from the "failed" program path to alternative ones is desired. What we introduce is just such a feature, called a *reset* procedure.

A *reset* procedure derives its effect from its lexical context in much the same way as an *escape* procedure, previously used in 2.(1) and described in [2, 9]. In addition to the effects of an *escape*, a *reset* procedure also undoes all changes produced by code executed since its enclosing procedure was invoked. We require that this enclosing procedure be an *action* procedure so as to isolate the recovery of the process executing it from other processes. An *action* procedure then becomes the unit of recovery. Consider the skeletal program of 3.(1).

3.(1)   x: **action**
           y: **reset** (a);
              .
              .
              .
              end y;
           z: **procedure;**
              b: local variable;
                 .
                 .
              † y (b);
              end z;
              .
        ‡ z;
              .
              end x;

We assume that the call (‡) to procedure "z" is executed in action "x". Both "x" and "z" modify the process state by means of, e.g. updating variables global to "x". However, "z" encounters some difficulty it cannot cope with and realizes that some of the changes made have been erroneous. It, therefore, calls "y" at (†), passing some information via argument "b". When "y" is called, all changes to variables global to "x" are erased and the local variables of "x" are re-initialized. Only those changes produced by "y" will be detectable subsequently. When "y" terminates, it returns control to the caller of "x", exactly as if "y" had been an *escape* procedure.

We should offer a word of caution concerning the argument(s) to a *reset* procedure. If an argument is a variable passed by reference, the *reset* procedure will not see its value at the moment of call but rather its value after recovery, i.e. the value the variable had when the enclosing action was entered. Passing arguments by value does not, of course, have this potential confusion.

An Example: Recovery Blocks

We illustrate the use of *reset* procedures by programming an implicit recovery mechanism, i.e. Randell's recovery blocks [10]. Basically, a recovery block is a control structure that consists of two main components.

1. an "acceptance test" that must be satisfied on exit from the recovery block, i.e. it is a boolean expression that must evaluate to *true*.
2. a set of alternative bodies that are executed to produce the desired effects. The first alternative body is executed and the acceptance test evaluated. If *true*, the recovery block is complete. If *false*, recovery takes place, returning the block to its initial state after which the next alternative body is executed, etc.

A syntax for recovery blocks is:

3.(2)   **ensure** ⟨boolean expr⟩
      by ⟨procedure⟩
      {**else by** ⟨procedure⟩} *
      else error;
      end;

The procedure of 3.(3) provides the recovery semantics required of a recovery block. The resetting in "ensure" prior to the execution of the first alternative can be avoided if the invocation of "recover(1)" is replaced by most of the body of "recover". This results in duplicate code. Since there are no effects to be undone at "recover(1)", little if any cost is involved in this initial resetting.

Many other applications should exist for *reset* procedure, including some in which information of a more essential nature than illustrated for recovery blocks is passed from the rejected control path to its alternative. Sussman and McDermott [11] present a cogent argument for this, though advocating a very different mechanism for accomplishing it.

3.(3)   ensure: **action** (accept: **boolean function,**
      alternative: **array of procedure**);
      recover: **reset** (j: **integer**);
          alternative (j);
          if accept **then return;**
          else
        if j < highbound (alternative) † **then**
          recover (j + 1);
        else error; ‡
        end recover;
      recover (1);
      end ensure;

† highbound is a function that returns the upper bound of a vector, i.e. its maximum index.
‡ error might designate an **escape** or a **reset** procedure.

4. Summary

Atomic actions have been explored as a means of structuring multiple process programs. *Action* procedures were suggested as a way of introducing atomic actions into a programming interface. Synchronization was achieved by means of the *await* statement, without exposing any underlying queueing or making explicit the acquisition and release of resources. Together, *action* procedures and the *await* statement make multiple process programming very little more difficult than sequential programming.

Because atomic actions isolate a process from the rest of the system, recovery involving restoring a process to the initial state of an uncompleted atomic action is particularly simple. *Reset* procedures were introduced to provide the user with explicit control over recovery and to permit the passing of some information from a rejected control sequence to its explicitly requested alternative.

Acknowledgements. This work was immensely aided by my frequent interactions with members of the System Reliability Project at the University of Newcastle upon Tyne. Particular thanks are due to B. Randell who stimulated my interest in this area and carefully critiqued an earlier draft of this paper; and to P. M. Melliar-Smith whose many informative discussions of this subject greatly enhanced my understanding of it.

References

1. Brinch Hansen, P. Operating System Principles, Prentice Hall, Englewood Cliffs, N.J., U.S.A. 1973.
2. Clint, M. and Hoare, C. A. R. Program Proving: Jumps and Functions, Acta Inf. 1 (1972) 214−224.
3. Dahl, O.-J., Myhnhaug, B., and Nygaard, K. The SIMULA 67 Common Base Language, Norwegian Computer Centre, Oslo, Publication S-22 (1970).
4. Dennis, J. B. and Van Horn, E. C. Programming semantics for multiprogrammed computations. Comm. ACM 9, 3 (March 1966) 143−155.
5. Dijkstra, E. W. Co-operating Sequential Processes, in Programming Languages (Ed. F. Genuys), Academic Press, New York, 1968.
6. Eswaren, K. P., Gray, J. N., Lorie, R. A., and Traiger, I. L. On the notions of consistency and predicate locks in a data base system. IBM Research Report RJ1487, December 1974.
7. Gray, J. N., Lorie, R. A., Putzolu, G. R., and Traiger, I. L. Granularity of locks and degrees of consistency in a shared data base. IBM Research Report RJ1654, September 1975.
8. Hoare, C. A. R. Monitors, an operating system structuring concept. Comm. ACM 17, 10 (October 1974) 549−557.
9. Landin, P. A. A correspondence between AL-GOL 60 and Church's lambda-notation: part I. Comm. ACM 8, 2 (February 1965) 89−101.
10. Randell, B. System structure for software fault tolerance, Sigplan Notices 10, 6 (June 1975) 437−449. [Also Chap. 1]
11. Sussman, G. J. and McDermott, D. V. Why conniving is better than planning. MIT A. I. Memo No. 255A, April, 1972.

A Formal Model of Atomicity in Asynchronous Systems

E. Best and B. Randell

Summary. We propose a generalisation of occurrence graphs as a formal model of computational structure. The model is used to define the "atomic occurrence" of a program, to characterise "interference freeness" between programs, and to model error recovery in a decentralised system.

1. Introduction

Atomic actions have long been recognised as an important programming concept. The ideas behind atomic actions can be traced back at least to Floyd's seminal paper [5] in which he proposed to characterise programs by their input/output relations. Our own interest in atomic actions stems from the awareness [18] that they could help in generalising the concept of a recovery block [17] for concurrent programs. We use the term in the same way as in [11]: by intuitive definition, an atomic action is a piece of program that enjoys the status of a simple "primitive" with regard to its environment, while it may however possess a "complicated" internal structure.

The concept of an atomic action is related to the so-called inductive assertion method for proving properties of programs (see for example [12]). In this technique an assertion can be proved invariant by showing that it holds initially and that its validity is preserved over successive portions of a program. This technique, which has been well-established for sequential programs, can be generalised to concurrent programs using atomic actions: to establish the invariance of an assertion one has to prove that it holds initially and that its truth is preserved by every action. Examples of correctness proofs for concurrent programs using this method include [1, 2] and [3].

Another area of application is that of shared database systems where atomic actions are usually called "transactions" [4, 7, 19]. The invariant property to be preserved in a database is usually called its "consistency". Transactions typically are short sequential user programs which individually preserve database consistency; one of the tasks of a database manager is to ensure that they occur atomically so that the consistency of the database is maintained at all relevant times.

In this paper we base our discussions on the use of a simple programming language consisting of the usual constructs (assignment, etc.) augmented by the parallel operator ‖ and the angular bracket facility to express atomic actions [3]. The semantics of the parallel operator partly depends on the semantics of the atomic actions used in connection with it, but could intuitively be expressed as "execute as much as possible in parallel". For example, the program

$$\langle s := s + 1 \rangle \| \langle s := s + 1 \rangle$$

is taken to indicate the (possibly partly parallel) execution of two "primitive" incrementations of s, so that its net effect should be to increase s by 2 rather than by any other value (i.e. the result should be $s = s_0 + 2$ where s_0 is the initial value of s).

We consider atomic actions in the first place as a programming tool rather than "a hardware feature" or "a synchronisation method". As such, atomic actions serve to build new "primitives" out of given "primitives". It therefore stands to reason that atomic actions be allowed to be the sub-actions of larger atomic actions [18], although such nesting of atomic actions has sometimes been forbidden [3].

For instance, the program

$$\langle\!\langle s := s + 1 \rangle | \langle s := s + 1 \rangle\!\rangle \| \langle s := 2* s \rangle$$

differs from the program

$$(\langle s := s + 1 \rangle \| \langle s := s + 1 \rangle) \| \langle s := 2* s \rangle$$

in that the set of possible results is $\{s = 2* s_0 + 2, s = 2* s_0 + 4\}$ for the former and $\{s = 2* s_0 + 2, s = 2* s_0 + 3, s = 2* s_0 + 4\}$ for the latter. Thus as opposed to, say, [4] where the atomicity of straight sequences of primitives is considered at only one leve of nesting, we shall in the sequel not put any restrictions on either the depth of nesting of atomic actions or the degree of their internal concurrency. It will be shown that this generality introduces non-negligible complications.

The salient properties of atomic actions have frequently been characterised by what is known as the "serialisability" property [4], expressed in [11] as follows: "Actions are atomic if they can be considered, as far as their environment is concerned, to be indivisible and instantaneous, such that the effect on the system is as if they were interleaved as opposed to concurrent". In [3] we find: "We require all accesses to shared variables to be part of an atomic action and postulate that the net effect of our concurrently operating processes is as if atomic actions are mutually exclusive, i.e. the execution periods of atomic actions don't overlap." And in [2] we read: "Atomic actions ... can be implemented by ensuring between their executions mutual exclusion in time."

These characterisations raise a number of questions. Firstly, atomicity which on the face of it is a "local" property of a single action is being expressed by serialisability which is a "global" property of a set of actions. In this paper we shall deal with this question by defining and comparing a variety of "local" and "global" atomicity criteria. Secondly, mutual exclusion seems but one, in general unnecessarily restrictive, way of implementing atomicity; in a shared data base, for instance, the proposition that all transactions be mutually excluded is unacceptable [7]. We shall in this paper regard any method which ensures the truth of our atomicity criteria as a valid implementation of atomicity. Thirdly, the "as if" clause in two of the above characterisations tends to blur the distinction as to whether atomicity is a static or a dynamic property. In this paper, by taking executions of atomic actions as our basic formal objects, we shall give purely dynamic atomicity criteria.

The formal model of computation we are using is that of occurrence graphs [8]. The present paper is in fact a direct successor of [14] where the use of occurrence graphs for the purpose of characterising atomicity has first been suggested. An occurrence graph serves to model a single computation as a set of interdependent events. Event dependencies may arise through usage of data (as in all of our examples), but other types of dependencies such as producer-consumer relationships can be modelled as well. Atomicity is represented by "collapsing" parts of an occurrence graph, i.e. by reducing a subgraph to a single event. In order to accommodate graph collapsing we generalise the occurrence graph model to that of "structured occurrence graphs".

The first part of the paper, comprising Sect. 2 and 3, is organised as follows. The occurrence graph model is introduced in Sect. 2.1 and Sect. 2.2 shows how atomicity can be represented by graph collapsing. This leads to "structured occurrence graphs", defined in Sect. 2.3. Using structured occurrence graphs we derive a "global" atomicity criterion (in essence a generalisation of serialisability, Sect. 3.1), a "local" atomicity criterion (interference-freeness, Sect. 3.2) and a "context-independent" atomicity criterion (Sect. 3.3) which we consider to generalise the notion of "two-phase executions" [4] (Sect. 3.4). A series of propositions establishes the precise relationship between these atomicity criteria.

In the second part of this paper (Sect. 4) we examine the topic of error recovery in a decentralised system, such as, for example, a multi-process message passing system. Our starting point is the assumption that during the activity of such a system recovery points have been established which may function as local fall-back points, so enabling the system to revert to an earlier valid state. We deal with two questions arising in this situation: (a) in the event of the detection of an error, which are the relevant "recovery lines", i.e. sets of recovery points to which the system can revert; and (b) following the detection of an error, which parts of the surrounding activity must be treated as suspect, in the sense of possibly being prey to the same error.

We shall show that the structured occurrence graph model can be adapted to deal with these questions. In Sect. 4.1 we extend the occurrence graph model to that of "recovery graphs" providing for the representation of recovery points. In Sect. 4.2 we define the "units of recovery" as those events which describe the activity "find the appropriate recovery line" atomically, and we show that this defines a structured occurrence graph. In Sect. 4.3 we examine in particular the question of whether or not a recovery point can be invalidated as a consequence of an error detected in a different part of the system, which leads to a classification of different types of recovery points.

We conclude this paper by putting our atomicity criteria inot perspective (Sect. 5). In particular, we discuss the connection between what we have called "interference" in Sect. 3.2 and other related properties, such as data dependency and information flow. We also outline different possible implementation strategies for atomic actions.

2. A Model of Computational Structure

2.1. Occurrence Graphs

We define an occurrence graph as a pair $G = (E, B)$, where E is a non-empty set and $B \subseteq E \times E$ is a (possibly empty) relation over E. We use occurrence graphs to describe computations, whereby the elements $e \in E$ are interpreted as the events of the computation and the elements $b \in B$ are interpreted as "conditions" holding between events and indicating an ordering of events as described below. Pictorially, events are represented as squares and conditions are represented as arrows between squares, as for example in

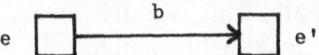

We define $e = \text{tail}(b)$ and $e' = \text{head}(b)$ iff $b = (e, e')$. We call a sequence $(e_0, \ldots, e_n)$, $n \geq 1$, of events a (directed) path from e_0 to e_n iff $e_i B e_{i+1}$ for $0 \leq i < n$. A path is called a cycle iff $e_0 = e_n$. A path is called "simple" iff its constituent events, except possibly the two endpoints e_0 and e_n, are distinct. We write $e < e'$ ("e before e'") iff $e B^+ e'$, i.e. iff there is a path from e to e'. We write $e \leq e'$ iff $e < e'$ or $e = e'$, and e and e' are said to be "concurrent" iff neither $e < e'$ nor $e' < e$. In Fig. 1, for example, $e_1 < e_1$, $e_2 < e_3$ but e_3 and e_4 are concurrent.

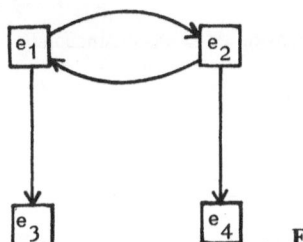

Fig. 1

We call an occurrence graph acyclic iff for no $e \in E$, $e < e$; i.e. iff it does not contain any cycles[1]. The structure $(E, <)$ derived from an acyclic occur-

---

1 There is a close connection between the occurrence graph model and the occurrence net model as defined in [6]. Occurrence nets are triples (B, E, F) where B and E are disjoint non-empty sets (with the same interpretation as above) and $F \subseteq E \times B \cup E \times B$ is a relation, such that

$$\forall b \in B: |F(b)| \leq 1 \quad \text{and} \quad |F^{-1}(b)| \leq 1, \quad \text{and} \tag{1}$$

$$F^+ \text{ is irreflexive.} \tag{2}$$

rence graph is a partial ordering of events. In contradistinction to [8] we allow (for the moment) occurrence graphs to be cyclic because we wish to attach a particular significance to cycles.

We next define the notion of an "immediate predecessor". Care must be taken in this definition because our graphs may be cyclic. Usually [15] an event e is called an "immediate predecessor" of another event e' if $e < e'$ but for no e'', $e < e'' < e'$. By this definition, in Fig. 1 e_1 is not an immediate predecessor of e_3, nor is e_2 an immediate predecessor of e_4. This is contrary to our subsequent intentions; we therefore define immediate predecessors slightly differently.

We call a path from an event e to an event e' a "(proper) extension" of another path from e to e' iff the former contains the same events in the same order as the latter, and besides also at least one other event. In Fig. 1, for example, (e_1, e_2, e_1, e_3) is a proper extension of (e_1, e_3). We call a path "maximal" iff it cannot be properly extended. In Fig. 1, for example, both (e_1, e_2, e_1, e_3) and (e_2, e_1, e_2, e_4) are maximal paths.

We require all occurrence graphs under consideration to satisfy the property that every path can be extended to a maximal path. This is a discreteness property which we subsequently refer to as the "maximality axiom". It is always satisfied for finite graphs.

We finally define $e \in E$ to be an "immediate predecessor" of $e' \in E$ (or e' an "immediate successor" of e), and write $e \lessdot e'$, iff there exists a maximal path $(e_0, \ldots, e_n)$ in which e and e' are neighbours, i.e. $e = e_i$ and $e' = e_{i+1}$ for some $i \in \{0, \ldots, n-1\}^2$. Note that by this definition, e_1 is an immediate predecessor of e_3 in Fig. 1 because they are neighbours in the maximal path (e_1, e_2, e_1, e_3); similarly, e_2 is an immediate predecessor of e_4.

As an example of the use of occurrence graphs to describe computations, we consider a simple program operating on a doubly linked list. Let the list

---

Every acyclic occurrence graph (E, B) in which $B \neq \emptyset$ can be considered an occurrence net

$(B, E, \{(e, b), (b, e') \mid b \in B \text{ and } e = \text{head}(b) \text{ and } e' = \text{tail}(b)\})$

satisfying the somewhat stronger property

$$\forall b \in B: |F(b)| = |F^{-1}(b)| = 1. \tag{1'}$$

Conversely, every occurrence net satisfying (1') can be considered an acyclic occurrence graph

$(E, \{(e, e') \mid e, e' \in E \text{ and } e F^2 e'\})$.

We use occurrence graphs rather than occurrence nets because the permit the collapsing operation to be described more easily

2 The following lemma shows that this definition agrees, for acyclic graphs, with the usual one referred to above.

Lemma 1. (i) $e < e'$ and $\neg \exists e''$: $e < e'' < e'$ implies $e \lessdot e'$.
(ii) *For acyclic graphs, the converse of* (i) *also holds*

consist of a "start" pointer, an "end"pointer and two proper elements "x" and "y" in the following current state:

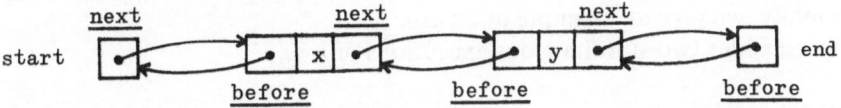

Fig. 2

The algorithm for removing a list element pointed to by a pointer p can make use of concurrency in the following way:

$$\textbf{rem}\,(p){:}p_1 := p.\textbf{before} \parallel p_2 := p.\textbf{next};$$
$$p_1.\textbf{next} := p_2 \parallel p_2.\textbf{before} := p_1,$$

where p_1 and p_2 are local pointer variables.

Every execution of *rem* thus consists of executions of its four constituent assignments in some valid order, the validity of the order being determined by the semantics of the semicolon and the $\parallel$ operator. With the abbreviations

$e_1 = $ execution of "$p_1 := p.\textbf{before}$",
$e_2 = $ execution of "$p_2 := p.\textbf{next}$",
$e_3 = $ execution of "$p_1.\textbf{next} := p_2$",
$e_4 = $ execution of "$p_2.\textbf{before} := p_1$",

the following two occurrence graphs describe two possible (valid) executions of *rem*:

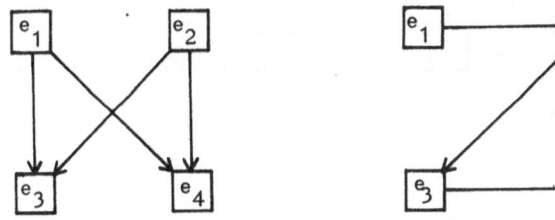   **Fig. 3**

The two executions differ in that in the first one, the pairs of events (e_1, e_2) and (e_3, e_4) both occur concurrently whereas in the second one, $e_1, \ldots, e_4$ occur in linear order. The first execution, in fact, is maximally concurrent in the sense that any more concurrent execution would no longer be a valid execution of the program.

2.2. Collapsing of Subgraphs

We represent programmer-defined atomic actions by "collapsing" the sub-graphs corresponding to their executions into single events, thus giving them

271

an "instantaneous" appearance. Through the collapsing operation we obtain from a given occurrence graph a new one which describes the same computation on a different level of abstraction. Before defining the collapsing operation formally, we give an example of its use.

Let us consider two simultaneous executions of *rem*,

rem $(x) \parallel$ **rem** (y)

of the two elements x and y of the list as shown in Fig. 2, where at first, *rem* is not specified as atomic. As in the previous section, let $e_1^x, \ldots, e_4^x$ and $e_1^y, \ldots, e_4^y$ denote the executions, respectively, of the four assignments in *rem* (x) and *rem* (y). The following Figure shows three possible executions of the simultaneous removal, all of which can be shown to be maximally concurrent:

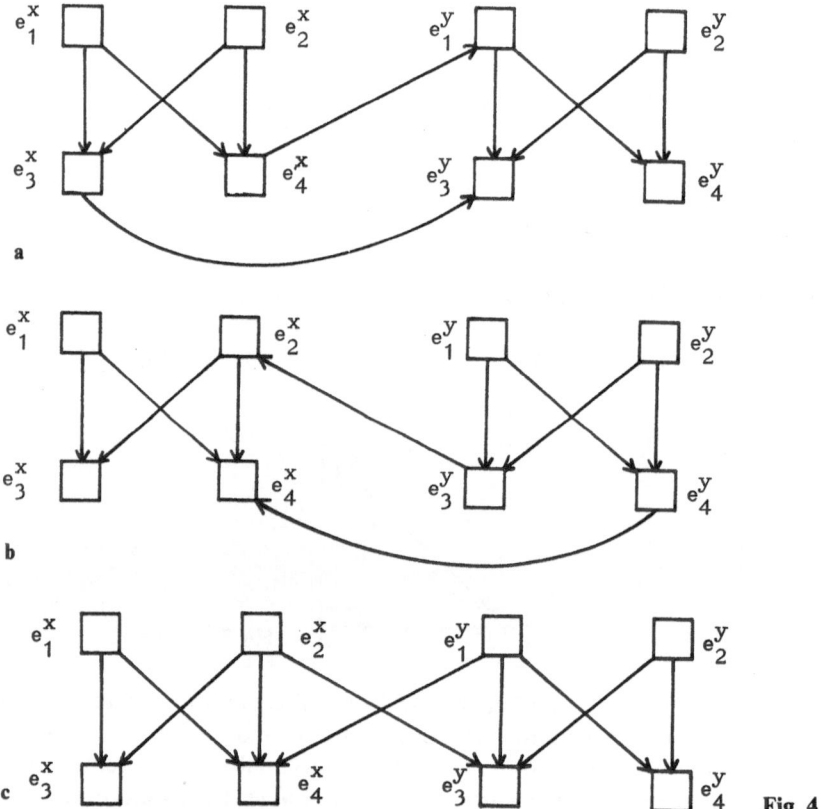

Fig. 4

As in these three executions the e_i^x and e_i^y occur in different order, they may denote different actual assignments (for instance, e_4^x denotes the setting of "*y.before*" to "start" in the first execution, while it denotes the setting of "end.*before*" to "start" in the second execution). Nevertheless, as can easily be verified, the first two executions both have the same overall effect of

272

producing the empty list whereas, by contrast, the third execution leaves the list in the following state:

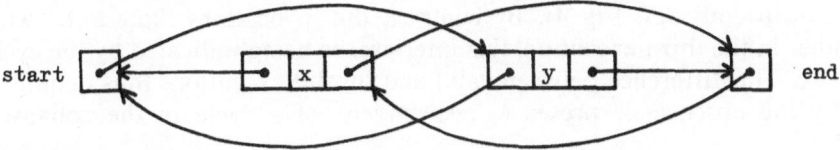

start   x   y   end

Fig. 5

Let us now consider the parallel program

$$\text{at-}\mathbf{rem}\,(x) \,\|\, \text{at-}\mathbf{rem}\,(y).$$

with the "remove" operation specified as an atomic action:

$$\text{at-}\mathbf{rem}\,(p):\ \langle p_1 := p.\,\mathbf{before} \,\|\, p_2 := p.\,\mathbf{next};$$

$$p_1.\,\mathbf{next} := p_2 \,\|\, p_2.\,\mathbf{before} := p_1 \rangle.$$

This means that the simultaneous removal is to have the effect of two proper individual removals, so that of the possible orderings of events shown in Fig. 4, only the first two are to be allowed.

We represent the programmer's actomicity specifications in the following manner:

e_1 e_2

e_3 e_4 $\Rightarrow$ at-rem

Fig. 6

When this collapsing is applied to the occurrence graphs shown in Fig. 4, the following can respectively be obtained:

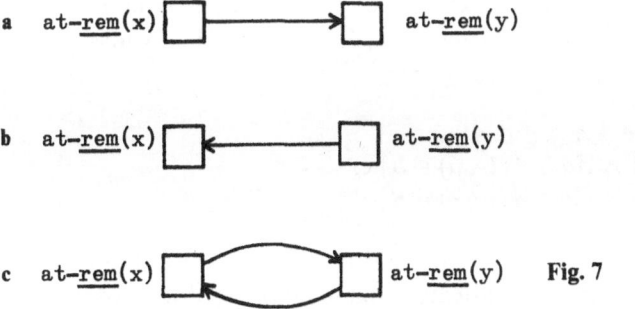

a   at-rem(x) $\longrightarrow$ at-rem(y)

b   at-rem(x) $\longleftarrow$ at-rem(y)

c   at-rem(x) $\longleftrightarrow$ at-rem(y)   **Fig. 7**

273

Figure 7 shows how the invocations of at-*rem* (x) and at-*rem* (y) are related to each other when they are seen as atomic events. In the first two executions, these events occur in strict order, although some of their constituent events occur concurrently (cf. Fig. 4). By contrast, the invocations "interfere" with each other in the third execution, this interference being indicated by the cycle in Fig. 7c. The difference between valid and invalid executions thus manifests itself by the absence or presence, respectively, of a cycle in the collapsed graphs.

We now define the collapsing operation formally. Let an occurrence graph $G = (E, B)$ and a non-empty subset $E' \subseteq E$ be given. We define the subgraph A generated by E' as the set E' together with all arrows that have both endpoints in E'. Formally,

$$A = (E', B') \quad \text{where} \quad B' = \{b \in B \,|\, \text{tail}\,(b) \in E' \wedge \text{head}\,(b) \in E'\}.$$

We also denote the set of events E' generating the subgraph A by $\mathring{A}$.

As A is again an occurrence graph, all the definitions relating to occurrence graphs can be transferred to subgraphs; in particular, a "before" relationship $<_A = B'^+$ can be defined for A which may not coincide with $< = B^+$ on A. Note also that A may be disconnected and/or that B' may be empty. We usually

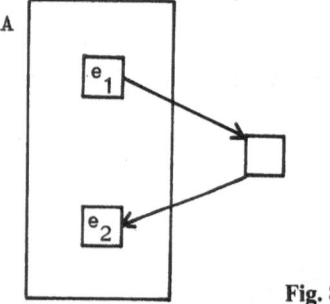

A

Fig. 8

enclose the set E' of events in question in a rectangle. For example, in Fig. 8 A is disconnected, B' is empty and $e_1 < e_2$ in G but not $e_1 <_A e_2$ in A.

We define the "collapsing" of A as the construction of a new graph $G\,[A]$ from G such that A is replaced by a single new event and all arrows leading into and out of A are replaced by arrows ending and starting, respectively, with the new event. We assume the new event to be uniquely named and call it "A" for the purpose of this definition. Formally, $G\,[A] = (E\,[A], B\,[A])$ where

$$E\,[A] = (E \backslash \mathring{A}) \cup \{A\}$$
$$B\,[A] = \{(e, e') \in B \,|\, e \notin \mathring{A} \wedge e' \notin \mathring{A}\} \cup$$
$$\{(e, A) \,|\, e \notin \mathring{A} \wedge \exists a \in \mathring{A} : (e, a) \in B\} \cup$$
$$\{(A, e) \,|\, e \notin \mathring{A} \wedge \exists a \in \mathring{A} : (a, e) \in B\}.$$

In the remainder of this section we present two simple facts about the collapsing operation. The first one indicates that collapsing does not tear the

274

graph apart, in the sense that paths leading into and out of a subgraph A in G change into paths ending and starting with A, respectively.

Lemma 2. $\exists a \in \dot{A} : e < a$ in $G \Leftrightarrow e < A$ in $G[A]$
$\exists a \in \dot{A} : a < e$ in $G \Leftrightarrow A < e$ in $G[A]$.

The proof of Lemma 2 follows immediately from the definition of the collapsing operation.

Our next lemma shows that the order of collapsing two disjoint subgraphs is immaterial. We call two subgraphs A and A' of G disjoint iff $\dot{A} \cap \dot{A}' = \emptyset$.

Lemma 3. *If A and A' are disjoint subgraphs of G then A' is a subgraph of $G[A]$, A is a subgraph of $G[A']$, and $G[A][A'] = G[A'][A]$.*

An example is furnished by Figs. 4 and 7 above.

2.3. Structured Occurrence Graphs

In the previous section, we have shown how the dynamic structure arising from programmer-defined atomic actions can be represented by collapsing the subgraphs corresponding to their executions. Generalising this in the present section, we use "structured occurrence graphs" to model the (dynamic) nesting of atomic actions to arbitrary depth. We define structured occurrence graphs to consist of a "basic occurrence graph" on which a "nested structure" is imposed.

The basic occurrence graph describes the computation to such a degree of detail that its events can be decreed basic without further justification; it may be helpful to think of them as being "system-defined". As we shall take cycle-freeness as our "basicness" criterion, we postulate that the basic graph be acyclic; any cycle in the basic graph would indicate an event being its own cause.

The nested structure imposed on the basic graph captures the dynamic structure arising from the programmer's atomicity specifications. At the most basic level, the computation is seen to consist of "small" basic events, interconnected as described by the basic graph. At the most abstract level, it can be viewed as a single event comprising all of its constituent activities (as if the entire user program was enclosed by outermost atomicity brackets). Depending on the depth of nesting, there may be a variety of intermediate levels of abstraction. In keeping with [18] we consider the (dynamic) overlapping of atomic action as contrary to their nature, so that we are considering "tree structures" only.

Formally, let an acyclic occurrence graph $G = (E, B)$ given which we refer to as the "basic graph", E being the set of "basic events". We define a "tree structure over G" to be a finite collection T of sets of events such that

(T 1) $E \in T$ and $\{e\} \in T$ for all $e \in E$
(T 2) $\forall E_1, E_2 \in T : E_1 \cap E_2 = \emptyset \vee E_1 \subseteq E_2 \vee E_2 \subseteq E_1$.

The sets in T, which we call "(atomic) activities", model the executions of atomic actions. (T1) is motivated by the above remarks concerning the most abstract and the most basic level, while (T2) ensures the absence of overlapping.

For instance, with $E_1 = \{e_1^x, \ldots, e_4^x\}$, $E_2 = \{e_1^y, \ldots, e_4^y\}$ and $E = E_1 \cup E_2$,

$$T = \{\{e_1^x\}, \ldots, \{e_4^y\}, E_1, E_2, E\}$$

is a tree structure over the occurrence graph shown in Fig. 4c. We represent T pictorially by enclosing its constituent sets in rectangles:

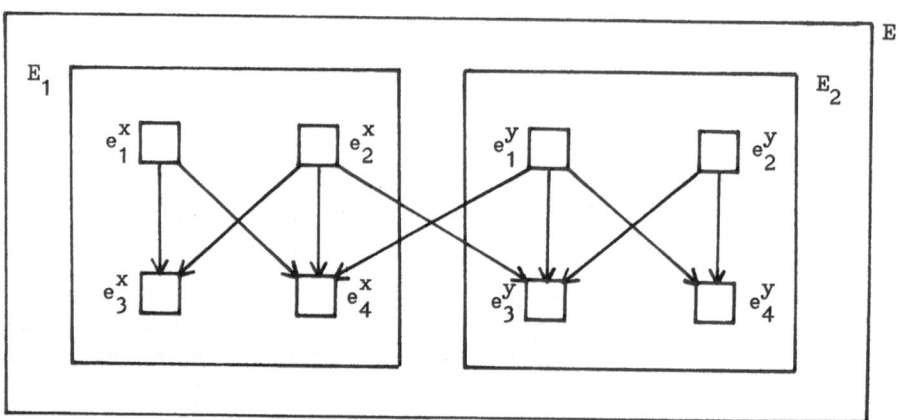

Fig. 9

This structuring represents the programmer's specification of *rem* as an atomic action and an implicit outermost atomic action.

We call a pair (G, T) where G is an acyclic occurrence graph and T is a tree structure over G, a "structured occurrence graph", and we define its structure tree as follows. The nodes of the tree are the activities in T, and a node E' is called a "parent" of another node E'' iff E' is the smallest superset of E'' in T. As a consequence of (T1) and (T2), there is a unique smallest superset for all sets in T except E, and the "parent" relationship therefore defines a tree with root E and leaves $\{e\}$, $e \in E$. For $E' \in T$ we define the set of "sub-activities" of E',

$$\mathring{E}' = \{E'' \in T \,|\, E' \text{ is parent of } E''\}.$$

Our next aim is to capture the notion of a structured occurrence graph describing a computation at different levels of abstraction. To this end we define levels of abstraction formally and then associate an occurrence graph with each level. Such a graph describes how the events of this level are related to each other, generalising the remarks made following Fig. 7 in the previous section.

276

For a given structured occurrence graph (G, T), we call a subset $L \subseteq T$ a "level (of abstraction)" iff

(L1) $E = \bigcup \{E' \mid E' \in L\}$

(L2) $\forall E_1, E_2 \in L: E_1 \cap E_2 = \emptyset \vee E_1 = E_2.$

(L1) requires that all basic events are considered and (L2) requires that none of them is considered more than once. Levels can be visualised as "cuts" through the structure tree. For our example shown in Fig. 9 we derive the following structure tree and five levels of abstraction $L_0, \ldots, L_4$ (where for simplicity the leaves of the tree are labelled with the names of the basic events they represent):

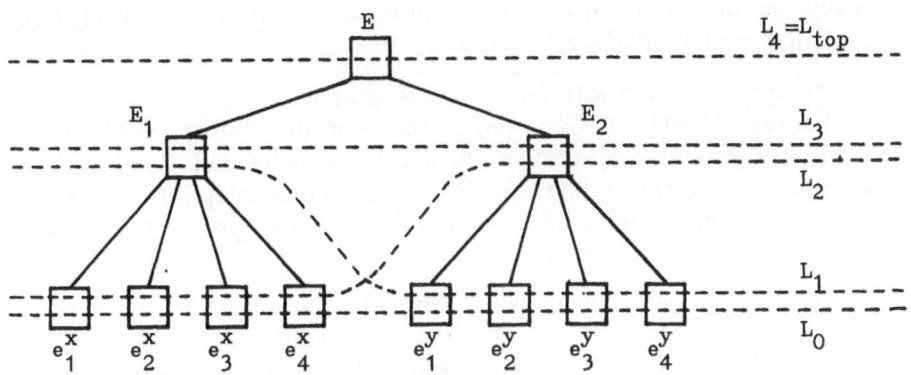

Fig. 10

We further define:
the "basic level" $L_0 = \{\{e\} \mid e \in E\}$,
the "most abstract level" $L_{\text{top}} = \{E\}$, and,
for any $E' \in T$ the level $L_{E'} = \{E'\} \cup \{\{e\} \mid e \in E \setminus E'\}$
containing E' and all basic events outside E'.
We define $L' \subset L$ for two levels L' and L iff

$$L' = (L \setminus \{E'\}) \cup \mathring{E}' \quad \text{for some} \quad E' \in T,$$

i.e. iff L' arises from L by substituting the sub-activities of E' for E'. We also write $L' = [E'] L$ in this case; for instance, $L_1 = [E_2] L_3$ in Fig. 10. We call L "more abstract" than L' iff $L' \subset L$, where $\subset$ is the transitive closure of $\subset$. The $\subset$ relationship turns set of levels into a lattice with L_0 as the minimal element and L_{top} as the maximal element. For our example we have the following lattice:

277

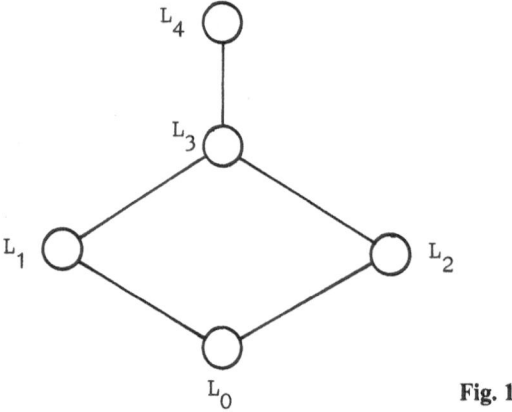

Fig. 11

Finally we define the occurrence graph associated with a level L by induction over the lattice of levels as follows.

(O1) The graph associated with L_0 is the basic graph.

(O2) Whenever $L' = [E'] L$, G' is the graph associated with L' and A is the subgraph of G' generated by $\mathring{E}'$, then the graph associated with L is $G'[A]$. We give the new event of $G[A']$ the name "E''", so as to make step (O2) repeatedly applicable; the events of the graph associated with L are thus just the activities in L.

As a consequence of Lemma 3 which shows that the order of collapsing disjoint subgraphs is immaterial and the requirement that all activities be non-overlapping, (O1) and (O2) properly define an occurrence graph for each level. For our example we obtain the following five level graphs:

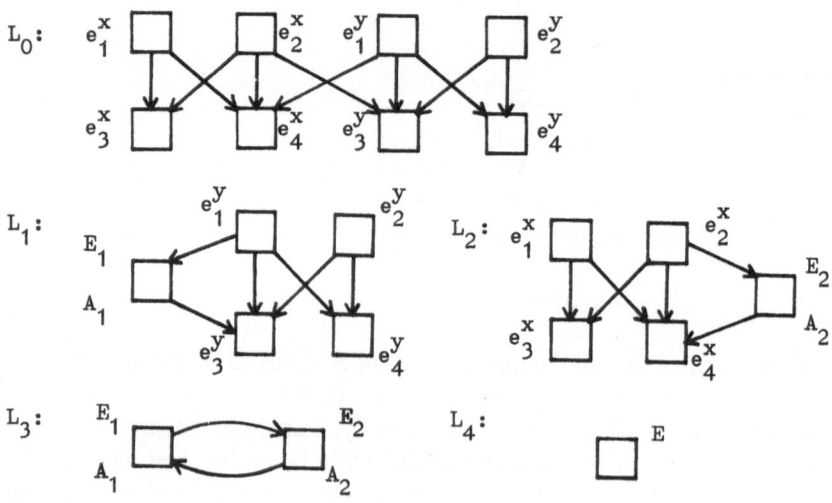

Fig. 12

278

Due to the association of an occurrence graph with every level, all concepts defined for occurrence graphs (the < relationship, for example) now become level-dependent. In the sequel we use the phrase "at level L" in order to avoid confusion about which level is meant.

If the convention of regarding basic events as trivial subgraphs is introduced, a one-to-one relationship between activities $E' \in T$ and subgraphs (generated by $\mathring{E}'$ if E' is non-basic) can be established. We therefore use the term "activity" for subgraphs $A_1, A_2, \ldots$ as well and extend all definitions accordingly. In particular, $L' = [A] L$ means that A is a subgraph at L' which is collapsed at L; L_A denotes the level containing A and all basic events outside A; and an activity A is said to "contain" another activity A' iff A' is a descendant of A in the structure tree.

We use structured occurrence graphs in Sect. 3 for the purpose of characterising atomic occurrences and in Sect. 4 for the purpose of describing the units of recovery in a decentralised system.

3. Atomicity of Activities

3.1. Cycle-Freeness and Serialisability

As exemplified in the previous section, we characterise atomicity dynamically by the absence of interference. Naturally, interference pertains not to activities in isolation but to the way in which they are related to each other. Consequently in our characterisation, which can be found in Sects. 3.1 and 3.2, we take into account the computation as a whole.

We take the characteristic (dynamic) property of atomicity to be that events are partially ordered on all levels of abstraction induced by atomicity specifications (not just the basic level). Thus we define a structured occurrence graph and the computation it describes to "satisfy atomicity" iff all of its level graphs are acyclic.

This definition generalises the "serialisability" criterion [4]. Under some very weak conditions [10] which are assumed to hold, every partial order can be "serialised" (i.e. extended to a linear order). Therefore for each acyclic occurrence graph $G = (E, B)$ a graph $G_{\text{lin}} = (E, B_{\text{lin}})$ can be found such that $B^+ \subseteq B_{\text{lin}}^+$ and E is linearly ordered under B_{lin}^+. More generally we have:

Proposition 1. *A structured occurrence graph (G, T) satisfies atomicity if and only if the basic graph G can be serialised such that the resulting structured occurrence graph (G_{lin}, T) describes a linear order on all levels.*

Proof. Assuming that (G, T) satisfies atomicity, we may serialise the basic events by processing the structure tree in the following way. Starting with the root of the tree we arrange all subactivities of non-basic activities in linear order, which is possible by assumption. This process stops when all basic events have been reached. Eventually all level graphs describe a linear order.

Conversely, assume that (G, T) does not satisfy atomicity. Then there exists a cycle at some level, the events of which cannot be serialised.

The term "serialisation" is perhaps misleading in that it may suggest that atomicity can only be implemented by actual strict sequencing (i.e. mutual exclusion in time) of the atomic actions of a program. This is not true according to our criterion which allows for the parallel execution of independent atomic actions. Even if atomic actions fail to be independent a partly concurrent execution does not necessarily violate atomicity, as demonstrated previously.

On the other hand, it may be suggested that strict sequencing always implements atomicity. However, programs such as the following cannot be serialised, i.e. are not implementable:

$(x, y) := (0, 0)$;
$\langle x := 1; \textbf{do } y = 0 \rightarrow \textbf{skip od} \rangle \| \langle y := 1; \textbf{do } x = 0 \rightarrow \textbf{skip od} \rangle$.

Typically, in such programs the successful termination of one atomic action depends on the progress of others in a cyclic manner. To prohibit this, it seems reasonable to postulate that atomic actions always terminate (this is indeed one of the key axioms in [16]).

3.2. Interference-Freeness and Atomic Occurrences

In this section we take a closer look at "interference". We define an event e to interfere with an activity A if it occurs strictly after part of A and strictly before another part of A. We define A to "occur atomically" if it is not interfered with in this fashion.

For example, in Fig. 13 we have $e_2^x < A_2 < e_4^x$ at L_2, which means that the event A_2 interferes with A_1 (though none of the constituent basic events of A_2 does!):

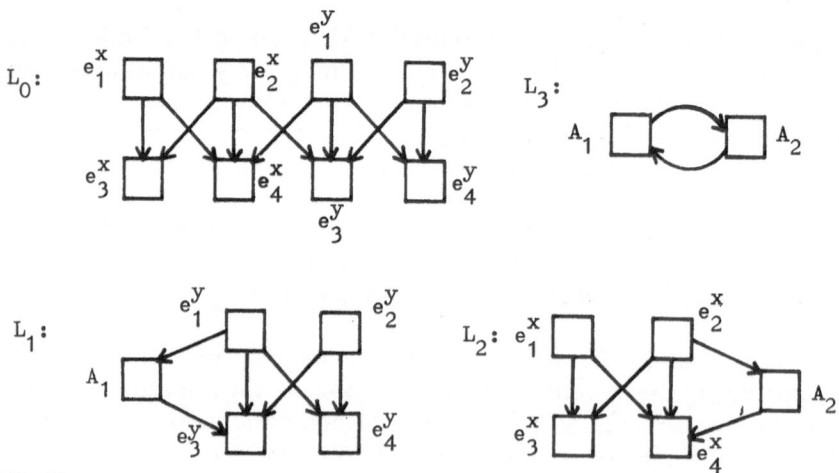

Fig. 13

280

This can also be characterised by the fact that at L_3, A_1 and A_2 stand in a cyclic relationship which disappears when A_1 is opened, i.e. at L_2; we take this as the basis for our formal definition below. We first remark that an activity may be in a cycle even though (intuitively) it is an atomic occurrence, and illustrate this point with an example.

We consider the program

$$\langle s := s + 1 \rangle \| \langle s := s + 1 \rangle,$$

assuming each assignment to consist of an event "r" of reading the value of s followed by an event "w" of overwriting s with the value of $s + 1$. Consider the following atomicity-violating (and hence invalid) execution:

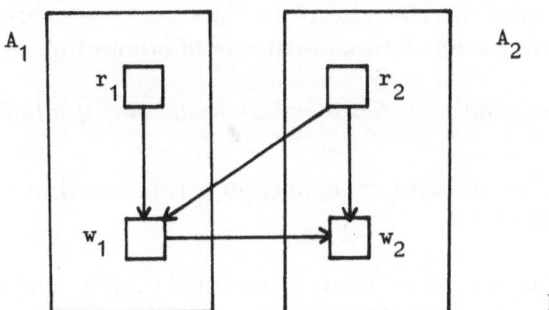

Fig. 14

giving rise to the following four level graphs:

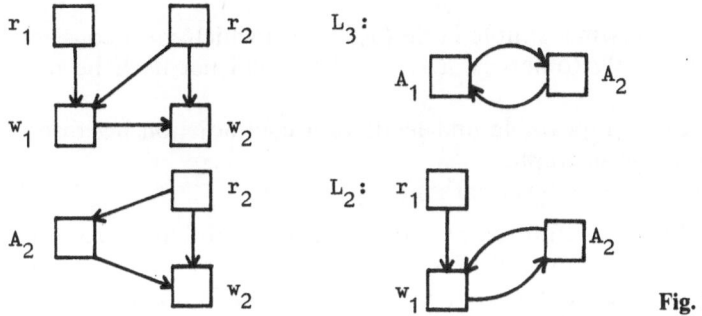

Fig. 15

Intuition suggests that A_1, though contained in a cycle at L_3, occurs atomically because it is not interfered with by other activity.

Generalising these examples, we define inductively that for a given structured occurrence graph (G, T),

(A1) Basic events occur atomically.
(A2) An activity A occurs atomically iff
    (a) $\forall a \in \acute{A}$: a occurs atomically, and
    (b) for all levels L, whenever $e < A < e$ at L then $\exists a \in \acute{A}$: $e < a < e$ at $[A] L$.

281

This definition signifies that if (A2b) is violated for some level L and event e then e is one of the outside activities that interfere with A, making it non-atomic.

(A1)–(A2) define the atomic occurrence of a single activity and can therefore be called a "local" atomicity criterion, in contrast to the "global" cycle-freeness criterion defined in the preceding section. These two criteria are inter-related as follows:

Proposition 2. (i) *If for no level either A or one of the activities it contains is involved in a cycle then A occurs atomically.*

(ii) *Let $e < e$ at L; then $\exists A: e \leqq A \leqq e$ at L and A does not occur atomically.*

Proposition 2(ii) is a weak converse of (i); as the example shown in Figs. 14/15 demonstrates, the immediate converse of (i) does not necessarily hold true. We also have the following immediate consequence of proposition 2:

Corollary. *A structured occurrence graph satisfies atomicity if and only if all of its activities occur atomically.*

Proof. (i) If neither A nor any of the activities contained in it is involved in a cycle then (A2b) cannot be violated for A.

(ii) Let $e < e$ at L.

Because of the maximality axiom, there exists a maximal simple cycle $(e = A_0, \ldots, A_n = e)$ at L.

Suppose that all of the A_i occur atomically.

This means that there exist $a_i \in A_i$ such that $a_0 < \ldots < a_n$ and $a_0 = a_n$ at $[A_0] \ldots [A_{n-1}] L$.

Again we choose a maximal simple cycle $(a_0, \ldots, a_n)$ which must consist of sub-activities of the A_i only (otherwise $(A_0, \ldots, A_n)$ would not itself be maximal).

This argument is thus repeatable and leads to a contradiction because of the cycle-freeness of the basic graph.

Hence for some i, A_i does not occur atomically, q.e.d.

We finally show that our definition remains intuitively valid also in a more complicated example than considered so far.

In this example, A_1 occurs atomically according to our definition (A1)–(A2) even though it is contained in four cycles at L_3, one of which (namely the one not including e_1 or e_2) disappears when A_1 is opened, i.e. at L_2. It is however perfectly in line with intuition that A_1 should be defined to occur atomically, while A_2 is clearly a non-atomic occurrence, being interfered with by A_1 and even by all basic events in A_1.

3.3. Context-Independence and Inherently Atomic Occurrences

As characterised in the preceding sections, the atomic occurrence or otherwise of an activity depends not only on its internal structure but also on its environment at large. We now show that there is a sense in which an activity can

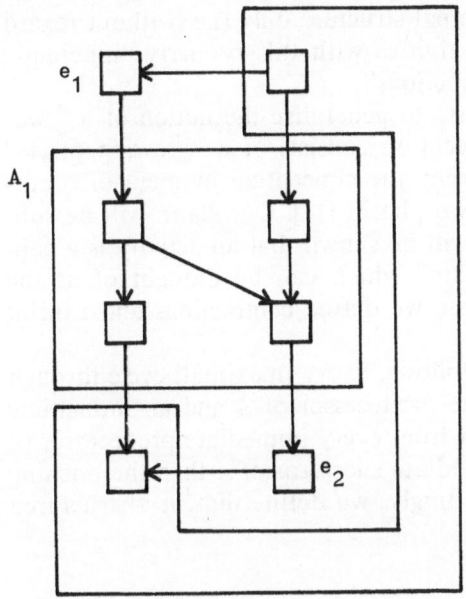

Fig. 16

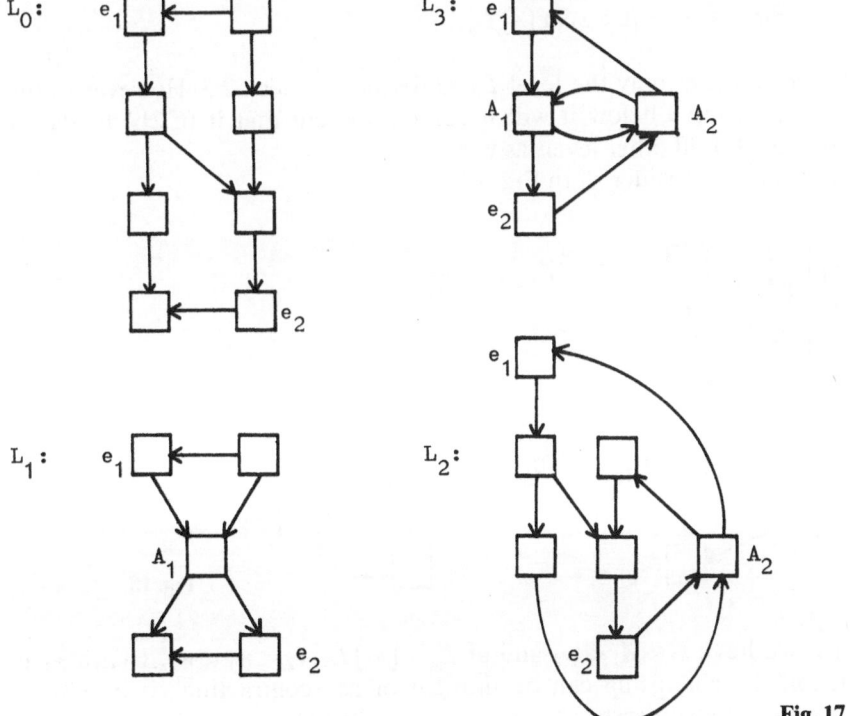

Fig. 17

be called "atomic" by virtue of its internal structure only (i.e. without regard to the entire computation). We call activities with this property "inherently atomic occurrences" or, for short, "contractions".

We consider the contraction property to generalise the notion of a "two-phase" execution [4]. A two-phase execution consists of a "growing phase" followed by a "shrinking phase", whereby the conceptual moment of occurrence of the activity lies between the two phases [11]. Our claim will be substantiated in the next section where it will be shown that an activity is a contraction iff it contains an "internal state" which can be thought of as the moment of its occurrence. In this section we define contractions and exhibit their relation to atomic occurrences.

Our definition can be motivated as follows. Every (maximal) cycle through A must also pass through an immediate predecessor of A and an immediate successor of A. If A is so structured that from every immediate predecessor of A a path leads through $\dot{A}$ to every immediate successor of A then the opening of A can never break that cycle. Accordingly, we define that in a structured occurrence graph (G, T),

(C1) Basic events are contractions.
(C2) An activity A is a contraction iff
    (a) $\forall a \in \dot{A}: a$ is a contraction, and
    (b) whenever $e_1 < A < e_2$ at L_A
    then $\exists a \in \dot{A}: e_1 < a < e_2$ at $[A] L_A$.

In (C2b) we consider only the level L_A as defined in Sect. 2.3. However in the proof of Proposition 3 below it will become apparent that if (C2b) holds for L_A then it holds for all other levels as well.

As an example, consider A_1 in Fig. 18:

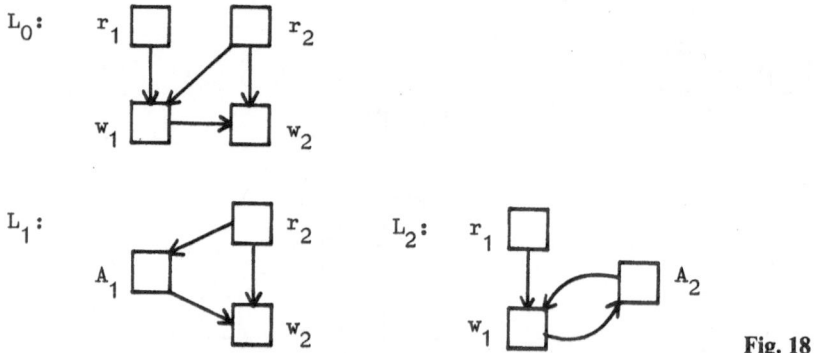

Fig. 18

At $L_1 = L_{A_1}$ we have $r_2 < A_1 < w_2$ and at $L_0 = [A_1] L_1$, $r_2 < w_1 < w_2$. Hence A_1 is a contraction. Its collapsing can be thought of as "contracting" it into w_1 — hence the name. By contrast, $w_1 < A_2 < w_1$ at L_2 but $w_1 \not< w_1$ at L_0; hence A_2 is not a contraction.

With the definition (C1)–(C2) we have the following:

284

Proposition 3. (i) *Contractions occur atomically.*

(ii) *If A is not a contraction then a structure T' can be defined containing the same subtree rooted at A as is contained in T, such that A does not occur atomically in (G, T').*

Proposition 3 (ii) is again a weak converse of (i), signifying not that non-contraction occur non-atomically, but that based just on the internal structure of a non-contraction, nothing can be inferred about its atomic occurrence.

Proof. (i) Let $e < A < e$ at L.

Because of the maximality axiom, there exists a simple cycle $(e, \ldots, A_1, A, A_2, \ldots, e)$ such that $A_1 \lessdot A$ and $A \lessdot A_2$ at L.

Because $A_1 \lessdot A$ at L, by repeated applications of Lemma 2 one sees that A_1 must contain a basic event d_1 such that $d_1 < A$ at L_A.

Again because of the maximality axiom, there exists a basic event e_1 with $d_1 \lessgtr e_1 \lessdot A$, which is also contained in A_1 (otherwise A_1 would not immediately precede A at L).

Similarly, A_2 contains a basic event e_2 such that $A \lessdot e_2$ at L_A.

Property (C2b) for A requires the existence of an $a \in \hat{A}$ such that $e_1 < a < e_2$ at $[A] L_A$.

For this a we also have, again by Lemma 2: $e \leqq A_1 < a < A_2 \leqq e$ at $[A] L_A$.

(ii) Since A is not a contraction there exist basic events e_1, e_2 outside A such that for no $a \in \hat{A}$, $e_1 < a < e_2$ at $[A] L_A$.

We define T' as containing $\{e\}$ for all $e \in E$, E, the entire subtree rooted at A and the set $\{e_1, e_2\}$.

T' is a tree structure and A does not occur atomically in (G, T').

In practical terms, Proposition 3 signifies the following. Suppose that a programmer wishes to use a set of system synchronisation primitives to ensure the atomic occurrence of his program, but cannot rely on any system-provided implementation of atomicity. Then he must ensure the contraction property (for example by employing the simple two-phase protocol [4], or by using more knowledge about the system to derive more complicated and efficient protocols [20]), in order to prevent unwanted interference which may arise due to the lack of system-provided safeguards. In this way, Proposition 3 can be seen as a generalisation of the result contained in [4].

3.4. Two-Phase Occurrences

We have seen that in the structured occurrence graph shown in Fig. 18, A_1 is a contraction and the event w_1 can be thought of as the conceptual moment of the occurrence of A_1. We now show that it is characteristic for a contraction to contain a "state" which can be thought of as the moment of its occurrence. The following example serves to illustrate this point:

In this example, A_1 is a contraction while A_2 is not. The broken line through A_1 represents a "cut" with the property that from every immediate predecessor of A_1 (e_1 or e_2) to every immediate successor of A_1 (e_3 or e_4) there is a path

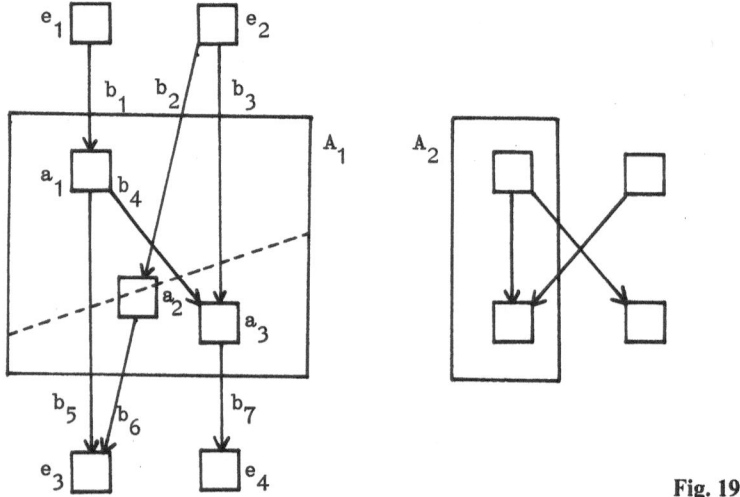

Fig. 19

which crosses this cut. No cut with this property can be found for A_2. Following [6] we interpret cuts as "states" of an activity and we go on to show that an activity A is a contraction iff it contains a cut with the property just mentioned.

To define states formally, let an occurrence graph $G = (E, B)$ and a subgraph $A = (E', B')$ of G be given. We first define

$\qquad B^> := \{b \in B \mid \text{tail}\,(b) \notin \acute{A} \wedge \text{head}\,(b) \in \acute{A}\}$
$\qquad$ (the set of arrows leading into A), and
$\qquad {}^<B := \{b \in B \mid \text{tail}\,(b) \in \acute{A} \wedge \text{head}\,(b) \notin \acute{A}\}$
$\qquad$ (the set of arrows leading out of A).

$B^>$ and ${}^<B$ can be considered the interface between A and its environment. The relation $<_A = B'^+$ (see Sect. 2.2) can be extended in a natural way to elements of the set

$$X = \acute{A} \cup B' \cup B^> \cup {}^<B:$$

if $x, x' \in X$, define $x <_A x'$ iff a directed path inside A leads from x to x'. Two elements $x, x' \in X$ are said to be "A-concurrent" iff neither $x <_A x'$ nor $x' <_A x$. We call a subset $C \subseteq X$ an "A-state" iff its elements are pairwise A-concurrent and it is a maximal set with this property (for instance, the A_1-state shown in Fig. 19 is $C = \{b_3, b_4, b_5, a_2\}$).

We are now ready to state:

Proposition 4. *Condition* (C2b) *in the definition of a contraction* (Sect. 3.3) *can be equivalently replaced by:*

(C2b') *There exists an A-state C at* [A] L_A *such that whenever* $e_1 < A < e_2$ *at* L_A *then* $\exists c \in C: e_1 < c < e_2$ *at* [A] L_A.

286

Proof. (C2b′) implies (C2b):

Let an A-state C be given and let $e_1 \lessdot A \lessdot e_2$ at L_A and $e_1 < c < e_2$ at $[A] L_A$ with $c \in C$.

Because C is a subset of X and hence contains only elements in A or bordering on A, one of the following must hold:

either $c \in A$, in which case (C2b) is satisfied with $a = c$;
or $c \in B$ and head $(c) \in A$, in which case $e_1 < $ head $(c) < e_2$;
or $c \in B$ and tail $(c) \in A$, in which case $e_1 < $ tail $(c) < e_2$.

Conversely, (C2b) implies (C2b′):

Because every path from $b_1 \in B^>$ to $b_2 \in B^>$ must include tail $(b_2) \notin \dot{A}$, the elements of $B^>$ are pairwise A-concurrent.

We define C_0 as the first A-state including $B^>$; formally,

$$C_0 = \{x \in X \mid \forall b \in B^>: x \text{ is } A\text{-concurrent to } b$$
$$\text{and } \neg \exists x' \in X: x' <_A x\}.$$

In the example shown in Fig. 19, $C_0 = B^> = \{b_1, b_2, b_3\}$.

The elements of C_0 are pairwise A-concurrent by definition, and C_0 is maximal because no $x'' \in X$ concurrent to all elements of C_0 can have an A-predecessor $x' <_A x''$ in X.

We show that C_0 satisfies the requirements of (C2b′).

Let $e_1 \lessdot A \lessdot e_2$ at L_A.

Because A is a contraction,

$$\exists a \in \dot{A}: e_1 < a < e_2 \quad \text{at } [A] L_A.$$

Every path from e_1 to a must contain a pair of neighbours (e_i, e_{i+1}) with $e_i \notin \dot{A}$ and $e_{i+1} \in \dot{A}$.

Hence $c = (e_i, e_{i+1}) \in C_0$ and $e_1 < c < e_2$ at $[A] L_A$, q.e.d.

The A-state C which exists by (C2b′) can be thought of as a "moment of occurrence" of A. C is by no means unique; in the proof of Proposition 4, the set C_1 defined as the last A-state including $^<B$ would have done a similar service as C_0. C_0 and C_1 are in fact the "first" and "last" A-states, respectively, which satisfy the property required in (C2b′).

Thus, in general, the occurrence of a contraction A can be viewed as consisting of the occurrences of its immediate predecessors, C_0, all intermediate A-states, C_1, and its immediate successors, in that order. In other words, A occurs quasi-sequentially, again illustrating the context-independence of its atomic occurrence.

287

4. A Model of Recoverability in Decentralised Systems

4.1. Recovery Points and Recovery Graphs

In this section we outline how the framework set up in Sect. 2 can be adapted to model error recovery in a decentralised system. We assume that in a given system, as part of a strategy for providing a degree of fault tolerance, certain states have been checked (for correctness or a similar property) and saved, so that the system can fall back on these states if need be; such states are called "restorable states" [14] or "recovery points" [18]. As before, we represent the activity of the system by an occurrence graph, indicating restorable states by a special type of condition.

A decentralised system may at any time contain several independent active components, any one or more of which may independently discover an error and invoke recovery, so that in each case the problem arises as to which recovery points should be chosen to fall back on. This is one of the questions to be dealt with in the remainder of this paper. We also extend the occurrence graph model slightly to indicate those active states, again by introducing special conditions.

We use the term "recovery graph" to denote an occurrence graph which may contain (besides normal conditions) also restorable conditions and active conditions. Pictorially, we represent restorable conditions by double arrows and active conditions by arrows "dangling" from an event (waiting to be connected to another event):

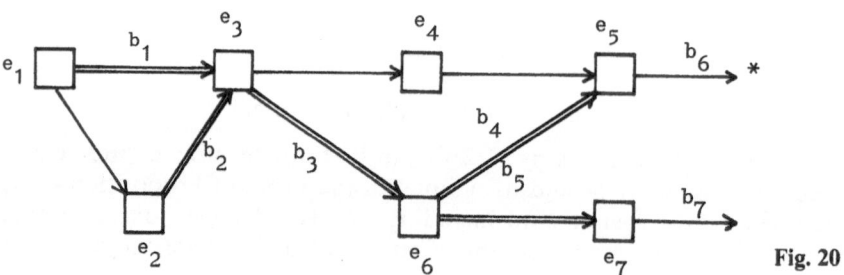

Fig. 20

This example represents a computation having started at e_1, having established the recovery points $b_1 - b_5$ and at present consisting of two strands of activity at b_6 and b_7.

By the asterisk we indicate the fact that an error has just been detected in the active component represented by b_6. It stands to reason that in this situation all of the activity having sprung from e_3 must be abandoned, because no proper restorable state lies between e_3 and b_6. Hence the nearest fall-back line (or "recovery line") in this example is the set of recovery points $\{b_1, b_2\}$, all later activity being suspect; we may represent actual recovery in the model by erasing the subgraph generated by $e_3 - e_7$ and making b_1 and b_2 the new active conditions from which further activity can spring [14].

288

In the remainder of this section we will discuss the following two questions. In case an error is detected in an active component of a system described by a ("basic") recovery graph, (a) which is the nearest recovery line, and (b) which portion of the graph should be treated as suspect as a consequence of the error detection? Question (a) is dealt with in Sect. 4.2 while question (b) is addressed in Sect. 4.3.

4.2. Error Propagation and Recovery Collapsing

Our aim is to determine the nearest recovery line in the event of an error being detected (which we represent by marking the corresponding active condition as "invalid"). We first define the propagation of error information by considering the three types of conditions separately:

(R1) e $\square\!\!\!-\!\!\!\xrightarrow{\ \ b\ \ }$

If the active condition b is invalidated (representing, for instance, the failing of an acceptance test [17]) then its input event e should also be invalidated as a consequence.

(R2) e $\square\!\!\!-\!\!\!\longrightarrow\!\!\!\square$ e'

Suppose e and e' are connected via a non-restorable condition. The invalidation of e' should entail the invalidation of e ("backward error propagation") and the invalidation of e should entail the invalidation of e' ("forward error propagation" or "chasing" [14]).

(R3) e $\square\!\!=\!\!\!\Longrightarrow\!\!\square$ e'

Here only forward error propagation is possible; the invalidation of e should be propagated to e' but not vice versa, because the recovery point between e and e' functions as a local fall-back.

Rules (R1)–(R3) can be thought of as giving the meaning of the different types of conditions introduced in Sect. 4.1 in the context of error recovery. We have:

Lemma 4. *In a recovery graph, an event e' becomes invalidated as a consequence of another event e being invalidated if and only if there is an undirected path between e and e' in which all restorable conditions point towards e'.*

Example:

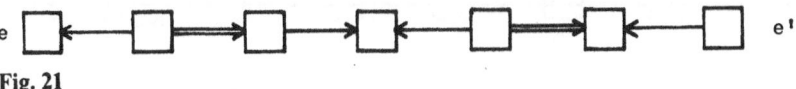

Fig. 21

Repeated applications of (R2) and (R3) show that, indeed, the invalidation of e eventually spreads to e'.

In particular, if a recovery graph contains a cycle then an invalidation of any one event of the cycle entails the invalidation of all events of the cycle. Generalising, we define a "unit of recovery" to be a maximal set of events with the property that the invalidation of any one of the events in this set is propagated to all of the events in the set. In our example (Fig. 20) there are three units of recovery, E_1, E_2 and E_3 as indicated in the next Figure:

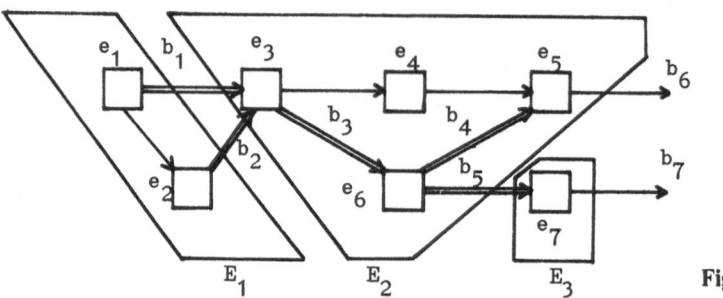

Fig. 22

As we can see, the units of recovery afford a disjoint covering of the basic graph. This is true in general, as the next lemma shows:

Lemma 5. *For any two units of recovery E_1 and E_2, either $E_1 \cap E_2 = \emptyset$ or $E_1 = E_2$.*

Proof. Suppose $e \in E_1 \cap E_2$.

Because both E_1 and E_2 are units of recovery, the invalidation of e entails the invalidation of both E_1 and E_2 and the maximality property implies

$$E_1 = E_2.$$

Lemma 5 implies that, in the terms of Sect. 2.3, the set containing all basic activities $\{e\}$, all units of recovery, and the set E, forms a tree structure over the basic recovery graph, in which the set of all units of recovery determines a level of abstraction. We call this the "recovery level". For our example we obtain:

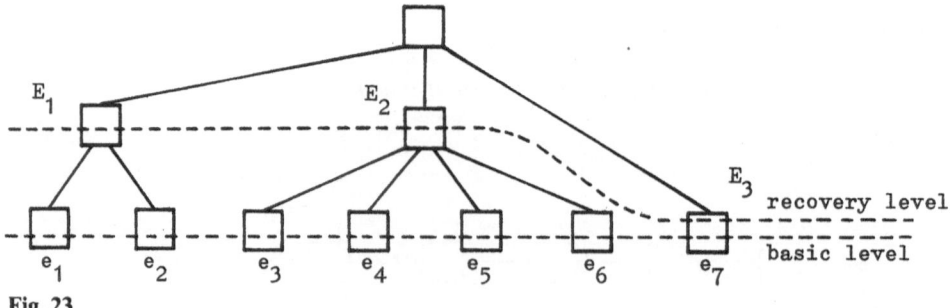

Fig. 23

The graph associated with the recovery level (which we call the "recovery collapsed graph") can be defined as in (O1)–(O2) of Sect. 2.3, except that provisions have to be made for restorable and active conditions. Because as a consequence of our definition, all conditions leading into or coming out of a unit of recovery must be either restorable or active, it is reasonable to introduce the rule that these properties are retained in the recovery collapsed graph. For our example (compare Fig. 22) we therefore obtain:

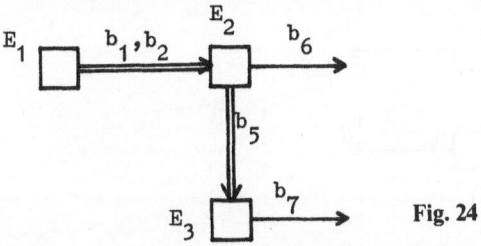

Fig. 24

Recovery collapsing can alternatively be described by the following two rules:

(R4) Collapse all parts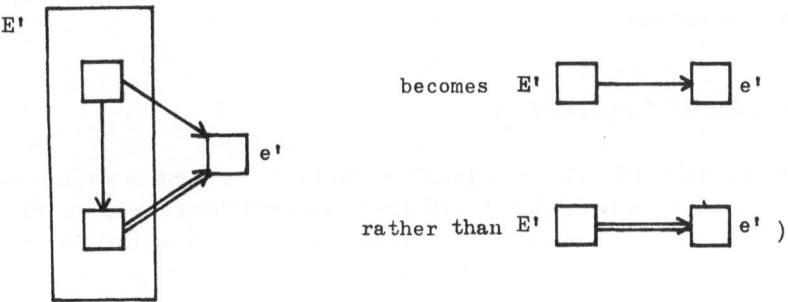

of a recovery graph into a single event, whereby ordinary conditions have precedence over restorable conditions (this means that, say,

becomes E'

rather than E')

(R5) Collapse all cycles into single events.
We then have:

Proposition 5. *A set of events is a unit of recovery if and only if it can be reduced to a single event by repeated and exhaustive applications of* (R4) *and* (R5),

which can be proved by applying Lemma 4. Proposition 5 indicates that exhaustive application of (R4) and (R5) to the basic recovery graph will be an automatic way of producing the recovery collapsed graph.

From our definitions it follows that the invalidation of an active condition is propagated at least throughout the unit of recovery it is attached to, i.e. its input event at the recovery level, but is not propagated to the input conditions of that unit of recovery. Thus we can define for every active condition its "(nearest) recovery line" to consist of the input conditions of its input event at the recovery level.

In our example, the recovery line of b_6 is $\{b_1, b_2\}$ and the recovery line of b_7 is $\{b_5\}$:

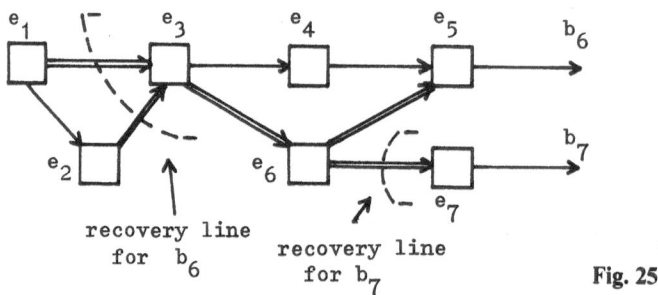

Fig. 25

The recovery collapsed graph thus helps to answer the question posed at the beginning of this section. The events of the recovery collapsed graph can also be interpreted as describing the activity "find the nearest recovery line" as single atomic events. Note however that upon invalidation of an active condition, possibly more than just the unit of recovery it is attached to have to be invalidated, as exemplified above (Fig. 25) where the invalidation of b_6 is propagated not only to $e_3 - e_6$ but also to e_7. We examine this situation more closely in the next section.

4.3. Classification of Recovery Points

Precisely which portion of a recovery graph becomes invalidated as a result of an active condition being invalidated is of course entirely determined by rules (R 1)–(R 3) of the previous section. The "chase protocols" described in [14] give a practical means of computing this portion of the graph. As has been demonstrated, this portion may in general comprise more than a single unit of recovery. In our example this was due to the existence of the restorable condition b_5 which, depending on the location of the detection of an error, in one case (if the error is detected at b_7) functions as a recovery line and in another case (if the error is detected at b_6) as a useless recovery point (compare Fig. 26). The existence of such restorable conditions is a consequence of the asymmetry in rule (R 3). In this section we characterise such conditions and derive a criterion for their absence.

In a recovery graph we distinguish three types of restorable conditions (compare Fig. 26):

– conditions which can never belong to a recovery line, such as b_3 and b_4 in our example; such conditions are called "irrelevant" [14];

292

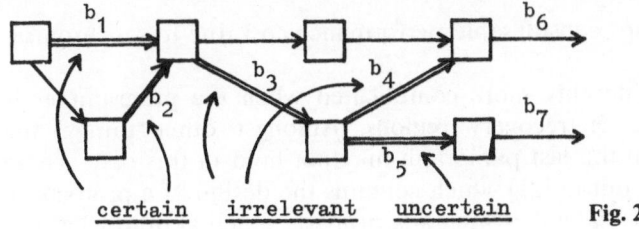

certain   irrelevant   uncertain   Fig. 26

— conditions which can never be invalidated as a consequence of rules (R1)–(R3), such as b_1 and b_2 in our example; such conditions may be called "certain";
— all others, such as b_5 in our example; these conditions may be called "uncertain".

We can characterise these types of conditions as follows:

Proposition 6. *A restorable condition is irrelevant if and only if it is absorbed at the recovery level.*

A restorable condition is uncertain if and only if it is contained in the recovery level but would be absorbed by recovery collapsing if all active conditions were joined to a common output event.

Thus, in Fig. 26, b_3 and b_4 are absorbed at the recovery level and b_5 becomes absorbed at the (imaginary) recovery level if b_6 and b_7 were joined to an (imaginary) event.

If the recovery graph does not contain any uncertain conditions then the units of recovery are precisely those portions of the graph that have to be invalidated as a result of an error detection; hence, in this case the recovery collapsed graph describes as a single atomic event not only the activity "detect the nearest recovery line" but also the activity "determine the suspect environment of the error".

The absence of uncertain conditions can be guaranteed by the simple requirement that at the recovery level, the output conditions of an event are either all active or all restorable. In order to meet this requirement, two (or more) components which are actively engaged in a single unit of recovery would have to be synchronised upon establishing a recovery point: either all components establish a new recovery point, or none does. Such synchronisation requirements are typical for fault tolerance schemes providing constraints on the forward propagation of errors. The scheme described in [17], for instance, requires a "conversation" (that is, in effect, a unit of recovery) to have a single well-defined point of exit. [9] and [7] describe "two-phase commit protocols" (not to be confused with the two-phase protocols of [4]) which serve a similar synchronisation purpose.

Finally, we consider "certain" conditions. If, for any two certain conditions, $b_1 < b_2$, then recovery will always stop at b_2. Thus, under the assumption that no influence other than rule (R3) destroys b_2, b_1 might as well be discarded. This assumption, therefore, makes "chasefree" recovery conceptually quite

293

simple, albeit at a perhaps considerable performance cost due to synchronisation as above.

Things become considerably more complicated when the programmer is allowed the nested use of recovery regions. Amongst other things, the assumption mentioned in the last paragraph may not hold in this case. These complications are sorted out in [21] which contains the design of a protocol to determine recovery point "safety", which is a property much akin to what has been defined as recovery point "irrelevance" above.

5. Concluding Remarks and Notes on Further Work

In this paper we have introduced a formal model of computational structure, that of structured occurrence graphs (Sect. 2). We have also investigated the use of structured occurrence graphs; firstly, in Sect. 3, as a conceptual tool to characterise interference-freeness and atomic occurrences. Secondly, in Sect. 4 we have used structured occurrence graphs as a means of modelling error recovery in a decentralised system. Here we have concentrated on precise characterisations of the notions of a "unit of recovery" and a "recovery line" when the activity of the system is described by a recovery graph.

Hopefully, our model of recovery could also be used as a practical means for achieving a degree of fault tolerance in a decentralised system. The idea would be to keep an occurrence graph in store (in some form) as a record of the history of the system, to be processed in the way described in Sect. 4 either as a consequence of an error being detected, or prior to that as a precautionary measure.

The "chase protocols" described in [14] can be seen as a first step towards making this scheme a practical one. In [13] a design is described which refines the "chase protocol" strategy, and a number of protocols are also given for discovering and deleting recovery points which are irrelevant in the sense described in Sect. 4.3. In [21] a variety of optimisation techniques are applied to obtain a practical implementation of recovery collapsing for a system of communication processes, under the complicating assumption that processes may be involved in nested recovery regions and may declare their commitment to their respective recovery points unilaterally.

As defined in this paper, the structured occurrence graph model has been based on the unexplained notion of dependency between events. Some tacit assumptions have been made about event dependency, for example that it is a transitive relationship. In the remainder of this section we discuss some issues related to event dependency and the semantics of atomic actions which in our opinion need further exploration.

We first observe that the notion of event dependency we are interested in does not necessarily coincide with what might be called an intuitive and simple notion of "information flow". This can be seen by considering a pair of actions which overwrite (but do not read) a common variable. In that case, due to the write-dependencies between the two actions, an example of an

294

atomicity-violating execution can well be constructed, even though there is no exchange of information between the two actions, at least not in the simple and intuitive sense that one action generates the value of a variable which is then read by the other action.

This remark may be related to the following characterisation of atomicity which has been claimed in [11] to be equivalent to the serialisability property: "An action is atomic if the process performing it does not communicate with other processes while executing the action". Our arguments indicate that the equivalence between this characterisation and serialisability must be questioned, unless "communication" is understood as referring to the same dependency relation as we are interested in.

How then can "event dependency" be positively determined? We think that the concept of maximal concurrency can be employed. In a maximally concurrent execution (such as the first one shown in Fig. 3 and the ones shown in Fig. 4, Sect. 2), all event dependencies are significant; otherwise a more concurrent execution could be found. Thus we would claim that the dependency relation could be characterised by the two statements that (a) in a maximally concurrent execution all event dependencies are significant, and (b) in a given execution, a dependency between two events is significant if it does not disappear if the given execution is transformed into a maximally concurrent one.

Thus we have reduced the notion of dependency to the equally unexplained notion of maximal concurrency. We believe that in order to determine the latter an analysis of the detail of the interaction between the program and its variables is essential. Let us, for instance, consider two 2-bit variables $x, y \in \{0, 1, 2, 3\}$ and the program

$$x := 2* (y \bmod 2) + x \bmod 2.$$

A detailed analysis shows that this program, *in effect,* reads only bit 0 of y and writes into bit 1 of x (see Fig. 27).

Let us then consider the parallel program

$$\langle x := 2* (y \bmod 2) + x \bmod 2 \rangle \| \langle y := 2* (x \bmod 2) + y \bmod 2 \rangle$$

and let us assume that each program consists of two reads (of x and y, respectively) followed by a single write. In this case *no* significant cross-dependencies exist because of the way in which the two programs access the two variables x and y:

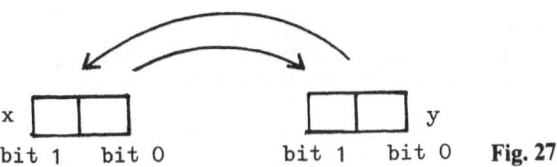

x   bit 1   bit 0   bit 1   bit 0   y   **Fig. 27**

Hence in a maximally concurrent execution all dependencies between the two programs would disappear. This example shows that the semantic interaction between the program and its variables may vary considerably from what it appears to be syntactically, entailing difficulties in the determination of maximally concurrent executions.

We believe that the exact relationship between event dependence, maximal concurrency and information flow needs much further exploration. In the occurrence graphs which we use to formulate our atomicity criterion, if we do not assume that all dependencies are significant, then the atomicity criterion may be "too strong" in the sense that an execution which on the face of it does violate atomicity, nevertheless cannot lead to incorrect results, because some of the dependencies of a cycle may be insignificant. However, the other and more important direction of this statement always holds: if an execution does not violate atomicity then it can never lead to an incorrect result (unless, of course, one of the actions has itself been programmed incorrectly).

Finally, we would like to reconsider our example of the doubly linked list and draw attention to the fact that the damage done by the atomicity-violating execution shown in Fig. 4c (leading to the corrupt final state of the list shown in Fig. 5) is not completely irreparable. If, starting with the corrupt final state, either $rem(x)$ or $rem(y)$ is first "undone" by executing it in reverse order and then "redone", a correct final state can be obtained.

This suggests an alternative implementation of atomicity. Rather than avoiding cycles from the outset one could try to cope with cycles. An "exception mechanism" would be waiting for a violating of atomicity to occur and then take action along the lines described in the last paragraph. This would require the capability to undo an action, as well as (possibly) the "chasing" of corrupt information as described in Sect. 4.3, again highlighting a connection between atomicity and error recovery.

Unfortunately there seem to be difficulties in generalising the undoing and redoing method suggested above. The example of the parallel addition (see the discussion relating to Fig. 14) cannot as easily be analysed as the linked list example. It might be another interesting future task to determine those properties which make the doubly linked list behave so "nicely" in this situation.

Acknowledgements. The authors wish to express their great indebtedness to their colleagues in the Project on Reliability and Integrity of Distributed Systems in Newcastle. In particular, the comments by Pete Lee, Santosh Shrivastava and Graham Wood have led to numerous improvements in this paper. This work was done with the financial support of the Science Research Council of Great Britain.

References

1. Best, E.: Proof of a concurrent program finding Euler paths. In: Proceedings of the MFCS'80. Lecture Notes in Computer Science, Vol. 88. Berlin Heidelberg New York: Springer 1980
2. Dijkstra, E. W.: Finding the correctness proof of a concurrent program. Proceedings of the Koninklijke Nederlandse Akademie van Wetenschappen. Series A, Vol. 81 (2), 1978

3. Dijkstra, E. W., Lamport, L., Martin, A. J., Scholten, C. S., Steffens, E. F. M.: On-the-fly garbage collection: an exercise in cooperation. CACM **21**, 966–975 (1978)
4. Eswaran, R., Gray, J., Lorie, R., Traiger, I.: On the notions of consistency and predicate locks. CACM **19**, 624–633 (1976)
5. Floyd, R. W.: Assigning meanings to programs. Applied Mathematics, Vol. 19, Providence: AMS 1967
6. Genrich, H. J., Stankiewicz-Wiechno, E.: A dictionary of some basic notions of net theory. Proceedings of the Advanced Course on General Net Theory. Lecture Notes in Computer Science, Vol. 84, pp. 519–531. Berlin Heidelberg New York: Springer 1980
7. Gray, J. N.: Notes on data base operating systems. In: Operating systems. Lecture Notes in Computer Science, Vol. 60, pp. 394–481. Berlin Heidelberg New York: Springer 1978
8. Holt, A. W.: Final Report of the project on information systems theory. Applied Data Research ADR5606, and USAF – Rome Air Development Centre, RADC-TR-68-305, 1968
9. Lampson, B. W., Sturgis, H.: Crash recovery in a distributed data storage system. Xerox PARC Report, 1978
10. Handbook of mathematical logic (J. Barwise, ed.). Amsterdam: North Holland (1977)
11. Lomet, D.: Process structuring, synchronisation and recovery using atomic actions. Proceedings of the ACM Conference on language design for reliable software. Sigplan Notices **12**, 128–137 (1977). [Also Chap. 4]
12. Manna, Z.: Mathematical theory of computation. New York: McGraw Hill 1974
13. McDermid, J. A.: Checkpointing and recovery in distributed systems. Second International Conference on distributed computing systems. IEEE Computer Society Press, pp. 271–282 (1981)
14. Merlin, P., Randell, B.: State restoration in distributed systems. In: FTCS-8, IEEE Toulouse, pp. 129–137, 1978. [Also Chap. 6]
15. Ore, O.: Theory of graphs. American Mathematical Society, Colloquium Publ. Vol. XXXVIII, Rhode Island, 1962
16. Owicki, S., Lamport, L.: Proving liveness properties of concurrent programs. Op. 57, Stanford University/SRI, 1980
17. Randell, B.: System structure for software fault tolerance. IEEE Trans. Software Engrg. **SE-1**, 220–232 (1975). [Also Chap. 1]
18. Randell, B., Lee, P. A., Treleaven, P. C.: Reliable computing systems. In: Operating systems. Lecture Notes in Computer Science, Vol. 60, pp. 282–391. Berlin Heidelberg New York: Springer 1978
19. Rhotnie, J. B., Bernstein, P. A., Fox, S., Goodman, N., Hammer, M., Landers, T. A., Reeve, C., Shipman, D. W., Wong, E.: Introduction to a system for distributed databases (SDD-1). ACM Transactions on Database Systems **5**, 1–17 (1980)
20. Silberschatz, A., Kedem, Z.: Consistency in a hierarchical database system. JACM, **27**, 72–80 (1980)
21. Wood, W. G.: Recovery control of communicating process in a distributed system. TR/158, Computing Laboratory, University of Newcastle upon Tyne, November 1980. [Also Chap. 6]

Reliable Resource Allocation Between Unreliable Processes

S. K. SHRIVASTAVA and J.-P. BANÂTRE

Abstract. Basic error recovery problems between interacting processes are first discussed and the desirability of having separate recovery mechanisms for cooperation and competition is demonstrated. The paper then concentrates on recovery mechanisms for processes competing for the use of the shared resources of a computer system. Appropriate programming language features are developed based on the class and inner features of SIMULA, and on the structuring concepts of recovery blocks and monitors.

Index Terms. Concurrent processes, error recovery, monitors, recovery blocks, reliable programs, resource allocation, software redundancy.

I. Introduction

The realization that even a well-designed and tested system is likely to contain residual faults has increasingly led designers to consider the application of redundancy techniques to software construction. Recently a program structure called a recovery block has been developed that allows redundancy, in the form of standby spares, to be added systematically and efficiently to computer programs to make them more reliable [1], [2]. The essence of this scheme is that it provides a facility for a computation to be backtracked to an earlier state, if an error is detected, and proceed again using a possibly different algorithm.

In this paper we extend this idea to apply to the error recovery problems of concurrent processes of an operating system sharing the limited resources of a computer system. A very general overview of the problem we wish to tackle here can be obtained by considering the progress of a process in an operating system. Suppose that during its "forward motion," the process is generating results entirely by assignments to variables in its private space. If an error is detected, the "reverse motion" of this process to a prior state is easily performed – the undoing of assignments is equivalent to the restoration of prior values. However, the actions of a process can be quite diverse – for instance, control of a peripheral. In general then, during its forward motion this process will generate results by recording them in various resources, such as storage locations, input-output equipment. Since many of the resources involved will usually be shared between processes, the process under consideration will occasionally be interacting with other processes during its progress. If an error is detected, the reverse motion of this process is no longer as easy as before and it may become necessary to provide algorithms for undoing the effects of previously done operations. Just as the process interacts with other processes during its forward motion, it may also interact during its reverse motion. It is thus seen that when programming for processes that are capable of backtracking, apart from programming for their normal forward progress, we must also be prepared to program for their reverse progress. The important point to note is that appropriate programming language tools must be provided to cope with this additional complexity in a systematic manner, otherwise resulting programs are likely to be even less reliable than versions with no redundancy. We believe that the programming language features developed in this paper meet the above criterion; however, the reader must be the ultimate judge.

The paper is structured into seven sections. Since recovery blocks play a prominent role in this paper, they are discussed in Section II where the role of exception handlers is also described. It is necessary to understand the main error recovery problems between interacting processes before appropriate programming language features can be developed. For this reason, we discuss the recovery problems in Section III and then in Section IV, we discuss the recovery requirements for a class of problems for which language features are to be developed. In Section V we describe how recovery blocks can be introduced into resource allocation algorithms implemented using monitors. A program structure called a *port* is developed in Section VI. A port provides facilities for specifying how a resource should be used and what recovery actions a reversing process should undertake. Finally, in Section VII, we briefly discuss some implementation details and summarize the work presented.

II. Error Recovery

A. Recovery Blocks and the Recovery Cache

A system can contain residual faults both in the hardware and software. Therefore, when an error is detected, quite often it is not possible to determine the sources of the fault; backward error recovery then is the only sensible solution. The recovery action consists of restoring a prior state of the computation and proceeding again in the hope of avoiding the fault. By using a different algorithm, after the restoration, a measure of fault tolerance against software faults can be obtained. A recovery block is a program structure embodying backward error recovery.

A recovery block consists of a conventional block which is provided with a means of error detection (an acceptance test) and zero or more standby spares (alternatives). Its structure is shown in Fig. 1.

ensure ⟨acceptance test⟩ **by**
    ⟨primary block⟩
    else by
    ⟨alternative 1⟩
        . . .
    else by
    ⟨alternative n⟩
    else error;   **Fig. 1**

As discussed in [1], [2], the primary and the alternatives represent different algorithms for producing acceptable results, the primary block representing the preferred algorithm. After the execution of the primary block, the acceptance test (a Boolean expression) is evaluated to check that the results produced are acceptable. If so, the statement following the recovery block is executed; otherwise the state of the computation is restored to that at entry to the recovery block, and the first alternative is tried, and so on. If during the execution, some error is detected (e.g., division by zero) then this is also regarded as the failure of the primary block or the current alternative, as the case may be, and the same recovery actions are taken as in the case of the failure of the acceptance test (this behavior is explained further in Section II-B). If the primary and all the alternatives fail then this is regarded as a failure of the current recovery block; further recovery may be performed by the enclosing recovery block, if any (recovery blocks can be nested to any degree).

State restoration is achieved with the help of a device called the recovery (or recursive) cache. Since recovery blocks may be nested, the cache is organized as a stack and contains entries for recovery blocks entered but not yet exited. Upon entry to a recovery block, recovery data are collected by treating global variables as follows: the value of a global variable is "cached" just before the first update in that recovery block is performed. Subsequent updates to that variable in that recovery block need not be cached. To undo the effects of operations other than assignments, the designers of the recovery block scheme presented their initial ideas on the concept of "recoverable procedures" [1]. Such a procedure has a "normal" procedure body that performs a given operation and a "reverse" procedure body to be executed when reversal of that operation is desired. These ideas are developed further in this paper.

At this point we introduce two simple facilities (not present in the original proposals [1], [2]) in the recovery block scheme. The first facility will turn out to be of a great use when programming reverse operations. We assume that a Boolean flag "errorflag" is associated with each process in the system that indicates whether this process is going forward or backward. It will be the responsibility of the recovery cache management system to update this flag properly. We make this flag accessible to programs in a read only mode. Recovery blocks can also be used to provide a more conventional form of "check point and restart" facility as shown below, where "retry" means "execute again the previous block."

ensure ⟨at⟩ by begin . . . . . . **end else by retry else by** . . . . . . **else error**;

This type of recovery block usage will provide fault tolerance against certain types of transient hardware faults only and should really be used when a programmer has a complete (and hopefully justified) confidence in the adequacy of the design of the primary block.

Complete details of the recovery block scheme and its cache are presented in [1]. Many of the theoretical ideas on structuring complex systems using recovery blocks are given in [2] while practical details of an implementation of simple recovery blocks are presented in [3].

B. On Faults, Errors, and Exceptions

The recovery block approach we have just discussed is a means of coping with residual faults in a system (such faults can be termed "unanticipated faults"). Quite often, when designing a particular algorithm, it is possible to anticipate the exact consequences of certain abnormal situations that might occur. Therefore a programmer, if he wishes, can take appropriate steps in his programs to deal with these anticipated abnormal situations. The discipline of coping with such situations is usually called exception handling [4], [5]. One can therefore say that exception handling is a technique for dealing with "anticipated faults" and is complementary to recovery blocks (the relationship between recovery blocks and exception handling is explored in [6]; note also that it is argued in [4] that the role of exception handling need not be just confined to the one we are assuming here). Throughout this paper, we will implicitly assume the use of exception handlers and confine our attention to coping with unanticipated faults only. When we say that "an error is detected at a particular point in a program" we mean that "an abnormal situation has occurred (an exception has been raised) for which no exception handler is available." Thus, if a division by zero exception is raised while executing a recovery block, this will not cause the failure of the primary block or the current alternative if an exception handler for this exception has been provided. Of course, if the action of the handler involves stopping the program from running by raising an "abort" exception, then this exception will invoke the recovery actions of the recovery block as explained earlier.

III. Error Recovery Problems Between Interacting Processes

A. General

Concurrent processes in an operating system are said to be loosely coupled, that is, most of the time their activities are independent of each other but sometimes they exchange information. Consider now the recovery problems associated with process interaction. Assume that a process passes some information to some other process(es) (i.e., sends a message or modifies the environment common to them). While this operation may be "acceptable" to the information generating process, in general we cannot afford to throw away the recovery information associated with this operation (i.e., the cache entries corresponding to this operation which we assume is inside a recovery block) until the other concerned processes have "accepted" the passed information. These processes will however react in their own time; thus the recovery information may have to be preserved for a long time. What should the first process do in the meantime?

On the one hand, if it were allowed to proceed with its computation, during which there may be further interactions involved, then there would be the risk of a domino effect [2], that is, a reversal in one process may give rise to an avalanche of reversals in other processes. On the other hand, if its progress were halted, pending acceptance of the information by the receivers, then there would be the risk of seriously reducing the asynchronism in the system. One particular solution would be to choose a larger unit of recovery such that it encompasses all the interactions between the concerned processes. The limitations of this solution are that 1) it has lost the generality of the recovery block approach which allows a programmer to choose an arbitrary "grain of recovery," and 2) quite often, the number of processes that will interact at a given time is not known in advance. It is thus seen that the control of processes and management of recovery information can become an extremely complex problem, and a general solution that allows processes to interact arbitrarily and yet provides recovery from unanticipated faults does not appear to be possible. What seems possible however, is to develop mechanisms for different classes of interactions. We have found the classification of interactions into interference, cooperation, and competition, as defined in [7], to be the most suitable. Interference includes those interactions that are unacceptable or unanticipated. This will happen when processes are simultaneously allowed to modify shared data. Mechanisms which allow processes to operate on shared data without interference (e.g., P and V operations on semaphores) are simple and implemented at a very primitive level; we shall assume here that they operate reliably. We shall also assume that programming language features are available (e.g., monitors [9]) to ensure that these mechanisms are used properly so that the operations on shared data are free from interference. Cooperation occurs when processes explicitly wish to exchange information with each other, while competition occurs when processes have no explicit desire to exchange information, but nevertheless they do so as they must share resources. These two forms of interaction are discussed below in some detail.

B. Cooperation and Competition

Consider a two-level system in which the lower level manages all the resources to be shared by the processes of the system (see Fig. 2). To be specific, we assume that the resource allocation algorithms have been implemented using monitors [9]. So the processes wishing to acquire or release these resources invoke appropriate monitor procedure calls. In the lower level, the processes are competing for the shared resources. When these resources are used privately by processes [Fig. 2(a)] then, at the higher level, these processes appear to be logically independent: the interface hides the competition. On the other hand, the processes of Fig. 2(b) are cooperating, as the acquired resources are explicitly being used for information exchange (as shown by the heavy arrows). We thus see that competition is a lower level activity with respect to cooperation. We consider first the recovery problems of cooperating processes.

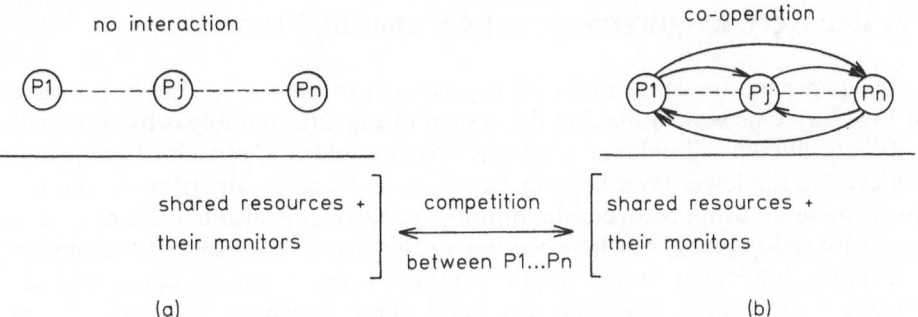

Fig. 2. **a** Private use of shared resources. **b** Shared use of shared resources

In general, cooperating processes are capable of exchanging arbitrary information (in the sense that a process can update a shared file in a manner it thinks fit or can send any message to other processes). This implies that, in general, only the receivers can verify the sent information. For this reason, in the conversation mechanism of [2], when processes enter a conversation (i.e., start exchanging information inside a common recovery block), they are allowed to exit from it only when all the concerned processes pass their acceptance tests (implying they are satisfied with the information exchange). Obviously, this restriction can reduce the degree of asynchronism in the system. As an example, consider the simple case of error recovery between producing and consuming processes coupled via a bounded buffer as described in [8]. If the "production of a message" and its "consumption" are programmed as a conversation, then it is no longer possible for the producer to race ahead of the consumer. Whether the conversation mechanism can be complemented by other mechanisms, which would allow the producer to race ahead, remains to be seen and we are currently investigating this area.

. Considering competition [i.e., the interaction in the bottom levels of Fig. 2(a) and (b)], we find that processes using a given monitor interact only through the monitor's shared data. This case is easier to deal with than cooperation (where the acquired resources are used for information exchange) for the following reason: the only information that processes exchange is that necessary to achieve harmonious resource sharing and this is determined by the monitor procedures. Thus it is no longer possible for processes to exchange arbitrary information using a monitor's shared data. As a result, when a process performs an operation on a monitor's shared data (i.e., executes a monitor procedure body) it should be in a position to assert the "global acceptability" of the shared data. This means that this form of interaction need not be structured as a conversation. We have exploited this property in the design of *recoverable monitors* to be described later.

IV. Recovery Requirements for Competing Processes

In this paper we are concerned with competing processes only, that is, processes of Fig. 2(a). One way of making the system of Fig. 2(a) reliable is by systematically introducing redundancy using the recovery block approach. Reliability is achieved in the lower level by making resource allocation algorithms reliable — this is done by using recoverable monitors (clearly, it is also beneficial to have hardware redundancy, but here we ignore this aspect and concentrate only on software redundancy). In the upper level, the codes of the processes will also contain redundancy. Since at this level these processes are logically independent, their recovery actions are also independent. If a process, after acquiring and using a resource, wishes to backtrack to an earlier state where this resource was not acquired, then it is necessary 1) to release the resource, and 2) to undo any effects owing to the use of the resource. We study these recovery actions in a greater detail below.

Figure 3 shows a recovery block where "units" is a *recoverable monitor* (i.e., a monitor whose procedure bodies are coded as recovery blocks — precise details of which are to be discussed in Section V) managing a pool of units — a process can acquire a unit, use it, and release it. The actual use of the acquired unit is performed inside a *forward procedure* "q" which specifies how the resource is to be used. There is also a *backward procedure* "undoq" that specifies how to undo any effects of the resource use (precise details of the program structure that provides facilities for defining such procedures need not concern us just now; they will be discussed in Section VI). We see that the execution of "q" is preceded by a "prelude" (concerned with resource acquisition) and followed by a corresponding "postlude" (concerned with the release of the resource).

Let an error occur while performing an operation. We consider recovery actions, other than restoration of prior values, that might be needed.

```
forward procedure q (...);
  begin ... use of one unit ... end;

backward procedure undoq;
  begin ... undo the effects of use ... end;
  ...
ensure ⟨at⟩ by "recovery block R"
  begin "primary block"
        units.acquire (...); "prelude"  ← (a)
        ...  ← (b)
        q (...);  ← (c)
        ...  ← (d)
        units.release (...); "postlude"  ← (e)
        ...  ← (f)
  end else by "first alternative" ...
```

Fig. 3

Error at point "a": This means that the primary and all the alternatives of "acquire" of the recoverable monitor "units" have failed and obviously this gives rise to the failure of the primary block of recovery block R; the alternative block must now be tried — no special recovery actions are necessary (note that if "acquire" is successful, i.e., no error at "a," the net result is the appropriate update of the monitor variables).

Error at point "b": The problem here is how to undo the effects of "acquire." Clearly it is possible to restore the state of the monitor variables but this would mean backtracking all those processes that have performed operations on "units" after the process under consideration performed "acquire." This is not necessary since simple reasoning tells us that all that is required is to release the acquired unit. The justification for this reasoning is as follows: a monitor (or any other SIMULA-like class object) is an abstract data type providing abstract operations over an abstract space — monitor variables being a concrete representation of this space. It is the abstract state of the object that is of concern to a calling process and it is only necessary to restore the abstract state when reversing — this does not necessarily mean restoring the concrete state. Thus, by releasing the unit (i.e., by calling "release") we ensure that the operation "acquire" can continue to provide the abstraction "a unit will be made available within a finite time." To summarize, the backtracking process must execute the postlude.

Error at point "c": Procedure "q" specifies how the acquired resource is to be used. The object of this use is to produce side effects the computation desires. We may regard a call on "q" as performing an abstract indivisible operation such that no side effects are produced if the execution of "q" fails. The recovery action is the same as at "b" discussed previously.

Error at point "d": The backward procedure "undoq" must be executed to undo the effects of the use of the acquired unit. As an example, consider that the forward procedure is for printing a file on the acquired line printer. Then the backward procedure for "unprinting" might be to send a message to the operator's console to ignore that printed file. This example also illustrates that resources needed for "undoing" may not be the same as that for "doing." After executing the backward procedure "undoq," further recovery actions needed are the same as at "b."

Error at point "e": This error, implying that resources cannot be returned is much more serious than the others discussed so far. This is because if the process is allowed to backtrack, it will eventually try to undo the prelude by executing the postlude (which it was unable to execute in the first place). A failure in a postlude is therefore regarded as a collapse of the recovery mechanism and the only sensible strategy is for the process to ignore this error and continue, hoping that a degraded service can still be provided.

Error at point "f": Since the postlude has been executed, the only effect that needs undoing is that due to "q" — this may be done by calling "undoq." Pro-

```
b: buffer;                              b: buffer;
...                                     ...
pool.acquirebuffer (b);                 pool.acquirebuffer (b);
    put some information                    put some information
    in the acquired buffer;                 in the acquired buffer;
ensure ⟨at⟩ by                          ensure ⟨at⟩ by
    begin                                   begin

        ...                                     ...
        pool.releasebuffer (b);
        ... ←
    end else by                             end else by
    begin                                   begin

        ...                                     ...
        pool.releasebuffer (b);             end ...

        ...
    end ...                                 else error;
                                            pool.releasebuffer (b);
                                            ...

            (a)                                     (b)                    Fig. 4
```

vision must be made for acquiring the necessary resources needed for undoing (in particular, it may be necessary to reacquire the released resource).

Error while backtracking: Any error detected while backtracking is quite serious since it means that the system will be unable to return to a consistent state. Again, a sensible strategy is to continue operation with the hope that some form of service may still be given.

We conclude this section by pointing out an important class of errors which can occur if proper program structuring is not used. In Fig. 4(a) a buffer is acquired from a shared pool of buffers and its release is done inside a recovery block.

If an error occurs at the point shown by the arrow (i.e., after the release), the execution of the alternative is meaningful only if the released buffer is acquired again, however, this cannot be guaranteed. This problem is not present in Fig. 4(b) where the acquired resource is released outside the recovery block concerned with its use.

We have identified the required recovery actions for a process using the shared resources of a system. From this discussion it is clear that if we can syntactically specify "prelude," "use," "unuse," and "postlude," then it is possible to design an appropriate recovery strategy. It is then only necessary to extend the recovery cache mechanism such that the cache processing includes this strategy.

In the next section, we describe how recovery blocks may be introduced in monitors. Such "recoverable monitors" are a means of making resource allocation algorithms reliable. A program structure called a *port* is next developed which provides facilities for specifying 1) a prelude and postlude, that is, how the calls on recoverable monitors are to be made for acquiring and releasing resources, and 2) how the acquired resources are to be "used" and "unused." The recovery cache management necessary to support recoverable monitors and ports is discussed in Section VII.

V. Recoverable Monitors

Recoverable monitors are a means of adding redundancy to the resource allocation algorithms. Bearing in mind the discussion in Section III-B on competition, we can say that the acceptance test of a monitor entry procedure (i.e., a procedure which may be called from outside the monitor) should test for the "global" acceptability of that operation, that is, test that not only is the result of that operation acceptable to the calling process, but also that it will be acceptable to subsequent calling processes. The state of a monitor after the acceptance test of one of its operations has been passed is called its consistent state. Briefly stated then, a recoverable monitor is used by processes as follows: the calling process will expect to find the monitor in a consistent state (say δ_1); after the execution of the appropriate procedure body, assuming it passes the acceptance test, it will leave the monitor in a (possibly different) consistent state (say δ_2). In case the test fails (or an error is detected during execution), δ_1 is restored and the next alternative is tried; if none exists then the process will get an error return and will have to take its own appropriate recovery action. We can ensure that a calling process finds a monitor in a consistent state by making sure that 1) a monitor is initialized to a consistent state, and 2) the executing process leaves the monitor in a consistent state before any other process is given entry. Some care is needed in order to observe the second condition. Fig. 5 shows an alternative of a monitor procedure body with a synchronizing operation such as a "wait" or "resume process." Assume also that s1 and s2 are statements updating monitor variables.

The danger now is that, as a result of the synchronizing operation, control may be given to some other process before the state of the monitor has been validated by the acceptance test. For example, if the synchronizing operation is a "signal" [9], then the awakened process (if any) will immediately be allowed to enter the monitor. It is thus clear that such operations must not be performed from inside a recovery block. A recovery block used in a procedure with syn-

```
ensure ⟨at⟩ by
   ... else by
   begin s1;
           wait/resume operation;
           s2
   end else by
   ...
```

Fig. 5

```
entry procedure procname (...);
  begin
    ⟨variable declarations⟩
             [s1]
    ['wait operation']
    ⟨recovery block⟩
    ['resume process operation']
  end;
```

Fig. 6

chronizing operations must be placed, as shown in Fig. 6, where operations inside square brackets are optional and "s1" is an operation without side effects.

Fortunately, in a majority of cases, as the examples of [9], [10] show, a "wait" operation is the first operation before side effects are produced and "resume" operations are the last operations in a procedure, so the above structuring should not prove to be too restrictive. The proof guided methodology presented in [9], [10] also indicates how acceptance tests may be constructed. In Section VII, we briefly discuss recovery cache details to support these monitors.

VI. Ports

A program structure called *port* is developed here which, as the name suggests, acts as a gate through which one or more ways of using a resource are made available to a process. In this section we shall see how the language features for recovery actions, discussed in Section IV, are incorporated into this program structure.

A systematic method of allowing processes to use the shared resources of the system is to create virtual resource objects out of real resources; a process can then create a "local instance" of a given virtual resource object when it wishes to use that resource. Hoare has shown that the SIMULA language's *class* and *inner* concepts [11] can be elegantly used for the above purposes [12]. The port structure to be described in this subsection follows directly from his ideas; however, their application to recoverable processes is believed to be new.

Let us suppose that we wish to create a virtual disk; we will consider the write operation of this disk in more detail (a Concurrent Pascal [13] like language is assumed). Let "diskinout" be a class that defines all the control operations on a disk:

```
type diskinout = class
  begin
    machine code routines to perform disk head
    movement, reading, writing etc.
  end;
```

308

For this disk, a resource allocation algorithm is implemented which allocates diskpages (where a diskpage is a sector on a track) to requesting processes and also controls the movement of diskheads as suggested in [9] (recovery blocks in the procedure bodies are now shown):

```
type diskresource = recoverable monitor
   begin var pageset: set of diskpage; "pool of free pages"
   ... other variables ...
   entry procedure move (p: diskpage);
      {use algorithm of [9] to queue the request
         to move heads to the track of 'p'}
   entry procedure move to write (var p: diskpage; var found: boolean);
      {if pageset not empty then {acquire a free page and queue
      the request for head movement; found := true}
      else found := false}
   entry procedure releasepage (p: diskpage);
      {pageset := [pageset] + [p]}
   entry procedure releasehead;
      {use algorithm of [9] to service the next request}
      ...
   end diskresource;
```

A few words are in order here regarding the procedure "move to write": this procedure is called when a process wishes to acquire a free page to write on it. We can anticipate that occasionally the disk will become full. For this reason we have chosen not to treat the "disk full" event (i.e., when "found" is set to "false") as an error condition requiring backward error recovery provided by a recovery block.

A class "diskcontrol" can now be written that provides virtual operations through ports (*entry* means that instances of that type can be created outside). Here, "writepage" provides a "write" operation for writing on the acquired page; "readpage" provides a "read" operation; "releasepage" is a port for releasing a page (this is needed, for example, when a process wishes to delete a file) and "update" provides a "rewrite" operation for updating a previously acquired page. Only the "writepage" port is programmed, the rest are similar. At this stage, ports may be regarded as identical to classes.

```
type diskcontrol = class
   begin var inout: diskinout;
              resource: diskresource;
      entry type writepage = port
         begin var p: diskpage; found: boolean;
            entry procedure write (c: corepage; var possible: boolean;
                                       var pp: diskpage);
```

```
            begin
                possible := found; if found then begin
                use 'inout' to write from 'c' to 'p';
                pp := p end
            end write;
          resource.move to write (p: found); "prelude"
                inner;
          resource.releasehead; "postlude"
        end writepage;
      entry type readpage = port (p: diskpage)
        begin ... end readpage;
      entry type releasepage = port
        begin ... end releasepage;
      entry type update = port (p: diskpage)
        begin ... end update
end diskcontrol;
```

Assuming there is one disk unit, an instance of type "diskcontrol" will be declared global to all user processes:

```
diskuse : diskcontrol;
```

and a process wishing to perform a write operation will proceed as follows (where "c" has been declared as a corepage, "f" a Boolean, and "p" as a diskpage):

```
... using diskwrite: diskuse.writepage do
begin ... diskwrite.write(c, f, p); ... end; ...
```

A local instance of port "writepage" is created and then its "write" operation is called. The term *using* emphasizes the fact that, because of the *inner* statement, the execution of the statement following *do* will be enclosed by the prelude-postlude of the port. We thus see that a port can be regarded as the modus operandi of a resource, taking on the responsibility of acquiring and releasing that resource and providing appropriate operations for the use of the resource. A clear separation between resource acquisition and resource use now allows us to introduce the kind of error recovery discussed in Section IV.

A. Recovery Features in Ports

The port schema with the recovery features is shown below. The following points should be noted:

```
[entry] type ⟨name⟩ = port (formal parameters)
        "entry is an optional feature"
```

begin ... local variable declarations ...

... procedures/forward entry procedures; one such
forward entry procedure is shown below ...
forward entry procedure ⟨name⟩ (formal parameters);
begin ... **end;**
... other procedures/forward entry procedures ...
[backward entry procedure ⟨name⟩;
"this procedure is optional"
begin ... **end;]**
S1; **inner;** S2
"Si are statements; where,
S1 is the prelude and S2 is the postlude"
end "of port definition"

1) Only a port is allowed to contain forward procedures and a backward procedure. The "forward" prefix dictates that only a forward going process may call that procedure.

2) The backward procedure is parameterless and can only be called by a process while reversing. Its role is purely to undo the effects due to the calls on the forward procedures (the local port variables may be used to record the information needed by the backward procedure, as illustrated by the "writepage" and "printop" examples to follow).

3) None of the procedures of a port are allowed explicit access to monitors.[1] Only the prelude and postlude can contain monitor calls. Whether these monitors are conventional or contain recovery blocks (recoverable monitors) is irrelevant from the point of view of a port. By insisting that only the prelude and postlude may contain monitor calls, we guarantee that the role of resource handling is confined to these program parts only.

We shall now see how to make the "writepage" port recoverable. The "use of the resource" is programmed as a *forward entry procedure* and "unuse of the resource" is programmed as a *backward entry procedure*. In our example we can assume that "unuse" consists of clearing the written disk page (say, writing all zeros in it). We note also that this "unuse" requires the disk resource. The port "writepage" with recovery features is now shown below (to make this example more interesting, we have also put recovery blocks in the bodies of the procedures, albeit with "retry" as the only alternative).

entry type writepage = **port**
begin var p: diskpage; found, acquired: boolean;
forward entry procedure write
(c: corepage; **var** possible: boolean; **var** pp: diskpage);

---

1 A procedure can, of course, declare a local instance of some port and thus have implicit access to monitors used in that port.

```
        begin possible := found; if found then
          begin pp := p; ensure ⟨good writing⟩ by
              begin write from 'c' to 'p' end else by
              retry else error
          end
        end write;
      backward entry procedure unwrite;
        begin var ct: corepage; if found then
          begin initialize 'ct' with zeros;
              ensure ⟨good writing⟩ by
              begin write from 'ct' to 'p' end else by
              retry else by retry else error
          end
        end unwrite;
      if ∼ errorflag then begin "process is going forward"
                              acquired := true;
                                resource.move to write (p, found)
                      end else
                begin "process is going backward"
                    if found then begin acquired := true; resource.move (p)
                              end else "a page was not
                    acquired so no resources are needed for undoing"
                    acquired := false
                end "prelude"
        inner;
      if found & errorflag then resource.releasepage (p);
      if acquired then resource.releasehead "postlude"
    end writepage;
```

The meaning of the various new constructs is explained with the help of the program shown in Fig. 7 (the particular recovery structure of this figure has been chosen deliberately to explain the semantics of port; it is not intended to show a typical use of "writepage").

We now consider various possible execution sequences (for failures, only the recovery actions other than restoration of prior values are described):

1) *AT3 passed:* This means that the recovery block R3 has produced acceptable results. The execution steps were the prelude of "diskwrite", then the recovery block, followed by the postlude. As the process is going forward (i.e., errorflag=false), "move to write" will be called in the prelude; assuming the disk is not full (found=true), only the diskheads will be released in the postlude (we assume that a process retains the page after acquiring it).

2) *Error at point "i":* The alternative of R3 must now be tried. Before that, the backtracking process calls the backward procedure "unwrite" of port "diskwrite" to undo the effects of write. Note that a failure at "i" implies that the procedure "diskwrite.write" was executed satisfactorily, but nevertheless the process failed after that. No recovery capability is available if the primary and

```
ensure AT1 by "recovery block R1"
  begin
        .

            ensure AT2 by "recovery block R2"
              begin var c: corepage; found: boolean; p: diskpage;
                .

                .

                using diskwrite: diskuse.writepage do
                ensure AT3 by "recovery block R3"
                  begin
                    .

                        diskwrite.write (c, found, p);
                        . ← (i)
                        .

                  end else by
                  begin
                        . ← (j)
                        .

                        diskwrite.write (c, found, p); ← (k)
                        . ← (l)
                        .

                  end else error;
                . ← (m)
                .

            end else by
            begin
                .

                using diskwrite: diskuse.writepage do
                .

                .

            end else error;
          . ← (n)
          .

  end else by
  begin
      .

      .

  end else by
      .

      .
```

Fig. 7
```
```

all the alternatives of "unwrite" fail. In this case, as discussed in Section IV, the process will ignore this failure and continue its operation.

3) *Error at point "j":* The alternative of R2 must now be tried. Before this is done, the process, as it backtracks, releases the resources by executing the postlude (as errorflag=true, if the process had acquired a page then it will be released).

4) *Error at point "k":* The process was unable to write properly (from the code of "write" we see that two attempts were made to write); the recovery action is the same as at "j."

5) *Error at point "l":* Before the alternative of R2 can be tried, the backtracking process must undo the effects of "write" and also release the resources. This is done by calling "unwrite" and then executing the postlude.

6) *Error at point "m":* Before the alternative of R2 is tried, "unwrite" is executed between the prelude and postlude. The reasoning for this action is as follows: clearly it is necessary to undo the effects of "write," but the required resources have been released. It is therefore necessary to execute the prelude and subsequently the postlude to acquire and release the resources. [2] The local variable "found" of the port is used to record whether a page was acquired by the forward going process. If "undoing of actions" were not our aim, we would have expected the port object "diskwrite" to be destroyed after the execution of the postlude. However, since we want to introduce the feature of programmed recovery actions, it is no longer possible for port objects to follow this scope rule (see the Appendix for the scope rule for ports).

7) *Error at point "n":* Recovery actions are the same as at "m."

B. Some Remarks on the Remaining Ports of "diskcontrol"

Rather than programming the remaining ports of "diskcontrol" (readpage, releasepage, and update) we discuss here some of their interesting features and leave the task of programming to the interested reader. The port "readpage" does not need a backward procedure for undoing the effects of a diskread operation. This is because the recovery cache will automatically store the previous contents of the "corepage" as it is updated by the diskread operation. An interesting problem arises while programming "update" port. If we assume that it has a "rewrite" procedure for overwriting the contents of a disk page, then clearly the previous contents of the disk page must be stored in a local port variable so that the effect of "rewrite" can be undone, if desired. From the cache storage's point of view, this may prove to be costly (especially when updating random access files) and a practical solution is as follows: the operation of "update" port is made unrecoverable (i.e., no attempt is made to save the previous contents of the disk page; no backward procedure is needed) and recovery is provided at the file level rather than at the disk page level. File level

---

2 If the process had not acquired a page then no resources are needed for undoing, so the variable "acquired" is used to record whether a resource was acquired in the prelude.

recovery can be provided by ensuring that the filing system always creates a backup file before a user is allowed to update that file. The same arguments hold for the "releasepage" port.

Two (often conflicting) factors influence the task of deciding whether to make operations of a port recoverable: 1) the "grain of recovery" desired, and 2) the recovery information storage requirements. In a hierarchically structured system, a fine grain of recovery can be obtained by introducing recoverability in most of the levels of the system while a larger grain of recovery can be obtained by introducing recoverability in only the top few levels. The latter approach is likely to demand appreciably less recovery cache storage than the former one. As an example, the overheads of providing a fine grain of recovery by making "write" operation of "writepage" recoverable as shown here may be acceptable in a situation where a time critical process acquires pages incrementally.

C. Another Example

As another example, suppose that we want to make printing of files reliable (especially tolerant against transient printer faults). A port "printop" is programmed as shown. It provides a "printpage" operation for printing a page. A process can acquire the printer, print the desired number of pages (by repeatedly calling "printpage") and then release the printer. If during printing, the process detects an error (we assume that this activity is being done inside a recovery block) and backtracks, the effect of the printing is "undone" by the operator message to ignore the number of pages printed for the user (note that the backward procedure of a port is called only once while recovering – see the Appendix for more details). Exception handling techniques may be used in the procedures "newpage" and "printpage" for dealing with certain exceptional events from the printer, such as, "printer not online;" such exception handlers are not shown in the program. To deal with unanticipated faults in the printer (e.g., accidental switching off of the printer during printing) a timer is used in the "printpage" and "newpage" procedures. It will be left to the calling program to deal with the "time out" exception (when raised).

```
type printer = class (number: integer)
  begin var pc: pcontrol; "a class providing primitive printer operations"
         pa: paccess; "a recoverable monitor for exclusive access
                                                    to the printer"
  entry type printop = port (id: name)
    begin var count: integer; acquired: boolean;
      forward entry procedure newpage;
        begin set timer; use 'pc' to prepare the printer to
               start on a new page; clear timer
        end;
```

```
forward entry procedure printpage (c: corepage);
    begin set timer; use 'pc' to print the contents of 'c'
        on the printer; count := count + 1; clear timer
    end;
backward entry procedure undo;
    begin using operator: console.output do
        operator.send ('ignore any current output of
                    user', id, 'on printer', number,
                    'consisting of', count, 'pages')
    end;
    if errorflag then acquired := false else
        begin acquired := true; count := o; pa.acquire end; inner;
    if acquired then pa.release
    end printop
end printer;
```

Let us assume a "printerprocess" whose job is to print user files. We assume two printers:

mainprinter : printer (1); auxiliary printer : printer (2);

The printer process prints on the "mainprinter" but if unable to do so, prints on the "auxiliaryprinter" (a printer which is mainly for the use of the computer operators). The code of "printerprocess" is as shown below. It is assumed that the most likely cause of error is the printer, so the second printer is tried in the first alternative of R1. If this fails as well, a message is sent to the operator (who could ask the user to try later). The above process should provide a service despite faults in 1) the printers, 2) disk, or 3) the program itself. Assume for example that the main printer becomes temporarily faulty. Then the printer process will 1) release that printer, 2) tell the operator to ignore the partially printed file, and 3) start printing the file on the auxiliary printer. There will also be a process for printing files requested by the operators. The code of this process will be similar to that of "printerprocess" except that the auxiliary printer is the preferred printer.

In the code of "printerprocess" we have chosen to regard the "time out" exception raised by the timer of port "printop" as unanticipated – such an exception will invoke the recovery actions of R1. It is also possible to provide an exception handler in the code of "printerprocess" (and, if desired, to do away with the recovery block R1). The actions of such a handler might be to release the acquired printer and to acquire another printer for printing the file. As it happens, this recovery action can be obtained automatically; hence our decision of not providing a "time out" exception handler.

In this example, we have assumed that both the printers have their own work loads and only occasionally work load sharing is done. The system has not been designed to work smoothly in the presence of permanent printer faults. Suppose a few more printers become available. Then a simple method (requiring minimum changes in program modules) of introducing fault-tolerance

316

against permanent printer faults is to modify the code of the monitor "paccess" such that 1) it now handles a pool of printers rather than just one printer, and 2) it provides facilities for adding and removing printers to and from the pool. Programs can now be developed easily that would allow an operator to remove a suspect printer from service or to add a printer back into the system.

```
         "assume an object 'r' that maintains a queue of print requests"
                   filename, username: name;
                   map: corepage; "to store file map" found: boolean;
                   length: integer; "indicates file length"
       cycle r.getrequest (filename, username);
          ... using f: filemaster.fileop (username) do
          f.open (filename, map, length, found);
          if found then
                   ensure ⟨good printing⟩ by "recovery block R1"
                   using pr: mainprinter.printop (username) do
                   begin var c: corepage; i: integer;
                   pr.newpage; c := standard header;
                   pr.printpage (c);
                   for i := 1 to length do
                   begin using dr: diskuse.readpage (map (i)) do
                     dr.read (c);
                     pr.printpage (c)
                   end;
                   c := standard tail; pr.printpage (c)
                   end else by using pr: auxiliaryprinter.printop (username) do
                   {similar code as the primary block}
                   else by using operator: console.output do
                     operator.send ('unable to print file', filename,
                                      'of user', username)
                   else error;
                     ...
       end "cycle";
```

We hope that the reader will now share our belief that ports are a systematic method of providing reliable, recoverable operations on the shared resources of a system. Programming language rules for constructing ports are stated in detail in the Appendix. Finally we note that, thanks to the *inner* mechanism, resource acquisition and release are performed automatically around its use — this eliminates the problem illustrated in Fig. 4(a) since programs are restricted to the structure of Fig. 4(b).

VII. Implementation Notes and Concluding Remarks

We will assume that each process in the system has its own recovery cache. We have described briefly, in Section II, the cache mechanism (i.e., how the recovery information is stored in the cache) for the case of assignments to private variables. The extensions needed to support recoverable monitors and ports are now described.

1) *Recoverable monitors:* Upon entry to the recovery block of a procedure (see Fig. 6) of such a monitor, copies of the monitor's variables are stored in the cache of the calling process in the usual manner and, if the primary (current alternative) fails, the cache is used to restore the state of the monitor – again in the usual manner. If the acceptance test is passed, these variables are popped off the cache – they are no longer needed.

2) *Ports:* When an object of type port is created inside a recovery block by a process, the cache of the process should record details of its use (e.g., prelude executed, prelude plus a forward procedure executed, etc.). This can be done by reserving a block of storage in the cache (as soon as a port object is created) where the above-mentioned details can be recorded. Precise rules for the caching of port variables and calling of the backward procedure are given in the Appendix. When an error is detected, the port information can be processed to provide the necessary recovery actions (as discussed with reference to Fig. 7).

The ideas presented in this paper are currently being implemented on our PDP11/45; the language chosen to incorporate these ideas is Concurrent Pascal [13]. In this experiment, recovery caches will be implemented as a part of the interpreter. The Concurrent Pascal system, as developed by Brinch Hansen's group, consists of a kernel (which implements processes, monitors, and the synchronizing primitives) and an interpreter (which acts as a simple stack machine). The storage organization is shown in Fig. 8. The virtual address space of each process is divided into a private segment and a segment that is common to all the processes. The common segment contains the virtual code (to be executed by the interpreter) and the shared variables (monitors). The task of

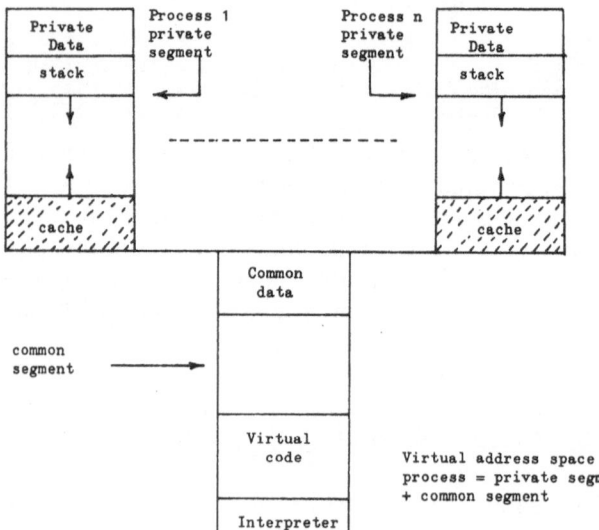

Fig. 8. Concurrent Pascal system

318

implementing the features of this paper reduces mainly to the modification of the interpreter. The shaded areas in Fig. 8 show the place of recovery caches. We hope to report our experience once the implementation exercise is over.

To conclude: after discussing the basic error recovery problems between interacting processes, we have developed recovery mechanisms to solve a subset of these problems – that of concurrent processes competing to use the shared resources of a system. Recoverable monitors were developed to make resource allocation algorithms reliable (i.e., to make process interaction for competition reliable). A program structure called port was developed that provided facilities for specifying 1) how a process should call on a (recoverable) monitor to acquire and release resources (when going forward or backward), and 2) how a process should "use" and "unuse" a given resource. Recoverable monitors and ports both impose a strict (but conceptually simple) discipline on how a programmer should think about resource allocation and recovery; this is essential if the recovery problems are to be kept manageable.

Appendix
Further Aspects of Ports

The remaining rules for structuring ports are given here. 1) Let p1; p2; ...; pn be a prelude; then only pn may be a monitor call for resource acquisition. Operations p1; ...; pn−1 must be recoverable, that is, for pi, $1 \leq i \leq n-1$, a) pi produces no side effects, or b) pi is an assignment operation, or c) pi is a call on a recoverable operation of some port. The postlude is compulsorily executed only if the prelude has been executed completely. Thus, if a process fails while executing pi, $1 \leq i \leq n$, then the postlude will not be executed; rather, the process will backtrack undoing all pj, $1 \leq j \leq i-1$; hence the requirement that p1; ...; pn−1 be recoverable. It is a programmer's responsibility to ensure that a prelude's role is confined to resource acquisition and that of the corresponding postlude to the release of the acquired resource. In the majority of cases, preludes and postludes are simply monitor calls for acquiring and releasing.

2) By creating a local instance of a port, a process, in effect, manipulates shared resources which are "permanent" objects. In principle therefore, the capability for undoing the effects of this manipulation should be maintained as long as the resource objects live. Since this is not a practical proposition, it is necessary to define a commitment discipline. It is suggested here that once a program successfully terminates, the effects produced by it (if any) should be regarded as committed (that is, automatic recovery capability is discarded).

Following this suggestion, the scope rule for ports is: port objects are treated as if they have been created in the outermost recovery block of the program under consideration (it is this scope rule that enables us to call upon the services of the port for undoing at point "m" or "n" in Fig. 7). The following exceptions to this rule should be noted.

a) If a port object is created inside a forward procedure, then it is treated as a local object of that procedure. This is because once such a procedure has been executed, it becomes the responsibility of the backward procedure to undo any effects.

b) If a port object is created inside a backward procedure, then it is also treated as a local object of that procedure (this is because "undoing" is never "undone").

c) If a port object is created in a prelude or postlude then it ceases to exist after the execution of that prelude or postlude.

3) In a port, only the bodies of procedures may contain recovery blocks.

4) While executing the inner statement which is enveloped by the prelude and postlude, the local port variables are treated as global variables by the recovery cache (i.e., on an assignment to such a variable, the previous value is cached, if necessary, in the current recovery region of the cache). However, when the execution of this statement ends, these cached entries are discarded. Consider the following program:

```
...
using A : B.C do
ensure AT1 by "Recovery block R1"
begin ...
      A.op1;
   ensure AT2 by "Recovery block R2"
   begin ...
      A.op2; A.op4;

         ...
   end else by
   begin ...
      A.op3; ...
   end else error
end else by ...
```

If, say, the primary block of R2 fails AT2, then, after calling the backward procedure, the states of port variables will be restored like those of any other global variables. After exiting from R1, the local port variables become inaccessible to the forward going process, so all the cached entries corresponding to them are discarded.

5) A backward procedure is called only once (if appropriate) while recovering. In the example of rule 4), if the primary block of R2 fails the acceptance test then despite the fact that two calls on forward procedures have been made, only one call on the backward procedure will be made. If R2 fails, then the recovery action of R1 will also include a call on the backward procedure (since R1 has also used a port operation).

Acknowledgement. Discussions with members of the Highly Reliable Computing Systems Project at the University of Newcastle upon Tyne were of great value. Our special thanks go to B. Randell, P. A. Lee, T. Anderson, and J. S. M. Verhofstad. Acknowledgement is due also to the referees whose critical comments led to the improvement of this paper.

References

1. J. J. Horning, H. C. Lauer, P. M. Melliar-Smith, and B. Randell, "A program structure for error detection and recovery," in Lecture Notes in Computer Science, vol. 16. New York: Springer, 1974, pp. 177 – 193. [Also Chap. 2]
2. B. Randell, "System structure for software fault tolerance," IEEE Trans. Software Eng., vol. SE-1, pp. 220 – 232, June 1975. [Also Chap. 1]
3. T. Anderson and R. Kerr, "Recovery blocks in action: A system supporting high reliability," in Proc. 2nd Int. Conf. Software Eng., Oct. 1976. [Also Chap. 2]
4. J. B. Goodenough, "Exception handling: Issues and proposed notation," Commun. Ass. Comput. Mach., vol. 18, pp. 683 – 696, Dec. 1975.
5. D. L. Parnas and H. Wurges, "Response to undesired events in software systems," in Proc. 2nd Int. Conf. Software Eng., Oct. 1976.
6. P. M. Melliar-Smith and B. Randell, "Software reliability: The role of programmed exception handling," in Proc., ACM Conf. Language Design for Reliable Software, Mar. 1977, pp. 95 – 100. [Also Chap. 3]
7. J. J. Horning and B. Randell, "Process structuring," ACM Comput. Surveys, vol. 5, pp. 5 – 29, Mar. 1973.
8. D. L. Russel and T. H. Bredt, "Error resynchronization in producer-consumer systems," in Proc. 5th ACM Operating System Symp., Nov. 1975, pp. 106 – 113.
9. C. A. R. Hoare, "Monitors: An operating system structuring concept," Commun. Ass. Comput. Mach., vol. 17, pp. 549 – 557, Oct. 1974.
10. S. K. Shrivastava, "Systematic programming of scheduling algorithms," Software – Practice and Experience, vol. 6, pp. 357 – 370, 1976.
11. O. J. Dahl, B. Myhrhaug, and K. Nygaard, "The SIMULA 67 common base language," Norwegian Computing Center, Oslo, Norway, Publ. S-22, 1970.
12. C. A. R. Hoare, "The structure of an operating system," in Proc. Int. Summer School Language Hierarchies and Interfaces, Munich, Germany, Aug. 1975.
13. P. B. Hansen, "The programming language Concurrent Pascal," IEEE Trans. Software Eng., vol. SE-1, pp. 199 – 207, June 1975.

Concurrent Pascal with Backward Error Recovery: Language Features and Examples

S. K. SHRIVASTAVA

Summary. The programming language Concurrent Pascal has been extended to include some language features that facilitate the writing of fault-tolerant software. As a result, it is possible now to (1) write operating systems witn a measure of fault-tolerance, and (2) for such an operating system to support fault-tolerant user programs. The paper describes these language features and illustrates their use with the help of a few working examples.

Key Words. Fault-tolerant software   Operating systems   Concurrent Pascal
Sequential Pascal   Error recovery   Recovery blocks   Ports

Introduction

A computer system can contain faults in either the hardware or the software or both. As a consequence of this, when an error is detected while executing a program, it is often not possible to locate accurately the fault that caused the erroneous situation. When writing fault-tolerant software (defined to be software that produces acceptable results despite faults in the hardware and software), one recommended practice therefore is to classify erroneous or abnormal situations encountered into those that were anticipated and the rest as unanticipated [1]. For example, suppose a programmer's task is to develop an input—output program module for a certain peripheral. He can classify a number of situations as 'abnormal' — these may include 'peripheral device not connected to the computer', 'parity error', etc. Suppose that his tested and debugged program still contains design faults as a result of which a 'division by zero' exception is detected during the program execution — such a situation will be considered as an unanticipated abnormal situation if no provision for coping with it has been provided. It can be appreciated that special purpose routines can be written for coping with anticipated abnormal situations, and many programming languages provide facilities for writing such 'exception handlers' (e.g. ON units in PL1). In contrast, any technique for coping with unanticipated situations has to be sufficiently general such that it can (hopefully) deal with all of the erroneous situations that were not foreseen by the programmer.

The best known technique for coping with unanticipated erroneous situations is the so-called backward error recovery technique which consists of abandoning the state of the computation in progress and 'rolling it back' to a prior state which is believed to be error free. After the rollback, the computation is resumed again with the hope of avoiding the offending fault. Furthermore, if after the rollback, a different algorithm is used for producing results, then a measure of tolerance against design faults can also be obtained.

Some work has been done at Newcastle in the area of constructing fault-tolerant software that makes use of backward error recovery [4–6]. This paper describes further effort in this direction: the programming languages Concurrent and Sequential Pascal [2, 3] have been extended to include some backward error recovery features. As a result it is now possible to write operating systems with a measure of fault tolerance and with the capability of supporting fault-tolerant user programs. In this paper, these language features are described and their use illustrated with the help of a few working examples. A companion paper [10] describes the implementation of these features.

Language Features for Error Recovery

Design Decisions and Objectives

Backward error recovery involves the restoration of a prior state. A decision was taken that the state to which a computation should be backtracked will be indicated by the programmer – the term recovery point will be used to refer to such a state – and that the task of restoring the state will be performed automatically by a recovery system that is part of the system that is supporting the computation. In order to appreciate what is involved when state restoration is performed, consider the progress of a computational process supported by an operating system. If the actions of the process, after a recovery point has been specified, is to produce its results entirely by updating its private variables, then the act of state restoration involves undoing the updates which merely consists of restoring the prior values of the updated variables – the recovery system can be designed to perform this task easily. However, the actions of a process can be arbitrarily complex; suppose the process is involved in the control of some input–output equipment. Under such a situation it may become necessary for the programmer to specify what should constitute the undoing of the input–output control operations (e.g. if the action was unwind a tape for accessing a particular file, the action needed for undoing might be to rewind the tape). A design decision was therefore taken that for all the actions other than assignments, for which recovery is desired (actions for which recovery is provided will be termed recoverable actions) the programmer must specify the appropriate routines for undoing the effects resulting from the actions; it will be the responsibility of the recovery system to invoke appropriately these programmer- specified recovery routines when state restoration is required.

So far, the state restoration of a single process has been discussed. For interacting processes, errors can propagate from one process to other; this may mean that when an error is detected, it becomes necessary to restore the state of a group of interacting processes. Many problems arise when state restoration of a group of processes is required [5, 6]; it is sufficient to note here that such a situation should be avoided as far as possible. There are, fortunately, some important cases where a certain degree of interaction between processes can be allowed and yet the error recovery of processes can be made independent from each other. Such processes are said to belong to the class of independently recoverable processes.

Definition: A group of processes is said to be independently recoverable if (a) no interaction between them takes place; or (b) they make private use of shared resources, that is, any interaction is solely for competition; or (c) they make shared use of the resources, but any information exchange that takes place is compensatable.

Statements (b) and (c) above need some explanation. If processes are only competing and making private use of shared resources (i.e. interaction is restricted to that necessary for acquiring and releasing the resources) then if the state of a process is to be restored to that at its recovery point, it is necessary to undo any effects due to any resource use and to release these resources — these actions need not affect the rest of the processes. Assume that a process A passes a message to some process B (i.e. A and B make shared use of a resource — say a buffer) and later it is necessary to restore the state of A. Then the message from A to B is said to be compensatable if it is possible for A to undo any effects due to that message by sending a corrective message to B; B can process this message as a part of its normal activity, therefore it is not necessary to restore the state of B.

The objective of the work to be described here was to develop and implement language features necessary for the recovery of independently recoverable processes. When the work began (late 1975), a program structure called recovery block [4, 5] had already been proposed by my colleagues as means for error detection and backward error recovery. Hence it was decided to develop and implement further language features within the framework of recovery blocks. An abstract data type called port was later developed by J. P. Banatre and myself [6]. A port provides facilities for programming recoverable actions of independently recoverable processes. In what follows, an understanding of recovery blocks and the language Concurrent Pascal will be assumed; in addition, a familiarity with the ideas presented on ports [6] will be helpful to the reader.

Recovery Blocks and Ports

The Pascal system of Brinch Hansen [3] consists of the language Concurrent Pascal which is intended for writing operating systems supporting concurrent processes. Each of the processes of such an operating system is capable of executing a sequential program (written in either Concurrent Pascal or Sequential Pascal). The task of the concurrent program — the operating system — mainly consists of providing, to the sequential programs, appropriate 'abstract' operations on the resources of the system. The backward error recovery capability has been provided to the sequential programs of processes in the form of recovery blocks. Sequential Pascal was first extended with recovery blocks [7] and later the similar exercise was performed for Concurrent Pascal. The notation for the recovery block as incorporated in these two languages is shown in Fig. 1.

```
ENSURE ⟨acceptance ⟩ BY
    ⟨statement⟩ 'primary'
ELSE–BY
    ⟨statement⟩ '1st alternative'
    – – –
ELSE–ERROR;
    – – –
```

Fig. 1. Recovery block notation for Concurrent and Sequential Pascal

```
TYPE ⟨port name⟩ = PORT (...formal access right parameters...)
    – – – port variable declarations – – –
    PROCEDURE ENTRY ⟨procedure name⟩ (...formal parameters...);
        BEGIN – – – use of the acquired resource – – – END;
    – – – other procedures – – –
    REVERSE PROCEDURE;
        BEGIN – – – undo use of the resource – – – – END;
BEGIN
    ⟨statement⟩ 'prelude, concerned with resource acquisition'
    INNER;
    ⟨statement⟩ 'postlude, concerned with the resource release'
END;
```

Fig. 2. A port data type

The language Concurrent Pascal was further extended with data type port, making it possible for a concurrent program (operating system) to provide arbitrarily complex recoverable operations to sequential programs (e.g. recoverable updates on random access files). The notation for port data type as embodied in Concurrent Pascal is given informally in Fig. 2.

A port is a system type (in the Concurrent Pascal report [3], data types PROCESS, CLASS and MONITOR are referred to as 'system type') and its properties closely match those of a class. A port differs from a class in the following ways:

1. In a port, recovery blocks can only be used within its procedure bodies.
2. A port contains a nameless and parameterless routine of a kind 'reverse procedure' whose body specifies undoing of actions. A reverse procedure cannot be accessed by any program component. Only the recovery system can access it (see the following subsection entitled Recovery semantics of ports).
3. The initial statement of a port contains an inner statement that splits the initial statement into a 'prelude' and a 'postlude'.
4. A port cannot be initialized by an init statement. Let PN be a variable of type port. Then PN can be initialized and its entry routines made use of as follows:

    USING PN (– – actual access rights parameters – –) DO S; where S is a statement that can contain calls on entry routines of PN. The above USING statement defines the access rights of the port (just like the init statement). The inner statement of PN is textually replaced by S and the body of PN is executed (this has now the effect of executing the sequence 'prelude; S; postlude').

325

```
TYPE SENDER = PORT (CON: CONSOLE; I: INTEGER; RES: RESOURCE)
  PROCEDURE ENTRY OUTPUT (L: LINE);
    BEGIN CON. SEND (L, I) END;
  REVERSE PROCEDURE;
    BEGIN CON. SEND ('IGNORE MESSAGE NUMBER', I) END;
  BEGIN
    RES.ACQUIRE; 'acquire the terminal'
    INNER;
    RES.RELEASE 'release the terminal'
  END;
                   _ _ _ _ _
MESSAGE: SENDER;
                   _ _ _ _ _
ENSURE 'acceptance test' BY
                   _ _ _ _ _
USING MESSAGE (TERMINAL, J, UNIT) DO
  BEGIN
                   _ _ _ _ _
                   MESSAGE.OUTPUT(L);
                   _ _ _ _ _
  END;
                   _ _ _ _ _
ELSE–BY            _ _ _ _ _
```

Fig. 3. A port example

It can be appreciated that a port can specify facilities for acquiring a resource, using it, undoing the effects of the use and releasing the resource. A
simple example should further clarify these ideas.

Example: Assume that it is required to construct a recoverable message
sending facility between a process and an operator. The process can send a
numbered message to the operator; should it be necessary to restore the state of
the process such that 'unsending' of the message is required, a compensating
message 'ignore the message' can be sent. A port with these facilities is shown
in Fig. 3, where two data types, a class CONSOLE (for sending a message) and
a monitor RESOURCE (for acquiring the operator's terminal), have been assumed to be provided.

Recovery Semantics of Ports

As mentioned earlier, state restoration is carried out automatically by a recovery system. The actions of the recovery system are: (1) to carry out recovery actions arising from the use of ports, if any, and then (2) to restore the state of
global variables updated in the recovery block in which the error was detected.
In this section, the recovery actions arising from the use of ports will be explained with reference to Fig. 4. Let an erroneous situation be detected at one
of the following points while executing the program of Fig. 4.

326

```
- - -
PN: PRT; 'Port instance'
- - -
ENSURE - - BY
BEGIN
   - - -
   USING PN(- - -) DO  'U1'
   BEGIN
      - - - 'a'
   PN.PROC1 (- -);
      - - - 'b'
   PN.PROC2 (- -);
      - - - 'c'
   END;
      - - - 'd'
   USING PN (- - -) DO  'U2'
   BEGIN
         - - -
      PN.PROC1(- - -);
   END;
         - - - 'e'
END ELSE-BY
      - - - - -
```

Fig. 4. A program to illustrate recovery semantics of ports

Error Detected at Point 'a'
An error has been detected after the execution of the prelude of PN, that is, after the acquisition of some resource. Since the state is to be restored to the point where this resource was not acquired, it must be released; this is done by executing the postlude (note that it becomes the programmer's responsibility to ensure that preludes and postludes are for resource acquisition and release respectively).

Error Detected at Point 'b'
The reverse procedure of PN is called and then the postlude is executed.

Error Detected at Point 'c'
The actions are the same as at 'b'. Note that, while recovering, a reverse procedure is called as many times as the number of times the corresponding using statements that contains calls on the port procedures have been activated in the recovery block in question.

Error Detected at Point 'd'
Let AB(Ui) represent the state of the variables and parameters of port AB after the execution of the using statement Ui. Then the recovery action is: starting with port PN in the state PN(U1), execute the sequence 'prelude; reverse procedure; postlude'.

327

```
PROGRAM JOB (------);

ENSURE -- BY
BEGIN

        JOB (---); 'execute a sequential program'

END ELSE–BY
```

Fig. 5. Typical Concurrent Pascal program

Clearly, it is necessary to execute the reverse procedure. However, the necessary resources have been released (as the postlude has been executed). It is therefore necessary, starting with the port in the appropriate state, to re-execute the prelude and subsequently the postlude.

Error Detected at Point 'e'
Starting with port PN in state PN(U2), the sequence 'prelude; reverse procedure; postlude' is executed; then starting with PN in the state PN(U1), the same sequence is executed. The same actions would be undertaken if the acceptance test of the recovery block failed.

Some Additional Remarks on Recovery Features

1. If a failure occurs while restoring the state of a process, then, conceptually this is regarded as a collapse of the recovery system since no assurance about continued service can be given.
2. The recovery blocks of a concurrent program and a Sequential Pascal program are not regarded as nested. Consider the following typical program (Fig. 5) in Concurrent Pascal where the concurrent program is making use of the PROGRAM statement to execute a sequential program (written in Sequential Pascal). The Sequential Pascal program can make use of recovery blocks, but they would not be regarded as nested within that of the concurrent program. Thus, Sequential Pascal programs represent independent modules from the point of view of recovery.
3. Two standard functions have been provided in Concurrent Pascal.
   (a) Boolean function ERRORFLAG. The true value indicates that the state of the calling process is being restored by the recovery system and the false value indicates that the process is normally executing its program.
   (b) An integer function RLEVEL. The value returned indicates the current degree of nesting of recovery blocks in the calling process.
   RLEVEL = 0 indicates that the process is not executing within a recovery block.

Examples

Three complete working examples will be used to illustrate how ports may be used to provide recoverable actions. The main aim of these examples is to illustrate the basic principles involved and as such the programs have been made as simple as possible. Thus, not much effort should be needed to understand these programs and the reader can concentrate upon their recovery aspects.

Producer – Consumer: Recovery by Compensation

This example illustrates what is known as recovery by compensation [8]: a process has passed some messages to other processes and later it becomes necessary to restore the state of the sending process to the state where these messages were not sent; the abstraction of 'unsending a message' can be provided by sending a corrective message to the receivers. If the receivers have been programmed to cope with corrective messages, then any recovery actions of the sender can be made independent.

Assume that there is a 'producer' process that is sending integer-valued messages to a 'consumer' process. The function of the consumer is to output the total sum of values received from the producer once the last message has been received from the producer. The objective is to make any recovery actions of the producer independent from those of the consumer. For simplicity it is assumed that only the producer has any recovery capability. Let us assume that the producer has sent two messages, values $+X$ and $+Y$, to the consumer. If an error is detected by the producer such that the state of the producer is to be restored to that before these two messages were sent, then if as a part of the recovery actions of the producer, compensating messages of values $-Y$ and $-X$ can be sent to the consumer, the consumer can still produce the correct result. Thus, the messages sent by the producer will have the property of recoverability. Figure 6 shows the complete Concurrent Pascal program for the above processes, with a port SENDER that provides recoverable message sending facility to the producer. A monitor MANAGER is needed to synchronize the sending and receiving of messages between the producer and the consumer.

The program for the producer process (lines 66 – 84) shows that the producer has access to a monitor of type MANAGER, and that a variable SEND of type SENDER has been declared. The program includes a recovery block with one alternative (lines 72 – 81), with the primary deliberately designed to fail the acceptance test. In the primary, the port variable SEND is used to send three messages (values $+1$, $+2$ and $+3$) to the consumer. So, when the primary fails the acceptance test, the automatic recovery action undertaken (before the alternative can be executed) must include sending of compensating messages (values -3, -2 and -1). The alternative merely sends one message (value $+9$). Lastly, a message of value 0, with LAST = TRUE, indicating that it is the last message, is sent to the consumer.

The program for the consumer (lines 87 – 105) is simple: the consumer has access to a monitor from which it receives messages. When the last message is received, the total sum is printed on the console (for simplicity, it is assumed that the sum does not exceed the value 9). Finally, appropriate instances of the data types are created (lines 109 – 110) and processes initialized with access to the same monitor (line 112). Figure 7 shows the console output produced by

```
1  TYPE IODEVICE=(TYPEDEVICE,DISKDEVICE,TAPEDEVICE,PRINTDEVICE,
2                                                  CARDDEVICE);
3  TYPE IOOPERATION=(INPUT,OUTPUT,MOVE,CONTROL);
4  TYPE IOARG=(WRITEEOF,REWIND,UPSPACE,BACKSPACE);
5  TYPE IORESULT=(COMPLETE,INTERVENTION,TRANSMISSION,FAILURE,
6                   ENDFILE,ENDMEDIUM,STARTMEDIUM);
7  TYPE IOPARAM=RECORD
8                   OPERATION:IOOPERATION;
9                   STATUS:IORESULT;
10                  ARG:IOARG
11              END;
12 TYPE OUT=CLASS;
13 PROCEDURE ENTRY PRINT(C:CHAR);
14 VAR
15    PR:IOPARAM; DV:IODEVICE;
16    CH:CHAR;
17    BEGIN
18      PR.OPERATION:=OUTPUT; DV:=TYPEDEVICE;
19      CH:=C; IO(CH,PR,DV)
20    END;
21 BEGIN   END;
22
23 TYPE MANAGER=MONITOR;
24 VAR
25    BUFFER:INTEGER;
26    FULL,B:BOOLEAN;
27    SENDER,RECEIVER:QUEUE;
28 PROCEDURE ENTRY SEND(I:INTEGER;LAST:BOOLEAN);
29    BEGIN
30      IF FULL THEN DELAY(SENDER);
31      BUFFER:=I; B:=LAST; FULL:=TRUE;
32      CONTINUE(RECEIVER)
33    END;
34 PROCEDURE ENTRY RECEIVE(VAR I:INTEGER; VAR LAST:BOOLEAN);
35    BEGIN
36      IF NOT FULL THEN DELAY(RECEIVER);
37      I:=BUFFER; LAST:=B; FULL:=FALSE;
38      CONTINUE(SENDER)
39    END;
40 BEGIN  FULL:=FALSE   END;
41
42 TYPE SENDER=PORT(MAN:MANAGER;I:INTEGER;LAST:BOOLEAN)
43 VAR
44    VALUE:INTEGER; COMPENSATE:BOOLEAN;
45 REVERSE PROCEDURE;
46    BEGIN END;
47 BEGIN
48    IF ERRORFLAG THEN
49      BEGIN
50         COMPENSATE:=TRUE;
51         MAN.SEND(VALUE,LAST)
52      END ELSE
53    BEGIN
54      VALUE:=-I; COMPENSATE:=FALSE;
55      MAN.SEND(I,LAST)
56    END;
```

Fig. 6. Recovery by compensation

```
57          INNER;
58     IF ERRORFLAG AND NOT COMPENSATE THEN
59          MAN.SEND(VALUE,LAST)
60 END;
61
62
63
64
65
66 TYPE PRODUCER=PROCESS(M:MANAGER)
67 "RECOVERY DATA SPACE=" +1000
68 VAR
69     SEND:SENDER; I:INTEGER; LAST:BOOLEAN;
70 BEGIN
71     LAST:=FALSE;
72     ENSURE (I=9) BY
73     BEGIN
74     FOR I:=1 TO 3 DO
75     USING SEND(M,I,LAST) DO ;
76     END ELSE BY
77     BEGIN
78       I:=9;
79       USING SEND(M,I,LAST) DO ;
80     END
81     ELSE ERROR;
82     LAST:=TRUE;
83     USING SEND(M,0,LAST) DO ;
84 END;
85
86
87 TYPE CONSUMER=PROCESS(M:MANAGER)
88 VAR
89     CONSOLE:OUT; I:INTEGER;SUM:INTEGER;
90     CH:CHAR;
91     LAST:BOOLEAN;
92 BEGIN
93     LAST:=FALSE; SUM:=0; INIT CONSOLE;
94       WHILE NOT LAST DO
95     BEGIN
96       M.RECEIVE(I,LAST);
97       IF NOT LAST THEN SUM:=SUM+I
98       ELSE
99       BEGIN
100          IF SUM > 9 THEN SUM:=0;
101          CH:=CHR(SUM+48);
102          CONSOLE.PRINT(CH)
103        END
104     END
105 END;
106
107
108 VAR
109     M:MANAGER;
110     PR:PRODUCER; CR:CONSUMER;
111 BEGIN
112     INIT M,PR(M),CR(M)
113 END.
114
```

Fig. 6 (continued)

331

```
SYSTEM READY

PROCESS 2 SYSTEM LINE 73 A. T. FAIL
9
```
Fig. 7. Output of the example of Figure 6

this program. As expected, the producer process (process 2) fails the acceptance test once, and an appropriate message is printed on the console (the run time system has been designed to print an indication of all run time detected errors [10]). The last line of Fig. 7 shows that despite the recovery action by the producer, the consumer produces the correct result (value 9) thus indicating that the port data type SENDER does provide the desired abstraction of recoverability.

Next, let us consider how the above-mentioned recoverability has been provided by the port SENDER (lines 42−60). As it happens, in this example, all the necessary port actions can be provided in the prelude (lines 47−56) and the postlude (lines 58−59), as such, this port has no entry procedures and the body of the reverse procedure is null. So, assuming the 'SEND' is a variable of type SENDER, it is necessary to execute the following statement to send a message (see line 79):

$$\text{USING (M, I, LAST) DO} \quad ;$$
$$\qquad\qquad\qquad\uparrow\quad\uparrow$$
$$\qquad\qquad\qquad(1)\quad(2)$$

Consider now the following three mutually exclusive situations:

(a) *No error is detected.* This represents the normal case. As the executing process is 'going forward', ERRORFLAG = FALSE will hold and the prelude statements on lines 53−56 will be executed (the message will be sent) followed by the execution of the postlude which has in this situation no effect.

(b) *Error detected at point* (1). This means that the error has been detected after the execution of the prelude by the forward going process (i.e. after the execution of statements on lines 53−56). The recovery action then consists of executing the sequence 'reverse procedure; postlude'. Since an error has been detected, ERRORFLAG = TRUE will hold and the net effect of the execution of the postlude will be to send the appropriate message for compensation. Note how the variable VALUE is being used to record the recovery information.

(c) *Error detected at point* (2). This means that the error has been detected after the execution of the USING statement (e.g. an acceptance test has failed). The recovery action consists of (see the discussion on Error detected at point 'd' in the section Recovery semantics of ports): with the port variables (VALUE and COMPENSATE) in their states just after the execution of this USING statement, execute the sequence 'prelude; reverse procedure; postlude'. As ERRORFLAG = TRUE will hold, statements on lines 49−52 of the prelude will be executed and the appropriate compensating message will be sent.

The Dining and Vomiting Philosophers

The second example illustrates how a port may be used for providing recoverable resource allocation and use between a set of competing processes. The well-known five dining philosopher's problem (due to Dijkstra [9]) has been modified to include recovery capability. (In what follows, it will be assumed that the reader is familiar with this problem and its solution.) In order to appreciate what recovery actions would be needed, consider the life cycle of a philosopher (Fig. 8). Assume that eating consists of printing a message to that effect on the console. Let 'x' represent the recovery point — the state to which a philosopher is to be restored in case an error is detected. If an error is detected at point (1) then recovery action consists of releasing the forks. If an error is detected at point (2) then the philosopher must 'uneat' (vomit!) which consists of printing a message to that effect on the console, and then release the forks. If an error is detected at point (3), then the philosopher has only to vomit — no forks are needed for this purpose — only the console is needed for message printing. We thus see that resources needed for 'doing' need not be the same as those needed for 'undoing'. Our task is to design a port with the appropriate prelude and postlude (for fork acquisition and release), an entry procedure (for eating) and a reverse procedure (for vomiting).

The complete Concurrent Pascal program listing is given in Fig. 9. The data types of interest are: FORKS (a monitor for acquiring and releasing forks), RE-SOURCE (a monitor for the exclusive access to the console), INOUT (a class for inputting or outputting a line of text on the console), MANAGER (a port for providing recoverable resource allocation and use as discussed previously) and PHIL (a process). Five processes of type PHIL (PH0 to PH4) are created and initialized with appropriate access rights. A number of recovery blocks have been included in the code of PHIL with some deliberate faults to illustrate recovery actions. These are (a) a fault that will cause a range error detection (line 145) in the primary of the recovery block in procedure EATS (line 137); (b) an acceptance test failure after the execution of the primary of the recovery block starting on line 155.

A sample output produced by this program is shown in Fig. 10. In order to understand this output, the following two points should be borne in mind: (1) All the run-time error messages produced by the system include the number of the executing process; in this example philosopher 0 is process 2, philosopher 1

```
cycle
   think;
       x ←    recovery point
   acquire forks;
            ← (1)
   eat;
            ← (2)
   release forks;
            ← (3)
end
```

Fig. 8. Life of a philosopher

333

```
1 CONST NL='(:10:)'; LENGTH=72;
2
3 TYPE FORKS=MONITOR
4     VAR AV: ARRAY (,0,,4,) OF INTEGER;
5         WT; ARRAY(,0,,4,) OF QUEUE;  J: INTEGER;
6  PROCEDURE ENTRY GET(I; INTEGER);
7     BEGIN
8           IF AV(,I,) <> 2 THEN
9               DELAY(WT(,I,));
10              AV(, (I+4) MOD 5,):=AV(,(I+4) MOD 5,)=1;
11    AV(,(I+1) MOD 5 ,):= AV(,(I+1) MOD 5,)=1;
12            IF AV(,(I+3) MOD 5,)=2 THEN
13                              CONTINUE(WT(,(I+3) MOD 5,));
14        END;
15  PROCEDURE ENTRY GIVE(I; INTEGER);
16      BEGIN
17            AV(, (I+1) MOD 5 ,):= AV(, (I+1) MOD 5 ,) +1;
18            AV(,(I+4) MOD 5,):= AV(,(I+4) MOD 5,)+1;
19            IF AV(, (I+1) MOD 5 ,) = 2 THEN
20                              CONTINUE(WT(, (I+1) MOD 5 ,));
21      END;
22  BEGIN FOR J:=0 TO 4 DO AV(,J,):=2 END;
23
24 TYPE FIFO=CLASS(LIMIT:INTEGER)
25    VAR HEAD,TAIL,LENGTH; INTEGER;
26 FUNCTION ENTRY ARRIVAL;INTEGER;
27    BEGIN
28          ARRIVAL:=TAIL;
29            TAIL:= TAIL MOD LIMIT +1;
30            LENGTH:=LENGTH+1;
31    END;
32 FUNCTION ENTRY DEPARTURE: INTEGER;
33    BEGIN
34              DEPARTURE:=HEAD;
35            HEAD:= HEAD MOD LIMIT +1;
36            LENGTH:=LENGTH=1;
37    END;
38 FUNCTION ENTRY EMPTY:BOOLEAN;
39      BEGIN EMPTY:=(LENGTH=0) END;
40 BEGIN HEAD:=1;TAIL:=1;LENGTH:=0 END;
41
42 TYPE RESOURCE=MONITOR
43    CONST NUMB=5;
44    VAR FREE:BOOLEAN;
45    Q: ARRAY (,1,,5,) OF QUEUE; NEXT: FIFO;
46 PROCEDURE ENTRY REQUEST;
47    BEGIN
48       IF   FREE THEN FREE:=FALSE ELSE
49       DELAY(Q(,NEXT,ARRIVAL,));
50    END;
51    PROCEDURE ENTRY RELEASE;
52      BEGIN
53         IF NEXT,EMPTY THEN FREE:=TRUE ELSE
54              CONTINUE(Q(,NEXT,DEPARTURE,));
55      END;
```

Fig. 9. Dining and vomiting philosophers

```
56      BEGIN FREE:=TRUE;INIT NEXT(NUMB) END;
57
58 TYPE LINE= ARRAY (.1,.LENGTH .) OF CHAR;
59 TYPE IOOPERATION=(INPUT,OUTPUT,MOVE,CONTROL);
60
61
62
63
64
65 TYPE IODEVICE= (TYPEDEVICE,DISKDEVICE,TAPEDEVICE
66                         ,PRINTDEVICE,CARDDEVICE);
67 TYPE IOARG= (WRITEEOF,REWIND,UPSPACE,BACKSPACE);
68 TYPE IORESULT= (COMPLETE,INTERVENTION,TRANSMISSION,
69                      FAILURE,ENDFILE,ENDMEDIUM,STARTMEDIUM);
70 TYPE IOPARAM= RECORD
71                  OPERATION:IOOPERATION;
72                  STATUS:IORESULT;ARG:IOARG
73                  END;
74
75 TYPE INOUT = CLASS(ACCESS:RESOURCE)
76  PROCEDURE ENTRY WRITE(TEXT:LINE);
77   VAR PR: IOPARAM; I: INTEGER; C: CHAR;DV: IODEVICE;
78           BEGIN  ACCESS.REQUEST;
79           PR.OPERATION:= OUTPUT;
80           DV:= TYPEDEVICE;   I:= 0;
81           REPEAT
82               I:=I+1;C:=TEXT(.I,);IO(C,PR,DV);
83           UNTIL (C=NL) OR (I=LENGTH);
84             ACCESS.RELEASE;
85           END;
86  PROCEDURE ENTRY READ(VAR TEXT: LINE);
87    VAR PR: IOPARAM; I: INTEGER; C: CHAR; DV: IODEVICE;
88           BEGIN  ACCESS.REQUEST;
89           PR.OPERATION:= INPUT;
90             DV:= TYPEDEVICE;  I:= 0;
91           REPEAT
92                   I:=I+1;IO(C,PR,DV);TEXT(.I,):=C;
93             UNTIL (C=NL) OR (I=LENGTH);
94                   ACCESS.RELEASE;
95             END;
96 BEGIN    END;
97
98 TYPE MANAGER=PORT(CONS:INOUT;FRKS:FORKS;I:INTEGER)
99    VAR ACQ:BOOLEAN;
100     PROCEDURE ENTRY EAT;
101     BEGIN
102       CASE I OF
103       0:CONS.WRITE(' PHIL0 EATING(:10:)');
104       1:CONS.WRITE(' PHIL1 EATING(:10:)');
105       2:CONS.WRITE(' PHIL2 EATING(:10:)');
106       3:CONS.WRITE(' PHIL3 EATING(:10:)');
107       4:CONS.WRITE(' PHIL4 EATING(:10:)')
108       END
109     END;
110     REVERSE PROCEDURE;
```

Fig. 9 (continued)

335

```
111     BEGIN   CASE I OF
112       0:CONS.WRITE(' PHIL0 VOMITING(:10:)');
113       1:CONS.WRITE(' PHIL1 VOMITING(:10:)');
114       2:CONS.WRITE(' PHIL2 VOMITING(:10:)');
115       3:CONS.WRITE(' PHIL3 VOMITING(:10:)');
116       4:CONS.WRITE(' PHIL4 VOMITING(:10:)')
117       END
118     END;
119      BEGIN
120        IF ERRORFLAG=FALSE THEN
121        BEGIN ACQ:=TRUE;FRKS.GET(I) END
122        ELSE ACQ:=FALSE;
123        INNER;
124        IF ACQ THEN FRKS.GIVE(I)
125     END;
126
127
128
129
130
131
132 TYPE PHIL =PROCESS(FRKS;FORKS;I;INTEGER;ACCESS:RESOURCE);
133 "RECOVERY DATA SPACE=" +1000
134 VAR   CONS:INOUT;
135       TEXT:LINE;XX:ARRAY(.1..2.) OF INTEGER;
136       MANG:MANAGER;
137       PROCEDURE EATS;
138       BEGIN
139         USING MANG(CONS,FRKS,I) DO
140         BEGIN
141           ENSURE TRUE BY
142           BEGIN
143           MANG.EAT;
144             CONS.READ(TEXT);
145             IF TEXT(.1.) <> 'F' THEN XX(.3.):=0;
146           END ELSE.BY
147           MANG.EAT
148           ELSE.ERROR
149         END
150     END;
151 BEGIN
152     INIT CONS(ACCESS); WHILE TRUE DO
153 BEGIN
154     XX(.1.):=10;
155     ENSURE (XX(.1.)=10 ) BY
156       BEGIN
157         XX(.1.):=123;
158         ENSURE (XX(.2.)=15 ) BY
159           BEGIN
160             XX(.2.):=15;EATS
161           END ELSE.ERROR
162       END ELSE.BY
163         XX(.2.):=10
164     ELSE.ERROR
165     END
166 END;
```

Fig. 9 (continued)

336

```
167 VAR
168 SETOFFORKS: FORKS;
169 PH0,PH1,PH2,PH3,PH4: PHIL;
170 A,B,C,D,E: INTEGER;
171   UNIT:RESOURCE;
172   BEGIN
173     INIT UNIT,SETOFFORKS;
174     A:=0; INIT PH0(SETOFFORKS,A,UNIT);
175     B:=1; INIT PH1(SETOFFORKS,B,UNIT);
176     C:=2; INIT PH2(SETOFFORKS,C,UNIT);
177     D:=3; INIT PH3(SETOFFORKS,D,UNIT);
178     E:=4; INIT PH4(SETOFFORKS,E,UNIT);
179 END.
180
```

Fig. 9 (continued)

```
SYSTEM READY
 PHIL0 EATING
 PHIL2 EATING
FFF


PROCESS 2 SYSTEM LINE 156 A.T. FAIL
YYY


PROCESS 4 SYSTEM LINE 145 RANGE ERROR
 PHIL0 VOMITING
 PHIL2 VOMITING
 PHIL0 EATING
 PHIL2 EATING


PROCESS 4 SYSTEM LINE 156 A.T. FAIL
FFF


PROCESS 2 SYSTEM LINE 156 A.T. FAIL
PHIL2 VOMITING
 PHIL3 EATING
 PHIL1 EATING
 PHIL0 VOMITING
FFF


PROCESS 3 SYSTEM LINE 156 A.T. FAIL
YYY


PROCESS 3 SYSTEM LINE 145 RANGE ERROR
PHIL4 EATING
 PHIL3 VOMITING
 PHIL1 VOMITING
```

Fig. 10. An output of the example of Figure 9

337

is process 3 and so on; (2) in procedure EATS, after calling the port procedure MANG.EAT, the executing process acquires the console to read a line of text from the user at the console (line 144). If the user's input does not begin with 'F' then a range error will be detected (line 145).

The output shows that initially philosophers 0 and 2 (i.e. processes 2 and 4 respectively) are eating (both have called procedure MANG.EAT, line 143). Process 2 now has the console and is waiting for user input, process 4 obviously is waiting for the console to be free. When the user types 'FFF', the execution of EATS finishes successfully, and the recovery block starting on line 158 is exited successfully. However, the acceptance test of the enclosing recovery block (line 155) fails and a message − − − LINE 156 A.T. FAIL is printed (indicating that the execution of the block beginning at line 156 has failed the acceptance test). Before the alternative beginning at line 163 can be tried, the recovery action must include vomiting − for this the process must acquire the console. The console, however, is in the possession of process 4 (philosopher 2) which is waiting for a user input. Figure 10 shows that the user typed 'YYY' which caused a range error message to be printed. The console now becomes free and is acquired by process 2 to print 'PHIL 0 VOMITING'. The reader should be able to trace the subsequent events that caused the output of Fig. 10.

This simple example also illustrates that just as a process can compete with other processes for making use of shared resources during its 'forward motion', it can also compete for the resources during its 'backward motion'.

Recoverable File Updates

The last example illustrates one way whereby ports can be used quite elegantly to provide recoverable operations to Sequential Pascal programs. In most multi-user operating systems, a job control language is used, among other things, for specifying resource requirements for a job; these resources are first acquired before executing the job. A simplified version of such a scheme can be implemented using ports as follows:

Let A, B and C represent the ports that provide the operations on resources that a user program requires. In this situation the following program suggests itself.

```
                 − − − −
PROGRAM JOB (−−−);
                 − − − −
USING A (−−−) DO
USING B (−−−) DO
USING C (−−−) DO
BEGIN
                 − − −
         JOB (− −); 'execute a sequential program'
                 − − −
END;
                 − − −
```

338

The necessary resources are automatically acquired and released around the execution of a sequential program.

Let us assume that the facility of recoverable file updates is to be provided to Sequential Pascal programs, so that such programs may update files from within a recovery block. Minor changes were made to the SOLO operating system [3] for this purpose. The following simplifying assumptions were made: (i) make use of the existing SOLO filing system, (ii) only one file may be opened for recoverable updates, (iii) Sequential Pascal programs do not make use of nested recovery blocks and (iv) recovery is to be provided at a page level, that is, sequential programs are given the facility of modifying file pages.

The changed part of the SOLO concurrent program is shown in Fig. 11 (an understanding of the SOLO operating system is required to appreciate this example). A port FILEMANAGER has been programmed that makes use of the DATAFILE data type for file manipulations (read, write, open and close). In the prelude of the port, a file called RECOVERY is first opened (this file will record the previous contents of updated pages) followed by the opening of the file whose name is supplied by the user; in the postlude, these files are closed. The WRITE procedure of the port records the previous contents of the page to be updated in file RECOVERY before performing the update. The reverse procedure makes use of RECOVERY file for restoring the page contents.

Figure 12 shows a simple test program with a recovery block that updates a file in its primary algorithm and prints a modified page on the console. After the termination of this program, the file should be in its original state; this was verified by printing the file on the line printer.

It is hoped that these illustrative examples will have convinced the reader that ports provide a systematic method for designing recoverable operations and that the extended version of Concurrent and Sequential Pascal can be used for programming fault-tolerant systems. Ports in conjunction with recovery blocks represent only one method of introducing backward error recovery in a system. The reader wishing to pursue the subject of backward error recovery further may find the ideas presented in Ref. [11] of interest, where many of the fundamental aspects of recoverability are discussed.

Lastly, a few words on the performance of this system are in order here. In the Concurrent Pascal system (designed by Brinch Hansen and his colleagues [3]) both the concurrent and sequential programs are interpreted by a simple stack machine programmed to run on a PDP 11/45. The automatic recovery system was implemented as part of this interpreter which doubled its size from 1K to 2K words. A recent performance study [12] has shown us that when no ports are used (i.e. only the assignments are recoverable), the time needed to collect and maintain recovery data is upto about 11 per cent of the execution time of the program with no recovery facilities. If a program uses a few ports, we do not expect the overheads to be significantly larger than 11 per cent. The design of this experimental recovery system, which is described in a companion paper [10], demonstrates that it is not too difficult to support automatic recovery features by a programmed interpreter, and the details of the interpreter given in that paper can be used for designing appropriate hardware for real (as against experimental) fault-tolerant systems.

```
857 "##################
858    FILENAME
859 ##################"
860
861 TYPE FILENAME = CLASS
862 VAR ID : IDENTIFIER;
863 PROCEDURE ENTRY SPECIFY(ID1:IDENTIFIER);
864 BEGIN ID:=ID1 END;
865 PROCEDURE ENTRY GETNAME(VAR ID1:IDENTIFIER);
866 BEGIN ID1 := ID END;
867 BEGIN END;
868
869 "########################
870 FILEMANAGER PORT
871 ########################"
872
873 TYPE FILEMANAGER =
874 PORT(DATAF1:DATAFILE;DATAF2:DATAFILE;FN:FILENAM
875 VAR
876    PA:ARRAY(.1..MAPLENGTH.) OF INTEGER;
877    RLENGTH:INTEGER;
878    ID : IDENTIFIER;
879    FOUND : BOOLEAN;
880 PROCEDURE ENTRY WRITE(P:INTEGER;VAR BLOCK:PAGE);
881 VAR
882    TPAGE:PAGE;
883 BEGIN
884    RLENGTH:=RLENGTH+1;
885    PA(.RLENGTH.):=P;
886    DATAF2.READ(P,TPAGE);
887    DATAF1.WRITE(RLENGTH,TPAGE);
888    DATAF2.WRITE(P,BLOCK)
889 END;
890 PROCEDURE ENTRY READ(P:INTEGER;VAR BLOCK:PAGE);
891 BEGIN
892    DATAF2.READ(P,BLOCK)
893 END;
894 REVERSE PROCEDURE;
895 VAR TPAGE:PAGE;I:INTEGER;
896 BEGIN
897    IF RLENGTH > 0 THEN
898    FOR I:=1 TO RLENGTH DO
899    BEGIN
900       DATAF1.READ(I,TPAGE);
901       DATAF2.WRITE(PA(.I.),TPAGE)
902    END
903  END;
904 BEGIN
905    RLENGTH:=0;
906    DATAF1.OPEN('RECOVERY    ',FOUND);
907    IF FOUND THEN
908    BEGIN
909       FN.GETNAME(ID);
910       DATAF2.OPEN(ID,FOUND);
911       IF FOUND THEN
```

Fig. 11. Recoverable file updates

```
912        BEGIN
913            INNER;
914         DATAF2.CLOSE;
915         END;
916     DATAF1.CLOSE
917     END
918 END;
919
920
921
922
923 "###############
924 #  JOBPROCESS   #
925 ###############"
926
927
928 TYPE JOBPROCESS =
929 PROCESS
930   (TYPEUSE; TYPERESOURCE; DISKUSE; RESOURCE;
931    CATALOG; DISKCATALOG; INBUFFER, OUTBUFFER; PAGEBUFFER;
932    INREQUEST, INRESPONSE, OUTREQUEST, OUTRESPONSE; ARGBUFFER;
933    STACK; PROGSTACK);
934 "PROGRAM DATA SPACE ="+14000
935
936 CONST MAXFILE = 2;
937 TYPE FILE = 1..MAXFILE;
938 VAR
939
940 FILES : ARRAY(.FILE.) OF DATAFILE;
941 FN : FILENAME;
942 FILEMAN;FILEMANAGER;
943 OPERATOR; TERMINAL; OPSTREAM; TERMINALSTREAM;
944
945 INSTREAM, OUTSTREAM; CHARSTREAM;
946
947
948 CODE; PROGFILE1;
949
950 PROGRAM JOB(VAR PARAM; ARGLIST; STORE; PROGSTORE1);
951 ENTRY READ, WRITE, OPEN, CLOSE, GET, PUT, LENGTH,
952    MARK, RELEASE, IDENTIFY, ACCEPT, DISPLAY, READPAGE,
953    WRITEPAGE, READLINE, WRITELINE, READARG, WRITEARG,
954    LOOKUP, IOTRANSFER, IOMOVE, TASK, RUN;
955
956 PROCEDURE CALL(ID; IDENTIFIER; VAR PARAM; ARGLIST;
957    VAR LINE; INTEGER; VAR RESULT; RESULTTYPE);
958 VAR STATE; PROGSTATE; LASTID; IDENTIFIER;
959 BEGIN
960   WITH CODE, STACK DO
961   BEGIN
962     LINE:= 0;
963     OPEN(ID, STATE);
964     IF (STATE = READY) & SPACE THEN
965     BEGIN
966       PUSH(ID);
967       IF ID <> 'DO            ' THEN
968
            Fig. 11 (continued)
```

341

```
969        BEGIN
970          FN.SPECIFY(PARAM(.2.),ARG);
971          USING FILEMAN(FILES(.1.),FILES(.2.),FN) DO
972          JOB(PARAM,STORE)
973        END ELSE JOB(PARAM,STORE);
974        POP(LINE, RESULT);
975      END ELSE
976      IF STATE = TOOBIG THEN RESULT:= CODELIMIT
977                        ELSE RESULT:= CALLERROR;
978      IF ANY THEN
979      BEGIN GET(LASTID); OPEN(LASTID, STATE) END;
980    END;
981 END;
982
983
984 PROCEDURE ENTRY READ(VAR C: CHAR);
985 BEGIN INSTREAM.READ(C) END;
```

Fig. 11 (continued)

```
131 "PREFIX PROCEDURES NOT SHOWN"
132 "##########################"
133
134 PROGRAM FILEUPDATE(VAR PARAM;ARGLIST);
135 VAR
136    I,J:INTEGER; BLOCK:PAGE;
137 BEGIN
138    ENSURE (J=3) BY
139    BEGIN
140      J:=1; GET(J,BLOCK);
141        FOR I:=200 TO PAGELENGTH DO
142        BLOCK(.I.):='X';
143      PUT(J,BLOCK);
144      J:=2; GET(J,BLOCK);
145      FOR I:=300 TO PAGELENGTH DO
146        BLOCK(.I.):='Y';
147      PUT(J,BLOCK);
148      FOR I:=1 TO PAGELENGTH DO
149      DISPLAY(BLOCK(.I.))
150    END ELSE_BY
151      J:= 9 DIV 3
152    ELSE_ERROR
153 END.
```

Fig. 12. A Sequential Pascal test program for the example of Figure 11

Acknowledgements. This work was supported by the Science Research Council (UK) and was carried out as a part of the Highly Reliable Computing Systems project at Newcastle University.

342

Appendix

Implementation Restrictions

The following restrictions (in addition to those given elsewhere [3]) in the implemented version of Concurrent and Sequential Pascal with recovery [7, 10] should be noted:

1. Real and pointer variables are not supported.
2. For a given port, its prelude, postlude and procedures represent the smallest unit of recovery such that no recovery is possible should an error be detected while executing any one of them. As a result of this restriction, it is not meaningful to use recovery blocks in the bodies of port procedures.
3. The variables of the initial process of a concurrent program are unrecoverable.
4. The body of the initial process of a concurrent program can not contain recovery blocks.

References

1. P. M. Melliar-Smith and B. Randell, 'Software reliability: the role of programmed exception handling', Proc. of ACM Conference on Language Design for Reliable Software, Sigplan Notices, **12**, No. 3, 95 – 100 (1977). [Also Chap. 3]
2. P. Brinch Hansen, 'The programming language Concurrent Pascal', IEEE Trans. on Software Engineering, **1**, No. 2, 199 – 207 (1975).
3. P. Brinch Hansen, The Architecture of Concurrent Programs', Prentice-Hall Inc., Englewood Cliffs, N.J., 1977.
4. J. J. Horning et al., 'A program structure for error detection and recovery', Lecture Notes in Computer Science, **16**, 177 – 193 (1974). [Also Chap. 2]
5. B. Randell, 'System structure for software fault tolerance', IEEE Trans. on Software Engineering, **1**, No. 2, 220 – 232 (1975).
6. S. K. Shrivastava and J. P. Banatre, 'Reliable resource allocation between unreliable processes', IEEE Trans. on Software Engineering, **4**, No. 3, 230 – 241 (1978). [Also Chap. 4]
7. S. K. Shrivastava, 'Sequential Pascal with recovery blocks'. Software – Practice and Experience, **8**, 177 – 185 (1978). [Also Chap. 2]
8. C. T. Davies, 'Recovery semantics for a DB/DC system', Proc. of ACM National Conference, 136 – 141 (1973).
9. E. W. Dijkstra, 'Hierarchical ordering of sequential processes', Acta Informatica, **1**, No. 2, 115 – 138 (1975).
10. S. K. Shrivastava, 'Concurrent Pascal with backward error recovery: implementation', Software – Practice and Experience, **9**, 1021 – 1033 (1979). [Also Chap. 4]
11. T. Anderson, P. A. Lee and S. K. Shrivastava, 'A model of recoverability in multi-level systems', IEEE Trans. on Software Engineering, **4**, No. 6, 486 – 494 (1978). [Also Chap. 5]
12. S. K. Shrivastava and A. Akinpelu, 'Fault-tolerant sequential programming using recovery blocks', Proc. of 8th Intl. Conference on Fault-tolerant Computing, France, IEEE Cat. No. 78CH1286-4C (1978). [Also Chap. 2]

Concurrent Pascal with Backward Error Recovery: Implementation

S. K. SHRIVASTAVA

Summary. The implementation of backward error recovery features requires the support of a run time subsystem (called the recovery system) that is responsible for performing the task of state restoration. The recovery system implemented to support the recovery features of Concurrent Pascal includes, for each process, a recovery cache for recording appropriate recovery data. This paper describes the details of the recovery system that was implemented as a part of the interpreter of Brinch Hansen's Concurrent Pascal system.

Key Words. Recovery blocks   Recovery cache   Concurrent and Sequential Pascal   Error recovery   Ports

Introduction

As has been discussed in a companion paper [1], the backward error recovery capability, in the form of recovery blocks, has been made available to the sequential programs of concurrent processes that are programmed in Concurrent Pascal. The environment of a sequential program includes the 'abstract' objects that have been made available by the corresponding process. Those objects that are intended to be operated on from within a recovery block must be made recoverable such that if recovery is invoked, their states are automatically restored. This state restoration is carried out by a recovery system that is part of the run time system that supports the processes. If an operation on an abstract object in effect amounts to the updating of store locations within the private address space of a process, then the recoverability of such an operation is easily obtainable: all that is necessary is for the recovery system to record, in some data structure, the addresses of the locations and the prior values in those locations; the recovery is carried out by appropriately restoring these values. This is how the originally proposed recovery cache (the data structure to record the addresses and values) is intended to work in conjunction with recovery blocks [2]. However, if an operation on an abstract object amounts in effect to operations other than update of private store locations then, in general, recovery of such an operation can be difficult to automate. The solution adopted in the extended version of Concurrent Pascal is to program such operations by making use of the abstract data type port; a port contains a reverse procedure for specifying the 'undoing' of operations. The recovery cache can be extended such that it can be made to contain enough information about ports used within a recovery block so that if recovery is invoked, this information can be made use of for automatically executing reverse procedures and related programs. The extensions that were made to recovery cache and their associated processing algorithms to support recovery as required by port objects is the main subject of this paper.

The recovery system which maintains a recovery cache for each process has been implemented as a part of the interpreter of Brinch Hansen's Concurrent Pascal system [3] available on a PDP 11/45. The implementation exercise was carried out in two parts. In the first part, the language Sequential Pascal was extended with recovery blocks and the interpreter was modified so as to make assignments recoverable [4]. In the second part, Concurrent Pascal was extended with recovery blocks and ports and the interpreter was further modified in a manner to be described below. In the description that follows, I shall assume that the reader is familiar with recovery cache details described elsewhere [2] and the way caches were implemented for Sequential Pascal with recovery blocks [4].

Preliminary Details

To set the scene, the Concurrent Pascal system, as developed by Brinch Hansen's group, together with the initial modifications that were made to it for maintaining recovery caches supporting recoverable assignments as required by Sequential Pascal programs with recovery blocks, will be briefly described.

The system consists of a kernel and an interpreter that executes both sequential and concurrent programs. The kernel implements processes, synchronizing primitives, basic input and output and a virtual storage system. The overall run time system is depicted in Fig. 1. The virtual address space of a process is divided into a private segment and a segment that is common to all the processes. This common segment contains the data necessary for resource sharing (monitor variables), virtual code (the code produced by the Concurrent Pascal compiler), the interpreter code, the current process head (containing the state vector of the current process) and the interpreter table (that has, for all the interpreter instructions, appropriate pointers to the interpreter code).

When the kernel selects a process for running, its state vector is copied into the current process head and the control is handed over to the interpreter. The current process head also acts as the interface between the kernel and interpreter. The interpreter implements a simple stack machine; the stack is maintained by the interpreter in the private segment of the selected process (see Fig. 1). The interpreter can also execute the virtual code produced for a Sequential Pascal program – such a code is stored as 'private data' of the process.

It was a relatively straightforward task to modify the interpreter so as to support a recovery cache for each of the processes in the system; Figure 1 shows how recovery caches were placed in the private segments. The interpreter was extended with virtual instructions 'enter recovery block', 'acceptance test pass' and 'acceptance test fail', and the virtual instructions that performed assignments (e.g. copyword) were modified to record in the cache, if necessary,

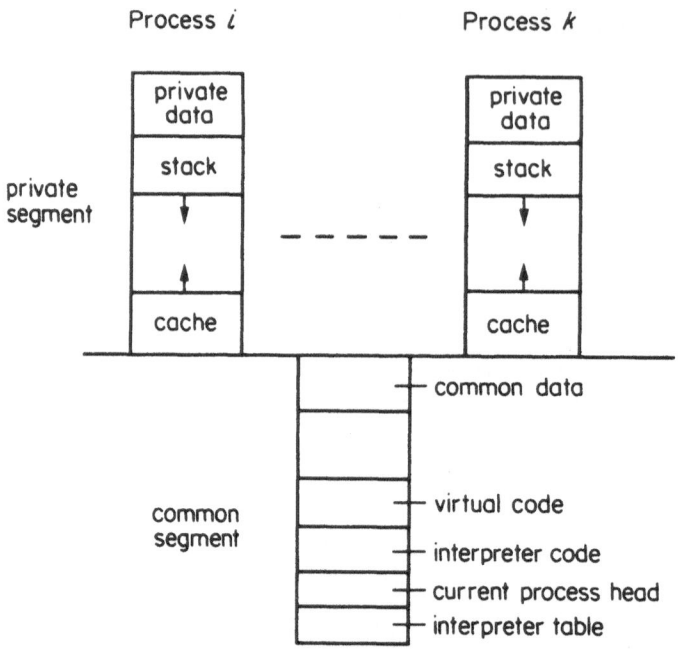

Process i Process k

address space of process i = private + common segment

Fig. 1. The Concurrent Pascal system

prior values. The interpreter incorporates a number of consistency checks for detecting abnormal situations (e.g. range error, stack limit); when such a situation is detected by the interpreter, a jump is made to an 'exception handler' which copes with the situation. The original system had no fault tolerance capability, hence the action of the exception handler was: if the program being interpreted is a Sequential Pascal program then abort the execution of that program; however, if the program is the Concurrent Pascal program then stop the system. The logic of the exception handler was modified to include cache processing for state restoration of a Sequential Pascal program (see Fig. 2, which presents a simplified picture of the exception handler described more fully elsewhere [4]).

The variable 'nest' counts the nesting of recovery blocks for the process (nest, together with a few other recovery block book-keeping variables are maintained by the interpreter as a part of the state vector of each process). If 'nest > 0' is true then recovery capability exists and state restoration is carried out by the procedure 'restore'. The action of 'restore' is simply to appropriately copy back the values recorded in the current region of the recovery cache. When ports were added to Concurrent Pascal, it was necessary to modify the procedure 'restore' to include the execution of reverse procedures and other related programs. It was also necessary to modify the organization of the recovery cache, as described next.

346

```
exception: var recovery: boolean;
            recovery: = false;
        while nest > 0& ~ recovery do
        begin
                with the recovery data of the current recovery block do
                begin
                        restore;
                        if an alternative exits then
                        begin
                        interpreter instruction counter: = start
                        of the code of the alternative;
                        recovery: = true
                        end else
                        begin
                        nest: = nest − 1; prepare recovery cache
                        for the processing of the recovery data of
                        the enclosing recovery block
                        end
                end
        end;
                if ~ recovery then
        begin
                if abnormal termination & program = concurrent then
                        stop;
                restore stack; return
        end;
```

Fig. 2. Exception handling by the interpreter

The Recovery Cache Structure

In order to appreciate what recovery information should be recorded in the recovery cache of a process, assume that the primary of recovery block R2 (see Fig. 3) fails the acceptance test. Then, (i) the reverse procedure of A must be executed, (ii) starting with B in state B(U2), the sequence 'prelude; reverse procedure; postlude' must be executed (B(U2) stands for the state of the variables and parameters of port B after the execution of the using statement U2) and (iii) the state of updated global variables must be restored. Thus the cache must record for each recovery block that has been entered but not yet exited: (a) addresses of any reverse procedures to be executed, (b) sufficient information about ports that have been used so that actions of type (ii) above can be performed, and finally, (c) the usual address-value pairs for restoring updated 'words' (all the variables are mapped by the interpreter onto store words, so restoring a variable is equivalent to restoring the appropriate words).

With the above requirements in mind, the cache structure which was used originally [4] was modified to that depicted in Fig. 4(a). As before, for all the recovery blocks entered but not yet exited, there are 'barriers' in the cache with which the appropriate recovery data can be associated; all of the barriers are linked together and the 'cachbr' entry in the process head points to the topmost barrier (corresponding to the innermost recovery block). The variables 'next'

347

```
ENSURE ... BY 'R1'
BEGIN
     ...—(1)
   USING A (...) DO 'U1'
   BEGIN
            ...—(2)
     ENSURE... BY 'R2'
     BEGIN
            ...—(3)
       USING B(...) DO 'U2'
       BEGIN
            ...—(4)
         B. PROC (...);
            ...
       END;
            ...—(5)
       A. Proc (...);
            ...—(6)
     END ELSE_BY
            ...
     ELSE_ERROR; 'END OF R2'
            ...—(7)
   END;
            ...—(8)
END ELSE_BY
     ...
```

Fig. 3. A skeleton program with recovery blocks and ports

and 'number' indicate the alternative to be executed and the number of alternatives in that recovery block. The variables q, g, b and s are pointers used by the interpreter (next instruction, global variables, local variables and stack top respectively), these values are stored when a recovery block is entered. The variable 'type' records the type of the recovery block (see below). A linked list of 'port recovery data' is maintained and the variable 'ports' points to the first entry. For every 'using' statement executed in the recovery block, there will be a corresponding 'port recovery data' recorded in the cache; the contents of this data will be discussed shortly. Finally the variables 'reve1' to 'reve4' are pointers to any reverse procedures that need executing, as mentioned at the beginning of this section (a fixed number of entries was chosen for efficient lookup during cache processing; for all practical purposes, these four entries should be sufficient). The following two points about this organization should be noted:

1. When a recovery block is entered, 'barrier' to 'reve4' entries are put in the recovery cache with type = 0, ports = 0, and reve1 to 4 = 0 (a '0' for ports and revei is taken to mean a null value).
2. The value-address pairs and port recovery data are recorded incrementally — as assignments are performed and 'using' statements are executed.

The state vector (process head) of each process was extended to contain a few book-keeping variables necessary for the maintenance of recovery blocks. The starred entries in the current process head of Fig. 4 show these variables. As already stated, 'cachbr' points to the topmost barrier. The other variables

348

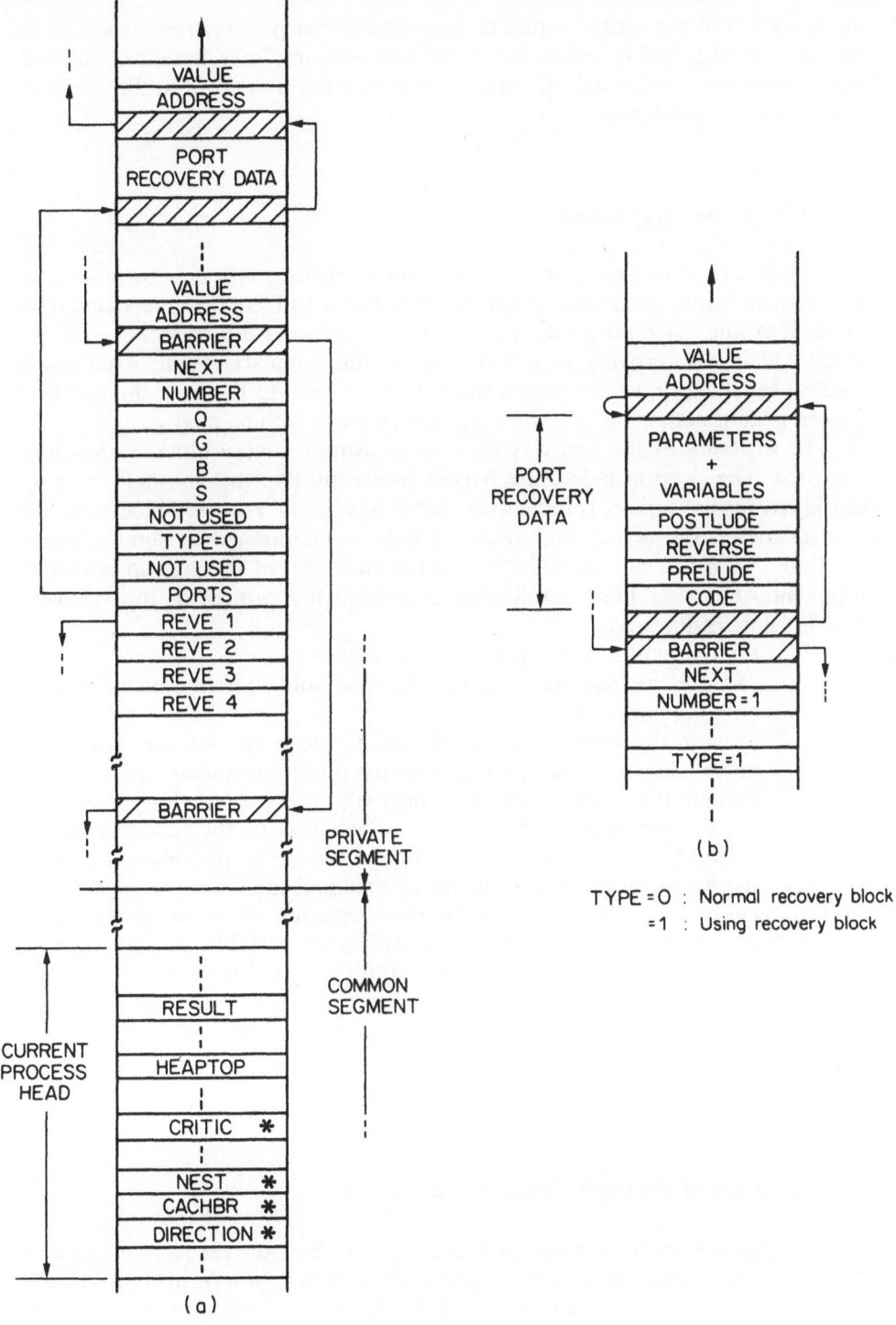

VALUE
ADDRESS
PORT RECOVERY DATA

VALUE
ADDRESS
BARRIER
NEXT
NUMBER
Q
G
B
S
NOT USED
TYPE = 0
NOT USED
PORTS
REVE 1
REVE 2
REVE 3
REVE 4

BARRIER

PRIVATE SEGMENT

COMMON SEGMENT

CURRENT PROCESS HEAD

RESULT
HEAPTOP
CRITIC *
NEST *
CACHBR *
DIRECTION *

(a)

VALUE
ADDRESS
PORT RECOVERY DATA
PARAMETERS + VARIABLES
POSTLUDE
REVERSE
PRELUDE
CODE
BARRIER
NEXT
NUMBER = 1
TYPE = 1

(b)

TYPE = 0 : Normal recovery block
      = 1 : Using recovery block

Fig. 4. Recovery cache organization: **a** recovery data for a normal recovery block; **b** recovery data for a using recovery block

are used as follows: 'critic' equal to zero means that port operations are to be recoverable (this will be explained in the next section); 'nest' indicates the nesting of recovery blocks and 'direction > 0 means the process is in the recovery mode, that is, 'going backwards'.

The 'Using' Recovery Block

The method by which the port recovery data is recorded will now be described. For a given 'using' statement, it was thought better to record any recovery data about it at one place rather than it being scattered over the enclosing recovery block and in the recovery blocks (if any) in the using statement. After many trials, a satisfactory way to record the data was found to be the technique that treated a using statement as a special recovery block with no alternatives.

The structure of the recovery data for a using recovery block is shown in Fig. 4(b). The portion below the barrier is exactly like the 'normal' recovery block except that type = 1, indicating that it is a 'using' recovery block. On top of the barrier, the actual port recovery data is maintained as shown, where 'postlude', 'reverse' and 'prelude' record the addresses of the appropriate code fragments and 'code' has the following meaning when processing this recovery data for state restoration:

code = 0: take no action on the port recovery data
$\quad$ = 1: execute the postulate (as the forward going process had executed only the prelude)
$\quad$ = 2: execute the reverse procedure and postlude (as the forward going process had executed prelude plus the port procedures)
$\quad$ = 3: execute the reverse procedure only (the process failed while executing the postlude − this implies a 'collapse' of the recovery mechanism, [5], as resources cannot be returned − so provide a degraded service by merely executing the reverse procedure).

Two actions are undertaken when the execution of a using statement finishes (e.g. the postlude has been executed): (1) the variables and parameters of the port are copied in the recovery data and (2) it is also taken to mean the exit from the using recovery block and the recovery data of this 'recovery block' are merged with that of the enclosing recovery block. In particular, the port recovery data is chained to enclosing recovery block's chain as indicated in Fig. 4(a).

The Dynamics of Recovery Cache Management

In order that the reader can get on overall view of how the recovery cache of a process is dynamically managed, a number of snapshots of a recovery cache are presented in Fig. 5 for the execution of the program of Fig. 3. Figure 5(1) to Fig. 5(4) show how barriers are placed and recovery data maintained for statements R1, U1, R2 and U2. From the recovery cache's viewpoint, R1 and R2

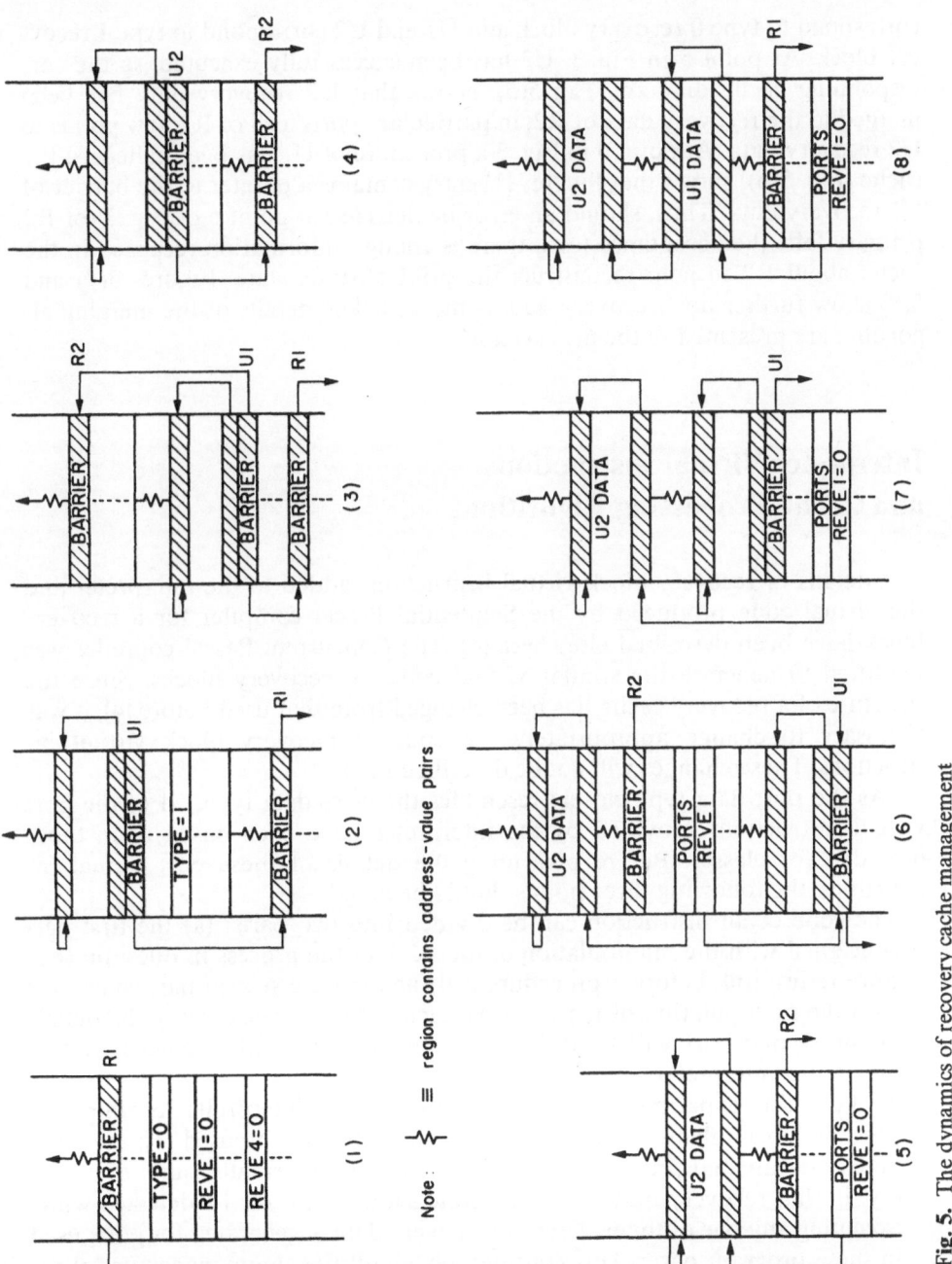

Note: ⋚ ≡ region contains address–value pairs

Fig. 5. The dynamics of recovery cache management

correspond to type 0 recovery block and U1 and U2 correspond to type 1 recovery block. At point 5 in Fig. 3, U2 has been successfully executed, so the corresponding cache diagram, Fig. 5(5), shows that U2 recovery data has been merged to the recovery data of R2; in particular, 'ports' cell of R2 now points to U2 recovery data. At point 6 in Fig. 3 a procedure of U1 has been called, so the cache [Fig. 5(6)] shows that the 'revel' entry contains a pointer to the barrier of U1 recovery data. Thus, should an error be detected at point 6 of Fig. 3 (or R2 primary fails the acceptance test), there is enough information recorded in the cache about R2 to help reconstruct the prior abstract state. Figures 5(7) and 5(8) show further how recovery data is merged. The details of the merging algorithm are presented in the next section.

Interpreter Virtual Instructions and Cache Processing Algorithms

The details of recovery block virtual instructions added to the interpreter and the virtual code produced by the Sequential Pascal compiler for a recovery block have been described elsewhere [4]. The Concurrent Pascal compiler was modified to generate the similar virtual code for recovery blocks. Since the structure of a recovery cache has been changed from that used before [4], it was necessary to change appropriately the code of recovery block virtual instructions. These changes will not be described here.

As the port data type closely resembles the class data type, all of the port virtual instructions provided by the interpreter have been based upon those provided for classes. Before presenting the details of these port virtual instructions, the following three points should be noted:

1. The code of an instruction can be divided into two parts: (a) the first part concerned with the manipulation of the stack of the process in question (e.g. store return link before a procedure call) and (b) the second part concerned with the manipulation of the recovery cache of the process. Only the details of the second part will be described here since it is this second part that makes this interpreter somewhat novel.

2. To keep this experimental implementation of the interpreter as simple as possible, an implementation restriction on ports was imposed [1]: the prelude, postulate and procedures of a port represent the smallest unit of recovery, in that recovery may not be possible should an error be detected while executing any one of them. Thus, no recovery data is generated for ports used in these program parts. This considerably simplifies the management of recovery data (at the expense of providing a coarser 'grain of recovery'). A variable 'critic' is maintained in each of the process heads of processes with the following meaning: 'critic > 0' implies generate no recovery data for a port and 'critic = 0' implies the opposite.

3. For the same reason as above, variables of the initial process were treated as unrecoverable, in that no recovery data is generated for them.

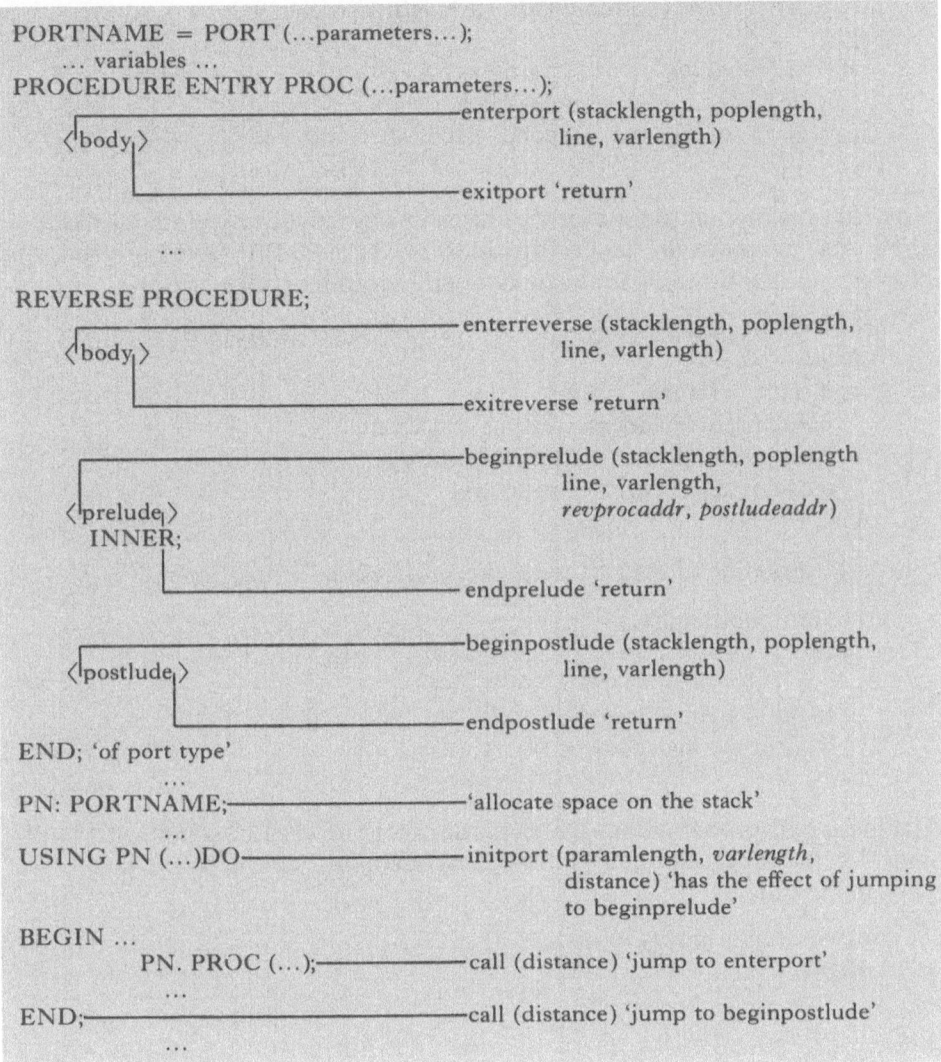

```
PORTNAME = PORT (...parameters...);
    ... variables ...
PROCEDURE ENTRY PROC (...parameters...);
    ┌──────────────────────────enterport (stacklength, poplength,
    │ ⟨body₁⟩                                  line, varlength)
    └──────────────────────────exitport 'return'

        ...

REVERSE PROCEDURE;
    ┌──────────────────────────enterreverse (stacklength, poplength,
    │ ⟨body₁⟩                                  line, varlength)
    └──────────────────────────exitreverse 'return'

    ┌──────────────────────────beginprelude (stacklength, poplength
    │                                          line, varlength,
    │ ⟨prelude₁⟩                               revprocaddr, postludeaddr)
        INNER;
    └──────────────────────────endprelude 'return'

    ┌──────────────────────────beginpostlude (stacklength, poplength,
    │ ⟨postlude₁⟩                              line, varlength)
    └──────────────────────────endpostlude 'return'
END; 'of port type'
        ...
PN: PORTNAME;─────────────────'allocate space on the stack'
        ...
USING PN (...)DO──────────────initport (paramlength, varlength,
                                          distance) 'has the effect of jumping
                                          to beginprelude'
BEGIN ...
        PN. PROC (...);───────call (distance) 'jump to enterport'
        ...
END;──────────────────────────call (distance) 'jump to beginpostlude'
        ...
```

Fig. 6. Port virtual instructions

Figure 6 shows the port virtual instructions and how they are planted by the Concurrent Pascal compiler around appropriate program bodies. For the sake of completeness, all the parameters of the instructions have been shown; however, only the underlined parameters are used explicitly for cache management, the rest are for stack management (stacklength indicates storage to be reserved on the stack, poplength indicates the storage to be reclaimed and so on).

The execution of a 'using' statement is started by the interpreter executing the 'initport' instruction. The recovery cache manipulation part of this instruction is shown below.

353

```
procedure initport (paramlength, varlength, distance);
begin      ...
    if critic = 0 then
    {create on the cache, recovery data
    for type 1 recovery block; code: = 0; nest: = nest + 1}
    end;
```

The next instruction to be executed after this is the 'beginprelude' instruction (note that 'revprocaddr' means the address where 'enterreverse' instruction is stored, a similar meaning is attached to 'preludeaddr', 'postludeaddr'):

```
procedure beginprelude (-, -, -, -, revprocaddr, postludeaddr);
    begin      ...
        if critic = 0 then
        {store prelude address, reverse procedure
        address and postlude address in the port
        recovery data; critic: = critic + 1}
    end;
```

The last instruction of the prelude is the 'endprelude' instruction:

```
procedure endprelude;
    begin

            ...
        critic: = critic − 1;
        if critic = 0 then code: = 1
    end;
```

Calling a port procedure has the effect of executing 'enterport' followed by the code for the procedure body followed by 'exitport' which returns the control back to the caller:

```
procedure enterport (-, -, -, - );
    begin

            ...
        critic: = critic + 1
    end;
```

```
procedure exitport;
    begin

            ...
        critic: = critic − 1;
        if critic = 0 then
        {if the current recovery data is
        of type 1 and refers to the port whose procedure has been called then
        code: = 2
            else {select an empty reve i cell
                and put in it a pointer to the barrier of appropriate type 1
                recovery data; make 'code' of this type 1 recovery data = 2}}
    end;
```

354

The algorithms for the instructions 'enterreverse' and 'exitreverse' are the same as those of 'enterport' and 'exitport' respectively. Finally, the algorithms for the instructions 'beginpostlude' and 'endpostlude' are given:

```
procedure beginpostlude;
   begin      ...
      if critic = 0 then
      {code: = 3; critic: = critic + 1}
   end;

procedure endpostlude;
   begin

            ...
      critic: = critic − 1;
      if critic = 0 then
      {copy from the stack, the actual port
      parameters and variables to the port
      data area in the cache; code: = 4;
      if nest > 0 then merge else discard}
end;
```

As noted earlier, successful execution of a using statement is treated as the using recovery block passing its 'acceptance test'. Hence in the instruction 'end-postlude', a call is made either to procedure merge (for merging recovery data to the enclosing recovery block's recovery data) or to procedure discard for throwing away the recovery data. The algorithm for 'merge' is given below:

```
procedure merge;
begin
   with all reve i of the recovery data of the just executed recovery block do
      {if the enclosing recovery block's recovery data has no reve j with
      the same value as revei and revei is not pointing to the barrier
      of the enclosing recovery block's recovery data then copy reve i to
      any unused reve j};

   with all the entries of the just executed recovery block's recovery data do
      {if the entry is a port recovery data then add it and link it
      to the port recovery data of the enclosing recovery block's
      recovery data;
      if the entry is a value−address pair and the variable is
      global and there is no entry for it in the recovery data of
      the enclosing recovery block then add it to the recovery data
      else throw it away;}
      update heaptop and cachbr;
end;
```

The last algorithm to be described here is that of procedure 'restore' which performs the task of state restoration. This procedure is called from within the exception handler of the interpreter (see Fig. 2). The procedure processes the current recovery data as follows:

```
procedure restore;
  begin
    critic: = critic + 1;
  while any port data left do
  {select the first unprocessed port data; copy the
  parameters and variables on the stack; execute
  the sequence 'prelude; reverse procedure; postlude';
  mark this port data as 'processed'; restore stack};
  with all reve i entries do
  {if reve i ≠ null then extract the reverse procedure
  address and execute the procedure};
  if the recovery data is of type 1 then
      case code of
  0:;
  1: execute the postlude;
  2: execute 'reverse procedure; postlude';
  3: execute reverse procedure;
      end 'case';
  appropriately select 'address—value' pairs and
  restore the prior values; restore the interpreter
  registers S, B, G and Q;
  critic: = critic − 1
  end;
```

A few remarks on this algorithm are in order.
1. By incrementing 'critic' at the beginning, it is made certain that no recovery data will be generated while executing any programs.
2. The order in which the various 'undo effects' programs are executed is not necessarily the reverse of the order in which the 'produce effects' programs were executed (this may turn out to be a weakness of this implementation and a revision of the method of recording recovery data will be needed to introduce the necessary changes).

A few changes were made to the error reporting routines of the kernel such that the identity of a process is appended at the beginning when an error message from the interpreter is printed on the console. Examples of such messages appear in a companion paper [1].

Conclusion

It can be seen that the structure of a recovery cache and its processing algorithms have become much more complicated than the scheme presented earlier [2]. This must be judged against the fact that it is now relatively straightforward for a concurrent program — an operating system — to offer abstract recoverable operations on arbitrary resources to user programs. In the absence of such a facility, ad hoc measures will have to be incorporated in concurrent and user programs. The resulting increase in complexity is likely to adversely affect the reliability of the system.

The size of the original interpreter was about 1K words. The size of the modified interpreter is about 2K words. This modest increase in the size of the interpreter was made possible by (a) making maximum use of the already existing 'class' virtual instruction codes for port virtual instructions, and (b) relying more on the use of subroutines as against macros. The modifications to the interpreter have been performed in such a manner that programs that do not use recovery blocks and ports are not affected; in particular, the SOLO operating system [3] and the supporting programs can be used for developing concurrent and sequential programs with recovery. The system that has been described here must be regarded as experimental since, for example, any realistic fault-tolerant system will include a high degree of hardware redundancy (this system has none). Nevertheless, this experimental system can be used as a basis for the design of more appropriate hardware; in particular, there is no reason why the interpreter described here could not be implemented by microprogramming.

Acknowledgements. Acknowledgement is due to P. C. Treleaven who made the necessary changes to the Concurrent Pascal compiler and to P. A. Lee whose criticisms on all aspects of this work proved to be of great value. This work was supported by the Science Research Council (UK) as part of the Highly Reliable Computing Systems project at Newcastle University.

References

1. S. K. Shrivastava, 'Concurrent Pascal with backward error recovery: language features and examples', Software — Practice and Experience, **9**, 1001 – 1020 (1979). [Also Chap. 4]
2. J. J. Horning et al., 'A program structure for error detection and recovery', Lecture Notes in Computer Science, **16**, 177 – 193 (1974). [Also Chap. 2]
3. P. Brinch Hansen, The Architecture of Concurrent Programs, Prentice-Hall Inc., Englewood Cliffs, N. J., 1977.
4. S. K. Shrivastava, 'Sequential Pascal with recovery blocks', Software — Practice and Experience, **8**, 177 – 185 (1978). [Also Chap. 2]
5. S. K. Shrivastava and J. P. Banatre, 'Reliable resource allocation between unreliable processes', IEEE Trans. on Software Engineering, **4**, No. 3, 230 – 241 (1978). [Also Chap. 4]

A Framework for Software Fault Tolerance in Real-Time Systems

T. ANDERSON and J. C. KNIGHT

Abstract. Real-time systems often have very high reliability requirements and are therefore prime candidates for the inclusion of fault tolerance techniques. In order to provide tolerance to software faults, some form of state restoration is usually advocated as a means of recovery. State restoration can be expensive and the cost is exacerbated for systems which utilize concurrent processes. The concurrency present in most real-time systems and the further difficulties introduced by timing constraints suggest that providing tolerance for software faults may be inordinately expensive or complex. We believe that this need not be case, and propose a straightforward pragmatic approach to software fault tolerance which is believed to be applicable to many real-time systems. The approach takes advantage of the structure of real-time systems to simplify error recovery, and a classification scheme for errors is introduced. Responses to each type of error are proposed which allow service to be maintained.

Index Terms. Concurrency, error classification, real-time systems, software fault tolerance, software reliability.

I. Introduction

A great deal of research is currently being performed on techniques for the production of better quality software. This research is particularly important for systems where the consequences of any noncompliance of software with its requirements may be disastrous. The failure of an unmanned space mission could cause the loss of extremely expensive equipment before the successful completion of mission objectives. Of even greater concern is the possibility that human lives could be endangered, for example, by the failure of a digital avionics system for a commercial air transport.

Many critical systems operate in real time. This means that inputs may be expected and/or outputs must be generated according to some real-time schedule. For example, an avionics systems may send commands to control surfaces every tenth of a second of real time. Of course, the traditional problems associated with software arise in real-time systems; the necessary outputs may be produced when they are needed, but they may be incorrect. However, the requirement for operation in real time presents difficulties over and above those normally encountered. For example, execution of a real-time program may successfully produce the output demanded by the program's specification but fail to do so within the imposed real-time deadline.

For some embedded real-time systems, belated (or even erroneous) outputs may not constitute an immediate problem. The inertial characteristics of attached physical equipment may absorb temporary aberrations so long as subsequent outputs are valid and generated on time. Nevertheless, a missed deadline can be taken as strong evidence that problems may exist in the operation of a system, and that much more serious consequences could ensue. In critical systems such anomalies should not be ignored. Of course, if a system is designed specifically to permit occasional delayed outputs, a missed deadline need not be considered anomalous. However, when a deadline is missed in such a system it will be very difficult to determine whether the delay results from the design or is in fact a harbinger of system failure. Such uncertainty is not acceptable for critical systems.

There are two approaches to the construction of software which must exhibit behavior that is highly reliable (that is, complying with its specification most of the time). Avizienis [2] called these approaches fault intolerance and fault tolerance. Fault intolerance, better referred to as fault elimination or fault prevention, embraces all the various techniques which try to ensure that software contains no faults. For example, requirements definitions, precise specifications, design and programming methodologies, proving, and testing can all contribute to an attempt to eliminate the presence of faults from software. Experience has shown that although the adoption of these techniques can be beneficial, a reduction in the incidence of faults and certainly not their complete elimination is all that can be expected. Fault tolerant software incorporates techniques which attempt to ensure that acceptable service is maintained by coping with the faults which remain despite the use of fault prevention measures. Elements are introduced into a system which, in the absence of faults, could be omitted without affecting the behavior of the system.

This paper discusses the application of fault tolerance techniques to real-time software. Real-time systems are modeled as a set of cooperating sequential processes with constraints on their execution time. Each process corresponds to the execution of a program which is part of the system, and provides some subset of the necessary system outputs. Programs are usually executed periodically and, for a given program, the intervals between initiations are almost always the same length of time. An executive ensures that processes of the system are dispatched at the appropriate time and monitors whether each process completes execution within its allotted time.

The approach to fault tolerance presented here can be applied to any practical real-time system for which the previous model is appropriate, and does not demand special-purpose hardware facilities for its implementation. It is not designed for or limited to any specific project but suggests techniques which can be tailored for any particular cyclic real-time application. Using this approach, systems can be constructed which will continue to provide adequate responses in real time under circumstances where faults in the software would normally cause a loss of service. It will be necessary to construct software above and beyond that which has been traditionally considered sufficient. The additional costs may be substantial but must be regarded as unavoidable, as are the costs incurred from the redundancy necessary to provide hardware fault tolerance. Software which does not include every facility to enhance reliability is unacceptable in the critical applications being considered here.

None of the techniques proposed here are intended to cope with hardware faults (although tolerance to some hardware faults may be obtained nevertheless). Hence, it is assumed that the software is executed on hardware of sufficiently high reliability. Furthermore, to assist in achieving reliable operation, the hardware should include facilities such as high resolution clocks and memory protection.

The work reported here was motivated by the need for reliability in flight software but the techniques have relevance in other real-time applications where the cost of failure is high; for example, the operation of a nuclear power plant or the monitoring of hospital patients.

Previous work in the area of fault tolerant real-time software has been reported by Campbell et al. [3], Hecht [9], and Kopetz [12]. It is likely that certain military real-time systems have made some use of software fault tolerance, but in most cases such systems have not been described in the open literature. One exception is SAFEGUARD [19].

Campbell et al. considered a system of independent primary processes which individually must provide their respective service within their own time limits. To guard against a primary process not completing in the required time it was suggested that an alternate process be available for each primary process, which would be able to provide a degraded service in substantially less time than is required by the primary process. The deadline imposed on the primary is such that there is always sufficient time to execute the alternate should this prove necessary.

Hecht has made various specific suggestions for incorporating fault tolerance in the software of practical flight control systems. In particular, he advocated the use of recovery blocks [16] augmented by error detection using an interval timer, and the provision of a back-up scheduler which would maintain only critical system functions.

Kopetz presented an abstract model of computation and used it do develop probability models of reliability. Real-time systems were handled as a special case and it was shown that various forms of redundancy in such systems lead to substantial increases in reliability.

Substantial hardware fault tolerance was built into the SAFEGUARD system together with limited software fault tolerance. Software error detection took many forms including range and plausibility checks on data. Once detected, software errors were usually handled by suspending the erroneous process if possible, by operator intervention, or by resetting the entire system. Some critical programs were equipped with specialized error recovery code. The techniques used in SAFEGUARD were rather specific to the needs of that particular project.

II. Characteristics and a Model of Real-Time Systems

Consider a set of programs with names $P1, \ldots, Pn$ and a set of distinct times $T1, \ldots, Tm$ which represent timing constraints (on some appropriate scale). Let G be a finite, acyclic, directed graph with exactly one node with in-degree zero called the frame beginning node and exactly one node with out-degree zero called the frame ending node. Each node of G is labeled with either a program name or a timing constraint, and more than one node may be labeled with the same program name. No two nodes are labeled with the same timing constraint. An arc of G can only connect two nodes with different types of label. Thus, G is a bipartite graph. The frame beginning and frame ending nodes are both labeled with timing constraints. If there is a path in G from a node labeled Ti to a node labeled Tj, then Ti must be less than Tj. Nodes labeled with program names have in-degree and out-degree one. G is referred to as a synchronization graph. Clearly, such graphs are connected.

The need to respond promptly to changes in the external environment dictates that real-time systems have an iterative nature. This repetitive attribute may be implicit if the systems is interrupt driven (as are many sequence control systems), but otherwise is usually exhibited explicitly in the form of cyclic system operation. A synchronization graph can be used to represent the process structure of cyclic real-time systems.

A synchronization graph represents the process structure of a real-time system. It shows which programs must be executed, and when each must start and finish. A node labeled with a program name indicates the execution of that program and therefore represents a process. Where no ambiguity arises, the phrase "process P" will sometimes be used in the remainder of this paper in place of the phrase "execution of the program named P." A node labeled with a timing constraint is a point of process synchronization (with other processes and/or the outside world) and the node label specifies the elapsed time by which this synchronization must occur. A node labeled with a program name P is connected to two nodes labeled with timing constraints. The graph indicates that the program named P must begin execution at the time specified at the node with an arc to the node labeled P, and must complete execution at or before the time specified at the node with an arc from the node labeled P.

Arbitrarily complex real-time systems can be modeled using such graphs but the resulting graphs may be inordinately large. However, we have found that the simple repetitive structure of many practical real-time systems allows their operation to be modeled as cyclic traversals of acceptably sized graphs, beginning each cycle with the unique node labeled by the earliest timing constraint (the frame beginning node) and ending with the unique node labeled by the latest timing constraint (the frame ending node). More complex systems often exhibit a natural modularity which can be represented using nested synchronization graphs. A part of the system can be represented as a separate synchronization graph and this used as a node in a graph representing the entire system.

The time period corresponding to a single iteration of the synchronization graph for a system is referred to as a frame. The length of a frame in real time (the frame time) is usually quite short (normally less than one second) since frequent outputs from the system are required for smooth operation. This means that any given process will only exist for a short time (at most a frame) which may be contrasted with the characteristics of a general-purpose operating system. Many real-time systems operate with some programs being executed more frequently than others. Such systems are said to operate with multiple frame rates or multiple iteration rates. This can be modeled either by nested syn-

361

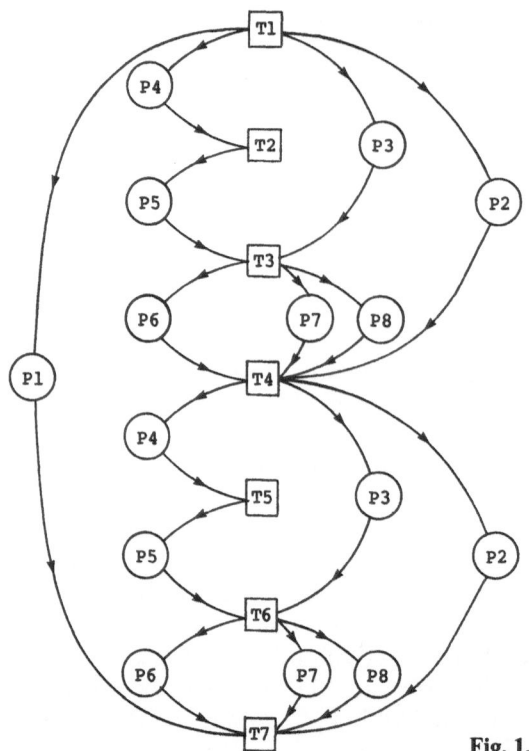

Fig. 1. An example of a synchronization graph

chronization graphs or by labeling several nodes with the same program name and using a series of timing constraints to show limits on sequential executions.

An example of a synchronization graph is shown in Fig. 1. The program names are $P1$, $P2$, ..., $P8$ and the timing constraints are $T1$, $T2$, ..., $T7$. It is convenient to depict the time labeled nodes of the graph in a linear sequence in order to show the relationship of the timing constraints. Programs $P1$, $P2$, $P3$, and $P4$ begin to execute concurrently at time $T1$ and $P4$ must complete by time $T2$. Program $P5$ begins at $T2$ and both it and $P3$ must complete by $T3$. At $T3$, programs $P6$, $P7$, and $P8$ begin, and they, together with $P2$, must complete by $T4$. All programs except $P1$ then repeat this execution sequence with new timing constraints $T5$, $T6$, and $T7$. Thus, this example includes multiple rates of iteration. Time $T7$ is the final constraint and programs $P6$, $P7$, and $P8$ must complete at this time, as must $P1$ and $P2$. The entire execution sequence is then repeated an arbitrary number of times. All timing constraints are incremented by $T7 - T1$ at the end of each iteration. $T1$ is the frame beginning node, $T7$ the frame ending node, and $T7 - T1$ the frame time.

Although Fig. 1 is a simple example, observations of practical systems suggests that they can be modeled adequately with extremely simple graphs. Fig. 2 is the synchronization graph of a slightly modified form of the software for the Annular Suspension Pointing System (ASPS) [23]. (The ASPS is a computer

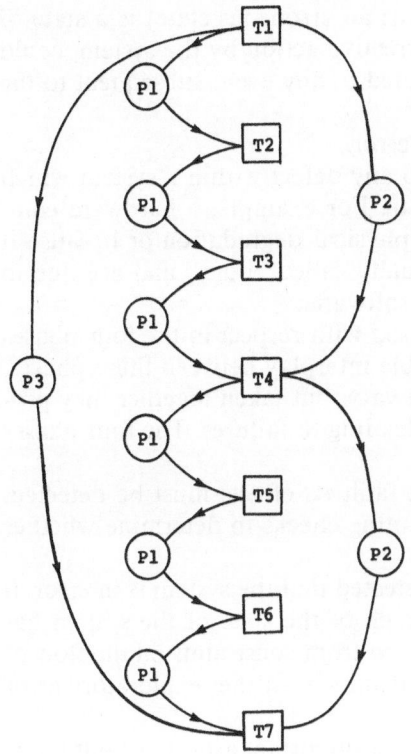

Fig. 2. Synchronization graph of the ASPS system

controlled pointing system which provides extremely accurate pointing of experiments to be carried on the Space Shuttle.)

The concurrency exhibited in practical real-time systems, such as ASPS, is usually limited and predefined. Parallel execution of processes is not uncommon, but the degree of parallelism is restricted and takes the same form during each frame. In principle, processes are being created as required but in a rigid predefined manner. There are none of the complex resource management problems which arise in systems where processes may be created arbitrarily. Interprocess communication is fairly simple and often identical in every frame.

III. Principles of Fault Tolerance

Detailed discussions of the general principles of software fault tolerance may be found elsewhere [1], [17]. Only an overview is given here.

In what follows, definitions derived from those given by Melliar-Smith and Randell [15] for fault, error, and failure are adopted. Specifically:

1) a FAILURE occurs whenever the external behavior of a system does not conform to that prescribed by the system specification,

2) an ERROR (more accurately known as an erroneous state) is a state of the system which, in the absence of any corrective action by the system, could lead to a failure which would not be attributed to any event subsequent to the error,

3) a FAULT is the adjudged cause of an error.

The term "fault" will be used to refer to any defect within a system which causes the system to enter an erroneous state. For example, a hardware component may malfunction either because of physical degradation or because it was badly designed. Software faults are usually called "bugs" and are due to mistakes in the design or construction of the software.

Fault tolerance techniques can be discussed with respect to the four phases summarized below. There can be considerable interplay between these phases, and the order in which they are applied can vary, but taken together they provide a capability for preventing faults from leading to failures. The four phases are as follows.

1) ERROR DETECTION: To tolerate a fault its effects must be detected. Clearly, this can only be achieved by performing checks to determine whether any erroneous situation has arisen.

2) DAMAGE ASSESSMENT: Having detected that the system is in error, it will usually be necessary to identify how much of the state of the system has been corrupted. The assessment may be derived from constraints on the flow of information in the system, or based on the outcome of further exploratory error checking.

3) ERROR RECOVERY: Probably the most important aspect of fault tolerance is the provision of an effective means of transforming an erroneous state of the system into a well defined and error free state. Methods for achieving this transformation can sometimes make good use of the information retained in the erroneous state, but it can be more secure to simply discard the erroneous state and reset the system either to some prior state (a recovery point) or other pre-designated state.

4) CONTINUED SERVICE: In order to enable the system to continue to provide the service required by its specification, further action may be needed to ensure that the fault whose effects have been obviated does not immediately recur and thus ruin the whole approach. Unless the fault was transient and will not recur in any case, it must either be rectified or circumvented. These actions are usually referred to as repair and reconfiguration, respectively.

Fault tolerance techniques have received widespread application in hardware [4], but are relatively little used in software. This is largely because the techniques adopted in hardware systems are intended to cope with anticipated faults resulting from physical degradation, and as such are inappropriate for software faults. Faults in software are present from the outset; their characteristics are those of design faults and as such their consequences are difficult to assess in advance. Techniques suitable for providing tolerance to software faults have not been proposed until comparatively recently [5], [10]. In order to cope with unpredictable damage to the state of the system, the strategies adopted for the four phases of fault tolerance described above must operate as generally as possible.

Thus, it is advocated that error detection should be achieved by checking that the system is functioning acceptably. It is not suggested that the more conventional approach of checking for specific malfunctions should be discarded, but that negative checks of this type should be supplemented by positive acceptability checks.

An automated exploratory approach to damage assessment would be difficult in an unanticipated error situation. Decisions about the extent of damage are more appropriately based on assumptions of how the system is structured and the apparent severity of the error.

A similar approach to error recovery entails mistrusting any of the state information considered to be damaged and avoiding the use of recovery techniques which rely on such information. In order to recover from the unpredictable situations which can ensue from design faults, it is necessary to adopt the more drastic alternative of replacing all suspected parts of the system state together with any other parts which must be replaced for consistency. This may involve substantial processing and consequent delay. To minimize this penalty, hardware implemented state restoration mechanisms have been proposed [14].

Finally, in order to achieve continued service after recovery has taken place, some means of preventing a repetition of the original fault must be found. An estimate of the location of a software fault will be needed so that the module containing the fault can be replaced by a stand-by spare. Given the nature of software faults, it is clear that the spare module must be of independent design.

The technique of recovery blocks [16] is based directly on the above principles whereas N-version programming [5] uses an NMR voting check for error detection and replicated states to obviate the need for explicit error recovery; neither technique is directly applicable to other than a single sequential process.

IV. Fault Tolerance in Concurrent Systems

While considerable success has been achieved in devising mechanisms to provide fault tolerance in the software of sequential systems, difficulties arise when systems of communicating concurrent processes are considered, particularly if real-time constraints are imposed. Suggestions in this more difficult area have involved major assumptions about the nature of the concurrency in the system. Randell [16] assumed that processes could be synchronized with respect to the discarding of recovery points, and suggested a technique of "conversations" between processes. Shrivastava [20], [22] considered processes which communicate solely in order to share scarce resources, and Russell [18] examined producer/consumer systems. In a slightly more general but much more complex approach, Kim [11] assumed that interprocess communication takes place through monitors and that inputs to a process are considered to be valid by the receiving process.

The basic problem is that if processes can communicate at will then whenever one process establishes a recovery point (for state restoration purposes) it is advisable for all other processes to do the same. If this is not done, system-wide consistent state restoration may only be possible by rolling back the activity of the system to an arbitrarily earlier point in time. This is the domino effect [16] and an example is shown in Fig. 3. Both processes must rollback to point A in order to recover because of the communication which takes place and the way in which recovery points are established. All of the above approaches are aimed at avoiding the heavy overhead incurred with large numbers of recovery points or extensive rollback.

As was discussed earlier, the process structure of real-time systems contains many synchronization points which are usually associated with timing constraints. Synchronization points occur within the process structure where a subset of the processes are synchronized, and at frame boundaries where all of the processes are synchronized. In fact, much of the synchronization of processes in a real-time system stems from the need to synchronize with the external environment, rather than from any inherent needs of the processes themselves. Thus, much more synchronization occurs than would be found in concurrent systems that do not operate in real time. This means that although real- time systems are concurrent, they have a characteristic which is highly desirable if recovery points are to be provided without excessive overhead. The provision of fault tolerance need not involve any changes to the process structure. Such systems are particularly amenable to the application of a modified form of the conversation technique mentioned above.

A set of processes which participate in a conversation may communicate freely among themselves, but with no other processes. Processes may enter the conversation at different times but, on entry, each must establish a recovery point (see Fig. 4). All processes must leave the conversation at the same time since if an error is detected in any participant, every process in the conversation must restore its recovery point and try again. If the conversation structure is used to provide recoverability in a general concurrent system, the necessary state restoration can be automated using a recovery cache [10], which is a form of mechanized incremental checkpoint. It can be used for both sequential and concurrent software. The recovery cache frees the software designer from the need to specify what has to be recorded, saves only a minimum of recovery

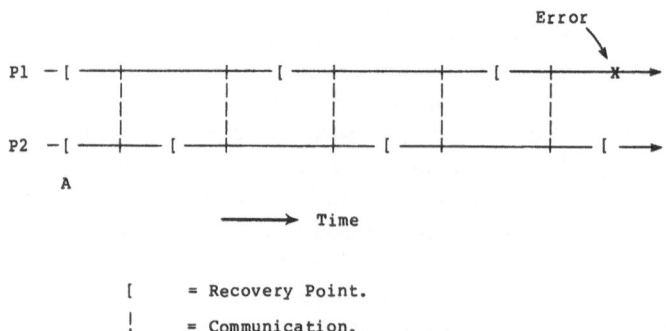

Fig. 3. The domino effect

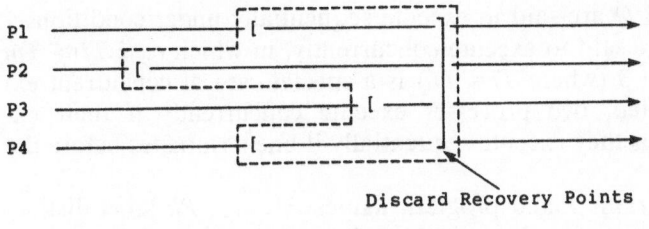

Discard Recovery Points

Time

Fig. 4. A conversation

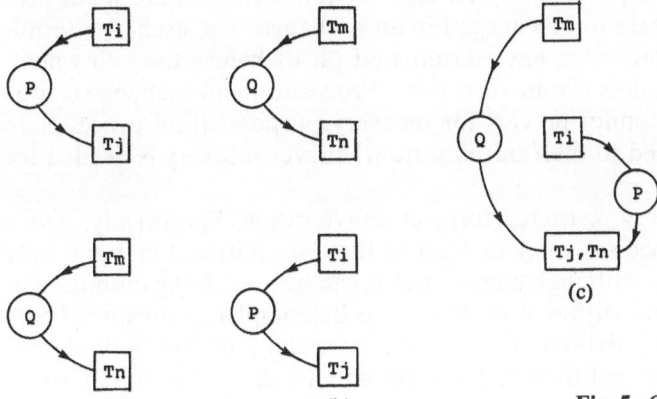

(a)

(b)

(c)

Fig. 5. Communications restrictions

data, and maintains the illusion that a complete checkpoint has been taken. Although this is conceptually straightforward, if a recovery cache is not supported in the underlying machine then extensive processing will be necessary to simulate its operation. Presently available computers do not provide a hardware recovery cache although an experimental version has been built for a PDP-11 [14]. Except in particularly simple cases, the overhead of a software recovery cache is likely to be prohibitive.

The successful implementation of software fault tolerance in a real-time system is greatly facilitated by imposing the following restriction on communication between processes of the system. Let timing constraints Ti, Tj, Tm, and Tn and program names P and Q label nodes of a synchronization graph with arcs defined by the ordered pairs (Ti, P), (P, Tj), (Tm, Q), and (Q, Tn). Necessarily, Ti is less than Tj and Tm is less than Tn. Communication is only permitted under the following mutually exclusive conditions:

1) from P to Q if $Tj \leq Tm$,   [see Fig. 5(a)]
2) from Q to P if $Tn \leq Ti$,   [see Fig. 5(b)]
3) between P and Q if $Tj = Tn$ [see Fig. 5(c)].

Note that condition 3 implies $j = n$ also. Since timing constraints are distinct, if $Tj = Tn$ they are the same node of the graph.

367

The processes P and Q are said to execute sequentially under conditions 1 and 2, and otherwise are said to execute concurrently, in which case $Tj > Tm$ and $Tn > Ti$. Condition 3 (where $Tj = Tn$) is a special case of concurrent execution. Informally stated, two processes execute concurrently if their executions overlap, whereas they execute sequentially if one terminates before the other begins.

Let the timing constraint T and program names $P1, \ldots, Pk$ label distinct nodes of a synchronization graph with arcs defined by the ordered pairs $(P1, T), \ldots, (Pk, T)$. Processes $P1, \ldots, Pk$ execute concurrently but are allowed to communicate because condition 3 is satisfied. If a recovery point is established for each of the processes when they are initiated then the set of processes $P1, \ldots, Pk$ are said to be engaged in an exchange. The exchange terminates when all of the processes have terminated (at or before time T) whereupon all the recovery points can be discarded. Processes in an exchange can be regarded as a single (atomic) process for recovery purposes if all processes in the exchange are restored to their initial state whenever recovery is needed for one process.

An exchange is a very restricted form of conversation. Specifically, it is a conversation which processes enter as soon as they are initiated and exit only when they all terminate. Although conversations can be nested, the definition of an exchange requires two different exchanges to be completely disjoint. These restrictions are imposed deliberately to take advantage of the natural synchronization inherent in real-time systems. By stipulating that communication between concurrent processes can only occur when the processes are members of the same exchange, a straightforward implementation of recovery for a real-time system can be constructed.

The unrestricted framework of conversations could be used as a basis for recovery in real-time systems, but exchanges are proposed here as a simpler alternative imposing stricter control on interprocess communication. Observation of typical cyclic real-time systems suggests that these restrictions are easily satisfied and are acceptable in order to facilitate the provision of recovery. Conversations provide more flexibility, but to take advantage of this involves imposing additional synchronization points on processes and necessitates the implementation of a more complex recovery mechanism.

Cyclic real-time systems often have characteristics which enable recovery for exchanges to be efficiently implemented in software, without the assistance of any special-purpose hardware. Because of the iterative nature of these systems, the initial state of a process at a specific synchronization point can be expected to be very similar for each frame. In the simplest case, the initial state of a process will always be the same. All that is required to restore the initial state if recovery is invoked is a simple reset. By storing constants to set up the initial state in read-only memory, the reset can be easily, and efficiently, achieved by means of software. Even if the initial state contains frame dependent values, state restoration by software will still be viable so long as the quantity of data involved is limited, and the relevant variables are known a priori. By preserving the initial values of the frame dependent variables at each iteration, recovery can be implemented by a fixed reset followed by a selective update using the preserved values. Thus, for many practical real-time systems, error recovery hardware will not be necessary.

One potential limitation of state restoration as a recovery technique concerns interaction between a system and its environment. Restoring the internal state of a process does not suffice to undo the effects of outputs from the process which have been acted upon externally to the system, or to regenerate inputs from the environment which the process has consumed. Although error recovery can simulate the reversal of time within the system, such abstractions are not available in the "real" world of the external environment.

Inputs to a process are not likely to pose a major problem. In many systems, input values will be sensor readings, in which case the values available after recovery may well be preferred to the original values (and since they may differ slightly, a recurrence of the error may be avoided). If necessary, however, input values can easily be recorded and retained for use in the event of recovery.

Outputs to the external environment are a much more serious problem. In some situations an erroneous output can be compensated by subsequent outputs, for example, when adjusting an aircraft's control surfaces. But in other situations, compensation may be impossible, for example, if an aircraft's fuel has been jettisoned inadvertently. The difficulties here are, in principle, insoluable. Once a system has generated erroneous outputs it has failed, and while fault tolerance techniques may be able to prevent a recurrence of the failure, nothing can be done to prevent a failure once it has occurred! (Remedial action may be undertaken but can only mitigate the consequences of the failure.) This suggests that a process should not release an output to the environment until all internal checks have been completed [21], that is, not until the process in committed in the sense that recovery will not be invoked for that process. A particularly simple strategy is to defer the transmission of outputs to the environment until the end of each frame.

V. Error Classification

For the purpose of discussing the recovery mechanisms, errors will be classified according to a set of definitions. This classification is based on the apparent seriousness of the situation arising from a fault. It is not appropriate to classify faults in this way since similar faults occurring at different points in a system can generate erroneous states with different degrees of severity. The definitions are as follows.
1) INTERNAL Error: An error that can be adequately handled by the process in which the error is detected.
2) EXTERNAL Error: An error that cannot be adequately handled by the process in which it is detected, but whose effects are limited to that process.
3) PERVASIVE Error: An error that cannot be adequately handled by the process in which it is detected and which results in errors in other processes.

The incidence of errors will be classified according to the following definitions.

1) PERSISTENT: An error is persistent if the frequency of occurrence of the associated fault exceeds some predetermined threshold.
2) TRANSIENT: An error is transient if it is not persistent.

As an example, suppose process P performs a division by zero, and has provision for recovery from this error. If this recovery is successful, then the error is considered to be internal. Such an error has no impact on the rest of the system. Internal errors may be transient or persistent, but this is of no immediate consequence to the rest of the system. However, a persistent internal error may eventually lead to an external or pervasive error.

If division by zero occurs within P but no error handler is provided, the service provided by P can only be maintained with the assistance of software which is not part of P. The error is then external, provided that no erroneous information has been propagated from P to other processes. Such an error is persistent if it recurs frequently, and it is likely that more extensive recovery will be required for persistent external errors than for transient ones.

Finally, suppose process P enters an erroneous state by, for example, setting to zero a variable which should always be positive. If, before this situation is detected, process P uses this variable in communication with other processes and they enter erroneous states as a result, then the error is pervasive.

Given this classification scheme for errors, it is necessary to be able to determine which class an error falls into once it has been detected. This enables appropriate recovery techniques to be invoked reflecting the extent of the damage incurred by the system. In practice, classifying an error can only be attempted since it will be impossible to classify all errors correctly. For example, the first occurrence of a persistent error is likely to be classified as transient. Similarly, an error could occur which was in fact pervasive, but if the consequent damage to the other processes was not detected, the this pervasive error would be indistinguishable from an external error. There is nothing that can be done about this problem other than to try to minimize its impact. Some form of recovery will be invoked even when an error is wrongly classified and this may still be sufficient to ensure continued service from the system.

VI. Error Detection and Damage Assessment

When software is being executed on a hardware implemented interface, the various checks built into the hardware may be supplemented by assertions in the software. These assertions may be in the processes themselves or in the executive software.

A check which is performed in hardware may reveal an error by detecting an invalid usage of the interface; for example, division by zero, a protection violation, or an attempt to execute an invalid operation code. A software assertion may reveal an error by detecting an illegal use of program data; for example, range checking, array bound checking, or checks on invariant relationships between variables. Timing errors are detected when a timing constraint specified in the software is violated. They form an important class of errors detected by supplementary software checking.

If error detection is to be followed by recovery and continued service, there must be time available after detection and before the outputs are actually required. In the particular case of signaling timing errors this means that deadlines must be imposed on the primary process which allow time for recovery and the execution of at least one alternate [3]. This is an important point for system designers to keep in mind.

It is assumed in the following discussion that whenever an error is detected, either by hardware or software checking, an interrupt is raised and control passes to a system error handler. On being invoked in response to the detection of an error, the error handler must make a determination of the extent of the damage to the system state, and then initiate appropriate error recovery measures. In the approach proposed in this paper, damage to the system is implicitly assessed by the error handler classifying each error as being internal, external, or pervasive. For external and pervasive errors, the recovery technique applied is also dependent on whether the error is deemed to be transient or persistent.

In order to classify errors with reasonable accuracy, it will be necessary for the error handler to retain information concerning the error history of processes in the system. No information need be maintained by the system for internal errors since such errors are considered to be completely localized difficulties for which the recovery applied by the process involved is adequate (this does not preclude an individual process from maintaining a private error history, for example, to identify persistent internal errors).

Whether an error in a process can be considered an internal error or not will be very system dependent. The error handler makes this determination on the basis of two questions.

1) Is the particular error one for which processes are permitted to attempt local recovery?
2) Does the process in which the error occurred have the means of attempting local recovery for this particular error? For example, did the designer include a suitable exception handler?

If local recovery is permitted and available, then the error handler allows the process to initiate its own recovery capability (such as exception handling or recovery blocks). Only if this recovery apparently succeeds is the error finally classed as internal. Otherwise, the error will be dealt with as an external or pervasive error.

An error can be suspected to be pervasive if multiple non-internal errors occur in a single frame. A persistent external error is suggested if an external error recurs frequently in a particular process. Frequent recurrence of pervasive errors indicates a persistent pervasive error. Quantification of "multiple" and "frequent" in the above yields a well-defined classification algorithm for use by the error handler.

It is suggested here that if an external error has occurred in a frame, then any further occurrence of a noninternal error in that frame should be classified as a pervasive error. It is preferrable for the error handler to err, if at all, on the side of caution.

	4	0	0	0	0	0	0
Process	3	0	1	1	1	0	0
Number	2	0	0	0	0	0	0
	1	0	0	0	0	0	0
		Frames					

Fig. 6. Error matrix example

The simple iterative structure of many existing real-time systems suggests that a less rigid approach can be adopted toward determining the persistence of an external error. A straightforward frequency test seems appropriate, for example, an external error in process P could be considered persistent if an external error in P had occurred either in each of the n previous frames, or in p of the q previous frames (where n, p, and q are integers selected by the system designer). A stricter version of the same test might be considered necessary to detect recurring pervasive errors.

The information needed by the error handler in order to classify errors is most simply maintained by recording the recent error history of the processes in a bit matrix E, called the process error matrix, whose row index ranges over the processes of the system and whose column index runs from zero to q, where q is the value employed in the frequency test above. At the beginning of a frame, all the elements in column zero of E are set to zero. If a noninternal error occurs in process Pi, then the column zero, row i element of E is set to one. At the end of each frame, a one place logical right shift is applied to each row of the matrix. Thus, a value of one in position Eij indicates the occurrence of a noninternal error in process Pi in the jth preceding frame to that which is current. Fig. 6 shows an example of a process error matrix as it might appear at the beginning of a frame for a system of four processes in which process 3 has experienced errors in each of the last three frames. It may be convenient to record the incidence of pervasive errors in a supplementary bit vector which records, for each of the last q frames, whether a noninternal error occurred in two or more processes.

VII. Recovery and Continued Service

A. Internal Errors

Recovery from internal errors is only attempted for those errors for which explicit provision has been made in the system design. Techniques for internal recovery by a process include ad hoc repair as a part of a local exception handler [8] such as a PL/I "ON" unit, or a more general approach such as the systematic state restoration employed by recovery blocks. Continued service is provided in an arbitrary fashion following recovery in an exception handler and more systematically by the alternates in a recovery block under the constraint of having to satisfy the acceptance test. It is inappropriate to discuss the response to internal errors in greater detail because in any given set of circumstances, recovery is highly dependent on the structure of the individual processes involved.

It is important to be aware that the processing of internal errors may be unsuccessful and provision must be made to detect this situation and signal an external error. Detection is trivial when using recovery blocks since it corresponds to exhausting the set of alternates. It is more difficult with exception handling because consistency checks of the recovery must be programmed explicitly. Signaling the external error may take any form which is appropriate for the system involved.

B. External Errors

The recovery used for external errors will depend upon whether or not the process is engaged in an exchange. For a process which is not, a suitable state can be restored by a simple reset mechanism as discussed in Section IV. Under software control, values of input data for the process can be established in preparation for execution of a suitable alternate.

For a process engaged in an exchange, the recovery can be similar but must involve all the processes in the exchange. A suitable initial state must be established for each so that alternates can be executed for each.

It has been suggested [9] that in most real-time systems there are certain processes in which any error leads to a system failure which is critical. Such processes are called critical processes. Other processes are not critical in that if they are in error, the resulting system failure is not critical. An example of the former might be a process responsible for engine throttle settings, while an example of the latter might be a process which provides noncritical information for display. Classification of processes in this way is the responsibility of the system designer but it must be borne in mind that a process may be regarded as noncritical in the presence of transient external errors but may have to be regarded as critical in the presence of persistent external errors. For example, an external error occurring in a process providing information such as fuel level or engine temperature for display, may cause the display to blink or present erroneous information for an instant if the error is transient. This is probably of no concern. However, a persistent error in that process could lead to a complete loss of the information and may require termination of whatever mission is in progress.

Three general approaches to recovery and continued service are possible following the detection of an external error. They are as follows.
1) No special processing. The error is ignored and the system continues trying to provide service.
2) Provision of behavior that is acceptable in the short term but is inferior to that intended from the process in which the error is deemed to have occurred.

3) Provision of behavior equivalent to the intended behavior of the process in which the error is deemed to have occurred.

Approach 1 could be considered for processes which are classified as non-critical but for no others. It is not recommended even under these circumstances since there is always the danger that an untreated error could have unanticipated side effects.

Approach 2 corresponds to the use of recovery blocks as proposed by Hecht [9]. Although it was suggested in the context of timing errors, this approach is equally applicable to other external errors. The occurrence or a fault in a primary process is handled by the execution or an alternate providing degraded service. It is interesting to note that several simple alternates are possible. In particular, in real-time systems with short frame times it is often acceptable to reuse the outputs of the previous frame as the outputs for the frame in which the error occurred. This is known as the "skip-frame" strategy. Another possibility is some form of extrapolation based on data from several previous frames. For example, an acceptable output might be generated by adding the difference between the outputs of the two previous frames to the output of the previous frame.

Such simple strategies are attractive but great care must be exercised in their use if interprocess communication is taking place. If the communication is between processes which execute sequentially, outputs which are satisfactory for receiving processes must be generated by the alternate. If the communication is between processes which execute concurrently, the process which is in error will have been involved in an exchange and so it is necessary to perform state restoration for all processes in the exchange. For example, suppose a set of processes are designed to produce commands to control surfaces of an aircraft and they communicate in an exchange while performing their calculations. If one of them is in error, the outputs of all of them will have to be mistrusted. Alternates for all of the processes in the exchange will have to be used in such cases. Although the skip-frame strategy seems simple, in practice it may not be because much more processing is needed than simply the preparation of a suitable output for a single process.

Approach 3 is similar to approach 2 but assumes that nondegraded outputs must be generated on every frame regardless of the occurrence of faults. In practice this approach will be required only rarely in the treatment of transient external errors. Most real-time systems seem able to operate acceptably despite momentary degradation of service and, if an external error is truly transient, approach 2 will often be appropriate. If an external error is persistent, repeated use of approach 2 is very likely to result in system failure eventually. For example, repeated use of the skip-frame strategy amounts to the system repeatedly ignoring changes in the external environment. The primary intent of most real-time systems is prompt response to changes in the external environment.

Hecht [9] has proposed the design of a real-time executive which will remove a defective process from the system and replace it by a new version. Using the model and error classification scheme proposed here, this amounts to responding to a persistent external error by replacing the relevant process with a substitute. This substitute should be completely equivalent in its interfaces to the rest of the system but constructed differently so that, hopefully, it will not become erroneous under the circumstances which caused the original process to become erroneous. It is worth noting that even when a defective process has been removed, it can still serve as a stand-by spare in case the substituted process is found to be defective under different circumstances at a later time.

Thus, provision of continued service depends on whether the external error is transient or persistent. Both types can occur and so provision must be made for both. This suggests that every primary program should be supplemented by at least one alternate program capable of providing degraded service to cope with transient external errors and another version of the primary program to cope with persistent external errors.

C. Pervasive Errors

Pervasive errors are the most serious of the error classes. The notion of critical and noncritical processes does not apply in the presence of a pervasive error. The fact that the error is pervasive means that, in the absence of fault tolerance, failure of critical processes is very likely even if the process error matrix E only indicates the occurrence of errors in supposedly noncritical processes. So much damage has probably been done that critical processes will almost certainly enter erroneous states.

Strategies are limited by the gravity of the situation. The error will be classified initially as transient and the only practical approach to continued service is to use the simple skip-frame strategy discussed above. The time required to attempt the execution of more elaborate alternates for many processes is almost certainly unacceptable. If the error is indeed transient then the skip-frame strategy is probably adequate anyway.

If the error turns out to be persistent and pervasive then it is extremely unlikely that the system will be able to provide any acceptable service. Treatment of the error during its initial transient classification will have attempted to ensure that acceptable service was maintained but such treatment cannot continue. The only viable automatic treatment for persistent pervasive errors is complete replacement of the software. If provisions for recovery and continued service have been made for external errors, there will be a second version of each process available and the replacement of each process by the second version amounts to total software replacement. Once again, recovery can be handled by a simple reset.

VIII. Conclusion

A classification scheme for errors and a technique for the provision of software fault tolerance in cyclic real-time systems have been presented. The technique is considered to be evidently practicable because of its relatively simple approach. It has been argued that many real-time systems have characteristics which make them particularly amenable to the inclusion of fault tolerance using this technique.

In summary, the technique requires that the process structure of a system be represented by a synchronization graph which is used by an executive as a specification of the relative times at which programs are to be executed and the way in which they will communicate during execution. Communication between concurrent processes is severely limited and may only take place between processes engaged in an exchange. A history of error occurrences is maintained by an error handler. When an error is detected, the error handler classifies it using the error history information and then initiates appropriate recovery action.

There are costs associated with the provision of fault tolerance; both in the implementation and operation of a system. Operational overhead is less important because it can be traded for an increase in hardware resources. However, the additional costs in design and construction of the software may be substantial. If two versions of a primary process are to be provided they must both receive equal care and attention in their preparation. It might be expected that this would more than double the total cost of the software but Gilb [6], [7] has argued that producing two versions of a software module should only cost about 10 percent more than a single version.

It must be remembered that in such critical systems as commercial air transports, the software cost is not a substantial portion of the total development cost. Copies of the software for additional aircraft cost nothing and so, for an entire fleet, the cost of producing high quality fault tolerant software may be insignificant compared to the total cost of producing the aircraft. Irrespective of the cost, in many cases the need for the utmost reliability dictates the need for fault tolerant systems.

Acknowledgement. It is a pleasure to acknowledge the very helpful comments on an earlier version of this paper which the authors received from B. Randell, R. H. Campbell, and the referees.

References

1. T. Anderson and P. A. Lee, Fault Tolerance, Principles and Practice, Englewood Cliffs, NJ: Prentice-Hall Int., 1981.
2. A. Avizienis, "Fault tolerant systems," IEEE Trans. Comput., vol. C-25, pp. 1304–1312, Dec. 1976.
3. R. H. Campbell, K. Horton, and G. G. Belford, "Simulations of a fault tolerant deadline mechanism," in Dig. Papers, FTCS, Madison, June 1979, pp. 95–101.
4. W. C. Carter, "Hardware fault tolerance," in Computing Systems Reliability – An Advanced Course, T. Anderson and B. Randell, Eds. Cambridge Univ. Press, 1979, pp. 211–263.
5. L. Chen and A. Avizienis, "N-version programming: A fault-tolerance approach to reliability of software operation," in Dig. Papers, FTCS, Toulouse, June 1978, pp. 3–9.
6. T. Gilb, "Parallel programming," Datamation, vol. 20, pp. 160–161, Oct. 1974.
7. T. Gilb, Software Metrics. Cambridge: Winthrop, 1977.
8. J. B. Goodenough, "Exception handling: Issues and a proposed notation," Commun. Ass. Comput. Mach., vol. 18, pp. 683–696, Dec. 1975.

9. H. Hecht, "Fault tolerant software for real-time applications," Comput. Surveys, vol. 8, pp. 391–407, Dec. 1976.

10. J. J. Horning et al., "A program structure for error detection and recovery," in Oper. Syst., Proc. Int. Symp (Lecture Notes in Comput. Sci.), vol. 16, E. Gelenbe and C. Kaiser, Eds. Berlin: Springer-Verlag, 1974, pp. 171–187. [Also Chap. 2]

11. K. H. Kim, "An approach to programmer-transparent coordination of recovering parallel processes and its efficient implementation rules," in Proc. Int. Conf. Parallel Processing, Detroit, MI, Aug. 1978, pp. 58–68.

12. H. Kopetz, "Software redundancy in real-time systems," in Proc. IFIP Congress 74, Stockholm. Amsterdam: North-Holland, Aug. 1974, pp. 182–186.

13. P. A. Lee, "A reconsideration of the recovery block scheme," Comput. J., vol. 21, pp. 306–310, Nov. 1978. [Also Chap. 2]

14. P. A. Lee, N. Ghani, and K. Heron, "A recovery cache for the PDP-11," IEEE Trans. Comput., vol. C-29, pp. 546–549, June 1980. [Also Chap. 2]

15. P. M. Melliar-Smith and B. Randell, "Software reliability: The role of programmed exception handling," in Proc. Conf. Language Design for Reliable Software, SIGPLAN Notices, Raleigh, vol. 12, Mar. 1977, pp. 95–100. [Also Chap. 3]

16. B. Randell, "System structure for software fault tolerance," IEEE Trans. Software Eng., vol. SE-1, pp. 220–232, Mar. 1975. [Also Chap. 1]

17. B. Randell, P. A. Lee, and P. C. Treleaven, "Reliability issues in computing system design," Comput. Surveys, vol. 10, pp. 123–165, June 1978.

18. D. L. Russell, "Process backup in consumer-producer systems," in Proc. 6th Symp. Oper. Syst. Principles, Nov. 1977, pp. 151–157.

19. "SAFEGUARD data-processing system," Bell Syst. Tech. J., vol. 54, special supplement, 1975.

20. S. K. Shrivastava, "Concurrent Pascal with backware error recovery," Software – Practice and Experience, vol. 9, pp. 1001–1020, 1021–1023, Dec. 1979. [Also Chap. 4]

21. S. K. Shrivastava and A. A. Akinpelu, "Fault tolerant sequential programming using recovery blocks," Comput. Lab., Univ. Newcastle, Tech. Rep. 122, Mar. 1978. [Also Chap. 2]

22. S. K. Shrivastava and J.-P. Banatre, "Reliable resource allocation between unreliable processes," IEEE Trans. Software Eng., vol. SE-4, pp. 230–241, May 1978. [Also Chap. 4]

23. "AGS Software Requirements Document," Sperry Flight Syst. Div., Sperry Rand Corp., Phoenix, File 5121.8085.14.6-1, 1979.

Chapter 5
Multilevel Systems

Introduction

A well known principle advocated for the construction of complex software systems is to structure the system into a hierarchy of interfaces (levels of abstraction). An interface may be characterized by the objects made available on that interface together with operations for manipulating them. In the literature, one frequently encounters diagrams such as that depicted in Fig. 1 (a), which is intended to indicate that a program such as P_j makes use of objects provided by the underlying interface L_i. The function of P_j is to maintain the interface L_j; that is, the (abstract) objects available on L_j have their concrete implementations in P_j. Since we are concerned with the provision of fault tolerance in computer systems, it is instructive at this point to re-examine the recovery block scheme of Chap. 2 as a two level system (see Fig. 1 b). The program P_0 implements the recovery cache scheme, thereby providing *recoverable store words* on interface L_0. An 'update a word' operation available on interface L_0 has its concrete implementation in program P_0, and essentially involves P_0 recording (if necessary) the prior value of the word in the cache before performing the update. Similarly, the operation 'recover' available on L_0 is implemented by P_0 by restoring the prior values of the relevant words. Thus the abstraction of backward recovery available to programs running over L_0 is supported by normal 'forward' actions of program P_0. We can take this idea further, and construct another interface L_1 that provides new sets of recoverable objects – this naturally leads us to the concept of multilevel recovery systems.

The three papers of this chapter explore fundamental ideas on the provision of recovery in multilevel systems. The work reported here owes its origin to the paper by Randell (see the second paper in Chap. 1) and the doctoral research work of Verhofstad [1]. In the first paper, Anderson, Lee and Shrivastava examine the nature of multilevel systems and propose a classification consisting of (i) *interpretive,* and (ii) *extended interpretive* multilevel systems and then go on to examine various issues concerned with the provision of recoverability in such systems. An example of an interpretive system with two levels is the machine

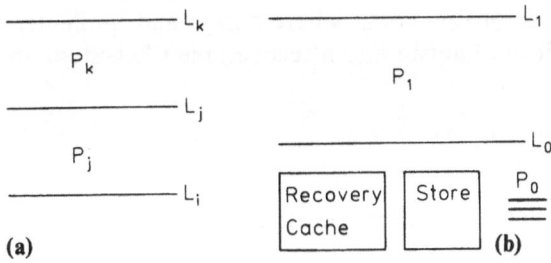

(a)　　　　　　　　　　　　(b)　　　**Fig. 1 a and b.** Multilevel systems

379

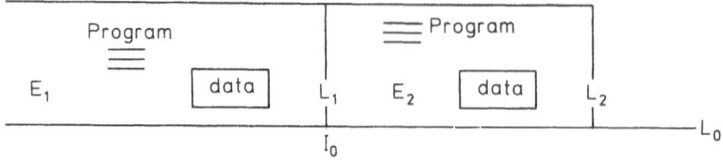

Fig. 2. Extended interpreter multilevel system

interface (L_0) supported by a microprogram (the interpreter for L_0) and a Pascal interpreter written over L_0, that maintains a new interface L_1 for executing Pascal programs. In an extended interpretive system, an interface L_i has many behavioural properties in common with L_{i-1}. As an example, consider a machine interface L_0 over which an operating system kernel has been implemented giving a new interface L_1. It is more appropriate to regard L_1 as an *extension* of L_0, since L_1 provides most of the 'machine instructions' of L_0, and in addition provides certain new objects (such as processes and semaphores). Anderson et - al. reserve the diagramatic notation employed in figure 1 for interpretive systems and use a different notation to depict an extended interpretive system (see Fig. 2). In Fig. 2, interface L_0 is supported by the interpreter I_0 and interface L_1 is an extension of L_0 and is maintained by the extension program E_1 and the interface L_0. Turning our attention to the provision of backward recovery on a given interface, Anderson et al. propose two types of recovery schemes, namely, *disjoint* and *inclusive*. The former recovery scheme is applicable to both types of multilevel systems while the latter scheme can only be applied to extended interpreter multilevel systems. The paper then goes on to discuss the strengths and weaknesses of the two recovery schemes. In the second paper, Anderson and Lee illustrate various aspects of the two recovery schemes by considering the design of a simple file system structured into three levels.

The last paper of this chapter, by Shrivastava, applies the concepts of multilevel recovery to distributed systems. The provision of backward recovery is of particular interest in distributed systems where failures such as lost messages and node crashes can introduce inconsistencies in stored data. Shrivastava considers the design of robust object managers that have recoverability and crash resistance properties. It is assumed that a program can invoke operations exported by a remote object by making use of *remote procedure calls*. Programs are taken to be atomic actions (see Chap. 4), and since a multilevel system structure is assumed, a user program (the 'outer most' atomic action) turns out to be composed from 'inner' atomic actions, giving rise to a nested atomic action computation. The concept of multilevel recovery and in particular its application to distributed systems forms the basis of some of the experimental work reported in the sixth chapter of this book, where design and implementation of a remote procedure call mechanism and a recoverable file system are presented.

Reference

1. J. S. M. Verhofstad, "The construction of recoverable multilevel systems", Ph. D. thesis, The University of Newcastle upon Tyne, 1977.

A Model of Recoverability in Multilevel Systems

T. ANDERSON, P. A. LEE, and S. K. SHRIVASTAVA

Abstract. Backward error recovery (that is, resetting an erroneous state of a system to a previous error-free state) is an important general technique for recovery from errors in a system, especially those errors which were not foreseen. However, the provision of backward error recovery can be complex, particularly if the implementation of the system is "multilevel" and recovery is to be provided at a number of these levels. This paper discusses two distinct categories of multilevel system, and then examines in detail the issues involved in providing backward error recovery in both types of system.

Index Terms. Error recovery, interpreters, multilevel systems.

Introduction

The demand for ever more powerful, flexible, and convenient interfaces to computational systems has led to the construction of increasingly complex hardware and software intended to support such interfaces. Unfortunately, the complexity inherent in the design and construction of these systems has been, and is, a major source of unreliability in their operation. Thus, attempts have been made to limit and master complexity by means of various design and implementation methodologies. In particular, approaches involving structuring a system into a hierarchy of interfaces (or levels of abstraction) are often advocated, and have been adopted in the construction of some systems; for example, the THE multiprogramming system [5] and the VENUS operating system [8]. While such "multilevel" approaches are certainly laudable, it is widely recognized that complex systems will, in general, always contain residual design faults; for some systems, specifically those with a high reliability requirement, there is a need for tolerance of such faults. Residual design faults are by their nature unanticipated and unanticipatable and, in consequence, are particularly difficult to deal with. However, backward error recovery is an important general technique for recovery from the errors caused by such faults, and involves resetting the state of the system to a previous (and hopefully error-free) state. Given this recovery capability, it may be possible to enhance the reliability of the system by invoking recovery when erroneous situations are detected.

This paper is concerned with the issues involved in the provision of backward error recovery to independent sequential processes in multilevel systems. After identifying two distinct categories of interface support for multilevel systems, a model of the implementation of backward error recovery for each category is developed and examined in depth. Techniques for error detection and fault treatment are not covered: Randell et al. [11] discuss these topics and both backward and forward error recovery in some detail.

381

Multilevel Systems

Many systems can be described as multilevel in that a hierarchy of abstract interfaces (or levels) can be discerned in their implementation. An abstract interface may be conveniently thought of as being characterized by a language providing objects and operations to manipulate those objects. A useful notion is that of the state of an interface, which may be regarded as the set of the current states of the objects provided by that interface.

Computational systems are usually sufficiently complex that numerous interfaces could be delineated within the implementation of such a system. However, examination of the implementation will usually enable certain significant interfaces to be identified. The most significant interfaces arising in the implementation of a system are those interfaces supported by interpretation, as described below.

In Fig. 1, each interface Li is implemented by means of a program Ii which is executed on the interface Li − 1. Every interaction with the interface Li (corresponding to the execution of an operation in the program Ii + 1) is, in fact, directly supported by means of the program Ii. Any "abstract" object available in Li has a "concrete" representation as a set of objects in Li − 1 which are managed by Ii and held in a data area maintained for this purpose by Ii. The program Ii is referred to as an interpreter for Li.

Example: An APL interpreter is a program which, after loading, is executed on an interface characterized by a machine language and supports an interface characterized by (the internal representation of) APL source code.

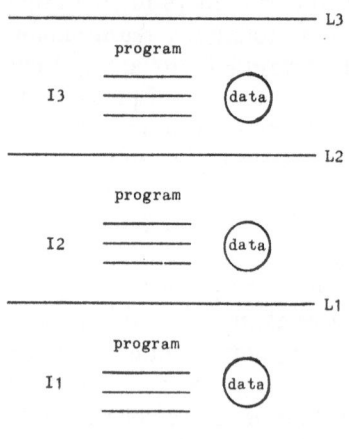

Fig. 1. Interpretive multilevel system

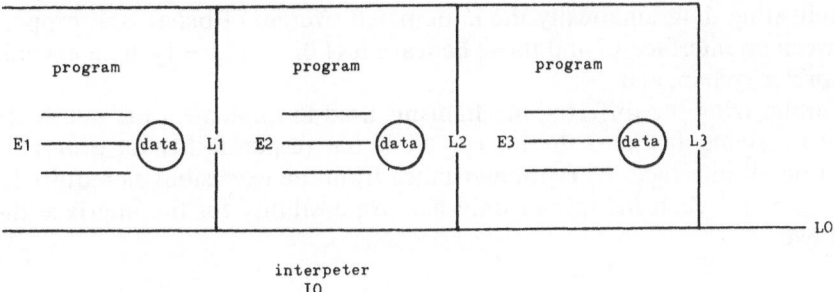

Fig. 2. Extended interpreter multilevel system

A further category of interfaces is important in the implementation of multilevel systems and usually occurs in the following circumstances. If the implementer of a system is presented with an interface Li − 1 and wishes to provide an interface Li such that Li and Li − 1 have many behavioral properties in common, then it may not be necessary to support Li by means of another level of interpretation. If Li − 1 makes available sufficiently powerful extension facilities, it will be possible to provide Li by generating an extension of Li − 1. Run time subroutine or procedure mechanisms can be regarded as a commonly available, though limited, interpreter extension facility, whereby new operators can be built up as programmed sequences of those originally provided. More powerful mechanisms could allow the addition of new types and even notations, as well as permitting the removal of features of the original interface. Ideally, the extension facilities would still be available in Li so that further extensions could be made if required.

Note that the above discussion refers to extending an interface at run time; indeed, all of the interfaces considered in this paper should be regarded as existing at run time, and not merely present in a source program before perhaps being thrown away during compilation.

In Fig. 2 the interface L0 is supported by an interpreter I0 which provides extension facilities. Each interface Li (i = 1, 2, 3) is constructed as an extension of the interface Li − 1, the extension being implemented by means of a program Ei, which is executed on the interface Li − 1. The program Ei is referred to here as an interpreter extension. Every interaction with the interface Li is first examined by the underlying interpreter I0, which determines whether that interaction is directly supported by I0 itself or, if not, which of the available interpreter extensions (Ej, j ≦ i) does support that interaction. Thus the interactions of a program may be supported by any lower extensions or by the underlying interpreter. Any "abstract" object available in Li, other than those directly supported by I0, has a "concrete" representation as a set of objects in one of the interfaces Lj (j < i). This set of objects is managed by Ej + 1 in a data area maintained for this purpose by Ej + 1.

The extended interpreter multilevel system of Fig. 2 is portrayed differently to the interpretive system of Fig. 1 with the intention of:

1) Indicating diagramatically the anticipated overlap of behavioral properties between an interface Li and those beneath it (L0, . . . , Li − 1) in an extended interpreter system, and

2) Emphasizing the differing mechanisms used to implement the interfaces of the two systems. In Fig. 2 the interpreter I0 has responsibility for programs executed on all interfaces Li (with assistance from the extensions as required), whereas in Fig. 1 each interpreter only has responsibility for the interface directly above.

Example: The nucleus of most operating systems can be regarded as an interpreter extension which provides a user interface from the underlying hardware interface by removing certain privileged instructions and adding a set of "operating-system" call instructions. A collection of system procedures often provides a further extension. Specifically, the programming language Concurrent Pascal [3] provides a facility whereby an operating system (written in Concurrent Pascal) can make available procedures that can be invoked by user programs (written in Sequential Pascal). The Concurrent and Sequential Pascal programs are both executed by the same underlying interpreter, and the procedures which are made available to the user programs can be regarded as interpreter extensions.

The potential advantage to be gained from using an interpreter extension to implement a new interface (when this is possible) in preference to a further level of interpretation is in avoiding the overhead that the latter entails. Whenever an interaction on the new interface could be directly supported by the underlying interpreter, an interpreter extension implementation will ensure that this direct support is available. Both techniques can, of course, be used in the same multilevel system; for example, in Fig. 1 an interpreter Ii could be implemented by first extending Li − 1 to a more convenient interface before constructing an interpreter for Li. However, it should be noted that to a program being executed on an interface it is completely immaterial whether that interface is implemented by an interpreter extension or not − this difference can only be determined from an examination of the details of the implementation of an interface, and not merely from the properties of the interface itself.

Recovery on an Interface

Before the problems of recovery in multilevel systems can be considered, it is necessary to introduce terminology and discuss the recovery of a program at one level in a system.

In this paper, recoverability is taken to mean the ability to recover an earlier state of an interface, thereby undoing the effects of operations that were performed on the interface. This ability is referred to as backward error recovery; backward error recovery necessitates the recording of recovery data, which can be used to restore an earlier state of the interface.

To be more specific, this paper considers recovery mechanisms which make the following features available to programs executed on an interface.

1) The interface supports both recoverable and unrecoverable objects.
2) Recovery points can be established which ensure that the current state of the recoverable objects of the interface is (at least conceptually) recorded so that it can be restored if necessary.
3) Recovery points can be discarded with the effect that information maintained for recovery to those recovery points is discarded.

Clearly, a recoverable object is one for which recovery is provided. In contrast, unrecoverable objects are objects for which state restoration is not available or appropriate for recovery. As such, unrecoverable objects can also be used to model the effects of the external environment — for example, an external clock. Verhofstad [14] has discussed the provision and uses of both recoverable and unrecoverable objects. For simplicity, this paper will regard communication between processes as being unrecoverable. Techniques by which a measure of recoverability can be provided for process interactions in a single-level system have been discussed by Davies [4], Randell [10], and Russell [12].

A recovery point is said to be active from when it is established until it is discarded. The term recovery region will be used to refer to the period for which a recovery point is active (this will usually correspond to a section of the text of a program). A further useful notion is that of the recovery environment associated with a recovery point. The recovery environment is that set of recoverable objects which are available on the interface at the time a recovery point is established. In a program, the recovery environment would consist of the set of recoverable variables that were in existence at the time the recovery point was established, but would exclude those created subsequently.

It is assumed that in a general recoverable system a program can have more than one recovery point active. When an active recovery point is discarded, some commitment occurs, to the extent that recovery to that recovery point is no longer available. Various different strategies can be adopted for determining the order in which active recovery points should be discarded and, in consequence, the recovery regions of a program may partially or totally overlap. Fig. 3(a) illustrates a program with partially overlapping recovery regions; Fig. 3(b) illustrates a program with totally overlapped regions.

Example: A programming language construct called the recovery block has been introduced by Horning et al. [7]. This construct enables a program to establish recovery points, while constraining recovery regions to be properly nested. Russell [12] has discussed an example in which recovery regions are not nested.

The model of recovery presented in this paper makes no assumptions about the extent to which recovery regions overlap. However, it is worth noting that discarding one out of a number of active recovery points may involve much more than merely discarding the associated recovery data, since otherwise recovery to the remaining recovery points may be compromised.

It is possible that although two recovery points are simultaneously active, their respective recovery environments may have no objects in common with each other. Such recovery environments are said to be disjoint. The notion of

385

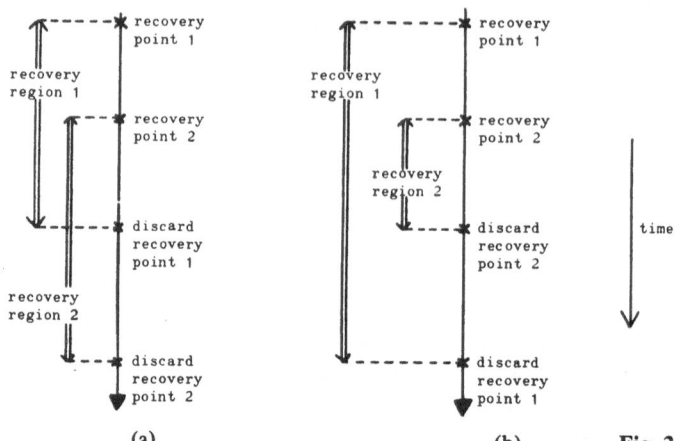

Fig. 3. Multiple recovery points

disjoint recovery environments has little significance when recovery of a program on a single interface is considered, but will be returned to when recovery in multilevel systems is described.

The previous discussion has been concerned with the recoverable objects of a program. The question remains as to what happens to any unrecoverable objects used by a program within a recovery region. Clearly, the answer is that no recovery data will be generated for such objects; consequently, if recovery is invoked, the current state of the unrecoverable objects will prevail. If in these circumstances some form of restoration of the unrecoverable objects is required, then the program would have to perform this restoration itself. It would, therefore, have to record some information specifically for this purpose. The terminology introduced by Verhofstad [14] refers to the data structure used to hold this information as the log. Since the log contains information to be used by the program for recovery, this information must not be lost when recovery is invoked.

Having discussed recovery on a single interface, and distinguished between interpreters and interpreter extensions as techniques for supporting the interfaces of a multilevel system, it is now possible to consider the problems of providing recoverability to such interfaces.

Recovery in Interpretive Multilevel Systems

The first problem to be considered is that of providing recoverability to an interface completely supported by an interpreter (such as Li and Ii in Fig. 1). If the recovery features previously identified are to be supported, then the interpreter must include programs and their data structures such that all information necessary for the recoverability of that interface is maintained. (Clearly, this is true for any of the features supported by the interpreter.) Those programs which are concerned with providing recoverability will be termed recovery programs.

386

There will, in general, be three distinct recovery program parts concerned with the following actions:
1) recording recovery data;
2) performing recovery;
3) performing commitment.

There are several strategies that could be adopted for the recording of recovery data. The simplest method is that of recording a complete checkpoint, in which the state of all of the objects within the current recovery environment is recorded when a recovery point is established. Although this is the simplest approach, it has the disadvantage that the state of all of the objects in the current recovery environment has to be recorded, despite the possibility that many of those objects might not be changed. This disadvantage is often mitigated in practical systems by only recording recovery data for those objects that are updated; for example, the COPRA system [9] attempts to assess in advance which objects fall into this category. Alternatively, recovery data can be recorded dynamically (that is, the state of an object is saved just before that object is updated) in what may be termed an incremental checkpoint.

Example: A highly optimized technique for recording recovery data (in conjunction with recovery blocks) was proposed by Horning et al. [7]. This technique, called the recursive/recovery cache, consisted of recording incremental checkpoints in such a way that a minimum of recovery data were maintained.

Audit trails [2] are a further strategy for providing recoverability, where the recovery data essentially provide a log [6] of the operations that were performed on the objects.

Whatever technique is employed for recording recovery data, it must only ensure that recovery and commitment can be performed as required. The concepts discussed in this paper are independent of the strategy adopted for recording and committing recovery data.

In Fig. 4, L1 is a recoverable interface supported by an interpreter I1 which contains recovery programs and their data structures. The mapping of the data space of I2 to its concrete representation in that of I1 is also indicated.

Changes to the objects in the data space of I2 are implemented (by I1) as changes to their concrete representations in the data space of I1. It is the responsibility of the recovery program of I1 to ensure that appropriate information is recorded as recovery data. Should it be necessary to restore the objects of I2, the recovery program of I1 uses these recovery data to update the concrete representations such that the objects of I2 have the appearance of having been restored. It may also be observed that backward error recovery is provided to I2 by means of normal (forward) computation of the recovery program part of I1, as noted by Randell [10].

It is important to observe that any recovery environment on L1 is disjoint from those on L0. Thus an active recovery point at one level is completely independent of those in other levels. (This point will be returned to subsequently when recovery in extended interpreter systems is discussed.) It should be clear that the provision of recoverability in L1 does not imply that higher interfaces are also recoverable. For L2 to be recoverable, I2 would have to include recov-

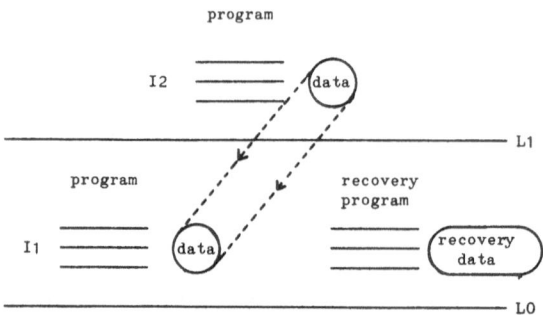

Fig. 4. Recovery structures in an interpreter

ery program and data to support that recoverability, just as I1 does to support the recoverability of L1. Use that I2 makes of the recovery features of L1 in order to provide a more reliable mode of support to L2 is completely independent of whether or not I2 itself provides recovery features in L2. (It may be possible for an interpreter to use the recovery facilities provided to it to achieve a more direct implementation of recoverability for the interface it supports. However, the implications and implementation of such a scheme are not at all straightforward.)

For I1 to provide unrecoverable objects in L1 is very simple. For these objects I1 records no recovery data. The only impact that the presence of unrecoverable objects in L1 has on I2 is that, if such objects are used within recovery regions by I2, then obviously their prior values could not be restored in the event of recovery actually being invoked. Consequently, I2 will have to log its own data for recovery, as discussed in the previous section.

Example: The EML system described by Anderson and Kerr [1] has exactly the structure shown in Fig. 4. In this system, the underlying interface L0 was that provided by (PDP-11) hardware, while the interface L1 was supported by an interpreter which emulated a high-level abstract machine architecture. The interpreter implemented a recovery cache mechanism, enabling programs executing on L1 to make use of recovery blocks.

In summary, the recoverability of a hierarchy of interfaces in an interpretive system is straightforward in concept.

Recovery in Extended Interpreter Multilevel Systems

This section considers the problems of recovery in a multilevel system implemented by a sequence of interpreter extensions. It is assumed that the underlying interface presented to the interpreter extensions (for example, L0 in Fig. 5) supports both recoverable and unrecoverable objects, and permits recovery points to be established and discarded.

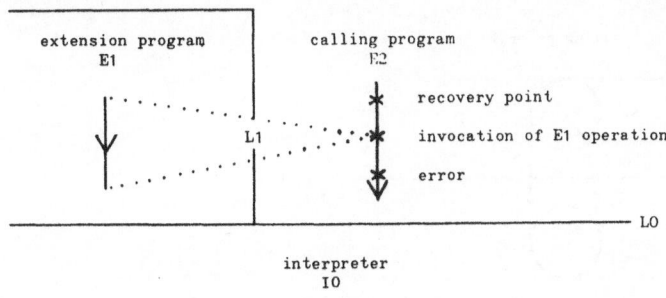

Fig. 5. Invocation of an interpreter extension

The principal objective of an interpreter extension is, as its name suggests, to extend an interface with new kinds of abstract object. Clearly, it is desirable for an extension to also provide recovery features for these abstract objects; it should extend the recovery features of the existing interface to include these objects. Issues concerning the provision of recoverability for the new objects require closer examination, since two distinct forms of organization for their recovery can be identified. These two organizations are termed the disjoint recovery scheme and the inclusive recovery scheme. The difference between the schemes stems from the two ways in which an extension is regarded as fitting into a multilevel system; namely, where the extension is a) considered to be a part of the underlying interpreter (disjoint from any calling program), or b) considered to be an inclusive component of the calling program. The main consequence of this distinction is in the treatment of the recoverable objects used by an extension; specifically, whether or not they are regarded as being within a recovery environment of a calling program. These issues are examined in depth in the rest of this section.

Consider the situation depicted in Fig. 5, which will be used as an example in the following discussions. This system has an interpreter extension E1 which is (indirectly) invoked by a program E2. Both of these programs are interpreted by I0, the underlying interpreter. The calling program has established a recovery point, and subsequently invoked an operation supported by E1. To E2, this operation appears to be indivisible, as do any of the operations interpreted directly by I0. (Indeed, E2 should not be able to distinguish between an operation supported by I0 and one supported by E1.)

In this example, it is assumed that all objects in the abstract data space of E2 are recoverable, and that some of these are maintained by the extension E1, while the rest are maintained by the interpreter I0. This is indicated in Fig. 6 by dividing A2, the abstract data space of E2, into two parts; these two parts have concrete representations A1 (in E1) and C2 (in I0), respectively. In fact, A1 is in the abstract data space of E1 and has its own separate concrete representation C1, which, in this example, is maintained solely by I0.

At some time following the return from the extension program E1, an error has been detected in E2 (Fig. 5); consequently, E2 has to be backed up to the

389

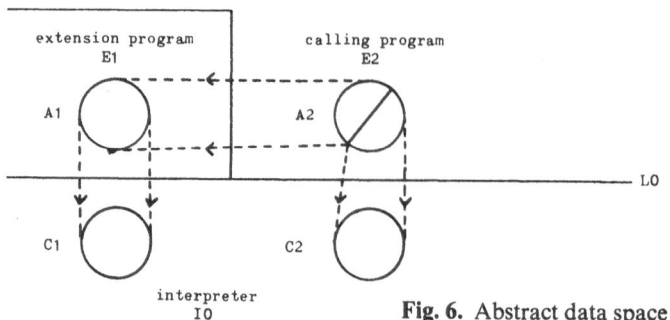

Fig. 6. Abstract data space mappings

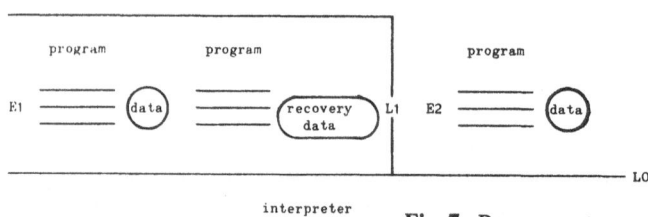

Fig. 7. Recovery structures in an interpreter extension

recovery point it had previously established. In order to achieve this backup, the recoverable objects used by E2 must be restored to their previous (abstract) state.

Certainly, I0 can restore those objects it is directly maintaining on behalf of E2 (i.e., those whose concrete representation is C2 in Fig. 6). The question arises as to how the abstraction of recoverability is provided for the objects used by E2 which are supported by the extension E1.

Consider first the situation in which this support is achieved through the use of unrecoverable objects (i.e., A1 in Fig. 6 contains unrecoverable objects only). In this situation it will be necessary for the extension to provide both recovery programs and data (as shown in Fig. 7) so that it can restore the abstract state of the relevant E2 objects. These recovery programs will need to be automatically invoked (by I0) as required. For example, in a complete checkpointing scheme, when the calling program establishes a recovery point, I0 would record a checkpoint and then invoke the recovery program of the extension so that it could also record a checkpoint of those objects it was maintaining for the program.

In a more general situation, an extension may well make use of both unrecoverable and recoverable objects for its implementation of new recoverable objects. A second question therefore follows; namely, should the recoverable objects used by the extension be regarded as being within a recovery environment of the calling program, and, in consequence, should they be included in the recovery data recorded by the underlying interpreter for the calling program? By analogy with the interpretive multilevel system discussed in the previous section, the answer would be no — in an interpretive system the recovery

390

environment of one level is completely independent of that of the level above. If this view is adopted for extended interpreter systems, the recoverable objects used by an extension should not be regarded as being within a recovery environment of the calling program. An extension would therefore be completely responsible for all of the recovery of the objects it was maintaining. Indeed, this would be the behavior expected if the underlying interpreter itself provided the features of the extension. To obtain this behavior in an extended interpreter system, it is only necessary to stipulate that the recovery environments of a program be disjoint from those of any supporting extensions. The scheme of recovery which exhibits this property in an extended interpreter system is referred to as the disjoint recovery scheme. When a program establishes a recovery point, the disjoint recovery scheme must ensure that the recovery environment of that recovery point only encompasses the abstract objects available on the interface, and not any of the objects used to implement those abstract objects. Thus, for example, referring to Figs. 5 and 6, when E2 establishes a recovery point, 10 will only record recovery data for those recoverable objects represented in C2, and not for any of those represented in C1. (E1 will, of course, be invoked to record recovery data for objects it is maintaining for E2.)

However, the disjoint recovery scheme does not prevent an extension from establishing its own recovery points. In this situation, any recoverable objects used by the extension within a recovery region would behave normally. When the local recovery point was discarded, all of the recovery data being maintained for the recovery point would be discarded.

Generalizing, the recovery in a multilevel system implemented by interpreter extensions with the disjoint recovery scheme would be as follows. Following the detection of an error in program Ei, the underlying interpreter would restore all of the recoverable objects that it was directly maintaining for Ei. The interpreter would then signal all of the extensions that could be called directly by Ei (in the set E1, . . . , Ei − 1) so that they could perform recovery for any objects they were directly maintaining for Ei. Following the completion of these actions, the program Ei will have been recovered and can be restarted as necessary. Conceptually, the interpreter also has to signal all of the directly accessible extensions in E1, . . . , Ei − 1 whenever program Ei creates or discards a recovery point, so that the extensions can, in a manner similar to that of the underlying interpreter, record or commit the necessary recovery data for the program Ei. Optimizations of this conceptual organization are clearly possible.

A significant chracteristic of the disjoint recovery scheme is that the behavior of an extension with respect to both recoverable and unrecoverable objects is uniform, in so far as the state restoration of the new abstract objects is concerned. The scheme also models the recovery behavior of the well-understood multilevel interpreter system.

However, the scheme does have a disadvantage which becomes apparent if the recoverable objects used in an extension are reconsidered. As discussed previously, one of the main aims of an interpreter extension is to extend a given interface without incurring the inefficiency of reimplementing all of the features it did not wish to change (as would happen in an interpreter system). However, as far as the recoverable objects used in the disjoint scheme are concerned, the extension will have to reimplement some form of recovery for these recoverable objects, even though that supplied by the underlying interface may have been exactly what was required. For example, if the interface L0 in Fig. 6 provided recoverable objects only, the extension E1 would still have to reimplement recoverability for E2, even though restoration of A1 by I0 is equivalent to the restoration of the corresponding objects in A2.

It is this apparent inefficiency which leads to an alternative answer to the question concerning the behavior of the recoverable objects used in an extension; namely, that the recoverable objects used in an extension are regarded as being within the recovery environment of the calling program, and are therefore automatically restored when the calling program is backed up. This recovery scheme is called the inclusive recovery scheme.

An example of the behavior of the inclusive recovery scheme can be obtained by reconsidering the system depicted in Figs. 5 and 6. The recoverable objects in A1 (Fig. 6) are then regarded as being within the recovery environment of the calling program E2. Consequently, when E2 establishes a recovery point, any recovery data generated for the recoverable A1 objects will be maintained with the recovery data associated with E2. (Of course, the extension still has local recovery features available to it.) When the calling program E2 is backed up, the extension E1 can assume, when it is invoked by I0, that any recoverable objects used by it will have been automatically restored; to maintain its abstractions, E1 therefore needs only to change, as necessary, the unrecoverable objects used in the concrete state. As in the disjoint case, the underlying interpreter I0 will have to signal the extension to obtain this recovery.

If the recoverable objects used by an extension were all objects supported directly by the underlying interpreter (as was the case in Fig. 6), then only this signal would be required. However, in general, some of the recoverable objects used by an extension may themselves be implemented by lower extensions (i.e., to the "left"), as indicated in Fig. 8.

If E3 were backed up, then E2 would be signaled to perform any recovery actions on the unrecoverable objects it used on behalf of E3. However, E2 would expect all of its recoverable objects to be recovered automatically, although some of them had been implemented by E1.

Clearly, therefore, when a program Ei is backed up, all of the lower extensions E1, ..., Ei − 1 will be required to return the abstract objects they are

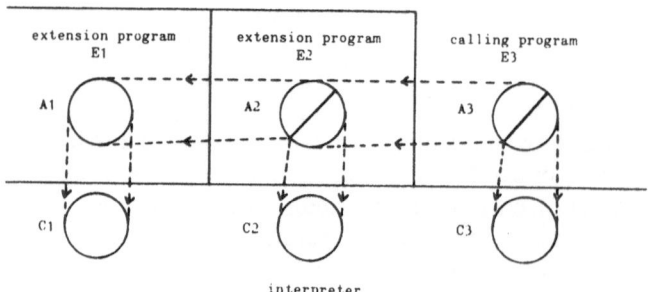

Fig. 8. Multilevel abstract data space mappings

392

maintaining to their prior states, and the underlying interpreter I0 must ensure that this occurs, signaling all of the relevant extensions until all of these restorations have been completed. At this point, execution of the program Ei can be resumed. As before, the underlying interpreter will (conceptually) have to signal the extensions E1, . . . , Ei − 1 whenever a program Ei establishes or discards a recovery point.

Example: Suppose that (as depicted in Fig. 8) a program E3 makes use of objects provided by E2 and I0, but makes no direct use of any objects provided by E1. In this situation, a significant distinction between the two recovery schemes can be exemplified. In the inclusive scheme, recovery of E3 would result in the recovery programs of both E2 and E1 being invoked by I0, whereas in the disjoint scheme, recovery of E3 would result in the recovery program of E2 being invoked but not that of E1.

The signaling of extensions in a "left" to "right" order (i.e., least to most abstract) seems to be the most natural order. Certainly, the interpreter I0 will be aware of this order, because each extension would have to be identified to the interpreter when it was created, so that it could be subsequently invoked. In fact, the ordering of the signaling is only significant in two somewhat improbable cases: first, if the unrestored values of recoverable objects were of interest to the recovery implemetation of an extension; and second, if the extension wished to update a recovered object. In the disjoint recovery scheme discussed previously, the signaling order would have no effect, because each extension is responsible for all of its recovery, and does not depend on any lower extensions to achieve this automatically.

The main advantage of the inclusive recovery scheme is that mentioned previously; namely, that an extension can rely on the automatic recovery of any recoverable objects that it uses an extension which only used recoverable objects would not therefore have to provide any programs or data for recovery purposes. Note that, unlike the disjoint scheme, the behavior of the extension with respect to its recoverable and unrecoverable objects is not uniform.

An important disadvantage of the inclusive recovery scheme stems from the fact that it is difficult (although not impossible) for this scheme to model the behavior of the disjoint scheme; one specific situation in which it is incorrect for the inclusive recovery rules to apply is when the extension is executing the recovery program parts discussed previously. Although these program parts are executed by an extension on behalf of a higher level program, their recovery environments must be regarded as being local to the extension (that is, disjoint from recovery environments of the higher level program) in contrast to the normal situation for the inclusive scheme. The need for this behavior can be illustrated by considering that part of the recovery program which records recovery data. If the data structures used to hold this recovery data were taken to be within the recovery environment of the calling program, then any backing up of that program would result in those data structures being automatically recovered, thus erasing the recovery data stored by the extension.

The desired behavior could be achieved in two ways: first, by the extension (or the underlying interpreter) ensuring that the recovery program parts of an extension did not make use of any recoverable objects that were within the recovery environment of the calling program (for example, by constructing the recovery data structures from unrecoverable objects); and second, and more generally, by the underlying interpreter being able to distinguish between the programs and recovery programs of an extension, and thus determining when to apply the disjoint recovery rules. Note that these problems do not arise in the disjoint recovery scheme since all programs (including recovery programs) exhibit the required behavior.

It would appear, therefore, that an implementation of the inclusive recovery scheme would also be required to provide the features of the disjoint scheme, at least for use as previously described. Given this requirement, the availability of these features of the disjoint scheme could be extended to allow them to be used, as required, by any extension, since there may be other situations in which the inclusive recovery rules are not appropriate or convenient.

Conclusions

This paper has investigated the issues involved in the provision of recoverability in multilevel systems implemented both by interpreters and by interpreter extensions. In particular, recoverability in extended interpreter systems has been examined in detail, and two recovery schemes (disjoint and inclusive) described. The disjoint recovery scheme models the recovery behavior which is obtained in a multilevel interpretive system. As such, it shares advantages and disadvantages of interpretive systems. These are, respectively, conceptual simplicity and the inability to automatically inherit and make use of the recoverability of lower level objects. To avoid this disadvantage, the inclusive recovery scheme was suggested. However, it was shown that this scheme needs the features of the disjoint scheme for use in the recovery program parts of extensions.

It seems appropriate, therefore, that an underlying interpreter should be able to support both of these recovery schemes for the efficient implementation of recovery in multilevel systems.

It is of interest to relate the recovery schemes discussed in this paper to two experimental multilevel recoverable systems using interpreter extensions that have been implemented at the University of Newcastle upon Tyne, since these motivated our investigations. In one experimental system [14] a first extension implements a recoverable single-user filing system; subsequent extensions can be built on top of this filing system. This experimental system implements the inclusive recovery scheme, and relies on programmer discipline to ensure that the recovery program parts of the extensions do not generate any recovery information. Disjoint recovery is not available to the implementers of extensions.

The other recoverable system uses the disjoint recovery scheme to provide for recoverable resource allocation between many competing processes [13]. This system provides a facility whereby a program can create recoverable resource objects (called ports); creation of such an object is equivalent to establishing a new extension. The scope rules of ports ensure that the recovery environment of a port is disjoint from that of the creating program. Inclusive recovery is not available to the implementers of ports.

Experimentation with these systems should shed further light on the adequacy of the two recovery schemes for implementing recoverable multilevel systems by means of interpreter extensions. However, neither system includes facilities for recovery from process intercommunication, and any such intercommunication (for example, from one user of the filing system to a subsequent user) is regarded as unrecoverable. Work is in progress to extend the model presented in this paper to encompass systems providing recovery for communicating processes and shared objects. Appropriate architectures for implementing recoverable multilevel systems are also being examined.

Acknowledgement. We would like to express our gratitude to our fellow members of the Reliability Project, which is sponsored by the Science Research Council of Great Britain, at the University of Newcastle upon Tyne. In particular, we wish to thank R. Kerr, and acknowledge the many discussions that took place between the authors and J. Verhofstad in the initial stages of the preparation of this paper.

References

1. T. Anderson and R. Kerr, "Recovery blocks in action," in Proc. 2nd Int. Conf. Software Engineering (San Francisco, CA, Oct. 1976), pp. 447–457. [Also Chap. 2]
2. L. A. Bjork, "Generalised audit trail requirements and concepts for data base applications," IBM Syst. J., vol. 14, pp. 229–245, 1975.
3. P. Brinch Hansen, "The programming language Concurrent Pascal," IEEE Trans. Software Eng., vol. SE-1, pp. 199–207, June 1975.
4. C. T. Davies, "Recovery semantics for a DB/DC system," in Proc. 1973 ACM National Conf. (Atlanta, GA, Aug. 1973), pp. 136–141.
5. E. W. Dijkstra, "The structure of the "THE" multiprogramming system," Commun. Ass. Comput. Mach., vol. 11, pp. 341–346, May 1968.
6. J. N. Gray, "Notes on data base operating systems," in Lecture Notes in Computer Science 60. Berlin: Springer, 1978, pp. 393–481.
7. J. J. Horning et al., "A program structure for error detection and recovery," in Lecture Notes in Computer Science 16. Berlin: Springer, 1974, pp. 177–193. [Also Chap. 2]
8. B. H. Liskov, "The design of the Venus operating system," Commun. Ass. Comput. Mach., vol. 15, pp. 144–149, Mar. 1972.
9. C. Meraud, F. Browaeys, and G. Germain, "Automatic rollback techniques of the COPRA computer," in Proc. 6th IEEE Int. Symp. Fault-Tolerant Computing (Pittsburgh, PA, June 1976), pp. 23–29.
10. B. Randell, "System structure for software fault tolerance," IEEE Trans. Software Eng., vol. SE-1, pp. 220–232, June 1975. [Also Chap. 1]
11. B. Randell, P. A. Lee, and P. C. Treleaven, "Reliability issues in computing system design," Comput. Surveys, vol. 10, pp. 123–165, June 1978.
12. D. L. Russell, "Process backup in producer-consumer systems," in Proc. 6th Symp. Operating Systems Principles (West Lafayette, IN, Nov. 1977), pp. 151–157.
13. S. K. Shrivastava and J.-P. Banatre, "Reliable resource allocation between unreliable processes," IEEE Trans. Software Eng., vol. SE-4, pp. 230–241, May 1978. [Also Chap. 4]
14. J. S. M. Verhofstad, "The construction of recoverable multi-level systems," Ph.D. dissertation, University of Newcastle upon Tyne, 1977.

The Provision of Recoverable Interfaces

T. ANDERSON and P. A. LEE

Abstract. The recovery block scheme has been proposed as one method of providing fault tolerant software, and is dependent on the availability of recoverable interfaces so that any damage caused by an erroneous program can be repaired by backward error recovery. However, it is clear that the interface provided by the hardware in any practical system will contain unrecoverable objects. This paper investigates a method of structuring a system into multiple levels so that a level of software can "hide" the unrecoverable features of an interface and provide a new interface with recoverable objects to programs needing facilities for backward error recovery. The paper discusses this organisation of recovery in such a system.

Introduction

In order to attain a high level of reliability the designer of a system will attempt to ensure first that the system does not contain faults, and second that those faults which it does contain (since the first objective will not be achieved) are tolerated and do not cause the system to fail. An important element in any measures for fault tolerance is a means of *error recovery*, that is of transforming a state of the system which (due to some fault) is erroneous to a state from which the system can continue to provide its specified service.

Many of the erroneous states which can occur in the operation of a system can be anticipated. In consequence it may well be possible to construct specific error recovery measures to rectify such errors. Indeed, most of the work on tolerance for faults in the hardware of computer systems has catered only for predicted error situations caused by (anticipated) component failures. Techniques for coping with component failure can be embodied in the hardware itself [Avi75], or in the software of a system in the form of exception handling routines [Goo75]. However, faults in the design of a system can lead to erroneous states which are unanticipated and cannot be predicted. Of course, faults in software are always due to deficiencies in design and in consequence the techniques which have been quite effective in averting system failures due to hardware faults are inadequate and inappropriate as a defence against software faults.

Any technique for providing recovery in an unanticipated situation must be of a very general nature and should not place undue reliance on an erroneous state caused by a design fault. One such technique is to abandon the erroneous state and restore the objects in the system to the values which pertained in some prior state. This approach has been termed "backward error recovery" [Ran78] since an earlier state is restored and some system activity is in consequence abandoned. Backward error recovery is an important technique, for if it is employed in a system then recovery can be obtained from the effects of a wide class of faults, including those of design. Successful restoration of a prior state ensures the elimination of all errors generated by any fault which occurred after that earlier state; thus a powerful fault tolerance capability can be provided.

Consider, for example, the interface between the "hardware" and "software" of a computer system. The hardware machine interprets the machine language programs comprising the software of the system, and provides various abstract objects such as registers, words of memory in main storage, pages of data on disc, and I/0 devices. One of the aspects of providing fault tolerance at the software level is to provide backward error recovery for the objects manipulated by the programs. (Objects for which backward error recovery is provided will be termed "recoverable" in this paper.) The recovery cache has been proposed [Hor74] as a mechanism for providing, by hardware, recovery for those objects that reside in the main store of the machine, and it has been demonstrated that this is a feasible and efficient technique [And76, Shr78, Lee79]. However, the optimised checkpointing strategy employed by the recovery cache is less appropriate for the provision of backward error recovery for most of the other objects supported by the hardware interpreter, particularly for those objects which interact with the external environment of the system.

This paper describes an approach to the construction of complex systems which involves structuring a system into a hierarchy of interfaces or levels such that a higher level can provide recoverable abstract objects which it implements from the (relatively) concrete objects available from a lower level. Examples of systems in which a hierarchical multi-level approach has been adopted have been described in the literature [Dij68, Lis72]; a detailed examination of a model of recovery in multi-level systems has also been published [And78]. This paper considers the way in which a multi- level recoverable system could be designed and illustrates the approach by means of a simple example. Some useful observations on the practical details of the approach are made.

Basic Recovery Concepts

First, consider the simple case of a program running on a given interface L. The term *recoverability* is, as indicated above, taken to mean the ability to recover an earlier state of the objects available on an interface, thereby undoing the effects of operations that were performed on those objects. To provide such backward error recovery necessitates the recording of *recovery data* which can be used for this state restoration. Correspondingly, programs which manipulate the recovery data are referred to as *recovery programs*.

In the rest of this paper it will be assumed that the following basic recovery features are available to programs executed on an interface:

(i) The interface provides both *recoverable* and *unrecoverable objects*.

(ii) A program can establish *recovery points* which ensure that the current state of the recoverable objects of the interface is (at least conceptually) recorded as recovery data.

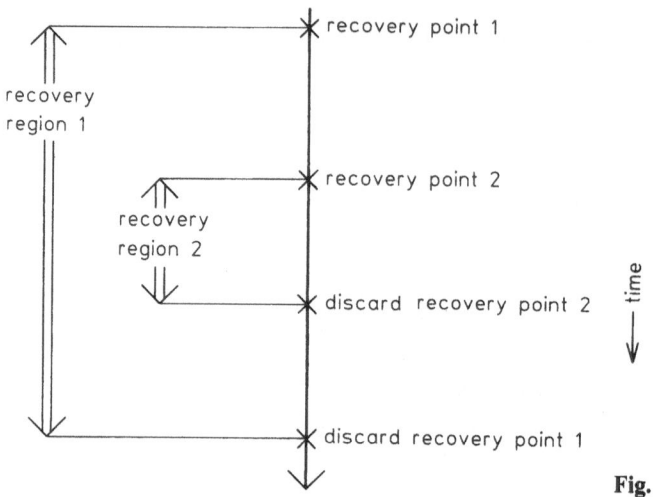

Fig. 1. Multiple recovery points

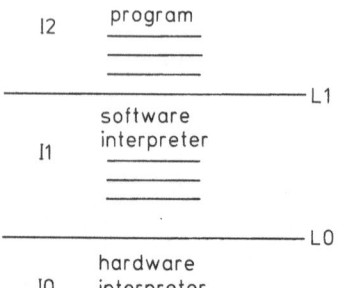

Fig. 2. Interpretive multilevel system

(iii) Recovery points can be discarded with the effect that recovery data maintained for recovery to those recovery points is discarded.

A recovery point is said to be *active* from when it is established until it is discarded. The term *recovery region* will be used to refer to the period for which a recovery point is active (Fig. 1 shows two nested recovery regions).

Multi-Level Systems

A systematic method of designing a complex computer system is to adopt a hierarchical approach: starting from a given hardware interface L0, a first layer of software is added to obtain a more attractive interface L1; this process is repeated to obtain L2, and so on. The resulting system is termed *multi-level* in that a number of interfaces, or levels, can be discerned in its implementation.

The most powerful and general method of providing a new interface is to use *interpretation* techniques. For example, a new level L1 can be constructed from an existing hardware interface L0 by providing a software-implemented interpreter I1 (which is, of course, executed on L0). This is depicted in Fig. 2.

The characteristic feature of this approach is that an interpreter has complete responsibility for the support of the new interface — every operation performed by a program I2 on objects available on L1 in Fig. 2 is directly supported by I1. The design of a multi-level system can be simplified by the adoption of interpretation techniques because the implementation of each of the levels supported by interpretation is completely independent of the implementation of the underlying levels. For example, in Fig. 2 the recoverability of the objects available on L0 has no direct bearing on the recoverability of objects available on L1. Any recovery features available on L1 have to be explicitly provided by I1.

The major practical disadvantage with interpretation is in the substantial overhead which it incurs. Indeed, if it is desired that a new interface L1 is to have many features in common with the underlying interface L0 then interpretation can be a costly technique to utilise. There is an alternative to full interpretation: if the hardware machine makes available sufficiently powerful *extension* facilities then it may not be necessary to support new interfaces by further levels of interpretation; instead, these may be provided by extending the hardware provided features. Figure 3 illustrates a computer system in which the hardware-provided interface L0 (itself supported by a hardware-implemented interpreter I0) provides extension facilities. Each new interface Li (i = 1, 2) is constructed as an extension of Li − 1, the extension being implemented by means of a program Ei which is executed on the interface Li − 1.

Each program Ei is referred to as an *interpreter extension*. Every interaction with the interface L2 is first examined by the underlying interpreter I0, which determines whether that interaction is directly supported by I0 itself or, if not, which of the interpreter extensions (E1, E2) does support that interaction. Thus, the interactions of a program may be supported by any lower extensions or by I0. The layout of Fig. 3 is intended to indicate that interfaces L0, L1 and L2 have many behavioural properties in common.

Example: The nucleus of most operating systems can be regarded as an interpreter extension which provides a user interface from the underlying hardware interface by removing certain privileged instructions and adding a set of 'operating system call' instructions.

The potential advantage to be gained from using an interpreter extension to implement a new interface (when this is possible) in preference to a further level

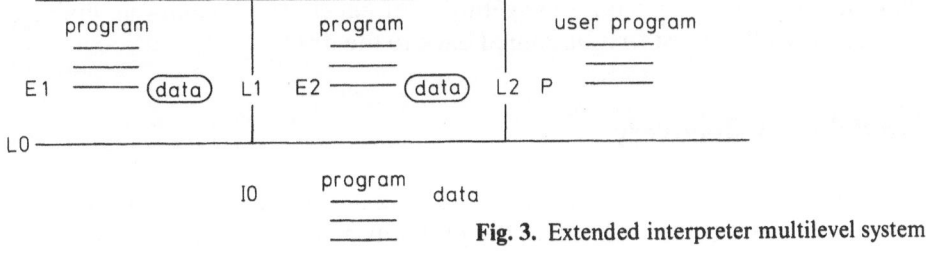

Fig. 3. Extended interpreter multilevel system

of interpretation is in avoiding the overhead that the latter entails. It should be noted that to a program being executed on an interface, it is completely immaterial whether that interface is implemented by an interpreter extension or not.

As discussed above, the advantages of full interpretation in the implementation of multi-level systems may be diminished by the overheads incurred, and it is likely that many practical multi-level systems will be constructed using interpreter extensions. Thus the rest of this paper concentrates on the provision of recoverable interfaces by means of a hierarchy of interpreter extensions. In order to illustrate the discussion a simple example multi-level system will be presented.

A Simple File System

The example system in which the provision of recoverable interfaces is to be considered is a rudimentary filing system; it supports only a single file for use by a single user. The implementation of the system is as depicted in Fig. 3, and has the following characteristics.

L0: Among the objects available on L0 are variables held in main memory, and disc pages held on secondary storage. The disc is accessed by means of the operations 'readdisc' and 'writedisc'. These objects and the operations to manipulate them are supported by the underlying interpreter I0.

L1: The interpreter extension E1 extends L0 by providing operations to acquire and release disc pages (operations 'getdiscpage' and 'releasediscpage'), maintaining a list of the free disc pages in main memory.

L2: The second interpreter extension E2 prevents the user program P from directly accessing the disc pages. Instead, P is given access to a file; the user views this file as an indexed sequence of lines of text, with operations 'openfile', 'closefile', 'readline' and 'writeline'. The concrete representation maintained by E2 for the file consists of a set of the unrecoverable disc pages, a copy (called 'pagebuffer') of the most recently accessed disc page, and an array of disc page addresses (called 'filemap'). The objects pagebuffer and filemap are held in main memory. Each entry in filemap points to one of the disc pages currently representing the file. When P accesses the file, either to read or write a line, the access is actually applied (by E2) to pagebuffer. If the line in question is not present, because pagebuffer is empty or contains the wrong disc page, then the relevant disc page is copied into pagebuffer (if pagebuffer contains an updated disc page then this must first be copied back to the disc).

Provision of Recovery

If backward error recovery is to be provided to a program in a system with interpreter extensions then whenever the program manipulates a recoverable ob-

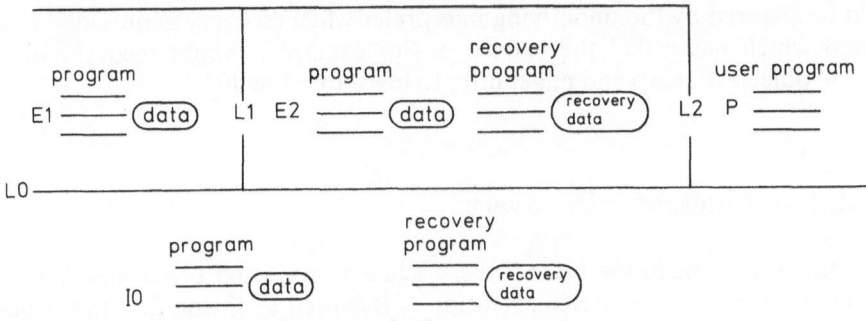

Fig. 4. Recovery structures in an extended interpreter system

ject within a recovery region, it must be ensured that the necessary recovery data is recorded. If the recoverable object is supported by the underlying interpreter then the recovery data will be maintained by the interpreter. Similarly, an interpreter extension may need to record recovery data so that it can provide recovery to any recoverable objects it supports.

It will be assumed that the underlying interpreter I0 of the file system example provides recovery for variables in main memory, but not for disc pages (that is, words of main memory are recoverable and disc pages are unrecoverable). Although the first extension (E1) provides no recovery features, the second extension (E2) is intended to provide a recoverable file; since the file is implemented on disc as well as in main storage, E2 will have to include recovery programs and data, as is depicted in Fig. 4.

In order that an extension, such as E2 in Fig. 4, can perform the necessary actions for recovery, the underlying interpreter must invoke the extension whenever a program using that extension establishes or discards a recovery point as well as whenever recovery is required. When recovery is required for P (the user of the file system) then the extension E2 must restore the prior state of the file and the interpreter I0 must restore those variables of P which are held in main memory.

The basis of one method by which E2 could provide recovery for the file is as follows: whenever P establishes a recovery point, E2 must ensure that the disc pages which represent the file are not subsequently overwritten. When pagebuffer is to be copied back to the disc, instead of overwritting the original disc page, an unused disc page is acquired and pagebuffer is written to this new page. Clearly, the appropriate entry in filemap must be changed to point to the new disc page, and in consequence the disc address of the old disc page must be recorded as recovery data by E2.

An interpreter extension can itself make use of recoverable objects, either in conjunction with its own use of recovery points or simply for convenience in representing objects maintained by the extension.

In the file system, the objects filemap and pagebuffer used by E2 are recoverable since they reside in main storage. The question which will now be considered is whether recoverable objects used by an interpreter extension

401

should be restored by the underlying interpreter when recovery is provided to a program which has called the extension. For example, should recovery of P cause the objects filemap and pagebuffer to be restored by I0?

Disjoint and Inclusive Recovery

The distinction between the two recovery schemes discussed below stems from the way in which an interpreter extension is regarded as fitting into the structure of the system. As its name suggests, an interpreter extension is an extension of an underlying interpreter and could therefore be regarded as being a part of that interpreter (at least conceptually), and hence independent (or disjoint) from any calling program. If the extension and calling program are regarded as disjoint components of the system it seems legitimate that recovery for one should not imply that any recovery is required for the other. In consequence an extension would be wholly responsible for the recovery of objects it was maintaining. A scheme of recovery for multi-level systems having these characteristics in termed a *disjoint recovery scheme*.

If disjoint recovery is adopted for the file system then the objects filemap and pagebuffer would not be restored to their prior states by I0 when recovery is provided to P. E2 must still be able to restore the prior state of the file — but this is easily achieved. The recovery data recorded by E2 simply needs to indicate which filemap entries must be restored and the disc addresses to which they should be reset (that is, the address of the old disc pages discussed in the previous section). Using this information, E2 can reset filemap to its state at the time the recovery point was established and can also release the new disc pages that had been acquired. Note that pagebuffer need not be restored. The recovery program of E2 merely empties pagebuffer since any subsequent access of the file by P will result in a disc page being copied into pagebuffer. All of these actions ensure that the file is restored to the abstract state which existed when P established the recovery point. This example also illustrates that provision of the abstraction of recovery for an object does not imply that an exact prior state of that object must be restored; there may be many concrete states which have the same abstract state. The disjoint recovery scheme can take advantage of this, as illustrated here, when providing recovery. (A more detailed elaboration of the file system program of E2 with disjoint recovery is supplied in the Appendix.)

There is a second way in which an extension may be regarded as fitting into the structure of the system. Instead of taking an extension to be disjoint from a calling program an alternative is to regard the calling program as being inclusive of the extension, the extension then being regarded as a nested component of the calling program. It then seems natural that recovery of the calling program should also include recovery of the extension. In consequence an extension would only need to record and maintain recovery data relating to the use of any unrecoverable objects it manipulates on behalf of a calling program; recovery of any recoverable objects used by the extension would be automatically

402

provided by lower extensions or by the underlying interpreter. A scheme of recovery for multi-level systems having these characteristics is termed an *inclusive recovery scheme.*

If inclusive recovery is adopted for the file system then when recovery is invoked for P, the prior states of filemap and pagebuffer will be automatically restored by I0. As with the disjoint scheme, E2 must acquire new disc pages to avoid overwriting the disc pages which represented the file at the time the recovery point was established. Automatic restoration of filemap thus ensures that the file is restored to its prior state, and the recovery program of E2 merely has to release the newly acquired disc pages, the addresses of which would have been recorded as recovery data (see the Appendix for a more detailed description).

One complication which arises with inclusive recovery concerns the recovery data maintained by the extension (such as the addresses of newly acquired disc pages in the file system). If this data is retained in recoverable objects (perhaps to enhance the recovery capabilities of the extension itself) then this information would be lost if the objects were restored by the underlying interpreter before the recovery program of the extension was executed. This difficulty can be avoided in a number of ways. The simplest, but least acceptable, approach is to stipulate that the recovery data of an extension must be maintained in unrecoverable objects; unfortunately the recovery programs of the extension are then unable to derive any local benefit from the recovery capability of the underlying interpreter. The most general solution is to allow an extension to specify that the provisions of disjoint recovery should be applied to the objects it uses to hold recovery data. The code presented in the Appendix assumes that this strategy is being employed. Alternatively, it may be possible to ensure that the recovery programs of an extension are executed before recovery is provided by the underlying interpreter. In a multi-level system this implies that when recovery is required for a program, the underlying interpreter must invoke the recovery programs of all relevant extensions in order from right to left, that is from "most" to "least" abstract. (The adoption of this strategy would also allow minor optimisations of the code presented in the Appendix to be made.)

General Comments on The Recovery Schemes

At a superficial level, there would appear to be only minor differences between the implementation of recovery in the example system utilising disjoint or inclusive recovery. Certainly, it would be wrong to try to draw firm conclusions about the usefulness of either scheme based on this simple example. It is claimed that both schemes provide exactly the same abstraction of recovery to the user of the file (P) and, as expected, it is necessary to investigate the implementation of this abstraction in E2 to distinguish the schemes.

As far as recovery is concerned, the implementation of the disjoint scheme naturally has to do more work than that of the inclusive scheme. However, in this example the extra work turns out to be relatively minor because, since the disjoint scheme gives full control over recovery, it is possible to adopt a reasonably efficient method of restoring a concrete state of the file in order to provide the abstraction of recovery. Thus, for example, pagebuffer does not need to be restored to the state that pertained when P established a recovery point. In contrast, with the inclusive scheme, pagebuffer is restored automatically without cost (strictly, at the cost of recovery data in the lower machine). The disjoint scheme does incur the cost of the disc access to reset pagebuffer when the file is next accessed by P. It should also be noted that if the 'getdiscpage' and 'releasediscpage' procedures of E1 were made recoverable by E1 then there would be no need whatsoever for a recovery program in E2 with the inclusive recovery scheme. However, the recoverability provided by E1 would have no impact on the recovery program of E2 in the disjoint scheme.

On the other hand, the disjoint scheme has to checkpoint information maintained in main memory about the file status when a recovery point is established. In the current example there is minimal information; a more practical file system which maintained other state information (time, data altered, owner, size, . . .) would necessitate the recording of additional information as recovery data of the disjoint scheme.

The example also highlights the problems of recording recovery data in recoverable objects with the inclusive recovery scheme. Anderson, Lee and Shrivastava [And78] stated that the natural order for recovery of the extensions is from least to most abstract. However, it has been shown that providing recovery in the reverse order would provide the desired effect and would simplify the system in that the objects used to hold recovery data would not need to be specially identified and dealt with. Indeed, the recording of recovery data may be simplified by the adoption of this strategy.

It is likely that extensions themselves contain faults. It should be noted that neither recovery scheme precludes an extension from establishing its own local recovery points as part of its fault tolerance strategies. Indeed, this may be considered necessary to provide reliable extension operation, although the simple example presented here contains no such strategies.

Summary

By discussing the details of the provision of backward error recovery in a very simple file system, the salient characteristics of two schemes of recovery in multi-level systems have been presented. The disjoint scheme gives complete control over recovery to an extension but only at the price of having to re-implement recovery when that provided by the underlying interpreter could have been adequate. The inclusive scheme enables an extension to take advantage of the recovery provided by the underlying interpreter in providing its own recovery capability, but is complicated by the need to obtain disjoint recovery for its recovery data. A practical solution to this problem has been discussed. The example system also illustrates how unrecoverable features of a low level interface can be eliminated by replacing them with recoverable abstract objects in a new interface. A reasonably detailed elaboration of the file system program of E2 is attached as an Appendix.

Acknowledgements. We are indebted to our fellow members of the Reliability Project, which is sponsored by the Science Research Council of Great Britain, at the University of Newcastle upon Tyne. We would also like to thank one referee for providing helpful comments on an earlier draft of this paper.

References

[And76] T. Anderson and R. Kerr, "Recovery blocks in action" proc. 2nd Int. Conf. on Software Engineering, San Francisco, Oct. 1976, pp. 447−457. [Also Chap. 2]

[Avi75] A. Avizienis, "Architecture of fault-tolerant computing systems". Proc. of 5th IEEE Int. Symp. on Fault-tolerant Computing, Paris, June 1975, pp. 3−16.

[And78] T. Anderson, P. A. Lee and S. K. Shrivastava, "A model of recoverability in multilevel systems". IEEE Trans. on Software Eng., Vol. SE-4, Nov. 1978, pp. 486−494. [Also Chap. 4]

[Dij68] E. W. Dijkstra, "The structure of the "THE" multiprogramming system". Commun. Ass. Comput. Mach., Vol. 11, May 1968, pp. 341−346.

[Goo75] J. B. Goodenough, "Exception handling: issues and a proposed notation". Commun. Ass. Comput. Mach., Vol. 18, Dec. 1975, pp. 683−696.

[Hor74] J. J. Horning et al., "A program structure for error detection and recovery". Lecture Notes in Computer Science 16, Springer, Berlin, 1974, pp. 177−193. [Also Chap. 2]

[Lee79] P. A. Lee, N. Ghani and K. Heron, "A recovery cache for the PDP-11". Digest of papers, FTCS-9, Madison, June 1979. [Also Chap. 2]

[Lis72] B. H. Liskov, "The design of the Venus operating system". Commun. Ass. Comput. Mach., Vol. 15, March 1972, pp. 144−149.

[Shr78] S. K. Shrivastava and A. A. Akinpelu, "Fault-tolerant sequential programming using recovery blocks". Digest of papers, FTCS-8, Toulouse, June 1978, p. 207. [Also Chap. 2]

Appendix

The code which follows is written in a Pascal-like language. The procedures which are made available to the user program P (as operations) are distinguished by the keyword *entry*. To make it clear to the reader which operations are provided by the extension E1 and which by the interpreter I0, invocation of such operations will be prefixed by "E1." and "I0." respectively. The *establishrp, discardrp* and *recover* procedures are those which it is assumed are automatically invoked by I0 as noted in the paper.

The declarations of a number of procedures have been omitted for brevity. The tasks performed by procedures readline, convert, put-in-cache and extract-from-cache should be clear from their names and invocations. Procedures initialise-cache and tidy-up-cache are merely to allow for any necessary updating of the housekeepingvars of the cache. Procedure cacheing-required determines whether recovery data must be entered in the recovery cache, according to whether the disc page which would have been overwritten is one which represented a part of the file at the time the recovery point was established.

As a further simplification, recovery in the example is only considered for a single recovery point. The elementary modifications necessary to cope with multiple nested recovery regions are left as an exercise for the interested reader.

Code is presented for E2 with disjoint recovery, and then for E2 with inclusive recovery.

Disjoint recovery in E2

```
constant
filemapaddr = ...; "address of disc copy of filemap"

type filemapindex = (1 ... N);
     discaddress   = ...;
     cacheentry    = record oldpage: discaddress;
                              index: filemapindex
                     endrecord;
     line = ...;

var filemap: array [filemapindex] of discaddress;
    pagebuffer: array [1 .. M] of line;
    activepageno: (0 ... N); "filemapindex of file page in pagebuffer"
    writtento: boolean;
    status: (open, closed) initially closed;
    cache: record
                housekeepingvars: ...;
                oldfilestatus: (open, closed);
                region: array [1 ... P] of cacheentry;
           endrecord;

entry procedure openfile;
begin if status = open then signalerror else
  begin
  I0.readdisc (filemapaddr, filemap): "read filemap"
  activepageno := false; status := open;
  end;
end openfile;

entry procedure closefile;
begin if status = closed then signalerror else
  begin if writtento then copybackpagebuffer;
  "assume filemap has been written to"
  I0.writedisc (filemapaddr, filemap);
  status := closed;
  end;
end closefile;

entry procedure writeline (lineno: integer, linecontents: line);
var pageno: filemapindex;
    displacement: integer;
begin if status = closed then signalerror else
  begin convert (lineno, pageno, displacement);
  getpage (pageno);
```

```
      pagebuffer [displacement] := linecontents;
      writtento := true;
      end;
   end writeline;

   procedure getpage (pagenumber: filemapindex);
   begin if pagenumber = activepageno then return;
   if writtento then copybackpagebuffer;
   I0.readdisc (filemap [activepageno], pagebuffer);
   activepageno := pagenumber;
   writtento := false;
   end getpage;

   procedure copybackpagebuffer;
   var newpage: discaddress;
   begin if cacheing-required then
      "record recovery data"
      begin newpage := E1.getdiscpage;
      "cache old disc page address & its filemapindex"
      put-in-cache (filemap[index], index);
      "reset filemap to point at new page"
      filemap[index] := newpage;
      end;
   I0.writedisc (filemap[index], pagebuffer);
   end copybackpagebuffer;

   "recovery procedures — establish a recovery point,
   recover, and discard a recovery point"

   procedure establishrp;
   begin if (status = open) & writtento then
   "ensure disc copy represents current file state"
   I0.writedisc (filemap[activepageno], pagebuffer);
   initialise-cache;
   cache.oldfilestatus := status; "checkpoint status"
   end establishrp;

   procedure recovery;
   var index: filemapindex;
       oldpage: discaddress;
   begin "reset the necessary in-core variables"
   if status = closed then openfile
                      else activepageno := 0;
   for each entry in cache.region do
      begin extract-from-entry (oldpage, index);
      "discard new page"
      E1.releasediscpage (filemap[index]);
      filemap[index] := oldpage; "reset filemap"
      end for loop;
```

```
if cache.oldfilestatus = closed then closefile;
tidyup-cache;
end recovery;

procedure discardrp;
var index: filemapindex;
    oldpage: discaddress;
begin for each entry in cache.region do
   begin extract-from-entry (oldpage, index);
   E1.releasediscpage (oldpage); "discard old page"
   end for loop;
tidyup-cache;
end discardrp;
```

Inclusive recovery in E2

"Type and var declarations as before except for the code"

```
type cacheentry = record oldpage: discaddress;
                         newpage: discaddress;
              endrecord;

...

var recoverycache cache: record
                         housekeepingvar: ...;
                         region: array [1 ... P] of cacheentry;
                         endrecord;

entry procedure openfile; ...      "as before"
entry procedure closefile; ...     "as before"
entry procedure writeline (...); ... "as before"
entry procedure readline (...); ... "as before"
procedure getpage (...); ...       "as before"

procedure copybackpagebuffer;
var newpage : discaddress;
begin if cacheing-required then
   "record recovery data"
   begin newpage := E1.getdiscpage;
   "cache old and new disc page addresses"
   put-in-cache (filemap[index], newpage);
   filemap [index]: = newpage; "reset filemap"
   end;
I0.writedisc (filemap[index], pagebuffer);
end copybackpagebuffer;

procedure establishrp;
begin initialise-cache;
end establishrp;
```

```
procedure recovery;
var oldpage, newpage: discaddress;
begin for each entry in cache.region do
    begin extract-from-entry (oldpage, newpage);
    E1.releasediscpage (newpage); "discard new page"
    end for loop;
tidyup-cache;
end recovery;

procedure discardrp;
var oldpage, newpage: discaddress
begin for each entry in cache.region do
    begin extract-from-entry (oldpage, newpage);
    E1.releasediscpage (oldpage); "discard old page"
    end for loop;
tidyup-cache;
end discardrp;
```

Structuring Distributed Systems for Recoverability and Crash Resistance

S. K. SHRIVASTAVA

Abstract. An object-oriented multilevel model of computation is used to discuss recoverability and crash resistance issues in distributed systems. Of particular importance are the issues that are raised when recoverability and crash resistance properties are desired from objects whose concrete representations are distributed over several nodes. The execution of a program at a node of the system can give rise to a hierarchy of processes executing various parts of the program at different nodes. Recoverability and crash resistance properties are needed to ensure that such a group of processes leave the system state consistent despite faults in the system.

Index Terms. Atomic actions, backward error recovery, commitment, concurrency, consistency, crash resistance, distributed systems, exception handling, message passing, recoverability, secure storage.

I. Introduction

Consider a computing system consisting of a number of autonomous computers (referred to as nodes) connected by a communication system that allows the various nodes to exchange information with each other. Each node of such a system will provide one or more services (e.g., data retention, document printing, compiling, text editing) and a user computation running on any node can make use of such services by suitable use of the communication system. Such a system will be called a *distributed system*. When a user computation running on a given node invokes a legitimate service call to some other node, there can be many reasons why that service might not be available; for example, the communication link between the nodes is perhaps faulty or the server node has "crashed" and so on. For these, and many other reasons, it is quite possible for a user computation to arrive at such a state from where further meaningful progress is not possible. Such a state of affairs can be highly undesirable in a system where node services are constantly being shared between various computations, since a computation that has not terminated satisfactorily could leave part of the system state inconsistent. Under the assumption that, if a computation (that begins when the system state is consistent) terminates properly, then it will leave the (possibly new) system state consistent, we require the following abstract property from all programs to guarantee consistency in the presence of faults: the computation invoked for a program either terminates or that invocation has no affect on the system state. The above abstraction can be maintained if the system can be structured to provide *recoverability* such that the current state of an unsatisfactory computation can be abandoned in favor of a prior state.

In this paper we shall examine some of the fundamental issues that are involved when this so-called backward error recovery facility [1] is to be provided

410

in a distributed system. The contributions of this paper are that: 1) it attempts to describe the underlying concepts on the means of achieving recoverability in distributed systems using a multilevel model of system developed earlier [6]; 2) the relationship between recoverability and "crash resistance" is discussed and treatment of abnormal situations during the execution of programs is examined in depth; and 3) as a result, problems such as a) exploitation of recoverability facilities of remote nodes, b) construction of recoverable and "crash resistant" objects whose concrete representations are spread over several nodes, and c) treatment of abnormal situations during recovery can be understood and their various solutions can be formulated and evaluated. These ideas, it is hoped, will not only help the reader in critically reviewing any existing systems (e.g., [2], [3]), but will also provide a framework for formulating arbitrarily complex recovery strategies and their implementations.

II. Preliminary Details

Atomicity and Message Passing

We shall view the system as consisting of a collection of abstract objects. An abstract object consists of abstract data and a set of abstract operations that manipulate the data — these operations are the only means of data manipulation. The term object manager will be used to refer to the provider of the corresponding abstract object. As is well known, in any system a hierarchy of abstract interfaces (or levels) can be discerned. Any given level is characterized by the abstract objects made available on that level together with their associated operations for their manipulations. We say that an object is in a consistent state (or simply consistent) if it satisfies some specified invariant properties. An interface is said to be in a consistent state if all of its objects are consistent. Consider now a number of programs $P1$, $P2$, ..., Pn written to run on a given interface (level) Li. These programs are in fact providing abstract operations for the next interface $(Li + 1)$ — the higher level of abstraction. In order that the invocations of these programs preserve the consistency of interface $Li + 1$, these programs must satisfy the following two properties.
1) If execution of any program Pj is considered in isolation, then Pj terminates and $Li + 1$ remains consistent.
2) If programs Pj, ..., Pm are executed concurrently, then these executions are interference free.

Programs that satisfy property 2) are referred to as atomic actions [4]. These two properties are necessary and sufficient for the maintenance of consistency in a concurrent environment. We shall not prove this here, the interested reader is referred to [3] — [5]. From now on we shall only consider programs that are atomic actions (the terms "program" and "atomic action" will be used synonymously). If programs are manipulating objects that are shared, then it is necessary for them to follow some appropriate locking protocol on these objects [3], [5]. We shall further assume that some such protocol is being observed.

411

We shall now consider a distributed system at a sufficiently high level of abstraction such that processes at different nodes have message sending facilities for interprocess communications with the following properties. A process can send a message to a named receiver at a given node using a "send" primitive. Successful execution of this primitive implies that the message has been delivered to the receiver. Either a "time_out" or "process_missing" exception can be raised during the invocation of a "send." If the "time-out" interval has been set properly, raising of that exception can be taken to mean that most probably that message was not sent. The process missing exception implies that the named receiver no longer exists. A process can also wait for a message; a time-out exception is associated with this "wait." We assume some sequence numbering scheme for these messages such that a "request" and its "reply" can be properly matched. Such a message system can be used neatly to implement a remote procedure call mechanism [2]:

> send_message (processname, node, message)
> [for all exceptions: invoke backward recovery]
> **repeat**
> receive_message (processname, node, result)
> [for all exceptions: invoke backward recovery]
> **until** sequence numbers match;

$- - - - -$

In the above algorithm, the sent message indicates the work to be performed at the remote node and the received message contains the result. From now on it will be assumed that a procedure "remote_call" that implements the above algorithm exists at each node, so allowing a process to access remote objects:

> remote_call (processname, node, message) **returns** result
> [for all exceptions: invoke backward recovery]

Note that the above use of backward recovery guarantees that an invocation of "remote_call" either produces the results or no side effects are produced. This necessarily requires the capability of "undoing" any work done at a remote node — how this can be achieved will be discussed in subsequent sections. It may also be noted that "remote_call" of this paper differs from that proposed by Lampson and Sturgis [2] in two important ways: 1) in [2], no backward recovery facility (other than crash recovery, see later) is available; 2) as a consequence of this, an exception during a send operation is dealt with by resending the message. Thus, a single invocation of a remote call procedure can result in repeated executions at the remote node; so it is meaningful to invoke only the idempotent operations at remote nodes. No such restriction is necesssry here.

In order to facilitate access of remote objects, two primitive operations are made available to a process (where the unable exception means that most probably that operation was not performed):

> 1) create_worker (workerj, Nodei)
>   [unable exception: $- - - - -$]
> 2) delete_worker (workerj, Nodei)
>   [unable exception: $- - - - -$]

412

A process can create a "worker process" at a remote node so that remote calls can be directed to it for accessing objects at that node. Any suitable response to the unable exception in the first operation is acceptable (e.g., retry, create at some other node); the same is not true for the second case, we shall discuss the reasons shortly.

Recovery Semantics

Using the terminology and concepts developed for an earlier paper [6], for a process to have the abstraction of backward error recovery (henceforth termed recovery) made available at a given level of abstraction requires the following.

1) The process can establish a recovery point, thus indicating the start of a new recovery region (see Fig. 1). This implies that, if necessary, the states of any recoverable objects modified in that region can be restored automatically to those at the beginning of the region. The following notation will be assumed:

    establish_recovery_point (control)

where "control" specifies the point where the flow of control should be after state restoration (e.g., for a recovery block [7], "control" could be the starting address of the next alternative).

2) The process can discard a recovery point, thus indicating the end of a recovery region. As shown in Fig. 1, a process can successively establish recovery points giving rise to nested recovery regions [6]. We assume that a restore(j) primitive is available for recovering to the jth recovery point. In the rest of the paper, the term "detection of an error" will be used to mean "the detection of an erroneous situation (exception) that necessitates the invocation of backward recovery."

To cope with situations where the abstraction of recovery can no longer be maintained (this may happen, for example, as a result of a physical breakdown of the memory system that is storing recovery information) we assume the existence of a "stronger," manual recovery facility that can restore prior states of objects and some relevant processes. The term crash recovery is typically used to refer to this action of state restoration [2], [3]. For the time being we will consider the provision of automatic recovery only and return to the subject of crash recovery later, in Section IV.

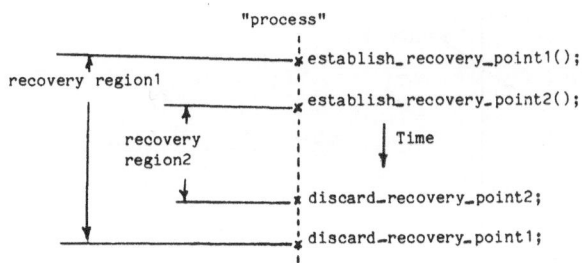

Fig. 1. Multiple recovery points

413

III. Recoverability Issues

Multilevel Architecture to Support Recovery

The establishment of a recovery point by a process entails notification to all those object managers (whose services will be used by the process) that are providing the abstraction of recoverability so that the managers can commence recording appropriate recovery data. When an error is detected, all these managers must be appropriately notified so that they can use their recovery data for providing the abstraction of recovery. The following three notifications must be handled by an object manager: 1) record_recovery_data, 2) discard_recovery_data, and 3) recover. Note that it is being assumed that after a "record" notification, any number of operations on that object can be invoked — the effects of all of these can be undone by a single "recover" notification.

For recovery to be automatic, it is clear that these notifications must be performed automatically on behalf of the process in question. A logical organization for how this may be done will now be briefly discussed (for the time being only a single node accessing local objects will be considered).

Referring to Fig. 2, it is assumed that interface $L0$ (that is being maintained by a set of programs $I0$ known as the interpreter for $L0$) provides some recovery facilities (see below) to programs that run over it. A number of object managers have been programmed on $L0$ thereby successively extending $L0$ to Li [6]. Thus, a program Pj cannot only use most of the operations of $L0$, a number of additional operations — those provided by the programmed managers — have also been made available to it. Consider now the execution of some program, say Pj. Every invocation of an operation on interface Li is first examined by $I0$ which determines whether that operation is directly supported by itself or if not, which of the managers (also referred to as extensions in [6]) does support it — the operation of that particular manager is then invoked by I0 ("M.op(...)" in this particular case). We shall now make the assumptions that L0 supports the abstraction of processes and that $I0$ maintains some data per level for the

```
erp:  establish_recovery_point
drp:  discard_recovery_point
```

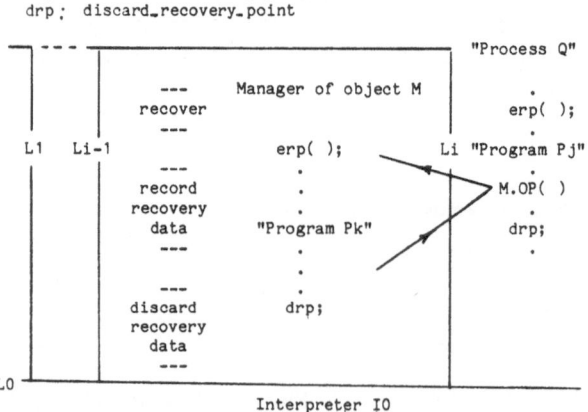

Fig. 2. A hierarchy of interfaces

414

purposes of recovery for each process. We shall refer to this data by process name.level.recovery data. Then, when a process such as Q executes an operation "establish_recovery_point," this results in $I0$ making an appropriate entry in Q.level.recovery data, thus signifying the start of a new recovery region at that level. Note that recovery regions of programs such as Pj and Pk are independent from each other, despite the fact that they "belong" to the same process (Q in Fig. 2); this is because they are at different levels of abstractions. The invocation of an operation such as "M.op(. . .)" results in $I0$ executing the following program (for simplicity, in the following algorithms it has been assumed that $I0$, itself has no recovery capability and also that it is not providing any recoverable objects):

```
begin
      if M is recoverable then
      search the current recovery region of
      Q.level.recovery data for object name M;
      if not found then
      begin record the name M in Q.level.recovery data;
            invoke M.record_recovery_data (j, level);
      end
            invoke M.op (...)
end
```

In the above figure, "i" will be the level number of Q when it executes M.op(. . .). Whenever $I0$ invokes recovery data associated operations (on behalf of the caller) of an object manager, the level number of the caller is also implicitly supplied. This number may be utilized for the management of recovery data by a manager in a manner similar to that done by $I0$. The first parameter of "record_recovery data" operation specifies the number of the current recovery region.

The invocation of operation "discard_recovery_point" by Q results in $I0$ executing the following program:

```
begin
      for all object names recorded in the
      current region of Q.level.recovery data do invoke
      object name.discard_recovery_data (level)
      ----- delete recovery data no longer needed -----
end
```

Finally, when Q executes restore(m) primitive, this results in $I0$ executing the following program:

```
begin
      prepare the set of object names that appear in
      Q.level.recovery data in region m to the current region;
      for all the elements of the set do
      invoke objectname.recover (m, level); delete recovery
      regions m to the current one
end
```

Structure of Atomic Actions

As stated before, programs such as recover, *Pk*, *Pj* (Fig. 2) are all atomic; in this subsection we will study their fine structure. To start with, it is clear that an atomic action should be made recoverable such that when an error is detected, capability for undoing all the effects produced by that action exists. Further, to avoid interference, all of the shared objects to be accessed must be locked appropriately and to prevent the domino effect [10], these locks must be held until the end of the action. Lastly, any worker processes created should be deleted at the end of the action. Bearing these in mind, the following structure for a recoverable atomic action suggests itself (Fig. 3).

A few remarks are in order here.

1) A recovery point is established at the beginning of an action and is discarded just before objects are unlocked − any number of intermediate recovery points can be established and discarded within an action.

2) Once the outermost recovery point has been discarded, all of the objects updated by the program become committed − their states cannot be restored.

3) All of the operations after the final "discard" (termed the commit operations) are unrecoverable and must succeed for the action to terminate properly. A sensible strategy for handling exceptions during this period is therefore to retry the commit operations a few times before giving up by executing the fail primitive of *I0* [see remark 5)]. So the unlock and delete operations must be designed such that repeated executions produce the same effect as a single execution.

4) Default exception handlers are associated with the recovery regions of the action to invoke recovery whenever exceptions are raised for which no programmer provided handlers are available (Fig. 3 illustrates the handler for the outermost region). Fig. 3 also shows that a "not done" exception is signaled to the caller if the action cannot produce the desired result (of course, the specification of this action includes "not done" as an exception that can be signaled).

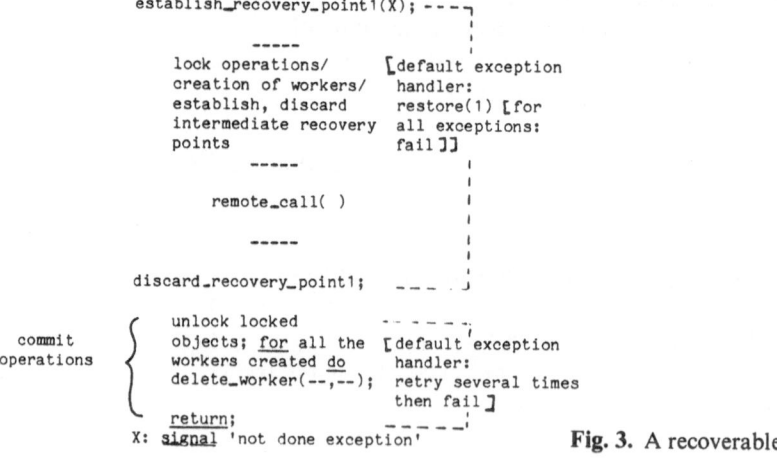

Fig. 3. A recoverable atomic action

416

Note that to maintain consistency, the above exception is signaled after recovery [9]. If the specification of an action precludes signaling of any exceptions, then the statement at label X should be replaced by the "fail" primitive (see below).

5) When some of the objects accessed by an action are in inconsistent states and (or) no recovery is available then the "fail" primitive of $I0$ can be executed to transfer control to the interpreter indicating inability to proceed further. Assuming that $I0$ can signal "failure exception" to the caller, the typical response of $I0$ is to signal a failure exception. When failure exceptions are raised, interfaces Li (Fig. 2) cannot be guaranteed to be consistent and a degraded service is likely to be available. Consistency can be restored by utilizing the crash recovery procedure for that node (to be discussed in Section IV).

6) If any unrecoverable objects are used inside a recovery region then their states must be explicitly restored during recovery — the code for this can be suitably incorporated in exception handlers that invoke recovery.

7) If remote recoverable objects are accessed from within a recovery region then these objects must be restored automatically (like local recoverable objects) during recovery; how this may be performed will be discussed shortly.

8) Finally, if an atomic action is not making use of any recovery facilities — it is unrecoverable — then the handler that normally invokes "restore" should simply invoke "fail."

Assuming the above structure for recoverable atomic actions, two issues now remain to be discussed in this section on recoverability, namely, 1) steps taken by an object manager to provide the abstraction of recoverability and 2) the treatment of remote objects. We shall consider these two issues in turn. In the rest of the paper, for simplicity, wherever it is necessary to show the program text of atomic actions, only the essential details will be shown.

Disjoint and Inclusive Recovery Schemes

The object M of Fig. 2 will be used for illustrative purposes. Let us assume that the concrete implementation of M is on three local objects A, B, and C and that A and B themselves are recoverable. The task of the object manager is thus to provide a recoverable object M constructed out of two recoverable and one unrecoverable objects.

It has been shown that there can be two ways of supporting recoverability of objects: by either using the disjoint recovery scheme or the inclusive recovery scheme [6]. The interpreter $I0$ is said to support the *disjoint recovery scheme* if, in Fig. 2, objects A and B appear as recoverable "locally," that is, only to the programs of the manager of M such as Pk. This means that recovery regions of Pk are disjoint (nonnested) from those of Pj. Thus, when an error is detected in Pj, $I0$ will automatically execute the recover program of the manager of M, the same is not done for those of A and B. It is entirely the responsibility of the manager of an object to provide the abstraction of recoverability. It can be seen that we have been implicitly assuming the disjoint recovery scheme so far (see the subsection on multilevel architecture).

The interpreter *I0* is said to support the *inclusive recovery scheme* if, in Fig. 2, objects *A* and *B* appear recoverable "globally." This is achieved by regarding the recovery regions of *Pk* as included (nested) within those of *Pj*. Thus, when an error is detected in Pj, I0 will execute "recover" operations of the managers of *M*, *A*, and *B*. This means that an object manager, in order to provide recoverability, need only be concerned with the unrecoverable objects it is managing. The "recover" program of *M* under the two schemes can be used to illustrate the difference:

recover(*n*) "disjoint scheme": _ _ _ _ _

                   restore states of *A, B* and *C*
                   using data stored in the *n*th
                   region of "recovery data"

                   _ _ _ _ _

recover(*n*) "inclusive scheme":

                   _ _ _ _ _

                   restore state of *C* using
                   data stored in the *n*th
                   region of "recovery data"

                   _ _ _ _ _

The above example would seem to indicate that the inclusive scheme provides an easier means of structuring recoverable objects than the disjoint scheme. However, as has been discussed elsewhere [6], inclusive scheme does need the features of disjoint scheme (i.e., nonglobal recovery) during the execution of programs with recovery features that manipulate recovery data (in the above example, if recovery data of *M* is stored on recoverable objects, then when an error is detected in *Pj*, these data must not be restored). Thus, its implementation by *I0* is much more complex. In a distributed system, an implementation of inclusive scheme is even more complex because of the following additional difficulty. Assume objects *A* and *B* are on remote nodes. If an error is detected in *Pj*, *I0* must invoke "recover" operations of *A* and *B*: this cannot be performed easily since the abstraction of remote object access in certainly not available at the level of *I0*. For these reasons, the disjoint recovery scheme appears as most suitable in a distributed environment. In the rest of the paper, unless otherwise stated, we shall be assuming such a recovery scheme. To exploit the recoverability of existing objects however, is an important advantage of the inclusive scheme; we shall later present a method whereby a process can exploit the recoverability of remote objects in a manner that models the inclusive scheme.

Treatment of Remote Objects

Remote objects are accessed by creating workers at appropriate nodes and then sending messages to them for object access. We will require that 1) "create _worker" operation be recoverable (i.e., workers be deleted during recovery) and 2) if messages are sent to access recoverable objects, then messages for restoration be sent during recovery. We shall consider two cases to explain the structuring to be proposed: 1) program Pj (Fig. 2) accesses an object Z located at a remote node (say Ni); and 2) object M's concrete representation is also distributed − A (recoverable object) on some remote node (Ns), B (recoverable object) on the local node (N local), and C (unrecoverable object) on another remote node ($N1$). During the execution of Pj by Q a worker (say wi) will be created at Ni; when Q starts executing Pk workers $w1$ at $N1$ and ws at Ns will be

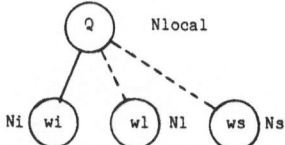

Fig. 4. Process hierarchy for the execution of program Pj

created. Workers $w1$ and ws will be destroyed when the execution of Pk finishes; wi will be destroyed when the execution of Pj finishes. Fig. 4 shows the master-worker process hierarchy (dotted lines indicate that the life times of $w1$ and ws are not the same as that of wi).

We assume that process creation and deletion operations are provided by an object referred to as the "remote object handler." The remote object handler implements the following facilities on behalf of its users (such as process Q of Fig. 4): whenever a process establishes (discards) a recovery point, messages to that effect are sent to the relevant workers of that process; if a process recovers to ith recovery point, messages to that effect are sent to the relevant workers, and any workers that were created in the now deleted recovery regions are destroyed. If the worker processes respond appropriately to the above messages then it is clear that recoverable objects can be utilized effectively by remote users. An indication of how the remote object handler implements the above mentioned facilities will now be given.

1) When a process establishes a recovery point, the "record_recovery_data" program of the remote handler will be automatically invoked by $I0$; this program is designed such that messages to establish a recovery point are sent to all the workers.

2) If a process executes "restore(j)," then the "recover" program of the remote handler will be invoked by $I0$; this program contains the code to send "restore" messages to appropriate workers.

More details of these and other operations of the remote handler are presented in the Appendix.

Next we shall study the actions of a worker. A worker acts as a command interpreter for its master. Logically, therefore, a worker can provide the abstraction of recoverability to its master exactly as the interpreter $I0$ and other object managers at the master's node do, namely, by appropriately recording recovery data and to use these data when recovery is desired. The point to note is that backward recovery of a master can be supported by a worker by its normal forward actions.

419

An undesirable property of this is that a worker has to implement the recoverability of all of the objects it accesses on its master's behalf — even if these objects are recoverable (this is, of course, the disadvantage of the disjoint recovery scheme). A further disadvantage — and this is more serious — is that a worker, in general, does not "know" the objects it will be called upon to access; implementing recoverability under such a condition can be very difficult. The question then arises as to how can a worker effectively use the recoverability features of its local node? One way to achieve this goal is for a worker to support the recoverability of the master by invoking its — the worker's — own recoverability:

```
"actions of a worker process"
cycle
    receive_message ( ) [time out exception: kill]
if message is establish recovery point then
{result := OK; establish recovery point (resume)}
else {execute command in the message; prepare answer}
[for all exceptions: result := exception type;
  goto resume]
resume: send_message (master, Nmaster, result)
[for all exceptions: kill]
end "cycle"
```

When a worker receives an establish recovery point command, it responds by creating its own recovery point, with flow of control at "resume." If the received command is "restore," the worker will execute this command, thus invoking its own recovery. As a result of this, all the recoverable objects updated by the worker are restored appropriately and the worker sends a message to master indicating that the recovery has been performed. This scheme makes the program of a worker simple and the existing recovery facilities are efficiently utilized as in the inclusive recovery scheme. Note that it is now a master's responsibility to maintain, if so desired, any recovery information for those objects that are unrecoverable at a worker's node.

The worker reports all the abnormal conditions encountered to its master. However, if during sending or receiving of a message exceptions are raised, then this is taken to mean either a collapse of the worker-master communication facility or the master's node. The worker's response is to destroy itself using the kill primitive provided by the underlying interpreter $I0$ which can implement it as follows:

```
begin "kill primitive"
    construct the set of object names (if any) recorded
    in calling process.level.recovery data in
    recovery region 1 to the current one;
for all these object names do
    invoke objectname.recover (1, level);
    delete all the information maintained for the calling process
end
```

No exceptions are signaled during the execution of "kill." In particular, if some recover program fails (fail instruction is executed), $I0$ does not signal "failure" to the caller (since the caller is being destroyed) rather, the execution of "kill" is continued. So, the net effect is that the calling process is killed, with as much state restoration performed as possible.

It is now perfectly straightforward for an object manager whose concrete representation is distributed to implement recoverability. Thus, the "record_recovery_data" operation of object M (mentioned at the beginning of this subsection) can be programmed as

record_recovery_data:

        -----

        create workers at Ns and N1;
        use "read" operations on A, B and C and
        record data in recovery data;
        destroy workers at Ns and N1;

An alternative technique that models the inclusive scheme is also possible whereby worker processes can be created to exploit the recoverability facilities of their nodes. Under this scheme, worker processes are created by an object manager at the beginning when its "record" operation is called for the first time by a process. All the operations of the manager use these workers which are destroyed in the "discard" operation when the outermost recovery region is discarded. Algorithms needed under this scheme should be fairly obvious to the reader; a sample algorithm is given below as an example:

record_recovery_data:

        -----

        if workers not created for calling
        process **then** create workers at Ns and N1;
        send message to establish recovery point to worker at Ns;
        invoke read operations on B and C
        (using worker at N1) and record data in recovery data;

Note that if the local node above supports the inclusive recovery scheme, then there would be no need to record any recovery data for B; also note that it is much more difficult in this technique — and this follows as the inclusive scheme is being modeled — for programs of an object manager to use recovery features for local recovery (this can be appreciated if the reader considers the problems encountered if the above program itself wants to use recovery facilities). Such problems are not encountered in the previous case: the object manager can record recovery data on recoverable objects and use recovery features in its programs without any complications. Lastly, it should be noted that the framework proposed here is sufficiently general in that objects that store recovery data need not be local.

IV. Crash Resistance Issues

Atomic Actions with Crash Recovery Features

A distributed system is subject to independent failure modes of its components – communications equipment and computers. The communication facility between a pair of nodes is said to have "crashed" if the nodes, while perhaps able to exchange messages with other nodes, cannot do so with each other. A node crash occurs if the interpreter of that node ($I0$) cannot maintain the interfaces ($L0, \ldots, Li$) in "acceptable" states, where the acceptability criterion is chosen by some external monitoring agency (say an operator). We shall make the following assumption when a node crashes: all the data stored in the system (except that stored on a secure storage, see below) are in an inconsistent state. Consider now our previous example of a process (Q) executing a program Pj that accesses a local object M at N local and a remote object Z at Ni. Suppose during the middle of the execution of Pj, node Ni crashes. While it is certainly possible to restore M to its prior state, the same cannot be said about Z whose recovery data must be regarded as corrupt. How can Z (and other objects at Ni) be restored to a consistent state? A solution to this problem is to provide crash resistant storage (henceforth referred to as a secure storage) facilities such that states of objects and processes can be stored on it ("secured"). Appropriate crash recovery procedures can then be introduced for bringing objects and processes back to their secured states. In a distributed system it is also necessary to synchronize the "securing of objects" such that objects at various nodes remain consistent with respect to each other.

An ingenious protocol (known as the two phase commit protocol) for achieving the above goal has been developed by many workers [2], [3], [12]–[14]. The protocol is to ensure that a given atomic action is allowed to terminate successfully only if all of the updated objects have been secured. A familiarity with this protocol will be assumed in the rest of this section. Just as we have taken the view that an object manager is responsible for providing recoverability, it will be assumed that it is also responsible for providing the necessary crash resistance features. We shall discuss some logical details of an interpreter that provides primitive facilities for suitably automating securing of objects.

In the discussion on recoverability, it was assumed that any program at any level i ($i > 0$) can make use of recoverability features provided by $I0$. Can the same be said about securing of objects? For example, is it meaningful for program Pk (Fig. 2) to secure objects used by it and for program Pj not to use secure facility? A little reflection on the reader's part will show that it only makes sense for a process to use securing facilities in its programs at the highest level of abstraction – this will ensure a proper flow of control after a crash recovery. Such a program then makes use of this facility in the manner shown below. Before commitment begins, a "secure" primitive of the interpreter is invoked. The parameters of the primitive specify the restart point and some relevant state information for the process after a crash recovery. Successful execution of this primitive implies that the current states of all of the updated objects have be-

```
                secure (crash_start, S);           [default exception handler: kill;]
crash_start:    discard_recovery_point;            "commit operations"
                unlock locked objects;             [default exception handler:
                for all the workers created do      retry the operation;]
                delete_workers (--, --);
                kill;
```

Fig. 5. Using secure primitive in an atomic action

come crash-proof (i.e., can be recreated if crashes occur). Once commitment begins, all of the operations must be completed (Fig. 5). It is possible that node and communication facility crashes can occur such that these actions take a long − possible infinite − time to complete. So, a distributed system should be sufficiently reliable to reduce the chances of such an event happening to a small probability (see the discussion on the General's Paradox in [3]). As stated before, commit operations are unrecoverable, so the only recovery action to take in case exceptions are raised is to retry that operation. Also, any crashes during the execution of commit operations can imply repeated executions of some of these operations. These factors must be borne in mind when these operations (discard, unlock, delete, kill) are implemented. The last commit action of the executing process − the absolute master process − is to kill itself, thus signifying the end of the action (a generalization enabling the process to execute another atomic action is certainly possible).

Multilevel Architecture to Support Crash Resistance

As a part of the process record of each process, the interpreter $I0$ at a node maintains a variable "state" that can take on the values "unknown" (initial value) "secured" or "committed." The "secure" primitive can be implemented by $I0$ as

```
secure (I, s):  begin
                use calling process.level.recovery data
                to construct the set of all object names recorded;
                with the process record of the calling process
                do {instruction counter := I; state := secured}
                write the set of object names, s and
                process record on to the secure storage;
                for all object names in the set do
                invoke object name.securestate;
                end
```

As before, the above is a simple logical organization that ignores any efficiency issues. It is assumed that $I0$ has access to some local secure storage facility which provides atomic read/write operations.

423

The implementation of the "discard" operation by I0 is slightly modified as

```
discard_recovery
point:              begin
                    if process record.state = not
                    committed then {"as before"}
                    if process record.state = secured then
                    {process record.state : = committed;
                      update "state" on the secure storage appropriately}
                    end
```

Finally, a new operation "crash_restore" is provided by I0:

```
crash_restore: begin
                    for all the securable objects
                    do invoke object name.crash_recover;
                    create processes and their recovery data using data stored
                    in secure storage "only processes in state = secured or
                    committed are recreated"
                    end
```

Crash recovery of a node thus consists of invoking the above operation which has the effect of bringing all the objects (that are "securable," see below) of that node to their latest secured states. Also, processes with state "secure" or "committed" are recreated. Crash restore should be a protected operation, not accessible to any object managers.

Making Objects Crash Resistant

In order to maintain a "securable" object, an object manager needs to provide two additional operations — securestate and crash_recover — that are invoked automatically by I0. Each object manager associates a variable "object_state" with its recovery data; this variable can take on one of the following values: unknown (initial value), secured, or committed. So far we have been assuming that an object manager records, in its recovery data, enough information necessary for the creation of specific prior states. In order to implement the secure-state operation, it is also necessary for the manager to record enough information for recreating the current state of the object. We assume that this information is recorded as a part of the recovery data (the two parts of recovery data are known as "undo" and "redo" parts [3], [14]).

Just as an object can be either recoverable or unrecoverable, it is also possible for it to be either "securable" or "unsecurable" (i.e., either resistant to crashes or not). Thus, an object can possess any one of the following properties:

Object Type	Properties of the Object	Comment
1	unrecoverable and unsecurable	object state cannot be automatically restored to that at a recovery point (if any); no crash resistance.
2	recoverable and unsecurable	object state can be automatically restored to that at a recovery point (if any); no crash resistance.
3	unrecoverable and securable	object state cannot be automatically restored to that at a recovery point (if any); object state can be made crash resistant.
4	recoverable and securable	object state can be automatically restored to that at a recovery point (if any); can be made crash resistant.

Clearly, it is desirable, at least for the "higher level objects" (those that are used in application programs) to be of type 4. The task of an object manager is, in general, to construct an abstract object that is recoverable and securable out of objects each of which can be of any of the above four types. (Note that details presented in Section III show that $I0$ only maintains recovery data for recoverable objects, so construction of type 3 objects would not be possible unless minor modifications are made to the algorithms of $I0$.) The disjoint and inclusive recovery schemes discussed in the previous section provide an appropriate framework for formulating and evaluating various possible implementations if these schemes are extended for securability in an obvious manner. It is interesting to observe that the inclusive scheme is preferable when crash resistance is desired. This follows from the fact that a secure operation is, by its very nature, "global," and that a crash recovery operation involves only a given node. However, it would be awkward to have a scheme that supported disjoint recovery and inclusive crash recovery. As an example, consider the object manager M of Fig. 2 (assume as before, that the concrete representation is on objects A, B, and C and further that they are local objects). Under the disjoint scheme, if process Q executing Pj invokes "secure( )" primitive, then $I0$ will only invoke "secure" operation of M (even if A and B were securable):

```
securestate:         - - - - -
            record "redo" information in recovery
            data for objects A, B and C;
            object_state := secured;
            record recovery data in a secure storage;
                     - - - - -
```

Note that the secure storage used by an object manager need not be a local object — it is perfectly possible for a manager to use some remote secure storage. The operation "crash_recover" can be programmed under the disjoint scheme as

425

```
crash_recover:          -----
                update recovery data from that stored on secure storage;
                construct states of A, B and C using "redo" data;
                if object_state = committed then object_state: = unknown;
                -----
```

The operation "discard_recovery_data" will include the following operations:

```
discard_recovery_data:
                -----
                delete 'undo" data no longer needed;
                if object_state = secured then
                {object_state := unknown; make object_state = committed
                for the secured recovery data}
                -----
```

One final point to note is that in the disjoint scheme, the interpreter $I0$ must invoke crash recover operations of objects in "low level to high level object" order. This will ensure, in the example under consideration, that the state of say, A, as constructed after the invocation of the crash recover operation of M, will not be affected even if that operation of A is also invoked by $I0$.

The case when the concrete representation of an object is distributed over several nodes needs a few words of explanation. As before, assume that M's implementation is distributed as follows: B at N local, A at Ns and C at $N1$. Then an operation such as "securestate" would be similarly coded as above except that workers will need to be created at the beginning of the operation (and destroyed at the end). It is easy to see that if N local crashes, the crash recovery procedure for that node will bring A, B, and C to their consistent states. But what happens if a node such as Ns crashes? There are four particular cases to consider:

1) Ns crashes (and remains crashed) before the invocation of an operation of M,
2) Ns crashes during the execution of an operation of M,
3) Ns crashes — but is "up" again — during the execution of an operation of M, and
4) Ns crashes and is recovered in between two calls on M.

The first three cases are easy to deal with since a time-out exception or process missing exception will be raised when an attempt is made to perform some operation on object A at Ns by a program such as Pk. A typical sequence of action that will take place is as follows: the default handler of Pk will execute "restore" to invoke backward recovery; this recovery will fail (as A cannot be accessed) so a failure exception will be raised during the execution of "restore;" the exception handler for restore (see Fig. 3) will execute fail — this has the effect of signaling "failure" to the caller (Pj). Case 4) can be detected only if consistency checks are incorporated in the programs of M. The following structure then suggests itself for all except the crash recover program of an object manager whose concrete representation is distributed:

```
                 -----
create workers at the relevant remote nodes
perform consistency checks on the
relevant remote objects; if ~ OK then
{crash_recover; fail} else
-- normal operations of the program --
                 -----
```

Note that if consistency checks detect an error then the crash recover procedure
of that manager is explicitly invoked to restore consistency. It is clear that the
crash recover program of the manager of M will succeed in restoring consistency of M only if nodes Ns and $N1$ are up and communication lines are working.
Nevertheless, we would like to make the crash recover operation of interpreter
$I0$ at N local in no way dependent on these factors (recall that the crash restore
program of $I0$ will contain a call on M.crash recover). This problem can be
solved if the crash recover programs of object managers with distributed implementations follow the philosophy of "restoring as much consistency as possible." Thus, this program for M can be designed as follows (assuming secure
storage is at N local):

```
crash_recover: create_worker (ws, Ns)
               [for all exceptions: goto X]
               using secure storage, restore object A at Ns;
               X: create_worker (w1, N1)
               [for all exceptions: return]
               using secure storage, restore object C at N1;
                 -----
```

Assuming that the rest of the programs of M follow the style indicated earlier,
eventually M will be restored to consistency. For the sake of simplicity, it has
been assumed here that the above programs themselves do not make use of any
recovery facilities. Lastly, the scheme discussed towards the end of the last section (for modeling the behavior of the inclusive scheme) can also be used to exploit the securability, if any, of remote objects. An evaluation of advantages
and shortcomings of this approach is left as an exercise to the interested reader.

Algorithms for "secure" and "crash_recover" for the remote object handler
are given in the Appendix.

Crash Resistance of Worker Processes

Finally, crash recovery aspects of a worker process will be described. The modified algorithm for a worker is as shown (the function "process_state" provided
by $I0$ returns the state of the calling process). Exception handling during message send and receive operations needs a few words of explanation. If a worker
is in a secured or committed state, then it must deliver its response to the just
executed command to its — the worker's — master. Therefore, a time-out exception during a "send" results in a retransmission. A process missing exception
during a send operation results in the worker destroying itself, unless it is in a

427

committed state: it then has little choice other than to retransmit the message. A similar reasoning applies to the handling of exceptions during a "receive" operation. The reader is encouraged, at this point, to try out a few crash recovery situations to convince himself that 1) if the master process executing an application program cannot "secure," then all of the processes created (and still alive) eventually destroy themselves undoing all of their work, and 2) if the master does "secure" itself, then it will be able to complete its commit actions (subject to the infinite delay possibility):

"actions of a worker process"

```
cycle
    wait: receive_message ( );
    [time_out exception: case process_state of
                        committed: goto wait;
                        secured: prepare 'ok' message; goto resume;
                        unknown: kill
                    end]
    if message = "establish_recovery_point" then
    {result := OK; establish_recovery_point (resume)}
    if message = "secure" then secure (wait, s)
    else {execute the command in the message; prepare answer;}
    [for all exceptions: result := exception type; goto resume]
     resume: send_message (master, Nmaster, result);
    [time_out exception: if process_state = committed or
                        secured then goto resume else kill
    process_missing exception: if process_state = committed
                    then goto resume else kill]
end "cycle"
```

Since we admit the possibility that the execution of an application program can give rise to a hierarchy of processes of arbitrary depth with master-slave relationships (with one absolute master), the relevant algorithms of $I0$ concerned with crash recovery (secure, crash_restore, etc.) have been designed to treat all processes symmetrically.

V. Concluding Remarks

In this paper we have discussed, using an object-oriented multilevel model of computation, how the abstractions of recoverability and crash resistance can be provided in distributed systems. The approach consists of 1) equipping the underlying machine at each node with some primitive facilities for supporting recoverability and crash resistance, and 2) designing object managers that provide appropriate operations necessary for the maintenance of the above abstractions; these operations are hidden from the users of the objects. The topics that were discussed included a) structure of atomic actions with particular reference to treatment of exceptional situations; b) suitability of disjoint and inclusive recovery schemes for the construction of recoverable objects with localized and distributed implementations; and c) additional issues that are raised when the above objects are also required to be crash resistant; in particular it was shown that some care is needed for objects with distributed implementations.

Some directions for future work will be discussed in the remaining part of this section. The crucial assumption that was made in this paper was that necessary to make recovery actions of processes independent from each other, namely, that a process does not use objects that are in uncommitted states. While this can be quite satisfactory for many applications, there can be situations where the resulting decrease in concurrency can seriously degrade performance. Davies and Bjork's important work on spheres of control [15]–[17] points the way whereby uncommitted objects can be made accessible to other processes in a controlled manner. The control exercised is such that whenever an error is detected, the number of processes that must take recovery actions is known a priori. A different approach has been suggested recently [11] where no such control is exercised; rather, when an error is detected, the set of processes affected is constructed dynamically. It is not clear at present to what a degree these ideas, together with the necessary crash resistance features, should be incorporated in a system. An interesting question arises as to what happens when recovery is desired after commitment. Any recovery actions undertaken in such a situation are essentially based on an examination of current system state; here again the work of Davies and Bjork on this so-called postcommital recovery provides guidelines for future work. The reader wishing to pursue this subject further may find the review papers [1], [8] of interest.

No mention was made here about how the recoverability and crash resistance features of object managers can be incorporated in programming languages that support abstract data types. One effort in this direction (for a centralized system) is described in [18], [19] where implementation details of a recovery system supporting many of the features mentioned here are also described. Whether the work described there can be extended easily so as to be applicable to distributed systems remains to be seen.

Appendix

Algorithms for the Remote Object Handler of a Node

A remote object handler itself relies on the message handling facility (mentioned earlier) for creating and destroying worker processes. We assume that each node has a "creator" process to which requests for process creation or deletion can be sent. We further assume that every remote object handler maintains a data structure for every process (that utilizes its services) in which information regarding workers created in a given level by the calling process is recorded. We shall refer to such a structure by "processname.level.workerlist."

Such lists can be operated upon as follows (it is assumed that the following programs themselves do not make use of any recovery facilities and further, all these programs have default exception handlers that execute "fail"):

record _ recovery _ data:

- - - - -

put a marker in calling process.level.workerlist signifying the start
of a new recovery region for the program at that level; record in this region
of calling process.level.workerlist names and nodes of any workers
created so far in that level; **for all** these workers **do**
      remote _ call (wi, Ni, establish _ recovery _ point)
      returns result

- - - - -

create _ worker (wi, Ni):

- - - - -

remote _ call (creator, Ni, create (wi))
returns result [for all exceptions: **signal** unable]
if there is a recovery region for calling process.level.workerlist **then**
remote _ call (wi, Ni, establish recovery point)
returns result; - - -
record worker name and its node in the worker list; record worker created;

- - - - -

detete _ worker (wi, Ni):

- - - - -

remote _ call (creator, Ni, delete (wi))

- - - - -

discard _ recovery _ data:

- - - - -

for all workers recorded in the current region of calling
process.level.workerlist **do**
remote _ call (wi, Ni, discard recovery point)
returns result

- - - - -

recover (j):

- - - - -

for the set of workers recorded in the jth to the current region of calling
process.level.workerlist **do**
    remote _ call (- -, - -, restore (j))
    returns result; - - -
    for the set of workers created in the jth to current region of calling
    process.level.workerlist **do** delete_worker ( ); delete j to the current
    region; - - - - -

The remote object handler records on behalf of each process, the names of
worker processes and their nodes that are created during the execution of a re-

coverable atomic action at a given level. Thus for action Pj (Fig. 2), the handler will record, in a region specially maintained for process Q, wi, Ni. When Q starts executing Pk, the handler will record (in a different region) $w1$, $N1$ and ws, Ns. If the execution of Pk ends, $w1$ and ws will be destroyed and when the execution of Pj ends, wi will also be destroyed. Note how messages for establishing recovery points are automatically sent to workers. Thus, if after creating a worker, a "master" progressively establishes n recovery points, n messages to that effect will be sent to the workers in appropriate order by the remote handler. For an explanation of the "fail" primitive, see the subsection entitled "Structure of Atomic Actions" of Section III.

Finally, crash resistance associated operations are shown below:

securestate:

-----

for all the worker names recorded in calling
process.level.workerlist **do**
remote_call (--, --, secure)
returns result; ---
calling process.level.workerlist.state := secured;
copy workerlist to a secure storage

-----

crash_recover:

-----

create workerlists using the data on secure storage;
"only lists with state = secured are constructed"

The following additional operation is needed in the logic of "discard" operation presented above:

discard_recovery_data:

----- "as before";
if calling process.level.workerlist.state = secured
then delete the workerlist;

Acknowledgement. The work described in the section on recoverability has benefitted greatly from long discussions with P. A. Lee. Acknowledgement is also due to F. Cristian for clarifying certain issues regarding exception handling. Papers by B. Lampson, H. Sturgis, and J. N. Gray introduced me to the subject of crash resistance. It was B. Randell who suggested the idea of combining their work with the work done at Newcastle on multilevel recovery and atomicity. Numerous versions of this paper were typed by J. Lennox.

References

1. B. Randell, P. A. Lee, and P. C. Treleaven, "Reliability issues in computing system design," ACM Comput. Surveys, vol. 10, pp. 123–165, June 1978.
2. B. Lampson and H. Sturgis, "Crash recovery in a distributed data storage system," Tech. report, Xerox Parc.

3. J. N. Gray, "Notes on data base operating systems," in Lecture Notes in Computer Science, vol. 60. Berlin: Springer, 1978, pp. 393–481.
4. E. Best and B. Randell, "A formal model of atomicity in asynchronous systems," Comput. Lab., Univ. Newcastle-upon-Tyne, Tech. Rep. 130, Dec. 1978; Acta Informatica, 16, pp. 93–124, 1981. [Also Chap. 4]
5. K. Eswaran, J. N. Gray, R. Lorie, and I. Traiger, "On the notions of consistency and predicate locks in a data base system," Commun. Ass. Comput. Mach., vol. 19, pp. 624–633, Nov. 1976.
6. T. Anderson, P. A. Lee, and S. K. Shrivastava, "A model of recoverability in multilevel systems," IEEE Trans. Software Eng., vol. SE-4, pp. 486–494, Nov. 1978. [Also Chap. 5]
7. J. J. Horning, H. C. Lauer, P. M. Melliar-Smith, and B. Randell, "A program structure for error detection and recovery," in Lecture Notes in Computer Science, vol. 16. Berlin: Springer, 1974, pp. 177–193. [Also Chap. 2]
8. T. Anderson, P. A. Lee, and S. K. Shrivastava, "System fault tolerance," in Computing Systems Reliability. Cambridge, England: Cambridge Univ. Press, 1979, pp. 153–210.
9. F. Cristian, "Exception handling and software fault tolerance," in Proc. 10th Int. Symp. Fault-Tolerant Comput., Japan, Oct. 1980. [Also Chap. 3]
10. B. Randell, "System structure for software fault tolerance," IEEE Trans. Software Eng., vol. SE-1, pp. 220–232, June 1975. [Also Chap. 1]
11. P. M. Merlin and B. Randell, "State restoration in distributed systems," in Proc. 8th Int. Symp. Fault-Tolerant Comput., Toulouse, June 1978, pp. 129–134. [Also Chap. 6]
12. J. Brenner, "A general model for integrity control," ICL Tech. J., vol. 1, pp. 71–89, Nov. 1978.
13. G. Colliat and C. Bachman, "Commitment in a distributed data base," in Database Architecture, G. Bracchi and G. Nijssen Eds. North-Holland, 1979.
14. B. G. Lindsay et al., "Notes on distributed data bases," IBM, San Jose, CA, Tech. Rep., 1979.
15. C. T. Davies, "Recovery semantics for DB/DC systems," in Proc. ACM Nat. Conf., 1973, pp. 136–141.
16. C. T. Davies, "Data processing spheres of control," IBM Syst. J., vol. 17, no. 2, pp. 179–198, 1978.
17. L. A. Bjork, "Recovery scenario for a DB/DC system," in Proc. ACM Nat. Conf., 1973, pp. 142–146.
18. S. K. Shrivastava and J. P. Banatre, "Reliable resource allocation between unreliable processes," IEEE Trans. Software Eng., vol. SE-4, pp. 230–241, May 1978. [Also Chap. 4]
19. S. K. Shrivastava, "Concurrent Pascal with backward error recovery," Software – Practice and Experience, vol. 9, pp. 1001–1033, Dec. 1979. [Also Chap. 4]

Chapter 6
Distributed Systems

Introduction

Distributed systems provide new possibilities for the construction of high performance computer systems; at the same time, however, they present reliability problems not normally encountered in centralised systems. The eight papers of this chapter report both theoretical and experimental work in the area of reliability in distributed systems.

The first four papers address the problem of recovery in distributed systems. Recovery based on atomic actions, as discussed by Randell in the second paper of Chap. 1 ('conversations') or by Lomet (first paper of Chap. 4), may be regarded as a 'planned approach' since the setting and discarding of recovery points is coordinated by the processes involved in a given atomic action. The paper by Shrivastava in Chap. 5 describes how such atomic actions can be constructed in a distributed system. Consider now a different approach to recovery whereby no attempt is made by interacting processes to coordinate the setting of recovery points. When an error is detected, it is then necessary to construct a *consistent set* of recovery points dynamically. As it turns out, the construction of such a set − termed a *recovery line* − really corresponds to the search for an as yet incomplete atomic action, which may be termed an 'unplanned' atomic action. In a distributed system where interactions between processes take place through messages, the construction of such an action is complicated because of the possibility of further interactions between processes during the search for a recovery line. Merlin and Randell discuss these aspects of recovery in a distributed system in the first paper of this chapter, and present an algorithm for constructing recovery lines. The algorithm basically involves the sending of 'fail' messages between nodes to prevent further interactions taking place. Consider now a related problem. Let there be a system of concurrent processes interacting through messages, in which each process is free to establish recovery points. When can a process safely *discard* a recovery point? Obviously, a recovery point should be discarded only when it is known that the process will never be recovered to that point. In the second paper Wood presents algorithms for determining when recovery points are 'safe' in this sense and shows the surprising complexity of this problem.

The third paper considers the problem of dynamically constructing 'larger' atomic actions (longer lasting atomic actions) out of 'smaller' atomic actions. A well known method of constructing an atomic action involves maintaining locks on all of the objects accessed by the action until the end of the action, at which time all the locks are released and the recovery capability of the action is also discarded (the action is then said to be committed). However, in the third paper Shrivastava presents a model in which not only can objects be released before termination of an action, but also the termination is not treated as the commitment of the action and discusses how the resulting flexibility can be utilised for the construction of larger atomic actions.

The fourth paper addresses the so called lost token problem for a ring of nodes. Distributed systems are often organised (either physically or logically) as a ring of communicating nodes with a single circulating control token which is utilised for synchronization purposes. If this token is lost due to some failure then the functioning nodes must insert a new token. Best and Panzieri present an algorithm for achieving this goal.

The remaining four papers of this chapter report on design and implementation efforts. A very convenient way of arranging interactions between a 'client' process and a remote 'server' process is to employ a remote procedure call (RPC) mechanism that converts a client's call into a request message directed at the server and the server's results into the corresponding reply message. Despite the apparent simplicity of the protocol, a careful design is required to cope effectively with failures (e.g. lost messages) without overly sacrificing performance. In the fifth and sixth papers, Panzieri and Shrivastava discuss various design issues for reliable RPCs and present a Unix-based implementation that embodies these ideas. This RPC mechanism formed the basis of a very interesting and practical distributed Unix system designed and built at Newcastle, which is the subject of the last but one paper of this chapter. The designers of this system, Brownbridge, Marshall and Randell, set out to construct a distributed Unix system which is functionally identical to a single Unix system. A new layer of software − termed the Newcastle Connection − was constructed that employs RPCs to handle system calls intended for remote machines. Since then, the Newcastle Connection software has been ported on to a variety of machines and distributed to numerous organizations. The distributed Unix system has proved to be an ideal vehicle for experimenting with a number of interesting ideas on system structuring which are summarised in the last chapter of this book. Finally, Jegado describes a recoverable file system constructed for Unix machines. The architecture of the system is described, which consists of (i) a message passing component, present in client and server machines; (ii) a distributed recoverable file manager component, present in client programs; and (iii) a local file manager component, present in server programs. Jegado discusses how the concepts of multilevel recovery (Chap. 5) can be applied in the design of a practical recoverable file system.

State Restoration in Distributed Systems

P. M. MERLIN and B. RANDELL

Abstract. This paper concerns an important aspect of the problem of designing fault-tolerant distributed computing systems. The concepts involved in "backward error recovery", i.e. restoring a system, or some part of a system, to a previous state which it is hoped or believed preceded the occurrence of any existing errors are formalised, and generalised so as to apply to concurrent, e.g. distributed, systems. Since in distributed systems there may exist a great deal of independence between activities, the system can be restored to a state that could have existed rather than to a state that actually existed.

The formalisation is based on the use of what we term "Occurrence Graphs" to represent the cause-effect relationships that exist between the events that occur when a system is operational, and to indicate existing possibilities for state restoration. A protocol is presented which could be used in each of the nodes in a distributed computing system in order to provide system recoverability in the face even of multiple faults.

1. Introduction

One important form of error recovery for fault-tolerance involves restoring a system, or some part of a system, to a previous state which it is hoped or believed preceded the occurrence of any existing errors, before attempting to continue normal processing. Such *backward error recovery* [RAN77] is illustrated in Fig. 1, which shows the history of a system which has suffered from a number of state restorations. (Dashed lines represent abandoned activity, dotted lines state restoration.) However, this method of describing, and illustrating, backward error recovery disguises many of the problems that exist in distributed computing systems (or in any system involving concurrent activities) in which the notion of "system state" (and for that matter of "previous") is by no means straightforward.

The present paper gives, in Section 2, a formal model of system behaviour which enables a precise definition to be given of state restoration in concurrent computing systems. A protocol is presented in Section 3 which could be used by

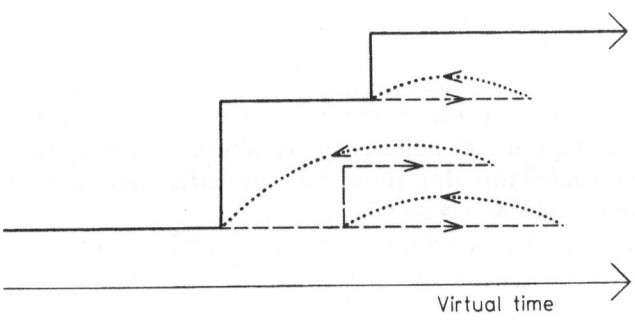

Fig. 1. State restoration in a sequential system

435

each of the nodes in a geographically distributed system in order to provide system recoverability in the face even of multiple faults. A proof of the correctness of this protocol is presented in [MER77a], together with a study of such matters as the problem of state restoration in the presence of contention for shared resources and the problem of reducing the amount of information about past system activity that has to be maintained for the use of such protocols.

2. Description of the Model

In this section we introduce the Occurrence Graph model of the dynamic behaviour of a concurrent system. Such graphs are similar to the Occurrence Nets (also called Causal Nets) described in [HOL68, PET76, PET77]. The main difference is that Occurrence Graphs are viewed as a dynamic structure which is "generated" as the system that it is modelling executes. The Occurrence Graph also contains certain additional features related specifically to the problem of state restoration.

2.1. The Occurrence Graph Model

We introduce the model using an example. Suppose that there exist files F1 and F2 (possibly at different locations) and a terminal T. The terminal requests that copies of the files be sent to a location where they will be merged into a single file F3, which replaces F1. A copy of F3 is also kept at the merging location for possible further use. Figure 2(a) represents the initial state of the system. In this model a condition (indicating a state of, for example, a given data structure, communication line, register, etc.) is represented by a "place", such places being denoted graphically by circles. Place 1 represents the existence of file F1, place 2 represents the existence of file F2 and place 3 represents the fact that the terminal is "ready to send" the requests. (In Fig. 2 the names F1, F2 and T are given only for convenience and are not part of the formal model.) The first event which takes place is the sending of the requests by the terminal. The result of this event is that the previous condition of the terminal (e.g. "ready to send" does not hold any longer, and that two new conditions, representing the requests to F1 and F2, are created. In the model, the occurrence of an event is denoted by a "bar". The new situation is shown in Fig. 2(b), where bar 1 represents the event of sending the requests, the input arcs of the bar indicate which conditions were necessary to generate the occurrence of the event (i.e. "caused" the event) and the output arcs point to the conditions resulting from this event. Bar 1 and its associated arcs thus show the cause-effect relationships between the occurrences of conditions 3, 4 and 5.

Assuming that, at this level of abstraction, copies of F1 and F2 can be acquired independently, different bars as shown in Fig. 2(c) will represent the perhaps concurrent events of copying the files. Bar 2 is generated by places 1 and 4, and this event results in the continued existence of the original file F1

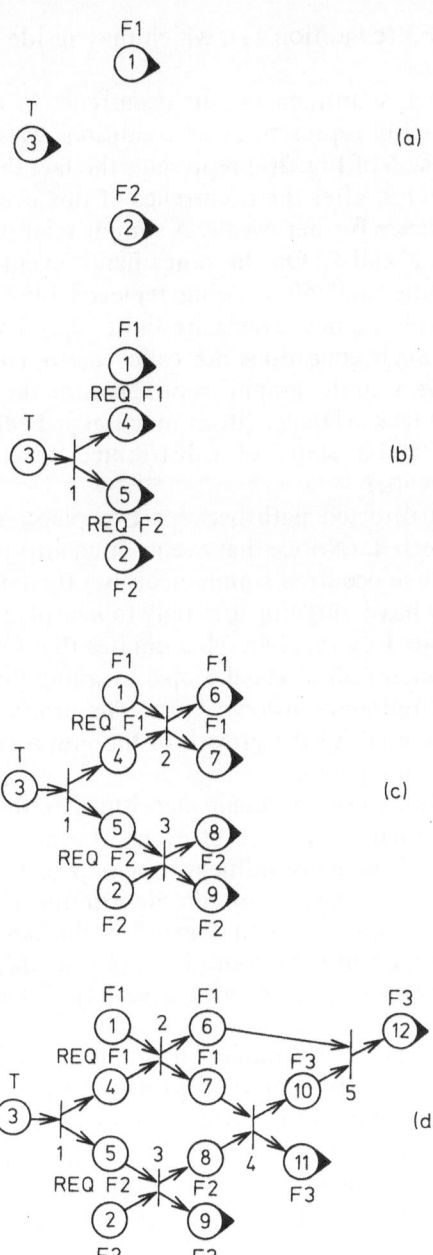

Fig. 2. The generation of an Occurrence Graph

(represented by place 6) and the sending of a new copy of F1 (represented by place 7) to the location where F1 and F2 will be merged. Bar 3 takes a similar action with respect to F2. Fig. 2(d) shows the entire Occurrence Graph model of the history of the cause-effect relationships between conditions and events for the *dynamics* of the given example. Bar 4 represents the merging of F1 and F2, and bar 5 the replacement of F1 by F3. The final result is F2 (condition 9),

437

F3 (condition 12) and another copy of F3 (condition 11), which may reside at different, indeed possibly remote locations.

In this model, we represent each place as influencing the occurrence of no more than a single event. Thus we explicitly represent those conditions which still hold after generating events, e.g. place 6 of Fig. 2(c) represents the fact that although file F1 (place 1) generates event 2, after the occurrence of this event the file is still available and able to influence further events. A similar relationship exists between event 3 and places 2 and 9. On the other hand, event 5 makes file F1 (place 6) unavailable while, and after, being replaced by F3. Hence the only conditions which may generate new events are those represented by places having no outgoing arcs. Such conditions are called *active conditions*, and are represented by *Active Places*; in the graphic representation these are, for convenience, indicated using a black triangle. (In as much as it is appropriate to refer to the instantaneous "global state" of a distributed system, this is what the set of active places represents.)

In the Occurrence Graph, there is a directed path between two places or bars if and only if they are causally connected. (Notice that events or conditions which are *not* causally connected could have occurred simultaneously.) By definition, when a new bar is created, it may have outgoing arcs only to *new* places representing conditions which are generated by this bar. This implies that Occurrence Graphs are acyclic (i.e. they contain no directed loops) meaning that no event or condition can be, directly or indirectly, its own cause. The progress made by a system or algorithm is represented by the growth of the graph (in our figures, towards the right-hand side of the page).

Notice that the Occurrence Graph does not represent algorithms (either hardware or programs) but rather the actual occurrence of events during execution and the pertinent conditions which actually influence them. The Occurrence Graph model is generated by the progress of the algorithmic execution, and from our point of view, many algorithms may generate the same Occurrence Graph. Depending on the actual timing of events, and, presumably, on the values of input data, a given algorithm may generate a variety of Occurrence Graphs.

In the Occurrence Graph model, each event is atomic. All conditions that are directly influenced by an event are explicitly connected to it by arcs and each condition has at most one incoming arc and at most one outgoing arc. The number of places and bars in a graph is allowed to be infinite. Similarly, there may be bars having an infinite number of incoming and/or outgoing arcs. There may also exist bars without incoming or outgoing arcs, representing, respectively, lack of causes or effects.

2.2. State Restoration

If an error is detected, a previous consistent state of the system should be restored at which it is possible to ignore those events and conditions which originally followed that state. By a "previous consistent state", we mean a state the system might have been in according to the cause-effect relationships between events and conditions, rather than one which had actually existed before. If the restored state is prior to the presumed set of events and conditions (i.e. the fault or faults) which caused the error, then the faults and their consequences can thus be effectively ignored.

State restoration is achieved by choosing the state to be restored, reactivating appropriate non-active conditions, and deactivating appropriate active conditions. The error detection, location of presumed faults, and reactivation and deactivation of conditions are performed by some "external mechanism" which is not considered as part of the system we model; we are only concerned with the effects that such mechanisms may have on the behaviour of the normal system.

Restoration of a condition can be achieved by the "external mechanisms" in different ways, e.g. having its original value "checkpointed", recomputing its value from related information provided by other conditions, etc. At the level of abstraction of the Occurrence Graph it only matters whether or not a condition is restorable, regardless of how such restoration can be done. In the Occurrence Graph, a restorable condition is represented by a *restorable place* which is graphically denoted by a double circle, as shown in Fig. 3. We assume that if at a certain point in time a condition is non-restorable it cannot become restorable later. (In [MER77a] we generalise to the case in which a restorable condition can become temporarily non-restorable.) Therefore, we assume that a single-circle place cannot become a double-circle place. The opposite is clearly possible, and it is called a *commitment* [RAN77], such as occurs when a checkpoint is discarded. A commitment has no impact on the regular execution of the system; it may only influence the possible consistent states to which the system can be restored.

The *reactivation* of a place can be performed, provided that the place is restorable and non-active. When a place is reactivated we want to ignore previous effects due to the place. This is represented in the Occurrence Graph by placing a black triangle in the place, replacing its outgoing arc by a dashed arc, and marking the bar to which it is connected by that arc with an "*". Such a bar is called an in *invalid bar* − our aim is to make it appear as if the event that it represents had never occurred. We show later how a subgraph including these invalid bars, and also invalid places (to be defined below), can be ignored without causing any inconsistencies.

The "external mechanisms" should be able to deactivate those conditions associated with activities which are to be ignored as a result of a state restoration. In the Occurrence Graph, the deactivation of an active place is represented by removing the black triangle from the place. However, also in this case, since a deactivation is performed by an "external mechanism" it does not correspond to the normal operation of the system and, therefore the situation of such a place is *invalid*. Hence, when a deactivation is performed, the place is marked as invalid by an "*".

In addition, any arbitrary sets of bars and places can be declared to be *invalid* by the "external mechanism" because of errors they are presumed to have caused. Our main goal is to find ways by which invalid places and bars can be ignored without causing any inconsistent behaviour by the system.

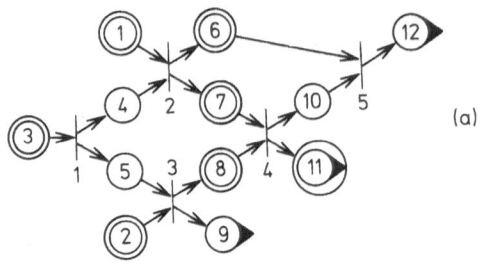

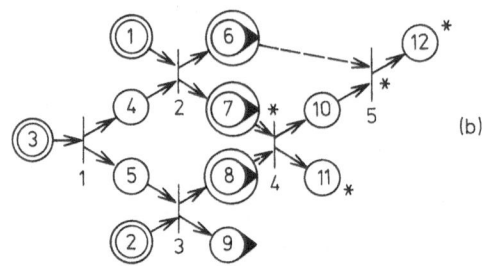

Fig. 3. Atomic state restoration

A *component* of an Occurrence Graph is a subgraph having no outgoing arcs of any kind to other subgraphs, and having no ordinary incoming arcs from other subgraphs. Incoming dashed arcs are permitted. Suppose that a component includes neither restorable nor active places. Such a component will never have an active place and therefore it will never be able to generate new bars. Since there are no outgoing arcs, the occurrence of the events and conditions of the component has no effect on the state of other parts of the system. Furthermore, since all incoming arcs are dashed, all places which are external to the component and which generated bars of the component have been re-activated afterwards. Therefore, with respect to other parts of the system, a component with neither restorable nor active places appears as if it never has occurred. Such a component is called an *Ignorable Activity*. Ignorable Activities can be freely deleted from the Occurrence Graph.

Suppose Fig. 3(a) is the Occurrence Graph of Fig. 2(d) including the marking of a set of restorable places. Since restorable marks cannot be added we assume that they existed initially. Suppose that an error is detected which is presumed to have been caused by the event represented by bar 5. Thus this bar is declared to be invalid. Hence, we have to find a way of producing an Ignorable Activity that includes bar 5. This can be done by deactivating places 11 and 12, reactivating 6, 7 and 8, and committing 11. The resulting Occurrence Graph is shown in Fig. 3(b), in which places 11 and 12 are invalid because they were deactivated, bar 5 is invalid by declaration and also because of the reactivation of 6, and bar 4 is invalid because of the reactivation of 7 and 8. The bars 4, 5 and the places 10, 11, 12 form an Ignorable Activity that includes all the invalid elements, thus the system is restored to a state it could have been in; in fact this is the state that was shown in Fig. 2(c). The Ignorable Activity can now be deleted from the Occurrence Graph.

A *Recoverable Activity* of an Occurrence Graph is a subgraph having no outgoing arcs of any kind to other subgraphs, and which is such that each incoming arc is either dashed, or ordinary and coming directly from a restorable place. This set of restorable places is called the *Recovery Line* of the Recoverable Activity. If all the places of a Recovery Line are restored, the arcs connecting the Recovery Line to the corresponding Recoverable Activity become dashed and the Recoverable Activity becomes a Component of the Occurrence Graph. Such a component can be turned into an Ignorable Activity by deactivating all active places and committing all restorable ones. Thus, a Recoverable Activity is a viable candidate for an Ignorable Activity, and in fact, *only* Recoverable Activities can be converted into Ignorable ones. Moreover all the bars which are invalidated by the reactivation of the Recovery Line, as well as the places which are invalidated by the deactivation of active places, will be included in the Ignorable Activity.

The construction of an Ignorable Activity is as simple as described above only when one can assume that the reactivation of the Recovery Line, the deactivation of active places and the commitment of restorable places can all be done atomically, i.e. when it can be assumed that there are no other changes in the Occurrence Graph while these operations are performed. The more complex case (and more realistic in many practical situations) where such an assumption cannot be made is discussed in Sec. 2.3.

We conclude this subsection by showing the two additional state restorations that can be performed in the system of Fig. 3(a). If the places 1, 2 and 3 are chosen as a Recovery Line and the rest of the graph is transformed into an Ignorable Activity, the system will be restored to the consistent state shown in Fig. 2(a). If the entire Occurrence Graph of Fig. 3(a) is considered a Recoverable Activity which is converted into an Ignorable Activity, then the entire graph will be ignored. Notice that any system can be definition be "restored" to such a consistent (albeit vacuous) state.

2.3. Decentralised State Restoration

State restoration involves the choice of a Recovery Line, the deactivation of each active place and the commitment of each restorable place of the corresponding Recoverable Activity, and the reactivation of each of the places of the Recovery Line. In many concurrent, and in particular distributed, systems it is not efficient or, in practice, even possible to perform all these operations atomically, i.e. assuming that other parts of the graph do not change while the operations are being performed. In such cases, each reactivation, each commitment and each deactivation is performed separately, and should all be coordinated in such a way as to ensure that, in spite of the possible changes which may occur in the graph between operations, the state restoration will be properly completed.

We illustrate the type of problems which may arise while performing decentralised state restoration by the following example. Suppose that in the example of Fig. 3(a) bar 5 is declared invalid, and a state restoration such as was de-

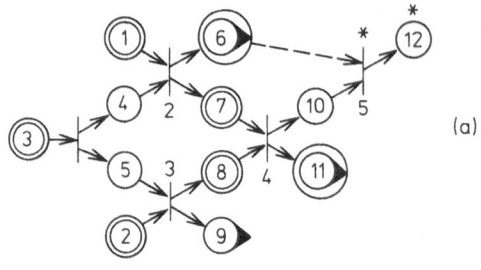

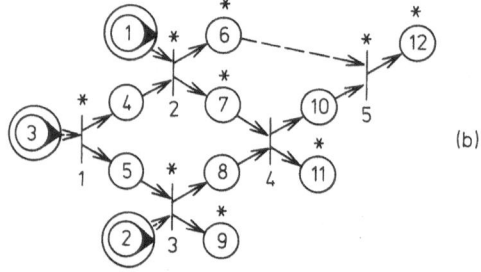

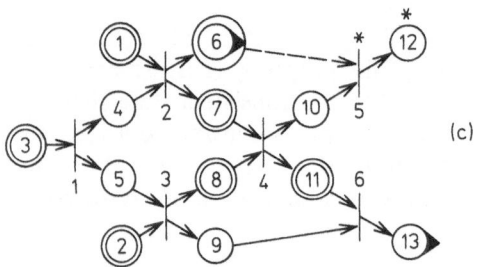

Fig. 4. Decentralised State Restoration

scribed in the previous subsection is initiated. Assuming that each restoration, each reactivation, and each commitment is performed independently, a possible intermediate state of the Occurrence Graph is shown in Fig. 4(a). This corresponds to the situation after the reactivation of place 6 and the deactivation of place 12. In this state, places 7 and 8 form a Recovery Line. To complete the restoration we need to reactivate them, and to deactivate and commit place 11. However, if in the meantime place 8 is committed then it cannot be reactivated and that restoration cannot be completed. Nevertheless, it is still possible to restore the system, albeit to the consistent state defined by the Recovery Line of places 1, 2 and 3. The resulting Occurrence Graph after such restoration is shown in Fig. 4(b). In this case, place 6 had to be deactivated in spite of the fact that it was reactivated as part of the state restoration. This would not be necessary if, for example, in Fig. 4(a) place 5 was restorable. In such circumstances it would be possible to restore the state of the system by choosing places 2 and 5 as a Recovery Line.

442

A Recovery Line may be lost not only by commitment of one of its members but also by the generation of new bars. For example, in Fig. 4(a) a new bar involving places 9 and 11 can be generated, as shown in Fig. 4(c), in which case places 7 and 8 no longer form a Recovery Line. (Such an occurrence is termed an "interaction commitment" in [RAN77].) More subtle situations could appear if the reactivated places generate new bars, possibly in conjunction with places which are from a Recoverable Activity in the process of restoration and are about to be deactivated.

Since in decentralised systems, there may be no central authority able to observe the entire Occurrence Graph, such an apparently simple task as that of determining a Recovery Line could be impossible, because while observing one part of the graph other parts may change. Section 3 describes a protocol which guarantees consistent state restoration in such a distributed system where arbitrarily many faults can be detected at different times in different parts of the system. The protocol also ensures that not only those elements which are declared invalid because of presumed faults, but also those elements which are invalidated by deactivation or reactivation operations, will ultimately be included in Ignorable Activities. The reader interested in a more formal discussion of Occurrence Graphs, of properties of such graphs, and of Recovery using Occurrence Graphs is referred to [MER77a].

3. A Decentralised Recovery Mechanism and the "Chase Protocols"

In this section we demonstrate the use of the Occurrence Graph model by discussing a protocol which guarantees consistent state restoration in decentralised systems.

Suppose a system is composed of a finite set of nodes communicating by means of messages through a set of prescribed virtual links connecting them. Such a system could be a packet switching network, a distributed application, or any other system where only message communication is permitted. In such a case there is no central means of performing atomic state restoration, and a decentralised recovery mechanism is required.

A node may send messages only to the nodes to which it is directly connected by a virtual link. Clearly, we abstract ourselves from the physical links, i.e. the virtual links could be provided by a lower level protocol. Each node can generate messages "spontaneously", or as a result of receiving messages. The dynamics of such a system can be modelled by an Occurrence Graph in which places represent messages and bars the generation of these messages. Copies of messages could be retained for recovery purposes, in which case the corresponding places will be marked as restorable. We assume that each node "remembers" that part of the history (i.e. the Occurrence Graph) which relates to it, and thus that between them the nodes "remember" the *structure* of the whole history but only the *content* of those messages explicitly marked as restorable.

3.1. Description of the Protocols

The system can freely generate new bars and places and commit restorable places, but the deactivation of active places and the reactivation of restorable non-active places are completely controlled by the recovery protocols that are described below. The protocol is independently performed for each bar and for each place. As described later, each protocol can be in either of two states, called the LIVE state and the DEAD state. The protocol for each bar or place can communicate with the protocols for those places or bars having incoming or outgoing arcs to it by sending and receiving a special message called FAIL. For simplicity of presentation, we will say that a bar or a place performs an action of its protocol (e.g. enters the DEAD state, sends a FAIL message, etc.) meaning by this that the mechanism that implements the protocol for that bar or place performs that action. We will first present the protocol informally, then give a formal definition.

Recovery is initiated when a bar or place is declared invalid as a result of a presumed fault. Obviously, such recovery can also be started when other recovery activities are already in progress in other elements of the Occurrence Graph. Initially, when a bar or place is created it is placed in the LIVE state. As described below in further detail, a bar or place declared invalid will become DEAD, and the DEAD state will propagate in all directions through the arcs of the Occurrence Graph by means of FAIL messages. This propagation stops when all the elements of the minimal Recoverable Activity that includes the invalid element are DEAD. The protocols guarantee that each DEAD place is neither active nor restorable, and that all the places which, though not included in the Recoverable Activity, have an ordinary outgoing arc to a bar of that Activity will be reactivated and the arc will be dashed. Thus each invalid element, together with all the DEAD elements caused by it, will become an Ignorable Activity. This guarantees recovery.

None of the operations performed on the graph (i.e. GENERATE, COMMIT, REACTIVATE, DEACTIVATE, INVALIDATE) can reduce the size of the minimal Recoverable Activity that includes a given element. In fact, the GENERATE, COMMIT and REACTIVATE operations can cause the size of the Activity to increase. Illustrations of this were given in Sect. 2.3, where the size of the minimal Recoverable Activity was shown to increase because a place of its Recovery Line is committed, and because the generation of a new bar nullifies the Recovery Line. There is also the simple possibility of growth by adding bars and places to a Recoverable Activity without changing the Recovery Line.

As mentioned above, the DEAD state is propagated by sending FAIL messages. Whilst this propagation is in progress, the minimal Recoverable Activity can grow because of operations performed on the graph. In such a case the DEAD state will propagate to the new (i.e. larger) minimal Recoverable Activity. Therefore, the propagation of the DEAD state could be "chasing" the growth of the minimal Recoverable Activity. In order to guarantee completion, it has to be assumed that the propagation will catch up the growth. There are many ways by which this can be guaranteed, such as giving higher priorities to

FAIL messages than to ordinary messages, bounding the number of ordinary messages the system can produce, or limiting their rate of production. We consider these mechanisms to be outside the scope of this paper, and we simply assume that the "chasing" will be successfully completed.

The propagation of the DEAD state from invalid elements having disjoint minimal Recoverable Activities is performed independently, and the state restoration of one does not affect the others. If several invalid elements have the same minimal Recoverable Activity, there is no effect on the propagation, except that now the propagation is started concurrently at several elements. If two elements have overlapping minimal Recoverable Activities, at least one of the elements will eventually have a minimal Recoverable Activity which encompasses the union of their minimal Recoverable Activities; ultimately state restoration will be consistently completed for this union. Similar comments apply to the situations which can arise if a minimal Recoverable Activity having invalid elements is enlarged (e.g. by a COMMIT or a GENERATE operation) with a subgraph which already includes invalid elements.

The protocol that each bar and each place executes is the following: If a LIVE bar is invalidated or if it receives a FAIL message, the bar will be placed in the DEAD state and FAIL messages will be sent to all places having incoming or outgoing arcs to this bar. If a LIVE place is invalidated, if such a place receives a FAIL message from its incoming arc (i.e. the event that caused it), or if it receives a FAIL message from an ordinary outgoing arc (i.e. one of the events that it caused) while being non-restorable, then FAIL messages will be sent by the place through all of its arcs independently of their direction, and the place will be left non-active, non-restorable and set to DEAD. If a LIFE restorable place receives a FAIL message from an ordinary outgoing arc, the place will remain LIVE and will be reactivated. Invalidations of bars or places in the DEAD state, as well as FAIL messages received by such bars or places are ignored.

The protocols for an arbitrary bar b and place p are summarised in Fig. 5 using a notation similar to those used in [BOC76] and [MER77b]. In this notation there is a finite state machine for each bar b and for each place p. Transition T1 is executed atomically by a 'b' machine whenever the predicate CONDITION1 is satisfied by b, and during the transition ACTION1 is performed. The transitions of a 'p' machine are executed in a similar way.

We assume that every FAIL message arrives at its destination within a finite, though arbitrarily long, time after it is sent. We assume also that FAIL messages, as well as notifications of invalidation, are received sequentially by the protocols (e.g. by queueing). This ensures that no more than one transition can be executed at each place at any given time. In [MER77a] a formal validation of the protocol is given together with a discussion of several improvements which can be made in the protocol.

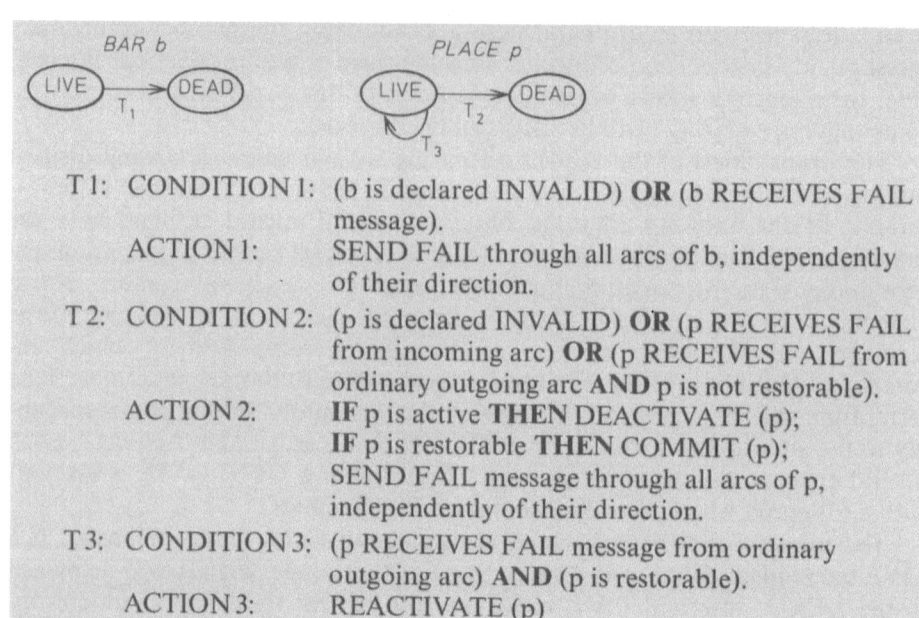

T1:   CONDITION 1:   (b is declared INVALID) **OR** (b RECEIVES FAIL
                     message).
      ACTION 1:   SEND FAIL through all arcs of b, independently
                     of their direction.

T2:   CONDITION 2:   (p is declared INVALID) **OR** (p RECEIVES FAIL
                     from incoming arc) **OR** (p RECEIVES FAIL from
                     ordinary outgoing arc **AND** p is not restorable).
      ACTION 2:   **IF** p is active **THEN** DEACTIVATE (p);
                     IF p is restorable **THEN** COMMIT (p);
                     SEND FAIL message through all arcs of p,
                     independently of their direction.

T3:   CONDITION 3:   (p RECEIVES FAIL message from ordinary
                     outgoing arc) **AND** (p is restorable).
      ACTION 3:   REACTIVATE (p)

Fig. 5. The "Chase" Protocol

4. Concluding Remarks

The ideas and techniques presented in this paper provide a basic model which can be either directly implemented or used as a reference for validation of other backward error recovery mechanisms for concurrent systems. However, much further work remains to be done.

In practical systems one could for example, expect the design of recovery protocols to take into account the planned constraints on information flow between entities of the system (e.g. using "conversations" [RAN75], rather than depend totally on such records as can be provided of the history of actual information flow. Such constraints result in a-priory knowledge of properties that the Occurrence Graphs of a particular system will possess, and which can be used to design more efficient protocols. Further study of practical constraints that will result in improved recovery protocols without unduly compromising system performance under normal conditions is clearly needed.

In many cases backward error recovery will be infeasible or insufficient, and some form of forward error recovery will be needed – this would involve the notion of "compensation" [BJO72, DAV77], i.e. the sending of additional corrective information to an entity which has previously received erroneous information, instead of requiring that the entity perform state restoration. Such strategies will involve considerations of the semantics associated with Occurrence Graphs, as well as their syntactic structure.

446

Acknowledgement. Development of the ideas contained in this paper has been greatly aided by discussions with numerous colleages in the Computing Lab. of the Univ. of Newcastle-upon-Tyne, particularly with Eike Best. Acknowledgements are also due to the UK Science Research Council for their financial support of this research.

References

[BJO72] L. A. Bjork, C. T. Davies, "The Semantics of the Preservation and Recovery of Integrity in a Data System", TR 02.540, IBM, San José, Cal., 1972.

[BOC76] G. V. Bochman, J. Gecsei, "A Unified Method for the Specification and Verification of Protocols", Pub. # 247, Dept. d'Informatique, Univ. of Montreal, 1976.

[DAV77] C. T. Davis, "Data Base Spheres of Control", TR 02.782, IBM, San José, Cal., 1977.

[HOL68] A. W. Holt, R. M. Shapiro, H. Saint, S. Marshall, "Information System Theory Project", Appl. Data Research ADR 6606 (US Air Force, Rome Air Development Center RADC-TR-68-305), 1968.

[LOM77] D. B. Lomet, "Process Structuring, Synchronisation and Recovery using Atomic Actions", Proc. ACM Conf. on Language Design for Reliable Software. Sigplan Notices 12, 3, 128−137, 1977. [Also Chap. 4]

[MER77a] P. M. Merlin, B. Randell, "Consistent State Restoration in Distributed Systems", TR 113, Computing Lab., Univ. of Newcastle-upon-Tyne, UK, 1977.

[MER77b] P. M. Merlin, A. Segal, "A Failsafe Loop-Free Algorithm for Distributed Routing in Data Communication Networks", Pub. 313, Dept. of Electr. Eng., Technion, Haifa, Israel, 1977.

[PET76] C. A. Petri, "Nichtsequentielle Prozesse", Rt. 76-6, GMD-ISF, Bonn, W. Germany, 1976.

[PET77] C. A. Petri, "General Net Theory", Proc. of the Joint IBM/Univ. of Newcastle-upon-Tyne Seminar on Computing System Design (B. Shaw, Ed.); Comp. Lab., Univ. of Newcastle-upon-Tyne, U. K., 1977, pp. 131−169.

[RAN75] B. Randell, "System Structure for Software Fault Tolerance", IEEE Trans. on Software Eng. SE-1, 2, pp. 220−232, 1975. [Also Chap. 1]

[RAN77] B. Randell, P. A. Lee, P. C. Treleaven, "Reliable Computing Systems", TR 102, Comp. Lab., Univ. of Newcastle-upon-Tyne, U.K., 1977.

Recovery Control of Communicating Processes in a Distributed System

W. G. WOOD

Abstract. The backward recovery of a computation to a previously existing state is a well-known method for attaining a degree of fault tolerance in digital systems.

In this paper a protocol is developed for the purpose of providing "unplanned" recovery control in a distributed system of communicating processes. The protocol has the property of ensuring that the whole system reverts to a consistent state in the event of one or more processes initiating recovery action and it supports the determination of recovery point *safety*; that is when a recovery point cannot possibly be recovered to. It provides recovery control that is "unplanned" in the sense that the consistent state to which the system reverts after the initiation of recovery action is not predetermined. It is determined dynamically when recovery action is initiated and is based on the recorded information flow between the processes.

The protocol is first developed for a model of computation in which each process independently implements a succession of single level, i.e. non-nested, recovery regions and where no restrictions are placed on inter-process message passing. The model is then extended to cover the case where processes may implement nested recovery regions. A development of the basic protocol which covers this case is presented and is shown to be significantly more complicated.

Introduction

The concept of backward recovery is now well-established as a means of preserving the integrity and/or consistency of fault-tolerant systems. First mooted in abstract terms by Bjork and Davies [1], the notion was given substance by Horning et al. [2] with their proposal of the recovery block scheme for constructing systems tolerant to software design faults. The concept, at least in limited forms, has also been widely adopted and put into general use in many transaction processing systems where data consistency is a critical requirement.

The basic principle of any scheme for providing system recoverability is that at various intervals a checkpoint of the system state is recorded. If at any time it is detected (perhaps belatedly) that the system has entered an inconsistent state, then the previously saved system state may be regenerated. The interpretation of inconsistency varies with the application, but generally may be characterised as violation of some invariant property which has been asserted for the system. The action taken after recovery to a consistent state also varies with the application: from system shut-down to retrying the computation.

In single process systems, or in multi-process systems under centralised control, it is simple to arrange that a global checkpoint of the system state may be taken at convenient points in time. This cannot be so easily arranged, however, in a distributed system under decentralised control.

448

Each component process in a distributed system must be responsible for recording its own state and it is the function of the *recovery control protocol* to determine a set of process states which together constitute a consistent state of the system. In general, an arbitrary grouping of process states will not compose a consistent state. They will be subject to *interference* with each other resulting from inter-process communications between the times at which the respective process states were saved.

Basic Definitions

A point in time at which the state of a process is saved for possible regeneration in the event of recovery action is called a *recovery point*. A process *expresses commitment* to a recovery point when it no longer requires the capability to initiate recovery action to that point. (Note that the process may still recover to the recovery point after commitment to it when it is requested to do so by other processes from which it has received information.) The period of process activity between the establishment of a recovery point and the commitment to it is called the *recovery region* associated with that point.

System Structures

As noted above, it is the function of the recovery control scheme to determine how a consistent system state may be compounded from a set of component process states. There are two fundamental strategies for approaching this problem, depending on whether the set is established a priori or a posteriori.

The former approach, which has been termed the *pre-planned* approach by Randell [5] and which forms the basis for the approach generally adopted in database management systems to ensure database consistency, relies on synchronisation between the processes and restrictions on inter-process communication. Processes which wish to exchange information agree to set up a *conversation,* on entry to which each participating process establishes a recovery point and within which communication with non-participating processes is prohibited. If any of the participating processes has cause to initiate recovery action within the conversation, then all must recover to the start of the conversation. On exit from the conversation, each participant must wait until it has been notified of the readiness of all other participants to leave the conversation before it may commit to its own recovery point and continue processing. Conversations may be nested (although database transactions normally are not) giving rise to the computation structure depicted in Fig. 1, where the boundaries of conversations are illustrated.

The clean system structure of the pre-planned recovery control strategy is achieved at the expense of processing speed and generality of communications. In constrast, the *unplanned* approach to recovery control sacrifices ease of recovery for speed and generality of computation. It dispenses with the

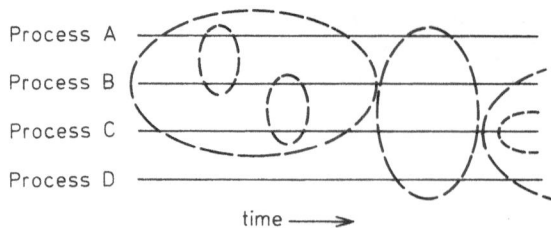

Process A

Process B

Process C

Process D

time ⟶   **Fig. 1**

restrictions of the planned approach, so that in general neither establishment of nor commitment to recovery points is synchronised among the processes, nor is any attempt made to restrict inter-process communication. Thus, during normal processing, no structure is imposed on the system. Only when a process has cause to initiate recovery action does the recovery control protocol seek, on the basis of observed information flow, to determine a set of recovery points to which the processes may be rolled back that represents a consistent state of the system; i.e. the system structure is imposed retroactively when required. Figure 2 depicts a typical history of computation in such a system, where vertical bars denote the bounds of recovery regions and arrows denote inter-process communications. The dashed lines define the set of recovery points to which the system will be rolled back in the event of each of the processes initiating recovery action. Such lines have been called *recovery lines* [5]. Note that not all processes need be represented on the recovery line – reflecting the situation where one process is not affected by recovery initiated by another.

Each of the two basic approaches to recovery control is appropriate for different applications (and there are several intermediate strategies). The pre-planned approach maps on to a transaction processing environment, whereas the unplanned approach is appropriate where the processes have a greater degree of functional identity and autonomy; for example in a distributed process control environment.

It is the latter of these two strategies, the unplanned approach, that we study in this paper. We first consider the case where the processes implement non-nested recovery regions, and derive a recovery control protocol which allows

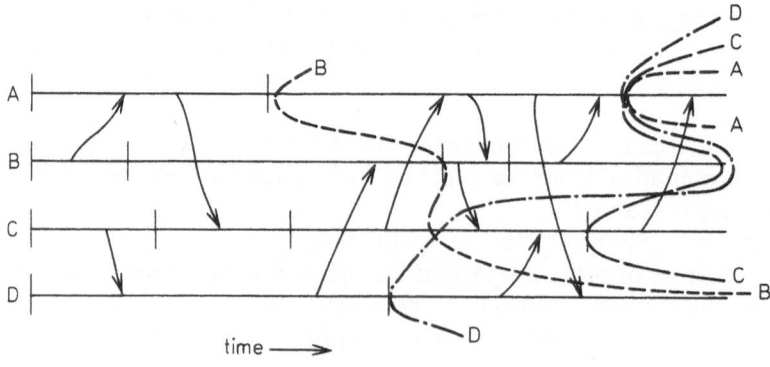

time ⟶   **Fig. 2**

450

determination of a consistent system state in the event of recovery action being initiated and also allows determination of when it is safe for processes to discard recovery points. We then extend the model to consider the case where the processes implement nested recovery regions and derive a recovery control protocol having the same two properties in this situation.

The Model of Computation

The basic model of computation assumed is as outlined above. Processes implement a succession of non-nested recovery regions, establishing a new recovery point immediately on commitment to the preceding one.

All inter-process communications take place via a message passing facility with the active participation of both the sending and receiving processes. All such communications are regarded as resulting in a flow of information from the sender to the receiver.

In many cases it is convenient to be able to regard this information flow as unidirectional, as denoted by the arrows in Fig. 2. However, using Kim's terminology [3], if the processes are "supicious" so that a process may blame the sources of its information when it finds itself to be in an inconsistent state, then information flow is considered to be bidirectional. This would be represented in our model as two essentially simultaneous unidirectional flows. In the following, without loss of generality, we shall assume unidirectional information flow in all inter-process communications. It is further assumed that information flow within processes is *total*; that is, all information sent out by a process is dependent on all information previously received by that process.

With this understanding, we can state that for any two processes P and P', if information flows from P to P' while they are inside recovery regions RR and RR' with associated recovery points RP and RP' respectively then recovery of P to RP must *invoke* recovery of P' to RP'.

It is in the context of this relationship that all references to system consistency should be understood. A set of recovery points (where, for the purposes of this definition, the current state of a process may be considered as a recovery point) represents a consistent state of the system if and only if there is exactly one member of the set associated with each component process of the system and there is no information flow from an event succeeding the establishment of one recovery point in the set to a corresponding activity preceding the establishment of one of the other recovery points; i.e. no information flow crosses the recovery line defined by the set.

In this study, we do not consider any impact on the system caused by malfunctioning of the message passing network. We see the problems of providing a reliable communications medium as being orthogonal to the problems being investigated here. In general, we assume total reliability of the message passing network, but the protocol will tolerate any interruption of finite duration to a process's activity or a communications line.

Definitions

D1) The most recently established recovery point of a process is said to be *active*.

D2) For any two recovery points RP and RP′ belonging to processes P and P′ respectively, RP is a *direct propagator* to RP′ if and only if information flows from P to P′ while RP and RP′ are the respective active recovery points of the two processes.

D3) For any two recovery points RP and RP′ belonging to processes P and P′ respectively, RP is an *indirect propagator* to RP′ if and only if: either RP is a direct propagator to RP′ or else, recursively, there exists a recovery point RP″ belonging to process P″ such that RP is a direct propagator to RP″ and RP″, or any recovery point in P″ succeeding RP″, is an indirect propagator to RP′. The indirect propagator relationship may be considered as the transitive closure of the direct propagator relationship if the definition of the latter is extended to make a recovery point a direct propagator to its immediate successor in the same process. (Note that P and P′ may be identical here. If so, then this is evidence that the "domino effect" [5] will be manifest in recovery of that process, since recovery to RP′ is a necessary consequence of recovery to RP).

D4) A recovery point RP is a *potential recovery initiator* (PRI) of a recovery point RP′ if an only if RP is active and is an indirect propagator to RP′.

D5) A recovery point which cannot possibly have recovery generated to it as a result of recovery action initiated anywhere in the system is said to be *safe*.

Thus in Fig. 3, after the history of information flow shown, the following relationships hold between the recovery points:

  A.1 is a direct propagator to D.1
  A.2 is a direct propagator to B.1
  B.1 is a direct propagator to C.1
  C.2 is a direct propagator to D.2
  B.1 is an indirect propagator to D.2
  A.2 is a PRI of B.1 and C.1 and D.2
  C.2 is a PRI of D.2
  A.1 and D.1 are safe.

Kim [3] and Russell [6] have used similar relationships to determine how to prevent the domino effect from arising. Our use of them will be in providing the desired recovery control.

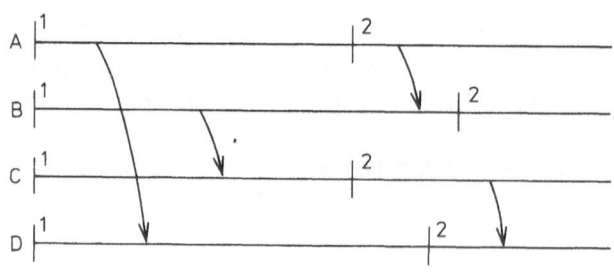

Fig. 3

We require the following two criteria to be satisfied by a recovery control protocol.

C1) It must ensure that the system reverts to a consistent state in the event of one (or many) processes initiating recovery action.

C2) It must support the determination of recovery point safety.

The first of these requirements may be seen as the useful, "productive" side of the protocol. The second is the garbage collection of the recovery points no longer required to ensure system consistency. In addition to these basic requirements, we seek to minimise the message passing and storage overheads associated with the protocol and to strive for conceptual simplicity.

As an aside, it is interesting to note that with respect to recovery control, a distributed system of communicating processes combines elements of decentralised and centralised control. The unit of control is the process, whereas the entities under control are recovery points. Processes are distributed throughout the system, but each maintains centralised control over all recovery points belonging to it. Thus the recovery control protocol can be expected to exhibit features of both centralised and decentralised control. It can exploit the simplifying assumption of total intra-process information flow to make inferences about relationships between recovery points which otherwise would have to be made explicit, involving greater message passing and storage requirements. In this context, one aspect of the recovery control protocol may be seen as an optimised implementation of the *"chase protocols"* devised by Merlin and Randell [4] as a scheme for providing recoverability in a totally decentralised system.

An Outline of the Recovery Control Protocol

It is quite clear that to satisfy the first of the criteria specified above, that of ensuring consistent system-wide recoverability, it is sufficient to maintain a record of the direct propagator relationship between recovery points. If each process is aware of the recovery points to which each of its own recovery points is a direct propagator, then it knows where it should invoke recovery in the event that it has itself to recover. It should invoke recovery to the appropriate points in all those processes to which the recovery point being recovered to, and all its successors in the same process, are direct propagators.

At first sight, it might appear that this relationship is sufficient also for the determination of recovery point safety: that a recovery point should not be declared safe until such time as it has been notified of the safety of each recovery point which is a direct propagator to it. Closer scrutiny reveals this tactic to be insufficient, however.

Consider the situation depicted in Fig. 4, in which process A has just expressed commitment to its recovery point A.1. This recovery point cannot be declared safe until A has been told by B that B.1 is safe, which cannot be stated until B has been notified of the safety of C.1, which depends on the safety of D.1, which in turn is waiting for the safety of A.1 to be declared. Thus, in the presence of *cycles* of dependencies, recovery point safety cannot be determined

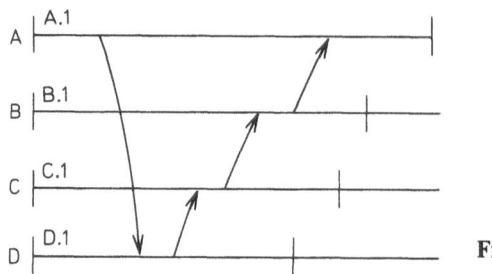

Fig. 4

solely by awareness of the direct propagator relationship, i.e. by knowledge of a recovery point's "neighbours". It is necessary to break cycles. This may be achieved by recording of the potential recovery initiator (PRI) relationship, D4 above. Then recovery point safety may be equated with having no PRI's.

In principle, a recovery point is safe when it has no PRI's. In practice, we desire a process to be able to declare a recovery point safe when the recovery control protocol leads the process to be aware of no PRI's for that recovery point. In a system under decentralised control in which message passing takes a finite length of time this desire is not immediately attainable. The PRI relationship between recovery points may be recorded by propagating throughout the system, according to the direct propagator relationship, messages telling of new PRI's resulting from some inter-process communication and messages proclaiming the commitment of processes to old PRI's. If this relationship is being recorded, then it is clear that when a recovery point does become safe, it will eventually receive messages which have the effect of placing the recovery point in a state such that it has no PRI's and will not thereafter gain any further PRI's. That is, a recovery point which becomes safe eventually will arrive in a stable state at which it is aware of no PRI's. We wish the relationship to hold good in the reverse direction also. We wish awareness of the absence of PRI's to signify a recovery point's safety. This can only be achieved if some sort of discipline is imposed upon the message passing network.

Consider the situation depicted in Fig. 5. Just before its commitment to B.1, B receives information from A, making A.1 a PRI of B.1 and therefore of C.1. B sends a message to this effect to C. It then commits to B.1 and sends a message proclaiming this to C, so that C may record the fact that B.1 is no longer a PRI of C.1. If the two messages sent from B to C arrive at C in a different order from that in which they are sent, then C.1 for a short period of time will be aware of no PRI's but then be notified of a new one. Under these circumstances, it is impossible to determine if and when C.1 becomes safe.

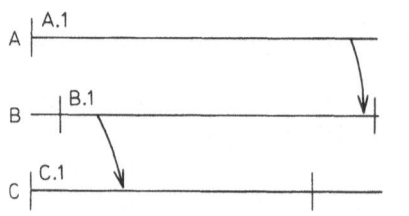

Fig. 5

However, by imposing a discipline on the message passing network so that all messages between each source-destination pair are always serviced in the order in which they are sent, it is possible to ensure that a process being aware of no PRI's for a recovery point implies the safety of that recovery point. This message serving discipline can be achieved simply by requiring that a process waits for each control message to be acknowledged before sending another, or else by associating an index with each source-destination pair. The source increments the index each time it sends a message to the particular destination and the destination only services the message which it expects next. In conjunction with some sort of time-out mechanism, this device could also serve to detect when messages get lost in the system.

As outlined above, the recovery control protocol involves recording the direct propagator and potential recovery initiator relationships between recovery points and using the former as a basis for providing system recoverability and the latter for determining recovery point safety. We now expand on these basic concepts.

Basic Operational Principles

In order to support the recovery control protocol, each process in the system maintains two linked lists: a PRI-list and a Prop-list. The PRI-list serves to record the identity of all potential recovery initiators of the process's recovery points. The Prop-list records the identity of all recovery points to which its own are direct propagators. Each time it establishes a new recovery point, a process sets up a *Recovery Display* for that point, comprising three pointers. These are:
(1) Recovery Context Pointer
(2) Prop-list Pointer
(3) PRI-list Pointer

The Recovery Context stores all the data necessary to enable the process to restore its state to that which existed at the time of the establishment of the recovery point. We are not concerned here about the form of the Recovery Context or how it is recorded.

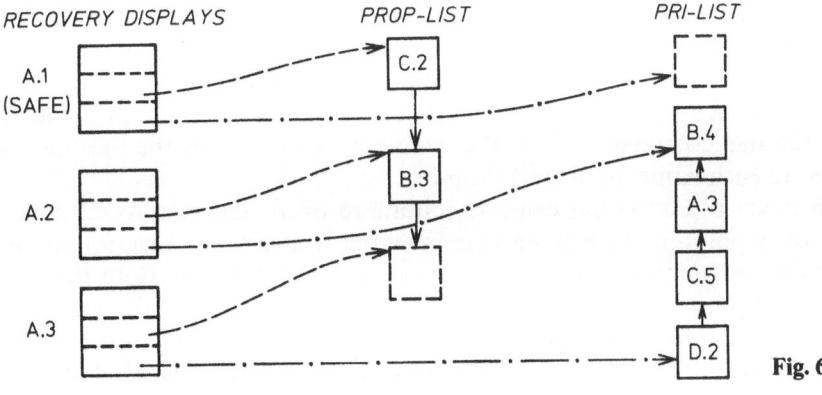

Fig. 6

455

The Prop-list Pointer is an index into the process's Prop-list, initialised to point to the tail of the Prop-list at the time the recovery point is established and never altered thereafter.

The PRI-list Pointer is an index into the process's PRI-list, initialised to point to the head of the list.

As will be described below, new entries are added to the Prop-list at the tail only, whereas new entries are added to the PRI-list at the point indicated by the PRI-list Pointer of the appropriate recovery point. Consequently, the data structures for recovery control associated with each process have the form illustrated in Fig. 6 which represents the lists that would be recorded by process A in Fig. 2.

In the following, we shall refer to the Prop-list and PRI-list of a recovery point, meaning that subsequence of the process's Prop-list (PRI-list) whose head is pointed to by the Prop-list (PRI-list) Pointer in the recovery point's Display.

There are four actions a process may perform which are significant with respect to the recovery control protocol. Three of these actions generate a recovery control message, a different message for each action. The general action taken on receipt of a recovery control message, whatever its type is to act upon the information contained in the message and then propagate it to each recovery point represented on the Prop-list of the recovery point to which the message was directed; i.e. to propagate the message to each recovery point to which the message recipient is a direct propagator.

Without going into too much detail, the principle of the recovery protocol for non-nested recovery regions may be summarised as follows (where each of the four significant process actions described below must be implemented atomically with respect to the rest of the system):

1) Whenever it establishes a new recovery point, a process adds that recovery point name at the head of its own PRI-list at the entry indicated by the PRI-list Pointer from the newly established recovery point's display. In other words, while it is live, a recovery point is its own PRI.

2) Whenever information flows from process P to process P', with respective active recovery points RP and RP', then the name P'.RP' is added at the tail of the Prop-list maintained by P and all of the PRI's of P.RP (including P.RP itself) are added at the head of the PRI-list of P'.RP'. These new PRI names are then propagated to each name on the Prop-list of P'.RP'.

3) Whenever a process P expresses commitment to a recovery point RP, it deletes that name from its own PRI-list and sends a message proclaiming the commitment to each name on the Prop-list of P.RP. On receipt of a message of this type, the name is deleted from the recipient's PRI-list and the message is propagated to each name on its own Prop-list.

4) Whenever a process has cause to initiate recovery action to its currently active recovery point, it sends a message invoking recovery to all names on the Prop-list of its active recovery point, resurrects its previous state from the Recovery Context, destroys the immediate PRI-list and Prop-list of the recovery point, re-establishes the recovery point (with a different name so that it may ignore subsequent recovery requests) and continues processing. The same actions

are performed on receipt of a message invoking recovery when the Recovery Display and Recovery Context for each recovery point succeeding the one to which recovery is invoked may be discarded, as may their immediate PRI-lists and Prop-lists.

Details of the protocol are presented in Appendix 1.

Observations and Optimisations

1) The point-to-point message servicing discipline ensures that all distinct messages emanating from a particular PRI will always be received at a given destination in the order in which they are originally sent. (This may be verified by structural induction. It depends on the fact that all messages, irrespective of type, received by a given recovery point are propagated to the same set of recovery points in the other processes − namely those on its Prop-list). Therefore receipt by a recovery point of a message proclaiming the commitment of a PRI is a guarantee that no further messages originating from that PRI will be received that have not already been received (over the same route as that by which the commitment message was propagated); i.e. it will receive no more new messages originating from that PRI.

2) The general action taken on receipt of a recovery control message, whatever its type, is to act upon it and then propagate the message. It follows that all information known to each recovery point is also known to all recovery points represented on its Prop-list. Hence, if a message is received containing information that is already known, for example two identical messages emanating from the same original source that have been propagated by different intermediaries, then that message may be ignored and it need not be propagated. The original message will have been propagated to all recovery points on the recovery point's Prop-list. As well as drastically reducing the message-passing overhead, this measure also ensures that messages are never propagated for ever around a cycle.

For example, in Fig. 7, notice of A's commitment to A.1 may be received by D.1 both via B.1 and C.1. The first of these messages to be received by D.1 will

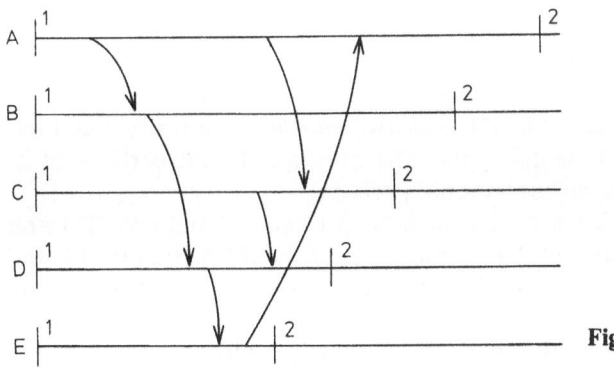

Fig. 7

457

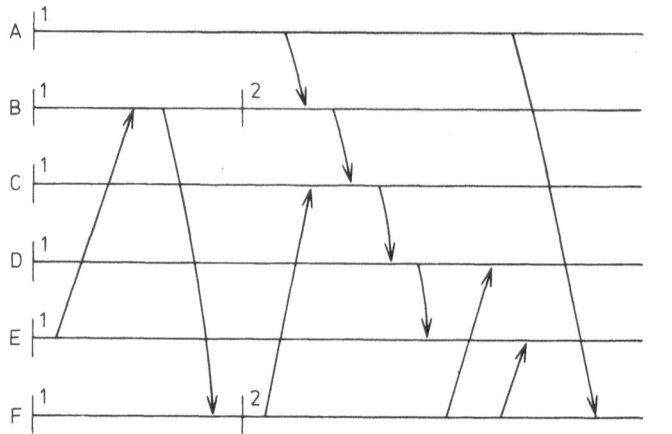

Fig. 8

be propagated to E.1. The second may be ignored. Note that E.1 would propagate the message back to A.1 where it would be ignored.

3) Conceptually, the recovery control messages of the protocol are sent between the recovery points of the system, because the dependency relationships to which they refer are defined between recovery points. In practice of course the messages are passed by the processes on behalf of the recovery points; but the significance of the centralised intelligence of processes extends beyond this.

All control messages are initiated as a result of process actions performed within the process's active recovery region. That is, all messages emanate from active recovery points and are propagated to all recovery points for which the message originator is a PRI, as determined by the dependency relationships maintained by the processes. There may be several recovery points in a single process which have the same PRI. The protocol ensures that they will all receive all messages emanating from that PRI; but this is not necessary. The earliest recovery point in a process having a particular recovery point as PRI *dominates* all succeeding recovery points in that process having the same property, in that all messages sent to the earliest recovery point will be propagated to all names held on the Prop-list of the later ones, its Prop-list subsuming all of theirs. It is therefore only necessary to record one instance of each PRI name in each process's PRI-list — so long as it is always associated with the earliest recovery point having the PRI in question. Then, if control messages are not directed to specific recovery points of processes, but rather just refer to the PRI from which the message has originated, the receiving process can associate the message with the appropriate recovery point on the basis of the PRI name. This may be thought of as sending a "*local broadcast*" message to a process and letting it use its intelligence as to which is the most appropriate (i.e. earliest) of its recovery points to which the message should pertain.

For example, in Fig. 8, A.1 is a PRI for both B.1 and B.2 and both F.1 and F.2. Notice of any action initiated by A conceptually should be sent to B.2 and F.2 and eventually propagated round to B.1 and thence to F.1 from where duplicate messages would be sent out to C.1, D.1 and E. 1 again. But if A were to send a local broadcast message to B and F which could then be directed straight to B.1 and F.1, the duplication of messages from B.2 and F.2 would be avoided.

4) We have just seen how processes need keep only one instance of each PRI name for all their recovery points. It follows that no matter how many times a process is represented on a recovery point's Prop-list, any message pertaining to that recovery point need be propagated once only to each process represented there.

This holds true even if messages are directed to the specific recovery points named on the Prop-list rather than taking advantage of the "local broadcast" capability, because the construction of the Prop-list ensures that all recovery points belonging to the same process must be held on the list in the order of their establishment. Therefore a message need be propagated only to the first representative of each process encountered on a Prop-list, this being the earliest, i.e. dominant, one.

5) Discarding of *unsafe* recovery points is also facilitated by the structure outlined above. If there is pressure on the amount of recovery data that may be stored at any one time, it is possible for a process unilaterally to discard any except its earliest unsafe recovery point: essentially by merging it with its precursor. This is done simply by:

(a) Associating the name of the recovery point being discarded with the Recovery Display of the preceding recovery point.

(b) Associating the PRI-list Pointer of the recovery point before the one being discarded with the entry indicated from the Display of the recovery point being discarded.

(c) Destroying the Recovery Context and Recovery Display of the point being discarded.

This is illustrated in Fig. 9 for the discarding of recovery point RP_{i+1}.

The significance of this capacity of unilateral discarding all but the earliest of a process's unsafe recovery points will be demonstrated in the following section when the safety of recovery points in nested recovery regions will be considered.

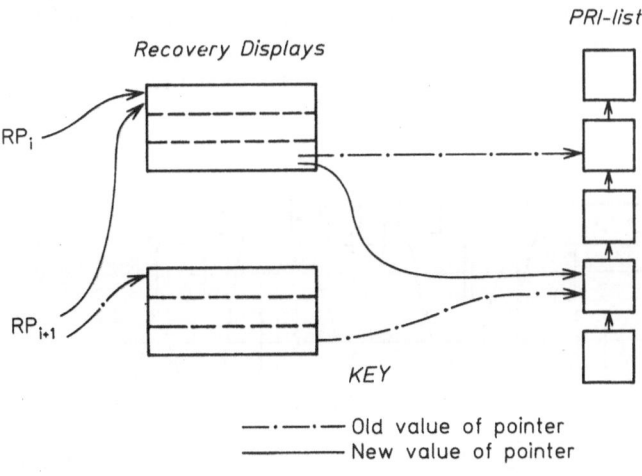

PRI-list

Recovery Displays

RP_i

RP_{i+1}

KEY

—·—·— Old value of pointer
————— New value of pointer

Fig. 9

Thus, in summary, a decentralised recovery control protocol for communicating processes with non-nested recovery regions can be made straightforward and efficient. A simple discipline on point to point message servicing enables strong inferences to be drawn concerning the existence of potential recovery initiators and recovery point safety. Details of the protocol are presented in Appendix 1.

Recovery Control in Nested Recovery Regions

There are several reasons why it may be thought desirable to implement nested recovery regions. The most obvious is that a nested structure maps naturally onto the calling hierarchy of procedures in most programming languages. It is often desirable to associate recovery regions with functional units, which normally correspond to procedures and functions in most computations. So the natural structure of the computation leads to nested recovery regions. Other reasons for implementing nested recovery regions might be to enhance the fault-tolerance capability by providing several levels of recovery fall-back, or simply to sub-divide natural recovery regions with a view to minimising the scope of recovery invoked from other processes after information flow. We make no comment on the validity of such reasoning here. We merely endeavour to find a recovery control protocol which fits the requirements in the nested case.

The model of computation to which we now direct our study is that of the previous section extended to allow processes to implement nested recovery regions. That is, a process is free to establish a new recovery point before expressing commitment to its previously established one. The recovery point to which a process expresses commitment is always the most recently established one to which it has not yet expressed commitment. This gives rise to a pattern of computation as depicted in Fig. 10. Angle brackets delimit external (level 0) recovery regions while square brackets delimit internal recovery regions.

When a process initiates recovery action, it recovers to the most recently established recovery point to which it has not yet committed. When recovery action in one process causes the invocation of recovery action in another, following information flow, then the invoked recovery should be to the latest recovery point preceding the inter-process communication over which the information

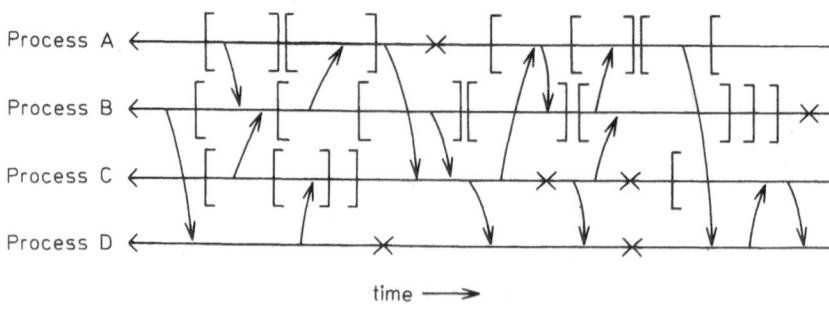

Process A

Process B

Process C

Process D

time ⟶

Fig. 10

460

transfer took place. Thus, in Fig. 11, recovery by A to A.1 should invoke recovery in B to B.1.1.1.

A simple scheme for the unilateral discarding of all but the earliest unsafe recovery points of a process by merging them with their predecessors was demonstrated in the preceding section. It is clear that the same scheme could equally well be applied to any recovery points which are nested inside other recov-

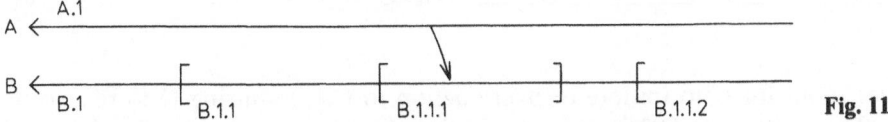

Fig. 11

ery regions. It follows that recovery point safety is only absolutely critical for the earliest outermost level recovery point in any process. All others may summarily be discarded by falling back to a preceding recovery point. For this reason, we shall confine our attention to the question of the safety of the earliest outer level recovery point of each process. We shall call this *critical recovery point safety*. This may be contrasted with the situation in which recovery regions are strictly nested in a computation with the outermost level recovery point never being committed to, always being available as the ultimate fallback point. We shall indicate briefly at the end of this paper how the question of recovery point *relevance* [4] in this situation, i.e. whether or not a recovery point lies on any recovery line, is a very similar problem to that of determining critical recovery point safety.

In determining critical recovery point safety, the commitment of processes to internal recovery points has no significance, since no information about the "validity" of any information passed within that recovery region may be inferred from this action. Only commitment to an outer level recovery point provides a guarantee that the source of some information will not initiate recovery action causing the invocation of recovery in a recipient of that information. It follows that it is only necessary to consider outer level recovery points as being potential recovery initiators and the commitment to internal recovery points need not be proclaimed to other processes.

There is no essential difference between the recovery control measures required to ensure system consistency in the nested case and those described in the previous section for controlling the non-nested situation. Basically, recovery action follows information flow according to the direct propagator relationship between recovery points, as previously. The only significant point to be noted is that two modes of recovery propagation are possible. There is direct propagation, as exemplified by the non-nested model, and *multi-phase propagation*, where a recovery point that previously has been committed to may be reactivated. Fig. 12 illustrates the possibilities.

If A initiates recovery action to A.1.1, then it will invoke recovery in B to B.1.1. Direct propagation of the recovery action by B would invoke recovery in C to C.1.1. But once C has rolled back to C.1.1 it must continue processing. This

461

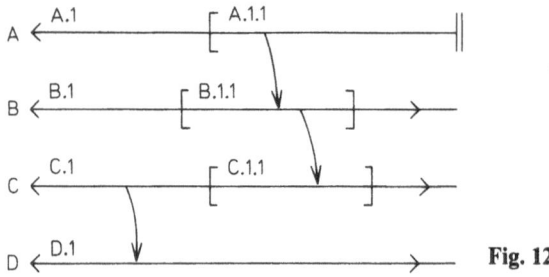

Fig. 12

leaves room for C to initiate recovery action to C.1, requiring D to recover to D.1. Thus, although D.1 is not directly threatened by recovery action initiated by A, it is threatened indirectly and should not be discarded while that threat exists. This requires that A.1 should be marked as a PRI for D.1. To generalise, all PRI's of internal recovery points must be treated as PRI's of the level 0 recovery point associated with the enclosing external recovery region.

The possibility of multi-phase propagation, however, prevents the "local broadcasting" to processes of control messages invoking recovery, as was used in the non-nested case. In the nested case, it is impossible for a process to determine to where recovery should be made solely from the identity of the original recovery initiator, because several intermediary recovery initiators may affect the issue. Figure 13 illustrates the point.

A.1 is a PRI for both D.1 and D.2. If A does initiate recovery to A.1.1, then D will definitely be required to recover as far as D.2. It may or may not have to recover to D.1, depending on whether C subsequently effects a second phase of recovery action. Thus, it has to be the responsibility of the sender of the recovery invocation message to name the recovery point to which recovery should be made by the message recipient. This is the action that was formulated for the non-nested case. It is just that the optimisation that was available there is not available in this instance.

We are led to the following redefinition of the terms introduced in D1 − D5 above, appropriately amended to apply in the nested case where the effects of multi-phase propagation must be considered.

A recovery point which has not yet been committed to is called *live*. The most recently established live recovery point of any process is said to be *active*. On commitment to it, a live recovery point becomes *dormant*.

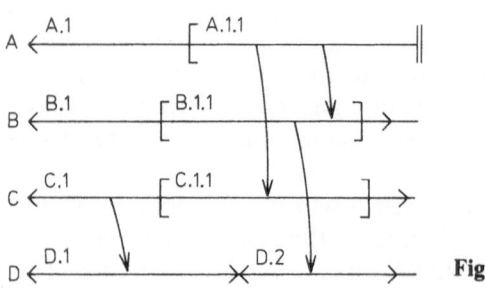

Fig. 13

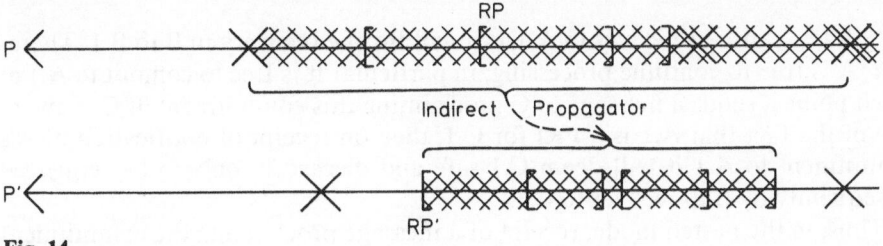

Fig. 14

A recovery point RP of process P is a *direct propagator* to a recovery point RP′ of process P′ if an only if information flows from P to P′ while RP is the active recovery point of process P and RP′ is the most recently established recovery point of P′.

RP is an *indirect propagator* to RP′ if and only if either RP is a direct propagator to RP′ or else, recursively, there exists a recovery point RP″ such that: RP is a direct propagator to RP″ and RP″, or any succeeding recovery point in the same process as RP″ or any preceding recovery point in the same external recovery region as RP″ is an indirect propagator to RP′.

It may be verified that recovery action initiated or invoked in process P to recovery point RP may (indirectly) cause recovery to be effected in process P′ to recovery point RP′ if and only if RP, or a recovery point succeeding RP in P, or a recovery point preceding RP in the same external recovery region is an indirect propagator to RP′ or to any recovery point contained within the recovery region defined by RP′. If any of these conditions hold, then RP′ is said to be *dependent* on RP.

This is illustrated in Fig. 14.

For completeness, all recovery points succeeding a recovery point in the same process are dependent on that recovery point and on each recovery point on which it is dependent. If RP′ is dependent on RP, then RP is said to be an *ancestor* of RP′ and RP′ is a *descendant* of RP.

An (outer level) recovery point RP is a *potential recovery initiator* (PRI) of another recovery point RP′ if and only if RP′ is dependent on RP and RP is still live.

With respect to the determination of recovery point safety, the nested case is significantly more complicated than the non-nested case. This derives from the fact that it is not necessarily true that a message proclaiming commitment to an outer level recovery point will be sent out to exactly the same set of recovery points as a message emanating from the same source which invokes recovery action. Figure 15 illustrates the critical conditions in their simplest form.

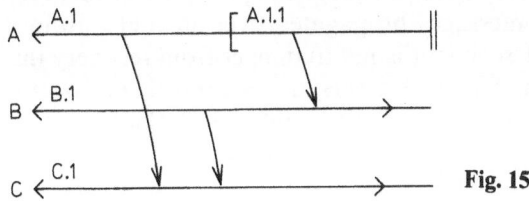

Fig. 15

If A has cause to recover to A.1.1, it will invoke recovery in B to B.1. Thereafter, A is free to continue processing; in particular it is free to commit to A.1 at which point it sends a message to C proclaiming this commitment. If C is aware only of the fact that A.1 is a PRI for C.1, then on receipt of notification of A's commitment to A.1 it will deem C.1 safe and discard it, only to be requested subsequently by B to recover to C.1.

Thus, in the nested mode, receipt of a message proclaiming the commitment of a PRI cannot guarantee the absence of invoked recovery action initiated by that PRI. The situation may be likened to a race condition in an asynchronous logic circuit — which must be avoided.

There are two alternative approaches to dealing with this situation. It is perhaps worth pointing out that the recording of internal recovery points as PRI's and proclaiming their commitment is not helpful, even although the situation described in Fig. 15 could be handled by this method. In general, the possible effects of multi-phase propagation (specifically, of multiple alternatives for multi-phase propagation from a single PRI) rule out any simple solution based on the recording of internal recovery points.

The Pessimistic Approach

The first approach relies on systematic preparedness for the type of critical conditions described above. Rather than just keeping a record of all the different PRI's of each recovery point as in the non-nested case, in this approach to recovery control in the nested case each process keeps track of all routes to its recovery points from their PRI's. The routes are expressed in terms of the names of intermediate message propagators. That is, thinking of the system as a directed graph with nodes as recovery points linked by the direct propagator relationship, this protocol attempts to keep track of all paths through the directed graph from each PRI node to each of its descendants. (The descendants record the information). Only when a "commitment" message from a PRI has been received over all paths linking the PRI to a descendant, i.e. only when the possibility of recovery action initiated by the PRI reaching the descendant has been completely eliminated, may the dependent recovery point be declared safe from that PRI. As the number of paths between two nodes in a directed graph in general is related exponentially to the number of nodes in the graph, the number of messages that this recovery protocol generates is prohibitively expensive.

We call this approach to a solution the "pessimistic" protocol, since it expects the worst: it makes systematic provision for what is in effect the worst possible eventuality. In the vast majority of cases, that is those in which the commitment to an outer level recovery point has not been preceded by recovery to an internal recovery point, the messages propagated over all routes from a PRI will all be identical: that the descendant is not in danger from recovery initiated by that PRI. In programming language terms, the pessimistic protocol is analogous to incorporating all exception handling facilities into the "standard algorithm" of a computation. In consequence, the efficiency of handling the standard conditions is drastically impaired.

The Optimistic Approach

In contrast to the pessimistic protocol, the alternative strategy, which we call the "optimistic" approach, distinguishes between the standard and exceptional situations and treats each differently. It incorporates just enough overhead in the standard algorithm to enable it to detect the exceptional condition, but makes separate provison for handling that exceptional contingency. Thus, in essence, it does not have to keep track of all paths from PRI's to their descendants.

The standard situation in this case is that commitment has not been preceded by recovery. Under these circumstances, the committing process is able to send out an *unconditional commitment* message informing its descendants that they are in no possible danger of being affected by some previous recovery action initiated by itself. The exceptional case is where commitment at the outer level has been preceded by internal recovery which has invoked further recovery elsewhere. When this is the case, we require of the protocol that no recovery point should be declared safe while there is danger that recovery action might be invoked to it.

A process expressing commitment to an outer level recovery point is aware when it has previously generated recovery to an internal recovery point and it is aware of where it has invoked recovery as a result of its own recovery action. It must warn all of its descendants of this situation, so that they do not mistakenly assume safety on notification of the commitment when they are in fact possibly endangered by the previously generated recovery action. Thus a *conditional commitment* message is used to proclaim a process's commitment to a PRI but at the same time warn of recovery action invoked to other specified recovery points. A descendant of the message originator will be endangered by the latter's previous recovery action if any of the recovery points specified in the conditional commitment message as having had recovery invoked to them is an ancestor of that descendant. In order to be able to detect the danger, each recovery point must keep a record of its ancestry. This may be implemented by a simple extension to the protocol for the non-nested case in which each recovery point was aware of its PRI's. An ancestor may be defined recursively as either a current or former PRI, or else an ancestor of a current or former PRI. So, by recording and propagating lists of former PRI's as well as current ones when information flows between processes, the PRI-list of the non-nested protocol can be transformed into an Ancestor List (Anc-list). This is the overhead in the standard algorithm which must be assumed in order to provide the foundations for the detection and handling of the exceptional condition. It will be shown that only one instance of each ancestor name need be retained on a process's Anc-list, just as in the non-nested case. (It will also be shown that the "local broadcast" optimisation is applicable for messages informing of new ancestors as the result of communications on the part of an existing one as well as for messages proclaiming conditional or unconditional commitment to active ancestors.)

There are two aspects to the determination of recovery point safety:
1) No recovery point should be marked safe which is not safe.

2) Every recovery point which is in fact safe should be determined as safe by the protocol "as soon as possible" — no recovery point should have to wait for ever to be declared safe.

The actions outlined above addressed the first of these requirements. The second implies that whenever the recipient of a conditional commitment message heeds the accompanying warning concerning the reactivation of one if its ancestors, then at some time later either it will itself be caught up in recovery

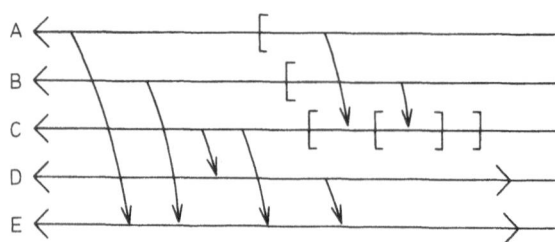

Fig. 16

action or else it will be informed that the danger has passed. In either case, it should not be left for ever awaiting one of these events. There are two situations in which a recovery point might conceivably be left waiting like this, which should therefore be avoided:

(1) The commitment message from a reactivated ancestor is not recognised — a recovery point may fail to match a message warning of recovery invoked in an ancestor with the corresponding commitment message from the reactivated ancestor.

(2) The commitment or recover message from a reactivated ancestor is not received, because the dependency relationship between the ancestor and descendant has been severed.

Due to the essential asynchrony of decentralised control, it is impossible to ensure any ordering between two independent messages directed to the same destination. It is therefore quite possible that a process which has had recovery to an internal recovery point invoked in it by another process will express commitment to the (outer level) reactivated recovery point before the invoking process has warned its descendants of the reactivation.

Descendants must expect to receive notification of the absence of danger (in the form of a commitment message — probably a conditional one) from an ancestor before they are even aware of the presence of that danger. And they must then be able to discern that the warning message, when it does eventually arrive, is already superfluous. On the other hand, that warning message must be distinguishable from other pertinent warning messages relating to the same ancestor and the commitment message must be distinct from messages proclaiming the ancestor's commitment to its normal activity. Indeed there is also the possibility that commitment messages will be received relating to the same ancestor's commitment with respect to reactivation from a different recovery invoker.

For example, if the situation depicted in Fig. 16 arises, it is possible that at some later time E might receive conditional commitment messages from both A and B warning of their activation of C.1. E might also receive, from both C and D, (distinct) messages proclaiming C's commitment to C.1 with respect to its normal activation, to its activation by A, and to its activation by B.

For this reason, it is necessary to associate an *activator index* with each recovery action which invokes recovery in other processes. This unique index is generated by the process effecting recovery and is quoted in the warning passed as part of the conditional commitment message for the index generator. It is al-

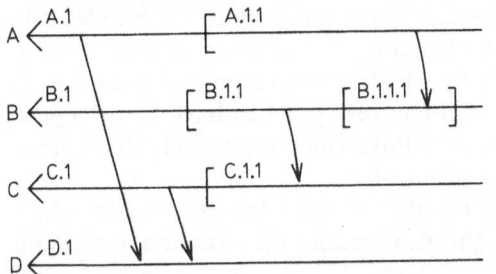

Fig. 17

so quoted in the "all clear" commitment message generated by the ancestor after its reactivation and subsequent commitment. In this way it is possible for a process to pair all warnings and reactions, irrespective of the order in which they arrive or the presence of other messages relating to the same ancestor. An analogy with the indices used between source/destination pairs to avoid races in point-to-point message flow might be drawn. So with each entry in a process's Anc-list are associated two linked lists – the Activator List, containing all activator indices that it has been informed of pertaining to that ancestor, and the Commitment List, containing the activator indices with respect to which it has been notified of commitment. For consistency, at the time of processes' normal establishing of outer level recovery points, an activator index is generated and this is quoted upon normal commitment. A critical (i.e. earliest extant outer level) recovery point will be safe when none of its ancestors in the Anc-list has an entry in its Activator List unmatched by a corresponding entry in its Commitment List. The recovery point (and its Anc-list) may then be discarded.

The second of the points noted above relates to the possibility of dependency relationships being severed by recovery action. Under normal circumstances, after recovery in one process has caused recovery to be invoked in another process via a path over which information transfer has taken place, then that path ceases to exist. However, this is unacceptable for the purposes of determining recovery point safety under the optimistic protocol.

Consider the situation depicted in Fig. 17 and a possible continuation of computation thereafter. When A commits to A.1, it may previously have recovered to A.1.1. Therefore the commitment message from A to D will be accompanied by a warning that A has invoked recovery of B to B.1.1.1. D's records reveal that B.1 is an ancestor of D.1, so it marks B.1 as having been activated by A (with the activator index quoted by A). But it is quite possible that B has previously initiated recovery to B.1.1 and therefore that the recovery action invoked by A has had no effect. D is unaware of this. All it knows is that

B.1 is an ancestor of D.1 and that A has claimed to have activated it; so it expects to receive some message emanating from B relating to this activation. If follows that B must retain knowledge of the connection between B.1.1 and C.1.1 even after that connection conceptually has been severed. Such connections are called *ghost connections* and the associated recovery points are *ghost recovery points*. B must add the index supplied to it by A to its list of activators of B.1 and include this index in its (conditional) commitment message, which must be sent out over the ghost connection to C.1.1.

Note that in the above example it would serve no purpose for B to let it be known that the connection between B.1.1 and C.1.1 had been severed, since D could not tell if this was the only path by which it was connected with B.1. To be able to determine this would require a recovery point to have knowledge of all paths by which it is connected to its ancestors, which is precisely the requirement we seek to avoid in the optimistic protocol.

The consideration applies not only to internal ghost recovery points. Outer level recovery points can also become ghosts. Consider the situation depicted in Fig. 18.

When A commits to A.1, it may warn D that it has previously invoked recovery in B to B.1, an ancestor of D.1. Even although the recovery action of B does not get propagated beyond C.1.1, D must be kept informed of events. It should be notified that B has committed to B.1 (with associated activator index as supplied by A.1.1), but warned of the recovery invoked to C.1.1. Thus recovery to an outer level recovery point must also be seen as (conditional) commitment to that point – and the commitment message must be propagated to all descendants, even although the invoked recovery action may not be propagated.

An optimisation of this procedure with respect to ghost recovery points is possible. Outer level ghost recovery points can never be reactivated. They are *dead*. If the (conditional) commitment message associated with recovery to an outer level recovery point expresses commitment with respect to all possible activators, then all its descendants may be made aware of its death. It is not then necessary for the dead recovery point to promulgate a commitment message each time it receives an activate (invoke recovery) message. Its descendants will ignore any warning messages which claim that their dead ancestor has been reactivated. The dead recovery point must however continue to propagate messages pertaining to its ancestors.

This ends the discussion of (2) above.

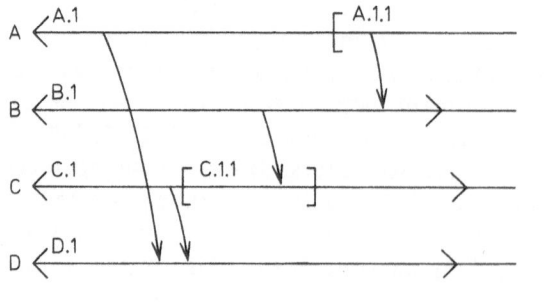

Fig. 18

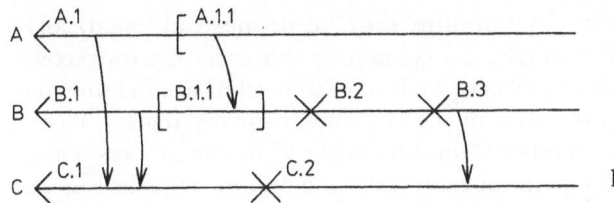

Fig. 19

We saw in the non-nested case how it was only necessary for a process to record one instance of any PRI for all of its recovery points, which was done by associating the PRI name solely with the earliest recovery point in the process having it as PRI. The same is possible in the nested case with the recording of recovery points' ancestors.

When a process invokes recovery in another process by sending it a "Recover" message, directed to a specific recovery point, the invoking process retains knowledge of this event to be included as a warning in its conditional commitment message. But "activation" of an outer level recovery point through recovery being invoked to it or to one of its internal recovery points automatically implies the "activation" of all succeeding outer level recovery points in the same process (due to the implicit intra-process information flow). The descendants of these successor recovery points must be made aware of the fact of their activation; i.e. processes having the name of any of these recovery points on their Anc-list must mark the activation on the relevant entries.

For example, in the situation depicted in Fig. 19 the conditional commitment of A to A.1 after having recovered to A.1.1 will warn C of the activation of B.1, but C must also be made aware of the activation of B.3. In general terms, this is not quite as straightforward as it might at first appear, since the recovery invoker is not aware of the identity of these successor recovery points and intra-process dependency is not a totally obvious relationship: due to the possible existence of dead recovery points. There are three possible methods by which the desired effect may be achieved.

1) Intra-process information flow could be treated in an identical manner to inter-process information flow, so that the message proclaiming the commitment (or death) of the recovery point in which the recovery was directly invoked could warn of the activation of its immediate successor in the same process as well as all other recovery points in other processes to which it is a direct propagator.

2) Recipients of the conditional commitment message warning of the activation of a recovery point to which recovery has been invoked could infer the activation of its successors. A linked list between the relevant (unique) entries in a process's Anc-list could describe the intra-process successor relationship, the links being established when new ancestors are added to the list. (All the intra-process ancestors of a recovery point are held on its own Anc-list and these may be linked at the time of establishing the recovery points. When one recovery point's Anc-list is added to another's as a result of an inter-process communication, ancestor names are not duplicated, but links to the new entries may be added to existing ancestors when new ancestor names are accepted).

469

3) Intra-process dependency relationships may be deduced automatically without the requirement for linked lists if a systematic nomenclature for recovery points is adopted. Successive recovery points at each level of nesting may be numbered incrementally from the start of the enclosing recovery region. Then, to name a recovery point, this number should be prefixed by the process name and the number of the recovery point of each enclosing region. Thus in Fig. 20 the systematic name for the arrowed recovery point would be P.2.2.2.2.

Process P

Fig. 20

However, there is another dimension to the relationship between recovery points belonging to the same process. It is determined by the incidences of recovery action between the time of the recovery points' respective establishment. This may be described by associating *version numbers* with recovery point names. Each process maintains its own version number which it increments each time it has cause to recover (thereby turning into ghosts perhaps several recovery points whose systematic names may later be reallocated when processing continues). The current value of the process's version number at the time a recovery point is established must be added to the recovery point's systematic name to make the name a unique identifier of that recovery point. This is described in Fig. 21 which illustrates the naming of recovery points over the duration of a period of a process's activity.

Then, the condition for an entry P.R(V) in the Anc-list of some process being affected when that process is informed of recovery invoked to P'.R'(V') is as follows:

$$P = P' \text{ AND } ((R \geq R' \text{ AND } V = V')$$
$$\text{OR } (R > R' \text{ AND } V > V' \text{ AND NOT } (P.R'(V) \in \text{Anc-list})))$$

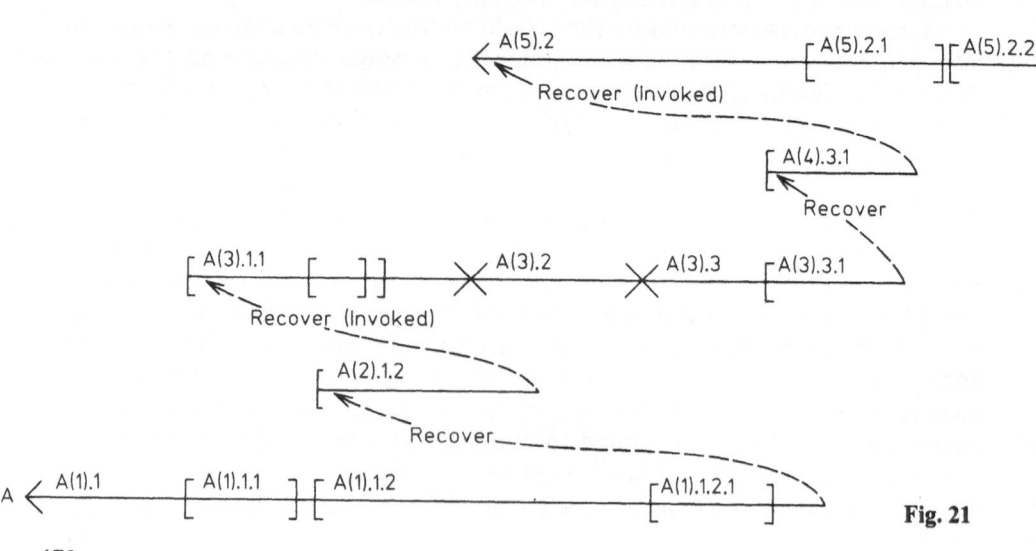

Fig. 21

470

That is, if R(V) is a succeeding recovery point in the same process as R'(V') and there is no evidence of recovery (death) having affected R'(V').

Although perhaps the least obvious, the last of these alternative solutions involves the least storage and message passing overhead.

Summary of the Optimistic Protocol

The salient features of the "Optimistic Protocol" for providing recovery control in a distributed system of communicating processes asynchronously implementing nested recovery regions may be summarised as follows.

1) Each process maintains a record of the ancestors of each of its recovery points, supported by the control messages issued as a consequence of inter-process information transfers.

2) Only one instance of each ancestor name is retained on a process's records.

3) Two types of commitment are supported: unconditional commitment, where commitment to an outer level recovery point has not been preceded by recovery to an internal one; and conditional commitment, where recovery to an internal recovery point prior to commitment at the outer level has caused recovery to be invoked in other processes. Warning of the recovery action invoked elsewhere is sent out with conditional commitment messages.

4) When a process receives a conditional commitment message which warns of recovery invoked to an ancestor of one (or several) of that process's recovery points, it marks its records with the information that the ancestor has been reactivated.

5) In order that all heeded warnings may be matched by a corresponding commitment message or by recovery action, it is necessary for processes to record a history of their recovery action by remembering ghost recovery points and their connections. Commitment messages must be propagated over ghost connections.

6) In order to maintain consistency between warnings of the activation of ancestors and notification of their commitment after activation, a unique index is associated with each activation. This is quoted in warning messages and on commitment. Processes associate an Activator List and a Commitment List with each entry in their records of their recovery points' ancestors. A critical recovery point may be declared safe when none of its ancestors has an entry in its Activator List unmatched by a corresponding entry on its Commitment List; i.e. it knows of no live ancestors.

Details of the protocol are presented in Appendix 3.

The logic of the Optimistic Protocol is fairly intricate, particularly in its optimisations on the conceptual model to reduce the message passing and storage overheads. We have attempted to present a reasoned argument in the above description of the protocol. There is not (yet) a formal proof of its correctness, but the reader is encouraged to verify (informally) that the following invariant features hold true for the protocol.

1) At any instant, each process is aware of all its recovery points' ancestors and of their activators, or else there is, or will be placed, a message in the system which will eventually reach it informing it of the addition of new ancestors or the activation of existing ones.

2) Commitment messages reach all descendants of the message originator.

3) All messages concerning the activation of an ancestor are matched, if not by recovery action, by messages proclaiming the commitment to that ancestor, and vice versa.

4) Processes can only receive messages originating from live ancestors of their recovery points (propagated perhaps by dormant ancestors), even though the message recipient may not know at the time of receiving the message that the message originator is in fact live.

5) When a process knows of no live ancestors for a recovery point it cannot receive messages originating from any ancestor of that recovery point. It follows that when all ancestors of a critical recovery point are known to be dormant (or dead), the recovery point may be declared safe.

6) All ancestors of a safe recovery point must themselves be safe.

Recovery Point Relevance

As promised, we return briefly to relate the results derived above for determining recovery point safety to the problem of determining recovery point irrelevance [4] in a totally nested system. It should be noted that in the non-nested case, recovery point irrelevance is equivalent to recovery point safety, but our consideration of critical recovery point safety in the nested case did not attempt to determine the status of internal recovery points.

It is not difficult, although beyond the scope of this paper, to map the protocols derived above onto the search for recovery point irrelevance. The only difference is that all recovery points must be treated identically, so that when information flow between processes takes place all enclosing recovery points of the message sender must be marked as active ancestors (PRI's) of the message recipient. It becomes obvious that the effects of multi-phase propagation of recovery make the detection of absolute irrelevance hopelessly complicated in the nested case. A far more practical exercise turns out to be the detection of *partial irrelevance* when multi-phase recovery propagation is discounted. This is of course perfectly reasonable, since recovery point relevance is not an absolutely critical issue. The only loss incurred as a result of incorrect determination of recovery point irrelevance is a longer than strictly necessary roll-back.

Conclusion

Decentralised recovery control of communicating processes with nested recovery regions requires more than just a straightforward extension to the protocol derived for similar systems with non-nested recovery regions. We have described two protocols for the nested case which meet the specified criteria of maintaining system consistency in the presence of recovery action and supporting determination of critical recovery point safety. The second of these protocols, the "Optimistic Protocol" has significantly better performance characteristics (in terms of message passing and storage requirements) than the first. This is due to the way it separates its treatment of the normal functioning of the system in the absence of recovery action from its handling of the exceptional conditions prevailing after a process has recovered to an internal recovery point.

Acknowledgements. This paper and the work reported herein have benefited much from the constructive criticism of my colleagues on the Reliability Project at Newcastle University, particularly Eike Best and Brian Randell. The financial support of the UK Science Research Council is also acknowledged.

Appendices
Recovery Protocol Implementation Details

Appendix 1

Non-Nested Case (with "local broadcast" optimisation)

Each process maintains two linked lists: a PRI-list and a Prop-list with pointers into them associated with each recovery point.

In the following, the subsequences of a process's PRI-list and Prop-list having as head the elements associated with a particular recovery point RP will called RP.PRI-list and RP.Prop-list respectively. The *immediate* PRI-list of a recovery point denotes that initial sequence of its PRI-list which is not included in the PRI-list of any preceding recovery point. Similarly, the immediate Prop-list of a recovery point denotes that initial sequence of its Prop-list which does not form part of the Prop-list of any succeeding recovery point. This is illustrated in figure A1.1. The general format of a recovery control message is as follows:

SOURCE	DEST	SEQ.NO.	TYPE	PRI_{INIT}	ARG-list

Network Flow Control Information   Process Recovery Control Information

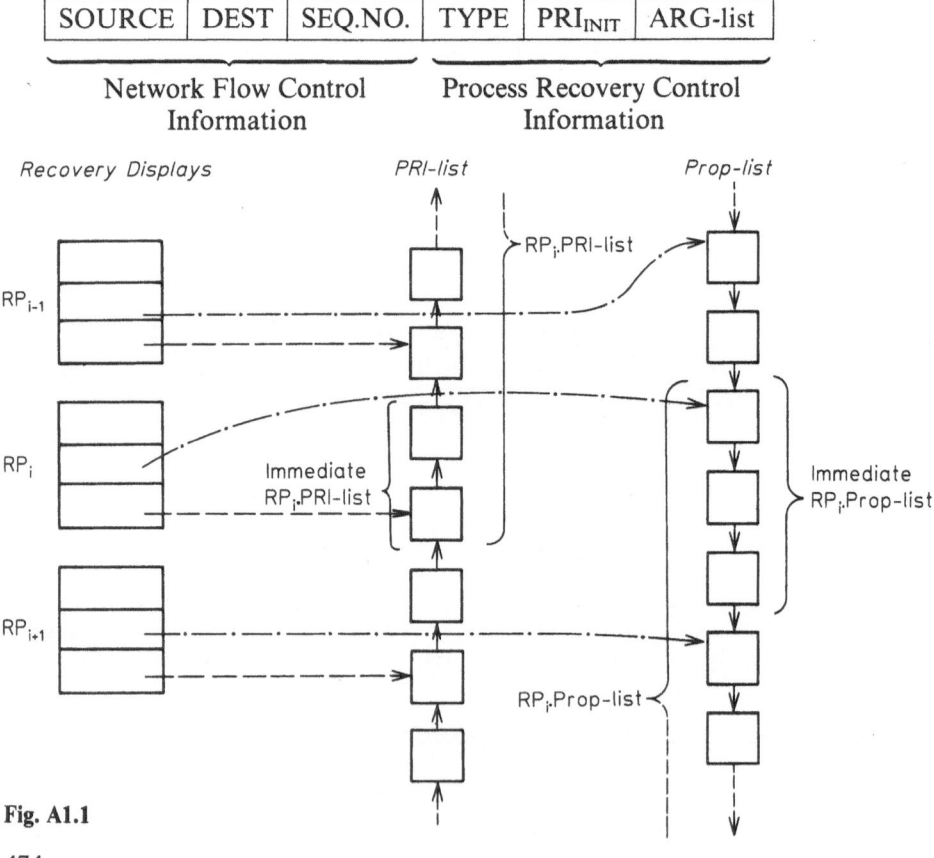

Fig. A1.1

474

The SOURCE and DEST name the transmitting and receiving processes respectively.

The SEQUENCE NUMBER is the unique point-to-point index associated with this SOURCE/DEST pair which enforces the message servicing discipline.

The message TYPE is one of three:

(1) Add new PRI's
(2) Proclaim Commitment
(3) Recover

The use and effect of these will be explained below.

The PRI_{INIT} names the recovery point from which the message originated (not necessarily the immediate source of this actual message, which may just have propagated it). This name is used by the recipient process as a key to index the recovery point to which the message pertains, namely the earliest one having that recovery point as PRI. Depending on the number of different PRI's, a process might maintain a separate index of PRI names to recovery points, or else might just search the PRI-list for the appropriate entry each time it receives a message.

The use of the ARGUMENT LIST (Arg-list) varies with the message type, as will be described below.

There are four process actions which are significant with respect to the recovery control protocol. All these actions and associated control measures must be performed atomically with respect to the other processes not participating in the action. The four significant actions are:

1. Establish New Recovery Point

When a process establishes a new recovery point it sets up a *Recovery Display* for that point, comprising three items:

(1) Recovery Context Pointer
(2) Prop-list Pointer
(3) PRI-list Pointer

The Recovery Context is used to contain sufficient data to allow the process state existing at the time of the recovery point establishment to be regenerated in the event of recovery to that recovery point.

The Prop-list Pointer is an index into the process's Prop-list, initialised to point to the tail of that list, and never altered thereafter as new entries are added at the tail.

The PRI-list Pointer is an index into the process's PRI-list, initialised to point to the head of the list. New entries are added to the PRI-list at the point indicated by the PRI-list Pointer of the appropriate recovery point.

The other action a process takes on establishing a new recovery point is to add an entry to the new recovery point's PRI-list which refers to that new recovery point, i.e. while the point is still live, it is its own PRI.

475

2. Participate in Inter-process Information Transfer

When two processes participate in the transfer of information between them, they also take the following control measures:

(1) The destination process tells the source the name of the former's currently live recovery point. (This information can be included in the message acknowledging receipt of the source's message).

(2) The source adds the destination process's name to the tail of its Prop-list.

(3) The source sends an "Add New PRI's" message to the destination, indexed by the name of the destination process's live recovery point and with, as Arg-list, the source process's PRI-list. The receiver's reaction to this message will be described below.

3. Recover

When a process wishes to initiate recovery to its currently live recovery point, it sends a "Recover" message to itself, indexed by the live recovery point name. The action taken when recovery is self-initiated is the same as when it is invoked from elsewhere, as will be described below.

4. Commit

When a process wishes to express its commitment not to initiate recovery to its currently live recovery point, it sends itself a "Proclaim Commitment" message indexed by the live recovery point name. Like recovery, the action taken by a process on its commitment to a recovery point is exactly the same as it takes on notification of someone else's commitment, as will be described below.

The action taken by a process on receipt of each of the three message types is now described in turn. The notation used is a form of pidgin guarded command language. Comments are enclosed by quote marks. The relationship "$<$" as defined between recovery points is used to denote "precedes in the same process".

1. Add New PRI's

"Received as a consequence of an inter-process information transfer. Arg-list is list of information sender's PRI's. PRI_{INIT} is name of information recipient."

"If PRI_{INIT} not represented on PRI-list, then must previously have received notification of commitment to PRI_{INIT}. Must also have received this message prior to notification of commitment".

> **if** $PRI_{INIT} \in$ PRI-list $\rightarrow$ let RP_{DEST} be earliest recovery point
> having PRI_{INIT} as PRI;
> **for each** name RP_{PRI} on Arg-list **do**

476

if $RP_{PRI} \in$ PRI-list $\rightarrow$ let RP_A be earliest rec. pt. having RP_{PRI} as PRI;
    if $RP_A \leq RP_{DEST} \rightarrow$ Remove RP_{PRI} from Arg-list
    □ $RP_A > RP_{DEST} \rightarrow$ Remove RP_{PRI} from RP_A.PRI-list;
                                      Add RP_{PRI} to RP_{DEST}.PRI-list
  fi
□   **else** $\rightarrow$ Add RP_{PRI} to RP_{DEST}.PRI-list
fi
od;
Propagate message with possibly depleted Arg-list to each process
represented on RP_{DEST}.Prop-list
□   **else** $\rightarrow$ skip
fi

2. Proclaim Commitment

"PRI_{INIT} is name of recovery point to which commitment has been expressed.
Arg-list is empty".

if $PRI_{INIT} \in$ PRI-list $\rightarrow$ Let RP_{DEST} be earliest recovery point
                                 having PRI_{INIT} as PRI;
                                 Delete PRI_{INIT} from RP_{DEST}.PRI-list;
                                 Propagate message to each process represented
                                 on RP_{DEST}.Prop-list.
□   **else** $\rightarrow$ skip
fi

3. Recover

"PRI_{INIT} is name of recovery point to which recovery has originally been
initiated. Arg-list is empty"

if $PRI_{INIT} \in$ PRI-list $\rightarrow$ let RP_{DEST} be earliest recovery point
                               having PRI_{INIT} as PRI;
                               Propagate message to each process represented
                               on RP_{DEST}.Prop-list;
                               Delete RP_{DEST}.Prop-list;
                               for each recovery point $RP_{REC} > RP_{DEST}$ **do**
                                   Delete Recovery Context for RP_{REC};
                                   Delete Immediate RP_{REC}.PRI-list;
                                   Delete Recovery Display for RP_{DEC}
                             od;
                               Resurrect Recovery Context for RP_{DEST};
                               Delete Immediate RP_{DEST}.PRI-list;
                               Rename RP_{DEST};
                               Reinitialise Recovery Display for new RP_{DEST}.
□   **else** $\rightarrow$ skip
fi

Appendix 2
The Pessimistic Protocol

We do not present implementation details for the pessimistic protocol for recovery control in the nested case, since it is obviously inferior in performance to the optimistic protocol. We merely point out the following salient features of the protocol.

(1) Each process maintains a record of all paths from PRI's to descendants – in terms of intermediate recovery point names as propagated in "Add New PRI's" messages.

(2) Each process must receive an explicit commitment with respect to each path from a PRI. Multi-phase recovery propagation is possible; so that when internal recovery points are destroyed in recovery action, a process must send compensatory commitment messages with respect to each path thus severed but not directly caught up in the recovery action. It does this at the same time as proclaiming the reactivated outer level recovery point as a new PRI.

(3) A process refrains from propagating a message when the path over which it already has been propagated includes the recovery point to which the message has been indirected, or a preceding recovery point in the same process.

Appendix 3
The Optimistic Protocol (with local broadcast optimisation)

Each process maintains two linked lists, the Prop-list and the Ancestor List (Anc-list). Prop-list entries are full recovery point names. Anc-list entires are of the form: NAME, ACTIVATOR LIST, COMMITMENT LIST.

The NAME is an outer level recovery point name.

The ACTIVATOR LIST (Act-list) is a list of the Activator Indices of the actions which claim to have activated that recovery point.

The COMMITMENT LIST (Com-list) is a list of the Activator Indices relating to the recovery point with respect to which notification of commitment has been received. Or it may contain the single entry '*' if the recovery point is dead.

As in the non-nested case, processes may maintain an index to their recovery points keyed by ancestor names to further enhance the speed of the local broadcast optimisation, or they may just search through the Anc-list on receipt of a message to find which of their recovery points is the earliest having the given recovery point as ancestor.

The format for recovery control messages is the same as in the non-nested case. As in the non-nested case, four process actions are significant with respect to the recovery control protocol. These are described below.

1. Establish Recovery Point

Each time a process establishes a new recovery point, it generates the appropriate systematic name for it (including version number) and sets up a Recovery Display comprising:

(1) Recovery Context Pointer
(2) Level
(3) Level 0 Pointer
(4) Ghost Indicator
(5) Prop-list Pointer
(6) Anc-list Pointer

The Level denotes the level of nesting of the recovery point.

The Level 0 Pointer is a pointer to the recovery display for the recovery point associated with the outer level recovery region enclosing this point.

The Ghost Indicator indicates whether or not the recovery point has been recovered beyond. It is initialised to hold the value 0, indicating that it is not a ghost, this value being changed to the appropriate activator index when it gets made a ghost, as will be described below.

When an outer level (level 0) recovery point is established, the process generates a unique activator index for it and adds an entry containing the name and index at the head of the new recovery point's Anc-list.

2. Participate in Inter-process Information Transfer

When information is transferred from one process to another, the communicants also perform the following control measures.

(1) The receiver of the data tells the sender the name of its most recently established recovery point (which need not be the currently active one).

(2) The sender adds this name to the tail of its Prop-list.

(3) The sender sends an "Add New Ancestors" message to the receiver, indexed by the outer level part of the recovery point name just given to it by the receiver (i.e. the receiver's outer level live recovery point). The argument of this message is the sender's complete Anc-list, minus those recovery points which it knows to be dead. The receiver's reaction to this message will be described below.

3. Initiate Recovery Action

When a process initiates recovery to its currently active recovery point, it sends a "Recover" message to itself, naming the active recovery point and associating with it the activator index which was generated on normal establishment of the currently live outer level recovery point. The effect of this message will be described below.

4. Commit

When a process expresses its commitment not to initiate recovery to its currently active outer level recovery point, it takes the following control measures. The notation is the same pidgin guarded command language as introduced in Appendix 1.

Let RP_{COM} be the recovery point to which commitment is being made; Let ANC_{COM} be the entry in RP_{COM}. Anc-list relating to RP_{COM};
Arg-list.Com-list := Nil;
Arg-list.Warn-list := Nil;

if Ghost Indicator (RP_{COM}) $\neq 0 \rightarrow$ Arg-list.Com-list := '*'
  ☐ **else** $\rightarrow$ **for each** index AI in ANC_{COM}.Act-list not matched
               by corresponding entry in ANC_{COM}.Com-list **do**
               Add AI to Arg-list.Com-list.
                 od
fi
if RP_{COM} is live $\rightarrow$ let RP_{SUC} be the next outer level recovery point
                               to be established.
  ☐ **else** $\rightarrow$ let RP_{SUC} be the outer level recovery point succeeding RP_{COM}
fi

"RP_{COM} may not be live if commitment is being made in conjunction with invoked recovery to an outer level recovery point".

for each recovery point RP_{INT}, $RP_{COM} \leq RP_{INT} < RP_{SUC}$ **do**
    Let GI = Ghost Indicator (RP_{INT});
    if GI $\neq 0 \rightarrow$ **for each** entry RP_{INV} on immediate RP_{INT}.Prop-list **do**
                Add $\langle RP_{INV}, GI \rangle$ to Arg-list.Warn-list;
                   od
    ☐ **else** $\rightarrow$ skip
    fi
od

Before describing the action taken on receipt of each of the three types of recovery control messages, some words of explanation on one aspect of the control measures associated with receipt of an "Add New Ancestors" message might be helpful.

As in the non-nested case, only one instance of each ancestor name is held on each process's Anc-list, associated with the earliest recovery point having the ancestor in question. This was straightforward in the non-nested case, but is more complicated here because there are further attributes associated with entries in the Anc-list beside the ancestor's name. There is the Activator List (Act-list) and the Commitment List (Com-list). The single instance of each ancestor name held on the Anc-list is the "representative" of perhaps many entries relating to the same ancestor which are associated with later recovery points. It is necessary that the sole instance assumes the "greatest lower bound" of the characteristics of all the entries is represents, with respect to the Act-list and Com-list.

For example, if an "Add New Ancestors" message is received with an argument which already is an ancestor of one (or several) of the recipient process's recovery points, and the message argument has different Activator and/or Commitment Lists to the Anc-list entry, what form should the resultant form in

Table A3.1

COMBINE	Index in Arg-list		
	$-C$	C	'*'
Index $\quad -C$	$-C$	$-C$	$-C$
in $\qquad$ C	$-C$	C	C
Anc-list $\quad$ '*'	$-C$	C	'*'

the Anc-list take? As implied above, the result must be "pessimistic" — it may not assume any property not exhibited by both the existing entries. If either entry (in the message Arg-list or process Anc-list) has an index in its Com-list which the other entry does not have, then the resultant entry must be without that entry in its Com-list. This is because the message which proclaimed the commitment to one of them may have been a conditional commitment accompanied by a warning referring to an ancestor of the other. Table A3.1 gives the definition of a function COMBINE which determines how the Com-list of the resultant entry in a recovery point's Anc-list should be formed in the above situation. The symbols C and $-C$ denote the presence and absence respectively of a given index in the Com-list of the function's arguments, namely the entry in the message Arg-list and the corresponding entry in the process Anc-list. The result denotes whether or not the index in question should be included in the Com-list of the resultant entry.

With respect to the Activator List of the two entries, the above question is not critical: it does not matter whether a given index is included in the Act-list of the resultant entry when it is represented in the Act-list of one, but not the other of the input entries. Whichever policy is adopted must be applied consistently throughout the system however.

The function COMBINE as defined in table A3.1 is applied irrespective of where the Anc-list entry is in relation to the recovery point to which the "Add New Ancestors" message applies. If the Anc-list entry is associated with an earlier recovery point, then that entry will be altered as defined by COMBINE. If the Anc-list entry is associated with a later recovery point then that entry is altered according to COMBINE, and then removed from that position in the Anc-list and added to the Anc-list of the recovery point to which the message applies. It is the Com-list generated by COMBINE which is then propagated in the message Arg-list.

We now describe the action taken by a process on receipt of a recovery control message of each of the three types.

1. Add New Ancestors

"ANC_{INIT} is recipient of information whose transfer caused this message. Arg-list is list of ancestors of information source."

> **if** $ANC_{INIT} \in$ Anc-list $\rightarrow$ let RP_{DEST} be earlier recovery point
> having ANC_{INIT} as ancestor;

481

for each name ANC_{ARG} on Arg-list **do**

if $ANC_{ARG} \in$ Anc-list → let RP_A be earliest recovery point

      having ANC_{ARG} as ancestor;

      Let ANC_A be entry in RP_A.Anc-list relating to

      ANC_{ARG};

      if $RP_A > RP_{DEST}$ → ANC_{ARG}.Com-list :=

        COMBINE (ANC_{ARG}.Com-list, ANC_A.Com-list);

        Delete ANC_A from RP_A.Anc-list;

        Add ANC_{ARG} to RP_{DEST}.Anc-list

      ◻ $RP_A \leq RP_{DEST}$ → TEMP := ANC_A.Com-list;

                ANC_A.Com-list :=

                COMBINE (ANC_A.Com-list,

                ANC_{ARG}.Com-list);

      if ANC_A.Com-list = TEMP →

          Delete ANC_{ARG} from Arg-list;

      ◻ **else** → skip

      fi

    fi

◻ **else** → Add ANC_{ARG} to RP_{DEST}.Anc-list

fi;

Propagate message with possibly diminished Arg-list to each process represented on RP_{DEST}.Prop-list, except for those ones which appear solely on the immediate Prop-list of ghost recovery points.

  od

◻ **else** → skip

fi

2. Proclaim Commitment

"ANC_{INIT} is recovery point to which commitment has been expressed. Arg-list = Commit List (Com-list) of activators of ANC_{INIT} + (perhaps) Warning List (Warn-list) of pairs $\langle RP_{INV}$, Activator Index of previously invoked recovery$\rangle$"

if $ANC_{INIT} \in$ Anc-list → let RP_{DEST} be earliest recovery point

               having ANC_{INIT} as ancestor;

  let ANC_A be entry in RP_{DEST}.Anc-list referring to ANC_{INIT};

  for each index AI on Arg-list.Com-list **do**

    if AI = '*' → ANC_A.Com-list := '*'

    ◻ AI $\in ANC_A$.Com-list → Delete AI from Arg-list.Com-list

    ◻ **else** → Add AI to ANC_A.Com-list

    fi

  od;

  for each name $P_{INV}.RP_{INV}$ (V_{INV}) on Arg-list.Warn-list **do**

  for each entry P.RP (V) on Anc-list (before RP_{DEST}.Anc-list) **do**

if $P_{INV} = P$ AND $((RP_{INV} \leq RP$ AND $V_{INV} = V)$ OR $(RP_{INV} < RP$ AND
$\qquad\qquad V_{INV} < V$ AND NOT $(P.RP\,(V_{INV}) \in$ Anc-list$))) \rightarrow$
$\qquad$ Let AI_{INV} be activator index paired with $P_{INV}.RP_{INV}\,(V_{INV})$
$\qquad$ in Arg-list. Warn-list;
$\qquad$ **if** $P.RP\,(V).$Com-list $=$ '*' $\rightarrow$ skip
$\qquad$ ▯ $\quad AI_{INV} \in P.RP\,(V).$Act-list $\rightarrow$ skip
$\qquad$ ▯ $\quad$ **else** $\rightarrow$ Add AI_{INV} to $P.RP\,(V).$Act-list;
$\qquad\qquad\qquad$ Mark tuple containing AI in Arg-list. Warn-list
$\qquad$ **fi**
$\qquad$ ▯ $\quad$ **else** $\rightarrow$ skip
$\qquad$ **fi**
$\quad$ **od;**
$\quad$ **if** unmarked $(\langle P_{INV}.RP_{INV}\,(V_{INV}),\,AI\rangle) \rightarrow$ Delete from Arg-list. Warn-list
$\quad$ ▯ $\quad$ **else** $\rightarrow$ skip
$\quad$ **fi**
od
▯ $\quad$ **else** $\rightarrow$ skip
fi

3. Recover

"$ANC_{INIT} =$ not used.
$\qquad$ Arg-list $= RP_{REC}$, name of recovery point to which recovery should be
$\qquad$ made, $+$ Recovery Index RI"

if Ghost Indicator $(RP_{REC}) \neq 0 \rightarrow$
$\quad$ **if** LEVEL $(RP_{REC}) = 0 \rightarrow$ skip;
$\quad$ "RP_{REC} is dead. Descendants know this"
$\quad$ ▯ $\quad$ **else** $\rightarrow$ Let RP_{REC0} be level 0 recovery point for region enclosing RP_{REC};
$\qquad\qquad\qquad$ Let ANC_{REC0} be entry in $RP_{REC0}.$Anc-list referring to RP_{REC0};
$\qquad\qquad\qquad$ Add RI to $ANC_{REC0}.$Act-list;
$\qquad$ **if** RP_{REC0} live $\rightarrow$ Enact Commitment to RP_{REC0}
$\qquad$ ▯ $\quad$ **else** $\rightarrow$ skip
$\qquad$ **fi**
$\quad$ **fi**
▯ $\quad$ **else** $\rightarrow$ Generate unique Recovery Index RI_{NEW};

Propagate "Recover" message with Index RI_{NEW} to first representative of each
process encountered on $RP_{REC}.$Prop-list, discounting all those which are on the
immediate Prop-list of ghost recovery points;

$\quad$ **for each** recovery point $RP_G \geq RP_{REC}$ **do**
$\quad$ **if** Ghost Indicator $(RP_G) = 0 \rightarrow$ Ghost Indicator $(RP_G) := RI_{NEW}$
$\quad$ ▯ $\quad$ **else** $\rightarrow$ skip
$\quad$ **fi**
$\quad$ **od;**

for each outer level recovery point $RP_0 \geq RP_{REC}$ **do**

   if Ghost Indicator $(RP_0) = RI_{NEW} \rightarrow$ let ANC_0 be entry in RP_0.Anc-list

                             referring to RP_0;

                             Add RI to ANC_0.Act-list;

                             Enact Commitment to RP_0

  ☐ **else** $\rightarrow$ skip

  fi;

  Discard immediate RP_0.PRI-list

od;

if LEVEL $(RP_{REC0}) \neq 0 \rightarrow$ let ANC_{REC0} be the entry in RP_{REC0}.Anc-list

                             referring to RP_{REC0};

                             Add RI to ANC_{REC0}.Act-list

  ☐ **else** $\rightarrow$ skip

fi;

for each recovery point $RP_G > RP_{REC}$ **do**

  Discard Recovery Context for RP_G

od

Discard RP_{DEC}.Prop-list;

Discard immediate RP_{REC}.PRI-list;

Increment process's version number;

Resurrect Recovery Context for RP_{REC};

Re-establish RP_{REC} with new version number;

"same as establishing completely new recovery point which happens to have same systematic name and Recovery Context as RP_{REC}".

fi

References

1. L. A. Bjork; C. T. Davies: "The Semantics of the Preservation and Recovery of Integrity in a Data System". IBM Technical Report TR 02.540 (December 1972).
2. J. J. Horning; H. C. Lauer; P. M. Melliar-Smith; B. Randell: "A Program Structure for Error Detection and Recovery". In Lecture Notes in Computer Science, Vol. 16 pp. 171−187. Eds. E. Gelenbe; C. Kaiser: Springer-Verlag, Berlin. [Also Chap. 2]
3. K. H. Kim: "An Approach to Programmer-Transparent Co-ordination of Recovering Parallel Processes and its Efficient Implementation Rules". Proc. 1978 Int. Conf. on Parallel Processing) (August 1978), pp. 58−68.
4. P. M. Merlin; B. Randell: "Consistent State Restoration in Distributed Systems". Technical Report 113, Computing Laboratory, University of Newcastle upon Tyne (October 1977).
5. B. Randell: "System Structure for Fault Tolerance". IEEE Trans. on Software Engineering, SE-1, No. 2 (February 1975), pp. 220−235. [Also Chap. 1]
6. D. L. Russell: "State Restoration in Systems of Communicating Processes". IEEE Trans. on Software Engineering SE-6, No. 2 (March 1980), pp. 183−193.

A short version of this paper was published in the Digest of papers, FTCS-11, pp. 159−164, June 1981.

A Dependency, Commitment and Recovery Model for Atomic Actions

S. K. Shrivastava

Abstract. Some ideas on the construction of user applications as atomic actions are developed. Atomic actions that last a long time pose several problems if conventional ideas on concurrency control and recovery are applied. What is required is some means of delaying commitment without sacrificing performance. A model is proposed in which it is possible for an action to release and process as yet uncommitable objects. The impact of this on recovery is also discussed.

1. Introduction

Much of the recent work in the areas of reliability and data integrity in distributed systems has been concerned with the provision of atomic transactions (atomic actions) [1 – 6]. Such an action is characterised by the serializable property [7]: it is the unit of concurrency control such that concurrent execution of actions is equivalent to some serial order of execution. For reliability purposes, it is also convenient to make it the unit of recovery such that an ongoing action that would have normally produced changes in the system state, can be terminated without producing any state changes – the action is then said to be recovered or aborted. By structuring user's interactions with the system as atomic actions with the above recovery property (henceforth termed *basic actions*) a powerful tool for maintaining the integrity of the shared data of the system is obtained. If during the execution of a basic action, some erroneous situation is detected such that further meaningful progress is not possible, then the recovery capability of that action is invoked for aborting the action. Refers. [2 – 5] describe numerous schemes for the construction of such actions in systems. For basic ideas on atomic actions, recovery and reliability, the reader's attention is drawn to the much cited paper of Randell et al. [8].

Given a user interface that provides the facilities for the construction of basic actions, the next question that naturally arises is, can user applications be constructed out of them with similar 'clean' properties? Unfortunately this does not appear to be easily possible for the following reasons:

(i) The relatively straightforward concurrency control technique that is typically used for the construction of basic actions (essentially the two phase locking scheme [7] with locks held till the end of an action) is not always practicable for the construction of 'bigger' atomic actions – actions that last for a longer time than a few seconds. Consider for example an insurance claim processing application where a client's claim can take as long as say six months to process. Logically, the claim processing can be regarded as an atomic action and yet it is absurd to assume that parts of the insurance data base will be kept locked for that long a period of time. Clearly a more sophisticated concurrency control technique is necessary.

(ii) The "all or nothing" property of a basic action is often not desirable, and sometimes impossible to achieve. This is because during the execution of an application, side effects might be produced that are either difficult or expensive to 'undo' or are potentially unrecoverable.

The above discussion is intended to suggest that a new set of mechanisms is needed to help construct arbitrary user applications out of basic actions. The model to be developed here is a step in that direction. The ideas to be described here are a further development (with occasional recasting) of the pioneering work on spheres of control by C. T. Davies and L. A. Bjork [9—13]. We begin by reviewing the essential ideas of their work. In the rest of the paper we shall concentrate upon "data processing" applications — those concerned with long term storage and manipulation of data (e.g. banking, office information systems); though the applicability of the ideas to other fields such as process control is not ruled out.

2. Basic Ideas on Commitment and Recovery

"As is true for the trapeze artist, so must data processing have a basis for further action, such basis being a commitment to prior action" — C. T. Davies [10].

Any atomic action can be viewed at a lower level as constructed out of more primitive atomic actions — this is illustrated in the 'trace diagram' of Fig. 1 which also introduce the diagramatic notation that will be used.

According to Fig. 1, actions E's constituents are actions A, B, C and D; the figure also shows the causal relationships between the actions. So, the execution sequence of actions A, B, C and D was 'A' followed by concurrent execution of 'B' and 'C' followed by 'D'. A line joining two actions is meant to represent the fact that outputs of the 'left' action are used by the 'right' action. So in Fig. 1, D gets its input from B and C and outputs of E are being used by F. Assume that time has advanced upto t2 and that an error is detected during the execution of C. Under such a circumstance, it is logically possible to abort C without affecting any other ongoing action (B in this case); in other words, C can be *recovered* ('backed out') *unilaterally*. What happens after C's recovery? The question must

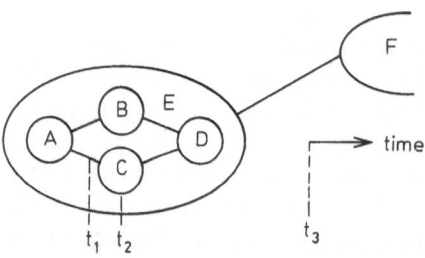

Fig. 1. Nested Atomic Actions

486

be resolved within the scope of E – the enclosing action. This leads us to the now well understood notion of nested recovery which will not be elaborated here.

As is well known, basic actions are equipped with the unilateral recovery capability with the property that this capability is discarded when a given action ends. This is a rather limited view of unilateral recovery. Assume that time has advanced up to t3; we note that as yet the outputs of 'E' have not been used. So, logically it is still possible to back out 'E' unilaterally (more precisely, since 'E' has terminated, the state changes produced by 'E' can be undone unilaterally). The question then arises as to when is it logically incorrect to back out an action? This leads us to the notion of *commitment*.

In our normal conversations when we say: "I am committed to ..." or "I have commitments ..." we imply that "others are depending on the promises made by me". The same idea needs capturing when we consider commitments of outputs produced by atomic actions. Informally, the outputs produced by a terminated action get *committed* when they are used as inputs to other actions. So for example, in Fig. 1, at time t1, no commitments have been made by A, (and A can be backed out unilaterally); at time t2, the outputs of A are committed, implying they cannot be 'with-drawn' unilaterally. Thus commitment guarantees 'input stability' [10]. A number of observations can now be made:

(a) When an action terminates, the output values produced by it have the status 'commitable' implying that other actions can use them. By embellishing the notation of Fig. 1 slightly, we can illustrate the idea further:

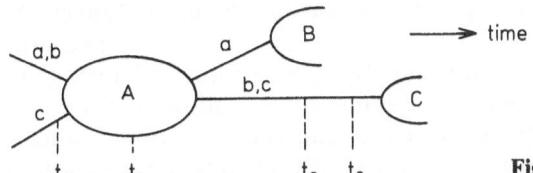

Fig. 2. Commitable and committed objects

Figure 2 shows that inputs to 'A' consist of objects a, b and c (shown as labels on the arcs). Henceforth the following convention will be used: upper case letters will denote actions and lower case letters will denote objects. We will assume that the function of an action is to produce 'new versions' of its input objects; so an action is a creator of new versions (for the sake of simplicity it is will be assumed that all objects are permanent). We shall refer to the specific version of an object by indicating its input (output) relationship to a given action:

a > A: The version of 'a' that is input to 'A';
A > a: The version of 'a' that has been created by 'A';

Note that in Fig. 2 A > a = a > B. So, from Fig. 2 we see that at time t2, the version a > B has been committed while the versions b > C, c > C are still only commitable.

(b) The notion of commitment is hierarchic in an obvious manner: at the level of abstraction of action E (Fig. 1) no commitments have been made at time t2; yet at a lower level, outputs of A have been committed.

(c) Next we illustrate the idea of dynamic control over commitment. So long as the criteria of serializability is observed, it is possible for an action to release versions of objects before the action ends (if two phase locking is used then objects can be released during the shrinking phase). Needless to say, this achieves a greater degree of concurrency at the cost of making recovery more complex. The early release of an object is illustrated in Fig. 3. Looking at Fig. 3(a) first, it is clear that even though 'B' starts using 'a' at time t2, a > B at t2 has not committed, since action A has not yet terminated.

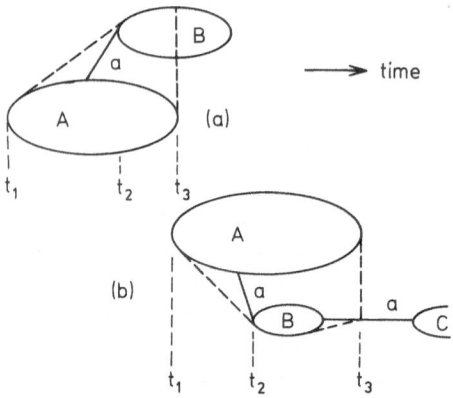

Fig. 3. Early release of objects

A different situation is illustrated in Fig. 3(b) where action B ends before action A. Here again, B > a will become commitable only after time t3. The dotted lines in Fig. 3 are intended to show action A's "sphere of influence" over commitment – only outside of this sphere are commitments allowed. From the point of view of recovery, 'A' can be recovered so long as no commitments have been made; however, a recovery after time t2 will also include the back out of 'B'.

Making uncommitted objects available to other actions in a controlled manner for performance reasons is the central theme of this paper and is explored further in the subsequent sections. In the rest of the paper we will assume that basic actions are the lowest level actions and concentrate upon the mechanisms suitable for the construction of actions composed out of basic actions.

3. Degrees of Dependencies and Commitment

Dynamic control over commitment, as discussed in the last section, is a technique that can be used to obtain a greater degree of concurrency than would otherwise be possible. We generalise that idea further here by introducing the concept of degrees of dependency. In our everyday life, it is common for us to make tentative decisions, inform the concerned parties of these decisions and later on either to cancel or to confirm those decisions (take the example of booking a seat on a plane). By making our tentative decisions public, we are essentially speeding up the process of achieving our objective, since the concerned parties can also perform some tentative processing that can await final confirmation. So far we have assumed that the status of an object is binary — commitable or noncommitable; by making it n-ary we can model the 'tentative' processing in a convenient manner.

3.1. Creator to User Dependency

With each version of an object we associate an abstract value that reflects the commitable status of that version: whether it is commitable and if not the chances of that version attaining the commitable status. This value is returned by a function 'Sc' when applied to a given version at a given time:

$Sc(A > a, t) =$

C1: the version of object 'a' as created by action 'A' will probably attain a commitable status at some time after 't';

C2: the version of object 'a' as created by action 'A' will most probably attain a commitable status at some time after 't';

Cm: the version of object 'a' as created by action 'A' is commitable.

The intuitive meanings associated with the values are given above. Formally, a given version (say, $A > a$) is said to be *commitable* at time t if the following condition is satisfied:

$Sc(A > a, t) = Cm$

Values C1 and C2 represent from minimum to maximum confidence in the fact that the given version of an object will eventually be commitable (it is possible to have many values between the interval C1 to Cm, but assuming only one value, C2, seems adequate). This is illustrated in Fig. 4. Assume that the version of 'a' at t0 is commitable and after time t1, 'a' can be released by 'A'. Since the processing of 'A' has not yet finished, 'a' can only be released with a low C_i value: C1. As 'A' nears the end of its processing, the chances of it being aborted decrease and hence the chances of $A > a$ attaining the commitable status increase, so far example, at t3, the status of 'a' can be C2, while at t4, it is Cm. The values C_i are useful to the user of a given object in deciding how much reliance it can place on that version of the object; this leads us to the complementary idea of user-creator dependency.

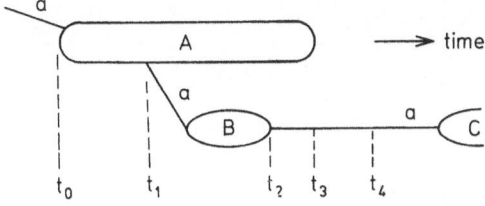

Fig. 4. Dependencies

489

3.2. User to Creator Dependency

Let C_i be the dependency value on some version $a > A$. If action A releases this object before termination, then in order that some control can be exercised over the dependency value of the version $A > a$, we introduce the concept of user-creator dependency. With each input object an action ('A' in this case) is using, we associate a variable 'Du' that can take on the following values (with their associated meanings):

$Du = U1$: $C1$ is the maximum dependency value that can be placed upon $A > a$;

U2: $C2$ is the maximum dependency value that can be placed upon $A > a$;

Um: Cm is the maximum dependency value that can be placed upon $A > a$.

Informally, 'U_i' values can be taken to represent the 'degree of importance' an action is attaching to its inputs since these values determine the commitability of the corresponding outputs.

The two dependency values (C_i, U_j) are related to each other in an important way; we can appreciate this by referring to Fig. 4 and asking the question what should be the value returned by $Sc(B > a, t3)$, given that the fact that 'B' used 'a' with a dependency value Um? Intuition tells us that it would be wrong for this value to be Cm, since 'a' as supplied to 'B' has not yet attained a commitable status. Before the relationship between them can be described formally, a few underlying assumptions about our model will be stated.

(a) Every output produced by an action is a function of all the inputs to that action.

(b) An action can assign in the beginning either U1 or U2 values to its inputs; as the action progresses these values can be changed. However, Um values can be assigned only at the termination time of the action.

(c) At the termination time of an action, all of the inputs to that action must have Um dependencies. That is, every action ultimately must have the capability of producing commitable versions of objects.

(d) An operation '*' is defined on the values C_i and U_j of an object:

$$C1 * Ui = C1$$
$$C2 * U1 = C1$$
$$C2 * U2 = C1$$
$$C2 * Um = C2$$
$$Cm * U1 = C1$$
$$Cm * U2 = C2$$
$$Cm * Um = Cm$$

The above equations are to be interpreted as follows: if an action acquires an object that has a dependency value C_i and uses it with a dependency value U_j, (the terms on the L.H.S. of the equation) then the value C_k (the term on the

490

R.H.S.) represents the *upper bound* on the the creator-user dependency on the new version of the object when it is released (made available to other actions). So, referring back to Fig. 4, and remembering that 'B' has used 'a' with Um, and $Sc(A > a, t3) = C2$, then $Sc(B > a, t3) = C2$. In words: action B has put maximum dependency on its input 'a', so the output version of 'a' as produced by 'B' can have as much chance of attaining a commitable status as the input version, namely, C2. Following this, it should be clear that $Sc(B > a, t4) = Cm$.

(e) The following three status values are of interest when an object 'a' is being used by an action 'A': (1) the creator-user dependency value Ci — this is the value associated with $a > A$; (ii) the user-creator dependency value Ua which is under the control of 'A'; and (iii) the creator-user value Cr — this is the value placed upon the the released version of the object $(A > a)$.

Let $Z = \{a, b, c, .., n\}$ be the set of input objects to action 'A' and let Ua, Ub, Uc, ..., Un be the dependencies placed on them by 'A' (see Fig. 5).
At some time tj, tj < te, 'A' releases some object 'c'; then the Cr value associated with 'c' must satisfy the following two conditions:

$$Cr = \min_{k \in Z} [Sc(k > A, tj)*Uc] \tag{1}$$

$$Cr < Cm \tag{2}$$

Cr is derived from the minimum of the the input Ci values and the user dependency value placed on the given object (Uc in this case); further, as the action has not yet terminated, Cr must be less than Cm.

Once an action ends, the dependency values on the versions created are given by:

$$Cr = \min_{k \in Z} [Sc(k > A, t)], \text{ where } t = > te \tag{3}$$

That is, the dependency value is determined by the smallest of the immediately preceding dependency values. So, from Fig. 4, at t3, $Sc(B > a, t3)$ will be, using (3), the same as $Sc(a > B, t3)$ (or using the 'output' notation, $Sc(A > a, t3)$); this value itself will be either C1 or C2 as determined by action A.

We can now see that the model allows a fine degree of control over commitability of objects. An action can acquire uncommitable objects and release them, still uncommitable, with a lower or same dependency value [as determined by condition (1)]. As actions terminate, these objects attain commitable status [as determined by condition (3)].

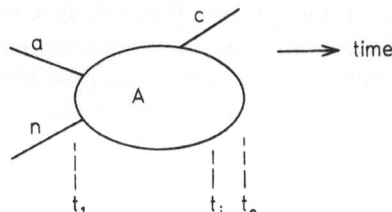

Fig. 5. An Atomic Action

491

3.3 Commitment

It is possible now to define 'commitment' formally in terms of the model: let a version of object 'a' be related to two actions A and B such that $A > a = a > B$; then this version is said to be *committed* at time 't' if the following two conditions hold:

(i) $Sc(A > a, t) = Cm$;
(ii) Action B has terminated on or before t or 'B' has placed a dependency value $Ui > U1$.

We can make several observations now:

(a) The commitment of a version of an object is only possible when that version acts as an input to some other action (subject to constraints stated above).

(b) The serializability property of atomic actions ensures that if 'a' at time tj is committed, then *all* the versions of 'a' prior to tj will also be committeed.

(c) A U1 dependency cannot cause a commitment. In many applications, a user has only a vague idea about the objects needed at the start of the application; more precise information becomes available as the application progresses in time. In such a case, the user would clearly wish to commit only those input objects that are strictly needed. This can be achieved by first acquiring the objects without causing any commitments (i.e. with U1 dependencies on them) and later on to convert the dependencies on the required objects to higher ones, while cancelling the remaining dependencies. It is indeed possible for an as yet uncommitted version of an object to be made available to a number of actions *simultaneously* − all of which have placed a U1 dependency; however, only one of the actions will be allowed to increase its dependency value and the rest of the actions must eventually cancel their dependencies (generalization for read locks is certainly possible). Delaying the commitment of objects as long as possible is a natural requirement for control over recoverability − we shall discuss this topic in the next section.

To conclude this section, a simple example will be used to illustrate the ideas introduced so far.

3.4. Example: Scheduling a Meeting

Designing a distributed calendar system represents a significantly challenging task [14]. We will consider the task of scheduling a meeting in the distant future between a group of people. Following the description given in [14], this task − an atomic action − can be seen to have the following phases: (a) the meeting organizer gets an agreement − without any obligations − for some possible meeting times; (b) after a while the organizer selects a possible meeting time − he would now certainly want to give the assurance that a meeting will be held at the specified time; (c) as the meeting time nears, the organizer confirms the meeting.

492

We shall assume some form of a distributed data base system where each person has a personal calendar system for keeping track of appointments and free time slots. So, making an appointment for a meeting essentially involves finding a few time slots on the various calendars as proposed options for a meeting and later on to fix one such time slot. Every user occasionally checks his calendar for meeting proposals – if a proposal is not acceptable the user can reject that option.

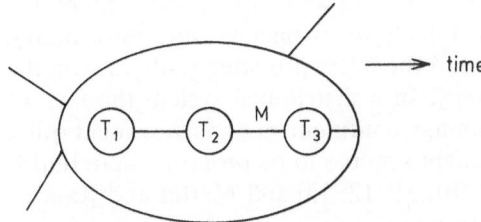

Fig. 6. Scheduling a meeting

The figure above shows how the scheduling of a meeting (in its simplest form) can be modelled. The organizer's activities are modelled as an action M (for meeting) which is composed out of – in this particular case – three basic actions T1, T2 and T3. The task of T1 is to select a number of possible meeting times, a U1 dependency is placed on the appropriate objects representing the time slots by action M (no commitment has as yet occurred). As time progresses, the meeting organizer wants to narrow down the choice to one 'most probable' meeting time – this is done by M trying to increase U1 dependencies to U2. Not all such attempts will succeed – users might have rejected some options (a user can reject an option by marking that time slot as occupied – committed – hence invalidating U1 dependencies). Assuming a time slot agreeable to everyone is found, (U2 dependencies can be placed upon them), T2 is scheduled to run – its task is to update the calendars appropriately – to indicate the chosen times; at the same time any superfluous dependencies are cancelled. After the termination of T2, M can release the meeting times which will have the dependency values C2 (assume that inputs to M are commitable). Finally, as the meeting time nears, T3 is run to confirm it. M then ends having placed Um dependencies on the chosen time slots and the meeting time is now released with status 'commitable' (dependency value Cm). Running the entire activity as an atomic action has the advantage that recovery requirements are known exactly (see the next section). In the absence of the surrounding action M, it will be difficult to maintain recoverability over the three basic actions.

The simple example discussed here is intended to demonstrate that interesting aspects of calendar management can be modelled using the ideas on dependencies and commitment developed in this paper. It is also worth noting that the state changes on objects are performed by the basic actions – the so-called 'atomic transactions' (needing stable storage and two phase commit termination algorithm) and these actions can be combined into bigger actions by exercising control over dependencies and commitment.

4. Recovery Management

It has been assumed throughout that a given action is constructed out of basic actions. If a basic action aborts, it raises a *failure exception* which must be handled by the enclosing action. There can be several such reasons — we shall enumerate them subsequently — for the detection of exceptions (or errors) during the execution of an action.

Following Randell [8], any recovery actions taken after the detection of an error can include the steps of damage confinement and damage assessment: the former is concerned with limiting the effects of erroneous state information from spreading further into the system and the latter provides guidelines on the selection of a particular recovery strategy. In a distributed system the lack of centralised control makes the task of damage confinement and assessment quite difficult [15, 16]. The recovery management scheme to be proposed here builds upon the work of Davies and Bjork [9, 10, 11, 12, 13] and Merlin and Randell [15]. We shall make a number of assumptions:

(1) A given application is structured as an atomic action (which itself is composed out of basic actions); within a computer system there may be a number of related applications.

(ii) Associated with an application are a number of 'audit routines' for consistency checking and determining — perhaps interactively with the user — the extent of backward recovery needed (in-process or post-process, see later).

(iii) The dependencies — who has used whose outputs — are being recorded and available for later inspection during recovery.

Let an error be detected during the execution of action C (see Fig. 7). If the audit routines assess the cause of the error (fault) to be within action C then any recovery action undertaken is known as *in-process* recovery; on the other hand, if it is assessed that the error has been caused owing to wrong inputs being supplied to C (i.e. outputs from A and B) then the recovery action undertaken is known as *post-process* recovery [12]. In-process recovery involves the action in which the error has been detected and possibly other actions that have used the outputs of this action. Post-process recovery in its simplest form, involves, in addition, the actions that have supplied inputs to the action in which the error has been detected.

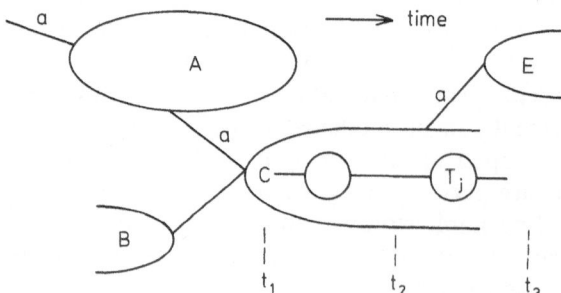

Fig. 7. Recovery

4.1. In-Process Recovery

Let an error be detected in action C (Fig. 7) at time t3 (current time) and let the recovery required be in-process. The audit routines might indicate Tj as the cause (e.g. Tj should not have been scheduled in the first place) in which case 'C' can be backed out up to Tj without affecting the dependent action E. However, if a back out beyond Tj is required, then it will be necessary to 'recall side dependencies' which in this particular case consists of cancelling the version $C > a$ (marking it as invalid). What happens to action E? There are two situations under which a back out of 'E' is required: (i) 'E' has placed a dependency value $Ui > U1$ on $C > a$; or (ii) 'E' has placed a dependency value U1 on $C > a$ and $E > a$ exists. We make it the responsibility of an ongoint action to make sure that any of its as yet uncommittable input object versions (i.e. versions with Ci values less than Cm) are still valid and to take the appropriate recovery action. By its very nature, it is always possible in the case of in-process recovery to back out the action such as C and all its dependent actions — in-process recovery represents the case when no commitments have been made.

4.2. Post-Process Recovery

Let current time be equal to t1 when an error is detected in C and further, the audit routines assess the output from action A as incorrect. Since $A > a$ is as yet uncommittable, this versions is cancelled (or marked as invalid) and 'C' is backed out (as discussed before). We make it the responsibility of on going actions to make sure that any uncommittable versions released by them are still valid. If for an action it is detected that one of its output has been marked invalid, then this represents the detection of an error which could lead to the invocation of either in-process or post-process recovery (within 'A' in Fig. 7).

Assume the same situation as before except that time has advanced up to t2 (Fig. 7) and that $A > a$ is still not commitable (because inputs to A have not yet attained a commitable status). The fact that 'A' has terminated makes no logical difference to the recovery actions required: indeed a suitable mechanisation might involve making 'A' 'active' again — purely for the purpose of invoking in-process or post-process recovery within 'A'.

Implicit in the discussion above was the assumption that 'C' has placed a dependency on $A > a$ that is greater than U1.

We now consider the case whereby the 'wrong input' of 'C' enjoys the status 'committed'. Under such a situation recovery — in addition to the back out of 'C' — is possible if the following conditions are met: (a) 'C' is the only user of $A > a$ (the case considered in Fig. 7; note that if read locks have been placed on $A > a$ then there could be multiple users); and (b) all the other outputs of 'A' are commitable only (not yet committed). It is possible then to perform recovery of 'A'.

If however the above two conditions are not met — thus implying that the outputs of 'A' have been committed by actions in addition to 'C' — then apart from backing out 'C' very little else can be achieved as far as backward recovery is concerned. Any further recovery actions are very much application dependent and involve running compensating actions [9]. Whether recovery by compensation can be modelled within the framework of this model remains to be seen.

A suitable mechanization of the recovery actions outlined above (determining whether conditions (a) and (b) hold) might involve 'chasing' as described by Bjork [9] and Merlin and Randell [15]: an attempt is made to prevent the as yet uncommitted outputs of 'A' from getting committed.

We conclude this section by enumerating various exceptions that could be raised during the execution of an action: (i) a basic action aborts; (ii) the user explicitly aborts the action; (iii) a request to increase one of the Ul dependencies fails; (iv) some of the inputs to the action become invalid; (v) some of the outputs produced by the action become invalid; and (vi) user supplied consistency checks reveal an error.

5. Concluding Remarks

In a recent paper [17] J. N. Gray stressed the need for 'nested transactions' for modelling long running applications. It is argued here that in addition to allowing actions to be nested, it is also necessary to provide some means of delaying commitments as far as possible without reducing the degree of concurrency. A model was proposed in which it is possible for an action to release (as well as process) as yet uncommitable objects. The following is a list of suggested areas for further research: (a) to test the suitability of the model by applying it to various applications (so far I have considered only simple test cases); (ii) to consider implementation issues − the work of Bjork [18] on 'audit trails' and that of Needham and Herbert on 'sequencers' [19] appears to be particularly helpful here in deciding how to record dependencies and schedule basic actions within an action; (iii) lastly, any relationship to other models − such as those for office systems [20] − needs to be explored.

Acknowledgements. Acknowledgement is due to Brian Randell with whom I have had many conversations on this subject. I had the pleasure of meeting Charles Davies on two occasions (first when he visited Newcastle in the summer of 1978 and secondly when I went over to the USA in the summer of 1979) during which time he was kind enough to explain many of his ideas on spheres of control to me. Earlier versions of this paper were read critically by Flaviu Cristian and Brian Randell. This work was supported partly by the Science and Engineering Research Council (UK).

References

1. D. B. Lomet, "Process Structuring, Synchronisation and Recovery Using Atomic Actions", ACM SIGPLAN Notices, Vol. 12, No. 3, March, 1977, pp. 128−137. [Also Chap. 4]
2. M. Hammer and D. Shipman, "The Reliability Mechanisms of SDD-1: A System for Distributed Databases", ACM TODS, Vol. 13, No. 2 December 1980, pp. 431−466.
3. B. Lampson and H. Sturgis, "Atomic Transactions", Lecture Notes in Computer Science, Vol. 105, Springer Verlag, 1981, pp. 246−265.

4. J. N. Gray, "Notes on Data Base Operating Systems", Lecture Notes in Computer Science, Vol. 60, Springer Verlag, 1978, pp. 398–481.

5. S. K. Shrivastava, "Structuring Distributed Systems for Recoverability and Crash Resistance", IEEE Trans. on Software Engineering, SE-7, No. 4, July 1981, pp. 436–447. [Also Chap. 5]

6. W. H. Kohler, "A Survey of Techniques for Synchronization and Recovery in Decentralised Computer Systems", ACM Computing Surveys, Vol. 13, June 1981, pp. 149–183.

7. K. Eswaran et al, "On the Notions of Consistency and Predicate Locks in a Data Base System", CACM, Vol. 19, Nov. 1976, pp. 624–633.

8. B. Randell, P. A. Lee and P. C. Treleaven, "Reliability Issues in Computing System Design", ACM Computing Surveys, Vol. 10, June 1978, pp. 123–165.

9. L. A. Bjork, "Recovery Scenario for a DB/DC System" Proc. of ACM Nat. Conf., 1973, pp. 142–146.

10. C. T. Davies, "A Recovery/Integrity Architecture for a Data System", Technical Report, IBM San Jose, TR02.528, May 1972.

11. C. T. Davies, "Recovery Semantics for a DB/DC System", Proc. ACM Nat. Conf., 1973, pp. 136–141.

12. C. T. Davies, "Data Processing Spheres of Control", IBM Systems Journal, Vol. 17, No. 2, 1978, pp. 179–198.

13. C. T. Davies, "Data Processing Integrity", Computing Systems Reliability, Cambridge Univ. Press, 1979, pp. 288–354.

14. I. Grief, "Notes on the Design of a Calendar System", Proc. Computer Networking Symposium, Dec. 1980, pp. 185–192.

15. P. M. Merlin and B. Randell, "State Restoration in Distributed Systems", Proc. of 8th Int. Symp. Fault-Tolerant Computing, June 1978, pp. 129–134. [Also Chap. 6]

16. W. G. Wood, "A Decentralised Recovery Control Protocol", Proc. 11th Int. Symp. Fault-Tolerant Computing, June 1981, pp. 159–164. [Also Chap. 6]

17. J. N. Gray, "The Transaction Concept: Virtues and Limitations", Proc. 7th Very Large Data Base Conf., Sept. 1981, pp. 144–154.

18. L. A. Bjork, "Generalized Audit Trail Requirements and Concepts for Database Applications", IBM Syst. Jr. No. 3, 1975, pp. 229–245.

19. A. J. Herbert and R. M. Needham, "Sequencing Computation Steps in a Network", ACM OP. SYS. Review, Vol. 15, December 1981, pp. 59–63.

20. C. A. Ellis and G. J. Nutt, "Office Information Systems and Computer Science", ACM Computing Surveys, Vol. 12, March 1980, pp. 27–60.

Fail-Safe Extrema-Finding in a Circular Distributed System

E. Best and F. Panzieri

In [2] an algorithm is given and analysed for finding the highest numbered node in a circular decentralised arrangement of nodes. We extend this algorithm to cover also the case in which nodes may enter a certain well-defined failure mode.

1. Introduction

We consider a circular arrangement of N nodes (numbered from 1 to N) in which nodes can receive messages from their immediate predecessors and pass messages to their immediate successors. Initially, no node can be assumed to have any knowledge about the distribution of the other nodes on the ring. We are requested to write an algorithm enabling node i to determine whether it is the one with the highest number, i.e. whether i = N. The following is the solution of [2], which is a simple and elegant improvement of an algorithm by Le Lann [5]:

```
1.1    !i;
1.2    do ?x;   {x is a local variable}
1.3        if  x < i → skip
1.4        □  x = i → "success"
1.5        □  x > i → !x
           fi
       od
```

Fig. 1. Basic algorithm BA

We use here a dialect of guarded commands [3] and CSP [4]. For our purposes, the construct *do . . . od* denotes an infinite loop, while the constructs

> if B1 → . . . □ B2 → . . □ B3 → . . . fi and
> if B1 then. . . else if B2 then . . . else if B3 then . . .

are equivalent. The input command ?x enables a node to receive a message from its predecessor, and the output command !x is used to pass a message to its successor.

BA works as follows. Initially, all node numbers start circulating (line 1.1). They keep circulating (lines 1.2 and 1.5) until they are taken out of circulation by being dropped at nodes with a higher number (line 1.3). Only the highest number complete a full circle and its eventual return to the sender indicates success (line 1.4). The program ends with node N executing "success" and all

498

other nodes waiting for more input. In [2] it is proved that BA necessitates 0(Nlog N) message passes in the average.

The fact that BA works with any numbering of nodes (as long as no two nodes have the same number) opens up the possibility, mentioned also in [2], that even if a node fails than the rest of the ring may continue to work satisfactorily. The authors had set out to investigate this possibility, with the objective of producing a fail-safe algorithm which matches BA in elegance and efficiency. In the remainder of this paper we describe three fail-safe variants of BA.

2. Failure Mode and Correctness Criteria

We consider what Chang calls "clean failures" in [1]. To be precise, we demand the truth of the following:

(F1) A failure leaves the circular nature of the network intact.
(F2) No messages can be destroyed by a failure.
(F3) Failed nodes do not recover.

The postulate (F1) is satisfied in many practical cases. For example, in a network using the Cambridge Ring [6] hardware, the failure of a node attached to the Ring does not affect the Ring itself. (F2) is a rather strong postulate: violations of (F2) may however lead to very tricky situations. It seems therefore, at first, reasonable to simplify the problem of postulating (F2). As to (F3), we believe that our solutions can be modified to cope with node recovery as well.

Let LIVE denote the set of all non-failed nodes (initially, $LIVE = \{1; ..,N\}$). Our task is to find an algorithm selecting the maximal number in LIVE. This can be described by the following two conditions:

(C1) If node i succeeds then $i = \max (LIVE)$.
(C2) Eventually, either $LIVE = \emptyset$ or some node succeeds.

Every algorithm satisfying $(C1) - (C2)$ for the failure mode $(F1) - (F3)$ shall in the sequel be called a "correct fail-safe algorithm". (C1) and (C2) can be viewed as the invariant and the termination condition, respectively, of such an algorithm.

We further propose that the correct algorithm should moreover match the basic algorithm in efficiency. We take as our efficiency criterion the average number of message passes (we are aware that there are other possible criteria, for example the time between the start and the execution of "success"; however, we do not consider these other criteria in this paper). Thus we require that

(E1) If no node fails then there should be a total of 0(N log N) message passes in the average.

Heuristic arguments which will become clear in the next section suggest that in general (i.e. if nodes fail) there should be no more than $0(N^2)$ message passes. Thus we state

(E2) The fail-safe algorithm should require 0(N²) message passes in the average (with any reasonable definition of "average").

3. Fail-Safe Algorithms

As long as the number max (LIVE) always remains on the Ring, the basic algorithm BA itself is a correct fail-safe solution. This suggests, firstly that there exists a correct solution similar to BA, and secondly that any solution should be capable of detecting the absence of max(LIVE) from the Ring and bring it back into circulation. Most of the design decisions to be taken in the sequel are based on these insights.

A few decisions can be taken straight away, greatly simplifying the search for a solution. We retain as a criterion for "success" the detection by a node of its own number as input. Further, when a node sees a smaller input it can argue that as long as it stays live the smaller number is insignificant, and therefore "skip" it. Greater inputs should be passed on unless they give definite information about other nodes having failed. Thus, lines 1.1 − 1.4 of BA remain unchanged while line 1.5 requires a modification.

We decide further that a node i should be responsible for the emission (and re-emission, if necessary) of its own number. Thus while other nodes may store the number i for their own purpose, they are not allowed to emit it other than passing it on immediately after receipt. This decision is taken mainly because failing this the complexity is greatly increased; however it may have to be reversed at a later stage.

Unless the node numbered N fails, BA works correctly. Our decisions imply, however, that when node N fails then the message N will return at least to the first live successor of N. This node can therefore detect the failure of N and take appropriate action. It can also deduce that its own number is no longer on the Ring and that all other live nodes have seen the message N.

This leads immediately to our first solution in which each node keeps track of the maximal number known to it and proposes itself each time it receives that maximal number again:

```
2.0   m := i;
2.1   !i;
2.2   do ?x;
2.3       if  x < i  →  skip
2.4       □  x = i  →  "success"
2.5       □  x > i  →  if  x < m  →  skip
2.6                    □  x = m  →  !i
2.7                    □  x > m  →  m := x
                       fi;
                       !x
          fi
      od
```

Fig. 2. Basic restart algorithm BRA

Proof: (sketch) We have to prove (C2) since (C1) is trivial. After the first round the variable m in all live nodes contains N and remains fixed. If max-(LIFE) is no longer on the Ring then the message N keeps circulating, causing the re-emission via 2.6 of all live node numbers. Thus, amongst others, the number max(LIVE) will eventually be back in circulation. Deadlock through overcrowding of the Ring cannot occur because whenever node i enters line 2.6, some other node either has failed or has taken a number off the Ring, compensating for the additional number to be put on the Ring by node i.

(E1) is clearly satisfied for BRA. The worst case failing behaviour is for nodes to fail one at a time in decreasing order, starting with node N. In this case BRA may require $O(N^2 \log N)$ message passes (N applications of BA), which strongly suggests that (E2) is satisfied for any sensibly defined "average" failing behaviour.

We have carried out a simulation study with different node arrangements, supporting this conclusion. In our simulation, a critical node (i.e. a node k such that the message k-1 is no longer on the Ring) was given a one-in-three chance of failing per cycle, which is hugely unrealistic. Even then, message passing averaged well less than N^2.

On the other hand, BRA is evidently inefficient in two respects. Firstly, the numbers of failed nodes other than N (if any) keep circulating unnecessarily. Secondly, line 2.6 may cause the re-emission of unnecessarily many node numbers. In the sequel we present two variants of BRA designed to partly overcome these inefficiencies.

We can attack the second inefficiency by keeping at each node a counter variable, storing the number of nodes known to that node as being candidates for selection, i.e. having a higher number. The counter should be decreased appropriately and re-emission should take place only if it is zero, i.e. the node in question is really a leading candidate. We propose the following as one possible solution:

```
3.0    (m, c) := (i, 0);
3.1    !i;
3.2    do ? x;
3.3        if  x < i  →  skip
3.4        □  x = i  →  "success"
3.5        □  x > i  →  if  x < m  →  c := c + 1; !x
3.6                     □  x = m  →  if  c > 0  →  c := c − 1
3.7                                  □  c = 0  →  !i
                                     fi;
3.8                                  !x
3.9                     □  x > m  →  (m, c) := (x, c + 1);
3.10                                 !x
                       fi
               fi
        od
```

Fig. 3. Restart algorithms with counting CRA

In CRA the count c is decremented each time the maximal message passes by. More refined strategies are possible, for example by inserting a conditional decrement in line 3.5; this would decrement c also if non-live non-maximal node numbers pass by. The correctness argument for these variants closely resembles the one given for BRA, while the message passing efficiency is slightly improved.

Finally, we present a solution in which nodes keep track of the numbers of all higher nodes (not just the maximum), thus enabling the extinction of non-maximal dead numbers. Each node i keeps a history of inputs $x > i$ in a sequence called H which is "updated" whenever the maximal number N passes by. Our objective is to enable a node receiving a number already contained in H to deduce that this node is dead. A node should therefore be able to recognise whether an input x is due to the failure of node x or to the re-emission of x. To this end we let a node re-circulate N *before* re-emitting its own number. It then follows that the "updating of H" should consist of removing from H all numbers up to and including N, and inserting N at the end of H. Because N thus remains in H, the condition for re-emission becomes "H={N}". The following is our proposed solution:

The size of the sequence H does not exactly correspond to the count c of CRA as more than one element may be taken out of H in line 4.12. The complete correctness argument for HRA will be again an extension of the one given above. The improvement introduced by HRA lies in line 4.15 where a non-maximal node number is not propagated further because it is known to be dead.

```
4.0   m := i;  H := ( );   {( ) is empty sequence}
4.1   !i;
4.2   do ?x;
4.3       if  x < i  →  skip
4.4       □ x = i  →  "success"
4.5       □ x > i  →  {(x ∈ H or x ≠ m) and (x ∉ H or x ≤ m)}
4.6               if  x < m  and  x ∉ H  →  H := H.x;
4.7                                        !x
4.8               □ x > m  and  x ∉ H  →  H := H.x;
4.9                                        m := x;
4.10                                       !x
4.11              □ x = m  and  x ∈ H  →  !x;
4.12                                       "update H";
4.13                                       if  H = {x}  →  !i
4.14                                       □ H ≠ {x}  →  skip
                                           fi
4.15              □ x < m  and  x ∈ H  →  skip
                  fi
          fi
      od
```

Fig. 4. Restart algorithm with history HRA

If, in retrospect, we compare the analogous parts 2.5−2.8, 3.5−3.10 and 4.5−4.15 of BRA, CRA and HRA, respectively, we can see the incorporation of message passing efficiency by making the emission of both x and i dependent on progressively more complicated conditions. Our simulation exercise indicates, however, that there is not a dramatic drop in message passing, so that the BRA rather than the other versions should be preferred on account of its simplicity, unless optimisation with respect to message passing is really crucial.

4. Concluding Remarks

We have described several variants of a decentralised extrema-finding algorithm capable of tolerating certain failures. The variants were designed so as to minimise message passing between nodes. Possible extensions of this work could include taking into account other efficiency measures, as well as generalising the algorithms to strongly connected networks which may not be cyclic (an extension of the basic algorithm in this way is described in [1].

We have also attempted to record the heuristic considerations that led to our solutions. A comparison with the well-established design methodologies for sequential programs may be of interest. We have applied the stepwise approach in the following way. The initial step from the basic algorithm to the fail-safe algorithm corresponds to an extension of the specifications: the new algorithm is fail-safe w.r.t. the original specifications if it is correct w.r.t. the extended specifications set out in section 2. The next step consists of finding a correct solution first and then transforming it into a more efficient one while retaining its correctness. Our specifications and correctness criteria are half-formal, but we would regard it as important that our arguments can (and should) be made completely formal for verification purposes. All of these techniques for goal-directed design, we believe, can be applied very advantageously in the design of distributed algorithms.

Acknowledgements. We wish to thank Graham Wood for the useful discussions we had during the preparation of this paper. We acknowledge the financial support of the Science and Engineering Research Council (U.K.) and of the Royal Signals and Radar Establishment (U.K.).

References

1. E. Chang, Decentralised Algorithms in Distributed Systems, TR-CSRG-103, Computer Systems Research Group, University of Toronto (October 1979).
2. E. Chang and R. Roberts, An Improved Algorithms for Decentralised Extrema-Finding in Circular Configurations of Processes, CACM 22/5 (May 1979), 281−283.
3. E. W. Dijkstra, Guarded Commands, Non-Determinacy and Formal Derivation of Programs, CACM 18/8 (August 1975), 453−457.
4. C. A. R. Hoare, Communicating Sequential Processes, CACM 21/8 (August 1978), 666−677.
5. G. LeLann, Distributed Systems − Towards a Formal Approach, Information Processing 77, North Holland, Amsterdam, 155−160.
6. M. V. Wilkes and D. J. Wheeler, The Cambridge Communication Ring, Proc. of Local Area Network Symposium, Boston, National Bureau of Standards, (May 1979).

The Design of a Reliable Remote Procedure Call Mechanism

S. K. Shrivastava and F. Panzieri

Abstract. In this contribution we describe the design of a reliable Remote Procedure Call mechanism intended for use in local area networks. Starting from the hardware level that provides primitive facilities for data transmission, we describe how such a mechanism can be constructed. We discuss various design issues involved, including the choice of a message passing system over which the remote call mechanism is to be constructed and the treatment of various abnormal situations such as lost messages and node crashes. We also investigate what the reliability requirements of the Remote Procedure Call mechanism should be with respect to both the application programs using it and the message passing system on which it itself is based.

Index Terms. Atomic actions, data communication, distributed systems, fault tolerance, local area networks.

I. Introduction

In this contribution we describe the design of a reliable Remote Procedure Call (RPC) mechanism which we have been investigating within the context of programming reliable distributed applications. In the following we consider a distributed system as composed of a number of interacting "client" and "server" processes running on possibly distinct nodes of the system; the interactions between a client and a server are made possible by the suitable use of the RPC mechanism. Essentially, in this scheme a client's remote call is transformed into an appropriate message to the named server who performs the requested work and sends the result back to the client and so terminating the call. The RPC mechanism is thus implemented on top of a message passing interface. Some of the interesting problems that need to be faced are: 1) the selection of appropriate semantics and reliability features of the RPC mechanism, 2) the design of an appropriate message passing interface over which the RPC is to be implemented, and 3) the treatment of abnormal situations such as node crashes. These problems and their solutions are discussed here. We shall concentrate primarily on the relevant reliability issues involved, so other directly or indirectly related issues such as type checking, authentication, and naming will not be addressed here.

The RPC mechanism described in the following has been designed for a local area network composed of a number of PDP 11/45 and LSI 11/23 computers (nodes) interconnected by the Cambridge Ring [1]; each node runs the UNIX[1] (V7) operating system. However, most of the ideas presented in here are, we believe, sufficiently general to be applicable to any other local area network system.

504

II. An Overview of Reliability Issues in Distributed Programming

In this section we briefly review the main reliability problems in distributed programming and discuss which of these problems need closer attention during the design of an RPC mechanism.

In this discussion we shall concentrate upon a distributed system consisting of a number of autonomous nodes connected by a local area network. A node in such a network will typically contain one or more processes providing services (e.g., data retention) that can be used by local or remote processes. We shall refer to such processes as "severs" and "clients," respectively. So an execution of a typical application program will give rise to a computation consisting of a client making various service requests to servers. These service requests take the form of procedure calls – if a server is remote then the calls to it will be remote procedure calls. In the rest of the paper we will assume the general and more difficult case of remote calls (note, however, that it is possible to hide the "remoteness" of servers by providing a uniform interface for all service calls). It can be seen that we have adopted a "procedure based" model of computation rather than a "message based" model. It has been pointed out that these two models appear to be duals of each other [2]. Bearing this in mind, we have chosen to support the first model because this allows us to directly apply the existing knowledge on the design and development of programs to distributed systems.

Let us ignore, for the time being, any reliability problems in the mechanization of a suitable RPC facility and concentrate upon the reliability problems at the application program level. The most vexing problems is to do with guaranteeing a clean termination of a program despite breakdowns (crashes) of nodes and communication subsystems. It is now well known that this can be achieved by structuring a program as an *atomic action* with the following "all or nothing" property: either all of the client's requested services are performed or none are [3] – [5]. Thus, a program terminates either producing the intended results or none at all. In a distributed system the implementation of atomic actions requires the provision of a special protocol, such as the *two phase commit* protocol [3], [4] to coordinate the activities of clients and servers. In addition, some recovery capability is also needed at each node to "undo" any results produced at that node by an ongoing atomic action that is subsequently to be terminated with null results. We shall not discuss here the details of how the various facilities needed for the provision of atomic actions can be constructed – they are well documented in the already cited references – but draw the reader's attention to Fig. 1 which shows a typical hierarchy of software interfaces. The point to note is that the atomic action software that supports $L3$ contains major reliability measures for application programs (undo capability, two phase commit). This has important consequences on the design of RPC – in particular in choosing its semantics and reliability capability.

The algortihm below, which shows the bare essentials of an RPC mechanism, will be used to illustrate the reliability problems.

```
          Client                    Server
                            cycle
       send (···);          →      receive (···);
       ---                         --
                                   "work"
                                   --
       receive (···);       ←      send (···);
                            end
```

The send and receive primitives provide a message handling facility (the precise semantics of which are not relevant in the following discussion). Suppose that the message handling facility is such that messages occasionally get lost. Then a client would be well justified in resending a message when it "suspects" a loss. This could sometimes result in more than one execution at the server. To take another case, suppose that the client's node crashes immediately after the server starts to perform the requested work. Suppose now that the client's node "comes up" again and the client reissues the remote call:

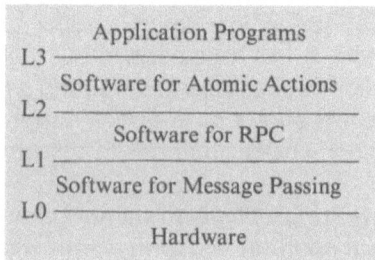

Fig. 1. Hierarchy of software interfaces

this again gives rise to the possibility of repeated executions at the server (the above situation can occur even if messages never get lost). If a client is not aware of the fact that repeated executions have taken place, then many of a server's executions will be in vain, with no client to receive the sent responses. Such executions have been termed *orphans* by Lampson and many ingenious schemes have been deviced for detecting and treating orphans [6], [7]. The above mentioned problems have led Nelson to classify the semantics of remote procedure calls as follows [7].

1) "Exactly Once" Semantics: If a client's call succeeds (i.e., the call does not return abnormally), then this implies that exactly one execution has taken place at the server; this is, of course, the meaning associated with conventional procedure calls.

2) "At Least Once" Semantics: If a client's call succeeds, then this implies that at least one execution has taken place at the server. Further subclassification is also possible (e.g., first one or last one) indicating which execution is responsible for the termination of a call.

To start with, it should be clear that out of the two, 1) has the more desirable semantics but is also the more difficult of the two to achieve. An approach that has been widely used (see, for example, [3]) is to adopt — for the sake of simplicity at the RPC level — the "at least once" semantics and to make all of the services of servers idempotent (that is, repeated executions are equivalent to a single execution). Thus the problems of repeated executions and orphans can be more or less ignored. The major shortcoming of this approach is that it is relatively difficult to provide servers with arbitrary services (e.g., a server cannot easily provide services that include increment operations); for this reason we have rejected this option in our RPC design and have chosen instead the "exactly once" semantics. This has been achieved by introducing sufficient measures at the RPC level to enable processes to reject unwanted messages arising during a call. This capability is not enough to cope with orphans, however, since as stated before, a client's crash can result in more than one remote call directed at a server when only call was intended. We treat orphans at the next level (in the software supporting L3, see Fig. 1) by insisting that all programs that run over L3 be atomic actions with the "all or nothing" property. In particular, this means that any executions at servers be atomic as well. This atomicity criteria implies that repeated executions at a server are performed in a logically serial order with orphan actions terminating without producing any results. This is the basis of the work presented in [5] where the techniques needed for the construction of level L3, given the existence of L2, are described (a broadly similar approach has, we understand, been independently developed by Liskov's group at the Massachusetts Institute of Technology [8]).

To sum up this section: 1) we have chosen the exactly once semantics for our RPC, 2) the main reliability feature needed at the RPC level is that necessary to discard any unwanted messages, and 3) any other reliability features necessary for ensuring proper executions of application programs are added not at the RPC level but at the next level concerned with the provision of atomic actions. In the design of the RPC mechanism to be presented we have followed the rule of keeping each level as simple as possible; this has been achieved by making reliability mechanisms application specific rather than general as argued in [9].

III. Communications Support for RPC: Datagram Versus Transport Service

The implementation of RPC requires that the underlying level support some kind of Interprocess Communication (IPC) facility. On the one hand, this facility could be quite sophisticated with features such as guaranteed, undamaged and unduplicated delivery of a message, flow control, and end to end acknowledgment. An interface supporting such features is usually said to provide a transport service for messages. On the other hand, the IPC facility could be rather primitive, lacking most of the above desirable properties. An interface supporting such an IPC mechanism is said to provide a *datagram service* [10].

Transport services are designed in order to provide fully reliable communication between processes exchanging data (messages) over unreliable media — they are particularly suitable for wide area pocket switching networks which are liable to damage, lose, or duplicate packets. The implementation of a "transport layer" tends to be quite expensive in terms of resources needed since a significant amount of state information needs to be maintained about any data transfer in progress. The initialization and maintenance of this state information, is required to support the abstraction of a "connection" between processes. To establish, maintain, and terminate a connection reliably is rather complex and a significant number of messages are needed just for connection purposes [11].

On the other hand, a datagram service provides the facility of the transmission of a finite size block of data (a message known as a datagram) from an origin address to a destination address. In its simplest form, the datagram service does not provide any means for flow control or end to end acknowledgments; the datagram is simply delivered on a "best effort" basis. If any of the features of the transport service are required, then the user must implement them specifically using the datagram service.

At a superficial level, it would seem that a good way to construct a reliable RPC would be to start with a reliable message service, i.e., a transport service. However, we reject this viewpoint and adopt the datagram service as the more desirable alternative. The argument for this decision is as follows. To start with, it must be noted that in the distributed system previously mentioned, the users are not given the abstraction of sending or receiving messages; rather only a very specific piece of software − that needed to implement RPC − is the sole user of messages. As such the full generality of the transport service is not needed. The provision of the transport service entails a considerable reduction of the available communication bandwidth (this is because of the overheads of connection management and the need for end to end acknowledgment). We may be able to utilize this bandwidth more effectively by reducing the need for connection management and acknowledgments as much as possible. This is indeed feasible in typical local area network since the underlying hardware − the Cambridge Ring in our case − provides a reliable means of data transmission. So a fairly reliable datagram service (whereby every datagram is delivered with a high probability to its destination address) can certainly be built on top of the hardware interface. Any additional facilities needed are then specifically implemented making the implementation of the RPC a bit more complex but highly efficient. Hence, we conclude that it is appropriate to give the software of the RPC mechanism the responsibility of coping with any unreliabilities of a datagram service. In the next section we will describe the specific datagram service to be implemented over the Cambridge Ring hardware in order to support our RPC mechanism.

IV. The Hardware and the Datagram Service

The Cambridge Ring hardware [12] provides its users with the ability to transmit and receive packets of a fixed size between nodes connected to the Ring − each transmitted packet is individually acknowledged. At the Ring level each node is identified by a unique station address. The following two primitive operations are available.

1) *transmit-packet* (*destination*: . . .; *pkt*: . . .; **var** *status*: . . .); where the acknowledgement is encoded as *status* = (*OK, unselected, busy, ignored, transmission-error*).

The meaning of "status" is as follows:

status = *OK*: The destination station has received the packet.

status = *unselected*: The packet was not accepted by the destination station because that station was "listening" to some other source station.

status = *busy*: The packet was not accepted by the destination station because that station was "deaf" (not listening to anyone). Note that either of the above two status conditions implies that the destination station is most likely to become available shortly.

status = *ignored*: The packet was not accepted because the destination station was not on-line. This indication can be taken to mean that there is little chance of packets being accepted by that station for a while.

status = *transmission-error*: The packet got corrupted somewhere during its passage through the Ring. This is the only case where the response of the destination station is not known.

It is worth mentioning here that the transmit primitive does not have a time-out response associated with it. As a consequence, the execution of this primitive will not return if the packet is not acknowledged due to a fault in the Ring hardware.

2) *receive-packet* (**var** *source*: . . .; **var** *pkt*: . . .).

The receive primitive allows for the reception of packets either from any source station on the Ring or from a specific source (a special operation is provided by the Ring for setting up a station in either of the modes). In either case, "source" will contain the identity of the sender with "pkt" containing the received packet. A curious aspect of the Ring is that each node has a parity error detection logic, but neither the sender nor the receiver of a packet get any indication when a parity error is detected in a packet (this does not matter all that much in reality as the probability of a packet getting corrupted has been shown to be very low).

We shall assume that all of the hardware components (e.g., Ring, processors, clocks) either perform exactly as specified or a component simply does not work (so, for example, for the Ring, a "send" or "receive" operation will not terminate). If this assumption were realistic, then the design to follow has some very nice reliability properties. However, unpredictable behavior of the hardware interface (i.e., a behavior that does not meet the specification) is likely to result in the same at the RPC/user interface to the extent that guaranteed behaviour cannot be promised.

The proposed datagram service will provide its users (processes) with the ability of: 1) sending a block of data to a named destination process, and 2) receiving a block of data from a specific or any process. We shall ignore here the fine details of how this may be implemented using the Ring operations described earlier; only the properties of the datagram service primitives will be described.

1) *send_msg* (*destination*: ...; *message*: ...; **var** *status*: ...); where *status* = (*OK, absent, not-done, unable*).

The message is broken into packets and transmitted to the home station of the destination process. If all these packets are accepted by the station, then "status = OK" will hold. Note that this only means that the message has reached the station, and not that it has been accepted by the destination process. If a packet is not accepted (possibly even after a few retries) by the station (packet level response is "unselected" or "busy"), then "status = not-done" will hold. A packet level response of "ignored" is translated as "status = absent" indicating that the destination process is just not available. The last two responses indicate that the message was not delivered. A time-out mechanism will be needed to cope with Ring malfunctions during the transmission of a message. The "unable" status holds either if the time out expires or if a packet level "transmission-error" response is obtained. The "unable" response indicates inability of the datagram layer to deliver a message properly (the message may or may not have reached the destination station).

2) *receive_msg* (*source*: ...; **var** *msg*: ...).

The above primitive is to receive a message from a specified "source" process. This primitive is implemented by repeatedly making use of the receive-packet (...) primitive. A time-out mechanism will be needed to detect an incomplete message transmission and Ring failures. Any corruption of the sent message can be detected if the sender includes a checksum in the message and appropriate computation is performed at the receiver; corrupted messages are simply discarded. So the receive_msg (...) primitive only delivers a "good" message (if any).

The receive_msg (...) primitive can also be used for receiving messages from any source by simply specifying "source" parameter as "any".

The datagram service described above is based on the Basic Block Protocol designed at Cambridge [13].

V. RPC Mechanism

A client invokes the following primitive to obtain a service from a server (where the "time-out" parameter specifies how long the client is willing to wait for a response to his request):

remote_call (*server*: ...; *service*: ...; **var** *result*: ...; **var** *status*: ...; *time-out*: ...);

where *status* = (*OK, not-done, absent, unable*)

and parameters and results are passed by value.

510

The meaning of the call under various responses is given below.

status = OK: The service specified has been performed (exactly once) by the server and the answers are encoded in "result."

status = not-done: The server has not performed the service because it is currently busy (so the client can certainly reissue the call in the hope of getting an "OK" response).

status = absent: The server is not available (so it is pointless for the client to retry).

status = unable: The parameter "result" does not contain the answers; whether the server performed the service is not known. The action of the client under this situation will depend typically on the property of the requested service. If the service required has the idempotency property, then the client can retry without any harm; otherwise backward recovery should be invoked to maintain consistency. How this is achieved is not relevant here; it is sufficient to observe, as noted in the section on reliability issues, that the consistency and recovery problems could be handled within the framework of the two phase commit protocol and atomic actions.

We believe that these responses are meaningful, simply understood, and quite adequate for robust programming. We shall show next that it is possible to design RPC with the above properties based on our datagram service despite numerous fault manifestations in the distributed system (including node crashes). A skeleton program showing only the essential details of the RPC implementation is depicted below which should be self-explanatory. The following two assumptions will be made in the ensuing discussion: 1) some means exists for a receiver process to reject unwanted (i.e., spurious, duplicated) messages; the next section contains a proposal for achieving this goal; 2) node crashes amount to that station being not on line. We now consider the treatment of various responses obtained during message handling.

```
        Client                      Server
remote-call (···) corresponds    cycle
to the following code:            –––
        –––                       repeat "get work"
    send_msg ( );         →       receive_msg (any, ···);
    "send service request"        until msg = valid;
                                  –––
                                  "perform work"
set (time-out);                   –––
repeat                            "send result"
    receive_msg ( );      ←       send_msg ( );
until msg = valid;                –––
        –––                       end;
```

1) *The Client Sends a Service Request*: Recall that a send_msg (...) can return the response "OK," "absent," "not done," or "unable." If the response is "OK," the control goes to the "set (time-out) statement. If the response is "absent," then the execution of remote_call (...) terminates with "status = absent."

If the response is "not-done," then the message is sent again. If after a few retries the same response is obtained, then the execution of remote_call (...) terminates with "status = not-done." A few retries can also be made if the send_msg (...) results in an "unable" response. If this response still holds after retries, then the execution of remote-call (...) terminates with "status = unable." Note that it is all right to send a message repeatedly. The server is in a position to discard any duplicates.

2) *The Client Waits for a Message*: The client prepares to wait for a response from the server. A time-out is set to stop the client from waiting forever; the maximum duration of the waiting is as specified in the last parameter of the remote_call (...). All the unwanted messages are discarded. A client may get such messages, for example, as a result of the actions performed by that node before it crashed and came up again. If a valid message is received, then the execution of remote_call (...) terminates with "status = OK" and "result" containing the answer. If the time-out expires, then the execution of the remote _call (...) terminates with 'status = unable" Note that "unable" response can be obtained for several reasons: server did not receive the message, server node crashed, or server's message not received because of a Ring fault.

3) *Server Waits for a Service Request*: Any spurious, in particular duplicated, messages are rejected. This guarantees that despite the possibility of repeated requests being sent by a client, only one service execution will take place.

4) *Server Sends the Reply*: If the execution of send_msg (...) results in an "OK" response, then the server is ready for the next request — it goes to the beginning of its cycle. Note that it is not guaranteed that the client will receive the reply, rather it implies that most probably the reply has reached the client. If the "send" operation gives rise to the "absent" response, then "unable" is signaled to the server. If the "send" operation gives rise to either a "not-done" or an "unable" response, then the message can be resent a few times before accepting defeat by signaling "unable" to the server. The reason for mapping all the three abnormal responses of send_msg (...) onto a single "unable" response is based on the belief that it is of little interest to a server as to why he was not able to deliver the result satisfactorily (this response means that most probably the client did not receive the reply). As before, any recovery actions of the server will be handled within the framework of atomic actions and the two phase commit protocol.

We conclude that the level concerned with RPC implementation provides three operations: 1) remote_call (...) — this is the client half of the program with the semantics discussed earlier; 2) get_work (...) — this corresponds to the repeat loop code of the server; and 3) send_result (..., status) — this corresponds to the code concerned with sending of the results, with status = (OK, unable), where the "absent," "not-done," and "unable" responses of send_msg (...) are all mapped onto "unable" response of send-result.

It should be noted that if fault manifestations are rare and messages are delivered with a high probability, then almost always, only two messages are required for RPC. This is not possible if the transport service is used for message passing.

VI. Generation of Sequence Numbers

In the previous section it was assumed that a receiver is always in a position to reject unwanted messages; this can be arranged by appropriately assigning sequence numbers (SN's) to messages. The problem of sequence numbering of messages is fairly complex if tolerance to node crashes is required. For example, it is necessary for a process of a node that has "come up" after a crash to be able to distinguish those incoming messages that have originated as a result of any actions performed before the crash. This typically requires maintaining relevant state information on a "crash proof" storage. This is a complicated and expensive process, so a scheme that has minimum crash proof storage requirements is to be preferred. A transport level is designed to cope with sequence numbering problems and users are not concerned with them; however, in our case they need to be generated explicitly within the RPC level. There can be three approaches to the generation and assignment of SN's.

1) SN's are unique over a given client-server interaction: this would be the approach implicitly taken by a transport level supported RPC. This is a fairly complex approach requiring the maintenance of a relatively large amount of state information that has to survive crashes [11].

2) SN's are unique over node to node interactions: rather than maintaining state information on a process to process basis, it is possible to maintain information on a node to node basis only. Clearly, it is less demanding than 1) above, in its requirements for crash proof storage.

3) SN's are unique over the entire system: if SN's are made unique over the entire network, then a very simple scheme suggests itself. A server need only maintain "the last largest SN received" in a crash proof storage (and as we shall see, even this requirement can be dispensed with). Further, all the retry messages are sent by a sender with the same SN as the original message. If a server accepts only those messages whose SN is greater than the current value of "last largest SN," then it is easy to see now that we have the server property assumed in the previous section (that of rejecting unwanted messages). A similar approach is necessary at the client's end.

We have chosen to incorporate the third method in our design because, as indicated above, coping with node crashes is comparatively easier in such a technique. Two of the best known techniques for the generation of network wide unique sequence numbers are based on: 1) the circulating token method of Le Lann [14], and 2) the loosely synchronized clock approach of Lamport [15]. In the former all of the nodes are logically connected in a ring configuration and an integer valued "token" circulates round the ring in a fixed direction. A node that wants to send a message waits for the token to arrive, then it copies its value, increments the value of the token, and passes it on to the next node. The copied value can be used for sequence numbering. In the latter method each node is equipped with a clock and each node is also assigned a unique "node number." A sequence number at any node is the current clock value concatenated with the node number. For "acceptable behavior" (see later) it is necessary that the clock values at various nodes be approximately the same at any given time. This is achieved as follows. Whenever a process at say

513

node n_i receives a message, it checks the SN of that messsge with the current SN of n_i; if SN (received) is greater or equal to SN (n_i), then the clock of n_i is advanced by enough ticks to make SN(n_i) greater than SN(received).

Out of the above two methods, we have adopted the second in our system for the following two reasons: 1) because of the kind of message facility we are using, it will not be easy for a node to find out whether its sent token has been received by the next node or not; as a result the detection of the lost token is not a straightforward process; and 2) the algorithm for the reinsertion of the token − which must ensure that only one token gets inserted − is rather complex. In comparison, as we shall see, Lamport's technique can be made to tolerate lost messages and node crashes in a straightforward manner. We shall next describe how we have incorporated Lamport's technique into our design.

The SN at a node at any time is constructed out of the time of day and calendar clock of the node and the Ring station number.

SN = | time and date | station number |

The SN of a node is maintained by a monitor [16] that provides the following two procedures:

get_SN(**var** *s_number:* . . .);

this procedure returns the SN

update_SN(*s_ number:* . . .);

The SN at the monitor is compared with passed sequence number and the clock of the node adjusted as described earlier. The SN's are used in the RPC algorithm as depicted below.

Client		Server
		begin
		llsn := get_SN ($\cdots$);
---		"llsn = last largest seq. no."
		cycle
i := get_SN ($\cdots$);		---
		repeat "get work"
send_msg ($\cdots$);	$\rightarrow$	receive_msg (any, $\cdots$)
"message includes i"		**until** msg $\cdot$ SN > llsn;
		llsn := msg $\cdot$ SN;

		"perform work"
set (time-out);		---
repeat		
receive_msg ($\cdots$);	$\leftarrow$	send_msg ($\cdots$);
until msg $\cdot$ SN = i;		"msg sent with SN = llsn"
---		---
		end;
		end;

Strictly speaking, in our system there is no logical requirement that the various clocks be "approximately the same." However, in the absence of such a situation, a client with a slower clock will have difficulty in obtaining services since his requests will stand a higher chance of rejection by servers. Hence, it is necessary that each node regularly receives messages from other nodes so that it can keep its clock value nearer to those of others. For this purpose we maintain two processes at each node (see below).

```
        Broadcaster                   Clock Synchronizer
cycle                           cycle
    delay (t);                      receive_msg (···);
    i := get_SN (···);              update_SN (msg · SN);
    for all remote nodes        end;
    do
        send_msg (···);
    "send message with SN = i
    to a clock synchronizer"
end;
```

The "broadcaster" process of a node regularly (say once every few minutes) sends its sequence number to all of the remote clock-synchronizer processes. A few retries can be made if a send operation returns a "not-done" or an "unable" response. If these responses persist or an "absent" response is obtained, then no further attempt is made to send the message to that clock-synchronizer in that cycle (at this level, a crashed node in no way affects the noncrashed nodes).

We shall now discuss how our sequence numbering scheme can be made to tolerate node crashes economically. We can avoid the need for any crash proof storage for our scheme by being careful during the start up phase of a node after a crash. In a centralized system, when the computer system is started up, the operator inputs the time and date to the system clock. This is not desirable in our system since careless clock updates can introduce problems. For example, entering "future time and date" will eventually affect the rest of the system in that all clocks will become "inaccurate" in the sense that they will not represent physical time (logically this is irrelevant). Also, entering a "past time and date" can result in the acceptance of wrong messages. We simply insist that the "clock-synchronizer" process be the only process (with one exception, see below) that can update the clock. So when a node comes up, eventually (within a few minutes) it will be able to get an appropriate clock value. An important requirement is that a node, when it comes up, should have its clock initialized to zero. The only drawback of the above scheme is that if all the other nodes are down (presumably a rare event), then our node will never get a clock value. This problem can be solved by giving some privileged user the authority for clock updates.

We conclude this section by summarizing the net effect of our sequence number assignment and generation scheme on the fault-tolerant behavior of our RPC mechanism: 1) since none of the state information of a call is maintained on a crash proof storage, a call does not survive a crash; 2) the clock

515

management scheme ensures that any messages belonging to a "crashed call" are ignored.

VII. Concluding Remarks

The design presented here is currently being implemented on our UNIX systems. At a superficial level it would seem that to design a program that provides a remote procedure call abstraction would be a straightforward exercise. Surprisingly, this is not so. We have found the problem of the design of the RPC to be rather intricate. To the best of our ability we have checked that all of the possible normal and abnormal situations properly map onto the responses of the "remote_call (. . .)," "get_work (. . .)," and "send_result (. . .)." Clearly, a formal validation exercise and experience with the completed implementation should expose any inadequacies in our design.

Note Added in Proof: The RPC is now operational; its implementation is described in the next paper of this chapter.

Acknowledgement. The authors' understanding of the subject matter reported here has been improved as a result of discussions with their colleagues at Newcastle; in addition, they have also benefited from informal contacts with other groups, most notably those at Cambridge, MIT, and Xerox.

References

1. M. V. Wilkes and D. J. Wheeler, "The Cambridge communication ring," in Proc. Local Area Network Symp., Boston, MA, Nat. Bureau of Standards, May 1979.
2. H. C. Lauer and R. M. Needham, "On the duality of operating system structures," in Proc. 2nd Int. Symp. on Operating Syst., IRIA, Oct. 1978; also in Oper. Syst. Rev., vol. 13, pp. 3 −19, Apr. 1979.
3. B. Lampson and H. Sturgis, "Atomic transactions," in Lecture Notes in Computer Science, Vol. 105. New York: Springer-Verlag, 1981, pp. 246−265.
4. J. N. Gray, "Notes on data base operating systems," in Lecture Notes in Computer Science, Vol. 60. New York: Springer-Verlag, 1978, pp. 398−481.
5. S. K. Shrivastava, "Structuring distributed systems for recoverability and crash resistance," IEEE Trans. Software Eng., vol. SE-7, pp. 436−447, July 1981. [Also Chap. 5]
6. B. Lampson, "Remote procedure calls," in Lecture Notes in Computer Science, Vol. 105. New York: Springer-Verlag, 1981, pp. 365−370.
7. B. J. Nelson, "Remote procedure call," Ph.D. dissertation, Dep. Comput. Sci., Carnegie-Mellon Univ., Pittsburgh, PA, CMU-CS-81-119, 1981.
8. B. Liskov, "On linguistic support for distributed programs," in Proc. Symp. Reliable Distributed Software and Database Syst., Pittsburgh, PA, July 1981, pp. 53−60.
9. J. H. Saltzer, D. P. Reed, and D. D. Clark, "End to end argument in system design," in Proc. 2nd Int. Conf. on Distributed Syst., Paris, France, Apr. 1981, pp. 509−512.
10. R. W. Watson, "Hierarchy," in Lecture Notes in Computer Science, Vol. 105. New York: Springer-Verlag, 1981, pp. 109−118.
11. C. A. Sunshine, and Y. K. Dalal, "Connection management in transport protocols," in Computer Networks, vol. 2. Amsterdam, The Netherlands: North-Holland, 1978, pp. 454 −473.

12. Science and Engineering Research Council (U.K.), "Cambridge data ring," Tech. Note, Sept. 1980.
13. R. M. Needham, "System aspects of the Cambridge ring," in Proc. 7th Oper. Syst. Symp., Dec. 1979, pp. 82–85.
14. G. Le Lann, "Distributed systems: Towards a formal approach," in Information Processing 77. Amsterdam, The Netherlands: North-Holland, 1977, pp. 155–160.
15. L. Lamport, "Time, clocks and the ordering of events in a distributed system," Commun. Ass. Comput. Mach., vol. 21, pp. 558–565, July 1978.
16. C. A. R. Hoare, "Monitors: An operating system structuring concept," Commun. Ass. Comput. Mach., vol. 17, Oct. 1974.

Reliable Remote Calls for Distributed UNIX: An Implementation Study

F. Panzieri and S. K. Shrivastava

Abstract. An implementation of a reliable remote procedure call mechanism for obtaining remote services is described. The reliability issues are discussed together with how they have been dealt with. The performance of the remote call mechanism is compared with that of local calls. The remote call mechanism is shown to be an efficient tool for distributed programming.

Introduction

We are currently in the process of implementing a UNIX* based distributed system with the objective of investigating various reliability issues in the design and implementation of such systems. Our current hardware configuration consists of a number of PDP11 computer systems (nodes) connected by the Cambridge Ring local area network [1]. Each node has at least 10 Mbytes of disc storage, runs the UNIX V7 operating system and supports a small group of users with broadly similar research interests. In this context, we envisage the distributed system as a loosely coupled system of largely autonomous nodes. This view has led us to assume that in such a system, users' accesses to system resources will be confined largely to those local to their nodes and further, any remote access will typically be concerned with file manipulations. It was our task to implement appropriate protocols for inter-process communications. Two design decisions were taken at the outset: (i) to provide a uniform interface to both local and remote objects, and (ii) to make no changes to the UNIX operating system. Since UNIX provides a procedure call based interface to all services (e.g. file open, close), it seems natural to provide access to remote services through a remote procedure call (RPC) mechanism. The implementation of such a remote call mechanism is the subject of this paper. In view of the second design decision, all of the implemented RPC software in effect runs as a UNIX application software, hence the RPC response can never be made as good as that from a local system call. To get reasonable remote responses, it was in our interest to cut down the RPC software to the barest minimum, thus implying the usage of simple communication protocols: an apparently conflicting requirement with that of achieving reliability. As the performance figures for the RPC show, we have managed to get acceptable response times for remote file accesses (the most likely use of the RPC); however this has not been achieved by compromising reliability.

---

* UNIX is a Trademark of Bell Laboratories

518

1. RPC Semantics and Reliability Requirements

An implementation of a RPC mechanism essentially involves sending the client's request as a message to the appropriate server and then receiving the server's response which constitutes the end of the call. Since the client and the server are on different machines, any good RPC mechanism must cope effectively with the problems arising from a crash of one of the machines and any unreliability of the underlying data communication facility. These problems and their solutions are discussed in [2, 3], and our particular approach to reliable RPC is described in [4]. Since the design of the RPC mechanism has already been described elsewhere [4], we shall not elaborate it here. However, for the sake of completeness, a very brief discussion on reliability problems and their solutions is presented here.

Figure 1 depicts the message exchanges for a call between a client and a server.

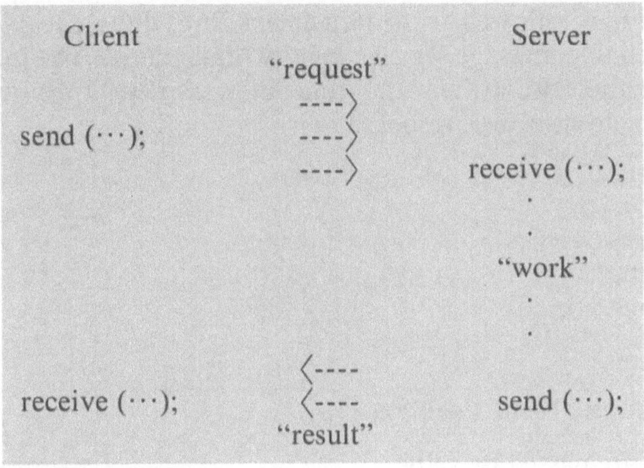

Fig. 1. Simple RPC

We assume that invocation of the message retry mechanism (in the interest of fault tolerance) can result in multiple messages directed at the destination. This can result in more than a single execution of "work" (orphan executions [2, 3]) at the server. A simple sequence numbering scheme can solve this problem since duplicate messages can now be recognised and hence rejected (reliability requirements R1 and R2):

R1: client's request message must include a sequence number (SN) which must match that of the corresponding result message (note: all retries of a message contain the same SN).

R2: SN's must survive node crashes.

We assume that recovery from a node crash involves starting up the node from some initial state. However, if SN's after a crash recovery of a client's node are the same as before the crash, then there is the possibility of a server confusing new requests with old ones and thus refusing to accept some of these requests. Worst still, there is the possibility of a client accepting a wrong result:

this could happen if the client's node crashes just after the 'call request' has been sent and, after the crash recovery, the client makes a request to the same server with the same SN, then the possibility of the client accepting the results from the previous call certainly exists. The above analysis indicates the need for the requirement R2. A crash of the client's node in the middle of a call can also result in an orphan; so requirement R3 is needed:

R3: a server must detect an orphan and cause its abortion before accepting a new call.

The above three reliability requirements must be met to ensure the 'exactly once' semantics of RPC (that is, a successful call implies one execution at the server and incomplete calls produce no interference). As discussed elsewhere [4], we employ a network wide unique sequence numbering scheme (based on the loosely synchronised clock approach [5]) to meet requirements R1 and R2 in the RPC level software. However we have chosen not to meet the requirement R3 at the RPC level; rather, such orphans are treated at a higher level: the 're-covery' level concerned with the maintenance of atomicity of user programs [6, 7]. These design decisions have allowed us to implement RPC quite cheaply based on a potentially unreliable message sending facility (datagrams). The following is the semantics of the RPC (where the 'timeout' parameter specifies how long the client is willing to wait for a response):

```
remote_call (server: . .;
             service: . .;
             var result: . .;
             var r_stat: . .;
             timeout: . .);
```

where 'r_stat' is of type 'status':

status = (OK, not-done, absent, unable);

and parameters and results are passed by value.

The meaning of the call under various responses is given below:

- status = OK: The service specified has been performed exactly once by the server and the answers are encoded in 'result'.
- status = not-done: The server has not performed the service because it is currently busy (so the client can certainly re-issue the call in the hope of getting an 'OK' response).
- status = absent: The server is not available (so it is pointless for the client to retry).
- status = unable: The parameter 'result' does not contain the answers; whether the server performed the service is not known (this response can be obtained when the timeout expires). If the service required has the idempotency property then the client can certainly re-issue the call without any harm; otherwise the services of the 'recovery' level must be invoked to undo any side effects produced before reissuing the call [7].

The RPC mechanism whose implementation is described in the rest of the paper meets the above specification provided the following conditions are met: (i) a node's hardware components (e.g. CPU, clock, ring interface) are working according to their specifications; (ii) the ring is working according to the specification; and (iii) the UNIX system of a node is also working according to the specification. If failure modes of these three subsystems were 'clean' (working or not working) then a failure of subsystem (i) or (iii) will constitute a node crash and has the net effect of all of the ongoing calls on that node not succeeding and any services provided by that node becoming unavailable; a failure of the Ring has the effect of all of the nodes becoming disconnected (so a node will be unable to obtain remote services). In practice of course, failures are rarely 'clean', nor are precise system specifications available. So, whenever it is suspected that a subsystem is not working properly, the best strategy is to convert that failure to a clean node or ring failure by switching off appropriate power supply or by stopping the operating system as the case may be. In the case of a crashed node, once it has been repaired, it can be inserted in the system dynamically: there is no need for either stopping the entire system to accomodate the new node or to specifically inform the live nodes that a new node has been added to the system.

2. RPC Implementation

This section describes the user interface supported by the RPC software and certain aspects of its implementation. The implementation has been performed in C language; however for the sake of readability, the algorithms have been described in a Pascal like language ('{' and '}' stand for '**begin**', '**end**' and comments are enclosed whithin quotes). But first, a few remarks of general interest are in order:

(a) The message passing system employed by the RPC mechanism uses a naming scheme based on 'port' numbers (integer values). A message is delivered to a given port at a given node; so the process that is 'attached' to that port becomes the recipient of the messages directed at that port. Some higher level 'name server' will typically be required through which various servers can publish their port numbers for receiving requests. The following two primitive operations are available:

(i) send_msg(destination: . . .;
                message: . . .;
                var msg_status: . . .));

where 'msg_status' is of type 'status', 'destination' is a record containing the node number (each node has a unique number) and the port number, and 'message' is an array of bytes. The response 'OK' implies that the message has been delivered to the appropriate port; while the response 'absent' means that the node is not connected to the ring. The response 'not-done' indicates that the message was rejected − possibly because the recipient is busy (so the sender can certainly retry). The response 'unable' indicates a ring malfunction during the transmission: the message may or may not have reached the destination.

(ii) receive_msg (at: port_number;
                   var node: source;
                   var message: . . .));

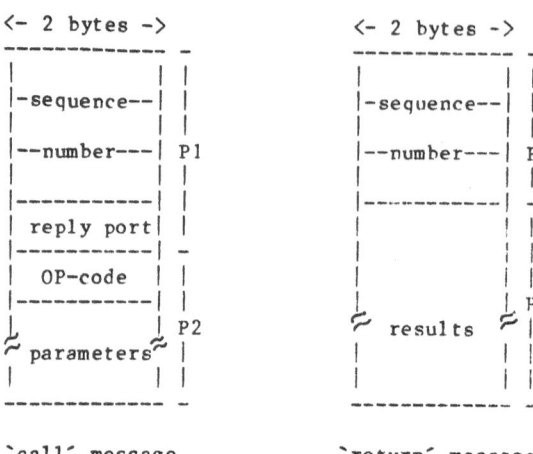

```
 <- 2 bytes ->                    <- 2 bytes ->
 -------------- -                 -------------- -
|            | | |               |            | | |
|-sequence--| | |               |-sequence--| | |
|            | | |               |            | | |
|--number---| P1                |--number---| P1
|            | | |               |            | | -
|-----------| | |               |-----------| |
| reply port| | |               |            | | |
|-----------| -                 |            | | |
| OP-code   | | |               |            | | | P2
|-----------| | |               |           | P2
|          | P2                 ~ results  ~ |
~ parameters~ |                 |            | | |
|            | | |               |            | | |
 -------------- -                 -------------- -

`call` message                   `return` message
   (a)                              (b)          Fig. 2. call and return message formats
```

This procedure receives in 'message' a message directed at port 'at' from the specified source 'node'. If source = 'any' then messages from any node directed at 'at' are accepted (in any case, 'node' will contain the node number of the sender).

(b) The sequence number (SN) used in a message is derived by concatenating the current value of the local clock of the node and the node number ($\langle$ clock value, node number $\rangle$); a function get_sn (. . .) has been implemented that returns a sequence number.

(c) The formate of call and return messages are shown in Fig. 2.

The caller supplied information includes the port number for receiving the reply, server operation and the necessary parameters. The maximum length of a message has been fixed to that necessary to return a page of data as a result.

2.1. User Interface

In addition to the 'remote_call (. . .)' operation available to clients, two operations — to be employed by the servers — are also provided by the RPC interface: (i) the operation 'get_work (. . .)' is used by a server to receive a call request, and (ii) the operation 'send_result (. . .)' is used by a server to send the results of the executed call.

The 'remote_call (. . .)' operation transfers an array of bytes (parameter 'service') to the named server (i.e. to the appropriate port) and returns an array of bytes (parameter 'result'). It is left to servers and clients to view these byte arrays as structured objects. A client's view of the 'call' message is the portion P2 of Fig. 2(a); the remote_call software constructs the portion P1 of the message, thus hiding unnecessary details of sequence numbering and reply port from the client. Similarly, a client only sees the portion P2 of the returned message (Fig. 2(b)). A number of 'pack' procedures have been provided for packing simple typed variables (integers, strings, etc.) onto an array of bytes; a complementary set of 'unpack' procedures are also available for constructing typed variables from an array of bytes. Here is a rather simplified description of how a client can perform a remote file read operation (assume that the client knows the node number and the port number of the file server).

In UNIX, a file read operation must specify the file descriptor (an integer value), the address of buffer for storing the data and the number of bytes to be read. The client needs the following variables:

```
var
    where  : "server address"
    fd     : integer;
    buff   : array [...] of char;
    index  : integer;
    nbytes : integer;
    service: array [...] of char;
    r_stat : status;
```

where the variable 'fd' should contain the file descriptor of the remote file (as a result of a remote open file operation performed by the client).

```
"remote_read implementation"
    ———
packint (0, service, index);
    "opcode 0: file read"
packint (fd, service, index);
packint (nbytes, service, index);
remote_call (where, service, buff, r_stat, timeout);
if r_stat = OK then
    begin
        "buff contains the result"
    end
else
    ———
```

Thus a 'remote_read' operation can be provided which is as easy to use as a local read. On the server's side, the server uses the 'get_work (...)' operation to receive an array of bytes; this array is suitably unpacked and then the requested operation is performed. The server then packs the results into an array of bytes which is then sent to the client's port using 'send_result (...)' operation.

2.2. Some Implementation Details

The program below shows those details of the 'remote_call (...)' that are to do with the provision of fault tolerance and mapping of message responses onto the status return of the call:

```
begin   "remote_call (...) implementation"
    ...
    sn := get_sn (...);
```

```
      at := get_port (...); "get port number"
      construct the message of figure 2 (a);
      retry := 0;
      done := false;
      repeat   "call request to server"
      { send_msg (server, msg, msg_status);
        case msg_status of
      ok:        { done := true}
      absent:    { r_stat := absent; return}
      not_done: { retry := retry + 1;
                      if retry = MAXTRY then
                      { r_stat := not_done; return}

                    }
      unable:    { retry := retry + 1;
                      if retry = MAXTRY then
                      { r_stat := unable; return}

                    }
            end  "case"
      } until   done;
      within time_out do
      { repeat
           receive_msg (at, server_node, result);
         until result.sn = sn
      } ⟨EXPIRED? (r_stat := unable; return)⟩
      r_stat := OK
    end;
```

In the current implementation, MAXTRY has been set to 10. A typical time-out period for a file read operation should be set by the user to a value ranging between 1 and 2 seconds, depending on the system load.

A server has to maintain certain global data which is initialised at the node start-up time. This data is the last largest sequence number (11sn) received from a given node, and is initialised to the current clock value of the server's node:

```
var 11sn: array [...] of sn;
    for i = 1 to maxnode do
      11sn (i) := get_sn (...);
```

Thereafter, the above data structure is utilised by the get_work (...) procedure to accept a valid request. The send_result (...) operation uses a similar technique to that of remote call (...) for transmitting the result.

```
procedure get_work (...);
  ...
begin
  repeat
     src := any;
```

```
        receive_msg (port, src, msg);
        sn := seq. no. in msg;
    until sn > 11sn (src);
    11sn (src) := sn;
    ...
end;
```

3. Clock Management

As stated before, a sequence number at a given node is constructed out of the current clock value and the unique node number. All the clocks of the system are kept loosely synchronised with each other so that they represent roughly the same physical time [5]. A simple way to achieve this objective was described in [4]. All that is necessary is for each node to maintain two processes: (i) a broadcaster process that regularly (say once every few minutes) sends its current time to the rest of the nodes; and (ii) a synchroniser process whose task is to receive the time sent by others and to advance its clock if it is behind that of a given sender.

Three practical problems were faced in the implementation of the above scheme.

(i) A client with a slow clock can experience difficulty in obtaining services from a server if the server relies on its own clock for deciding whether to accept or reject a request.

(ii) For the sake of efficiency, we would like that a broadcaster need only send its time to those nodes that are currently 'up'. The Cambridge Ring can accomodate up to 255 nodes, though our ring is currently rather sparsely populated. This suggests the need for a dynamically maintained 'up' list at every node such that if a new node is inserted in the ring, the broadcasters of the other nodes eventually discover this fact (and thus can start sending their times to the new node) and similarly if a node is removed from the ring, this fact is also discovered by the rest of the 'up' nodes.

(iii) The fact that clocks are always advanced implies that 'fast' clock errors will accumulate and in particular a runaway clock can advance the network time far ahead of the physical time. This suggests that a facility for setting clocks back is needed. Of course, this must be performed without compromising the security offered by the sequence numbering scheme.

The only way of avoiding problem (i) was to maintain the clock values of the other nodes at the server's node (the 'llsn' array mentioned in the last section). The solutions adopted to solve the remaining two problems will now be described. The solution adopted for setting back the clocks is quite practical if this operation were not invoked frequently (certainly true in our case as only a few adjustments are needed every month). When the clocks are being set back, users are likely to encounter some difficulty in obtaining remote services; however the system quickly stabilises (within a few minutes). The authority for setting clocks back is vested in the broadcaster of one node only — this special broadcaster will be referred to as the Time Lord. The Time Lord can send three types of messages:

synch: this is the normal message containing the current time;
goback: this message is a 'get prepared to set time backwards' message.
set: this message contains the new time.

All the other broadcasters can only send the 'synch' messages. The algorithms for a broadcaster (not a Time Lord) and a synchroniser of a node are as shown. Two shared variables 'dir' and 'uplist' are maintained and protected by a mutex semaphore.

```
     "shared variables"
var
   dir:    (forward, backward);
   uplist: array [1 ... maxnode] of (UP, DOWN);
   mutex: semaphore; "initially 1"

     "BROADCASTER ALGORITHM"
var retry: integer; done: boolean;
begin
   P (mutex);
   dir := forward;
   V (mutex);
   set_clock (0);   "initialise clock"
   for i :=  to max_node do
   begin
      retry := 0; done := false;
      repeat "send 'I am alive' synch message"
         send_msg (..., 0, msg_status);
         P (mutex);
         case msg_status of
      ok: {uplist (i) := UP; done := true}
      absent: {uplist (i) := DOWN; done := true}
      unable, notdone: {retry := retry + 1;
                           if retry = max then
                           uplist (i) := DOWN}
         end   "end case"
         V (mutex);
      until retry = max or done
   end "end of broadcaster initialisation program"
   cycle
      delay (t);   "wait for a minute"
      P (mutex);
      if dir = forward then
      {get_sn (...);
       send the sequence number as synch messages to all 'UP' nodes}
       V (mutex)
```

end "end cycle"
end; "end broadcaster"

"SYNCHRONISER ALGORITHM"
- - - local variables - - -
cycle
    receive_msg (prt, src, message);
    P (mutex);
    case message_type **of**
  goback: dir := backward;
  synch: {**if** dir = forward **then**
          {advance clock if necessary;
          if uplist (src) = DOWN **then**
            uplist (src) := UP}
      }
  set: {**if** dir = backward **then**
          {set_clock (message.time + 1 tick);
          dir := forward}
      }
    end "end case"
    V (mutex)
end; "cycle"

When a node comes 'up', the broadcaster of that node sends 'I am alive' messages to all the possible nodes in the system. The responses received from the send message operations are used for the construction of the 'uplist'. We have assumed that all the synchronisers have got the same port number, so a broadcaster's messages always go to synchronisers. Also, note that the synch message with time 0 will not affect local time at any node. A broadcaster only broadcasts its time if it is going forwards.

The synchroniser's task is to analyse the messages directed to it and act accordingly. The algorithm for the Time Lord is given below (the synchroniser at the Time Lord's node is identical to other synchronisers). The user at the Time Lord's node has to supply a GO BACK command which is caught by the Time Lord who then sends 'goback' messages to all the 'up' nodes. This has the net effect of stopping all the broadcasters. When the Time Lord gets the user supplied new time, it broadcasts it which has the net effect of initialising all the clocks. Note that no special action is needed for a node to set up its clock when it comes up − its synchroniser will get a clock value that will result in the update of the clock.

"TIME LORD ALGORITHM"
- - - "initialisation part, same as a BROADCASTER" - - -
cycle
  if GOBACK command from the user **then**
  { send ' goback' messages to all 'up' nodes, including own synchroniser;
    get a new clock value from the user;
    send 'set' messages to all the 'up' nodes, including own synchroniser
  } **else** {same as a BROADCASTER}
end;

Finally, all the servers must also discover the fact that clocks have been set back — so that they can adjust their llsn arrays (mentioned in Sect. 2.2); otherwise requests will continue to be rejected until such time as the 'new' time catches up. A simple means of performing this task is shown below — a slight modification to the get_work(...) procedure is needed. A 'reject' count is maintained and whenever this count exceeds a given value, (say 5), it is suspected that clocks have been put back, so the llsn array is initialised.

"modified get_work ( ) algorithm"

procedure get_work (...);
begin
   ———
  reject := 0;
  repeat
    src := any;
    receive_msg (port, src, msg);
    sn := seq. number in msg;
    if sn <= llsn (src) **then**
      reject := reject + 1;
  until sn > llsn (src) **or** reject = MAX;
  if reject = MAX **then**
  { sn := get_sn (...);
    for i := 1 **to** maxnode **do**
      llsn (i) := sn}
  else
    {llsn (src) := sn; reject := 0}
  ———
end;

A few remarks regarding the actual UNIX implementation are perhaps in order. In UNIX only files can be shared between unrelated processes; so the shared variables of our algorithms are kept in a file. This has not caused any performance problems since both the broadcaster and the synchroniser have very little active processing to perform. The maintenance of up lists and the facility of putting clocks back certainly add complications. Nevertheless the resulting algorithms are still fairly simple with very little message and computation overheads.

We conclude this section by pointing out two aspects of the clock management scheme: (i) let 'd' be the maximum clock drift, then the minimum crash recovery time of any crashed node must be greater than 'd' to guarantee that the SN's after a crash are greater than SN's before the crash; (ii) a crash of the Time Lord's node can not be tolerated when clocks are being put back. If crash recovery time is known, then the observation (i) indicates how much drift between clocks is tolerable, which in turn can be used to calculate how often clocks need be synchronised. Although we have not made a detailed study of clock drift, sending synchronising messages once every few minutes (say 2 min) results in only a small drift (2—3 sec per week) which appears acceptable.

4. Performance Measurements

This section presents some of the results obtained from initial tests carried out to assess the performance of the RPC mechanism. Our aim was to compare the data transfer rates as seen by the user for local and remote operations. The measurements were carried out between two PDP 11/45 computers and involved (for the distributed case) a program on one cpu to read 50 Kbytes of data from an already opened file on the other cpu. Various block sizes for the transfer were utilised: from 16 bytes to 512 bytes (one page). The standard 'time' facility of UNIX was used for obtaining the times which are accurate to a millisecond. The graph of Fig. 3 shows the results obtained, where 'local' figures refer to the results obtained when only one cpu was utilised.

From this graph it is seen that when the unit of transfer is a page of data, the inter machine transfer rate is about 40% slower than the local transfer rate. This degradation is tolerable since initial user experience indicates that most users have been unable to differentiate between a local file operation and a remote one. Some additional performance data are presented in table 1 (a block size of 512 bytes was used and the same file was used for the first test).

As a matter of interest, the data transfer rate obtained by utilising a high level virtual circuit based protocol (Byte Stream Protocol) was also measured: the result obtained − 1.46 KB/s as against 5.36 KB/s − confirms the opinion expressed in [3] that sophisticated protocols are often undesirable. The process to process data transfer rate (involving no disc accesses) for the distributed case appears to be rather small if one takes in account the fact that the Ring bandwidth is 1.25 Mbytes/sec! The reason for this is that the Ring itself transmits two bytes of data at a time and our Ring interfaces are interrupt driven. So transmission of a block of data involves considerable interrupt handling over-

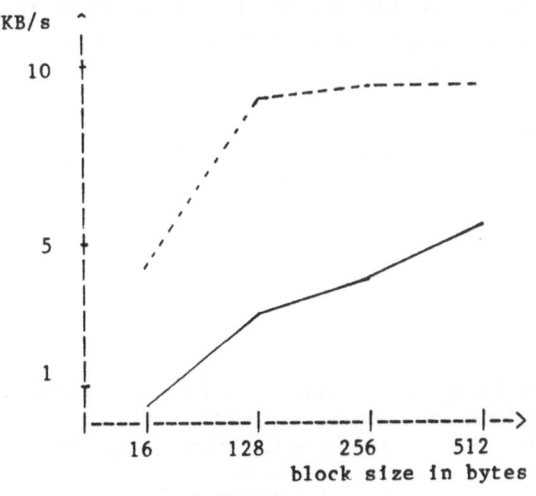

```
KB/s   ^
       |
 10    +
       |           ,-------------------
       |         ,-'
       |       ,'
       |      /
       |     /
       |    /
  5    +   /
       |  /
       | /              _____
       |/           ___/
       |         __/
  1    |      __/
       |     /
       T____/
       |----|---------|---------|---------|-->
         16    128       256       512
              block size in bytes
```

KB/s = Kilobytes/sec
---- = local read
———— = remote read

Fig. 3. Data transfer rate

Table 1. Additional performance data

Test	Local	Remote RPC	Remote BSP
Open; read; close	9.12 KB/s	5.36 KB/s	1.46 KB/s
Process to process (Unix pipe)	41 KB/s	7.4 KB/s	–
Open or close file	18 msec	60 msec	

heads (the maximum raw data transfer rate of the message passing system is about 8 Kbytes/sec). We are in the process of upgrading the interface hardware to provide the DMA (Direct Memory Access) access to cpu memory – this will considerably enhance the performance of the RPC mechanism.

The only part of the RPC mechanism that appears a bit complex is the clock management scheme needed to meet the reliability requirement R2 (see Sect. 1). However, as the clocks are only loosely synchronised (a node sends its time to the other 'up' nodes once every few minutes), processing overheads for keeping clocks approximately the same are not appreciable. Thus the cost of attaining reliability has been kept low.

5. Concluding Remarks

The RPC mechanism is operational and available to our colleagues for programming basic facilities of a distributed system (e.g. a file server at each node). As stated earlier, the RPC software does not prevent all the cases that can generate orphans. Our next task is to design a layer that supports the abstraction of atomic actions. This level will include the mechanisms for concurrency control, recovery and two phase commit [8] and as a result will deal effectively with any outstanding orphans.

Acknowledgements. This work was supported by the Science and Engineering Research Council (U.K.) and by the Royal Signals and Radar Establishment (U.K). The datagram facility was implemented by W. P. Sharpe of Science and Engineering Research Council. Acknowledgement is also due to our colleague L. F. Marshall whose knowledge of the UNIX system proved invaluable.

References

1. Wilkes M. V. and Wheeler D. J., "The Cambridge Communication Ring," Proc. of Local Area Network Symposium, Boston, National Bureau of Standards (May 1979).
2. Lampson B., "Remote Procedure Calls," in Lecture Notes in Computer Science Vol. 105, Springer Verlag, Berlin (1981).
3. Nelson B. J., "Remote Procedure Call," CMU-CS-81-119, Department of Computer Science, Carnegie-Mellon University (1981). Ph.D. dissertation
4. Shrivastava S. K. and Panzieri F., "The Design of a Reliable Remote Procedure Call Mechanism," IEEE Transactions on Computers (July 1982). (To appear). [Also Chap. 6]

5. Lamport L., "Time, Clocks and the Ordering of Events in a Distributed System," CACM Vol. 21(7), pp. 558–565 (July 1978).
6. Lampson B. and Sturgis H., "Atomic Transactions," pp. 246–265 in Lecture Notes in Computer Science, Vol. 105, Springer Verlag, Berlin (1981).
7. Shrivastava S. K., "Structuring Distributed Systems for Recoverability and Crash Resistance," IEEE Transactions on Software Engineering Vol. SE-7(4), pp. 436–447 (July 1981).
8. Gray J. N., "Notes on Data Base Operating Systems," pp. 393–481 in Lecture Notes in Computer Science, Vol. 60, Springer Verlag, Berlin (1978).

The Newcastle Connection or
UNIXes of the World Unite!

D. R. Brownbridge, L. F. Marshall and B. Randell

Summary. In this paper we describe a software subsystem that can be added to each of a set of physically interconnected UNIX or UNIX look-alike systems, so as to construct a distributed system which is functionally indistinguishable at both the user and the program level from a conventional single-processor UNIX system. The techniques used are applicable to a variety and multiplicity of both local and wide area networks, and enable all issues of inter-processor communication, network protocols, etc., to be hidden. A brief account is given of experience with such a distributed system, which is currently operational on a set of PDP11s connected by a Cambridge Ring. The final sections compare our scheme to various precursor schemes and discuss its potential relevance to other operating systems.

1. Introduction

The Newcastle Connection is the name that we could not resist giving to a software subsystem that we have added to a set of standard UNIX[1] systems in order to connect them together, initially using just a single Cambridge Ring. The resulting distributed system (which in fact can use a variety and multiplicity of both local and wide area networks) is functionally indistinguishable, at both 'shell' command language level and at system call level, from a conventional centralized UNIX system [1]. Thus all issues concerning network protocols and inter-processor communications are completely hidden. Instead, all the standard UNIX conventions, e.g. for protecting, naming and accessing files and devices, for inter-process communications, for input/output redirection, etc., are made applicable, without apparent change, to the distributed system as a whole.

This is done, without any modification to any existing source code, of either the UNIX operating system, or any user programs. The technique is therefore not specific to any particular implementation of UNIX, but instead is applicable to any UNIX look-alike system that claims, and achieves, compatibility with the original at the system call level.

In subsequent sections we discuss the structure of this distributed system, (which for the purposes of this paper we will term UNIX United), the internal design of the Newcastle Connection, the networking and inter-networking issues involved, some interesting extensions to the basic scheme, our operational experience with it to date, its relationship to prior work and its potential relevance to other operating systems.

---

1 UNIX is a trademark of Bell Laboratories

2. UNIX United

A UNIX United system is composed out of a (possibly large) set of inter-linked standard UNIX systems, each with its own storage and peripheral devices, accredited set of users, system administrator, etc. The naming structures (for files, devices, commands and directories) of each component UNIX system are joined together in UNIX United into a single naming structure, in which each UNIX system is to all intents and purposes just a directory. Ignoring for the moment questions of accreditation and access control, the result is that each user, on each UNIX system, can read or write any file, use any device, execute any command, or inspect any directory, regardless of which system it belongs to. The simplest possible case of such a structure, incorporating just two UNIX systems, is shown in Fig. 1.

With the root directory (/) as shown, one could copy the file *a* into the corresponding directory on the other machine with the shell command

　cp   /user/brian/a /../unix 2/user/brian/a

(For those unfamiliar with UNIX, the initial '/' symbol indicates that a path name starts at the root directory, and the '..' symbol is used to indicate the parent directory.)

Making use of the current working directory ('.') as shown, this command could be abbreviated to

　cp   a /../unix2/user/brian/a

If the user has set up the shell variable *U2* as follows

　U2 = /../unix2/user/brian

it could be called forth, using the $ convention, so as to permit the further abbreviation

　cp   a $U2/a

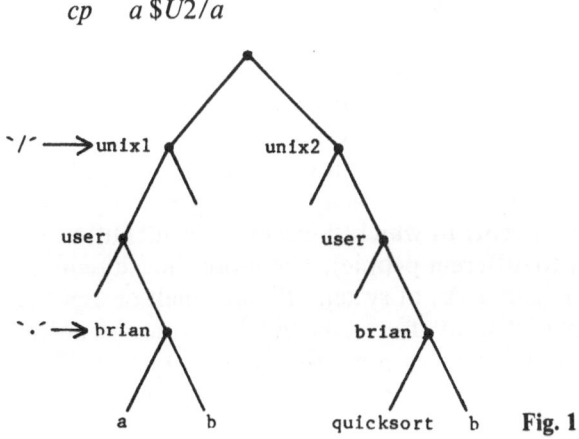

Fig. 1

All the above commands are in fact conventional uses of the standard 'shell' command interpreter, and would have exactly the same effect if the naming structure shown had been set up on a single machine, with *unix*1 and *unix*2 actually being conventional directories.

All the various standard UNIX facilities (whether invoked via shell commands, or by system calls within user programs) concerned with the naming structure carry over unchanged in form and meaning to UNIX United, causing inter-machine communication to take place as necessary. It is therefore possible, for example, for a user to specify a directory on a remote machine as being his current working directory, to request execution of a program held in a file on a remote machine, to redirect input and/or output, to use files and peripheral devices on a remote machine, etc. Thus, using the same naming structure as before, the further commands

cd /../unix2/user/brian
quicksort a > /../unix1/user/brian/b

have the effect of applying the quicksort program on *unix*2 to the file *a* which had been copied across to it, and of sending the resulting sorted file back to file *b* on *unix*1. (The command line

/../unix2/user/brian/quicksort/../unix2/user/brian/a > b

would have had the same effect, without changing the current working directory.)

It is worth reiterating that these facilities are completely standard UNIX facilities, and so can be used without conscious concern for the fact that several machines are involved, or any knowledge of what data flows when or between which machines, and of which processor actually executes any particular programs. (In fact, in our existing implementation, programs are executed by the processor in whose file store the program is held, and data is transferred between machines in response to normal UNIX read and write commands.)

2.1. User Accreditation and Access Control

UNIX United allows each constituent UNIX system to have its own named set of users, user groups and user password file, its own system administrator (super-user), etc. Each constituent system has the responsibility for authenticating (by user identifier and password) any user who attempts to log into that system.

It is possible to unite UNIX systems in which the same user identifier has already been allocated (possibly to different people). Therefore when a request, say for file access, is made from system 'A', of system 'B', on behalf of user 'u', the request arrives at 'B' as being from, in effect user 'A/u' — a user identifier which would not be confused with a local user identifier 'u'. It will be, in effect, this user identifier 'A/u' which governs the uses by 'u' of files, commands, etc., on machine 'B'.

534

Just as the system administrator for each machine has responsibility for allocating ordinary user identifiers, so he also has responsibility for maintaining a table of recognized remote user identifiers, such as 'A/u'. If the system administrator so wishes, rather than refuse all access, he can allow default authentication for unrecognized remote users, who might for example be given 'guest' status – i.e. treated as if they had logged in as 'guest', presumably a user with very limited access privileges.

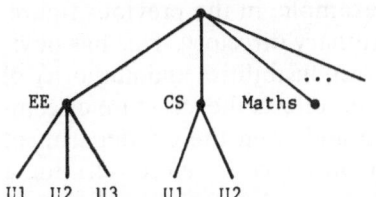

EE   CS   Maths

U1 U2 U3   U1   U2   **Fig. 2**

From an individual user's point of view therefore, though he might have needed to negotiate not just with one but with several system administrators for usage rights beforehand, access to the whole UNIX United system is via a single conventional log in. Subject to the rights given to him by the various system administrators, he will then be governed by, and able to make normal use of, the standard UNIX file protection control mechanisms in his accessing of the entire distributed file system. In particular there is no need for him to log in, or provide passwords, to any of the remote systems that his commands or programs happen to use. This approach therefore preserves the appearance of a totally unified system, without abrogating the rights and responsibilities of individual system administrators.

2.2. The Structure Tree

The naming structure of the UNIX United system represents the way in which the component UNIX system are inter-related, as regards naming issues. When a large number of systems are united, it will often be convenient to set up the overall naming tree so as to reflect relevant aspects of the environment in which the UNIX systems exist. For example, a UNIX United system set up within a university might have a naming structure which matches the departmental structure. With the naming structure as shown in Fig. 2, files in the system U1 in the Computing Science Department could be named using the prefix /../../CS/U1 from within the Electrical Engineering Department's UNIX systems.

Such a naming structure has to be one that can be agreed to by all the system administrators, and which does not require frequent major modification – such modification of the UNIX United naming structure can be as disruptive as a major modification of the structure inside a single UNIX system would be, owing to the fact that stored path names (e.g. incorporated in files and programs) could be invalidated.

The naming structure could, but does not necessarily, reflect the topology of the underlying communications network. It certainly is not intended to be changed in response to temporary breaks in communication paths, or of service from particular UNIX systems. (An analogy is to the international telephone directory – the U.K. country code (44) continues to exist whether or not the transatlantic telephone service is operational.) This issue is pursued further in Sect. 4 below.

One final point: UNIX systems can appear in the naming structure in positions subservient to other UNIX systems. For example, in the previous figure, CS might denote a UNIX system, not just an ordinary directory. This has obvious implications with respect to the respective responsibilities and authority of the various system administrators. If the structure reflects the structure of communication paths, it indicates that all traffic to and from the CS department flows via this particular UNIX system, which is in effect therefore fulfilling a gateway role.

3. The Newcastle Connection

The UNIX United scheme whose external characteristics were described above is provided by means of communication links, and the incorporation of an additional layer of software – the Newcastle Connection – in each of the component UNIX systems. This layer of software sits on top of the resident UNIX kernel, i.e. between the UNIX kernel and the rest of the operating system (e.g. shell and the various command programs) and the user programs. From above, the layer is functionally indistinguishable from the kernel. From below, it appears to be a normal user process. Its role is to filter out system calls that have to be re-directed to another UNIX system, and to accept system calls that have been directed to it from other systems. Communication between the Connection layers on the various systems is based on the use of a remote procedure call (RPC) protocol, [2] and is shown schematically in Fig. 3.

In fact a slightly more detailed picture of the structure of the system would of course reveal that communications actually occur at hardware level, and that the kernel includes means for handling low level communications protocols.

The Connection layer has to disguise from the processes above it the fact that some of their system calls are handled remotely (e.g. those concerned with accessing remote files). It similarly has to disguise from the kernel below it that

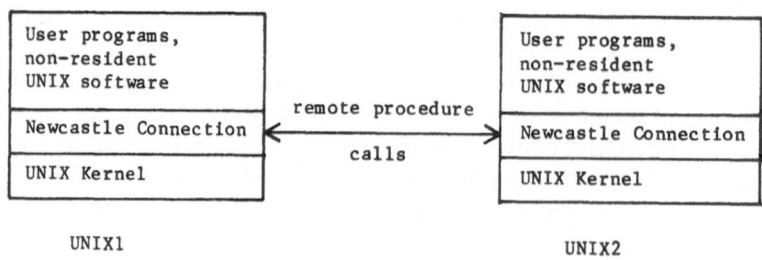

UNIX1   UNIX2   Fig. 3

536

the requests for the kernel's services, and the responses it provides, can be coming from and going to, remote processes. This has to be done without in any way changing the means by which system calls (apparently direct to the UNIX kernel) identify any real or abstract objects that are involved.

The kernel in fact uses various different means of identification for the various different types of object. For example, open files (and devices) are identified by an integer (usually in the range 0 to 19), logged on users by what is effectively an index into the password file, etc. Such name spaces are of course inherently local. The Connection layer therefore has to accept such an apparently local name and use mapping tables to determine whether the object really is local, or instead belongs to some other system (where it may well be known by some quite different local name). The various mapping tables will have been set up previously — for example when a file is opened — and for non-local objects will indicate how to communicate with the machine on which the object is located. The selection of actual communication paths, the management of alternative routing strategies, etc., are thus all performed by the Connection layer, and completely hidden from the user and his programs.

Such mapping does not however apply to the single most visible name space used by UNIX, i.e. the naming structure used at shell level, and at the program level in the *open* and *exec* system calls, for identifying files and commands, respectively. Rather, the Connection layer can be viewed as performing the role of glueing together the parts of this naming structure that are stored on different UNIX machines, to form what appears to be a single structure. A given UNIX system will itself store only a part of the overall structure. Taking the example given above in Fig. 1, *unix*1 will store all of the overall structure except those elements that are below *unix*2, and vice versa. Thus, copies of some parts of the structure will be held on several systems, and must of course remain consistent — a problem which would become severe if changes to these parts of the structure were a frequent occurrence.

It is essential for the mapping layer to be able to distinguish local and remote file accesses. The Newcastle Connection layer intercepts all system calls that use files and determines whether the access is local or remote. Local calls are passed unaltered to the underlying local kernel for service; remote calls are packaged with some extra information, such as the current user-id, and passed to a remote machine for service. The Connection uses its own local fragment of the UNIX United naming tree to resolve file names. Names are interpreted as a route through the tree, each element specifying the next branch to be taken. If the name can be fully interpreted locally, only a local access in involved. If a leaf corresponding to a remote system is reached, then execution must be continued remotely by making a remote procedure call to the appropriate system. Such leaves are specially marked with the address of the appropriate remote station. This address is given to the RPC as routing information. In some cases (examined in more detail in the next section) a request may be passed on through a number of Connections before being satisfied.

As well as accessing files using a name, a UNIX program can *open* a file and access it using the file descriptor returned from the *open* system call. When a file is opened the Connection makes an entry in a per-process table indicating

537

whether or not the file descriptor refers to a local or a remote file. The table also holds remote station addresses for remote file descriptors. Subsequent accesses using the descriptor refer to this table using the information there to route remote accesses without further delay.

The actual remote file access is carried out for the user by a file server process that runs in the remote machine. Each user has their own file server, and the initial allocation of these is carried out by a 'spawner' process that runs continuously. This latter process is callable (using a standard name) by any external user and, upon request, will spawn a file server (after carrying out some user/group mapping), returning its external name to the user that initiated the request. The user then communicates directly with this file server, which is capable of carrying out the full range of UNIX file operations. The user/group mapping is carried out to ensure that the access rights of the file server are in accord with those allowed to the external user by the local system manager, and consists of converting external names into valid local names. Nevertheless, a file server is still an extension of the environment of a user on a remote machine, and any relevant changes in the environment seen by a user must be mirrored by it. The most important of these is that when a user process 'forks' (that is, creates a duplicate of itself), all the remote file servers that it is connected with must also fork. This greatly simplifies the implementation of remote execution and signalling, as each user process only ever has to deal with a single remote file server.

Communication with the 'spawner' and the file servers always takes the form of a remote procedure call, the first parameter of all calls being a sequence number. This is used by the servers to detect retry attempts − if the received sequence number is the same as that of the last call, then it is a retry (the RPC scheme precludes calls being lost, so there is no need to check for continuity in the sequence).

4. Networking and Inter-Networking Issues

The various kernels provide mappings between the user-visible name spaces and the hardware name spaces − in particular between the names of what appear to be directories, and the hardware names of distant UNIX systems. It is important that this latter mapping be such that:

(i) The file naming hierarchy need bear no relationship to the inter-system communications topology

(ii) Modifications to the communications topology should be easy, as well as having no effect on the way in which any user or user program accesses anything.

File naming does, however, have some implications concerning protection and authentication − thus when a path is specified in an *open* command, checks are made against the permissions associated with each directory or file entry named explicitly or implicitly in the path, an activity that can require access to one or more distant UNIX systems. However it may not be necessary to repeat the same inter-system route when a file has been successfully opened, if some shorter route is available. For example, opening the file identified by the path

$/../Unix1/a/Unix1.3/b$

would involve accessing both *Unix*1 and *Unix*1.3, though subsequent reads and writes might not involve accessing Unix1, depending on the underlying communications topology.

Our approach to providing these facilities takes advantage of the fact that the UNIX and hence the UNIX United file (and device, etc.) naming hierarchy constitutes a set of stable system-wide distinct identifiers. Only one such set is needed, so given that we already have this set available at user level, we are not using the Xerox Ethernet approach, which we understand requires the different stations on a set of interconnected Ethernets to have built-in uniquely assigned identification numbers. Rather, when a UNIX system is introduced into, or physically moved within, a UNIX United system, it will have to be identified to the system using an identifier such as

UK/NEWCASTLE/DAYSH/REL/U5

This identification will remain valid no matter the geographical location of the machine.

Our approach also involves arranging that hardware names related to one machine do not permeate to other machines in the system. At the hardware level, each machine identifies the machines it is directly connected to simply by identifying the means of connection, i.e. by I/O device number, and has no means of identifying any other machines. The I/O device numbers remain private to each machine, though presumably all machines on a given network will use the same ring port or modem numbers for a given machine.

In Fig. 4, the kernel on machine *U*1 will make use of hardware addresses for accessing *P*1 (identifying the hardwired connection to be used) and *U*2, *U*3, *U*4, *U*5 and *CRS* (identifying the ring and the port number to be used). It will not have knowledge of any hardware addresses relevant to *P*2 or *N*. Similarly, if it is *U*2 that gets connected to a wide area network, say, then only this machine, of the ones shown, will contain any wide area network telephone numbers for other UNIX systems. (Questions of routing through the wide area network will of course not concern the kernel, which only has to deal with routing between UNIX systems, not network nodes.)

Each kernel therefore routes accesses to distant machines to an appropriate one of its adjacent neighbouring machines, which can then pass the request on further, through another wide or local area network, or a direct hard-wired connection, if necessary. (The routing information used is that held in the various special files which of course are accessed by means of the paths or the file descriptors specified by users and user programs.)

Means must be provided for modifying this routing information appropriately when a system is unplugged from one place in the overall network, and replugged into another — or indeed when any changes are made to the com-

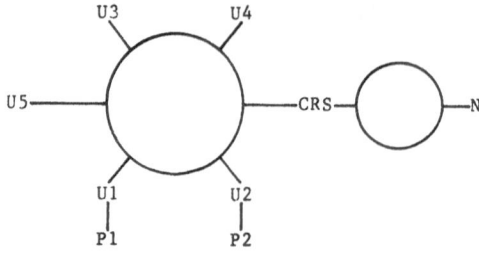

(a) Physical Structure

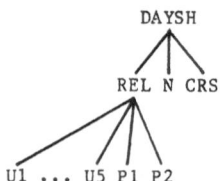

(b) Naming Structure   **Fig. 4**

munications topology visible at the Newcastle Connection level. (Changes within any of the networks are of no concern, rather the Newcastle Connection has to deal just with changes concerning hardwired machine links and inter-networking.)

We choose to separate the question of updating topological information from that of performance-oriented dynamic routing, and plan to ignore the latter issue (which in any case seems more suitable for networking than inter-networking). In fact some dynamic routing schemes do, almost as a by-product, cope with topological changes, but typically respond rather slowly to such changes [3]. A scheme such as that described by Chu [4], which arranges the immediate broadcasting of updates to routing tables when a topological change is notified (or perhaps discovered) seems much more appropriate to our needs, and is to be investigated. (Such a distributed approach can be contrasted, for example, with Cambridge's scheme of using a special machine on a ring as a name server, which has to be interrogated whenever an actual ring port number is needed, but thereby simplifies the table updating required when moving a machine from one port to another.)

As a message is passed from one machine to the next, the addressing information it contains (which will be described in terms of paths) will sometimes have to be adjusted, to allow for the fact that movement around the physical structure causes movement around the naming structure. Thus in Fig. 4, a message emanating from *P1*, intended for *P2*, will not have its addressing information changed as it travels through *U1* and *U2*, since from both systems, as from *P1*, *P2* would in effect be identified by the path /. ./*P2*. In contrast a message from *U4* to *N* would have its addressing information in effect changed from

540

$/../../N$ to$/../N$ as it passed through *CRS*. If system *N* had been made sub-servient to directory *REL* instead of *DAYSH* then *U4*, having a common parent directory with *N*, would in effect use the path $/../N$ to send a message to it. En route through *CRS*, this message would need this path to be changed to $/../$ *REL*$/N$, because *CRS* though physically closer to *N* is in fact more distant from it in naming terms. (In practice, file descriptors rather than paths would be used as addressing information − though the principle of changing the addressing information en route still applies.)

5. Extensions to the Basic UNIX United Scheme

We have found that the conceptual simplifications to the task of implementing a UNIX-based distributed computing system that the Newcastle Connection approach has provided have spurred us to produce a variety of extensions of, or variations on, the basic theme, some of which we have already started to implement.

The Connection layer can be regarded as isolating and solving the problems associated just with distribution − and, in turns out, is applicable to the case of distributed systems made from components other than complete UNIX systems. For example, one could connect together some systems which have little or no file storage with other systems that have a great deal − i.e. construct a UNIX United system out of workstations and file servers. Almost all that is necessary is to set up the naming tree properly.

Moreover since the Connection layer is independent of the internals of the UNIX kernel, it is not even necessary for the Connection layer to have a complete kernel underneath it − all that is needed is a kernel that can respond properly (even if only with exception messages) to the various sorts of system call that will penetrate down through, or are needed to support, the Connection layer. In fact the Connection layer itself can be economized on, if for example it is mounted on a workstation that serves as little more than a screen editor, say, and so has only a very limited variety of interactions with the rest of the UNIX United system. All that is necessary is adherence to the general format of the inter-machine system call protocol used by the Newcastle Connection, even if most types of call are responded to only by exception reports.

Thus the syntax and semantics of this protocol assume a considerable significance, since it can be used as the unifying factor in a very general yet extremely simple scheme for putting together sophisticated distributed systems out of a variety of size and type of component − an analogy we like to make is that the protocol operates like the scheme of standard-size dimples that allow a variety of shapes of LEGO children's building blocks to be connected together into a coherent whole.

In addition to the problem of distribution, we also have taken what are, we believe, several other equally separable problems, in particular those of (i) providing error recovery (for example in response to input errors or unmaskable hardware faults), (ii) using redundant hardware provided in the hope of masking hardware faults, (iii) the enforcement of multi-level security policies and

(iv) load balancing between the component systems, and plan to embody their solutions in other separate layers of software. Indeed, two significant extensions of UNIX United are already operational, albeit in prototype form. The first of these provides multi-level security, using encryption to enforce security barriers and to control permissible security reclassifications. The second uses file and process replication and majority voting to mask hardware faults – application programs are unchanged, though in fact running in synchronization on several machines with hidden voting. Further details of these and other extensions of the UNIX United scheme are the subject of separate papers.

6. Operational Experience

At the time of writing (July 1982) the basic UNIX United system is in regular use at Newcastle on a set of three PDP11/23s and two PDP11/45s, connected by a Cambridge Ring. The most heavily used facilities have been those concerned with file transfer and I/O redirection, for example in order to make use of the line printer and magnetic tape unit that are attached to one machine. The system is now also relied on for network mail, and for solving the problems of overnight file-dumping (of all machines, onto the one tape unit) and of software maintenance and distribution. As mentioned earlier, two prototype extensions of the system, concerned with security and hardware fault tolerance, respectively, are already operational, and work is under way on facilities for replicated files and on a distributed version of MASCOT [5].

A pre-release version of the Newcastle Connection has been provided to the University of Kent, where work has started on the (it is believed comparatively simple) modifications needed in order to use it to unite several VAX computers, running Berkeley UNIX, also over a Cambridge Ring. The incorporation of X25 network links, and the actual implementation of the mechanisms we have designed for inter-networking, have been delayed by problems beyond our control concerned with the provision of network connections, which it is hoped will be resolved soon.

A first analysis of the performance of the remote procedure call protocol [6] used by the Connection layer indicates that, subjectively, terminal users of the Newcastle system in general notice little performance difference between local and remote accesses and execution. This is despite the fact that the Cambridge Ring stations used are quite slow, being interrupt-driven devices, and perhaps indicates that such stations are reasonably well matched to the rather modest performance that UNIX itself can achieve on a small PDP11/23 used as a personal workstation, or on a PDP11/45 that is usually being used by a number of demanding terminal jobs. However a further and more extensive programme of performance monitoring and evaluation is planned, which would also include experiments with the DMA ring stations that we have recently obtained and, it is hoped, with more powerful computers than our current set of PDP11s.

The modest size of the Newcastle Connection reflects the need we had to make the system work on our small PDP11/23s, which provided a strong incentive to find simple well-structured solutions to the various implementation

542

problems. (In our view an overabundance of program storage space can have almost as bad an effect on the quality of a software system as does inadequate space – it is surely no coincidence that UNIX was first designed for quite modestly sized machines.) A program that made use of every facility provided by the Newcastle Connection would be increased in size by slightly more than 7K; however, it is very unlikely that this would ever be the case and a more usual figure would be an increase of 4 · 5K, the absolute minimum being 3K (including the code for the RPC interface).

7. Related Earlier Work

The Newcastle Connection, and the UNIX United scheme that it makes possible, have many precursors, and not just within the UNIX world.

The idea of providing a layer of software which aims to shield users of a set of interconnected computers from the need to concern themselves with networking protocols, or even the fact of there being several computers involved, is well-established. It is for example, what the IBM CICS System [7] does for users of various transaction processing programs, and what the National Software Works project [8] aimed to do for the users of various software development tools, running on a variety of different operating systems. Such layers of software are intended for somewhat specialized use, and run on top of specific sets of application programs. At the other end of the spectrum, such location- or network-transparency is also one of the aims of the Accent kernel, [9] on which operating systems can be constructed which use its 'port' concept as a means of unifying inter-process communication, inter-computer message passing, and operating system calls.

The dawning realization that the 'shell' job control language and the program-level facilities (i.e. system calls) of the UNIX multiprogramming system could suffice, and indeed would be highly appropriate, to control a distributed computing system can be traced in a whole series of distributed UNIX projects. The global file naming technique used in the early 'uucp' facilities [10] for interconnecting UNIX systems via standard telephone circuits can be seen as a special, but rather *ad hoc*, extension of the individual file system naming hierarchies, and had been copied by us in our Distributed Recoverable File System. [11] (The technique provides what is in effect a set of named hierarchies, rather than a single enlarged hierarchy.)

Rather better integrated with the standard UNIX file naming hierarchy are the facilities provided in the Network UNIX System. [12] This modification of standard UNIX provides a series of Arpanet protocols, which are invoked by means of some additional system commands, using what appear to be ordinary file names as the means of identifying which Arpanet host is to be communicated with. (The paper describing this system also speculates on the possibility of redesigning the shell interpreter so as to provide network transparency for commands and files at the shell command language level.) The Purdue Engineering Computer Network [13] is conceptually similar to the Network UNIX System, though based on hard-wired high speed duplex connections. It provides additional commands which invoke the services of special protocols for virtual terminal access and remote execution at the shell level, and also a means of load balancing through a scheduling program which takes responsibility for deciding which processor should execute certain selected commands.

The distributed system of interconnected S-UNIX personal workstations and F-UNIX file servers [14] goes further by providing each workstation user with an ordinary UNIX interface, without any additional non-standard commands, yet incorporating a distributed version of the UNIX hierarchial file store containing just his own local files plus all the files held on the file servers. This system is one of several built at Bell Labs using the Datakit virtual circuit switch — others are RIDE [15] and D/UNIX. [16] The RIDE system provides complete remote file access and remote program execution, but is based on a 'uucp'-like, rather than standard, UNIX naming hierarchy — it is however implemented merely by adding a software layer on top of the UNIX kernel, an approach which is highly similar to that we have since used with our Newcastle Connection technique. D/UNIX is a distributed system based on modified versions of UNIX which provide virtual circuits between processes, and a transparent file sharing scheme covering all the files on all the component systems.

A fully symmetrical means of linking computer systems together so as to give the appearance of a single UNIX-like hierarchical file store, and the standard shell command language, is also provided by the LOCUS system — the paper [17] describing this system also discusses its intended extension to provide remote program execution as well as remote file access. However, for all its external similarity to UNIX, the LOCUS system involves a completely redesigned operating system rather than a modification of an existing UNIX system, albeit an operating system which is also designed to have extensive fault tolerance facilities.

The penultimate stage in the evolution can be seen in the COCANET local network operating system, [18] a system which has been built using the standard UNIX system, and which comes very close indeed to our aim of combining a set of standard UNIX systems into a single unified system, and which certainly supports network-transparent remote execution as well as file access. However the COCANET designers have allowed themselves to make a number of changes to the UNIX kernel and would appear, from the description they give, not to have coped fully with user-id mapping. It would also appear that COCANET is designed specifically around the idea of having a relatively small number of machines linked by a single high-speed ring, and hence has a rather restrictive structure tree, which is viewed slightly differently from each machine. However many of the mechanisms incorporated in UNIX United are very similar to those used in COCANET.

It is thus but a comparatively small step from COCANET to UNIX United, and to the idea of the Connection layer resting on top of an unchanged UNIX kernel, replicating all its facilities exactly in a network-transparent fashion, and capable of making a distributed system involving large numbers of computers, connected by a variety of local and wide area networks. Incidentally, one can draw an interesting parallel between the Connection layer and what is sometimes called a 'hypervisor', the best-known example of which is VM/370 [19].

Each is a self-contained layer of software, which makes no changes to the functional appearance of the system beneath it (the IBM/370 architecture in the case of VM/370, which fits under rather than on top of the operating system kernel). However, whereas a hypervisor's function is to make a single system act as a set of separate systems, the Newcastle Connection (a 'hypovisor'?) makes a set of separate (though of course linked) systems act like a single system!

However, to our embarrassment, we have to admit that the idea of the Connection layer, of the basic UNIX United scheme, and of most of the extensions of the scheme, did not arise from careful study and analysis of these precursors. (Indeed it is clear that what was presented above as a more-or-less orderly evolutionary development path often involved parallel activity by several groups, and much accidental reinvention.) In fact we were not consciously aware of any of these systems (other than 'uucp' and of course DRFS) while the work that led to the Newcastle Connection was in progress. Indeed, by the time we learnt of LOCUS and COCANET, all the basic ideas and strategies to be incorporated in the Newcastle Connection had been worked out, though not all in full detail, and much of the system was already operational and in daily use. Rather we can trace the origins of our scheme to the existence of the plans for our remote procedure call protocol, and the idea, which we now know has occurred to many groups independently, of extending the UNIX 'mount' facility from that of mounting replaceable disk packs to that of mounting one UNIX system on another.

This idea arose at Newcastle in early December 1981 — within a week or so much of the UNIX United concept had been thought up and even roughly documented. A hesitant start at what was initially intended as just an experimental and partial implementation was made after Christmas, but within a month facilities related to accessing and operating on files remotely over the Cambridge Ring were in active use. Work proceeded rapidly, both on extending the range of UNIX kernel features that the Newcastle Connection mapped correctly, and on discovering, mainly via experimentation, some of the more arcane features of the kernel interface as implemented and used in V7 UNIX. At about this stage we found out about first the S-UNIX/F-UNIX and LOCUS systems, and shortly afterwards the COCANET and then the RIDE systems. These various papers were a considerable encouragement to us to continue our efforts, and also provided us with a useful perspective on our approach. In particular they strengthened our growing belief in the viability of an alternative. UNIX-based, approach to distributed computing to that based on the use of a variety of explicit servers, each with its own specialized service protocol. [20, 21]

Returning to the layered ('level of abstraction') aspect of UNIX United and its various extensions, this of course can be seen as being directly in the tradition pioneered by Dijkstra's seminal THE operating system [22] — a system which it now seems to be as unfashionable to reference as it was once fashionable. However, if only through our extensive work on multi-level structuring for purposes of fault tolerance, [23] we remain convinced that this approach to designing (and describing) systems is of great merit. It leads to designs which work well and which seem to us to be much easier to comprehend, and therefore have faith in, than those where little explicit thought has apparently been given to achieving any sort of separation of logical concerns, such as those of naming, communications routing, load balancing, recoverability, etc.

8. Why Just UNIX?

It is interesting to analyse just what it is about UNIX, and the linguistic interfaces it provides at shell and system call level, that make it so suitable for use as the model and basis for a network operating system. There seem to be six principle factors involved.

First, there is the hierarchical file (and device and command) naming system. This makes it easy to combine systems, because the various hierarchical name spaces just become component name spaces in a larger hierarchy, without any problems due to name clashes. The standard UNIX mechanisms for file protection and controlled sharing of files then carry over directly, once the problem of possible clashes of user identifiers is handled properly.

Second, there are the UNIX facilities for dynamically selecting the current working directory and root directory. In particular the ability to select the root directory — normally thought of as one of the more exotic and little needed of the UNIX system commands — seems to have been designed especially for UNIX United, since it provides a perfect way of hiding the extra levels of the directory tree that have to be introduced.

Third, and obviously vital, is the fact that UNIX allows its users, and their programs, to initiate asynchronous processes. This is used inside the Newcastle Connection, and also provides the means whereby even a single user can make use via the Newcastle Connection of several or indeed all of the computers that are involved in the UNIX United system. It also provides the means whereby slow file transfers (via low bandwidth wide area networks) can be relegated to background processing, and so still be organized using remote procedure calls.

Fourth, there is the fact that the UNIX system call interface is (relatively) clean and simple, and can easily be regarded as providing a small number of reasonably well defined abstract types. The task of virtualizing these types, so as to give network transparency, therefore remains manageable.

Fifth, there is the fact, even in this day and age still regrettably worthy of mention, that the original UNIX system, and all of its derivatives known to us, are written in a reasonably satisfactory high level language. Our method of incorporating the Newcastle Connection layer therefore merely involved recompiling relevant parts of the system, using a different subroutine library.

Finally, there is the well-established set of exception reporting conventions that are used in UNIX, for example, to indicate the reasons why particular system call requests cannot be honoured. When such a call has, via the Newcastle Connection, involved attempted communication with another UNIX system there are various other (quite likely) reasons, but they can be mapped onto the exceptions that the caller is already supposed to be able to deal with.

546

However it is unlikely that the idea could not be carried across to at least some other systems. Indeed a report by Goldstein et al. [24] implies that something similar is being bravely contemplated for IBM's MVS operating system, and some aspects of the idea are we understand commercially available as additions to the RSX/11 operating system – no doubt other examples exist. The one other system whose suitability for the Newcastle Connection approach has been considered at all seriously by us is DEC's VAX/VMS system. It would appear that it has many of the necessary characteristics though there could be problems with the way that devices are involved with its system of file naming.

This section would not be complete without any mention of what we regard as some shortcomings of the UNIX V7 specifications (at system call level): Firstly, the system of *signals* for asynchronous communication between processes could be improved. Allied to this, a general synchronous inter-process communication mechanism would be useful, allowing communication between numbers of unrelated processes. Some awkward features in the file protection scheme were encountered when constructing the file server. These were associated with the notions of *super-user* and *effective user-id*. Lastly, we found that the ability to have many directory entries (links), each naming the same physical file, was elegant in concept but severely limited in generality by the actual UNIX V7 implementation.

With respect to the programs that are provided with the UNIX system, very few difficulties were encountered in connecting them, except, that is, for the Shell. This program makes use of system facilities in non-standard ways, and its internal design is obscure to say the least. However, it has proved to be an excellent testbed for the system – if the Shell works you can be pretty sure that most other programs will!

9. Conclusions

The first of our internal memoranda on what we later came to call the Newcastle Connection described the idea as 'so simple and obvious that it surely cannot be novel'. And, as described above, it did turn out to have a number of precursors – in fact probably many more than we yet realize. However we take this as confirmation of the merits of the twin ideas of network transparency and of its provision by a single separate mapping layer, an approach whose ramifications we feel we have barely begun to explore. Certainly our present plan is to continue our programme of experimental implementations and applications, and to determine how well the Newcastle Connection (and UNIX) can withstand the weight of additional software layers containing the various reliability and security-related mechanisms that we have developed, hitherto in a rather fragmented fashion for various systems and languages.

One other point is worth stressing. It has for some years been well accepted that the structure and mechanisms of a multiprocessing operating system are very similar to those of a (good) multiprogramming system. What has now become clear to us, as a result of our work on UNIX United, is that this similarity can usefully extend also to distributed systems. The additional problems and opportunities that face the designer of a homogeneous distributed system should not be allowed to obscure the continued relevance of much established practice regarding the design of multiprogramming systems.

Acknowledgements. Many of our colleagues at Newcastle have had a part in the often apparently furious, yet always enjoyable, discussions out of which the Newcastle Connection scheme, and its internal design, evolved. Two colleagues in particular, Fabio Panzieri and Santosh Shrivastava, also deserve acknowledgements as designers and implementors of the Remote Procedure Call protocol on which we have relied so heavily. The X25 protocol software that we are planning to use was provided by Keith Ruttle of the University of York, who is being most co-operative with our efforts at burying his software in a way that he could hardly have foreseen or intended.

A special acknowledgement is obviously due to the creators of that famous Registered Footnote of Bell Laboratories, UNIX, much of whose external characteristics, if not detailed internal design, deserve the highest praise. Last but not least, we are pleased to acknowledge that our work has been supported by research contracts from the U.K. Science and Engineering Research Council, and the Royal Radar and Signals Establishment.

References

1. D. M. Ritchie and K. Thompson, "The UNIX time-sharing system', Comm. ACM, 17 (7), 365–375 (1974).
2. S. K. Shrivastava and F. Panzieri, "The design of a reliable remote procedure call mechanism', IEEE Trans. Computers, C-31, (7), 692–697 (1982). [Also Chap. 6]
3. A. S. Tanenbaum, Computer Networks, Prentice-Hall, Englewood Cliffs, N. J. (1981).
4. K. Chu, 'A distributed protocol for updating network topology information', Report RC 7235, IBM T. J. Watson Research Center, Yorktown Heights, New York (27 July 1978).
5. The Official Handbook of MASCOT, MASCOT Suppliers Association (5 December 1980).
6. F. Panzieri and S. K. Shrivastava, 'Reliable remote calls for distributed UNIX: an implementation study', Report 177, Computing Laboratory, University of Newcastle upon Tyne (June 1982). [Also Chap. 6]
7. J. Gray, 'IBM's customer information control system (CICS)', Operating System Review, 15 (3), 11–12, (1981).
8. R. E. Millstein, "The national software works: a distributed processing system', Proc. ACM 1977 Annual Conference, Seattle, Washington, 44–52 (1977).
9. R. Rashid, 'Accent: a communication oriented network operating system kernel', Operating Systems Review, 15 (5), 64–75 (1981).
10. D. A. Nowitz, 'Uucp implementation description', Sect. 37 in UNIX Programmer's Manual, Seventh Edition, Vol. 2 (January 1979).
11. M. Jegado, 'Recoverability aspects of a distributed file system', Technical Report, Computing Laboratory, University of Newcastle upon Tyne (February 1981). [Also Chap. 6]
12. G. L. Chesson, "The network UNIX system', Operating Systems Review, 9 (5), 60–66 (1975). Also in Proc. 5th Symp. on Operating Systems Principles.
13. K. Hwang, W. J. Croft, G. H. Goble, B. W. Wah, F. A. Briggs, W. R. Simmons and C. L. Coates, 'A UNIX-based local computer network with load balancing', Computer, 15, (4), 55–66 (1982).
14. G. W. R. Luderer, H. Che, J. P. Haggerty, P. A. Kirslis and W. T. Marshall, 'A distributed Unix system based on a virtual circuit switch', Operating Systems Review, 15, (5), 160–168 (1981). (Proc. ACM 8th Conf. Operating System Principles, Asilomar, Calif.).
15. P. M. Lu, 'A system for resource sharing in a distributed environment – RIDE', Proc. IEEE Computer Society 3rd COMPSAC, IEEE, New York, 1979.
16. J. C. Kaufeld and D. L. Russell, 'Distributed UNIX system', in Workshop on Fundamental Issues in Distributed Computing. ACM SIGOPS and SIGPLAN (15–17 December 1980).

17. G. Popek, B. Walker, J. Chow, D. Edwards, C. Kline, G. Rudisin and G. Thiel, 'LOCUS; a network transparent, high reliability distributed system', Operating Systems Review, 15 (5), 169–177 (1981) (Proc. ACM 8th Conf. Operating System Principles, Asilomar, Calif.).
18. L. A. Rowe and K. P. Birman, 'A local network based on the UNIX operating system', IEEE Trans. Software Eng., SE-8 (2), 137–146 (1982).
19. L. H. Seawright et al., 'Papers on virtual machine facility/370', IBM Systems J., 18 (1), 4–180 (1979).
20. M. V. Wilkes and R. M. Needham, "The Cambridge model distributed system', Operating System Review, 14 (1), 21–28 (1980).
21. E. Lazowska, H. Levy, G. Almes, M. Fischer, R. Fowler and S. Vestal, "The architecture of the EDEN system', Operating Systems Review, 15 (5), 148–159 (1981) (Proc. ACM 8th Conf. Operating System Principles, Asilomar, Calif.).
22. E. W. Dijkstra, 'The structure of the "The" multiprogramming system', Communications of the ACM, 11 (5), 683–696 (1968).
23. T. Anderson, P. A. Lee and S. K. Shrivastava, 'A model of recoverability in multi-level systems', IEEE Transactions on Software Engineering, SE-4 (6), 486–494 (1978) (also Report 115, Computing Laboratory, University of Newcastle upon Tyne). [Also Chap. 5]
24. B. Goldstein, G. Trivett and I. Wladawsky-Berger, 'Distributed computing in the large systems environment', Report RC 9027, IBM T. J. Watson Research Center, Yorktown Heights, New York (9 September 1981).

Recoverability Aspects of a Distributed File System

M. Jegado

Summary. The paper presents the recoverability features of a distributed file system which has been built as an extension of the UNIX[1] file system. The algorithm to achieve recoverability for the distributed files is discussed. The techniques implemented include: backward and forward error recovery, global and incremental recovery data recording. The paper outlines how these techniques can coexist to provide the abstraction of recoverability to a user of the distributed file system.

1. Introduction

The aim of the distributed file system described in this paper is to incorporate in the design of a real system some of the ideas on reliability and fault tolerance developed by a research project at the University of Newcastle upon Tyne, U.K. which is investigating the reliability and integrity of distributed computing systems [1–5]. Recent work documented in Ref. 5 and the availability of a Unix local network form the basis for an experiment in distributed systems.

Schemes for dealing with the damage that has been assessed as existing when an error is detected are usually classified into backward and forward recovery techniques. Backward error recovery depends on the provision of recovery points, [4] i.e. a means by which the state of a process can be recorded and later reinstated if required. The notion of a recoverable file system is used to mean that the state transformations performed on files can be recovered from by invoking the backward recovery capability of the system, providing the abstraction of recoverability to a user of the file system.

Although mechanisms to provide recoverability for local objects are well understood [6–9], mechanisms to provide recoverability in a distributed environment are more complex. In data bases the unit of recovery considered is referred to as a transaction [10]. However, the recovery capability of a distributed data base management system is generally not provided to support fault tolerance but rather to recover a transaction when an access conflict is detected, or when system crashes occur for example.

In contrast, the distributed recoverable file system (DRFS) described here can be used to support software fault tolerance, for instance, for use with the recovery block scheme [6]. The DRFS provides its users with the ability to establish recovery points. The grain of recovery is arbitrary and fixed by the user.

The DRFS provides some protection against crashes. A crash is an undesired event which causes the state of volatile storage in one machine to be reset

---

1 UNIX is a trademark of Bell Laboratories.

to some standard value [11]. The measure of crash resistance incorporated in the DRFS is discussed.

The paper is arranged as follows: in the next section we describe briefly the standard Unix file system and state our objectives. 'The third section presents the specifications of the DRFS. It introduces some preliminary definitions and explains the concurrency control mechanism. The global architecture of the system is described in Sect. 4 and we examine in turn the detailed implementation of the system components with particular emphasis on the implementation of recoverability. The last section addresses some aspects regarding exception handling and crash resistance.

2. Objectives

Before stating our objectives, we give an overview of some of the operations supported by the standard Unix file manager [12]. In response to an operation: *open (filename, mode)* the Unix file manager (UFM) returns a file descriptor which has associated with it a read/write pointer. The role of the file descriptor is to identify the file in subsequent operations such as *read*, *write* and *close*. The UFM simply considers a file to be a contiguous array of bytes. The read/write pointer defines the position from which a read or write operation begins in the array.

Our objective is to build an *extension* [1] of the UFM such that (i) it handles the distributed nature of the files, and (ii) it provides the abstraction of recoverability for the distributed files to the user processes.

The DRFS interface is designed to be as similar as possible to the UFM interface. A DRFS user accesses distributed files located on different sites (remote or local) in the same manner as local files can be accessed through the UFM. However, the geographical distribution of the files is visible to the user. A user has to specify when a particular named file is in fact resident on a remote machine. In Figure 1 we consider only a subset of the filing operations implemented since they are the most meaningful regarding recoverability.

```
dopen (machinename!lfname, mode) returns fd: int
        where mode = (Read, Write, R/W)
dclose (fd)
dwrite (fd, buffer, nbytes) returns nwritten: int
dread (fd, buffer, nbytes) returns nread: int
```

Fig. 1. Distributed recoverable file manager interface

The operations listed in Fig. 1 are prefixed by *d* (distributed). The exceptions that may be returned are not considered. The notation *fd* is a shorthand for file descriptor and *lfname* stands for local filename. Those operations, constituting the DRFS interface, are supported by a file manager which is called the distributed recoverable file manager (DRFM). A file can be opened several times in possibly different modes by the same user. However, for the

551

sake of simplicity of this presentation, we assume that a file can be opened only once within a transaction (Sect. 3).

All the operations provided on the DRFM interface are atomic in the sense that their invocation has an 'all or nothing' effect: either the standard state transition takes place or the state remains unchanged [3]. This is examined in further detail in the last section.

3. Specifications

3.1. Recovery Structure

The terms *establish recovery point* (*erp*), *discard recovery point* (*drp*), and *recovery region* have the same meaning as in Ref. 1. Recovery points can be nested and lead to nested recovery regions.

We define a transaction as a user program delimited by 'begin transaction' and 'end transaction' operations. A transaction consists of an arbitrary number of possible nested recovery regions. A particular case occurs when within a transaction no recovery point is established. This could correspond to a situation in which a user does not want to make use of recoverability, for example, for cost reasons. Another situation very likely in practice occurs when a recovery point is established at the beginning of the transaction and discarded at the end as illustrated in Fig. 2. Such transactions are termed recoverable transactions. [10]

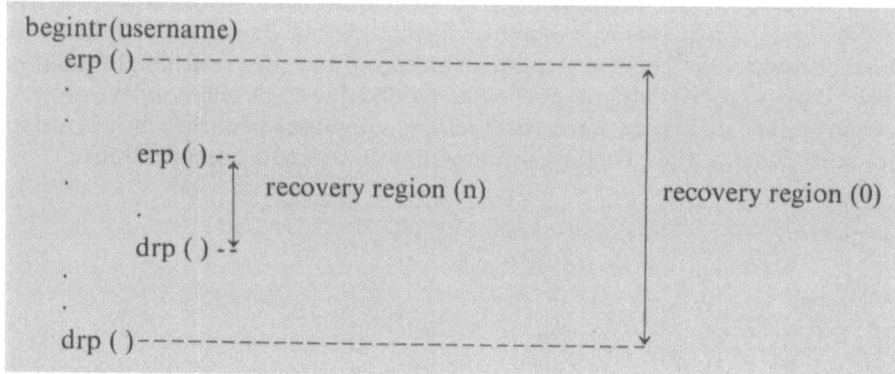

Fig. 2. Recovery structure in a user program

The *erp* operation returns a recovery point number (*rpn*) which permits identification of the recovery point. A user can invoke recovery to any active recovery point by the *restore(rpn)* operation. The recovery point *rpn* remains active after the *restore(rpn)* operation has been performed. The effect of the *restore(rpn)* operation is to recover from state transformations performed on files within the *rpn* recovery region. Note that files manipulated by the DRFS are the only recoverable objects provided. The user has to restore explicitly the state of any other objects used within the recovery regions in order to undo the whole effect produced within that recovery region [1, 5]. The *drp* operation discards the most recently established recovery point. We define *commitment* as taking place when an outermost recovery point is discarded, since after that time the state transformations performed on files cannot be recovered from by invoking the backward recovery capability of the system.

It is worth noting that the recovery discipline adopted does not enforce any particular structure with respect to the filing operations (Fig. 1). Constraints such as 'a file must be closed within the recovery region in which it was opened' are not imposed. A user can perform filing operations independently from the recovery structure.

In the rest of this paper, we assume for simplicity that transactions are recoverable transactions, that is compiled of a single outermost recovery region. Recoverable transactions have the property that their effects on the state of the distributed files can be undone by restoring the first recovery point.

3.2. Concurrency Control

In order to guarantee consistency in a concurrent environment, transactions are designed as atomic actions [4] which are implemented by an appropriate locking mechanism of the public (shared) files. The actual system does not provide a protection mode for the files such as the UFM and simply considers that all files are public. The locks granted within a transaction are held until commitment. This strategy enables the DRFS to construct planned atomic activities [4] and refer to the occurrence of the so-called 'domino-effect' by making recovery actions of transactions independent from each other. All locks are exclusive and the granularity of lock is the entire file. Note that transactions are well formed and respect two-phase locking [10].

The locking mechanism is decentralized so that the lock of a file is maintained at the site on which the file resides. The locking operations are not made visible to the user. The DRFS implements the locks internally. When a user performs a *dopen* operation on a file, the DRFS tries to grant the lock. If the lock cannot be granted an exception code: 'lock not granted' is returned. In this case, the user can wait and retry, or invoke recovery explicitly. Since the locking operations are themselves recoverable, a deadlock situation can be solved by recovery. However, no automatic provision for deadlock has been incorporated in the implemented system.

The locking strategy presented operates at a crude level, the main advantage being its simplicity. Alternative schemes are possible based for instance on unplanned recovery control [13]. The reader interested in the influence of different locking strategies on the degree of concurrency can refer to Ref. 4. Note that the scheme presented enables a transaction to begin by opening all the files which might be required, thereby obtaining all the locks which might be needed during the execution of the transaction. Therefore a user can either follow this policy or choose to acquire the locks during the execution as needed.

3.3. Crash Resistance

The DRFS incorporates some protection against crashes. When a machine crashes, the effects of the transactions which have not entered the commitment phase are undone. In other words the first recovery point established is made crash resistant. The specific problems regarding crash recovery during the commitment operation itself are not taken into account. Therefore the atomicity property of a transaction [5, 10, 11, 15] which has started commitment is not provided.

The crash resistance feature of the DRFS is achieved by keeping all the state modifications performed on file before commitment in volatile storage. Memory and temporary files are examples of such volatile storage, temporary files being deleted at system restart.

A user may decide to terminate a transaction before it is completed. For this purpose, we provide an additional operation: 'abort'. When a transaction is aborted no effect on the state of the files will take place.

4. Implementation

The implementation of the DRFS is distributed. On each machine a unique local file server process serves the requests related to the files residing on that machine. This process is implemented in the form of a local file manager (LFM) which is built on top of the UFM. The interface provided by the LFM is

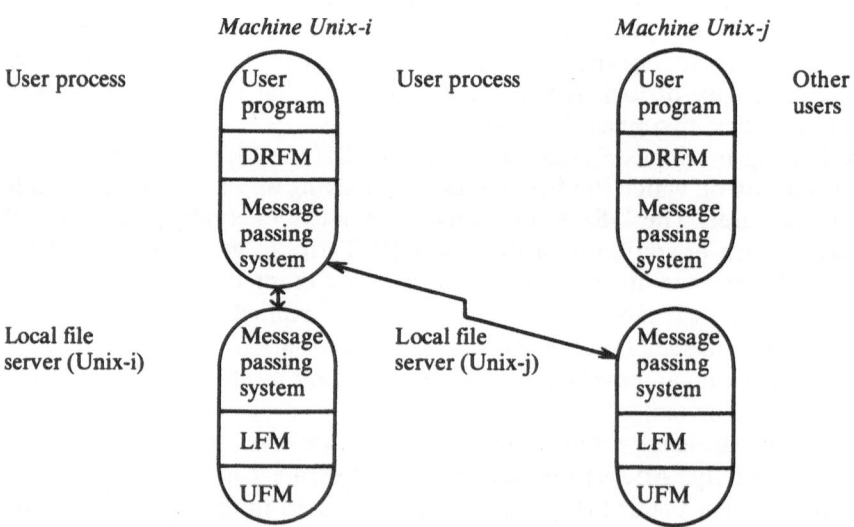

UFM: Unix File Manager
LFM: Local File Manager
DRFM: Distributed Recoverable File Manager

Fig. 3. Distributed Recoverable File System architecture

detailed further below. The set of active entities or processes present in the distributed system comprises the local file servers and the user processes. Note that a local file server process has an infinite life. The relationship between the components of the DRFS is depicted in Fig. 3.

The DRFM and the LFM communicate via a message passing system. However we can regard this communication as equivalent to distributed procedure calls which are meant to encompass both local and remote calls. The DRFM calls the procedures provided by the LFM at various sites. An extension of the system using a remote procedure call mechanism [16] has been implemented.

Accessing local files by the same mechanism as remote files has facilitated system testing. Most of the tests have been performed on a single machine, following which the decentralization to a physically distributed environment has not caused particular difficulties.

In order to limit communication overhead between the DRFM and the LFM, a paging mechanism is implemented. With each file descriptor allocated to a user, the corresponding current page is maintained at the DRFM level while the LFM performs block transfers. A subset of the filing operations provided by the LFM is given in Fig. 4.

The interface shown in Fig. 4 forms an internal interface between the DRFM and the LFM and is not visible to the user. The operations are prefixed by l which stands for local. The file descriptor (fd) returned in response to the 'lopen' operation

```
lopen(lfname, mode) returns fd: int
lclose(fd)
lwriteblock(fd, buffer, blockno)
lreadblock(fd, # buffer, blockno)
lcreat(lfname, protection) returns fd: int
lunlink(lfname)
```

Fig. 4. Local File Manager interface.

is not the fd returned to the user. The DRFS performs successive file descriptor mappings which are not considered in this paper.

The basic interactions that occur between the components of the DRFS are better illustrated by the following example. When a '$dopen(dfname, mode)$' operation is invoked within a transaction the DRFM isolates the machine name and the local file name from the distributed file name provided and invokes the '$lopen(lfname, mode)$' operation of the LFM. The LFM serves this request by using the service of the UFM.

We now examine in turn the fine structure of the DRFM and the LFM with particular emphasis on the implementation of recoverability.

4.1. Structure of the Distributed Recoverable File Manager

The DRFM is the 'controller' of a transaction. It co-ordinates the LFMs whose services are requested during the execution of a transaction. The question which arises regarding recoverability is: How can recoverability be achieved for the distributed files? The scheme presented by Shrivastava [5] gives a solution to this problem by using the recoverability capabilities of the remote objects managers in a manner that models the inclusive recovery scheme [1].

The DRFS follows this strategy. When a user establishes a recovery point, the DRFM *broadcasts* an 'establish recovery point' message to the LFMs which have taken part so far in the execution of the transaction. On reception of such a message, the LFM establishes its own recovery point, thereby using its own recovery capabilities. Similarly when a user performs a *restore* or *drp* operation a corresponding *restore*, *drp* message is broadcast.

As all the operations provided on the LFM interface are made recoverable, the DRFM does not have to maintain recovery information for the objects accessed through that interface. This greatly simplifies the implementation of recoverability in the DRFM since only the recovery information related to the objects maintained at the DRFM level has to be recorded.

We define a *session* as being the logical channel which links a DRFM to the LFM of a machine. A session is opened with an LFM when the machine name is referenced in the user program (Fig. 1). Only the first reference generates the opening of a session. The sessions are closed when the 'end transaction' operation is executed. When a session is opened, the DRFM sends for each active recovery point of the user, a corresponding 'erp' message to the LFM. The DRFM records *incrementally* the history of the sessions in a recovery cache type structure termed the *session* cache.

The DRFM also maintains some information related to each file descriptor allocated to the user (current page, read/write pointer, local file server name...). This information represents a small amount of data and is recorded *globally* when a recovery point is established in a recovery cache type structure termed the *file descriptor cache*. However, the contents of the current pages are not recorded. When a recovery point is established the current pages which have been written are flushed onto the disk storage by calling the *lwriteblock* procedure of the LFM. When recovery is invoked, the status of the current pages in the DRFM are set to: 'toread', meaning that the pages will have to be read by calling the *lreadblock* procedure of the LFM. It is worth noting that although the concrete state thus restored differs from the prior concrete state it satisfies the same abstraction [1, 3].

When the recovery data are recorded incrementally, the standard algorithms of an object manager have to handle the recovery data during their execution. However this technique may be necessary to limit the amount of recovery data stored. The advantage of recording the recovery data globally versus incrementally resides in that the former technique enables a clear distinction between the standard algorithms of an object manager and the recovery algorithms (*erp*, *drp*, *restore*).

In fact these techniques can coexist to make the recovery implementation more efficient. The DRFS is an example of such a use of a combination of techniques. The LFM provides the abstraction of recoverability mainly by recording the recovery data incrementally as explained in the following.

4.2. Structure of the Local File Manager

A local file server process executes the recovery and filing operations supported by the LFM on request from the DRFMs. The LFM maintains an execution context for each session opened with a DRFM consisting of two instances of a recovery cache type structure respectively the *undo cache* and the *commit cache*. The undo cache records the operations to be undone when a user invokes recovery. The commit cache records the identification of the files which are not in a committed state. The commit cache does not contain redundant data.

We now examine how recoverability is achieved for some of the filing operations supported by the LFM. The creation and deletion of files by the operation *lcreat* and *lunlink* are mentioned for the sake of illustration and not considered in further detail.

(i) *lwriteblock*. When this operation is performed, the original file is copied into a temporary file if no copy has been made previously. This copy is made in order to provide crash resistance (Sect. 3) and is maintained as the up-to-date version of the file, that is, all updates are performed on this copy. (Recall that temporary files use volatile storage and are deleted at system restart after a crash). When the copy is performed the file identification is recorded in the commit cache and the code (copy) in the undo cache.

The copy made would be sufficient for recovery purposes if recovery regions were not nested. As recovery regions can be nested, the LFM, to update a block, proceeds by: (a) reading the contents of the block from the copy; (b) cacheing it in the undo cache of the session's execution context; (c) updating the block in place on the copy. To avoid redundancy of recovery data, a block is not cached if it has already been cached within the current recovery region. In order to limit the amount of recovery data held in the undo cache, the prior contents of the block are not recorded directly in the undo cache but in a temporary file of the LFM called *block-pool*; the undo cache retains only the code (*lwriteblock*). The parameters associated with this code are: *fd*, blockno written, blockno allocated from the block-pool. The block-pool file is a shared data structure maintained by a monitor. Files which are lengthened are not considered for simplicity of this presentation.

(ii) *lopen*. This operation consists of two primitives operations which are (a) locking the file; (b) executing the open operation of the UFM. Hence the codes (*lock*, *open*) with appropriate parameters are recorded in the undo cache. If recovery is invoked, the file is closed and unlocked.

(iii) *lclose*. This operation consists of (a) executing the close operation of the UFM; (b) unlocking the file. Since the unlock operation must be delayed until commitment, the unlocking is not performed but the file identification is recorded in the commit cache while the code (close) is recorded in the undo cache. If recovery is invoked the file is reopened. Note that the execution of the open and close operations of the UFM are performed on the copy of the file if a copy has been made.

Maintaining a copy of a file to provide crash resistance may appear an inefficient solution. An alternative scheme would have been to maintain only a copy of the blocks which have been written. A file block mapping [7] could then associate to a blockno, either the original block if the block has not been modified, or the copy of that block if an update has been performed. However, apart from the simplicity of implementation, the first solution has the following advantages:

(a) It optimizes the normal execution of the *lreadblock* operation. No file block mapping has to be performed since the copy contains the up-to-date version of the file.

(b) It enables us to adopt the same solution for the *lcreat* and *lunlink* operations. The basic idea is to work on temporary files and not to perform state modifications in non-volatile storage before commitment. For instance, an *lcreat* operation results in a copy being created.

Indeed, although the solution retained is more simple, it may become inefficient both in terms of auxiliary storage required and with respect to performance issues when handling large files.

To summarize, the commit cache contains the identification of the files which are not in a committed state, whereas the undo cache contains the operation codes (locks, open, close, copy, writeblock) as necessary. A recovery cache is organized as a stack, which is subdivided into regions separated by barriers [6]. The algorithm executed by the LFM when recovery is involved by a user process is given in Fig. 5.

```
lrecover(rpn) =
i1)   Remove the barriers from the current recovery region to region rpn
      in the commit cache and the undo cache respectively.
i2)   Process the undo cache as follows:
          while (pop(operation) != barrier) {
          switch (operation) {
          case lock:     unlock;
          case open:     close;
          case close:    open;
          case copy:     delete copy;
          case wblock:   write the prior value of the block;
                         free (blockno allocated from block-pool);

          }
      }
i3)   Process the commit cache by removing the entries until the barrier is
      encountered.
i4)   Set current recovery region of rpn.
```

Fig. 5. Recovery algorithm of the local file manager

At commitment time, the entries in the undo cache are discarded and the commit cache is processed as follows. For each file identification recorded in the commit cache, the LFM determines what the state of the file after commitment should be. It then performs the necessary commit operations to effect the state transition from the actual state of the file to the post commitment state in non-volatile storage. For instance, the commit operations related to a file which has been successively opened, updated and closed are: rename the copy to be the original file name, delete the original file, free the blocks allocated from block-pool, and unlock the file.

The implementation of the LFM has shown how unrecoverable features of the lower level interface of the UFM can be concealed in an extension to provide new recoverable abstract files. In retrospect of this exercise it appears that the amounts of work vary a lot between the operations depending upon the facilities provided by the non-recoverable interface, and it is not clear, at this stage whether one could establish some properties of an 'ideal' non-recoverable interface such that the recoverable extension be built in the most efficient manner.

5. Exception Handling – Crash Resistance

In this section we examine in turn exception handling and crash resistance issues. As is emphasized in Ref. [2] exception handling forms the basic framework for fault tolerance strategies. Although neither our programming language nor the Unix operating system support an 'exception mechanism', we believe that some of the principles presented elsewhere [2, 3] can be used successfully when programming with more conventional tools.

In response to a request, a component may provide its normal service or signal an exception. Two reasons can lead a component to signal an exception: (i) an illegal request for service is made – an interface exception [2] – or (ii) the component fails to provide the standard service – 'not done' exception [5]. Before signalling an exception a component must revert to the external state it had prior to the request in order to enforce the atomicity of the operation invoked. As advocated in Ref. [2] a simple method of meeting this requirement is for a component to establish a recovery point when the request for service is received and then either discard or restore that recovery point as necessary. When an exception is signalled, the handler associated with the exception at the point of invocation of the request is activated. The handler can either attempt to mask the occurrence of the exception and proceed with execution or if nothing is successful, signal an exception to a higher level of abstraction.

The Unix operating system does not support backward error recovery as a basic mechanism, therefore consistency of the components of the DRFS is restored by forward error recovery. Indeed, the DRFM could establish a recovery point when an operation of its interface is involved, thereby using the backward recovery capability of the LFM which provides recoverable operations. However, this facility has not been used for the following reasons. Firstly the need to deal with recovery points established at several levels of abstraction has been avoided – the reader interested by this issue can refer to Ref. [1]. Secondly, the operations provided on the LFM interface being atomic, it was simple and more efficient to restore the consistency of the DRFM if necessary by forward error recovery.

If consistency cannot be restored successfully a 'failure' exception can be signalled, the task of restoration relying then at a higher level of abstraction.

However, the DRFS avoids to *propagate* 'failure' exceptions since on one hand it is desirable for the user not to have to provide two exception handlers to handle separately 'failure' and 'not done' exceptions. On the other hand, the recovery data which are recorded incrementally by a recoverable component can be inconsistent when a 'failure' exception is signalled. If the recovery data is inconsistent, backward error recovery situated at a higher level will fail therefore achieving no progress in restoring consistency.

Restoration of consistency by forward recovery within the LFM relies upon the assumptions made upon the atomicity property of the operations provided on the UFM interface. In the actual system, the UFM operations have been assumed to be atomic. However, the write operation should be considered as signalling 'failure' exception. The handler associated with this anticipated failure occurrence could then for instance attempt to mask it by relocating the whole file. We do not specifically consider communications failures. These failures result in 'not done' or 'failure' exceptions being signalled by the lower level message passing systems. When a 'not done' exception is signalled, an attempt to restore consistency is made and a 'not done' exception propagated, whereas if a 'failure' exception is signalled, it is assumed that consistency cannot be restored.

When consistency cannot be restored within the LFM or DRFM, the standard algorithms for maintaining the abstraction of recoverability are deemed to have failed. In order to guarantee consistency despite such failures, some redundancy is required and provided by the crash resistance features. Therefore, in such a situation the DRFS simulates a crash event by aborting the transaction.

In the following, we present some characteristics of the crash recovery protocol. When the LFM aborts a transaction, it cleans the session's execution context and returns an 'abort' answer to the DRFM. On reception of such a message the DRFM triggers the abort procedure which consists of cleaning up the transaction locally and broadcasting an 'abort' message to the other local file servers recorded in the session cache. On reception of an 'abort' message the LFM executes the abort procedure if the session is not already aborted. Should a local file server crash and a 'failure' exception being signalled by the message passing system within the DRFM, the abort procedure is triggered. Should a DRFM crash, a time-out mechanism set on each session at the LFM level enables to abort the session locally. As a simplification, the time-out mechanism is not implemented. Rather the session's context remains pending until the user launches a new transaction which requests services of this LFM. The opening of a new session then causes the abortion of the previous pending one. The protocol implemented is fairly simple and no 'crash-recovery' procedures are implemented. However it does not cope with exceptions being raised during commitment nor with crashes occurring at that time. An extension of the system to deal with these situations is under investigation.

6. Conclusion

In this paper we have discussed the recovery features of a distributed file system, detailing successively the structure of the system components. It has been shown that a combination of techniques such as global and incremental recovery data recording can make the implementation of recoverability more efficient. The fact that the system is geographically distributed has not complicated the design since local files are accessed in the same manner as remote files. The access is made through the message passing system interface which 'hides' the inter-machine dependencies. The system has been written in the high level language 'C' and is currently running on a local area network comprised of PDP 11/45 and LSI 11/23 machines connected through the Cambridge ring. The overall structure of the system is simple and in this respect sticks to the objectives of development of the first version.

A number of extensions are possible: (i) to investigate other concurrency control mechanisms; (ii) to improve the basic set of facilities provided in order to give to a user the same facilities as the Unix file system and to measure the actual overheads incurred.

Acknowledgements. A special debt of gratitude is due to P. A. Lee who launched the project by an internal communication and who continuously helped the author during the design and implementation. The author remains also grateful to F. Cristian for his valuable advice in modular programming and to S. K. Shrivastava and G. Wood for their useful comments.

This work has been carried out with the support of the Institut National de Recherche en Informatique et Automatique of France and the Science and Engineering Research Council of Great Britain.

References

1. T. Anderson, P. A. Lee and S. K. Shrivastava, 'A model of recoverability in multilevel systems', IEEE Trans. Software Engineering, SE-4, 486–494 (1978). [Also Chap. 5].
2. T. Anderson and P. A. Lee, Fault Tolerance – Principles and Practice, Prentice-Hall, 1981.
3. F. Cristian, 'Robust data types', Acta informatica, (1981). [Also Chap. 3].
4. B. Randell, P. A. Lee and P. C. Treleaven, 'Reliability issues in computing systems design', ACM Computing Surveys, 10, 123–165 (1978).
5. S. K. Shrivastava, "Structuring distributed systems for recoverability and crash resistance', IEEE Trans. on Software Engineering, SE-7, 436–447 (1981). [Also Chap. 5]
6. T. Anderson and R. Kerr, 'Recovery blocks in action', Proc. 2nd Int. Conf. on Software Engineering, San Francisco, October, 447–457 (1976). [Also Chap. 2].
7. F. Cristian, 'A recovery mechanism for modular software', Proc. 4th Int. Conf. on Software Engineering, Munich, 42–50 (1979).
8. P. A. Lee, N. Ghani and K. Heron, 'A recovery cache for the PDP-11', IEEE Trans. on Computers, C-29, 546–549 (1980). [Also Chap. 2].
9. J. S. M. Verhofstad, 'Recovery and crash resistance in a filing system', Proc. SIGMOD Conf., ACM, New York 158–167 (1977). [Also Chap. 2].
10. J. N. Gray, 'Note on data bases operating systems', Lecture Notes in Computer Science, 60, Springer, Berlin, 393–481 (1978).
11. B. Lampson and H. Sturgis, 'Crash recovery in a distributed data storage system', TR Xerox.
12. D. M. Ritchie and K. Thompson, 'The Unix time sharing system', CACM, 17, 365–375 (1974).

13. W. G. Wood, 'Recovery control of communicating processes in a distributed system', TR 158, Computing Laboratory, University of Newcastle upon Tyne, 1980. [Also Chap. 6].
14. D. Z. Badal, 'On the degree of concurrency provided by concurrency control mechanisms for Distributed Data Bases', Proc. Int. Symp. on Distributed Data Bases, North Holland Publishing Co., 1980.
15. H. E. Sturgis, J. G. Mitchell and J. Israel, 'Issues in the design and use of a distributed file system', Op. Sys. Rev., 14, 55−69 (1980).
16. S. K. Shrivastava and F. Panzieri, 'The design of a reliable remote procedure call mechanism', IEEE Trans. on Computers, July (1982). [Also Chap. 6].
17. T. Anderson and P. A. Lee, 'The provision of recoverable interfaces', Digest of Papers FTCS-9, Madison, June, 87−94 (1978). [Also Chap. 5].
18. B. Randell, 'System structure for software fault tolerance', IEEE Trans. on Software Engineering, SE-1, 220−232 (1975). [Also Chap. 1].

Chapter 7

Fault Tolerance and System Structuring

B. Randell

Abstract. We discuss a general approach to the design of fault-tolerant computing systems, concentrating on issues of system structuring rather than on the design of particular algorithms. Three forms of structuring are described. The first is based on the use of what we term "idealized fault-tolerant components". Such components provide a means of system structuring which makes it easy to identify what parts of a system have what responsibilities for trying to cope with what sorts of faults. The second is a "recursive structuring" scheme. It involves using complete computers as the basic idealized fault-tolerant components of a distributed computing system whose functionality matches that of its component computers. Finally we discuss a generalization of the usual concept of an "atomic action", which provides a means of structuring both forward and backward error recovery in distributed systems. These discussions are given in general terms, and also illustrated by brief accounts of recent and current work at Newcastle on the construction of UNIX-based fault-tolerant and distributed systems.

1. Introduction

The most straightforward way of constructing reliable computing systems would be to use only reliable components, and to put them together only in accordance with correct designs. In practice one often has to try to achieve reliability despite the unreliability of the hardware and software components used. Moreover (though this is less often admitted) one may well not be able to guarantee that the overall system design is absolutely faultless. Thus strategies aimed at fault avoidance or removal (prior to use of a system) must usually be complemented by strategies aimed at tolerating the presence of faults.

In this paper we will discuss a general approach to the design of fault-tolerant systems. Our approach concentrates on issues of system structuring rather than on the design of particular algorithms. This is because, with computing systems that have to meet complex and demanding specifications, the overall reliability levels achieved will depend crucially on the extent to which the system design can be kept simple. Thus, in our view, careful structuring is at least as important as are clever algorithms to the achievement of successful fault-tolerant system design.

This viewpoint has motivated research over the years at Newcastle, and has led us to a style of system design which is based on what we term "idealized fault-tolerant components". Such components provide a means of system structuring which makes it easy to identify what parts of a system have what responsibilities for trying to cope with which sorts of fault. Moreover, by taking complete computers as the basic idealized fault-tolerant components, one can make use of a "recursive structuring" scheme which simplifies many design issues. However these schemes of structuring the software and hardware comprising a system need to be used in such a way as to achieve an appropriate structuring of the complex asynchronous activities to which the system can give rise, in particular those related to fault-tolerance. In common with other groups, we have been investigating the use of so-called "atomic actions" for this purpose.

These three forms of structuring are described in Sect. 2, 3 and 4 below. The discussion is given in general terms, and is illustrated by brief accounts of recent and current work at Newcastle on the construction of UNIX-based fault-tolerant and distributed systems.

2. Idealized Fault Tolerant Components

Systems, and their components, can be regarded as performing operations in order to provide responses to requests. Within a system in which it is acknowledged that faults might exist these faults can, from the viewpoint of a given component, be grouped into three categories:

(i) faults within the component itself,
(ii) faults in the sub-components or co-existing components that a component makes use of, and
(iii) faulty requests made of the component by its environment, i.e. the enclosing component or the co-existing components with which it is interacting.

Potentially therefore, in a system which is intended to be fault-tolerant, each component should be designed to deal appropriately with each of these three very different situations. Ideally a component should seek to mask its own faults, and any unmasked faults in the components that it makes use of, so that it can appear fully reliable to its environment. In general, however, this will not always be possible. Thus each component should have pre-defined means of reporting to its environment that a fault has occurred, if it has been unable (or has not been designed) to mask the fault.

On the other hand a component cannot be expected to mask the faults (in its environment) that cause the component to be requested to perform an operation which is outside its specification. (A component which is designed, say, to calculate the square root of its input cannot be expected to produce a real result from a negative input.) However we would again argue that the component should have a defined means of reporting the problem back to its environment, where attempts to mask the fault would be appropriate.

Our notion of an "idealized fault-tolerant component" is concerned with these issues of fault reporting, and of the assignment of responsibility for attempts at fault masking. In this section we deal just with a single component and its interactions with its environment, deferring until Section 4 consideration of the structuring of systems constructed out of multiple components, and so capable of asynchronous behaviour.

What is significant about an idealized fault-tolerant component is that it implies a scheme for structuring systems which incorporate various means of tolerating various sorts of faults. The structuring scheme makes minimal assumptions about what sorts of fault cannot occur, and what sorts of fault masking will be achieved — the one requirement is, naturally, that faults do not invalidate the planned structure of components and their inter-relationships.

The scheme requires that, in general, each component should have identifiable, and in principle separate, means for dealing with the above three categories of fault. In hardware terms, we are in part arguing for a design based on self-testing components [1], since it is each component's responsibility to alert its environment when it cannot carry out a requested operation. In programming terms, our scheme is in fact a suggested discipline for exception handling. It is illustrated in Figure 1, in which local exceptions, failure exceptions and interface exceptions are the respective means by which the three categories of fault listed above are reported.

If a component either receives an abnormal response from an invocation of another component or detects an error or abnormal condition during normal activity, it should *raise* an exception and invoke appropriate fault tolerance measures. Recovery is an abnormal activity of the component and is continued until the component either returns to is normal activities or *signals* an exception. The relationship between the normal and abnormal activity of a component and the raising and signalling of exceptions is shown in Fig. 1. Note that an exception is raised within the component, but signalled between components. The flow of control of a computation within a component should change as the result of a raised exception. Such a modified or *exceptional flow of control* is distinguished from the normal flow of control. Within a program, exceptional flow of control is associated with code fragments that are called *exception handlers*.

Exceptions, software components, and exception handlers are associated by a *handling context*. If the fault tolerance measures provided by a handler are successful, the handler will provide a normal return, from the component which raised the exception, to the component which invoked that component. If the fault tolerance measures are unsuccessful or inadequate, a handler should signal a failure exception. Abnormal control flow continues in an exception handler of the invoking component.

An exception handler is a component and may have its own context, exceptions, and exception handlers. This permits the nesting of exception handling facilities. If an exception is raised within a component (or an exception handler) that does not have a context defining an appropriate handler, the component fails and a failure exception is signalled.

The scheme is based on the so-called "termination model" of exception handling [2]. In other words, we require that the operation that a component undertakes for a particular service request be terminated by the provision of a normal or abnormal response to the environment. Thus an operation cannot be resumed after the environment has dealt with an interface or failure exception -- the component can only be asked to start another operation.

With such a structuring scheme it is possible, and indeed desirable, to specify the interface between each component and its environment completely. This enables the design of the component to be based on just the interface specification, and so to be undertaken independently of that of its environment, even with respect to issues of fault tolerance. This is a very important advantage. When fault tolerance provisions have not been carefully structured

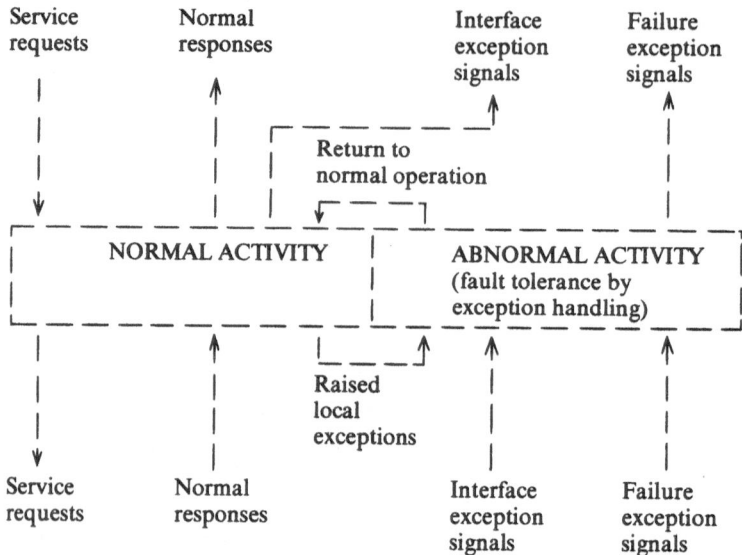

Fig. 1. An Idealized Fault Tolerant Component

their design can be very complex, to the point where the design itself is a source of unreliability.

One of the important tasks of a system designer using this structuring scheme will be to decide what sort of faults can and cannot occur, and what sorts of fault masking can be presumed to be successful. This is so as to determine what exceptions must be defined and what exception handlers must be provided. For example, a component using triple modular redundancy techniques to mask sub-component faults should in principle still have a way of reporting a failure exception to its environment for use if, say, no two of the triplicated components are in agreement. However in some circumstances it might well be decided that it is safe to disregard such a possibility, and hence to omit the provision of such an exception, i.e. to modify the specification of the interface between the component and its environment.

2.1. A Remote Procedure Call Protocol

The approach that we, and several other groups, have taken recently to the structuring of local area networking software can usefully be described in terms of idealized fault-tolerant components. Oversimplifying somewhat, the software can be regarded as being structured into two levels of component, with a third underlying level of component in the form of the network hardware. The lower level software component uses the hardware to provide message-passing facilities, which the upper level software uses to provide a remote procedure call facility.

Fig. 2. Communications Software Structure

It would have been possible to provide message passing over the local area network by a component which used a sophisticated protocol involving mechanisms for flow control, error correction and acknowledgements, etc., to give "guaranteed" delivery of undamaged and unduplicated messages. In such circumstances the temptation would have been to treat the message passing as being fully reliable, and to omit any provisions for signalling a communications failure exception to the upper level component.

In fact such a protocol would consume considerable processing and storage resources, since a significant amount of state information would have to be maintained about any data transfer in progress, in order to support the abstraction of a "connection" between processes. To establish, maintain and terminate a connection reliably is rather complex, and a significant number of messages would be needed just for connection purposes [3].

This would be quite appropriate for wide area packet-switching networks which are liable to damage, lose or duplicate packets. However it is not so appropriate for a local area network, such as the Cambridge Ring, because of the much greater (though still of course less than total) reliability of the underlying hardware. We therefore chose to provide message passing by direct use of the underlying hardware communications facilities, without trying to mask any of their faults. Instead the message-passing component merely signals an appropriate exception to the enclosing remote procedure call protocol software when necessary. (In fact, once an appropriate interface, *with adequate exception signalling*, has been defined it is practicable to support it by a variety of communications hardware and message-passing protocols. Thus we plan to support exactly the same message-passing interface when we use, instead of a Cambridge Ring, a wide area packet-switching network together with a connection-oriented protocol [4].)

The upper-level component therefore contains handlers for exception signals indicating that there has been a communications fault which the message-passing component has not masked, perhaps because it did not attempt to do so. This upper level of software, which provides the rest of the system with a remote procedure call facility, in any case has to deal with problems arising from computers crashing, and hence being temporarily unable to respond at all to messages.

The remote procedure call software in fact has responsibility for trying to ensure that remote procedure calls obey an "exactly once" semantics [5], i.e. that computer crashes and consequent re-sending of messages do not cause unintended repeated execution of a procedure. Being able to do this, it can also readily cope with failure exceptions from the message-passing component. This choice of structure (which is based on the so-called "end-to-end argument" [6]), has proved very satisfactory, since our "light-weight" remote procedure call protocol has proved to be as reliable as, and considerably more efficient than, an existing connection-oriented protocol for the Cambridge Ring [7].

3. Recursively Structured Systems

The notion of an idealized fault-tolerant component can be applied to many different aspects and levels of computing system design. An allied structuring technique that we have been investigating is aimed at the situation where one is taking complete computers as basic system components, and using them to construct a distributed computing system. This "recursive structuring" technique is expressed in the design rule:

A distributed system should be functionally equivalent to the individual systems of which it is composed.

In other words, one arranges to use, as the principal idealized fault-tolerant components of a computing system, computers whose external interface exactly matches that required of the system as a whole. Thus, if the distributed system is to provide facilities for parallel processing, the component computers must also provide (at least the appearance of) parallel processing. More importantly, each component computer's naming facilities (i.e. the means it provides to users for identifying its various constituent objects, such as devices, files, programs, etc.) must be independent of whether the computer is in fact an isolated (i.e. complete) system, or merely a component of some larger system. This characteristic is not common in the world of computing systems, despite the fact that it is well known elsewhere, for example in telephone systems. (The telephone numbers used in a company's internal telephone system need not be affected if the system becomes part of a national telephone system. National telephone numbers need not be changed if the country becomes part of the international telephone system, etc.)

Specifically, the component computer systems need to support a general "contextual naming" scheme for their various objects. In order for a system to be extensible, it should have means for introducing and entering (and leaving) new naming contexts. Such facilities are reasonably common. What is not so common is a system in which *all* names are context-relative. However this is essential, because of the requirement that a computer be usable in the same way when it is isolated as when it is within a larger system.

The mechanisms that one uses in order to build the overall distributed system out of the component computers must not affect the functionality of the system — they must, in other words, be transparent to the user of the system. These user-transparent mechanisms can however be designed to have beneficial effects on such aspects of the overall system as its capacity, reliability and security — qualities that we term *abilities*, so as to distinguish them from the logical *functionality* of the system.

The most important such mechanism is the one that enables a number of component computers to be linked together. The mechanism in fact provides what is often termed "network transparency", since the users of the distributed system will, in view of the design rule that has been followed, be shielded from all issues of inter-computer communication, networking protocols, etc. Note that this is a rather special form of network transparency since one must be able to repeat the construction process, and build a further larger distributed system using several first-level distributed systems as though they were basic component computers. A distributed system which is recursively structured in this way is — by definition — indefinitely extensible, at least in theory.

One can contrast this scheme of making a set of computers look like a single computer with the better known technique of using a virtual machine monitor, or "hypervisor", to make a single computer look like a set of computers. (With a so-called "recursive virtual machine monitor" [8], the subdivision can be performed repeatedly, in close analogy to the idea of repeated construction described above.) Both schemes can in fact be regarded as forms of virtualisation, as can user-transparent mechanisms for providing other so-called abilities, in particular reliability.

In a recursively structured computer system, the possible exceptions signalled by the overall system must be the same as the exceptions signalled by the component computers. However, by the use of redundant component computers, one can largely mask their faults, and hence greatly reduce the frequency with which the overall system has to signal failure exceptions. Thus although no change has been made with respect to functionality, the user-perceived reliability of the overall system can be significantly enhanced. This involves construction of a further virtualisation mechanism (e.g. to perform the synchronization and voting needed for triple modular redundancy) but this mechanism can be designed and constructed independently of the virtualisation mechanism that provides network transparency.

In fact one can envisage enhancing the ability of the overall system by means of a whole set of independently designed virtualisation mechanisms. This clear separation of logical concerns greatly reduces overall system complexity. Indeed the important point about a virtualisation mechanism is that its presence is, in a sense, always optional. Thus one can in principle use any selection of virtualisation mechanisms together, in order to obtain a system with the desired abilities.

3.1. UNIX United

The technique of recursive structuring underlies recent work at Newcastle which has resulted in the implementation of yet another distributed system based on UNIX. The system, which for purposes of description we will call "UNIX United", is a distributed system which is functionally equivalent to a conventional UNIX system running on a single processor. All the standard UNIX facilities, e.g. for protecting, naming and accessing files and devices, for input/output re-direction, for inter-process communication, etc., are applicable

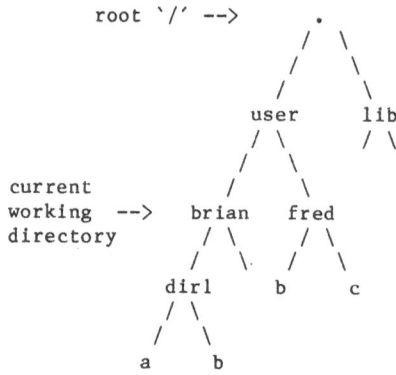

Fig. 3. A Typical UNIX Name Space

without apparent change to the system as a whole. UNIX is a particularly suit-ed to the use of the recursive structuring scheme, because of its very simple yet general scheme for naming files, devices and commands, in which directories serve as the required contexts.

Figure 3 shows part of a typical UNIX naming hierarchy. Files, directories, etc., can only be named relative to some known "location" in the tree. It so happens that UNIX provides two such locations, namely the directory which is designated as being the "current working directory" and that which is designated as the "root directory". Thus in the figure "/user/brian/dir1/a" and "dir1/a" identify the same file, the convention being that a name starting with "/" is relative to the root directory. Objects outside a context can be named relative to that context using the convention that ".." indicates the parent directory. (Note that this avoids having to know the name by which the context is known in its surrounding context.) The names "/user/fred/b" and "../fred/b" therefore identify the same file, the second form being a name given relative to the cur-rent working directory rather than the root directory.

The root directory is normally positioned at the base of the tree, as shown in the figure, but this does not have to be the case. Rather, like the current work-ing directory, it can also be re-positioned at some other node in the naming tree, *but this position must be specified by a context-relative name.* Thus all nam-ing is completely context-relative — there is no means of specifying an absolute

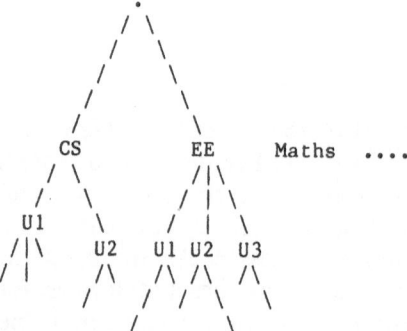

Fig. 4. A University-Wide UNIX United System

570

name, relative to the base of the tree, say. (The base directory can itself be recognized only by the convention that it is its own parent.) Moreover *all other means* provided for identifying any of the various kinds of objects that UNIX deals with, e.g. users, processes, open files, etc., can be related back to its hierarchical naming scheme. It is for these reasons that UNIX, in contrast to most operating systems, can be said to support a contextual naming scheme.

This simple and elegant scheme of context-relative naming has been taken advantage of in UNIX United by identifying individual component UNIX systems with directories in a larger name space, covering the UNIX United system as a whole. In Fig. 4 we show how a UNIX United system spanning an entire university might be created from the machines in various university departments, using a naming structure which matches the departmental structure. (This naming structure need bear no relationship to the actual topology of the underlying communications networks. Indeed this exact naming structure could be set up on a single conventional UNIX system.)

The figure implies that from within the Computing Science Department's U1 machine, files on its U2 machine will normally have names starting "/. ./U2" and files on the machine that the Electrical Engineering Department has also chosen to call "U2" will need to be identified with names starting "/. ./. ./ EE/U2". Indeed U2 and the directory structure beneath it might not be associated with a single machine. Rather it might be a UNIX United system, itself containing an arbitrary number of other UNIX United systems, unknown to U1 in CS.

The network transparency that UNIX United provides has been implemented merely by inserting a software layer, which we call the "Newcastle Connection", into an otherwise unchanged UNIX system. The positioning of the Connection layer is governed by the structure of UNIX itself. In UNIX all user processes and many operating system facilities (such as the 'shell' command language interpreter) are run as separate timeshared processes. These are able to interact with each other, and the outside world, only by means of 'system calls' – effectively procedure calls on the resident nucleus of the operating system, the UNIX kernel. The Connection is a transparent layer that is inserted between the kernel and the processes. It is transparent in the sense that from above it is functionally indistinguishable from the kernel and from below it appears to be a set of normal user processes. It filters out system calls that have to be re-directed to another UNIX system (for example, because they concern files or devices on that system), and accepts calls that have been re-directed to it from other systems. Thus processes on different UNIX machines can interact in exactly the same way as do processes on a single machine.

Since system calls act like procedure calls, communication between the Connection layers on the various machines uses a remote procedure call protocol (which is based on that discussed in Sect. 2.1 above), as portrayed in Fig. 5.

Various additional UNIX virtualisation mechanisms are being investigated. One that has already been implemented in prototype form makes use of triple modular redundancy techniques in order to mask hardware faults. This is designed as an additional transparent software subsystem (the Triple Modular Redundancy layer) in each of a number of UNIX machines on top of their Con-

571

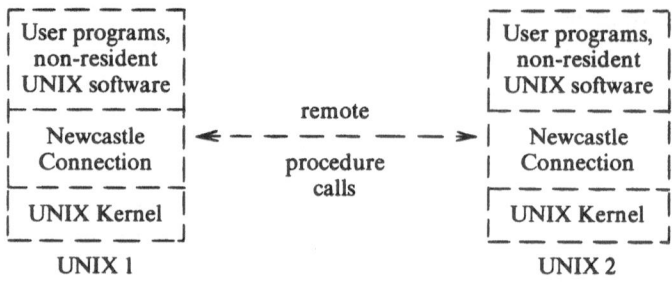

Fig. 5. The Position of the Connection Layer

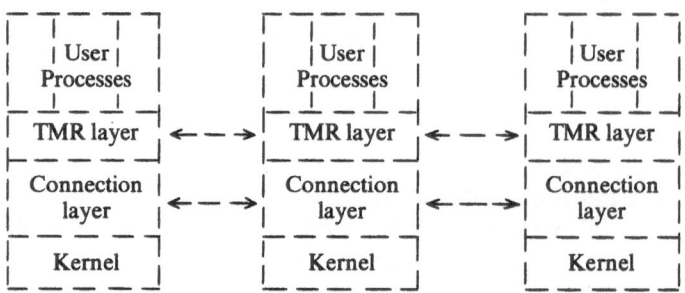

Fig. 6. Hardware Fault Masking

nection layers, as shown in Fig. 6. The TMR layer goes on top of the Connection layer because it can then rely on the latter to handle all problems relating to the physical distribution of processes, files, etc. Copies of a conventional application program and its files can then be loaded onto each of three machines and run so that file accesses are synchronized and voted upon. Any malfunctioning computer so identified by the voting is automatically switched out and in due course another switched in to replace it. (Being independent of the Connection layer, the TMR layer could, in principle, be used in a single conventional UNIX system. This would give a sort of "temporal triple modular redundancy", with three identical processes running in interleaved fashion on a single processor.)

4. Atomic Actions

The structuring techniques discussed so far have been concerned with the use of systems as components of larger systems, and in particular with the static structure of the software and/or hardware making up a computer system. We now turn our attention to the closely related topic of the dynamic structure of a system. By this we mean the structure of the perhaps complex activities that the components of the system give rise to when the system is operational. By so doing, we can deal with the issues raised by systems in which components can share subcomponents, so that there can be complex asynchronous behaviour, and in which the number of components can change. As always, our aim is to cope with complexity by finding means of treating various aspects of the system design independently of each other, even (or rather, especially) with regard to the problems of achieving fault tolerance. In this regard we now concentrate on error recovery techniques, i.e. the design of the exception handling mechanisms in a system built using idealized fault-tolerant components.

Error recovery techniques are aimed at allowing a system to continue operation and to resume normal computation. However other errors may well have been generated in the interval between the manifestation of a fault, and the moment of error detection. Successful fault tolerance must enable the system to continue to function despite error propagation during the time interval, which may be lengthy, between the first manifestation of a fault and the eventual detection of an error.

So-called "forward error recovery" aims to remove or isolate specific errors so that normal computation can be resumed [9]. It is accomplished by making selective corrections to a system state. Because recovery is applied to a state that contains errors, forward error recovery techniques require accurate damage assessment (or estimation) [10] of the likely extent of the errors introduced by the fault.

In contrast, "backward error recovery" aims to restore the system to a state which occurred prior to the manifestation of the fault. Using this earlier state of the computation, the function of the system is then provided by an alternate algorithm until normal computation can be resumed [11]. (In practice, the most recent restorable system state which is free from the effects of the fault may be difficult to determine. In order to find an appropriate system state, a search technique may be used involving iteratively attempting recovery from successively earlier restorable states until recovery is successful.) Because backward error recovery restores a valid prior system state, recovery is possible from errors of largely unknown origin and propagation characteristics. (All that is required is that the errors have not affected the state restoration mechanism.)

Forward and backward error recovery techniques complement one another, forward error recovery allowing efficient handling of expected conditions and backward error recovery providing a general strategy which will cope with faults a designer did not − or chose not to − anticipate. As a special case, a forward error recovery mechanism can support the implementation of backward error recovery [12].

If a system has but a single component, and the operations performed (for the environment surrounding the system) by this component can be regarded as having an instantaneous or indivisible effect on the state of the system, the system is said to be *sequential*. As long as the component, and all of its subcomponents, are not also part of any other system, then the system is *isolated*. The provision of forward or backward error recovery in such isolated sequential systems can be reasonably easy.

If on the other hand a system has a number of components, of which one or more subcomponents are shared, it will be possible for the system to give rise to perhaps very complex asynchronous and interacting activities. The provision of error recovery will be a much more difficult problem in such circumstances.

Nevertheless it is possible to limit this complexity, and hence facilitate the provision of error recovery, if one can arrange that the overall activity of the system is appropriately structured.

If an operation provided by a system is carried out by the system's components in such a way that there are no interactions between the set of components and the components of any other system, then we can say the operation has given rise to an *atomic activity*. (A more rigorous definition can be found in [13].) If a particular operation is always performed atomically, then we term it an *atomic operation* or, more commonly, an *atomic action* – a notion which has much in common with that of a "sphere of control" [14].

There are great advantages to structuring systems out of hierarchies of atomic activities. The temporary creation and then destruction of additional components within an atomic action can be dealt with reasonably easily. If a fault, resulting error propagation, and subsequent successful error recovery all occur within a single atomic action it is possible to ensure that they will not affect other system activities. Furthermore, if the activity of a system can be organized into atomic actions, fault tolerance measures can be constructed for each of the atomic actions independently. Thus, atomic actions provide a framework for encapsulating fault tolerance techniques within modular components. If all the operations on a system are atomic, then that system is an *atomic system*. Such systems may be used as components in the design and construction of other, more complex, systems as if their activities were primitive atomic actions. Systems that are designed explicitly so as to synchronize the activities of their components in order to form atomic actions have *planned atomic actions*. Systems may also give rise to *spontaneous atomic activities,* i.e. ones that arise fortuitously from the dynamic sequences of events occurring in a system. For the purposes of structuring fault tolerance measures, spontaneous atomic activities are of little value even if they can be easily identified as such.

Planned and spontaneous atomic activities represent the two opposite ends of a spectrum of error recovery techniques, depending on the extent to which explicit constraints are imposed upon inter-process communication. The conversation [15] is an example of a planned atomic activity with which backward error recovery is associated. The chase protocol scheme [16] associates backwards error recovery with a more spontaneous form of atomic activity dynamically determined by the protocol from past patterns of interprocess communication and available fault-tolerance provisions. Other error recovery techniques based on atomic activities that are more spontaneous than those of the conversation but less spontaneous than those of the chase protocol exist. For example, the two phase commit protocol [17] explicitly co-ordinates the activities of components leaving a "transaction" but does not require that the components be identifiable beforehand.

However the conversation, chase protocol and two-phase commit techniques concern themselves just with the use of backward error recovery in asynchronous systems. What is needed is a more general scheme for trying to ensure that a system behaves reliably in the presence of faults. The notion of reliability requires that a system have a specification against which the actual results of invoking its operations can be assessed. When an atomic action is executed, a well-defined state exists at the beginning and termination of its activity (although these states may not necessarily be instantaneously observable). The intended relationship between these states constitutes a specification for the atomic action which is independent of any asynchronous activity inside or outside the atomic action.

Such a specification is needed if general exception handlers are to be designed. (No such specification can be available for spontaneous atomic activities, which therefore can at most be used as a basis for backward error recovery.) Thus atomic actions provide a basis for structuring both forward and backward error recovery in asynchronous systems, provided appropriate exception handling rules can be devised. The following paragraphs describe our attempts to do this.

The raising of an exception within a fault-tolerant atomic action requires the application of abnormal computation and mechanisms to implement the fault tolerance measures. If the recovery measures succeed, the atomic action should produce the results that are normally expected from its activation. Atomic actions that explicitly return an abnormal result do so only due to the agreement of all their components. Thus we *associate exception handling contexts with atomic actions.*

An atomic action may contain internal atomic actions. If an exception is raised within an internal atomic action, then the fault tolerance measures of that internal atomic action should be applied. However, an internal atomic action may signal an exception. This exception is raised in the containing atomic action.

Whether one or several of the components carrying out an atomic action raise an exception, we would argue that *the fault tolerance measures necessarily involve all of the components involved in that atomic action.* (The fact that an exception has been detected invalidates the assumptions that the components can terminate normally and collectively provide the appropriate results. If some of the components are not required to change their flow of control to execute fault tolerance measures, they do not interact with the other components and hence should participate in a separate atomic action.)

Depictions of an atomic action in which a component raises an exception and each component of the atomic action changes its flow of control are shown in Figs. 7 and 8. (Comparing these figures to that given earlier of an idealized fault-tolerant component, the pair of arrows entering the atomic action corresponds to a service request being made of the system, the system being viewed as a fault-tolerant component containing two sub-components. Similarly, the pair of arrows leaving the atomic action corresponds to the provision of either the normal response, or an exception signal, by the system.) Although it is so implied by the diagrams, the activities involved in the start and the finish of the atomic action need not be closely synchronized – more sophisticated implementations are possible, though at the cost of increased complexity of error recovery.

Every component involved in the atomic action responds to the raised exception by changing to an abnormal activity. Each component changes to an exceptional control flow so as to execute a handler for that exception. This han-

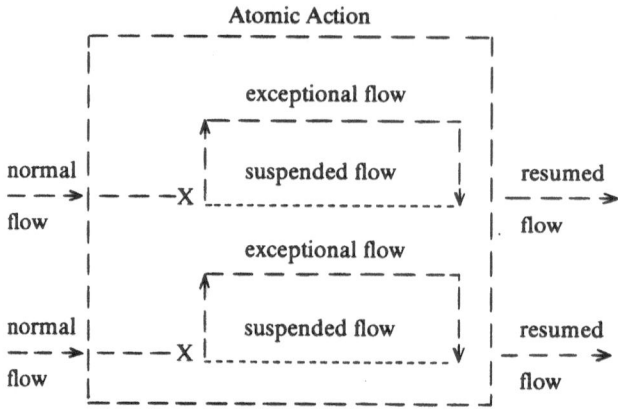

Fig. 7. Successful Error Recovery in an Atomic Action

dler either returns the component to normal activity or signals a further exception. (The change in control flow of a component that occurs as a result of a raised exception in a sequential system is a special case of the changes in control flow that should occur in an asynchronous system.) In Fig. 7, the recovery measures implemented by the exception handlers succeed and the normal control flow of the components is resumed. Figure 8 shows the control flow of the components involved in an atomic action when the exception handlers for the components cannot recover.

It is convenient to restrict signalled exceptions so that *each component (or exception handler) involved in an atomic action returns the same exception.* The signalling of the same exception ensures that the components agree on the abnormal result that should be returned to indicate the failure of the atomic action. (Note that an exception should be raised if two or more components try to signal different exceptions. The exception handlers for this exception should

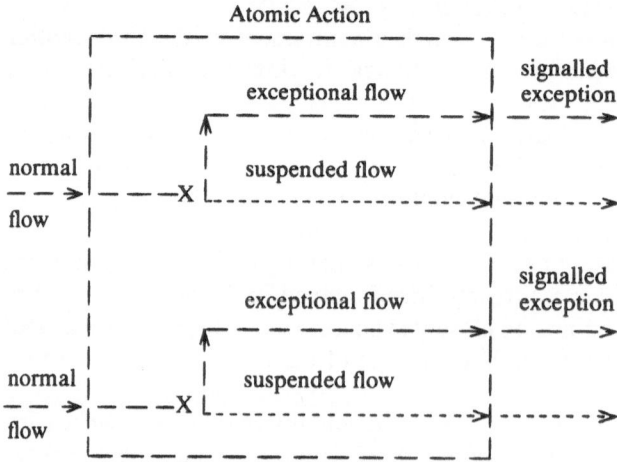

Fig. 8. Signalling an Exception from an Atomic Action

signal a failure exception.) An exception is raised in an atomic action if one of its internal atomic actions signals an exception. Signalling a single exception from an internal atomic action simplifies the selection of the appropriate exception handlers and recovery measures.

If *any of the components of an atomic action do not have a handler for a raised exception then all of the components should signal an atomic action failure.* However one will commonly arrange that an implicit handler, providing backward error recovery, is invoked by default, if no explicit handler is given.

Our scheme for using atomic actions to structure both forward and backward error recovery in asynchronous systems is described in greater detail in [18]. This deals with such further issues as the simultaneous raising of different exceptions by different components within an atomic action, and the problems of aborting an atomic action, for example in an attempt to avoid missing an imminent deadline.

4.1. Atomic Actions in UNIX United

Our initial experiments concerning the addition of atomic actions to UNIX United mainly address questions of overall system structuring, rather than the problems of implementing the full generality of the atomic action concept and of exception handling as described above. Thus we are concerning ourselves, at least in the first instance, solely with backward error recovery, in fact just at the level of file usage. It will be possible to nest atomic actions, and asynchronous activity will be supported, but only internal to an atomic action.

The fact that atomic actions are of equal relevance to users of a multiprogramming system, such as UNIX, as to users of a distributed system, prompts their provision in UNIX United by two separate, albeit related, mechanisms. The first of these effectively adds atomic actions to UNIX itself, in the form of three extra system calls:
(i)   Establish Recovery Point (i.e. start state-saving, and locking files),
(ii) Discard Recovery Point (i.e. discard saved state, and unlock relevant files), and

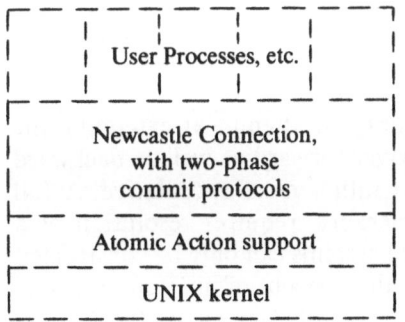

Fig. 9. Provision of Atomic Actions

577

(iii) Restore Recovery Point (i.e. go back to latest uncommitted recovery point).

This additional software is being implemented in the first instance as a separate layer, which will be interposed between the Connection layer and the kernel, as shown in Fig. 9 below.

The second mechanism provides network transparency for these additional calls. It is to be implemented by a modest augmentation of the Connection layer. (In the case of the Discard Recovery Point call, it might well be thought necessary to incorporate a simplified form of two-phase commit protocol, which would involve the provision of another system call "Prepare to Discard Recovery Point" by the Atomic Action layer. This should minimize the risk of having some but not all the component UNIX systems complete their Discard Recovery Point calls. In fact virtually all the facilities required within the Connection layer for two-phase commit already exist, being needed to support some existing UNIX system calls.)

5. Conclusions

The three forms of structuring that we have attempted to describe and justify here are just a modest generalisation and extension of various current approaches to the design and implementation of distributed and/or fault-tolerant computing systems. Nevertheless, we believe that they provide a surprisingly effective and constructive methodology for the design of such systems.

Certainly our experience with UNIX United provides what we regard as strong evidence for the merits of the first two structuring schemes. As reported in [19], a very useful distributed system, enabling full remote file and device access, was constructed within about a month of starting implementation of the Connection layer. Needless to say, the fact that — due to the transparency of the Newcastle Connection — it was not necessary to modify or in most cases even understand any existing operating system or user program source code was a great help! In only a few months this system had been extended to cover remote execution, multiple sets of users, etc. Distributed UNIX systems based on the Connection, using PDP11, VAX, M68000 or ICL PERQ computers, linked either by Ethernet or Cambridge Ring, are now operational at various sites. Moreover two prototype extensions of the system, for multi-level security and hardware fault tolerance, have been successfully demonstrated, and the design of others commenced.

The third structuring scheme described here, an attempt at extending the concentional concept of an atomic action to cover forward as well as backward recovery, and asynchronous systems, is as yet rather more speculative. A full implementation of the scheme, in all its generality, requires resolution of a number of design issues. In particular, practical systems can only be constructed if suitable notations are developed to express the concept of an atomic action. However we believe that the scheme provides a suitable framework for discussing general error recovery in asynchronous systems, and that it will be useful as a guide to the design and implementation of a variety of more specialised and/ or limited error recovery schemes.

Acknowledgements. The discussion of structuring issues presented in this paper owes much to the work of the author's many colleagues, at Newcastle and elsewhere, over a number of years. Recent work specifically on the Newcastle Connection and the Remote Procedure Call Protocol, however, has been mainly in close collaboration with Lindsay Marshall, Dave Brownbridge, Fabio Panzieri, Santosh Shrivastava and Jay Black. The work on error recovery in asynchronous systems has been largely carried out with Roy Campbell, of the University of Illinois, during the sabbatical year that he spent at Newcastle. This research has been sponsored by the U.K. Science and Engineering Research Council and the the Royal Signals and Radar Establishment.

References

1. W. C. Carter, "Hardware Fault Tolerance", pp. 211–263 in Computing Systems Reliability, ed. T. Anderson and B. Randell, Cambridge Univ. Press (1979).
2. B. H. Liskov and A. Snyder, "Exception Handling in CLU", IEEE Transactions on Software Engineering Vol. SE-5(6), pp. 546–558 (November 1979).
3. C. A. Sunshine and Y. K. Dalal, "Connection Management in Transport Protocols", pp. 454–473 in Computer Networks, Vol. 2, North-Holland, Amsterdam (1978).
4. F. Panzieri and B. Randell, "Interfacing UNIX to Data Communication Networks", Technical Report, Computing Laboratory, University of Newcastle upon Tyne (1983).
5. B. J. Nelson, Remote Procedure Call, Ph.D. Dissertation, Dept. Computer Science, Carnegie-Mellon Univ., Pittsburg, PA (1981).
6. J. H. Saltzer, D. P. Reed, and D. D. Clark, "End to End Argument in System Design", in Proc. 2nd Int. Conf. on Distributed Systems, Paris (509–512).
7. F. Panzieri and S. K. Shrivastava, "Reliable Remote Calls for Distributed UNIX: An implementation study", pp. 127–133 in Proc. Second Symp. on Reliability in Distributed Software and Database Systems, IEEE, Pittsburg (July 1982). [Also Chap. 6].
8. H. C. Lauer and D. Wyeth, "A Recursive Virtual Machine Architecture", ACM Workshop on Virtual Computer Systems, Cambridge, Massachusetts, pp. 113–116 (26–27 March 1973) (Also TR54, Computing Laboratory, University of Newcastle upon Tyne.).
9. P. M. Melliar-Smith and B. Randell, "Software Reliability: The Role of Programmed Exception Handling", Proceedings of Conference on Language Design For Reliable Software, Sigplan Notices Vol. 12 (3), Raleigh, pp. 95–100 (March 1977). (Also TR 95, Computing Laboratory, University of Newcastle upon Tyne.). [Also Chap. 3].
10. T. Anderson and P. A. Lee, Fault Tolerance: Principles and Practice, Prentice-Hall (1981).
11. J. J. Horning, H. C. Lauer, P. M. Melliar-Smith, and B. Randell, "A Program Structure for Error Detection and Recovery", pp. 171–187 in Lecture Notes in Computer Science 16, ed. E. Gelenbe and C. Kaiser, Springer Verlag (1974). [Also Chap. 2].
12. F. Cristian, "Exception Handling and Software Fault Tolerance", IEEE Transactions on Computers Vol. C-31(6), pp. 531–540 (1982). [Also Chap. 3].
13. E. Best and B. Randell, "A Formal Model of Atomicity", Acta Informatica Vol. 16, pp. 93–124 (1981). [Also Chap. 4].
14. C. T. Davies, "Data Processing Integrity", pp. 288–354 in Computing System Reliability, ed. T. Anderson and B. Randell, Cambridge Univ. Press (1979).
15. B. Randell, "System Structure for Software Fault Tolerance" IEEE Transactions on Software Engineering Vol. SE-1(2), pp. 220–232 (June 1975). (Also TR 75, Computing Laboratory, University of Newcastle upon Tyne.). [Also Chap. 1].
16. P. M. Merlin and B. Randell, "Consistent State Restoration in Distributed Systems", pp. 129–134 in Digest of Papers FTCS-8: Eight Annual International Symposium on Fault-Tolerant Computing Toulouse (June 1978). [Also Chap. 6].

17. J. N. Gray, "Notes on Data Base Operating Systems", pp. 393–481 in Lecture Notes in Computer Science 60, ed. R. Bayer, R. M. Graham and G. Seegmueller, Springer-Verlag, Berlin (1978).

18. R. H. Campbell and B. Randell, "Error Recovery in Asynchronous Systems", Technical Report, Computing Laboratory, University of Newcastle upon Tyne (1983).

19. D. R. Brownbridge, L. F. Marshall, and B. Randell, "The Newcastle Connection – or UNIXes of the World Unite", Software Practice and Experience Vol. 12(12) (Dec. 1982). [Also Chap. 6].